Atiyah's Accidents, Compensation an\

Since its first publication, *Accidents, Compensation and the Law* has been recognised as the leading treatment of the law of personal injuries compensation and the social, political and economic issues surrounding it. The seventh edition of this classic work explores recent momentous changes in personal injury law and practice and puts them into broad perspective. Most significantly, it examines developments affecting the financing and conduct of personal injury claiming: the abolition of legal aid for most personal injury claims; the increasing use of conditional fee agreements and after-the-event insurance; the meteoric rise and impending regulation of the claims management industry. Complaints that Britain is a 'compensation culture' suffering an 'insurance crisis' are investigated. New statistics on tort claims are discussed, providing fresh insights into the evolution of the tort system which, despite recent reforms, remains deeply flawed and ripe for radical reform.

Peter Cane has been Professor of Law in the Research School of Social Sciences at the Australian National University since 1997. For twenty years previously he taught law at Corpus Christi College Oxford. His main research interests are in the law of obligations, especially tort law; public law, especially administrative law; and legal theory. Recent publications include *Responsibility in Law and Morality* (2002) and *The Oxford Handbook of Legal Studies* (edited with Mark Tushnet) (2003).

Patrick Atiyah is one of the leading common lawyers of his generation. Until his early retirement in 1988 he was Professor of English Law at Oxford University. His published writings range widely over topics in tort law, contract law, legal history and legal theory; and include *The Sale of Goods* (11th edition with J N Harpers and H L McQueen, 2005), *The Rise and Fall of Freedom of Contract* (1985) and *The Damages Lottery* (1997).

The Law in Context Series

Editors: William Twining (University College London) and
Christopher McCrudden (Lincoln College, Oxford)

Since 1970 the Law in Context series has been in the forefront of the movement to broaden the study of law. It has been a vehicle for the publication of innovative scholarly books that treat law and legal phenomena critically in their social, political and economic contexts from a variety of perspectives. The series particularly aims to publish scholarly legal writing that brings fresh perspectives to bear on new and existing areas of law taught in universities. A contextual approach involves treating legal subjects broadly, using materials from other social sciences, and from any other discipline that helps to explain the operation in practice of the subject under discussion. It is hoped that this orientation is at once more stimulating and more realistic than the bare exposition of legal rules. The series includes original books that have a different emphasis from traditional legal textbooks, while maintaining the same high standards of scholarship. They are written primarily for undergraduate and graduate students of law and of other disciplines, but most also appeal to a wider readership. In the past, most books in the series have focused on English law, but recent publications include books on European law, globalisation, transnational legal processes, and comparative law.

Books in the Series

Anderson, Schum & Twining: *Analysis of Evidence*
Ashworth: *Sentencing and Criminal Justice*
Barton & Douglas: *Law and Parenthood*
Beecher-Monas: *Evaluating Scientific Evidence: An Interdisciplinary Framework for Intellectual Due Process*
Bell: *French Legal Cultures*
Bercusson: *European Labour Law*
Birkinshaw: *European Public Law*
Birkinshaw: *Freedom of Information: The Law, the Practice and the Ideal*
Cane: *Atiyah's Accidents, Compensation and the Law*
Clarke & Kohler: *Property Law: Commentary and Materials*
Collins: *The Law of Contract*
Davies: *Perspectives on Labour Law*
Dembour: *Who Believes in Human Rights?: The European Convention in Question*
de Sousa Santos: *Toward a New Legal Common Sense*
Diduck: *Law's Families*
Elworthy & Holder: *Environmental Protection: Text and Materials*
Fortin: *Children's Rights and the Developing Law*
Glover-Thomas: *Reconstructing Mental Health Law and Policy*
Gobert & Punch: *Rethinking Corporate Crime*
Harlow & Rawlings: *Law and Administration*
Harris: *An Introduction to Law*
Harris, Campbell & Halson *Remedies in Contract and Tort*

Harvey: *Seeking Asylum in the UK: Problems and Prospects*
Hervey & McHale: *Health Law and the European Union*
Lacey & Wells: *Reconstructing Criminal Law*
Lewis: *Choice and the Legal Order: Rising above Politics*
Likosky: *Transnational Legal Processes*
Maughan & Webb: *Lawyering Skills and the Legal Process*
McGlynn: *Families and the European Union: Law, Politics and Pluralism*
Moffat: *Trusts Law: Text and Materials*
Norrie: *Crime, Reason and History*
O'Dair: *Legal Ethics*
Oliver: *Common Values and the Public-Private Divide*
Oliver & Drewry: *The Law and Parliament*
Picciotto: *International Business Taxation*
Reed: *Internet Law: Text and Materials*
Richardson: *Law, Process and Custody*
Roberts & Palmer: *Dispute Processes: ADR and the Primary Forms of Decision-Making*
Scott & Black: *Cranston's Consumers and the Law*
Seneviratne: *Ombudsmen: Public Services and Administrative Justice*
Stapleton: *Product Liability*
Tamanaha: *The Struggle for Law as a Means to an End*
Turpin: *British Government and the Constitution: Text, Cases and Materials*
Twining: *Globalisation and Legal Theory*
Twining: *Rethinking Evidence*
Twining & Miers: *How to Do Things with Rules*
Ward: *A Critical Introduction to European Law*
Ward: *Shakespeare and Legal Imagination*
Zander: *Cases and Materials on the English Legal System*
Zander: *The Law-Making Process*

Atiyah's Accidents, Compensation and the Law

Seventh Edition

Peter Cane

Research School of Social Sciences
Australian National University

CAMBRIDGE UNIVERSITY PRESS

Cambridge, New York, Melbourne, Madrid, Cape Town, Singapore, São Paulo

Cambridge University Press
The Edinburgh Building, Cambridge CB2 2RU, UK

Published in the United States of America by Cambridge University Press, New York

www.cambridge.org
Information on this title: www.cambridge.org/9780521689311

Printed in the United Kingdom at the University Press, Cambridge

A catalogue record for this publication is available from the British Library

Library of Congress Cataloguing in Publication data

ISBN -13 978-0-521-68931-1 (paperback)
ISBN -10 0-521-68931-7 (paperback)

Cambridge University Press has no responsibility for
the persistence or accuracy of URLs for external or
third-party internet websites referred to in this publication,
and does not guarantee that any content on such
websites is, or will remain, accurate or appropriate.

Contents

Preface   xiv
List of abbreviations   xvii
List of tables   xxii
Table of legislation   xxiii
Table of cases   xxviii

Part One: The Issues in Perspective

1   Introduction: surveying the field   3

   1.1 Compensation for accidents   3
   1.2 Natural and human causes   6
        1.2.1 The issue   6
        1.2.2 Society's 'responsibility' for human causes   8
        1.2.3 Protecting reasonable expectations   9
        1.2.4 Egalitarianism and the problem of drawing the line   10
   1.3 Mixed systems in a mixed society   11
   1.4 Some facts and figures   18
        1.4.1 Accidents causing personal injury or death   18
        1.4.2 Death and disability from other causes   20
        1.4.3 The prevalence of disability   21
        1.4.4 The effect of disability on income   21
        1.4.5 Distribution and sources of compensation   22
        1.4.6 The more serious and the less serious   25

Part Two: The Tort System in Theory

2   Fault as a basis of liability   33

   2.1 The conceptual basis of tort law   33
   2.2 Negligence as a basis of liability   34
   2.3 The fault principle   35
   2.4 Negligence as fault   36
        2.4.1 A question of fact?   36
        2.4.2 The nature of negligence   40

2.4.3 Probability of harm   42
2.4.4 Likely magnitude of harm   43
2.4.5 The value of the activity and the cost of the
       precautions needed to avoid harm   45
2.4.6 The function of the negligence formula   46
2.4.7 Foreseeability   47
2.4.8 The objective standard of care   48
2.4.9 Negligence in design and negligence in operation 50
2.5 Conduct of the claimant   53
2.5.1 Contributory negligence   54
2.5.2 Volenti non fit injuria   61
2.5.3 Illegality   65

3   The scope of the tort of negligence   68

3.1 The nature of the duty of care   68
3.2 Specific duty situations   70
3.2.1 Common situations in which duties of care
       have been imposed   70
3.2.2 The distinction between acts and omissions 72
3.3 Nervous shock   84
3.4 Family claims   89

4   Departures from the fault principle   92

4.1 Fault liability and strict liability   92
4.2 'Procedural' devices   94
4.3 Breach of statutory duty   95
4.4 Contractual duties   99
4.5 *Rylands* v. *Fletcher*, nuisance and animals   100
4.6 Joint liability   101
4.7 Vicarious liability   102
4.8 Products liability   103
4.9 Proposals to extend strict liability   105
4.9.1 Dangerous things and activities   105
4.9.2 Railway accidents   106
4.10 Ex gratia compensation schemes   107
4.10.1 Vaccine damage   107
4.10.2 HIV   108
4.10.3 Hepatits C   108
4.10.4 Variant CJD   109

5   Causation and remoteness of damage   110

5.1 Introduction   110
5.2 Factual causation   111

	5.2.1 Proving causation	111
	5.2.2 Causing and increasing the risk of harm	112
	5.2.3 Omissions	115
	5.2.4 Multiple causal factors	116
5.3	Limits on the liability of factual causes	118
	5.3.1 Legal causation	118
	5.3.2 Damage not within the risk	125
	5.3.3 Foreseeability again	127
5.4	Conclusion	129

6   Damages for personal injury and death   130

6.1	The lump sum: predicting the future	130
	6.1.1 Personal injury cases	130
	6.1.2 Fatal cases	132
	6.1.3 Variation of awards after trial	135
	6.1.4 Suitability of lump sums	137
	6.1.5 Alternatives to lump sums	139
6.2	Full compensation	143
	6.2.1 Interest	145
	6.2.2 Lost earnings and support	146
	6.2.3 Medical and other expenses	149
6.3	Full compensation for lost 'earnings': is it justified?	152
	6.3.1 The earnings-related principle	152
	6.3.2 The hundred-per cent principle	156
6.4	Full compensation: the commitment in practice	157
6.5	Intangible losses	161
	6.5.1 Assessing intangible losses	161
	6.5.2 The tariff system	166
	6.5.3 Subjective factors	170
	6.5.4 Should damages be payable for intangible losses?	171
6.6	Overall maxima	173
6.7	Punitive damages	173

7   An appraisal of the fault principle   175

7.1	The compensation payable bears no relation to the degree of fault	175
7.2	The compensation bears no relation to the means of the tortfeasor	177
7.3	A harm-doer may be legally liable without being morally culpable and vice versa	179
	7.3.1 Collective liability	179
	7.3.2 The objective definition of fault	180
	7.3.3 Moral culpability without legal liability	182

	7.3.4 The fault principle and popular morality	183
7.4	The fault principle pays little attention to the conduct or needs of the victim	183
7.5	Justice may require payment of compensation without fault	185
7.6	It is often difficult to adjudicate allegations of fault	187
7.7	The fault principle contributes to a culture of blaming and discourages people from taking responsibility for their own lives	192

Part Three: The Tort System in Operation

8   Claims and claimants   201

8.1	Accident victims and tort claimants	201
	8.1.1 Cases reaching trial	201
	8.1.2 Cases set down for trial	203
	8.1.3 Actions commenced	203
	8.1.4 All tort claims	204
8.2	Why do people (not) make tort claims?	206
	8.2.1 Some research findings	206
	8.2.2 Alternative remedies	207
	8.2.3 Claims consciousness	209
8.3	Particular types of claims	214
	8.3.1 Road accidents	214
	8.3.2 Industrial injuries and illnesses	216
	8.3.3 Public liability claims	218
	8.3.4 Medical injuries	219
	8.3.5 Group claims	221

9   Tortfeasors and insurers   222

9.1	Defendants	222
9.2	Individuals as tort defendants	222
9.3	Employers and corporations as tort defendants	228
9.4	Insurers	233
9.5	The nature of liability insurance	234
9.6	Some problems of liability insurance	239
9.7	First-party insurance for the benefit of others	244
9.8	The impact of liability insurance on the law	245
	9.8.1 Statutory provisions	245
	9.8.2 The impact of insurance on the common law	248
9.9	The Motor Insurers' Bureau	255

10   Trials and settlements   260

10.1	The importance of settlements	260
10.2	Obtaining legal assistance and financing tort claims	261

10.3 The course of negotiations   268
    10.3.1 Individual claims   269
    10.3.2 Group claims   274
10.4 When negotiations break down   278
10.5 The time taken to achieve a settlement   281
10.6 The amount of compensation   284

Part Four: Other Compensation Systems

11   First-party insurance   291

11.1 Types of first-party insurance   291
11.2 First-party insurance compared with tort liability   295

12   Compensation for criminal injuries   300

12.1 Tort claims   300
12.2 Compensation orders   301
12.3 Other sources of compensation   303
12.4 Criminal injuries compensation scheme   304
    12.4.1 Justifications for the Scheme   304
    12.4.2 The scope of the scheme   309
    12.4.3 Comparison between the CICS and tort liability 316
    12.4.4 Administration   324
    12.4.5 Claims consciousness   326

13   The social security system   328

13.1 Foundations of the social security system   328
    13.1.1 Workers' compensation   328
    13.1.2 National insurance   330
13.2 The Beveridge Report and the 1946 Acts   331
13.3 Developments since 1946   333
13.4 The industrial injuries system   338
    13.4.1 The scope of the system   338
    13.4.2 Accidents and diseases   340
    13.4.3 Benefits   342
    13.4.4 Administration   351
    13.4.5 The tort system and the IIS compared   355
13.5 Non-work-related disablement   355
13.6 Preferences within State provision for the disabled   356
13.7 Income-support benefits   358
    13.7.1 Benefits   358
    13.7.2 Administration   360
13.8 Fraud and abuse   360

14   Other forms of assistance   363

14.1 The taxation system   363
14.2 Social services   365
      14.2.1 Employment   366
      14.2.2 Mobility   369
      14.2.3 Housing and residential accommodation   370
      14.2.4 Other social services   371
14.3 Conclusion   372

Part Five: The Overall Picture

15   A plethora of systems   377

15.1 The concept of over-compensation   377
15.2 The choice of compensation system   378
15.3 Subrogation and recoupment   380
15.4 Tort damages and other compensation   385
      15.4.1 General principles   385
      15.4.2 Tort damages and sick pay   387
      15.4.3 Tort damages and personal insurance   388
      15.4.4 Tort damages and charitable payments   389
      15.4.5 Tort damages and social security benefits   390
15.5 Criminal injuries compensation   394

16   The cost of compensation and who pays it   395

16.1 The cost of tort compensation   395
16.2 Costs not paid through the tort system   402
      16.2.1 The cost of social services   402
      16.2.2 The cost of the social security system   403
      16.2.3 Other sources of compensation   405
      16.2.4 Costs in perspective   405
16.3 The cost of criminal injuries compensation   406

17   The functions of compensation systems   408

17.1 Compensation   408
      17.1.1 Some preliminary questions   408
      17.1.2 The meaning of 'compensation'   411
      17.1.3 Compensation and compensation systems   414
17.2 Distribution of losses   415
      17.2.1 What should be distributed?   415
      17.2.2 How should it be distributed?   416
17.3 The allocation of risks   418
17.4 Punishment   419
17.5 Corrective justice   421

17.6 Vindication or satisfaction   422
17.7 Deterrence and prevention   424
    17.7.1 Rules and standards of behaviour   425
    17.7.2 Accident prevention via insurance   433
17.8 General deterrence   439
    17.8.1 The basic idea   439
    17.8.2 Ascertaining the costs of an accident   442
    17.8.3 Allocation of costs to activities   442
    17.8.4 Responsiveness of price mechanism   446
    17.8.5 Applying general deterrence criteria in practice   448
    17.8.6 General deterrence and existing systems   448
    17.8.7 An assessment of the value of the
           general-deterrence approach   453
    17.8.8 Conclusions about general deterrence   457

Part Six: The Future

18   **Accident compensation in the twenty-first century**   461

18.1 Where we are now and how we got here   461
18.2 Basic issues   467
    18.2.1 Strict liability or no-fault?   467
    18.2.2 Limited or comprehensive reform?   468
    18.2.3 Preferential treatment   472
    18.2.4 Assessment of compensation   474
    18.2.5 Funding   477
    18.2.6 Goals of the system   478
18.3 Proposals and schemes   484
    18.3.1 Road accident schemes   484
    18.3.2 Other schemes   487
18.4 The way ahead   488
    18.4.1 A social welfare solution   488
    18.4.2 A private insurance solution   493
18.5 Damage to property   495
18.6 The role of the insurance industry and the legal profession 496

Index   499

Preface

The seven years since I wrote the preface to the sixth edition have been ones of rapid and momentous change in the tort system, affecting most particularly the financing and settlement of personal injury claims. Some of these changes were foreshadowed in the previous edition; but it was hard to predict the precise contours of the revolution that was about to be triggered by the abolition of legal aid for most personal injury claims and the consequent growth of the claims management industry. Phrases such as 'compensation culture', 'blame culture' and 'insurance crisis' have become part of the common currency of public debate and political rhetoric in Britain. At the same time, social security provision for the disabled and compensation for victims of crime have continued to engage the concern and attention of the government and the public, both being under review as I write. Nor is it only in Britain that personal injury compensation looms large in legal and political debate. In the USA, for instance, asbestos and medical malpractice litigation are matters of intractable and acrimonious disagreement. In Australia, as a result of turmoil in the liability insurance industry, 'tort reform' became, for several months in 2002, the hottest issue in domestic politics, leading to the appointment of a committee to review personal injury law and, in its wake, major legislation in all jurisdictions. Despite widespread dissatisfaction with the tort system, the past decade has (ironically, perhaps) seen its further entrenchment in the political economy of personal injury compensation. Except at the margins, the thrust of public policy has been to make the tort system work better (whatever that might mean), not to replace it with something better.

Changes to the law, both in the areas already mentioned and in others such as the assessment of damages, have required substantial rewriting of various parts of the book. The opportunity of a new edition has also been taken to relocate the discussion of human and natural causes (which appeared in chapter 16 of the sixth edition) into chapter 1 where (I think) it sits more comfortably. In this edition, too, there is new discussion (particularly in chapter 4) of various forms of administrative compensation arrangements benefiting victims of hepatitis-C, black lung, vibration white finger and other chronic externalities of modern industrial and technological activities.

Moving away from law and procedure, undoubtedly the most important development since the last edition has been the increasing availability of reliable statistics about the tort system. The NHS Litigation Authority now publishes detailed information about the number and cost of medical negligence (and other personal injury) claims against NHS Trusts, and the Compensation Recovery Unit within the Department of Work and Pensions – as administrator of schemes for recouping the cost of social security benefits and NHS treatment from payers of tort compensation – produces robust estimates of the total number of tort settlements. The general picture that emerges is that tort claims have increased about threefold since the 1970s (assuming that figures produced by the Pearson Commission were reasonably accurate). The impact of this new information is most obvious in chapter 8; but its influence pervades many parts of the book. As yet, intelligence about the cost of compensation is more patchy and less reliable. In some areas – criminal injuries compensation, for instance – the facts are known. But the total cost of the tort system, for example, is a matter of considerable speculation and disagreement. Estimates of the total economic cost of personal injuries are even more problematic. There seems little doubt, however, that the turnover of the compensation 'industry' (broadly understood) runs into the tens of billions of pounds per annum – a significant amount by any standard.

As ever, the main aim of this book is to provide the reader with resources for standing back from tort law and the tort system and viewing them in a larger legal and social landscape. Whether placing tort at the centre of the picture in this way continues to be desirable is a difficult question deserving of serious attention. From the point of view of legal education, the approach still seems defensible because tort law is the only aspect of the political economy of personal injuries that the typical law student encounters. Whether the focus on tort has the same utility in the context of public policy debates is contestable. Tort law has an immanent ideology, and taking tort as a starting point may undesirably skew consideration of the basic question of how risks of personal injury ought to be distributed. Tort law and the tort system are (it seems) here to stay. The challenge is to imagine a dispensation to which tort can make a positive contribution in partnership with other principles and institutions of risk distribution. Only by doing this can we nurture the hope that the various components of existing compensation arrangements can be held in benign and creative tension. In the world of *realpolitik* the burning question is not how to get rid of tort but how to live with it.

When a book has had as long a life as this one, the passage of time effects much more than the law discussed therein. This edition will appear under the imprint of the third publisher of the Law in Context Series, in which this book was the first. In 1970 academics used pens, typewriters and 'dictaphones' to produce their manuscripts. Fax machines had not been invented, let alone personal computers, email and the internet. Thanks to the World Wide Web and other marvels of information technology, much of the research required to prepare a new edition of this book is more easily done at my desk in Canberra than it was a decade ago when I lived and worked in England. Even so, the help of colleagues based in England – especially Professor Richard Lewis and Professor Nick Wikeley – has been invaluable. Email has also enabled me to keep in frequent contact with Patrick Atiyah, whose characteristically forthright and original observations and opinions continue to provide inspiration and stimulation. The best form of thanks I can think of is to dedicate this edition to him with affection, admiration and respect.

Peter Cane
Canberra
April 2006

List of abbreviations

A	Atlantic Reporter (USA)
AC	Appeal Cases
All ER	All England Law Reports
ALR	Australian Law Reports
App Cas	Appeal Cases (19th C)
ATE insurance	after-the-event insurance
Australian Committee Report	*Compensation and Rehabilitation in Australia*, Report of the National Committee of Inquiry (Australian Government Publishing Service, Canberra, 1974)
Beveridge Report	*Social Insurance and Allied Services*, Report by Sir William Beveridge (Cmnd 6404, 1942)
BMLR	Butterworths Medico-Legal Reports
BTE insurance	before-the-event-insurance
C	claimant
CA	Claims assessor
Cal Rptr	California Reporter
Can BR	*Canadian Bar Review*
Cantley Committee Report	Report of the Personal Injuries Litigation Procedure Working Party (Cmnd 7476, 1979)
CFA	Conditional Fee Arrangement
Ch	Chancery Division Reports
CICA	Criminal Injuries Compensation Authority
CICB	Criminal Injuries Compensation Board
CICS	Criminal Injuries Compensation Scheme
Civil Justice Review	Report of the Review Body on Civil Justice (Cm 394, 1988)
CLR	Commonwealth Law Reports (Australia)
Cm	Command Paper (HMSO)
CMC	Claims management company
Cmnd	Command Paper (HMSO)

CNST	Clinical Negligence Scheme for Trusts
Conard, *Automobile Accident Costs and Payments*	A.F. Conard and others, *Automobile Accident Costs and Payments* (Ann Arbor, 1964)
CPR	Civil Procedure Rules
CRU	Compensation Recovery Unit
D	defendant
DCA	Department for Constitutional Affairs
DH	Department of Health
DLA	disability living allowance
DLR	Dominion Law Reports (Canada)
DPTC	disabled persons tax credit
DSS	Department of Social Security
DWA	disability working allowance
DWP	Department for Work and Pensions
ER	English Reports
F	Federal Reporter (USA)
FC	Family Credit
F Supp	Federal Supplement (USA)
Fisher Committee Report	*The Abuse of Social Security Benefits* (Cmnd 5228, 1973)
George	V. George, *Social Security: Beveridge and After* (London, 1968)
GLO	Group Litigation Order
HC	House of Commons
Harris 1984 Survey	D.R. Harris and others, *Compensation and Support for Illness and Injury* (Oxford, 1984)
HL	House of Lords
HMSO	Her Majesty's Stationery Office
How Much is Enough?	*Personal Injury Compensation: How Much is Enough?* Law Com. No. 225 (1994)
ICLQ	*International and Comparative Law Quarterly*
ICR	Industrial Cases Reports
IIAC	Industrial Injuries Advisory Council
IIS	Industrial Injuries Scheme
IPI	Income protection insurance
IRLR	Industrial Relations Law Reports
IS	Income Support
Ison	T.G. Ison, *The Forensic Lottery* (London, 1967)

J (after a surname)	Mr/Ms Justice
J.	*Journal*
JPIL	*Journal of Personal Injury Law*
JSSL	*Journal of Social Security Law*
KB	King's Bench Reports
KIR	Knight's Industrial Reports
Law. Com.	Law Commission Report
LGR	Knight's Local Government Reports
LJ (after a surname)	Lord/Lady Justice
LJ	*Law Journal*
Lloyd's Rep	Lloyd's Reports
LQR	*Law Quarterly Review*
LR	*Law Review*
LR . . . Ex	Law Reports (Exchequer) (19th C)
LS	*Legal Studies*
LSC	Legal Services Commission
MIB	Motor Insurers' Bureau
MR	Master of the Rolls
MVR	Motor Vehicle Reports (New South Wales)
NE	North Eastern Reporter (USA)
NHSLA	National Health Service Litigation Authority
NI	National Insurance
NSWLR	New South Wales Law Reports
NW	North Western Reporter (USA)
NY	New York Reporter (USA)
Osgoode Hall Study	A.M. Linden, *Report of the Osgoode Hall Study on Compensation for Victims of Automobile Accidents* (Toronto, 1965)
Osgoode Hall Study (Victims of Crime)	A.M. Linden, *Report of the Osgoode Hall Study on Compensation for Victims of Crime* (Toronto, 1968)
OPCS Disability Survey	Report 1: Martin, Meltzer and Elliott, *The Prevalence of Disability Among Adults* (HMSO, 1988) Report 2: Martin and White, *The Financial Circumstances of Disabled Adults Living in Private Households*

Report 3: Bone and Meltzer, *The Prevalence of Disability Among Children* (HMSO, 1989)
Report 4: Martin, White and Meltzer, *Disabled Adults: Services, Transport and Employment* (HMSO, 1989)
Report 5: Smyth and Robus, *The Financial Circumstances of Families with Disabled Children Living in Private Households* (HMSO, 1989)
Report 6: Meltzer, Smyth and Robus, *Disabled Children: Services, Transport and Education* (HMSO, 1989)

P (preceded by date in square brackets)	Probate Division Reports
PAI	Personal accident insurance
Pearson Report	Report of the Royal Commission on Civil Liability and Compensation for Personal Injury (Cmnd 7054, 1978, 3 volumes)
Piercy Committee Report	Report of the Committee of Inquiry on the Rehabilitation, Training and Resettlement of Disabled Persons (Cmnd 9883, 1956)
PMI	Private medical insurance
PPO	periodical payment order
Q.	*Quarterly*
QB	Queen's Bench Reports
QBD	Queen's Bench Division Reports (19th C)
QdR	Queensland Reports
R.	*Review*
REA	Reduced Earnings Allowance
RTR	Road Traffic Reports
Robens Committee Report	Report of the Committee into Safety and Health at Work (Cmnd 5304, 1972)
SCR	Supreme Court Reports (Canada)
SDA	Severe Disability Allowance
SF	Social Fund
SFO	Social Fund Officer
SLT	Scots Law Times
SSAT	Social Security Appeals Tribunal

SSCBA 1992	Social Security Contributions and Benefits Act 1992
SSAA 1992	Social Security Administration Act 1992
SSP	Statutory Sick Pay
Seebohm Report	Report of the Committee on Local Authority and Allied Personal Social Services (Cmnd 3703, 1968)
TRL	Transport Research Laboratory
TRRL	Transport and Road Research Laboratory
TSO	The Stationery Office
U.	University
UCLALR	*University of California at Los Angeles Law Review*
WAR	Western Australian Reports
WALR	Western Australian Law Reports
WFTC	working families tax credit
Wikeley, Ogus and Barendt's The Law of Social Security	N.J. Wikeley, *Wikeley, Ogus and Barendt's The Law of Social Security*, 5th edn (London, 2002)
Winn Committee Report	Report of the Committee on Personal Injuries Litigation (Cmnd 3691, 1968)
WLR	Weekly Law Reports
WN(NSW)	Weekly Notes (New South Wales)
WMA	Widowed Mother's Allowance
Woolf Reforms	Changes to civil procedure introduced in 1999 and embodied in the Civil Procedure Rules (CPR)
WP	Widow's Pension
Woodhouse Report	Report of the Royal Commission of Inquiry on Compensation for Personal Injuries in New Zealand (Government Printer, New Zealand, 1967)

List of tables

Table 1 Numbers of disabled persons in Great Britain by age and
degree of disability (thousands)   22
Table 2 Sources of income of family units containing a disabled
adult by severity of disability (per cent)   23
Table 3 Numbers of injured persons obtaining compensation
from different sources   23
Table 4 Cost of compensation paid from different sources to
injured persons and administrative costs of payments, average over
1971–6 (1977 currency values)   24
Table 5 Court waiting times in personal injury actions   202

Table of legislation

Administration of Justice Act 1970..226
Administration of Justice Act 1982 ....89n, 462
    s.1 ....90n
    s.2 ....149n, 382n
    s.5...349n, 390n, 393n
Animals Act 1971 ....72, 101, 248
    s.2(2)(b)..101n
    s.6 ....101n
Attachment of Earnings Act 1971..226n

Chronically Sick and Disabled Persons Act 1970................................365
    s.2...370
Civil Evidence Act 1995
    s.10..158
Civil Liability (Contribution) Act 1978..102
Civil Partnership Act 2004 ....89n
Civil Procedure Act 1997
    s.7 ....187n
Coal Industry Act 1975 ....357n
Companies Act 1989
    s.141 ....253n
Congenital Disabilities (Civil Liability) Act 1976 ....57, 72, 246, 462
Consumer Protection Act 1987...............................71, 103, 104, 105n,
                                                            124, 219
    Part I 99n, 103, 143n, 462, 467, 476, 489
    s.4(1)(e) 104n
Contracts (Rights of Third Parties) Act 1999 244–5
Courts Act 2003
    s.95–s.96...302n
    s.100 ....142n
Courts and Legal Services Act 1990
    s.58(4)(c) 265n

Criminal Damage Act 1971
  s.1(1)–(2) 311n
Criminal Injuries Compensation Act 1995 ....303, 307, 309, 381
  s.7A–s.7D 303
Criminal Justice Act 1988...308
Criminal Justice Act 1991
  s.18–s.21 ....178n

Damages Act 1996 ....159n
  s.2 ....142n
Damages (Scotland) Act 1976...90, 172n
Defective Premises act 1972
  s.4..72
Disability Discrimination Act 1995 ....368, 369, 370
  Part IV 370
  s.1(1) 368
Disability Living Allowance and Disability Working Allowance Act 1992 335
Disabled Persons (Employment) Act 1944......................................367, 368, 369
Domestic Proceedings and Magistrates' Courts Act 1978
  s.3(2) 155n
Domestic Violence, Crime and Victims Act 2004
  s.59 ....303n

Employers' Liability Act 1880 328–9
Employers' Liability (Compulsory Insurance) Act 1969...228n, 234, 246, 259, 297n

Factories Act 1961
  s.14..96
Fatal Accidents Act 1976.......................57, 58, 89, 90, 91, 132, 133, 134, 135, 136n,
                          137n, 141n, 143, 146, 147, 148, 149, 162, 171, 172n,
                          240, 245, 253, 318, 320, 323, 351, 381, 393
  s.1A..89n
  s.3(3) 134n
  s.3(4) 351n
  s.4 ....144, 245n, 351n

Health and Safety at Work etc Act 1974 98
  s.47(1)–(2) 98
Health Services and Public Health Act 1968..371n
Highways (Miscellaneous Provisions) Act 1961..72, 191
Housing (Homeless Persons) Act 1977 365
Human Rights Act 1998 194

Income and Corporation Taxes Act 1988
   s.263 ....364n
   s.265 ....364n
   s.327 ....364n
Industrial Assurance and Friendly Societies Act 1948..295
Industrial Injuries Act 1946 98

Law Reform (Contributory Negligence) Act 1945....................................36, 55, 245
Law Reform (Husband and Wife) Act 1962...72, 245, 255n
Law Reform (Miscellaneous Provisions) Act 1934..................36, 132, 147, 148, 245
Law Reform (Miscellaneous Provisions) Act 1971
   s.4...240
Law Reform (Personal Injuries) Act 1948 ....36, 245, 391, 392
   s.1(3) 245n
   s.2...390
   s.2(4) 150n
Legal Aid Act 1988
   s.13 ....268n
   s.16(6) 268n
   s.17 ....268n
Local Authority Social Services Act 1970 365
Lord Campbell's Act 1846 ....91, 132

National Assistance Act 1948
   Part III...365
   s.21–s.28...371n
National Health Service and Community Care Act 1990
   Part III...371n
National Insurance Act 1911...330, 331, 337, 343n
National Insurance (industrial Injuries) Act 1946..338

Occupiers' Liability Act 1957 ....36, 72, 248
Occupiers' Liability Act 1984 ....36, 72
Offences Against the Person Act 1861
   s.34 ....311n

Pneumoconiosis etc (Workers' Compensation) Act 1979.................................357n
Policyholders Protection Act 1975...242
Powers of Criminal Courts Act 2000 301
   s.130–s.134...301n

Race Relations Act 1976 368
Riot (Damages) Act 1886...295, 305n

Road Traffic Act 1988......................234, 246, 247, 248, 253n, 256, 257, 297n, 302n
   s.144 ....233n
   s.149(2) 61n
   s.149(3) 65n, 257n
   s.151(4) 257n
   s.153...232, 246, 247
   s.158 ....382n
Road Traffic (NHS Charges) Act 1999...382, 402

Sex Discrimination Act 1975 368–9
Social Security Act 1975 334
Social Security Act 1985
   s.23 ....108n
Social Security Act 1986 335
Social Security Act 1989 ....391, 392
Social Security Act 1990 335
Social Security Act 1998..352n, 360
   s.29 ....355n
Social Security Administration Act 1992 ....334, 351–2n
   Part IV..391
   s.10(1)(b) 340
Social Security (Contributions and Benefits) Act 1992................................334, 344
   s.94(3) 339n
   s.99 ....338n
   s.101...339, 340
   Sch.6..344n
Social Security (Incapacity for Work) Act 1994...336
Social Security (Recovery of Benefits) Act 1997 ....359n, 381, 383,
                                                              384, 393
   s.17 ....393n
Supreme Court 1981
   s.32A..136, 142, 283n

Tax Credits Act 2002
   s.10 ....358n
Third Parties (Rights Against Insurers) Act 1930 ....232, 246, 247

Unfair Contract Terms Act 1977...62, 244, 248
   s.2..61
   s.11(4) 248n

Vaccine Damage Payments Act 1979 ....108, 381

Welfare Reform and Pensions Act 1999 ....336, 347n
Workman's Compensation Act 1897 ....328, 330

Secondary legislation
Civil Procedure Rules...354n
  Part 19...276
  Part 36...280
  Part 45..265n
  Part 46..266n
  Part 72..225n
Damages (Variation of Periodical Payments) Order 2005............................142n
European Communities (Rights Against Insurers) Regulations 2002..........246n
High Court and County Courts Jurisdiction Order 1991............................201n
Management of Health and Safety at Work Regulations 1999
  reg.22(1) 98n
Motor Vehicles (Compulsory Insurance) (Information and Compensation
Body) Regulations 2003
  reg.11 ....256n
  reg.13 ....256n
Social Security (Claims and Payments) Regulations 1979
  reg.25 ....355n
Social Security Commissioners (Procedure) Regulations 1999....................354n
Social Security (General Benefit) Regulations 1982
  Sch.2..344n
Social Security (Recovery of Benefits) Regulations 1997 ....393n
  reg.2(2)(a) 351n
Vaccine Damage Payments Act 1979 Statutory Sum Order 2000................108n
Working Tax Credit (Entitlement and Maximum Rate) Regulations 2002
  reg.4(1) 358n

European legislation
Compensation of Crime Victims Directive 2004/80/EC................................312
European Convention on Human Rights 194
  Art.3 ....70n
  Art.6 ....70, 82, 83
  Art.13 ....70, 83
European Convention on the Compensation of Victims of Violent Crime...312
Fifth Motor Insurance Directive 2005...297n
Product Liability Directive...489
Working Time Directive 396n

New Zealand legislation
Accident Compensation Act 1972..16n, 153n, 156
Injury Prevention, Rehabilitation and Compensation Act 2001
  s.122 ....467n

Table of cases

AB v British Coal Corporation [2004] EWHC 1372 ....286n
AB v John Wyeth & Brother Ltd [1994] PIQR P109 ....277n
Adamson v Motor Vehicle Insurance Trust (1957) 58 WALR 56......................182n
Airedale NHS Trust v Bland [1993] AC 789 ....170n
Albert v MIB [1972] AC 301 259
Alcock v Chief Constable of South Yorkshire [1992] 1 AC 310.................87n, 88n
Allen v Distillers Co (Biochemicals) Ltd [1974] 2 All ER 365 ....137n
Arnold v Teno (1978) 83 DLR (3d) 609..77n
Ashton v Turner [1980] 3 All ER 890; [1981] QB 137 ....66n, 258n
Attia v British Gas [1988] QB 304..85n, 316n
Austin v Zurich Insurance Co [1945] KB 250 ....381n

Baker v Willoughby [1970] AC 476...116n, 380n
Banque Keyser Ullman v Skandia Insurance [1990] 1 QB 665...........................74n
Barker v St Gobain Pipelines plc [2004] EWCA Civ 545 ....114n
Barnett v Chelsea and Kensington Hospital Management Committee [1969]
    1 QB 428 ....78n
Barrett v Enfield LBC [2001] 2 AC 550...70, 82n
Barrett v Ministry of Defence [1995] 1 WLR 1217 ....80n
Berina (1888) 13 App Cas 1 ....57n
Beswick v Beswick [1968] AC 58..258n
Bevan Ashford v Geoff Yeandle (Contractors) Ltd [1998] 3 All ER 238 ....273n
Biesheuvel v Birrell [1999] PIQR Q40...173n
Bird v Pearce [1979] RTR 369..77n
Bolitho v City and Hackney HA [1998] AC 232...39n
Bolton v Stone [1951] AC 850 ....43n, 45, 186
Bond v Chief Constable of Kent [1983] 1 All ER 456 ....303n
Bradburn v Great Western Railway (1874) LR 10 Ex 1 ....388n
Bradley v Eagle Star Insurance Co Ltd [1989] AC 957.......................................253n
Bretton v Hancock [2005] EWCA Civ 404..247n
Brice v Brown [1984] 1 All ER 997..127n
Broome v Cassell [1972] AC 1027 ....419n

Brown v Roberts [1965] 1 QB 1 ....82n
Buckley v John Allen & Ford Ltd [1967] 1 QB 637 ....134n
Burmah Oil Co v Lord Advocate [1965] AC 75 117
Burns v Edman [1970] 2 QB 541..318n
Bux v Slough Metals Ltd [1974] 1 All ER 262 115

Caparo Industries plc v Dickman [1990] 2 AC 605.............................68n
Capital & Counties plc v Hampshire CC [1997] QB 1004...................79n
Capps v Miller *The Times* 12 December 1988....................................55n
Carmarthenshire County Council v Lewis [1955] AC 549 179
Cassidy v Ministry of Health [1951] 2 KB 343................95n, 180n, 232n
Caswell v Powell Duffryn Collieries [1940] AC 152.................54n, 111n
Cavanagh v Ulster Weaving Co [1960] AC 145 ....38n
Chadwick v British Railways Board [1967] 1 WLR 912................83n, 88n
Chaplin v Boys [1971] AC 356..254
Charlton v Forest Printing Ink Co [1978] IRLR 559...........................301n
Chester v Afshar [2005] 1 AC 134 ....115n
Chief Adjudication Officer v Faulds [2002] 2 All ER 961 ....341n
Chorlton v Fisher [2002] QB 578..247n
Clark v National Insurance Corporation [1963] 3 All ER 375.............237n
Clarke v Vedel [1979] RTR 26...257n
Clunis v Camden and Islington Health Authority [1998] 3 All ER 180..............67n
Cole v South Tweed Heads Rugby Football Club Ltd (2004) 217 CLR 469........79n
Colledge v Bass Mitchells & Butlers Ltd [1988] 1 All ER 536 ....388n
Connelly v RTZ Corporation plc [1998] AC 854 ....168n
Cooke v United Bristol Healthcare NHS Trust [2004] 1 WLR 251 ....160n
Cookson v Knowles [1979] AC 556 ....133, 145n, 159n
Cooper v MIB [1985] QB 575 ....257n
Corfield v Groves [1950] 1 All ER 488...258
Corrigan v Bjork Shiley Corp (1986) 227 Cal Rptr 247 ....168n
Cox v Hockenhull [1999] 3 All ER 577 ....132n
Creutzfeldt-Jakob Disease Litigation; Group B Plaintiffs v Medical Research
    Council (1997) 41 BMLR 157...87n
Crocker v Sundance Northwest Resorts Ltd [1988] 1 SCR 1186 ....79n
CSR Ltd v Eddy [2005] HCA 64...149n
Cutter v Eagle Star Insurance Co Ltd [1998] 4 All ER 417................247n

Daly v General Steam Navigation Ltd [1980] 3 All ER 696...............149n
Davie v New Merton Board Mills [1959] AC 604.............................249
Davies v Eli Lilley & Co [1987] 1 WLR 1136..................................267n
Davies v Swan Motor Co [1949] 2 KB 291.......................................55n
Davies v Taylor (No 2) [1973] 1 All ER 959.....................................279n
Davies v Whiteways Cyder [1975] QB 262......................................143

Davis Contractors v Fareham UDC [1950] AC 696 ....38n
Deep Vein Thrombosis and Air Travel Group Litigation (Re) 3
Deyong v Shenburn [1946] KB 227...75n
Dillon v Twin State Gas & Electric Co (1932) 163 A 111 ....116n
Dimond v Lowell [2002] 1 AC 384..265n
Dodds v Dodds [1978] QB 543...57
Donnelly v Joyce [1974] QB 454 ....151n
Donoghue v Stevenson [1932] AC 562...68, 71
Dooley v Cammell Laird [1951] 1 Lloyd's Reports 271 ....88n
Doughty v Turner Manufacturing Co [1964] 1 QB 518.....................................126
DP & JC v UK (2003) 36 EHRR 183 ....70n
Dunne v NW Gas Board [1964] 2 QB 806..419n
Dunnett v Railtrack plc [2002] 1 WLR 2434 ....274n

Eagle v Chambers (No 2) [2004] 1 WLR 3081 ....137n
Eley v Bedford [1972] 1 QB 155 ....391n

Fairchild v Glenhaven Funeral Services Ltd [2003] 1 AC 32............................113n
Finlay v Railway Executive [1950] 2 All ER 1969...280n
Fitzgerald v Lane [1989] AC 328 ....59n
Fletcher v Autocar Ltd [1968] 2 QB 322 ....251n
Flynn v Commonwealth of Australia (1988) 6 MVR 186 ....50n
Fontaine v Insurance Corporation of British Columbia.....................................94n
Froom v Butcher [1976] QB 268 55
Frost v Chief Constable of South Yorkshire [1999] 2 AC 455 ....87n, 88n

Gaca v Pirelli General plc [2004] 1 WLR 2683..388n, 389n
Gale v Motor Union Insurance Co Ltd [1928] 1 KB 359 ....378n
Gardner v Moore [1984] AC 548 ....258n, 315n, 379n
Gaskill v Preston [1981] 3 All ER 427...391n
Giambrone v JMC Holidays Ltd (No 2) [2004] 2 All ER 891 ....151n
Goldman v Hargrave [1967] 1 AC 645..83, 84
Goodburn v Thomas Cotton Ltd [1968] 1 QB 845..133n
Gorris v Scott (1874) LR 9 Ex 125 126
Gray v Barr [1970] 2 QB 626 ....319n
Gray v CICB (1998)...313n
Green v Russell [1959] 2 QB 226..244n
Gregg v Scott [2005] 2 WLR 268 ....114n, 117
Gregory v Kelly [1978] RTR 426..64n
Griffiths v British Coal Corporation [2001] 1 WLR 1493...............................393n
Griffiths v Brown *The Times* 23 October 1998..79n
Groves v Wimborne [1898] 2 QB 402..96n, 328n
Gurtner v Circuit [1968] 2 QB 587..258

Gwilliam v West Hertfordshire Hospitals NHS Trust [2003] QB 443.....248n, 250n

H v Ministry of Defence [1991] w QB 103 ....166n
Haigh v Ireland [1974] 1 WLR 43...98
Haley v London Electricity Board [1965] AC 778 ....42n
Hall (Arthur JS) & Co v Simons [2002] 1 AC 615..69n
Hall v Brooklands Auto Racing Club [1933] 1 KB 205 ....64n
Halsey v Milton Keynes General NHS Trust [2004] 1 WLR 3002 ....274n
Hamilton v Al Fayed (No 2) [2003] QB 1175...263n
Hardy v MIB [1964] 2 QB 745...319n
Harman v Crilly [1943] 1 KB 68..248n
Hartley v Birmingham CC [1992] 1 WLR 968 ....233n
Harvest Lane Motor Bodies, Re [1969] 1 Ch 457 ....253n
Hatton v Sutherland [2002] 2 All ER 1 ....87n
Hay v Hughes [1975] 1 All ER 257 ....147n
Hayden v Hayden [1992] 1 WLR 986...255n
Heil v Rankin [2001] QB 272 ....165n
Henderson v Merrett Syndicates Ltd [1995] 2 AC 145..78n
Hepburn v Tomlinson [1966] AC 451 ....244n
Hewson v Downs [1970] 1 QB 93 ....391n
Hill v Chief Constable of West Yorkshire [1989] AC 53 ....53n, 82n, 301n
Hinz v Berry [1970] 2 QB 40 ....85n
Hodges v Harland & Wolff [1965] 1 WLR 523 ....166n
Hodgson v Imperial Tobacco [1998] 2 All ER 672 ....275n
Hodgson v Trapp AC 807...391n
Hollis v Dow Corning Corp (1995) 129 DLR (4th) 609 ....115n
Holmes v Syntex Laboratories Inc (1984) 202 Cal Rptr 773...............................168n
Home Office v Dorset Yacht Co [1970] AC 1004................................52n, 81n, 301n
Horsley v MacLaren (The Ogopogo) [1971] 2 Lloyd's Reports 210............76n, 79n
Hosie v Arbroath Football Club Ltd [1987] SLT 122 ....83n
Hotson v East Berkshire HA [1987] AC 750...113n, 117
Houghton v Hackney BC (1961) 3 KIR 615 ....301n
Hudson v Ridge Manufacturing Co [1957] 2 QB 348...81n
Hunt v Severs [1994] 2 AC 350 ....151n, 158n, 255, 389n
Hunter v British Coal Corporation [1988] 2 All ER 97...88n
Hussain v New Taplow Paper Mills [1988] AC 514 ....388n

ICI v Shatwell [1965] AC 656 ....64n, 184n
IRC v Hambrook [1956] 2 QB 641..379n

Jaensch v Coffey (1983–4) 155 CLR 549...87n
Jefford v Gee [1970] w QB 130 ....145n

Jobling v Associated Dairies Ltd [1982] AC 794......................................118n, 380n
Jones v Dennison [1971] RTR 174 ....181n

Kars v Kars (1996) 187 CLR 354..255n
Kent v Griffiths [2001] QB 36..79n
Kingston v Chicago & NW Railway (1927) 22 NW 913...............................116n
Kirkham v Chief Constable of Manchester [1990] 2 QB 283.............66n, 67n, 79n
Kralj v McGrath [1986] 1 All ER 54 ....174n

Lamb v Camden LBC [1981] QB 625 ....128n
Lamb v Cotogno (1987) 164 CLR 1 ....174n
Lane v Holloway [1968] 1 QB 379..319n
Larner v British Steel plc [1993] ICR 551 ....96n
Leakey v National Trust [1980] QB 485 ....83n
Lee v Lee's Air Farming Ltd [1961] AC 12 ....338n
Lefevre v White [1990] 1 Lloyd's Rep 569...232n
Leversley v Thomas Firth [1953] 1 WLR 1206 ....97n
Lim Poh Choo v Camden Health Authority [1979] QB 196; [1980]
    AC 174...143, 148n, 252n, 416n
Lincoln v Hayman [1982] 1 WLR 488 ....391n
Lister v Romford Ice & Cold Storage Co Ltd [1957] AC 555 232n, 249n, 254, 381n
Longden v British Coal Corporation [1998] AC 653 ....388n
Lowe v Guise [2002] QB 1369 ....149n
Lubbe v Cape plc [2000] 1 WLR 1545...168n

McCafferey v Datta [1997] 1 WLR 870 ....280n
McCamley v Cammell Laird Shipbuilders Ltd [1990] 1 WLR 963....................388n
McGhee v National Coal Board [1972] 3 All ER 1008 ....112n
McGlinchey v UK (2003) 37 EHRR 41 ....70n
McHale v Watson (1964) 111 CLR 384 ....181n
McKew v Holand and Hannen and Cubitts (Scotland) Ltd [1969] 3 All ER
    1621...121n, 122, 128n
McNealy v Pennine Insurance Co [1978] RTR 285 ....233n
McWilliams v Sir William Arrol & Co [1962] 1 All ER 623 ....115, 117
Mahony v J. Kruschich (Demolitions) Pty Ltd (1985) 156 CLR 522..............122n
Mallett v McMonagle [1970] AC 168 ....159n
Meah v McCreamer (No 1) [1985] 1 All ER 367..............................67n, 123n, 300n
Meah v McCreamer (No 2) [1986] 1 All ER 943 ....67n, 300n
Medlin v State Government Insurance Commission (1995) 182 CLR 1..........122n
Metropolitan Police Commissioner v Reeves [2000] 1 AC 360 ....79n
Miller v Jackson [1977] QB 966...186n, 446
Mitchell (George) Ltd v Finney Lock Seeds Ltd [1983] 2 AC 803 ....62n
Mitchell v Mulholland [1971] AC 666 ....136, 159n

Monk v Warbey [1935] 1 KB 75 ....247n
Moriarty v McCarthy [1978] 1 WLR 155..161n
Morley v United Friendly Insurance plc [1993] 1 WLR 996.............................237n
Morrell v Owen *The Times* 12 December 1993...44n
Morris v Ford Motor Co [1973] QB 792 ....251n, 381n
Morris v KLM Royal Dutch Airlines [2002] 2 AC 628 ....168n
Morris v Murray [1991] 2 QB 6...64n
Morris v West Hartlepool Steam Co [1956] AC 552 ....38n
Mt Isa Mines Ltd v Pusey (1970) 125 CLR 383 ....88n
Mulcahy v Ministry of Defence [1996] QB 737..69n
Mulligan v Coffs Harbour City Council [2005] HCA 63.....................................81n
Murphy v Brentwood District Council [1991] 1 AC 398......................................82n
Murphy v Culhane [1977] QB 94 319
Murphy v Stone Wallwork Ltd [1969] 2 All ER 949..135n
Murray v Haringey Arena [1951] 2 KB 529 ....64n

Nabi v British Leyland (UK) Ltd [1980] 1 WLR 529..391n
Nagle v Rottnest Island Authority (1993) 177 CLR 423.....................................81n
Naylor v Payling [2004] EWCA 560 ....250n
Nettleship v Weston [1971] 2 QB 691...49n, 250n
Newton v Edgerley [1959] 1 WLR 1031...81n
Ng Chun Pui v Lee Chuen Tat [1988] RTR 298..94n
Nimmo v Alexander Cowan & Sons Ltd [1968] AC 107 ....96n, 97n

O'Dwyer v Leo Buring Wines [1966] WAR 67 ....50n
Oliver v Birmingham & Midland Omnibus Co [1933] 1 KB 35..........................57n
OLL Ltd v Secretary of State for Transport [1997] 3 All ER 897 ....79n
Osman v UK (2000) 29 EHRR 245...70
Owens v Brimmell [1977] QB 859 ....55n, 64n

Page v Smith [1996] AC 155 ....87n
Palfrey v Greater London Council [1988] ICR 437 ....391n
Paris v Stepney Borough Council [1951] AC 367 43
Parry v Cleaver [1970] AC 1 ....387, 388n
Paterson v Chadwick [1974] 2 All ER 772 ....233n
Performance Cars v Abraham [1961] 3 All ER 413 ....116n
Persson v London Country Buses [1974] 1 All ER 1251 ....257n
Phillips v Britannia Hygienic Laundry [1923] 2 KB 832.....................................96n
Phillips v William Whitely [1938] 1 All ER 566..65n
Photo Production Ltd v Securicor Transport Ltd [1980] AC 827 ....62n
Pickett v British Rail Engineering Ltd [1980] AC 136.......................................148n
Pickett v Motor Insurers' Bureau [2004] 1 WLR 2450 ....257n
Pigney v Pointer's Transport Services Ltd [1957] 1 WLR 1121 ....127n

Pitts v Hunt [1991] 1 QB 24...63n, 65n, 66n, 258n
Polemis, Re [1921] 3 KB 560...127
P's Curator Bonis v CICB (1996)..309n

R (Factortame) v Secretary of State for Transport, Local Government and
    the Regions (No 8) [2003] QB 381..262n
R v CICB, ex parte Clowes [1977] 1 WLR 1353...............................310–11
R v CICB, ex parte Ince [1973] 3 All ER 808 ....317n
R v CICB, ex parte Kent and Milne [1998] PIQR Q98.......................317n
R v CICB, ex parte Lain [1967] 2 QB 864 ....307n
R v CICB, ex parte Thompstone [1984] 1 WLR 1234.........................318n
R v CICB, ex parte Webb [1986] QB 184; [1987] QB 74 (CA)........310n, 311, 313n
R v Criminal Injuries Compensation Appeal Panel, ex parte Wade (2000)......313n
R v Daly [1974] 1 All ER 290 ....302n
R v Horsham Justices, ex parte Richards [1985] 2 All ER 1114 ....303n
R v Industrial Injuries Commissioner, ex parte Amalgamated Engineering
    Union (No 2) [1966] 2 QB 31 ....340n
R v Secretary of State for the Home Department, ex parte Fire Brigades'
    Union [1995] AC 513..309n
Rance v Mid-Downs Health Authority [1991] 1 QB 487......................66n
Randall v MIB [1968] 1 WLR 1900 ....257n
Rees v Darlington Memorial Hospital NHS TRust 69n
Reeves v Commissioner of Police of the Metropolis [1998] 2 WLR 401...........67n
Reffell v Surrey CC [1964] 1 WLR 358..429n
Regan v Williamson [1976] 1 WLR 305......................................134n, 147n
Reid v Rush & Tompkins [1990] 1 WLR 212 ....74n, 228n, 250n
Revill v Newbery [1996] QB 567 ....65n, 318
Roberts v Ramsbottom [1980] 1 All ER 7..49, 182n
Robinson v Post Office [1974] 2 All ER 737 ....128n
Rookes v Barnard [1964] AC 1129.........................174n, 419n, 420n
Rootes v Shelton (1967) 116 CLR 383...64n
Rylands v Fletcher...34, 100, 418

St Helen's Colliery Ltd v Hewitson [1924] AC 59..............................338n
Sarwar v Alam [2002] 1 WLR 125 ....264n
Saunders v Edwards [1987] 1 WLR 1116...66n
Sayers v Perrin [1966] QdR 89...127n
Schuster v New York (1958) 154 NE 2d 534.................................52n52n
Scottish Omnibuses v Wyngrove The Times 24 June 1966....................50n
Selfe v Ilford & District Hospital Management Committee The Times
    26 November 1970 ....78n
Shiels v Cruickshank [1953] 1 WLR 533..155n
Sidaway v Governors of Bethlem Royal Hospital [1985] AC 871 ....39n

Smith v Arndt (1997) 148 DLR (4th) 48..115n
Smith v Baker & Sons [1891] AC 325 ....63n, 328n
Smith v BEA [1951] 2 KB 893...245n
Smith v Leech Brain [1962] 2 QB 405...117n, 127n
Smoker v London Fire and Civil Defence Authority [1991] 2 AC 502..............389n
Stapley v Gypsum Mines [1953] AC 663 ....55n
State Rail Authority of New South Wales v Wiegold (1991) 25 NWSLR 500 ...123n
Stephen v Scottish Boatowners Mutual Insurance Association [1989]
    1 Lloyd's Reports 535 ....237n
Stovin v Wise [1996] AC 923 ....79n
Sturges v Bridgman (1879) 11 Ch D 852...445
Suosaari v Steinhardt [1989] 2 QdR 477..50n

Tame v New South Wales (2002) 211 CLR 317 ....89n
Tan Chye Choo v Chong Kew Moi [1970] 1 All ER 266....................................96n
Taylor v Bristol Omnibus Co [1975] 1 WLR 1054 ....393n
Thomas v Quartermaine (1887) 18 QD 685...54n
Thompson v Price [1973] QB 838..134n
Thurston v Todd (1966–7) 84 WN (NSW) (Pt 1) 231 160
Tomlinson v Congleton BC [2003] UKHL 47 ....81n
Topp v London Country Bus (South West) Ltd [1993] 1 WLR 976.................125n
TP & KM v UK (2002) 34 EHRR 42...70n
Transco plc v Stockport MBC [2004] 2 AC 1...100n

Union Carbide Corporation Gas Plant Disaster in India in December 1984,
    Re (1987) 809 F 2d 195 ....168n
US v Carroll Towing Co (1947) 159 F 2d 169...41n

Vairy v Wyong Shire Council [2005] HCA 62 ....81n
Van Oppen v Clerk to the Bedford Charity Trustees [1990] 1 WLR 235...250n, 293n
Versic v Connors (1969) 90 WN (NSW) (Pt 1) 33 ....128n
Vincent v Lake Erie Transportation Co (1910) 124 NW 221 ....185, 186
Vowles v Evans [2003] 1 WLR 1607 ....250n

W v Meah [1986] 1 All ER 935 ....300n
Wagon Mound (No 1) [1961] 1 AC 388...127
Wagon Mound (No 2) [1967] 1 AC 617 ....43n
Waite v North Eastern Railway (1858) El, Bl & El 719; 120 ER 679 ....57n
Ward v James [1966] 1 QB 273...166n
Warren v King [1963] 3 All ER 993n..137n
Warren v Scruttons [1962] 1 Llloyd's Rep 497...127n
Warriner v Warriner [2002] 1 WLR 1703 ....159n
Watson v British Boxing Board of Control [2001] QB 1134............................250n

Watson v Powles [1968] 1 QB 596..144n
Waugh v James Allan Ltd [1964] 2 Lloyd's Reports 1..182n
Wells v Wells [1999] 1 AC 345..158n, 159n
West v Shephard [1964] AC 326...171
White v MIB [2001] 1 WLR 481...257n
Widdowson v Newgate Meat Corporation [1998] PIQR P138............................94n
Williams v BOC Gases Ltd [2000] ICR 1181...389n
Williams v Grimshaw (1967) 3 KIR 610..301n
Wilsher v Essex AHA [1988] AC 1074...113n
Wilson v Ministry of Defence [1991] ICR 595...136n
Winward v TVR Engineering Ltd [1986] Business and Trading Law Cases
   366..50n
Wise v Kaye [1962] 1 QB 638...170n, 171
Withers v Perry Chain Co [1961] 1 WLR 1314..65n
Wood v Bentall Simplex Ltd *The Times* 3 March 1992..50n
Wooldridge v Sumner [1963] 2 QB 43..64n
Wright v British Railways Board [1983] 2 AC 773..145n
Wringe v Cohen [1940] 1 KB 229...101
Wyong Shire Council v Vairy [2004] NSWCA 247...81n

X v Bedfordshire County Council [1995] 2 AC 633...82n

Yuen Kun Yeu v Attorney-General of Hong Kong [1988] AC 175.........................82n

Z v UK (2002) 34 EHRR 97..70n

Part 1

The issues in perspective

1

Introduction: surveying the field

1.1 Compensation for accidents

This book deals with certain kinds of misfortune, and in particular with injury and damage arising from accidents. Although the term 'accident' is a convenient one, its meaning is not straightforward, and some further explanation of the way it is used in this book is necessary. First, the word 'accident' will be used to cover injury and damage inflicted intentionally (as when, for example, one person deliberately assaults another), even though neither the inflicter nor the victim may consider the injury to be 'accidental' in the normal sense. Secondly, the term will not be confined to the technical legal sense – in this sense, injury or damage would be accidental only if it was not a foreseeable consequence of a deliberate or negligent act.

Thirdly, we are sometimes reluctant to refer to injury or damage resulting from natural causes as accidental: we might hesitate to say that a house, the roof of which was blown off by a hurricane, was damaged 'by accident' (although we might say that a person hit by the debris suffered an accident); or we might hesitate to say of a person who died of leukaemia that they died accidentally (although if a person, while on holiday, contracts a rare viral disease and dies soon after, we might call the death an accident). Fourthly, the term 'accident' is often used to refer to injury and damage which is caused by a sudden, non-repetitive, traumatic occurrence; and in this sense it is contrasted with illness or disease, which often develops gradually and has no easily identifiable starting point. The distinction between 'traumatic' accidents and 'non-traumatic' diseases is of considerable practical and theoretical importance in the law,[1] and it will be mentioned at various points.

The scope of this book is not limited to any of these narrower senses of the word 'accident', although its primary focus is on injury and damage for which the law provides some compensation. As we will see, the law distinguishes in many ways, not only between injury and damage resulting from natural causes on the one hand, and human activity on the other (see 1.2); but also between injury and damage of

---

1 J. Stapleton, 'Compensating Victims of Disease' (1985) 5 *Oxford J. Legal Studies* 248; *Disease and the Compensation Debate* (Oxford, 1986). It has been held that suffering deep vein thrombosis as a result of long distance air travel is not an accident within the terms of the provision of the Warsaw Convention 1929 dealing with compensation: *Re Deep Vein Thrombosis and Air Travel Group Litigation* [2005] 3 WLR 1320.

the latter type according to whether the person responsible for it was in some sense at fault. We will be considering to what extent these distinctions are justified. The main questions to be addressed are: for what injuries and damage ought the law to provide compensation? what form should that compensation take? how should it be assessed? and who should pay for it? Important related issues include how compensation systems are administered and how the law seeks to reduce the amount of injury and damage inflicted.

This book is principally concerned with personal injuries and death, and only marginally with damage to property. The main reason for including some discussion of property damage is that it allows some illuminating contrasts to be drawn between different possible ways in which a compensation system can operate. The comparison, for instance, between the way in which tort law works in relation to personal injuries and the way fire insurance works in relation to damage to houses is so significant that it would be wrong to exclude all reference to property damage.

Just as the word 'accident' has a number of senses, the meaning of the term 'compensation' is also far from straightforward. Meanings of the word and the purposes of giving compensation will be considered in detail later (17.1). Here it is sufficient to note that lawyers generally think of compensation as a method of making good a 'loss', of replacing something of which a person has been deprived. Lawyers use the word 'loss' in a rather strange way to include many things that are not losses in a literal sense, such as pain. In the context of personal injury, death and accidental damage to property, compensation has two major purposes. First, it is designed to make good measurable financial losses such as out-of-pocket expenses, income that has been 'lost' in the sense that it can no longer be earned, and the cost of repairing or replacing property which has been physically damaged or destroyed. Secondly, it is designed to make amends for disabilities or loss of faculty, pain and suffering, or death of a close relative. Here also the lawyer thinks mainly of compensating in financial terms: even though the 'loss' has no measurable financial value, compensation in money can be, and is, given.

Another question closely related to those posed earlier is whether, as a society, we are making the most sensible use of the resources devoted to compensation for injury and damage. Even ignoring the controversial question of whether a larger share of national resources should be devoted to such compensation, we cannot fail to ask whether the resources already distributed to the injured and disabled are being sensibly allocated. Do we over-compensate some and under-compensate others? Is there any justification for compensating some people twice over and others not at all for basically similar misfortunes?

The answers to these questions cannot be found by looking at any one segment of the law. It is true that one large chapter of private law – tort law – appears to be central to the questions posed, and a significant part of this book is concerned with tort law. But to concentrate on this segment of private law to the exclusion of other relevant areas of the law would give a very distorted view of the way in which the problem of compensation for misfortunes is dealt with in our society. There are many other methods of compensation, such as the social security system and the criminal injuries compensation system, which deal with disability and bodily injuries. Personal accident insurance is also important – although it operates principally, but by no means exclusively, in the field of damage to property.

Besides being only a part of the picture, in practice tort law operates very differently from the way suggested by a simple statement of the relevant legal rules. The development of liability insurance altered the administration and financing of the tort system[2] out of all recognition. Because the vast majority of tort claims are settled out of court by the defendant's insurance company, the behaviour of insurance companies is at least as important to an understanding of the way the tort system is administered in practice as is the behaviour of lawyers and courts. In practice, most tort compensation is paid by insurers and not by the people who commit torts.

Yet there are very important issues at stake here. If the person responsible for injury or damage to another is not to pay the compensation, then who should pay it? Furthermore, once it is conceded that tortfeasors (i.e. people who commit torts) do not generally pay for the injury and damage they cause, other questions arise. For example, should compensation be assessed differently depending on who will pay it? Again, if the legally responsible party does not pay the compensation, why should people be entitled to compensation only if there is someone legally responsible for the injury or damage suffered? Recognition that most tortfeasors do not personally pay damages, and that most tort damages are paid either by the government or by insurance companies, points to the conclusion that damages are effectively paid for by society as a whole. But this recognition carries many other puzzles in its wake. In particular, it raises the question of the relationship between the welfare state and the tort system. Society's obligation to the injured and the disabled is, it might be thought, discharged by the provision of social security benefits, the national health service and personal health and welfare services. What, then, is the place of the tort system in all this?

In addition to questions of this kind, which arise from the practical operation of the tort system, many complex problems arise from the interrelation of the various systems of compensation operating simultaneously today. Should an injured person be compensated through one system or another? Should an injured person be allowed to collect compensation from more than one source? Should one compensation fund be entitled, having paid out compensation to an injured person, to recoupment from another fund? These questions have been dealt with to some extent by the courts in relation to the tort system. But they also arise in relation to compensation systems, which are rarely the subject of court proceedings. In order to see these issues in perspective and to discuss them rationally, it is necessary to look beyond the rules of tort law.

---

2 The phrase 'the tort system' refers to the relevant rules of tort law and the machinery for using those rules to obtain compensation.

This book is primarily concerned with compensation for injury and damage, but it is impossible to overlook completely the question of accident prevention. Compensation is nearly always second best; prevention should be the first aim. Law can play only a limited part in preventing injury and damage: the skills of mechanics, engineers, psychologists, managers and so on are probably much more relevant. Even when the law is invoked to prevent (or reduce) accidents, it is usually the criminal law which is used; and in our legal system the criminal law does not have a great deal to do with compensating people (although some would like to see this changed). This book does not profess to deal at length with the role of the criminal law in injury prevention, but the claim is often made that compensation systems also perform the incidental role of reducing or preventing accidents, and this subject is dealt with at length in chapter 17.

1.2   Natural and human causes

1.2.1   The issue

We noted earlier that the law draws a distinction between injuries and diseases according to whether or not they are caused by the actions (or inaction) of some human person. In the tort system this distinction marks the line between liability and no-liability because compensation for injury or illness will be recoverable in a tort action only if one of its immediate or proximate causes was the conduct of some human person other than the claimant. This is so even if the defendant to the tort action is a corporation. Normally there will be liability only if the person who caused the injury is identifiable.[3] The Criminal Injuries Compensation Scheme (see ch. 12) is also limited to injuries caused by someone other than the victim. By contrast, the social security system is not so limited in its coverage: it draws no distinction between disabilities with a human cause and disabilities resulting from 'natural causes'. Sickness and incapacity benefits (12.5) are available to all disabled people regardless of the cause of their disabilities. Industrial injuries benefits (12.4.3) are only available in respect of 'injuries arising out of and in the course of employment'; but while it is probably true that most such injuries can be traced to a proximate human cause, the claimant does not have to do this in order to qualify for benefits.

It is important not to confuse the distinction between natural and human causes with the distinction between traumatic injuries caused by accidents (in the sense of sudden, short-lived events), on the one hand, and illnesses and diseases, on the other. Many traumatic injuries (by which is meant injuries resulting from accidents as just defined) can be traced to a proximate human cause, but by no means all can: a person may be struck by lightning, or swept out to sea and drowned, or have a heart attack while driving and run into a roadside pole. Conversely, many illnesses and diseases cannot be traced to any proximate human cause; but one of the great advances in medical science in this century has been the discovery that very many diseases have

---

3 For an exception see 4.2.

human causes.[4] The most we can say is that a greater proportion of traumatic injuries are probably attributable to human causes than of illnesses and diseases; and that illness and disease account for a much greater proportion of human disability than do traumatic injuries (1.4.2). It is also true, as a generalization, that responsible human causes are much harder to identify in the case of many diseases than in the case of traumatic accidents. The result is that, in practice, a much greater proportion of victims of traumatic injuries receive tort compensation (and industrial and criminal injuries benefits) than do victims of illnesses and diseases. If proper attention were to be paid to the compensation of those disabled by disease, the distinction between human and natural causes would have to be abandoned.[5]

The distinction between human and natural causes can produce some striking results. Why, for example, should a child born disabled as a result of negligence, on the part of the doctor who delivered the child, be entitled to substantial compensation from the tort system, while the child born with similar *congenital* disabilities receives no common law damages; or why should a person blinded in a criminal attack be entitled to compensation from the Criminal Injuries Compensation Scheme while a person blinded by a 'natural' disease or by their own actions is entitled only to social security benefits? It has been suggested that 'the view that brain-damaged babies deserve more generous treatment than the congenitally disabled is rooted in the desire for accountability, not compensation'.[6] More generally, it might be argued that compensating victims of human causes at a higher level than victims of natural causes is a way of giving effect to notions of personal responsibility: a person should be required to pay compensation for injuries if, but only if, that person was in some sense responsible for the disabilities. But there are many ways of holding people accountable for their actions other than by making them pay compensation; and even if we accept that compensation for injuries caused by humans ought to be paid for by those who cause them, it does not follow that those injured and disabled by human causes should be treated more generously than those injured and disabled by natural causes.

Nevertheless, if compensation for disabilities was paid by individuals, the argument based on personal responsibility might have some force. However, we will see that most tort compensation is not paid by individuals but by insurers, corporations and the government, and in this light it is less clear why tort-type benefits should only be available to those injured by human action. On the whole, those disabled people who can recover tort damages or criminal injuries compensation are much better provided for financially than those disabled people who must rely on social security benefits alone. Can this be justified in the light of the fact that the tort system and the social security system are, in effect, both financed by the public at large: in the case of the tort system, by insurance premiums paid by potential tortfeasors, and in the case of the social security system, by all those who pay National Insurance contributions and taxes?

4 See Stapleton, *Disease and the Compensation Debate*.
5 Ibid.
6 P. Fenn, 'The No-fault Panacea' (1993) 100 *British J. of Obstetrics and Gynaecology* 103, 104.

1.2.2   Society's 'responsibility' for human causes

One possible answer to this is to say that society is 'responsible' for injuries, diseases and disabilities attributable to human conduct in a way in which it is not 'responsible' for naturally caused conditions because the former are, while the latter are not, caused by people, or by the organization of society in certain ways. What does this mean? It cannot mean that society is responsible for making good the consequences of – or, in other words, is under an obligation to compensate for – injuries with a human cause, because this begs the very question at issue. Society may also regard itself as 'responsible' for those disabled by natural causes in the sense that it regards itself as obliged to maintain them at a reasonable standard of living; and it would involve circular reasoning to justify different treatment of different classes of disabled people by pointing out that society 'accepts responsibility' for them in varying degrees.

We might say that society is responsible for disabilities with a human cause because it is 'at fault' or 'to blame' in respect of them. But this too is a difficult argument to sustain because the concept of 'fault' being used here is very different from the concept of fault we apply to individuals. We might say, for instance, that society is to blame for most road accidents because judges, magistrates, legislators, jurors, the media, highway authorities, and so on, pay insufficient attention to the 'massacre on the roads' and because, as a society, we devote insufficient resources to road safety and to developing safer alternatives to road transport. There is an important difference between this type of judgment and the judgment involved in a finding of negligence. The latter normally implies that the negligent party has paid too much attention to his or her own interests, whereas our system of social decision-making allows those in power to make decisions which are thought to be in the interests of society as a whole, even if they inflict injury or harm on some people. We may all share some of the blame for every road accident, but this is blame in a quite different sense from that embodied in the law of tort.

Another possible meaning of the 'responsibility' of society for disabilities with human causes might be found in the concept of cause. We might say that even if society is not to blame for such disabilities, it nevertheless causes them in a way in which it does not cause disabilities resulting from natural events. There are many illnesses and diseases for which human conduct is in some sense responsible. For instance, much bronchitis is caused by air pollution resulting from human activity, much cancer is caused by smoking (both active and passive), and many diseases are spread by the fact that people are brought into contact with one another in public transport and workplaces, as a result of the way in which society organizes itself. However, responsibility of this diffuse type is very different from the responsibility which attaches in tort law to the proximate human cause of an individual's disabilities, and so it can hardly explain why victims of proximate human causes are better treated by the law than victims of proximate natural causes. Of course, to say that society causes disabilities is to say that people cause them by their actions or inaction. But the human conduct being referred to is usually very much more remote, in a causal sense, from the disabilities than conduct which attracts tort liability. Sometimes it is said that society is responsible for the conduct of individual citizens as when, for example, it is alleged that social deprivation leads people into crime. Even assuming that such a connection could be demonstrated, it would not follow that society should bear the cost of compensating the victims of violence by individual criminals: the responsibility of the criminal is different from the responsibility of society.

There may be good arguments why society should compensate people disabled by human conduct, but these do not depend on the fact that such disabilities are caused by some members of society whether proximately or not, but on the fact that the disabled need help. Therefore such arguments cannot be used to justify different treatment for those disabled by human actions and those disabled by natural causes.

1.2.3   Protecting reasonable expectations

An important aim of a compensation system is to minimize the hardships that arise out of the disappointment of reasonable expectations, in particular, the expectation of regular future income (17.1.2.3). It might be thought that one of the reasons why the law distinguishes between human and natural causes is that human causes of disability tend to strike more suddenly and with little warning, whereas natural causes tend to operate more slowly, thus giving the victim more time to adjust his or her affairs and lifestyle to cope with the disability. However, on examination, this argument has very little force. It is true that being seriously injured or killed in a road accident, for example, is a sudden misfortune. But by no means all traumatic injuries are caused by human actions; even less are they all caused by anyone's fault, and yet the tort system compensates chiefly on the basis of fault. It is also true that some diseases have a gradually disabling effect, but others do not; and a person afflicted with a gradual disease is not necessarily better able, because the disease is gradual, to take steps to ameliorate the misfortune it brings in its wake. Besides, the nature of the disease as either sudden or gradual in effect is not related to whether it is caused by people or by nature.

Perhaps one factor which influences our attitude to whether disabilities from particular causes deserve compensation is the relative frequency of disability from that cause. Serious long-term disability (such as is apt seriously to disappoint expectations) caused by human activities is relatively rare in our society, and so we feel that those unfortunate enough to suffer from it ought to be compensated because they have probably planned their lives and entered commitments on the reasonable assumption that they will not be seriously disabled in this way. Thanks to advances in medical science, serious or prolonged disease and premature death resulting from natural causes are also relatively uncommon today, and people tend to plan their lives on the basis that these misfortunes will not befall them. This might encourage us to feel that compensation is as due here as in the case of disability from human causes.

This would suggest that any argument which justifies compensation on the basis of disappointment of expectations should focus not on the suddenness of the disability, but on its relative frequency and the extent to which people can reasonably be expected to guard against the risk of disability by personal insurance.

1.2.4   Egalitarianism and the problem of drawing the line

Underlying the idea that people ought to be compensated for rare and uncommon misfortunes but not for the common and widespread misfortunes which affect the lives of all or of a large proportion of us, are notions of social equality, that we should all have equal opportunities to enjoy life and to fulfil ourselves. Such notions may lead to the idea that people who suffer unusual losses ought to be helped by being compensated, and that the cost of that compensation should be spread or distributed amongst those members of society who have been fortunate enough not to suffer such losses. These ideas are vividly illustrated by the adoption of the principle of State compensation for war property damage during the Second World War. Sir Winston Churchill explained the genesis of the war damage scheme in his history of the War in the following terms: [7]

> Another time I visited Ramsgate. An air raid came upon us, and I was conducted into their big tunnel, where quite large numbers of people lived permanently. When we came out after a quarter of an hour, we looked at the still-smoking damage. A small hotel had been hit. Nobody had been hurt, but the place had been reduced to a litter of crockery, utensils and splintered furniture. The proprietor, his wife and the cooks and waitresses were in tears. Where was their home? Where was their livelihood? Here is a privilege of power. I formed an immediate resolve. On the way back in my train I dictated a letter to the Chancellor of the Exchequer laying down the principle that all damage from the fire of the enemy must be a charge upon the State and compensation be paid in full and at once. Thus the burden would not fall alone on those whose homes or business premises were hit, but would be borne evenly on the shoulders of the nation.

Here the justice of treating war damage as a charge on the State is clearly rested on the notion of equality. Few would disagree with these sentiments. The question is how far this principle can be extended. In his speech in the House of Commons introducing the War Damage Bill, Churchill pointed out that the principle of State compensation must be limited to direct loss from enemy action and not extend to indirect loss such as loss arising from business failure. But was there any sound reason for this limitation except that a scheme without it would be very expensive?

The difficulty is, of course, to distinguish between those misfortunes we expect people to bear and those which seem sufficiently unusual that their victims deserve our sympathy and financial help. We do not compensate people simply because

---

7 *The Second World War*, vol. II (London, 1949), 308. Churchill was one of the pioneers of social insurance: *Liberalism and the Social Problem* (London, 1909), 309, 315–16.

their natural abilities do not allow them to earn as much as some others, but we do compensate people whose earning power is reduced by a work accident (under the industrial injuries scheme) or by someone else's fault (by imposing tort liability). The social security system compensates earners for income loss resulting from illness or accident, but it does not compensate people who have never been able to work for their inability to do so. Again, people who suffer facial disfigurement in a work accident or as the result of a tort are compensated for their disability as such, but people born with serious facial disfigurement are not. Even if we entirely abandoned the distinction between human and natural causes as a criterion for compensating the disabled, it would not follow that we would compensate everyone whose abilities or endowments were less than normal or average. Some disabilities are just facts of life which we must all bear as best we can. At the end of the day, it might not be possible to draw and justify distinctions between the disabled on any more precise basis than that the notions of human individuality and personal responsibility require people to cope themselves with (or to compensate themselves for) certain types of differences between human beings which disadvantage some people compared with others. Few, if any, advocates of egalitarianism see this notion as justifying or requiring the elimination of all differences between individuals. Such distinctions are bound, however, to appear to some extent ad hoc and arbitrary.

1.3   Mixed systems in a mixed society

We live in a society based on a mixture of political and economic principles. Many aspects of people's lives are regulated by the State, and a significant proportion of people's money is spent by the State. On the other hand, people are entitled, within fairly broad margins, to spend the rest of their money on what they like and to arrange their affairs as they wish. British society runs according to a basic principle that the prices of goods and services should be fixed by supply and demand, so that prices reflect consumer preference; but at the same time, taxes and subsidies may deflect consumer preferences from the directions they would take entirely unaffected by the State's interference. Britain is a society in which there are great inequalities of income and wealth, and in which a substantial degree of inequality appears to be acceptable to many people; but at the same time some of the most extreme and glaring forms of inequality of income are reduced by the taxation and social security systems.

It is not surprising, therefore, that we have a variety of regimes for dealing with the problem of compensation for misfortune. Some misfortunes are so trivial that they are simply accepted as routine ups and downs of life; others are less trivial but are still regarded as something that individuals should protect themselves against, if they wish, by private insurance; still others are seen as sufficiently important to justify the State instituting a coercive system to ensure that compensation is paid to the victim by some other person; and yet others are so important that the State takes upon itself the burden of raising money to provide compensation or to assist victims with benefits in kind.

Obviously the choice of one regime rather than another raises fundamental political, economic and social issues. For instance, how far is a society justified in requiring people to protect themselves against misfortune? Or to put the question in another way, is society justified in instituting a system of compulsory insurance against certain misfortunes? If so, what provides this justification? Again, if some misfortunes are regarded as so serious and so deserving of the interference of the State that it is willing to shoulder the burden of paying compensation, how is this compensation to be funded? Should it be funded by an insurance system in which premiums vary according to the risk insured against, or by a system of flat-rate premiums? Or should the whole system be financed out of taxation? These questions in turn raise important issues about income redistribution.

As for the aim of reducing or preventing injuries, it might seem at first sight that it raises no fundamental political problems. Surely everything possible should be done to prevent at least those accidents that cause personal injuries. On further reflection, however, it will be seen that this is not so. Society does not try to prevent all accidents, even those that cause personal injury. As a society we often have to make choices between objectives: shall we permit such and such an activity even though we know it will cause injuries? In making choices of this nature, there is plenty of room for disagreement on ideological grounds. For instance, we may decide to prohibit or regulate certain types of activity by statutory or administrative machinery; alternatively, we may decide to leave them to be regulated by the operation of a free market.

For example, it is known that young drivers cause more accidents than older ones, and we may want to reduce the number of these accidents. How should this be done? One way is to fix an age below which people are not allowed to drive; this is 16 for a motorcycle, and 17 for a car. Another way is to use the law to require drivers to insure, but to let the market provide the insurance. In this way, young drivers will have to pay higher premiums because, as a group, they cause more accidents than older people, and the costs of road accidents are mostly paid for out of premiums fixed by normal insurance principles. In fact, of course, we use both methods: statutory regulation (fixed age-limits) and the market (variable insurance premiums), but the precise combination of these two methods is largely arbitrary. Why 16 or 17 as the appropriate age limits? And are the extra premiums for young people really 'fair'? If a young person is allowed to drive at all, might it not be urged that they should be treated like older and more experienced drivers?

The distinction between an individualistic and a more communitarian political philosophy affects the choice of compensation systems in many ways. Communitarians tend to favour active State participation in the provision of help and care to those in need, whereas individualists often advocate that the State should just provide a coercive mechanism (such as the tort system) for enabling injured persons to obtain compensation from their injurers if they choose to. Individualists often favour providing assistance in cash, which the recipient can then use as they choose, rather than assistance in kind.

The types and levels of compensation available to members of a particular society will also depend to a great extent on the wealth of that society. In a society which has ceased to depend on subsistence agriculture, the first need of an individual is an income, and loss of income is the loss which ranks highest for compensation purposes; although even in wealthy countries there is room for argument about whether income should be replaced in full, irrespective of the size of the income. If society can afford it, other 'losses' may also be recognized as worthy of compensation – such as loss of bodily function, pain and suffering; and perhaps at the end of the scale, mental distress from insult or indignity.

In Britain today we can in practice distinguish broadly between three different compensation systems according to the level of State involvement. First, there is personal accident insurance through which individuals buy protection against particular misfortunes. In practice – and this must be emphasized – to the extent that damage to property is compensated for, this is done almost entirely through personal insurance. People commonly insure against destruction of their houses by fire. Motor vehicles, too, are often insured comprehensively, which means that the owner will be compensated by their insurer for loss of or damage to the vehicle. Property used in the earning of profits, such as factories or offices, or plant and machinery, is often insured, not only for its own replacement value but also for loss of profit that might result from its being damaged or destroyed. Personal accident insurance can also be bought to provide protection against the risk of personal injury, although this is relatively uncommon. But the State does not force people to buy accident insurance, however prudent it would be to do so.

Despite the lack of direct State involvement in this area, the State does intervene indirectly in various ways. It provides the legal framework within which people can make insurance contracts and enforce them in the courts,[8] and the activities of insurance companies are regulated in certain respects. Many people depend greatly on insurance companies in arranging their affairs, and would suffer significant loss and misfortune if an insurance company failed. There is a great public interest in the solvency of insurance companies; although in Britain, while there are statutory provisions concerned with the solvency of insurance companies (imposing what are called 'capital adequacy requirements'), the way they fix premiums is not controlled.

Secondly, we will consider the compensation system based on tort liability and liability insurance. This system is concerned primarily (although by no means exclusively) with providing compensation for personal injury and consequent loss of income, pain and suffering, and permanent or partial disability; for the death of an earner, causing loss of support to dependants; and for the death of a spouse or a child

---

8 See generally M. Clarke, *Policies and Perceptions of Insurance in the Twenty-First Century* (Oxford, 2004).

who did not support anyone but whose death causes grief and anguish. Here, once again, the State provides the legal framework of rights and obligations and the system of courts to enforce these rights and obligations. In addition, in important areas the State has used its coercive power to require potential tortfeasors to take out insurance against the risk of their being held liable. Users of motor vehicles must insure against liability for personal injury (and property damage) caused by their cars, and employers must insure against liability to their employees for injuries suffered at work. The function of compulsory insurance is not really to protect the insured against the cost of liability but rather to ensure that the victim receives adequate compensation.

Tort compensation is, in theory, usually available only if the injury or damage was caused by someone's 'fault' – a very complex notion, which is examined in chapter 2. In practice, tort liability is further restricted: most successful tort actions arise out of road or industrial accidents. In fact, only a very small proportion of injury victims receive any tort compensation.

The third compensation system to be considered consists of schemes operated directly by the State. The National Insurance system primarily protects workers against income loss, and provides for various needs resulting from illness and unemployment; the industrial injuries scheme (13.4) deals with injuries suffered and diseases contracted at work; the Criminal Injuries Compensation Scheme (ch. 12) compensates the victims of criminal violence to the person. Income support benefits (13.7) provide basic assistance to persons in need who do not qualify for other benefits. In addition to cash benefits, the Welfare State provides a wide range of personal social services useful to those who suffer personal injury – the National Health Service, rehabilitation and employment services, residential accommodation and day centres, home helps and so on. Some groups of the disabled, especially blind people, enjoy special tax concessions. Most social security benefits are available to those with the relevant need, regardless of whether the need was the result of natural causes or human conduct; and, unlike most tort compensation, entitlement to social welfare benefits does not depend on proof that the need was the result of someone's fault.

This social welfare system has very little contact with the tort system or with private insurance systems, although the relationship between them causes problems. Should a person be able to claim both tort compensation and social security benefits? Suppose an injured person receives free medical treatment: can that person recover in a tort claim what it would have cost to have private treatment? Or suppose they have private treatment when free treatment was available: can the cost of the private treatment be recovered in a tort claim? And suppose private treatment is paid for by private insurance: can the cost of the treatment be recovered in a tort claim?

All these issues are dealt with fully later. Here the point to note is how little the tort system and the State welfare system have influenced each other. They are utterly different from each other in structure, philosophy and execution. Tort offers 'full compensation'; social security a good deal less. Tort pays compensation for pain and suffering; social security does not – though it does pay something for some disabilities. Tort compensates in money alone; welfare programmes provide a variety of benefits other than money. Tort pays lump sum compensation; social security payments are nearly all made periodically. Tort depends in practice on liability insurance; social security is financed by a mixture of personal (but compulsory) insurance and taxation. Tort claims are mainly dealt with by private institutions, the insurance companies; social security is administered by the State. The tort system is very much more expensive to operate than the social security system. Above all, tort claims are in the main confined to cases in which fault can be proved against someone covered by liability insurance; in the social security system fault is irrelevant.

As we will see, there are many defects in the tort system as a means of compensating for misfortune and disability; but questions of reform are, unfortunately, often discussed without proper attention being given to the complex interrelationship between these three types of compensation system. The Pearson Royal Commission on Civil Liability and Compensation for Personal Injury (which reported in 1978) paid lip-service to the need to plan reforms in the light of both the tort and the social security systems: 'It is clear to us [the Report said] that the two systems have for too long been permitted to develop in isolation from each other, without regard to the fact that, between them, they meet many needs twice over and others not at all.'[9] Unfortunately, as is explained more fully later, the Report did not seriously and systematically face up to the problems of integrating the two systems.

Fundamental questions of priorities arise both between the existing compensation systems, and between the existing systems and other forms of public expenditure. As an example of the latter, should more money be spent on compensating the injured and disabled and less (say) on schools or roads? This is a political question, and although lawyers must not ignore such issues, they are not legal questions and are not dealt with in this book. Also important is the question of whether society strikes the right balance between accident prevention and compensation for accidents. Would it be more cost-effective to devote a greater part of our resources to accident prevention, even at the expense of what we devote to compensation? If we spent more money on roads, would this enable us to save more than it costs in compensation for road accidents? These are economic questions, but if lawyers are to understand the role of the law properly it may well be necessary for them to consider such questions. They are touched on at various points in this book, though considerations of space, if nothing else, preclude fuller discussion.

Of greater concern to lawyers are issues concerning priorities between the existing systems. For example, should tort compensation continue to be 'full' when social security benefits are relatively low? Should a young childless dependent widow be entitled to be maintained out of tort compensation if her husband is killed by fault, while the social security system expects a childless widow of 44 to

---

9 Report of the Royal Commission on Civil Liability and Compensation for Personal Injury (Cmnd 7054, 1978) (Pearson Report), vol. 1, para. 271.

earn her living if her husband dies a natural death?[10] Should tort benefits continue to be paid for 'pain and suffering' and loss of amenities when social security
benefits for permanent disability are confined to industrial accidents? Should we
continue to allow people to recover compensation from more than one compensation system when many injured people are entitled, at most, to compensation from
one system? Is there any justification for paying more compensation for accidents
at work than for other accidents, as the social security system – but not the tort
system – does? Is there any justification for reducing the compensation payable to
a claimant when the loss is partly the claimant's own fault – which the tort system
does regularly but the social security system very rarely? Should we concentrate
more help on benefits in kind and less on financial assistance? How should the
cost of compensation systems be borne? Should the long-term disabled be treated
relatively more generously than those whose disabilities are short-lived? Should
those whose injuries result from someone's fault be treated more generously than
others? These and many other questions must be answered if our compensation
systems are to operate consistently with one another.

Forty years ago it seemed probable that the steady development of the welfare
state might well supplant the entire tort system in the foreseeable future. New
Zealand led the way with the total abolition of the tort action for damages for
personal injuries caused by accidents, and its replacement by a national accident
insurance scheme.[11] An Australian committee of inquiry advocated a still more
comprehensive scheme that would have brought accidental injuries and diseases
under one national system.[12] However, these proposals were never acted upon, and
are unlikely to be revived in any form in the foreseeable future.

In this country public dissatisfaction with the tort system as a means of
compensating accident victims began to be expressed in the 1960s. A move was
made in 1969 to persuade the Lord Chancellor to establish a Royal Commission
to examine the principles of liability for personal injury.[13] The proposal attracted
some interest among lawyers, and it was subsequently supported by a Committee
chaired by Lord Robens, which reported on Safety and Health at Work;[14] but there
was at first little public interest. However, in the early 1970s, widespread concerns about a spate of compensation claims for congenital defects attributed to
maternal use of the drug Thalidomide suggested significant public dissatisfaction
with existing compensation laws, and the result was the establishment in March

---

10 Bereavement allowance is a contributory benefit payable to bereaved spouses and civil partners
   without dependent children, between age 45 and retiring age, for a maximum of 52 weeks
   (12.4.3.3).
11 Accident Compensation Act 1972. The scheme has been considerably changed since it was first
   introduced: see further 17.1.2.
12 Australian Committee Report.
13 By means of a memorandum prepared by Professor Atiyah and subscribed to by 33 lawyers, par-
   liamentarians and others. See (1969) 119 New LJ 653 for the text of the memorandum and The
   Times, 5 July 1969.
14 See Report of the Committee into Safety and Health at Work (Cmnd 5304, 1972) (Robens
   Committee Report) paras. 448–50.

1973 of the Royal Commission on Civil Liability and Compensation for Personal Injury, chaired by Lord Pearson. The Commission reported in March 1978, but it rapidly became clear that the Report would not provide the basis for any wide-ranging reforms acceptable to the government or the public. The Report did not offer anything in the way of a blueprint for an integrated compensation system, nor even any serious strategy for developing the various existing systems in a co-ordinated fashion. It contained a very large number of recommendations, some of considerable value and some of which would have quite dramatic effects on the number of tort claims (for example, in minor injury cases); it also contained a great deal of valuable data about the operation of the tort system, much of which will be referred to in the relevant places in this book. But apart from leading to a few minor changes in the law, most of the Commission's work bore no fruit.

Renewed concern in the mid-1980s about the cost and delays of the tort system prompted the Lord Chancellor's Department to conduct a Civil Justice Review which led, *inter alia*, to a package of changes in the way personal injury actions were dealt with by the courts, and to the enactment of a provision authorizing the use of conditional fee arrangements for the financing of personal-injury tort claims. In the 1980s the Legal Aid Board (now called the Legal Services Commission) also began investigating and developing ways of facilitating multi-party personal injury actions by changes in legal aid rules and administration. However, the introduction of conditional fees eventually led (in 2000) to the withdrawal of legal aid for the bulk of personal injuries litigation. As a result of a recommendation of yet another inquiry into the civil justice system chaired by Lord Woolf (*Access to Justice*, 1996), major changes (colloquially called 'the Woolf reforms') were made to court procedure with a view to reducing expense and delays.[15]

In the late 1980s, too, considerable pressure built up for piecemeal substantive reform of the tort system. The medical profession, faced with rapidly increasing liability insurance premiums, started pressing for the partial replacement of the tort system with a no-fault compensation scheme for medical misadventure, but the introduction in 1990 of 'Crown (or "NHS") indemnity' (which means that health authorities now pay damages awarded against NHS hospital doctors) took the heat out of the campaign. Proposals by the Lord Chancellor's Department in 1991 for some form of no-fault compensation scheme for minor road accidents were shelved. In the past decade the Law Commission has examined many aspects of the assessment of damages for personal injuries, but this project assumed the continued existence of the tort system and the other compensation systems in their present form. So it seems clear that for the foreseeable future, the basic structure of the different compensation systems is likely to remain unchanged. Apart from anything else, the political climate is unpropitious for any

---

15 See 10.2 for more details about procedure, legal aid and conditional fees.

extension of the welfare state sufficient to render acceptable radical reform or abolition of the tort system.

1.4   Some facts and figures

Before we examine the various compensation systems in detail, it is worth attempting to paint with a broad brush a picture of the nature and extent of the social problems with which they deal. But, first, it is necessary to say something at a general level about the use of statistics. Wherever possible throughout this book, the results of statistical surveys and other empirical evidence are used to illustrate and support the analysis and argument. Those who, like me, have no training in statistics, are not equipped to test the quality of such evidence or the methodology by which it was generated. However, there are various reasons to be very cautious about drawing firm conclusions from such evidence. First, careful researchers are typically explicit about the shortcomings and defects of their methodology: there is a greater or lesser margin of error even in the most meticulous statistical studies. At the other end of the spectrum, however, figures are often given without any indication or explanation of how they were arrived at, arousing the suspicion that they are little more than 'guesstimates'. Such 'junk statistics' are often used for rhetorical or propaganda purposes, to promote a particular cause or point of view. Secondly, statistical information about particular topics often has to be derived from disparate sources that used different research techniques. So the consumer of statistical evidence has to be aware of the danger of comparing like with unlike (as it were). Thirdly, the world changes and life moves on. Statistics, even if highly trustworthy at the time they were collected, can go out of date and may become more or less worthless as the years pass. Fourthly, some important points about the validity of statistics will be obvious even to the innumerate. For instance, statistics about how many people are killed in road accidents, and about the circumstances of those deaths, are likely to be very accurate because most serious road accidents are witnessed, analysed and recorded in detail. By contrast, there has, until very recently, been no system for recording, and analysing the causes of, deaths in hospitals; and so estimates of how many such deaths are the result of negligence, or could have been avoided, are less reliable and more contested than the road fatality figures. Although it is highly desirable that analysis and critique of the law and practice of compensation systems be based on sound empirical evidence, for the foregoing reasons (amongst others) it is important to take a critical approach to the increasing volume of data relevant to the subjects discussed in this book.

1.4.1   Accidents causing personal injury or death

In 2003 about 11,300 deaths by accident were recorded in England and Wales. Some 3,200 deaths were the result of road accidents (roughly the same as the number of deaths by 'intentional self-harm'); about a hundred resulted from other transport accidents, and about 230 from work accidents.[16] Fires caused about 360 deaths. In 1987 it was estimated that as many as 1,000 people die each year as a result of mishaps associated with surgery.[17] In 2002–3 around 800 offences were recorded as homicide (that is, murder, manslaughter and infanticide). The number of deaths in any category should be distinguished from the risk of dying. Although, it seems, more people die in accidents in the home than on the roads, it has been estimated that the risk of dying in a road accident is ten times greater than that of dying in a home accident.[18]

The number of accidental injuries obviously depends on the definition of injury that is used. The Pearson Commission adopted a definition that included only those injuries that resulted in an absence from work of 4 days or more; and for those not at work, an injury of comparable severity. This is a convenient working definition because it fits in with the operation of the social security system which, in general, only provides benefits for those off work for more than 3 days; and it also matches the definition of workplace injuries reportable to the health and safety authorities. But the statistics that follow are gleaned from various sources, and it is not always clear what definition of injury has been used in their compilation. So they should be taken as giving only a very approximate idea of the incidence of accidental injury. Nevertheless, more recent figures have, where available, been used in preference to the Pearson figures because there is good reason to think that in some areas, at least, the Pearson figures may not represent the present position.

The Pearson Report found that there were some 3 million accidental injuries each year in Britain.[19] In 2004 some 278,000 people were recorded[20] as having suffered injury as a result of road accidents; and about 151,000 were reported[21] as having been injured as a result of work accidents. According to the Pearson Commission, some 55,000 people are injured each year as a result of violent crime. It has been estimated that about 11,000 victims of burns need medical treatment each year; and that a third of all accidental injuries requiring medical treatment occur in the

---

16 Like the total number of accidental deaths, the number of deaths on the road has dropped dramatically in the last 35 years from about 8,000 in 1971. For an examination of some of the reasons see R.B. Noland and M.A. Quddus, 'Improvements in Medical Care and Technology and Reductions in Traffic-Related Fatalities in Great Britain' (2004) 36 *Accident Analysis and Prevention* 103; R.B. Noland, 'Traffic Fatalities and Injuries: The Effect of Changes in Infrastructure and Other Trends' (2003) 35 *Accident Analysis and Prevention* 599. The number of employees killed at work dropped from 1,228 in 1961 to 227 in 2002–3 and 220 in 2004–5, largely as a result of changes in employment patterns away from high-risk industries.

17 *Confidential Enquiry into Perioperative Deaths* (Nuffield Provincial Hospitals Trust, 1987).

18 Report of HM Chief Medical Officer, *On the State of Public Health, 1995* (HMSO) – 1:1,000–10,000 as opposed to 1:10,000–100,000.

19 Pearson Report, vol. 2, paras. 16, 22.

20 Department for Transport, *Road Casualties in Great Britain 2004*, table 5c. This figure does not take account of unreported or unrecorded injuries, of which there are thought to be very many. We know, for instance, that road accidents gave rise to more than 400,000 successful personal injury tort claims in 2004–5: 8.3.1.

21 Reportable injuries are those that lead to an absence from work of more than 3 days or fall into one of a number of categories of 'major' injury. It has been estimated that less than half of reportable non-fatal injuries are reported. The 2003–4 Labour Force Survey estimated that there were around 363,000 reportable injuries in that year.

home.[22] It has also been estimated that in 2002 around 2.7 million people suffered injury 'serious enough to warrant a visit to hospital' as a result of accidents in the home; and that another 2.8 million or so suffered such injury in leisure accidents.[23] In 1994 it was suggested that 13,000 cases of permanent disability (and 27,000 deaths) a year may be 'due wholly or partly to medical intervention'.[24] More recent research in several countries suggests that 10% or more of patients admitted to acute-care hospitals suffer an 'adverse event' as a result of 'medical management', and that a significant proportion of these are 'preventable'.[25]

1.4.2   Death and disability from other causes

In order to keep the problem of accidental injury in perspective, it is necessary to appreciate that disabilities attributable to birth defects and to illnesses and diseases resulting both from natural causes and potentially actionable human activity (diseases caused by exposure to asbestos[26] and deformity caused by the drug Thalidomide are examples of the latter) are very much more widespread than those attributable to what we would normally think of as 'accidents'. In 2002, the male death rate from cancer in England was 275.3 per 100,000, and from circulatory disease, 385.2 per 100,000; while the male death rate from 'all accidents and adverse events' was only 23.1 per 100,000 and from road accidents, 9.2 per 100,000.[27] The Pearson

22 *Home Accident Surveillance System 20th Annual Report* (Department of Trade and Industry, 1996). A Department of Health report estimates that each year, 200,000 victims of non-fatal home and leisure accidents spend 4 or more days in hospital: *Preventing Accidental Injury – Priorities for Action* (2002), 5.

23 *24th (Final) Report of the Home and Leisure Accident Surveillance System, 2000–2002 Data* (DTI, 2003), HASS table 1 and LASS table 1 respectively. Research from the Netherlands estimates that three-quarters of injuries leading to medical treatment are the result of home and leisure accidents: S. Mulder *et al.*, 'Epidemiological Data and Ranking Home and Leisure Accidents for Priority Setting' (2002) 34 *Accident Analysis and Prevention* 695.

24 M. Ennis and C. Vincent, 'The Effects of Medical Accidents on Doctors and Patients' (1994) 16 *Law and Policy* 97, 99. A report in 1997 said that infections caught in hospital are solely responsible for 5,000 deaths a year and partly responsible for another 15,000; and that one-third of hospital infections are preventable: *The Times*, 16 September 1997.

25 E.g. C. Vincent, G. Neale and M. Woloshynowych, 'Adverse Events in British Hospitals: Preliminary Retrospective Record Review' (2001) 322 *Brit Med. J.* 517; G.R. Baker *et al.*, The Canadian Adverse Events Study: The Incidence of Adverse Events Among Hospital Patients in Canada' (2004) *Canadian Medical Association J.* 1678; National Audit Office, *A Safer Place for Patients: Learning to Improve Patient Safety* (HC 456, 2005–6). The whole issue of illness, injury and death as a result of medical mishaps has become politically very hot in recent years. In the UK, 2001 saw the establishment of the National Patient Safety Agency, one of the functions of which is to collect data on hospital-patient safety. Its first report, *Building a Memory: Preventing Harm, Reducing Risk and Improving Patient Safety*, was published in 2005. In years to come it should provide valuable data on the incidence of harm resulting from mishaps in hospitals. In Australia, the Australian Institute of Health and Welfare has recently begun collecting data on tort claims against hospital doctors: *Medical Indemnity National Data Collection: Public Sector* (2005).

26 It has been estimated that asbestos-related deaths will peak in 2020 at 3,300 a year. Asbestos will perhaps turn out to be the source of the largest single group of tort claims for illness as opposed to accident. Estimates of the total bill for asbestos compensation go as high as £8 billion. For a wealth of information about asbestos claims in the USA see S.J. Carroll *et al.*, *Asbestos Litigation* (RAND Institute for Civil Justice, 2005).

27 *Health and Personal Social Services Statistics, England*, table A3. Significantly fewer women than men died by accident: 16.8 and 2.8 per 100,000 respectively.

Commission estimated that only about 10% of disabled adults were disabled by injury;[28] and that not more than 1 or 2% of disabled children were disabled as a result of injury, by far the greater number having been disabled as a result of congenital defects, and rather under 10% having been disabled by disease.[29] Even among amputees, for instance, disease accounts for about 77% of the cases, and accidents for only about 18%.[30] In 2004 about 2.4 million people were in receipt of incapacity benefit, but in only about 147,000 cases was the recipient's incapacity attributable to 'injury, poisoning or other consequences of external causes' as opposed to disease and congenital defects.[31] On the other hand, disablement is much more likely to be the result of accident among those of working age than among the old.

Amongst victims of illness and disease, only a very small proportion are victims of disease caused by potentially actionable human activities; but the absolute number of deaths and disabilities attributable to such diseases is undoubtedly significant, and much greater than the number of deaths and disabilities attributable to accidents.[32]

1.4.3   The prevalence of disability

A great deal of information about the extent of disabilities in Britain became available as a result of a major government survey, the results of which were published in 1988–9.[33] This survey estimated that there are some 360,000 disabled children under 16 and 6.2 million disabled adults in Great Britain.[34] These figures by themselves are, however, apt to mislead because the survey adopted a wide definition of disability; and because a very large proportion of the disabled (80% of disabled men and 84% of disabled women) are over normal retiring age. For the purposes of this book, which is mainly concerned with lost income, figures relating to those of normal working age are more important. The survey classified the disabled into ten categories according to the severity of their disabilities, 1 representing the least degree of disablement and 10 the most severe disablement. Table 1 summarizes the findings of the survey.

1.4.4   The effect of disability on income

The OPCS Disability Survey found that the majority of disabled adults live in family units containing no earner. Only a minority of disabled adults under pension age were in paid employment, and the proportion of disabled people who

---

28 Pearson Report, vol. 2, para. 35; but the term 'injury' is not given a precise meaning: Stapleton, *Disease and the Compensation Debate*, 6.

29 Pearson Report, vol. 1, para. 1519; vol. 2, table 54.

30 *Aids for the Disabled* (London, 1968), para. 21.

31 *Social Security Statistics 2004*, Incapacity Benefit, table 4.

32 Stapleton, *Disease and the Compensation Debate*, 6–8.

33 OPCS Disability Survey Reports 1–6.

34 A follow-up study in 1996/7 put the number of disabled adults at more than 8.5 million (20% of the adult population): E. Grundy *et al.*, *Disability in Great Britain: Results for the 1996/7 Disability Follow-Up to the Family Resources Survey* (DSS Research Report No. 94, 1999). The distribution of the disabled according to severity was similar in the two studies.

Table 1. *Numbers of disabled persons in Great Britain by age and degree of disability (thousands)*

Age group	Categories 1–3	Categories 4–6	Categories 7–10
0–15	100	123	137
16–29	125	127	86
30–49	271	273	151
50–59	409	252	131
60–69	713	390	231
70+	1,158	916	858
Total	2,776	2,081	1,594
16–59	805	652	368

worked was much lower than that in the general population. The more disabled a person was the less likely that they would work. Only 2% of disabled adults under pension age in severity category 10 worked, whereas 24% in categories 5 and 6 worked, and 48% in category 1. On the whole, disabled adults in full-time employment earned significantly less than non-disabled adults. The mean equivalent income[35] of non-pensioner family units containing a disabled person was only 72% of that of non-pensioner family units in the general population. And whereas 34% of the former had income less than half the mean equivalent, only 23% of the latter did. The OPCS Disability Survey also found that 23% of families headed by a person under pension age and containing a disabled adult were in receipt of supplementary benefit under the social security system.[36] In 2005, about half of all recipients of income support under the age of 60 are disabled.[37] Table 2 shows the proportion of income received from various sources by family units containing a disabled person (as reported by the OPCS).

The effect of premature death on the income of the deceased's dependants is really impossible to ascertain from available statistics.

1.4.5   Distribution and sources of compensation

The Pearson Report estimated the number of injured persons who received compensation from various sources, and the relative proportions of society's total provision for the injured which was attributable to the various compensation systems. Of the total number of some three million persons suffering an injury (as defined by the Commission), only some 1.7 million, or about 55%, were estimated to receive any financial assistance at all. Some of these received compensation from more than one source, as set out in table 3.

---

35 The equivalent income reflects different amounts of income which different families require to maintain the same standard of living.

36 Which was the main income-support benefit at the time of the survey.

37 *Income Support Quarterly Statistical Enquiry, February 2005*, table IS 1.2.

Table 2. *Sources of income of family units containing a disabled adult by severity of disability (%)*

Severity category	1–2	5–6	9–10	all
Earnings	56	43	18	41
Benefits	30	48	73	49
Other	14	9	9	10

Table 3.[38] *Numbers of injured persons obtaining compensation from different sources*

Source of compensation	Number of new beneficiaries per annum (thousands)
Social security	1,550
Tort	215
Occupational sick pay	1,000
Occupational pensions	4
Private insurance (excluding life insurance)	200
Criminal injuries compensation	18
Other forms of compensation	150
All forms of compensation	1,700

Thus, of the estimated 3 million persons suffering some injury in each year, only some 215,000 (approximately 7%) received any compensation in the form of tort damages.[39] However, the total value of the damages paid to this 7% was almost half of the total value of the social security payments made to the million and a half recipients of those payments. When account is then taken of the administrative costs of the differing compensation systems, the position is even more striking, because the tort system is much more expensive to administer. The figures are set

38 Pearson Report, vol. 1, table 4. The last figure in this table takes account of double counting.
39 D.R. Harris and others, *Compensation and Support for Illness and Injury* (Oxford, 1984) (Harris 1984 Survey) found that 12% of its sample of accident victims obtained some damages through the tort system. This higher figure probably results from the fact that about 40% of the sample suffered 'lasting physical effects' as a result of their injuries. In other words, the sample contained a high proportion of cases involving injuries much more serious than those which met the Pearson definition. The more serious the injuries, the more likely it is (other things being equal), that tort compensation will be claimed and obtained. As we will see later (8.1.4), the number of successful tort claims today is around 750,000 per annum. However, we have no equivalent contemporary figure for the number of persons suffering personal injury (as defined by the Pearson Commission), and so it is impossible to say whether the increase in successful tort claims represents an increase in the proportion of injured persons who receive some tort compensation. According to an estimate made in 2000, some 11.2 million people a year suffer personal injury. If this is correct (and there is no way of knowing), the proportion who recover tort compensation is slightly lower than the Pearson estimate.

Table 4.[40] *Cost of compensation paid from different sources to injured persons and administrative costs of payments, average over 1971–6 (1977 currency values)*

Source of compensation	Annual payments (£s)	Administrative costs p.a. (£s)
Social security	421 million	47 million
Tort	202 million	175 million
Occupational sick pay	125 million	*
Occupational pensions	5 million	*
Private insurance (excluding life insurance)	51 million	*
Criminal injuries compensation	17 million	1.7 million**
Other forms of compensation	6 million	*

* No estimates provided by the Pearson Commission
** Estimates based on reports of Criminal Injuries Compensation Board

out in table 4, from which it will be seen that of the total cost of compensation paid (on average in each of the years 1971–6) of some £1 billion, the tort system accounted for no less than £377 million.

Thus 7% of the accident victims accounted for perhaps 37% of the total cost (payments plus administration) of the compensation paid out (making some allowance for the unestimated administrative costs). It must be pointed out at once that the 7% who received tort damages certainly included a disproportionate number of the more seriously injured, so that one would not expect the tort victims to have received only the same proportion of payments as their number bears to the whole. Nevertheless, it seems that, even allowing for this fact, the beneficiaries of the tort system came off remarkably well compared with all the other injured. Indeed, their position was even better than is indicated by this table because many of those who obtained payment of tort damages would also have been beneficiaries under one or more of the other compensation systems. For example, about three-quarters of those who received tort damages would also have received social security payments,[41] and many of these would also have received occupational sick pay.[42]

Furthermore, the vast majority of those who receive tort compensation are the victims of accidental injury. Only a very small number of those disabled from birth or by illness or disease receive tort damages, not only because very many such disabilities are the result of natural causes but also because, even if a particular victim's disability was the result of intentional or negligent human action, it will often be very difficult or impossible to prove this with the degree of cer-

40 Based on Pearson Report, vol. 2, table 158.
41 Concerning the present position regarding cumulation of tort damages and social security payments see 15.4.5.
42 Pearson Report, vol. 2, para. 52.

tainty the law requires. Most people disabled by illness or disease must rely on various social security benefits. So we have a situation in which (according to the Commission's estimates) a very small proportion of the disabled received about half of total compensation payments. Although we do not have equivalent contemporary statistics, there is no reason to think that the basic picture is significantly different today.

Preferential treatment of certain groups of the disabled does not end here. In addition to compensation for loss of income, those fortunate enough to be compensated under the tort system, the criminal injuries compensation system, or the industrial injuries scheme, may also receive compensation for 'loss of faculty', or the disability as such, regardless of whether it causes any loss of income. For example, a person who loses sight in one eye may receive up to £36,000 if there is a tort claim, or a disablement pension of around £36 per week if they qualify under the industrial injuries scheme, even if the claimant's earning power is quite unimpaired. A disabled person who cannot claim under any of these schemes will not receive any compensation for disability as such, even if they receive some compensation for loss of earning power. We will meet such distinctions between different groups of the disabled time and again, and it is necessary to ask whether there is any justification for them.

1.4.6   The more serious and the less serious

Of the very large number of injuries (even as defined by the Pearson Commission) it is clear that the greater number are of a relatively minor character; and, although statistics are lacking, the same is also certainly true of disabilities caused by diseases. For every person who is off work for months, hundreds are off work for weeks; and for every one off for weeks, scores are off for days. For every one who loses a leg or an arm or an eye, hundreds of others suffer nothing worse than scratches and bruises. For every person totally blind there are many more partially sighted. For every person who cannot walk, many more have difficulty in doing so. For example, in 2002–3 the rate of reported 'major' work injuries amongst employees was 113 per 100,000 whereas the rate of (less serious) injuries that caused an absence from work of more than 3 days was 501 per 100,000.[43] Of those who were absent from work as a result of a workplace injury suffered in 1989–90, 42% were away for only part of a day, 13.4% were away for between 4 and 7 days, and only 3.7% were absent for over 3 months.[44] The Pearson Commission found that most disablement pensions awarded under the industrial injuries (social security) scheme are paid for under a year; and only about 30% are still being paid 3 and more years after they are awarded.[45] Of the 245,000 recipients of disablement pensions in 1996, some 133,000 were assessed at 24% disabled or less; most recipients were assessed at between 20 and 54%. Only 12,000 were assessed

43 *Health and Safety Statistics Highlights 2002/3*, 30.
44 *Employment Gazette*, December 1992, 628, table 12.
45 Pearson Report, vol. 2, table 7.

at 65% disabled or above; and only 5% were assessed as between 85 and 100% disabled.[46] Of the 1,710 people assessed as suffering a prescribed disease under the industrial injuries scheme in the March quarter of 2005, 1,090 were assessed as less than 25% disabled, and only 420 were assessed as more than 55% disabled.[47] Similarly, of the persons who received tariff awards from the Criminal Injuries Compensation Authority in 2002/3, 60% suffered injuries assessed at the lowest 5 (out of 25) tariff levels, and only 3 out of more than 42,000 recipients of awards were assessed at the highest level.[48]

Translate bodily injuries into financial losses and the position is the same. For everyone who counts their losses in thousands of pounds there are many more who count their losses in hundreds of pounds. One survey among those who recovered damages in respect of industrial injuries found that 20% received less than £100 each, another 25% recovered between £100 and £249, while only 19% obtained more than £1,000.[49] The Pearson Commission's own survey among 3,302 injured persons showed that 19% had no income loss at all (after allowing for sick pay), that 67% incurred income loss of under £100 (1973 currency values), some 3.7% had losses of between £500 and £999, and only 2.2% had losses exceeding £1,000.[50] A study of insurance company payments, also made for the Pearson Commission, showed that in the month of November 1973, nearly half the payments were of less than £200, and only 1% exceeded £5,000.[51] The Harris 1984 Survey (based on data collected in 1976–7 from 169 persons who received tort damages) found that the mean amount of damages was £1,135 while half of the respondents received less than £500.[52] A large study conducted in the 1990s found that of 80,000 personal injury claims for which legal aid was granted 70% resulted in total damages of less than £5,000, and 80% in total damages of less than £10,000.[53]

It is plain that long-term disability and chronic sickness raise social and financial problems for the victim and the victim's family different in kind from those raised by short-term sickness or minor injuries.[54] Many (but by no means all) families can weather a short period of lost or reduced income without great hardship. Savings can be used; borrowing can be relied on; payment of bills deferred; expenditure can be cut down for short periods. So also minor disabilities that do not

46 *Social Security Statistics 1997*, table F2.05
47 *Industrial Injuries Disablement Benefit Statistics: Quarter ending March 2005*, IIDB 2.7. As we shall see later, even 100% disablement is far from representing complete helplessness.
48 Criminal Injuries Compensation Authority, *Annual Report 2002/3*, table 1.
49 TUC Evidence to the Pearson Commission, table 6 (1977 currency values).
50 Pearson Report, vol. 2, table 78.
51 Ibid., para. 522.
52 Harris 1984 Survey, 86–91.
53 Law Com. No. 287, *Pre-Judgment Interest on Debts and Damages* (2004), para. D33. The fact that the cases were legally aided probably means that they were not the very smallest in value.
54 Recent research confirms what might be expected, namely that the incidence of long-term health problems is much greater amongst accident victims than among the general population: Law Com. No. 225, *Personal Injury Compensation: How Much is Enough?* (1994), 53–9.

affect earning power can be tolerated and lived with, even though they may be permanent or long-lasting. But long-term or permanent income loss or reduction, or permanent disabilities, are far more serious.

On the other hand, it is also the case that although a very small proportion of accident victims suffer serious injury or heavy financial loss, they receive a very considerable proportion of total payments of compensation. For instance, claims for medical negligence in respect of birth-related brain damage represent only 5% of claims against the NHS, but account for more than 60% of total expenditure on medical litigation.[55] The Pearson Commission's study of insurance payments found that 1% of payments accounted for no less than 23% of the sums paid.[56] A recent survey of medical negligence cases found that the top 10% of successful claims by size of payment accounted for 76.1% of the total amount paid out, while the bottom 50% by size accounted for only 3.5% of the total paid.[57] Among the recipients of criminal injury awards in 1979–80, 2% (or 356 out of 17,460) received approximately £4.2 million, or 26.8% of the total sum paid out under the criminal injuries scheme during that year.[58]

One conclusion of vital importance can be drawn from these facts, namely that insistence on equal treatment for all cases is likely to prejudice satisfactory treatment of the more serious cases because the impact of long-term serious disability on people's lives is likely to be relatively much greater than the impact of short-term minor disability. To be satisfactory, a compensation system must achieve a proper financial balance between treatment of more serious cases, on the one hand, and of less serious, on the other. If we attempt to treat all cases alike, the paradoxical result is that we end up in practice by treating the more serious and deserving cases less generously. If one person is off work for 6 months and loses £10,000 in wages, and another person is off work for 2 days and loses £200 in wages, and we cannot afford to compensate them both in full, equality of treatment might suggest, for example, that we pay the first person £5,000 in compensation and the second person £100 in compensation. Yet this would probably cause much greater hardship to the first person than the second.

Moreover, we know that large sums can be saved by eliminating the smallest claims altogether. Although the smallest claims may not in aggregate be as great as the few much larger claims, they still represent a substantial proportion of the total sums paid out. They also account for a very large percentage of the administrative costs of any compensation scheme, since these costs are proportionate to the number of claims as well as to the size of the claims. Administratively it is likely to cost far more to process one hundred claims for £100 each than one claim for £10,000 (even though the cost of processing a claim for £10,000 will probably be greater than the cost of processing a claim for £100); and this is true whether

55 Department of Health, *Making Amends: A Report by the Chief Medical Officer* (2003), 47.
56 Pearson Report, vol. 2, para. 522.
57 P. Hoyte, 'Unsound Practice: The Epidemiology of Medical Negligence' [1995] *Medical LR* 53.
58 *CICB Sixteenth Report* (Cmnd 8081, 1980), para. 8 (latest available figure).

the administration of the system is in the hands of courts, insurance companies, the Department for Work and Pensions (DWP) or anyone else. Thus by refusing to pay any compensation to the person who has lost £100 we might be able to afford to pay very much more to the person who has lost £10,000, because for every one who has lost £10,000 there will be scores if not hundreds who have lost only £100. In the USA it has been calculated that the cost of workers' compensation programmes can be reduced by no less than 17% by the simple expedient of denying benefits for the first 7 days of incapacity unless the incapacity lasts more than 28 days.[59]

We shall see later that most of the compensation systems in operation today go some way to meet the point being made here by eliminating the smallest claims. Only the tort system clings to the principle of full compensation for all claimants. There is a good case not only for eliminating certain small claims but, in addition, for increasing the proportion of compensation payable in cases of more serious or lasting injury. Since the tort system professes to make full compensation for all injuries, it does not, in theory, allow the more seriously injured to be treated relatively more generously than the less seriously disabled. In practice, however, as we shall see later, the tort system does the converse and treats those with minor injuries relatively more generously than those with serious injuries. Sick pay schemes, also, understandably tend to be more generous to those off work for short periods than to those with chronic disability. Of existing compensation systems, only the social security system treats the long-term and more seriously disabled relatively more generously than those who suffer minor and short-term disabilities.

Another vital question, arising from these considerations, concerns the strategy for future improvement. There seems no doubt that in the long run society will, within the limits of its resources, gradually improve the provision it makes for the accident victim, the disabled and the sick. This has been happening for many years, and there is every reason to expect the process to continue. The crucial question, however, is whether the process is to continue along a broad front, with steady but necessarily slow improvement in the position of all those similarly placed; or, alternatively, whether some more fortunate groups among the afflicted are to be permitted to advance ahead of others similarly placed. For example, are tort victims to be permitted to continue reaping the great financial advantages of the tort action, as compared with those unable to recover tort damages? If so, is the value of tort damages to continue to be improved, as has been happening for some time, so that the disparity in treatment becomes even greater? Are accident victims to continue to receive favoured treatment as compared with victims of disease? Or, alternatively, are all those unable to earn an income because of incapacity to be treated equally, and perhaps not very generously at the outset, so that improvement will

59 *Report of the National Commission on State Workmen's Compensation Laws* (Washington, 1972), table 3.5.

come gradually for all? Are tort-type benefits to be provided for new classes of victims unable to prove fault? And if so, on what principle are these new classes to be selected, if indeed there is to be any principle at all other than that of giving most to those with the loudest voices? These are difficult questions to which we shall return at various points.

Part 2

The tort system in theory

2

Fault as a basis of liability

2.1 The conceptual basis of tort law

The aim of this Part is to explain the main features of tort law as a system for compensating for personal injuries and death, and to examine its main theoretical defects as a compensation mechanism. We will focus on tort law because most claims for damages for personal injuries and death are 'made in' tort; although occasionally such a claim may be 'made in' contract or based on some statutory cause of action. The boundaries of a legal subject are not set by divine prescript but by the custom of lawyers. Tort law as a separate legal subject is largely a product of the systematizing activities of academic lawyers in the nineteenth century. This body of law deals with a variety of social and economic problems that may be classified in a number of different ways, for instance, by looking at the interest of the person who complains of some injury: are they complaining about deprivation of liberty; injury to their person or feelings; damage to property, or the invasion of land; damage to reputation or invasion of privacy; injury to relations between members of a family; damage to trade or business? Alternatively, problems may be looked at in terms of the cause of the injury: who caused it; was it caused intentionally, maliciously, negligently or without 'fault' on the part of anyone; did the injured person play a part in causing the injuries?

A third way of classifying problems is according to the relationship between the claimant and the defendant. For example, the liability of an employer to employees could be isolated as a subject for legal treatment on its own, and so also could the liability of a manufacturer of products to a consumer injured by the use of the product. Similarly, the liability of a landowner to neighbours, and the liability of one road user to another, could be, and to a limited extent are, studied as separate parts of tort law.

The result of all this is that the conceptual structure of tort law is disorganized and ramshackle.[1] On the one hand, we have the tort of negligence, which is based on the blameworthy nature of the tortfeasor's conduct and which covers not only injury to the person and damage to property, but also, to some extent, purely financial loss. On

---

1 See generally P. Cane, *The Anatomy of Tort Law* (Oxford, 1997).

the other hand, we have a collection of 'specific' torts. Some of these are based on the interest they protect (e.g. defamation, malicious prosecution and wrongful imprisonment), others on the relationship between the parties (e.g. some types of nuisance, and the form of liability known as the rule in *Rylands* v. *Fletcher*) and yet others on a combination of the two (as with the 'economic torts' such as intimidation and interference with contractual relations). Much of tort law is judge-made, but there is an increasing number of 'statutory torts' created by legislation, such as 'strict' liability for defective products (which is discussed in ch. 4). Of all these torts, the tort of negligence is the most important for the purposes of this book because tort liability for death and personal injury is most commonly based on the rules of the law of negligence.

2.2   Negligence as a basis of liability

A loose synonym for 'negligence' is 'carelessness'. To behave negligently is to be careless. But lawyers also say that negligence is a 'distinct tort'. What this means is that damage caused by negligent conduct is generally actionable irrespective of the kind of activity out of which the damage arose. The tort of negligence thus extends over the whole sphere of human activity and is not confined, as are most other torts, to particular types of conduct or activity. It concerns the way in which activities are carried out, and not any particular activity; and it protects a variety of interests. However, in practice the law of negligence is largely concerned with certain consequences of two particular activities, that is, with bodily injury and, to a lesser extent, damage to property suffered on the roads and in the workplace.

Actions for damages for personal injuries constitute a significant proportion of all civil litigation in Britain today. Moreover, we know that for every action for damages for personal injuries that comes up for trial in court, another ninety-nine claims are settled by negotiation. The total amount of money that changes hands as a result of negligence cases (including settlements) is very large. It is true that the maximum amount involved in a single personal injury or fatal accident claim is relatively small compared with the maximum that may be involved, for example, in a single commercial claim arising out of an important contract; but the total value of personal injury and fatal accident claims is great. In quantitative terms, the tort of negligence is of great importance in the process of compensating people for unintentional personal injury.

The tort of negligence is said to consist of three elements: first, a duty to take care; secondly, a breach of that duty; and, thirdly, damage caused by that breach of duty. This third element can be subdivided into two further elements, namely that the tortfeasor's conduct must have been the 'cause in fact' of the damage; and, secondly, that it must have been the 'legal cause' of the damage. The second element ('breach of duty') is concerned with the definition of negligent (or, loosely translated, 'careless') conduct. Negligence is a species of 'fault', and it is with this that the remainder of this chapter deals. The other two elements of the tort are examined in later chapters.

2.3   The fault principle

Apart from negligence, the other main species of fault recognized by the law of torts are intention and recklessness.[2] To harm someone intentionally is to do some act with the aim thereby of inflicting injury, loss or damage on that person. To harm someone recklessly is to do some act realizing that it may result in injury, loss or damage to that person. Negligence consists of failure to take reasonable precautions against risks of injury to others that one ought to have foreseen and guarded against. Some claims for damages for personal injury or death arise out of intentional or reckless conduct, but the vast majority arise out of negligent conduct. In a few instances, as we shall see in chapter 4, a claim for damages for personal injury or death may be made against a person even if that person has not been at fault in any of the above senses. But in general, tort liability for personal injury and death is based on fault. To say that a person was at fault is to say that they should have behaved differently in some respect.

Traditionally, the fault principle is seen as having two aspects: it has generally been used both as a sufficient and (with a few exceptions) a necessary condition of and justification for the imposition of liability to pay tort damages for personal injuries and death. In other words, the principle asserts, first, that a person who causes injury, loss or damage to another by fault should be required to compensate that other; and, secondly, that a person who causes injury, loss or damage to another without fault should not be required to compensate that other. But, as we shall see, the fault principle, as it operates in tort law, also requires us to take account of any fault of the claimant (C)[3] that causes injury, loss or damage to C. We must, then, expand the first proposition as follows: a person who causes injury, loss or damage, *whether to themselves or to another*, should bear the burden of that loss or damage to the extent that it was caused by their fault. Of course, it is a corollary of the second proposition that a person who suffers loss as a result of events that were no-one's fault, must bear that loss personally unless compensation is available from some other source.

As between an individual claimant and an individual defendant, these two propositions stated in this general form seem perfectly just. But the fault principle suffers from serious defects, which will be examined in chapter 7.

The notion that tort liability should be based on fault has had a powerful influence on the minds of people generally and of lawyers in particular in the last century or more, and it still exerts great force. Even (proposed) schemes of 'strict' liability (or 'liability regardless of fault', e.g. product liability)[4] usually contain

---

2 See generally P. Cane, '*Mens Rea* in Tort Law' (2000) 20 *OJLS* 533.

3 For centuries, the party who initiates a legal claim under English law was called the 'plaintiff'. Now the term used is 'claimant'. In this book, the new term is used even in relation to events and cases in the long period before the change. In Scots law, the term for a plaintiff is 'pursuer' and for a defendant, 'defender'. Some of the cases discussed in this book originated in Scotland because the House of Lords is the final court of appeal for Scotland as well as England. But for the sake of simplicity, even in relation to such cases, the terms 'claimant' and 'defendant' will be used.

4 See further ch. 4.

numerous concessions to the fault principle. As we will see in due course, there have been many legal developments in the last 80 years or so which have been designed to facilitate the operation of the fault-based tort system of accident compensation. These include the system of compulsory third-party insurance to cover liability for road accidents, and of compulsory insurance to cover liability of employers to their employees. There is also a body called the Motor Insurers' Bureau (MIB) which is designed to fill the gap in the compulsory motor insurance system caused by failure of vehicle owners to insure in accordance with the legal requirements; in addition, the MIB accepts liability in some hit-and-run cases and in cases where the party at fault was insured but the insurer has become insolvent.

Much other legislation has been passed which has improved the operation of tort law as a compensation mechanism: the Law Reform (Miscellaneous Provisions) Act 1934 allows actions to be brought against the estate of a deceased negligent person; the Law Reform (Contributory Negligence) Act 1945 changed the law to allow claimants to recover some damages despite having contributed by their own negligence to the injuries suffered; the Law Reform (Personal Injuries) Act 1948 abolished the doctrine of common employment and enabled employees to sue their employers where they suffered injury as a result of the negligence of a fellow employee; and the Occupiers' Liability Acts of 1957 and 1984, among other things, simplified the law concerned with the negligence liability of occupiers of premises to visitors.

Outside tort law, too, there have been legal developments based on the idea that the fault principle provides a sound basis for a compensation system. Most notably, under the Criminal Injuries Compensation Scheme (discussed in ch. 12), entitlement to compensation depends on proof that someone was at 'fault' in the sense of having committed a criminal act against the claimant.

In the rest of this chapter, we will examine the nature of negligence as a species of fault.

2.4   Negligence as fault

2.4.1   A question of fact?

A requirement of success in an action based on the tort of negligence (or 'in negligence' as lawyers say) is proof that the defendant was negligent. 'Negligence' means failure to take that degree of care which was reasonable in all the circumstances of the case, or failure to act as a reasonable person[5] would have acted. The question of whether a person acted reasonably or not is often said to be a 'question of fact', but this is a misleading expression. It is necessary to distinguish between primary facts and inferences or evaluations. What actually happened; how an accident occurred;

---

5 The classic phrase is 'the reasonable man'. Without entering into a discussion of whether the standard of the reasonableness is gender specific, in this book the word 'person' is used instead of 'man'. For a brief discussion see Cane, *The Anatomy of Tort Law*, 43–4.

whether the claimant did this or the defendant did that; what part was played by third parties, and so forth – all these are questions of primary fact. Usually the judge decides what the primary facts of the case were after hearing the evidence. Sometimes there is no dispute about the primary facts: everyone agrees about what happened. Sometimes it is not possible to reach any satisfactory conclusion about the primary facts because the evidence is fragmentary – perhaps because the parties were killed in the accident, or because the defendant is the only person who knows what happened and takes refuge in silence, or for some other reason. In such circumstances the judge is still bound to make 'findings of fact'; that is, to determine, in accordance with certain rules of law, procedure and evidence, what facts shall be assumed to be the primary facts. The judge may hold particular facts to be established because the contrary has not been proved, or because of some legal presumption, or because they are reasonable inferences from what has been proved, or for some other reason.

When all findings of fact that are necessary or relevant have been made, the judge will proceed to the second stage of the negligence inquiry, which is that of making a judgment: given the findings of fact, was the defendant negligent? Although this is also often referred to as a question of fact, this is a somewhat unfortunate usage. It is quite true that in certain ways a finding of negligence is treated as a question of fact – for instance, a decision of this kind cannot technically constitute a precedent for future cases. But in many other respects a finding of negligence is treated rather like a decision on a question of law. For example, appeal courts are sometimes prepared to reverse such findings, while they are very reluctant to disagree with a trial court's findings of primary fact. It cannot be *proved* that a person was negligent; one can merely *argue* that the person was negligent and hope to persuade the judge by argument.

At all events, a finding that a defendant was negligent clearly involves making a value judgment on that person's conduct; and it is therefore necessary to discover what criteria are employed in the process of making that judgment. The conventional answer to this question invokes the somewhat mystical figure of the reasonable person. A person is negligent if they fail to take the degree of care that a reasonable person would or does take. But this raises the further question of what 'reasonable' means. Is the reasonable person black, coloured or white? Male or female? Young, middle-aged or old? Christian, Muslim or of some other, or no, religion? Rich, poor or averagely affluent? Perhaps none of these differences between people is relevant, for instance, to questions about how a reasonable person would drive a car, but some or all of them may be thought to be relevant in some contexts. To complicate matters further, what the law says is that people should behave in the way that a reasonable person *in their position* would behave. This formulation allows the court to invest the reasonable person with characteristics that the defendant actually possesses. For example, in an action against a surgeon, the standard of reasonableness is that of the reasonable surgeon, not the reasonable GP. However, it is largely up to the court to decide which of the characteristics of the defendant to attribute to the reasonable person. In fact, the reasonable person is an abstraction whose characteristics are invented by the judges. Lord Radcliffe once said that the reasonable person was 'the anthropomorphic conception of justice';[6] which, in the context of the tort of negligence, means that a person is negligent if they fail to take that degree of care which justice requires should be taken. However, this tells us nothing about the characteristics of the reasonable person except that they are a function of ideas of justice and sound behaviour about which people (and judges) might justifiably disagree.

Would it help to equate the reasonable person with the 'average person'? A statistician might reject the idea that there is such a person as the 'average person';[7] but in some contexts, at least, it may be possible to find out how people generally behave or react to given situations. Suppose, for instance, that an employee is injured by a machine in a factory, and alleges that it was negligent of the employer to use the machine without taking certain precautions. Is it any help to find out whether other employers do the same? Suppose we find that the great majority of employers who use this machine also do not take the allegedly required precautions. Is this not evidence that at least the 'average employer' would not regard it as necessary? The (legal) answer is that it is, and the courts give considerable weight to the practice of employers in this respect. The courts also give considerable weight to the practice of professional and business people in arriving at decisions on questions of negligence. To some extent decisions of this kind are probably based on the feeling that a person should not be blamed for doing what everybody else does, and a court may be reluctant to consider the issue of whether the common practice was itself negligent. But to some extent also, a decision of this kind may be based on acceptance by the court of the standards of the community, so that although a judge may personally feel that the common practice is unsatisfactory, he or she may subordinate that view to the practice of the community. In this way, the concept of the average person may be of assistance to judges in helping to set the standard of care in particular circumstances.

This does not mean that negligence consists simply of the failure to observe normal or usual precautions in a given situation or, conversely, that observance of normal or usual precautions cannot amount to negligence. The courts have never accepted that they are precluded from finding negligence even in the face of widespread and long-standing practice.[8] If it were alleged that a driver was negligent in driving across a road junction without stopping, it would not help much to prove that 90% of drivers did the same. On the other hand, where professional negligence is alleged, for example, against a doctor, the fact that the defendant observed the care or precautions customarily practised by a body of professional colleagues considered by the court to be reputable, will usually lead a court to hold that there has

---

6 *Davis Contractors* v. *Fareham UDC* [1950] AC 696, 728.
7 R. Powell, 'The Unreasonableness of the Reasonable Man' (1957) 10 *Current Legal Problems* 104.
8 *Morris* v. *West Hartlepool Steam Co.* [1956] AC 552; *Cavanagh* v. *Ulster Weaving Co.* [1960] AC 145.

been no negligence, even if a majority of members of the relevant professional group would have acted differently.[9] The effect of this latter approach is to give professionals, especially doctors, considerable protection from negligence liability. These examples show that at the end of the day the concept of reasonable conduct depends more on value judgments by courts than on observations about what people generally do.

Anyway, given the many differences in outlook and behaviour between people who live in our pluralistic society, the notion of the average person may, in many contexts, be very difficult to invest with any concrete meaning. There may be no relevant common practice that can be treated as reasonable behaviour, and people may genuinely disagree about what would constitute reasonable behaviour in particular circumstances. The standard of behaviour against which the defendant's conduct is measured is a standard decided on, and inevitably decided on, by judges.

Why does the law continue to utilize the largely fictional figure of the reasonable person? The answer appears to be, in order to obscure the role of the judge as policy-maker. Judges in this country have traditionally eschewed the role of policy-maker: they continue to proclaim that they are not concerned with policy but only with law, and it is possible that the public prefers it this way. For many people, 'impartial justice' means justice without policy. If a judge were to say to a defendant: 'You have failed to do what I think you should have done and that amounts to negligence', the defendant may come away thinking of the judge, 'Who are you to tell me that?' But if the judge says: 'You have failed to do what the reasonable person would have done, and that amounts to negligence', the defendant may come away with more respect for the judge and the law.

On the other hand, in recent decades many people have become more aware of the fact that judges in Britain are overwhelmingly white, wealthy, male, middle-aged or elderly, from highly or relatively privileged backgrounds, and Judaeo-Christian in upbringing or outlook even if not actively 'religious'. If it is correct to say that it is judges who decide what conduct is reasonable and what is not, then it may be hard to avoid at least a suspicion that the law embodies standards of reasonableness that may not reflect the views and expectations of many members of our society. This inevitably raises the further question of why such people, who are neither popularly elected nor democratically accountable, should be allowed to force their standards of justice and reasonableness on the rest of us. This is a difficult question that will not be addressed here. Whatever the answer, the question may lead us to ask, further, whether the issue of what sorts of conduct ought to entail liability to compensate for injury and damage should not be decided by the legislature rather than the courts.[10]

---

9 *Sidaway* v. *Governors of Bethlem Royal Hospital* [1985] AC 871; *Bolitho* v. *City and Hackney HA* [1998] AC 232.

10 See generally P. Cane, 'Taking Disagreement Seriously: Courts, Legislatures and the Reform of Tort Law' (2005) 25 *OJLS* 393.

2.4.2   The nature of negligence

One way of summarizing the points made in the previous section is to say that the issue of negligence or reasonable conduct is an issue of 'policy' which is little different from the sorts of policy decisions which public officials are continuously having to make. The judge's decision is often a far less momentous decision because the majority of litigated cases involve a microscopic analysis of conduct at a particular moment of time. But this is not always so, and there are occasions on which a judge may have to decide whether action taken 'on grounds of public policy' or 'in the public interest' was 'reasonable' – i.e. whether the judge agrees with the policy-makers. For instance, in the 1960s British Railways and the Ministry of Transport spent a great deal of time debating the desirability of replacing manually operated level crossings with automatically operated barriers. They took into account the financial savings that would result and the risk of possible accidents, and they decided on balance that the changeover was desirable. Subsequently an accident occurred at one of these crossings, which formed the subject of a public inquiry by a QC.[11] Had legal proceedings been brought, the judge would have had to determine a similar question to that which the railway authorities and the Ministry had already determined, though the question would have been couched in the language of 'negligence'.

In more recent years, major disasters such as the sinking of the *Herald of Free Enterprise* in Zeebrugge harbour, the fire in the King's Cross underground station, and the destruction of the *Piper Alpha* oil platform, have been followed both by public inquiries, which have investigated the causes of these tragedies and made recommendations as to how similar accidents might be avoided in the future; and also by tort claims brought by persons injured and relatives of those killed in these disasters. Such tort claims inevitably raise important policy issues about the desirable balance between safety and the commercial interests of entrepreneurs, and such inquiries often lead to the imposition of stricter safety standards by legislation or other government action. Tort actions in which claimants allege that they have been injured as a result of a defect in the design of a product may also raise fundamental policy issues about the proper balance between the safety of consumers, the profitability of manufacturing industry and the desirability of innovation in product design.

However, even though the issue of negligence is sometimes essentially an issue of 'desirability in the public interest', it does not follow that in deciding a case a judge will take into account all those factors that a public official or a Minister might take into account. A Minister may, for example, decide that a certain course of action is likely to win votes for his or her party, and that this consideration outweighs all others; a judge would not be influenced by such a consideration. In fact a judge is likely to take into account (whether explicitly or silently, consciously or subliminally) four main considerations: first, the degree of probability, judged as at

---

11 *Report of the Public Inquiry into the Accident at Hixon Level Crossing* (Cmnd 3706, 1968).

a point in time just before the accident occurred, that damage would result from the conduct which is complained of; secondly, the magnitude of the harm (once again judged as at a point in time just before the accident occurred) which was likely to result if the conduct complained of took place; thirdly, the value or utility of the object to be achieved by the conduct in question; and, fourthly, the burden in terms of cost, time and trouble, of taking those precautions against the risk of damage which the claimant alleges ought to have been taken.

A famous US judge, Learned Hand, once declared that negligence was a function of three variables;[12] on this view, negligence is shown where the burden of the precautions needed to avoid a risk of injury or damage occurring as a result of particular conduct is less than the product of the likely magnitude of the damage and the probability that the damage will occur. It has been argued that this is fundamentally an economic test,[13] as opposed to the essentially moral notion of fault embodied in the concept of reasonableness. If it can be shown that the expenditure of £X on avoiding or minimizing the risk of an accident will prevent accident costs of £X + Y, then it is clearly desirable that the £X should be spent. On the other hand, it is said, there is no point in spending £X to prevent accident costs which are less than £X. In some situations this is a useful perspective, and sometimes (although by no means always) it may even be possible to put actual figures on the probability of an accident occurring,[14] the damage likely to be caused if an accident does happen and the cost of precautions. But any attempt to reduce the whole law of negligence to the form of an algebraic equation must be dismissed because we will normally not be dealing with precisely measurable values. More importantly, how can we place a value on the object to be achieved? Significantly, perhaps, Learned Hand did not specifically mention this factor; and plainly it cannot be reduced to monetary terms in most instances. Suppose an ambulance driver is taking a seriously injured person to hospital and is driving faster than usual in order to arrive sooner and so give the injured person a better chance of survival. How do we put a value on the life of that person, and how do we compare it with the value of any lives that may be lost in an accident caused by the ambulance driver's speeding? Such things can only be the subject of a delicate personal judgment, and people may well differ in making such judgments.

The point is even stronger where, as often happens, the court is required to compare dissimilar things. Suppose a court is asked to say whether it is negligent to play cricket on a ground without a fence, so that balls are occasionally hit into the street. We might be able to assess with reasonable accuracy the likelihood of a ball being hit out of the ground and injuring someone, the likely severity of those

---

12 US v. Carroll Towing Co. (1947) 159 F 2d 169.
13 R. Posner, Economic Analysis of Law (4th edn, Boston, 1992), 163ff.
14 One of the easiest risks to quantify is death from various causes. It is also relatively easy to quantify the risk of being injured in a road accident, for example; but determining the risk of suffering specified injuries or being involved in a particular type of accident may be very difficult. Much will depend on whether reliable statistics are available.

injuries and the cost of taking precautions against this happening. But how can we compare the value of cricket as a pastime with the value of the safety of passers-by, and so decide whether playing cricket without a fence was negligent?

At this stage it might be thought that we reach the realm of purely subjective judgment; but it is often said that what judges ought to do at this point is to attempt to discern and give effect to community values. If a judge believes that the community has a high regard for the game of cricket, it is right, so the argument goes, to give it a high value when weighing it against the possibility of personal injury. The obvious weakness of this approach lies in the notion of 'community values'. In a pluralistic society, although there may be a core of issues on which many people hold similar views, there will be many more about which a variety of differing and more or less inconsistent views can be and are legitimately held. The value of the game of cricket is, perhaps, a good example. Furthermore, there may be occasions on which judges feel very strongly that widely held values are wrong or misguided, and there is nothing to stop a judge from trying to change such values by applying his or her own. In this way the courts may seek to mould opinion, and change the community's sense of values. However, as we have already observed, the legitimacy of such behaviour is questionable given the make-up of the judiciary and the unelected and unaccountable nature of the office of judge.

In making a finding of negligence the courts do not generally rely on factual or statistical or expert knowledge, at least where the facts do not clearly fall within the realm of scientific knowledge. Where allegations of professional negligence are made, for example, against a doctor, the courts do rely on expert witnesses to tell them what is accepted practice and what is not. But in many areas judges rely almost entirely on their own experience, hunch or instinct. Thus the probability of an event is almost invariably[15] decided without the assistance of statistical evidence; and the assessment of the amount of damage likely to be done and the burden of precautions is rarely reduced to arithmetical calculations. Even in cases in which hard facts could be adduced and measured, courts seem to discourage the use of empirical evidence. What is known in the USA as the 'Brandeis brief' is rarely used in this country. Reluctance to hear empirical evidence is partly the result of a desire not to prolong and complicate trials, and partly of a realization that the ultimate issue in a negligence action is not a factual one but requires a value judgment.[16]

2.4.3 Probability of harm

As we have just seen, four factors are taken into account in deciding whether a person has taken reasonable care: the probability that the claimant would suffer harm and

---

15 *Haley* v. *London Electricity Board* [1965] AC 778 is an exception; but even here the evidence used (about the number of blind people in London) was only indirectly relevant to the issue to be decided, namely whether the Board ought to have guarded against the possibility of a blind person falling into an excavation in the pavement.

16 For a discussion of the issues in an Australian context see K. Burns, 'It's Just Not Cricket: The High Court, Sport and Legislative Facts' (2002) 10 *Torts LJ* 234, esp. 247–54.

the likely magnitude of that harm, the cost of taking precautions to prevent it and the value of the activity which caused the harm. We will consider each of these factors in turn. First, probability. The most important thing to note here is that probability is relative. Some events are so probable that there would be no point in conducting one's life except on the assumption that the event will take place – for example, that the earth will continue to spin on its axis in its accustomed orbit round the sun.[17] Other events may be such remote possibilities that nobody would adjust their conduct because of them – for instance, that a major earthquake will occur in Britain. In between these extremes there is an infinite number of gradations, and these degrees of probability are reflected in the language of the courts. Events may be described as 'very probable', 'highly probable', 'quite likely', 'not unlikely'; events may be described, after they have happened, as 'remarkable' or 'extraordinary'; risks may, before the event, be stigmatized as 'remote' or 'fantastic' possibilities.

There is no fixed point at which the law requires people to take account of a possibility. The point is a moving one because negligence is a function of several variables. In other words, it may be negligent to disregard a very remote risk in one situation, but not negligent to disregard a much greater risk in another situation. We must consider alongside probability the other factors mentioned above – the utility of the conduct in question, the magnitude of the damage that may be done; and the burden of the precautions required to avoid the damage. In *Bolton v. Stone*, for example, the possibility that a cricket ball might be hit out of the ground and injure someone in the street had to be set against the fact that the chance of this happening was quite small; that the amount of damage, if any, which the ball was likely to do was limited; and that cricket could not be played without creating such a risk except at the cost of building a high and costly fence. Taking all these factors into account, the balance was held to be in favour of no liability.[18] On the other hand, *The Wagon Mound* involved the very remote chance that oil accidentally discharged from a vessel in a harbour might ignite on the surface of the water. Set against this the fact that, if it did ignite, very considerable damage could be done, the fact that a discharge of oil serves no useful purpose, and that the only precaution required to avoid it was the turning off of a tap, and the balance was held to be in favour of liability.[19]

2.4.4   Likely magnitude of harm

This is the second factor taken into account in deciding a negligence issue, and in some cases it may tip the scales. For example, in *Paris v. Stepney Borough Council*[20] it was held that an employer who knows that one of its workers has only one sound eye may be negligent if it fails to supply the worker with goggles for work involving a risk to the eyes, even though the risk is sufficiently remote that the employer

---

17 The distinguished mathematician, G.H. Hardy, once wagered 'his fortune till death' to a halfpenny that the sun would rise on the following day.
18 See *Bolton v. Stone* [1951] AC 850.
19 *The Wagon Mound (No. 2)* [1967] 1 AC 617.
20 [1951] AC 367.

would be justified in disregarding it in the case of a normally sighted worker. Similarly, it has been held that organisers of sporting events must take greater care for the safety of disabled than of able-bodied participants.[21]

There is some empirical evidence to suggest that people do take into account the magnitude of the damage which their conduct may cause in determining the degree of care with which they will perform some task. In an experiment conducted by the Road Research Laboratory in 1961[22] a group of motorists was asked to drive through three narrow gateways the pillars of which appeared to be made of plastic, wood and concrete respectively. It was found that they drove at the lowest speed and with the greatest care when the pillars appeared to be concrete, at the highest speed and with least care when the pillars appeared to be plastic. Unfortunately there was insufficient evidence to show whether lower speeds and greater care actually made any material difference to the accident rate.

In order to determine the magnitude of the harm it may be necessary to make judgments based on community values. Is the death of one individual a harm of 'greater magnitude' than the suffering of injury by a dozen others; or than the physical destruction of thousands of pounds' worth of property? Can the death of one individual ever be regarded as harm of greater magnitude than that of another or are all people equal for this purpose? Such questions are rarely discussed openly by courts or lawyers; and it may very well be that society's sense of values on such matters is not always wholly rational. As a society we tolerate many risks that could be avoided at manageable cost. Cars, for example, could be made safer if people were prepared to pay more for them;[23] roads could certainly be much safer if more money was spent on them, or if cars travelled at slower speeds. Many accidents could be avoided every year, but society is evidently not prepared to pay the cost of doing so. By contrast, if an individual is in actual and immediate peril, society may be prepared to devote very considerable resources indeed to saving that person's life. For example, the amount we are prepared to spend to save the lives of miners trapped underground is much greater, per life saved, than we are prepared to spend to avoid accidents in coal mines. Although it is hard to find any rational basis for this,[24] it is also hard to dissent from the way in which society reacts to these situations.

---

21 *Morrell* v. *Owen*, *The Times*, 12 December 1993.
22 *Research on Road Safety* (HMSO, 1963), 89–90.
23 People's attitudes to the risks of different types of transport may not correlate with the degree of danger involved. For example, many people have a much greater fear of flying than of motoring, even though flying is statistically much safer than motoring. 'Psychologists have identified . . . a tendency for people to judge a particular type of event as more likely to happen if particular instances of the event are easy to remember or, for whatever reason, "come to mind" more readily. Thus people tend to overestimate the frequency of widely reported causes of death': M.W. Jones-Lee, 'The Value of Transport Safety' (1990) 6 *Oxford Review of Economic Policy* 39, 53 n. 22. Such attitudes may affect the amount we are prepared to spend (or require to be spent) on reducing the risks involved in various modes of transport.
24 An attempt is made by C. Fried, 'The Value of Life' (1969) 82 *Harvard Law Review* 1415. One answer is that the time available in such circumstances to effect a rescue puts a limit on the amount which can be expended. It is sometimes suggested that people who carelessly get themselves into situations from which they need to be rescued should pay the cost of the rescue.

2.4.5   The value of the activity and the cost of the precautions needed to avoid harm

The negligence formula requires the harm caused by the allegedly tortious conduct to be weighed against the cost of the precautions which it is argued ought to have been taken and the social benefits flowing from the conduct. The more valuable an activity, the more uncompensated harm we might be prepared to accept as a cost of the continuance of that activity. So, for instance, in *Bolton* v. *Stone* the court (in effect) had to decide whether the playing of cricket on the ground in question was worth the risk of injury to passers-by in the street, given the probability and magnitude of the risk. Suppose that it would have cost so much to take precautions sufficient to remove the risk of injury to passers-by that people would not have been prepared to pay the entrance charges or membership fees needed to finance it, and so the cricket club would have had to close. In that case, the court would have had to decide how important the cricket club's activities were relative to the interest of passers-by in personal safety. In fact, the court did not address this issue directly, but found in the club's favour simply on the basis that the risk was very small. However, implicit in this decision was a value judgment that the playing of cricket under the conditions in question was worth the small element of risk to passers-by which it created.

In many cases, the taking of suitable precautions will not threaten the very continued existence of an activity, but may reduce the value of the activity. The speed at which motor vehicles are driven provides an example. Driving more slowly may reduce the risk of accidents and injury, but it may also reduce the value of driving as an activity. A court, confronted with the need to decide whether driving at a particular speed in particular circumstances was negligent or not, will need (implicitly at least) to weigh the advantages of higher speed against the greater safety and lower risk of driving more slowly. For instance, we might be prepared to allow emergency vehicles to drive at speeds we would not tolerate in other circumstances even though such speed increases the risk of accident and injury. On the whole, however, the risks attaching to the use of motor vehicles are great, and the sorts of precautions necessary to prevent the typical motor vehicle accident – such as driving a little more slowly, or giving a signal earlier, or sounding a horn, or waiting for the next straight stretch of road before overtaking – reduce the value of the activity only slightly. This is probably why the issue of reasonable care is rarely contested in relation to road accidents.

Of course, we cannot measure the value of an activity without first defining it, and this may not be a straightforward matter. The case of emergency vehicles illustrates the point. Transporting a desperately ill person to hospital, sightseeing by car, driving to work and long-distance trucking are all instances of the activity of using a motor vehicle. However, because of its special social value, we may be prepared to pick out the first and describe it as a different activity from the other three for the purposes of tort law. Conversely, we might treat sightseeing and driving to work as the same activity even though it could be said that the latter is more socially important than the former.

In practice, courts rarely decide the issue of negligence by reference to the nature and value of the defendant's activity. They tend to focus on the probability and magnitude of the risk and the cost of precautions. However, decisions about whether a defendant ought to have taken particular precautions to avoid particular risks often imply judgments about the value of the defendant's activity. For instance, courts are quite unwilling to hold medical practitioners negligent in respect of the way they treat their patients; and one reason for this approach is the high value implicitly placed on treatment of the sick. The courts often express a fear that too readily holding doctors negligent may cause them to practise 'defensive medicine'; that is, that they may be led to carry out or not to carry out particular procedures simply in order to reduce the risk of incurring legal liability and not in the interests of their patients. In other words, courts are quite willing to hold that precautions which claimants allege that doctors ought to have taken to avoid harm are so costly in terms of their effect on styles of doctoring that they would reduce the value of medical practice to an unacceptable extent. The social benefits of medical practice are thought to be worth more uncompensated harm than the social benefits of many other activities.

2.4.6   The function of the negligence formula

The allegation in a negligence action is basically that the defendant paid insufficient attention to the interests of others in deciding how to behave, and has pursued his or her own objectives at the risk of injuring other people or damaging their property. This is perhaps the foundation for the view that negligence is a moral fault. Whereas the individual looks at the matter primarily from their own point of view, the judge looks at the matter from the point of view of the public interest and the need to balance the interests of different persons. People are entitled to pursue their own interests and objectives even if by doing so they may endanger other people or their property to some degree. But there are limits to the extent to which people may do this, and the judge's task is to define those limits with the aid of the negligence formula. People may drive their cars at a 'reasonable' speed because the gain to them and the public from being allowed so to drive is at least worth the risk of the harm such driving may cause; but people are not allowed to drive at an 'excessive' speed because the additional gain that it brings does not outweigh the additional risk that it imposes on others.

There is another fundamental difference between the judge's task and that of anyone else who is called upon to decide between different courses of conduct, and that is the purpose for which the decision is to be made. When a person chooses a course of action, they do so prospectively, before engaging in one or other course of conduct. By contrast, a court always decides the negligence issue retrospectively: in a negligence action the judge has to decide what should have been done in the past, not what should be done in the future. The purpose of this inquiry is to decide whether compensation should be paid to those who have suffered injury or damage as a result of the chosen course of action.

What is the justification for imposing an obligation to pay compensation on the basis of a judgment that a person should have behaved differently in the past? There are two main arguments. The first is that negligent conduct can be stigmatized as blameworthy and from this it follows that a negligent defendant ought to compensate an innocent claimant for the latter's injuries. The second argument is that by holding past conduct to have been negligent and by requiring the negligent party to pay for loss caused by it, the law might have some deterrent effect on future behaviour. If, for example, a court were to hold that a cricket club had been negligent in not building a fence around its ground, this might have some influence on the future behaviour of that and other clubs. The assertion that the law can operate as a deterrent is, in theory, capable of being empirically tested, and if it proved unfounded then this second justification would collapse. Each of these arguments is discussed extensively later in this book (in ch. 17).

2.4.7 Foreseeability

Negligence is a form of fault. To say that someone was at fault in behaving as they did is to say that they should have behaved differently. To say that a person was negligent is to say that they should have taken certain precautions (which they did not take) to prevent harm to another. We have seen that the precautions which the law requires are those which the reasonable person would take in the light of the probability and magnitude of the harm in question, the cost of the precautions needed to avoid it and the value of the harm-causing activity. However, we cannot meaningfully or fairly say that a person should have taken such precautions unless we can also say that they ought to have known about the risk at the time when it is alleged that the precautions ought to have been taken. In the terminology of tort law, negligence is failure to take reasonable precautions against foreseeable risks of harm. Foreseeable risks are those the reasonable person in the defendant's position would have foreseen.

The concept of foreseeable risk is a difficult one because foreseeability is relative in three important ways. First, an event may be more or less foreseeable according to the detail in which the event is described. The fact that most houses are insured against fire is testimony to the foreseeability of damage to or destruction of a house by fire; but it would be a very different matter to say, after a fire has occurred, that anyone could or should have foreseen when, where and how it might break out. In general, the more detailed the description of an event, the less reasonable it would be to say that it should have been foreseen. For instance, it is reasonable to expect a person to foresee that if they drive negligently they may injure another road user. It would be much less reasonable to expect them to foresee (for instance) the sex or age of that other road user or the precise nature of the injuries suffered or the exact sequence of events that led to the accident and the injuries. When the law says that a person cannot be liable for negligence unless harm to the claimant was foreseeable, it does not mean that every detail of what happened must have been foreseeable. A person can be held liable for negligence provided they ought to have foreseen a risk of harm sufficiently great to justify taking the precautions which the claimant alleges ought to have been taken. The fact that the harm actually suffered by the claimant was greater than was foreseeable, or that it occurred in an unforeseeable way, will not relieve a person of liability provided it can be said that the person ought to have foreseen harm which would have justified the taking of the precautions in question.

A second way in which the concept of foreseeability is relative arises from the fact that what a person can foresee depends on what they know. A person who knows that a vessel is full of petrol vapour, for instance, is much more likely to foresee the destruction of the vessel by fire than a person ignorant of this fact. The foreseeability of particular events may also depend on the state of scientific and technical knowledge. This has proved particularly important in relation to negligence claims arising out of the use of pharmaceutical drugs and in litigation against cigarette companies. Since foreseeability depends on knowledge, the obvious question is, whose knowledge? The law's answer is, 'the knowledge which the reasonable person in the defendant's position would have had'. As we saw above, the concept of the reasonable person in the defendant's position rests ultimately on value judgments about the amount of care people ought to take for the protection of others.

A third reason why foreseeability is relative is that people vary in their attitude to risk. Some people are 'risk averse', others are 'risk-takers' and yet others are 'risk neutral'. The more risk averse a person is, the more likely they are to foresee remote risks of harm and to take precautions. By contrast, the more 'risk-taking' a person is, the less likely are they to foresee or guard against risks of harm in their activities. The courts have never explicitly considered the relationship between attitudes to risk and the legal concept of foreseeability. What is the 'reasonable person's' attitude to risk? Perhaps it is neutrality. The point is that one person might foresee a risk that would not occur to another. The law must, even if only implicitly, adopt some attitude to risk in applying the concept of foreseeability.

2.4.8   The objective standard of care

The question in a negligence action is not whether the defendant personally could have foreseen the harm or could have avoided it. The general principle is that the defendant's personal capacity to foresee and avoid harm is irrelevant. The judge must decide what the defendant *should* have done (which is what the reasonable person would have done), not what he or she *could* have done. Various reasons for this 'objective' approach can be identified. First, it would be difficult and time-consuming to determine the relevant capabilities of every defendant; secondly, it would be very difficult to tailor the notion of 'reasonable care' to the personal capabilities of each defendant; thirdly, to the extent that the legal concept of negligence is rooted in morality, it shares with morality the role of setting standards of conduct which people are expected to strive to achieve.[25] Fourthly, defining negligence in terms of what the defendant personally could have done would unduly sacrifice the interest of potential claimants in personal security and freedom from injury and damage to the freedom of potential injurers to engage in risky activities. The objective standard of care can be understood as the law's attempt to strike a fair balance between the competing interests in freedom of action and personal security that we all share.

The fact that the legal standard of care is objective should be distinguished from the issue of how demanding that standard is. For instance, prevalence of liability insurance has perhaps encouraged courts to impose standards of care which are beyond the reach of many people, because they know that in the typical case, the defendant personally will not have to pay any damages awarded. This last reason provides one of the explanations for the rule that a learner driver[26] or the inexperienced doctor must conform to the same standard of care as is required of experienced drivers or doctors, and the fact that physical disabilities are generally ignored in judging whether a driver was negligent:[27] if the defendant is insured against liability (as car-owners are required to be by law) then the law's aim of compensating persons injured on the road can be achieved without imposing intolerable financial strains on negligent drivers.[28]

Nevertheless, the law must pay some attention to what *could* have been done: it would be Kafka-esque to say that the defendant should have done something that could not have been done by anybody. Conversely if the defendant is a person claiming special skill, such as a doctor or other professional, the court will take into account, in deciding what should have been foreseen or what precautions should have been taken, the standards of conduct commonly achieved by people possessed of that skill or by members of that profession. Even so, the question in any particular case is not what degree of care the defendant was capable of exercising, but whether the defendant exercised the degree of care the law requires.

The objective nature of the legal definition of negligent conduct tells us something about the aims of the law of negligence: if the law's main aim was to reinforce some notion of personal fault, the law might pay more attention to the abilities of individual defendants, such as learner drivers. Again, if the main aim was to deter negligent conduct in the future, the law might take more account of the ability of individuals to avoid the sort of conduct in question. But the prime concern of the modern law of negligence as it applies to death and personal injuries, is to provide compensation for loss and injury suffered as a result of negligent conduct. In practice, such compensation nearly always comes out of an insurance fund. This is not to say that the legal notion of negligence is totally divorced from moral notions of

25 People who are incapable of exercising the required care should avoid situations in which their lack of capacity may produce adverse consequences.
26 *Nettleship* v. *Weston* [1971] 2 QB 691.
27 *Roberts* v. *Ramsbottom* [1980] 1 All ER 7.
28 See further ch. 9.

fault, nor that the law is not concerned to encourage care, but only that the goal of compensation is uppermost in modern law.

2.4.9   Negligence in design and negligence in operation

In practice, although not in legal theory, there is an important difference between negligence in the *operation* of an object or an activity and negligence in the *design* of an object or activity. The distinction is not always easy to draw, but in general terms it is much easier to establish negligence in operation than negligence in design.[29]

This is especially noticeable in the case of road accidents. There is no reason in theory why an injured person should not sue a motor manufacturer for the negligent design of a vehicle, or a highway authority for negligent design of a road junction or a roundabout, but in practice such actions would be unlikely to succeed. Bad vehicle design is undoubtedly a factor in the causation of many injuries, and in the USA it has been the source of much negligence litigation. So far in Britain no judgment in favour of a claimant in a motor accident case has been based on bad vehicle design.[30] One hardy litigant sued the manufacturers of a bus alleging that the failure to provide a central pillar on the platform was negligence, but the action failed in the House of Lords.[31] English courts are unwilling to decide cases on design issues of this sort and tend to base their judgments on other grounds.[32] This unwillingness appears also to be a feature of cases involving injuries caused by defective products in which negligent design is alleged: courts tend to decide such cases on the issue of failure to control or warn against the hazard rather than on that of negligent creation of the hazard.[33] In general there is a strong tendency to attribute injuries to some act or omission occurring close in time to the event causing injuries (such as speeding or failure to protect a worker from some health hazard) rather than to some design feature of the environment in which the act or omission occurs (such as the state of the road or the design of equipment).[34]

---

29 There are some Australian examples of successful design negligence claims: e.g. *O'Dwyer* v. *Leo Buring Wines* [1966] WAR 67 (design of a wine bottle stopper); *Suosaari* v. *Steinhardt* [1989] 2 QdR 477 (design of a trailer); *Flynn* v. *Commonwealth of Australia* (1988) 6 MVR 186 (design of a median strip). English examples are hard to find. One is *Winward* v. *TVR Engineering Ltd* [1986] Business and Trading Law Cases 366. The case of the Abbeystead pumping station in Lancashire (in which there was a methane gas explosion in 1984) is another: the Court of Appeal held that the station was negligently designed (*Guardian*, 19 February 1988) and the House of Lords refused the designers leave to appeal the decision (*Independent*, 10 June 1988). Another possible example is *Wood* v. *Bentall Simplex Ltd, The Times*, 3 March 1992 (design of a slurry tank). See also J. Stapleton, *Product Liability* (London, 1994), 251–2.
30 In 1992 an action was launched against Ford in respect of the design of centre rear seat-belts: *The Times*, 8 December 1992.
31 *Scottish Omnibuses* v. *Wyngrove, The Times*, 24 June 1966.
32 Perhaps the major exception to this generalization concerns obligations of employers to provide a 'safe system of work'.
33 J. Stapleton, 'Compensating Victims of Disease' (1985) 5 *Oxford J. of Legal Studies* 248, 253.
34 J. Reason, *Human Error* (Cambridge: Cambridge University Press, 1990), ch. 7. It is probably the case that both human behaviour (especially deliberately risky behaviour): D. Parker and S. Stradling, 'Influencing Driver Attitudes and Behaviour (No. 17)' (Driver Behaviour Research Group, University of Manchester, undated) and system design contribute to many

A number of factors may account for the lack of litigation on design issues. First, the fact, for example, that most cars are designed with the same basic defects might help manufacturers in that it would enable them to argue that they built all the customary safety features into their cars and that there is no reason why they should be required to do more. As we have seen, however, the courts have never accepted customary practice as completely precluding a finding of negligence, and there is nothing in law which would prevent a holding that customary design was negligent.

Another factor is that a decision by a court that a vehicle (or other product) was badly designed, though technically a decision about a 'question of fact', would effectively be a legislative act. If there has been negligence in the design of an article, there must have been negligence in the manufacture of all other articles made to the same design. When dealing with motor vehicles a court would doubtless be reluctant to make a decision of this kind, because in doing so it would be competing with the statutory powers of the appropriate Minister to make regulations prescribing requirements for the construction of vehicles. There is certainly no legal reason why a court should not declare a design to be negligent, even though a safer design has not been prescribed by regulation. But there are grounds for regarding the legislative powers of the Minister to be a more appropriate way of dealing with this sort of problem, partly because the Minister can take into account wider issues of public interest that would be ignored in the courts, such as, for instance, the effect of particular design requirements on the export trade, and the need to give the makers time to change their designs.[35] Similarly, if the courts were to hold that it is negligent of the Home Office to maintain 'open' prisons from which the inmates can easily escape and do damage, they would be pronouncing on complex and politically sensitive

accidents – although this distinction itself may be misleading because humans design faulty systems. It may also be the case that the relative contribution of these factors varies from area to area and activity to activity. But hard evidence may be difficult to find. For instance, one survey concluded that 'despite a wealth of literature . . . there is no reliable evidence either for or against a relationship between car crash injury risk and any . . . measure of fatigue or sleepiness [other than sleep apnoea] from current research': J. Connor, 'The Role of Driver Sleepiness in Car Crashes: A Systematic Review of Epidemiological Studies' (2001) 33 *Accident Analysis and Prevention* 31. Another study found that road improvements in the USA between 1984 and 1997 did not reduce, and may even have increased, the total number of injuries and fatalities. Reduction in total fatalities was attributed to factors such as increased usage of seat-belts and reduced alcohol consumption: R.B. Noland, 'Traffic Fatalities and Injuries: The Effects of Changes in Infrastructure and Other Trends' (2003) 35 *Accident Analysis and Prevention* 599. Yet another recent study concluded that there are so many methodological defects in studies of the causal role of 'psychological' factors in road accidents that we know have only 'a very vague knowledge of what psychological variables can actually predict accidents': A.E. af Wahlberg, 'Some Methodological Deficiencies in Studies on Traffic Accident Predictors' (2003) *Accident Analysis and Prevention* 473. For a thorough review of the research see Health and Safety Executive, *Differences in Accident Liability*, Contract Research Report 175/1998.

35 For the same reason there may be objections to allowing actions for damages in respect of faultily designed houses, although it appears that negligent design accounts for a significant number of accidents in the home (8% according to one inquiry: see *Personal Factors in Domestic Accidents: Prevention through Product and Environmental Design* (Consumer Safety Unit, DTI, 1983), 17 (reporting research by the Building Research Station in 1964).

issues about the design of the penal system which are more appropriately decided by the executive and the legislature.[36] There would be no such difficulty in a finding that prison officers had performed their custodial task negligently.

A third factor militating against judicial resolution of design issues arises from doubts as to whether courts are able to weigh the social costs and benefits of different designs and whether they ought to do so. For example, if it would cost £X to install a new safety device in all cars, are judges the right people to decide that everybody should pay £X more for their cars? Again, is a court the right body to decide how much a drug company should spend on testing a new drug to ensure its safety? The problem of balancing risks against gains in such cases is very difficult indeed, and probably beyond the resources of the courts. It would involve an assessment of the risk of accident – which may be difficult enough – but it would also involve consideration of how much the public gains through being able to buy cheaper cars or from the availability of a particular drug sooner rather than later, and less rather than more expensively.

A fourth relevant factor arises out of the fact that litigation which considers design issues is likely to be much more complex, lengthy and costly than litigation which concentrates on specific acts or omissions.

The question of whether the courts ought to be making decisions in 'design' cases that certain precautions to avoid loss or damage ought to have been taken is of particular importance in relation to actions against public bodies. Suppose, for example, that a local authority is sued in respect of a road accident on the ground that it should have installed traffic lights at a dangerous intersection; or in respect of someone's death by drowning at a dangerous beach because it neglected to provide warning flags or a lifeguard. Installing lights or providing lifeguards costs money. Furthermore, a decision that lights ought to have been installed at one intersection or a lifeguard provided on one beach might lead this and other local authorities to feel that in order to avoid liability in negligence it would be necessary to install lights at many dangerous intersections or to provide lifeguards on many dangerous beaches. To meet the cost of such precautions other public projects, such as the provision of new hospitals or extensions to schools, might have to be starved of funds if extra revenue cannot be raised. As a matter of constitutional theory, it is widely accepted that such policy choices between, for example, safer roads, better schools and more hospitals, ought to be made by elected representatives of the people and not by judges.

Another important example of this problem relates to the prevention of crime. Criminal attacks on individuals may sometimes be facilitated by inefficient police patrols or investigations; or by refusal of the police to protect someone who has been threatened by thugs or a vital witness in a case against a well-organized gang of criminals.[37] In England a court would be very unlikely to find the police negligent

---

36 *Home Office* v. *Dorset Yacht Co.* [1970] AC 1004.
37 See *Schuster* v. *New York* (1958) 154 NE 2d 534.

for failing to take adequate steps to prevent this or that crime, because questions about expenditure on the prevention of crime and about the level of policing are left to the police or their political masters.[38] The existence of a scheme, separate from the tort system, for the compensation of the victims of criminal injuries (the Criminal Injuries Compensation Scheme) provides the courts with another ground for refusing to impose negligence liability on the police, at least in respect of personal injury and death. The argument that the law of negligence might be used in this context to encourage the police to take greater care in detecting and preventing crime has been turned on its head: to hold the police liable would be, it is said, to risk 'overkill'; that is, it would tend to make the police unduly cautious in doing their job for fear of being sued rather than for any good operational reason. In other words, to impose liability too readily on the police or other public authorities would be to risk over-deterrence. The overkill argument is commonly used not only in actions against public authorities but also in actions against professionals. Its main weaknesses are that there is very little empirical evidence to support the idea that tort liability has the sort of effects the argument assumes; and that no court has ever defined in any meaningful way how much deterrence is too much.[39]

2.5 Conduct of the claimant

So far in this chapter we have been considering the notion of fault (in the sense of negligence) in relation to the conduct of the defendant. There are circumstances in which a claimant may be deprived of part or all of a damages award because of his or her own conduct. Circumstances in which we would say that a person's injuries were wholly or partly their 'own fault' are mostly[40] dealt with in the law by the 'defence' of contributory negligence. The defence of *volenti non fit injuria* (or 'assumption of risk'), by contrast, exonerates the defendant not because the claimant was at fault but because the claimant accepted the risk of injury; although in many cases, such conduct is little different from contributory negligence. Finally, the defence of illegality deprives the claimant of damages not because the injuries

---

38 *Hill* v. *Chief Constable of West Yorkshire* [1989] AC 53 (police owed no duty of care to a woman who was the penultimate victim of a serial rapist and murderer).
39 See further R. Dingwall, P. Fenn and L. Quam, *Medical Negligence: A Review and Bibliography* (Oxford, 1991), 44–51; M.A. Jones and A.E. Morris, 'Defensive Medicine: Myths and Facts' (1989) 5 *J. of Medical Defence Union* 40; D. Tribe and G. Korgaonkar, 'The Impact of Litigation on Patient Care: an Enquiry into Defensive Medical Practices' [1991] *Professional Negligence* 2; P. Cane, 'Consequences in Judicial Reasoning' in J. Horder ed., *Oxford Essays in Jurisprudence, Fourth Series* (Oxford, 2000); and 17.7.1.1.
40 The rule that a claimant must take reasonable steps to 'mitigate' (i.e. reduce to a minimum) their loss is also underpinned by some notion of fault. Contributory negligence is pre-accident fault, while failure to mitigate loss is post-accident fault. In relation to economic loss, the courts have adopted a general principle that people should take reasonable steps to protect themselves against such loss. This principle is used as the basis for denying tort liability for negligently caused economic loss.

were his or her own fault but because of an objection to compensating a person for loss or damage arising out of criminal behaviour.

2.5.1 Contributory negligence

Contributory negligence is failure to take reasonable care for one's own safety as opposed to failure to take reasonable care for the safety of others; or, put another way, failure to take reasonable precautions against risks of injury to oneself, of which one was aware or ought to have been aware. Until 1945, a finding that the claimant's injuries were wholly, or even partly, the result of his or her own (contributory) negligence was a complete defence in the sense that it resulted in the claimant receiving no damages at all. This defence was originally based on the same general idea of fault that justified liability for negligence, although the legal justification for the defence was expressed in terms of 'cause'.[41] It may also have been partly based on some idea of deterrence: people should be encouraged to take care for their own safety even when imperilled by the negligence of others. It has been argued that neither of these rationales is very satisfying.[42] As for the first, the kind of 'fault' which justifies liability is not the same as the kind of fault embodied in the notion of contributory negligence. The 'fault' of a defendant can, in a broad sort of way, be treated (in many cases) as involving self-interested or unsocial risk-taking at the expense of others. A claimant's 'fault' is not of this kind: such fault is not so much selfish as just foolish, and it is not clear that one can equate, or even compare, foolishness with selfishness. The second rationale is looked at in some detail later,[43] and it is enough to say here that the instinct for self-preservation is likely (in most circumstances) to be quite sufficient to deter most people from taking risks with their own safety. It is, therefore, not at all evident that the deterrent function of the doctrine of contributory negligence is of any real value.

   In the course of time, a rule that denied a negligent claimant any compensation however slight the claimant's fault and however serious the defendant's, appeared unjust and led the courts to invent devices to mitigate the effects of the doctrine. The courts did not feel able to take the sensible course of reducing the claimant's damages to reflect the fact that he or she was to some extent to blame. What was done, in suitable cases, was to deny that the claimant's contributory negligence had been a real cause of the loss, and to insist that the defendant's negligence was the 'sole' cause of the damage. The problem with this approach was that the claimant's negligence was always in some sense a cause of the damage, and so to say that the defendant's negligence was the sole cause only meant that the court was prepared to ignore the claimant's negligence and treat the defendant's negligence as solely responsible. The device for evading the contributory negligence doctrine was the

41 See e.g. Bowen LJ in *Thomas* v. *Quartermaine* (1887) 18 QBD 685, 694; and *Caswell* v. *Powell Duffryn Collieries* [1940] AC 152.
42 G. Schwartz, 'Contributory and Comparative Negligence: A Reappraisal' (1978) 87 *Yale LJ* 697.
43 See 17.7.1.2.

so-called 'last opportunity rule', i.e. the rule that the person who had the last opportunity to avoid the accident should be treated as its sole cause.[44] The courts were
never very happy with this rule, partly because it ran counter to prevalent ideas
about causation, and partly because it seemed such a crude method of mitigating
the harshness of the contributory negligence rule. Eventually the law became intol-
erably subtle and complex so that it was well nigh impossible to direct a jury in intelligible terms – and cases were still being tried by juries when these difficulties were
at their peak.

The Law Reform (Contributory Negligence) Act, enacted in 1945, empowered
the courts to apportion the responsibility for an accident, and to reduce the
damages awarded to a claimant who had been guilty of contributory negligence,
while not denying a remedy altogether. At first there were doubts about the extent
to which the Act had done away with the complexities of the old law,[45] but in practice the Act of 1945 has removed most of the difficulties from this part of the
law. Now the only questions that arise in the typical case are whether the claimant
acted negligently, whether the damage or loss was wholly or partly the result of that
negligence, and by how much (if at all) the claimant's damages should be reduced.
One of the few points of general application to arise since the passage of the 1945
Act has involved the application of contributory negligence rules to passengers in
cars. Failure by a passenger in a car to wear an available seat-belt is contributory
negligence,[46] and if it can be shown that the passenger's injuries would not have
occurred or would have been less serious if a seat-belt had been worn, the passenger must bear some share of the responsibility. In *Froom* v. *Butcher*[47] the Court of
Appeal laid down as a general guide that the claimant's damages should be reduced
by 25% in cases where the injuries would have been prevented altogether, and by
15% where they would have been less severe if an available seat-belt had been
worn. A passenger who consents to be driven by a driver clearly the worse for
alcohol may also have their damages reduced for contributory negligence.[48]

The Act of 1945 has greatly simplified the law of contributory negligence and
made it much fairer. Judging from the reported cases, it appears to work smoothly in
practice and few difficulties have been encountered in its application.[49] Nevertheless,
there are important questions about the whole doctrine of contributory negligence,
and about the relationship between the doctrine and liability insurance, to which
attention should be drawn.

44 See R.F.V. Heuston and R.A. Buckley eds., *Salmond and Heuston on The Law of Torts*, 21st edn
   (London, 1996), 486–8.
45 See e.g. *Davies* v. *Swan Motor Co.* [1949] 2 KB 291, 310; *Stapley* v. *Gypsum Mines* [1953] AC 663,
   677.
46 As e.g. is failure by a (motor) cyclist to fasten the chin strap of a crash helmet: *Capps* v. *Miller*, *The
   Times*, 12 December 1988.
47 [1976] QB 268.
48 *Owens* v. *Brimmell* [1977] QB 859; see N. Gravells, 'Three Heads of Contributory Negligence'
   (1977) 93 *LQR* 581.
49 For some evidence about the role of contributory negligence in the settlement of cases see Harris
   1984 Survey, 91–2.

2.5.1.1   The difference between negligence and contributory negligence

In the first place, it is important to understand the relationship between negligence and contributory negligence *in practice*. At first sight contributory negligence appears to be a sort of mirror image of negligence itself. There is an apparently satisfying balance in the idea of the negligence of the injurer being counterpoised by the negligence of the injured. But the practical effect of a finding of contributory negligence is very different from the effect of a finding of negligence. To find a defendant guilty of negligence shifts a loss away from the claimant and typically spreads it by means of insurance or other processes. A finding of contributory negligence usually has precisely the opposite effect, which is to leave part or all of the loss on the claimant, who will typically be without relevant insurance. Thus, reduction of damages for contributory negligence typically falls much more heavily on the claimant than liability for negligence bears on the defendant. In practice, negligent people do not pay for the consequences of their negligence; but contributorily negligent people do pay for the consequences of their contributory negligence. It is not too much to say that the only significant group of people who are called upon to bear the consequences of their negligence are accident victims themselves.[50]

This difference between the effect of a finding of negligence and the effect of a finding of contributory negligence may have influenced the courts in recognizing a very important legal distinction between negligence and contributory negligence. The test of negligence as applied to the conduct of claimants is more personalized than the test of negligence applied to defendants. In other words, the courts are more prepared to acquit claimants of negligence on grounds of their personal abilities and characteristics (and so avoid the need to reduce their damages) than they are to acquit defendants on such grounds (with the result that the claimant is deprived of compensation). In particular, the age of the claimant is taken into account in determining contributory negligence. A young person is only expected to show the degree of care which a person of that age should exercise, and the same may be true of an elderly person. The importance of this in practice can be gauged from the fact that young children and old people form a disproportionate number of the pedestrians killed and seriously injured in road accidents. In 2004, for example, the recorded casualty rate for pedestrians killed and seriously injured in road accidents was 9 per 100,000 for persons aged 30 to 39, but 23 per 100,000 for children aged 8–11, and 13 per 100,000 for those aged between 70 and 79.[51] The Pearson Report recommended that contributory negligence should not be available as a defence in road accident cases where the injured person is a child under the age of 12.[52] This would make very little difference to the practical position at present, though it is impossible to understand why this proposal should have been limited to road accident cases.

---

50 The point is well made by A. Tunc, *La Securité Routiere* (Paris, 1966), 31–7 and 'The Twentieth Century Development of the Law of Torts in France' (1965) 14 *International and Comparative Law Q.*, 1089,1100–1.

51 Department for Transport, *Road Casualties in Great Britain 2004*, table 30.

52 Pearson Report, vol 1, para. 1077.

2.5.1.2   Contributory negligence and family cases

At one time in the nineteenth century there was support for a doctrine of 'identification' under which one person might be so identified with the contributory negligence of another as to preclude the former from recovering damages even though personally free from fault. For example, a child who was accompanying his grandmother was severely injured at a station when his grandmother crossed the lines and both were struck by a passing train. It was held that as the grandmother had been found to be contributorily negligent the child could not recover.[53] Some such idea applies in claims under the Fatal Accidents Act 1976 where the claimant's damages must be reduced proportionately to any negligence on the part of the deceased contributing to the death. Under a provision of the Congenital[54] Disabilities (Civil Liability) Act 1976 the claim of a child for damages in respect of injuries suffered before birth can be met with defences available to the defendant against its mother. In general, however, the doctrine was thought unjust, and was rejected in 1888 by the House of Lords which held that a person was not to be affected by the contributory negligence of another unless the former was legally liable for that other's acts; for example, if the latter was the former's servant acting in the course of employment.[55]

But there are cases in which the lack of some such doctrine produces strange results in cases involving members of one family. Suppose that a person is injured by the negligent driving of their spouse; the injured spouse can recover damages from the other (in reality, from the insurer). The family as a whole will 'gain' from the award of damages and the negligent spouse may well share in these gains. Suppose, next, that one of the spouses is killed through the negligence of the other. In *Dodds* v. *Dodds*[56] a man was killed in an accident caused by his wife's negligent driving. The wife could not obtain damages for the loss of her husband, but it was held that their 8½-year-old son was entitled to damages against his mother for causing his father's death, and he was awarded £17,000 – paid, of course, by the insurers. In such a case the bulk of the capital would probably be retained under the control of the court until the child reached majority, but the income would probably be paid to the mother for the maintenance and education of the child. So in reality the negligent spouse would share the benefit of the award. On the other hand, we may baulk at allowing a tortfeasor to benefit directly from an award of damages in respect of the tort. In one case the question arose whether an injured claimant could be awarded damages representing the value of care rendered gratuitously to her by the tortfeasor (her partner). The House of Lords, having decided that when such damages are awarded, they are 'held on trust by the

---

53 *Waite* v. *North Eastern Railway* (1858) El, Bl & El 719; 120 ER 679.
54 Note that 'congenital' in this context means 'suffered as a result of events occurring before birth', not 'attributable to genetic factors'.
55 *The Bernina* (1888) 13 App Cas 1; see too *Oliver* v. *Birmingham & Midland Omnibus Co.* [1933] 1 KB 35.
56 [1978] QB 543.

claimant for the carer', held that an award under this head could not be made where the carer was the tortfeasor.[57]

On the assumption that the fault system is concerned with personal responsibility for harm, these results seem remarkable. On the other hand, if emphasis is put on tort as a mechanism for providing compensation rather than for compensating *on the basis of responsibility*, then the cases seem less strange (and the position under the Fatal Accidents Act 1976 seems the one which is out of line). There is no particular reason to deprive one family member of compensation on the ground that another faulty one will indirectly benefit thereby, when the damages will be paid by an insurer and when the real sufferer, if damages are not awarded, will be the innocent victim.

2.5.1.3   The assessment of contributory negligence

Even though the principle of reducing damages for contributory negligence may appear to be based on a simple idea about personal responsibility, the principle according to which the claimant's damages are reduced is far from obvious or straightforward. The claimant's damages will be reduced having regard not just to the degree of his or her fault – whether that be slight or gross – but according to the degree of the claimant's fault *relative* to that of the defendant. In addition, just as the amount of compensation which a negligent defendant must pay bears no relation to the degree of his or her fault where he or she alone is to blame, so also the amount of the loss which the claimant must bear when partly at fault depends not just on the extent of that fault, but also on the extent of the loss itself. Let us consider how all this works with a few illustrations.

First, a claimant who is 50% to blame for an accident in which they suffer a loss assessed at £10,000 will lose £5,000 as a result of their negligence. A claimant who is a mere 10% to blame for an accident in which the loss is assessed at £100,000 will lose £10,000 as a result of their negligence.

Secondly, a motorist who commits a trivial act of negligence and collides with a defendant who was driving with gross negligence will be held perhaps 10% to blame; but the motorist (guilty of the same trivial act of negligence) may be held 50% to blame if the defendant was no more negligent than the claimant. Yet the claimant's act of negligence is precisely the same in the two cases.

Thirdly, and similarly, a motorist who is driving with gross negligence will certainly be held very largely responsible and so recover very little if involved in an accident partly due (say) to the negligence of a pedestrian who crosses the road in front of the car; but if our motorist is fortunate enough to collide with another grossly negligent driver they will probably recover 50% of the loss.

Fourthly, the last illustration shows that two motorists driving with gross negligence will each recover 50% of their loss, assuming their negligence to be of a similar degree. If *three* negligent motorists all collide simultaneously due to the same degree of negligence, the responsibility of each for their own injuries will be assessed as if the negligence of the other two was that of a single defendant.[58] Thus each will recover 50% of their loss.

2.5.1.4   Contributory negligence and the fault system

Finally, and perhaps most seriously, the combination of the contributory negligence principle with the 'no liability without fault' principle produces the result that a person injured without fault on the part of anyone receives no tort compensation, whereas a person who may be very largely to blame for his or her own injuries can receive some tort compensation. Suppose that two workers are working side by side in a factory and are both severely injured, suffering losses assessed at, say, £100,000 each. Worker *A* is injured by gross negligence on their own part and slight negligence on the part of a fellow worker; worker *A* will recover perhaps 20% of the loss, i.e. £20,000, not of course from the fellow worker but from the employer or its insurers. Worker *B*, on the other hand, is injured entirely by 'accident'. Worker *B* will receive not a penny in tort compensation.

When we look at other compensation systems, we will see that there are many situations in which the aim of compensating victims of injury and damage is so paramount that it is thought unjustifiable to reduce the compensation because of fault on the part of the victim. Life insurance or fire insurance or comprehensive motor insurance would not be such attractive propositions if they did not provide protection against the risk of negligence on the part of the victim. The point is that however attractive the idea that no one should incur tort liability in the absence of fault on their part, the proposition that no one should receive compensation except for loss or damage attributable to the fault of another may seem much less attractive.

Nobody knows quite what is the quantitative effect of the law of contributory negligence. The Harris Survey found that in 26% of the cases studied in which tort damages were obtained, there was some reduction explicitly on the ground of contributory negligence.[59] In the survey of insurance claims handled in November 1973 conducted for the Pearson Commission, it was found that 26% of claims settled were disposed of on the basis of partial liability;[60] but this included cases settled without any payment at all. The cases settled with a partial admission of liability comprised about 31% of the number of cases in which some payment was made. None of these figures, however, tells us anything about the size of the discount made on account of contributory negligence. In an Australian survey it was found that the claimants who were found contributorily negligent lost 39% of their damages, but this does not tell us what proportion this bears to all tort recoveries.[61] In Scandinavia, where apportionment is permitted much as it is in England, it has been

---

58 *Fitzgerald* v. *Lane* [1989] AC 328.
59 For the results of the 1984 survey see Harris 1984 Survey, 91–2.
60 Pearson Report vol. 2, table 117.
61 *Australian Committee Report*, paras.130–1. The proportion of successful actions in which a reduction for contributory negligence was made was found to vary from 10 to 28% (the figures correlated jurisdictions and whether or not the claimant suffered permanent disability).

estimated that abolition of the defence would increase the cost of motor insurance by at least 7.5%.[62]

2.5.1.5   The usefulness of the doctrine

Does the doctrine of contributory negligence serve any useful purpose? From one point of view the answer must be 'no', at least in the law relating to personal injuries. Since tortfeasors are almost invariably insured against liability, the doctrine is not needed to spare an individual defendant the injustice of being made to compensate an injured person who was partly to blame for his or her own injuries. It operates, in effect, as a penal device: the contributorily negligent claimant is punished by being deprived of some of the compensation to which they would otherwise be entitled. Penal laws are usually justified on the grounds of their deterrent value, but it is very doubtful if the doctrine of contributory negligence has any deterrent value in personal injury cases. It is true (as has been argued)[63] that fairness may still seem to demand that if the claimant complains of the defendant's negligence, the former must be prepared to bring their own conduct onto the scales. The answer to this point surely lies in the effect of current insurance practice. When this is taken into account, ignoring the claimant's carelessness surely seems less unjust in the typical case where the claimant is uninsured and the defendant insured. The negligent defendant will not pay for their negligence, while the negligent claimant typically will pay for their own negligence, if the damages payable by the defendant are reduced for contributory negligence.

There is, however, a pragmatic argument that may favour the retention of the doctrine of contributory negligence in personal injury cases. If attention is confined exclusively to the tort system, the case for abolition appears to remain strong. But when the whole scene is surveyed, the case weakens. For it then becomes apparent that a claimant who recovers *any* tort damages is in a sense very fortunate compared with most other victims of accident and disease. As we saw in chapter 1, we are here talking of some 6.5% of accident victims, and a very much smaller proportion of those who suffer illness or disabilities from other causes. The financial provision made for this very small proportion of the disabled and injured is already generous by comparison with what is available to the others. It would seem wrong to improve it still further, even by abolishing doctrines unjust in themselves.

Certainly, so long as the tort system retains anything like its present structure, it would be undesirable to abrogate the defence of contributory negligence in relation to property damage. If the doctrine were swept away altogether it would mean that in many road accidents in which two motorists cause damage to their vehicles by their combined negligence, each would be entitled to claim in full from the other. Such a result might be acceptable in a personal injury claim, but if applied to all cases

62 J. Hellner, 'Tort Liability and Liability Insurance' in F. Schmidt ed., *Scandinavian Studies in Law 1962* (Stockholm, 1962), 131, 159 n. 9.
63 See Schwartz, 'Contributory and Comparative Negligence'.

of damage to vehicles, it would result in a considerable and wasteful recourse to tort liability and liability insurance, rather than to the personal accident insurance of the vehicle owner. Given that property damage-only accidents are six or seven times as frequent as personal injury accidents,[64] this would undoubtedly increase the cost of motor insurance by adding to the administrative cost.

2.5.2   Volenti non fit injuria

The defence of *volenti non fit injuria* is also sometimes referred to as the defence of '(voluntary) assumption of risk'. It has been associated with at least three types of case. In some cases it is indistinguishable from the defence of contributory negligence, except that it is used to deny liability altogether rather than as a ground for apportioning damages. In other cases the claimant agrees not to sue the defendant for any injury as a result of tortious conduct of the latter. In yet other cases a person is taken to have consented to the defendant acting in accordance with a standard of conduct lower than that normally required by the law. Failure to distinguish clearly between these three types of case has caused much confusion.

2.5.2.1   Volenti and agreement not to sue

Agreements not to sue for damages for death or personal injury caused by negligent conduct may take the form of a clause (called an 'exclusion clause') in a contract to which the claimant is a party, or of a written notice by which the claimant has expressly or impliedly agreed to be bound.[65] Such clauses or notices are (by virtue of s. 2 of the Unfair Contract Terms Act 1977) ineffective in any case where the defendant's liability arose in the course of carrying on a business. Nor can a defence of *volenti* be founded solely on such an agreement. Where the liability arose out of the sale or hire-purchase of goods, an exclusion clause will be ineffective against a claimant who did not acquire the goods in the course of a business (a 'consumer') whether or not they were supplied by the defendant in the course of a business. These provisions signal the importance we place on compensating people for personal injury and death caused by negligence, and they recognize the fact that individual consumers often have no choice whether or not to agree to exclusion clauses, even if they are aware of their existence.

Where a passenger in a motor vehicle suffers personal injury as a result of negligence of the driver, the passenger will not normally be bound by any agreement or understanding with the driver that the passenger will not sue the driver.[66] This is so regardless of whether the agreement is in the form of a contract term, or is based on a written notice or arose in some other way. The purpose of this provision is to

---

64 No precise figures for property damage-only accidents are available because there is no obligation to report these; this is an estimate of the Road Research Laboratory: *The Cost of Road Accidents in Great Britain* LR 79 (HMSO, 1967).

65 The most common example is where a landowner puts up a prominent notice addressed to persons entering their land.

66 Road Traffic Act 1988, s. 149(2).

prevent passengers being deprived of the advantages of the third-party liability insurance which users of motor vehicles must take out. Such insurance also covers liability for property damage (up to € 1 million),[67] and agreements to exclude liability for such damage are also ineffective.

In other contexts, however, the position with regard to negligent damage to goods is quite different. Damage to property does not so urgently cry out for compensation as death and personal injury; goods of significant value are often insured by their owner against the risk of damage; and significant property-damage claims are much more likely to be made by businesses (who are more able to look after their own interests) than by individuals. For these reasons, it is not so important to regulate the exclusion of tort liability for damage to property. Under the Unfair Contract Terms Act 1977, clauses which exclude liability for property damage can be effective if they are 'reasonable', except where the clause is contained in a contract for the sale or hire-purchase of goods to a consumer, in which case it will be ineffective. At least in relation to contracts between business concerns, the availability of insurance will be an important factor in deciding the issue of reasonableness.[68] It is not clear, however, to what extent the insurance factor will be held relevant in other cases. For example, will the courts hold that car-parking companies may reasonably exempt themselves from liability for negligent damage to cars on the ground that the owners can insure themselves and that many do so? There is a good deal to be said for the view that such an exclusion would not be unreasonable (at least if it did not extend to the first slice of damage, which is typically not recoverable under property insurance policies); otherwise prudent (insured) owners would be paying for damage to less prudent (uninsured) owners.

So far we have been discussing cases where the defendant has committed a tort and where the effect of the relevant agreement is to protect the defendant from liability. By contrast, sometimes the effect of the relevant agreement or consent by the injured person is to prevent conduct that would otherwise be tortious from amounting to a legal wrong. Examples are agreement to allow a person on to one's land, so preventing the entry from being a trespass; and agreement to bodily contact, or even to being hit, as in sports, where the agreement prevents the conduct amounting to assault. In this type of case it is usually said that the defendant's defence is one of *consent* to trespass or assault rather than assumption of the risk of trespass or assault; but the two defences are clearly related, and they have the same legal effect of depriving the claimant of a cause of action.

2.5.2.2   Volenti and contributory negligence

It is sometimes argued that a person who voluntarily does something that presents a risk of being injured by negligent conduct (such as taking a ride in a car driven by a drunk, or testing an explosive device without taking shelter) should not be

---

67 This provision was introduced in order to comply with EC law, and it was a retrograde step.
68 *Photo Production Ltd* v. *Securicor Transport Ltd* [1980] AC 827; *George Mitchell Ltd* v. *Finney Lock Seeds Ltd* [1983] 2 AC 803.

allowed to recover damages for any resulting personal injuries because that person has willingly or voluntarily 'assumed the risk' of being injured. This involves serious confusion of thought. In the first place, taking a risk will entail a willingness that the risk should occur only if the person taking it knew the nature and extent of the risk. So, for the defence of assumption of risk to succeed, the defendant must first prove that the claimant knew of the risk in some detail. But this is not enough[69] because willingly taking a known risk may be the result of a choice between evils, and not of indifference as to whether the risk materializes, or of a desire that it should materialize, still less of an intention to abandon the right to sue for damages should the risk occur. A pedestrian who crosses the road certainly incurs a known risk of being injured by a driver's negligence, and is willing to be injured in the sense of preferring to incur the risk rather than to stay permanently on one side of the road. But willingness to run this risk is no justification for barring an action against a negligent motorist who runs the pedestrian down.

Something more is needed to justify refusing damages to an injured claimant. Perhaps the additional factor is that the risk must be a very great one, either in the sense of very likely to materialize or in the sense that any resulting injury is likely to be very great, or both. In some circumstances, however – for example, where people in distress or danger are being rescued – the taking of great risks is felt to be justified, and a person who takes such a risk to effect a rescue will not be denied damages on the ground of assumption of risk. It seems then that the only remaining possibility is to treat the defence as confined to those cases in which the claimant ran a risk that was *unjustified or unreasonable in the circumstances*. If this is correct, the only difference between the defence of assumption of risk and that of contributory negligence is that in the former case the claimant must actually have known of the risk whereas in the latter case it is enough that the claimant knew *or ought to have known* of the risk. On this basis, in any case in which a defence of assumption of risk would be available, a defence of contributory negligence would also be available. If this is so, why do courts ever allow a defence of *volenti* to succeed and deny the claimant any damages at all when the defence of contributory negligence allows the court to reduce the damages awarded to the claimant by such proportion as it thinks fit? In the great majority of cases this discretion enables the court to achieve what it regards as a just solution, and consequently a defence of *volenti* rarely succeeds in this sort of case today.

There are two reasons why the defence survives. The first is that although the discretion to reduce a claimant's damages for contributory negligence is wide, it does not allow the court to award nothing[70] – which it may want to do if the claimant acted in a grossly negligent way. The second reason is that damages are apportioned for contributory negligence according to the relative degree of fault of the two parties, and cases occur in which the claimant has acted very unreasonably, so that

---

69 *Smith* v. *Baker* [1891] AC 325.
70 *Pitts* v. *Hunt* [1991] 1 QB 24.

the court wishes to award little or nothing, but in which the defendant has been equally or even more negligent. For instance, a passenger who consents to be driven (or flown)[71] by a person in a heavily drunken state is doing something very foolish indeed, but at the same time the court could hardly assess the defendant's share of responsibility as less than that of the claimant; so the court's power to reduce the damages the claimant will receive is limited in this kind of case.[72] The same is true of cases of joint negligent action, for example, where two workers together do something very negligent and injuries occur to one or both. It is in such cases that courts may be attracted to the defence of *volenti*.[73]

This is hardly satisfactory. The truth is that recourse to the defence of *volenti* in cases where the claimant has been injured partly by their own fault and partly by the fault of the defendant, flies in the face of the provisions of the apportionment legislation and of the case-law which has grown up around it. The main reason for these difficulties is undoubtedly the prevalence of liability insurance. It may be thought, for instance, that as between a drunken driver and a willing passenger, the main responsibility for injuries to the passenger should rest on the driver. But as between the willing passenger and some third party who will actually pay any compensation – an insurance company, or an employer vicariously liable, or the State – the passenger's responsibility may be thought to be great enough to justify awarding little or no compensation.

2.5.2.3 Volenti and standard of care

The classic example of the type of case we are concerned with here is that in which the claimant is injured while watching some sporting event – for example, by a flying puck at an ice hockey match;[74] or by a horse at a show-jumping contest;[75] or a by car at a race track.[76] The question in such cases is whether a person should be allowed to complain of conduct which would or might be negligent in a different place, or in a different context. Whether the defendant in such cases has failed to take reasonable care depends in part on whether the claimant is a willing spectator: for example, a spectator at a cricket match may be said to have accepted the risk of being hit and injured by a six, but a pedestrian on the street outside the playing field surely has not. Putting the matter another way, a driver who races round a race track at 100 m.p.h. in front of willing spectators is not driving negligently just because of the speed of the car; but it would be negligent to drive at the same speed on a public road.

Whether the consent of the claimant should be allowed to affect the standard of care required turns on ideas of personal responsibility. For example, it has been held that a woman who willingly goes to a jeweller to have her ears pierced cannot

---

71 *Morris* v. *Murray* [1991] 2 QB 6.
72 *Owens* v. *Brimmell* [1977] QB 859; also *Gregory* v. *Kelly* [1978] RTR 426.
73 E.g. *ICI* v. *Shatwell* [1965] AC 656.
74 *Murray* v. *Haringey Arena* [1951] 2 KB 529.
75 *Wooldridge* v. *Sumner* [1963] 2 QB 43; see also *Rootes* v. *Shelton* (1967) 116 CLR 383.
76 *Hall* v. *Brooklands Auto Racing Club* [1933] 1 KB 205.

complain if the conditions under which the procedure is done are less hygienic than those which exist at a doctor's surgery.[77] Or take the case of a woman who applied for a job knowing that she was allergic to a substance which the employers used, but not anticipating the extent of the risk she thereby faced. The employers also knew of the allergic condition, and the issue was whether the employers were under a duty not to employ the woman, assuming no precautions were possible. The court said, 'No'.[78] The result would be different, however, if an employer subjected its existing employees to a new risk: in such a case the fact that the employees 'willingly' went on working for the employer would not allow it to argue that they had in some sense accepted the risk.

The effect of a decision that the claimant willingly accepted a lower standard of care than might otherwise be expected will normally be to acquit the defendant of negligence and to deprive the claimant of any damages. Looking at these cases from another point of view, it may sometimes (but not always) be possible to argue that what the claimant has done is to take less than reasonable care for their own safety. When this is so, the better approach might be to hold that claimant contributorily negligent and to reduce the damages awarded rather than to deny compensation entirely.

2.5.3   Illegality

This defence is not of much importance in practice: a court which wants to penalize an injured person for being in breach of the criminal law at the time the injuries were suffered will usually be able to do so by allowing a defence of contributory negligence[79] or *volenti* to succeed. It does have a role in road accident cases where the court thinks that the claimant should recover nothing.[80] This result cannot be achieved under the apportionment legislation, and the *volenti* defence is not normally available in road accident cases.[81]

The defence is of theoretical interest because it raises in acute form the question of the proper role of tort law – is it to compensate the injured, or to give effect to judgments about fault by compensating injured persons in appropriate circumstances, or to deter culpable conduct? The situation is made more complicated by worries about the extent to which the courts would lower their prestige and credibility if they were to 'help' criminals by awarding them damages. A number of basic problems have troubled the courts. The first concerns the extent to which the civil law ought to be used as an adjunct to or reinforcement for the criminal law. The argument that it should be so used is a two-edged sword where both the claimant and the defendant were acting illegally at the time of the injuries. To deny compensation *might* deter the claimant from criminal activity in the future, but relieving the

---

77 *Phillips* v. *William Whitely* [1938] 1 All ER 566.
78 *Withers* v. *Perry Chain Co.* [1961] 1 WLR 1314.
79 E.g. *Revill* v. *Newbery* [1996] QB 567.
80 *Pitts* v. *Hunt* [1991] 1 QB 24.
81 Road Traffic Act 1988, s. 149(3).

defendant of liability for tortious conduct could hardly have a deterrent effect. A second point is that much modern 'criminal' legislation is in fact only regulatory; it is very often designed to co-ordinate human behaviour for the sake of efficiency or to set safety standards to protect people from their own carelessness or stupidity. Little, if any, stigma will attend breach by injured persons of many such laws; and so while deterrence of breach by means, for example, of a fine may be desirable, the unpredictable and usually much more serious sanction of the denial of a civil remedy may seem an unnecessary and unduly harsh sanction. Thus, in a number of cases the question of whether a plea of illegality should succeed has been said to depend in part on whether the 'public conscience' would be 'affronted' or the 'ordinary person shocked' if the claimant were allowed to recover.[82]

A third point relates to the allocation of resources: if a choice has to be made between allowing the claimant to recover from the defendant's insurer or, on the contrary, leaving the claimant in the position of needing to rely on social security benefits, it is by no means obvious that any good purpose is served by denying recovery against the defendant.

A fourth problem concerns the relationship between the illegal act and the injuries. In the formulation adopted above the issue was put in terms of whether the claimant was acting illegally *at the time* the injuries were suffered. But the defence is unlikely to succeed unless the fact that the claimant was acting illegally was in some fairly strong sense a cause of the injuries. The basic principle appears to be that the fact that the claimant was acting illegally at the time the injuries were suffered provides no answer to a claim for damages. If the rule were otherwise, many people who suffer personal injuries on the road or at work would recover no tort damages because breach of some traffic or safety regulation by the injured party is a common contributory cause of injuries. It is only in rather extreme cases that the courts have thought it right to relieve a negligent defendant of liability in order to express disapproval of illegal conduct on the part of the claimant.

Where the claimant and the defendant are *jointly* involved and co-operating in illegal activity, one approach is to bar the claimant from recovery only if the nexus between the act of negligence and the illegal activity is such that the standard of care owed in the particular circumstances could only be determined by taking into account the illegal nature of the activity in which the parties were engaged.[83] If a thief is injured when a companion plants explosives in an allegedly negligent way to blow a safe, the court will not inquire into whether the burglar alarm had sounded or whether the police were on their way or whether the furtive nature of the occasion made it inappropriate to apply to the defendant a standard of care which would be appropriate to a lawful activity. The reason for this approach appears to be one

---

82 E.g. *Kirkham* v. *Chief Constable of Manchester* [1990] 2 QB 283; *Saunders* v. *Edwards* [1987] 1 WLR 1116; *Pitts* v. *Hunt* [1991] 1 QB 24, 45–6 *per* Beldam LJ; but note the reservations of Dillon LJ at 56. See also *Rance* v. *Mid-Downs Health Authority* [1991] 1 QB 487 (public policy would not allow P to sue for loss of a chance to have an illegal abortion).

83 *Ashton* v. *Turner* [1980] 3 All ER 890; *Pitts* v. *Hunt* [1991] 1 QB 24 *per* Balcombe LJ.

of 'public policy', but it is not clear what the policy is: it may be that if the courts were to engage in such inquiries this would lower the respect felt for the courts; or some vague feeling that if things go wrong in the course of criminal activities, even if by the negligence of one of the criminals, the criminals deserve everything they get. To this extent the compensatory aim of the law is subordinated to other values. This is not altogether surprising because even when no-fault systems of motor accident compensation are adopted, there is often much dispute as to whether persons involved in criminal activities should be entitled to claim. The alleviation of need and suffering regardless of fault is clearly an important part of our morality, but it is unlikely that all elements of personal responsibility will ever be eliminated from popular views about the proper way to deal with non-criminal injuries.

So far we have been discussing cases in which the claimant's illegal conduct was not a consequence of the defendant's alleged tort. Suppose prison authorities negligently fail to prevent a person in their custody from committing suicide?[84] Should the person's dependants be allowed to recover from the prison authorities? Or suppose that as a result of injuries received in a car accident, a man's personality changes, he commits rape and is imprisoned?[85] Should he be allowed to recover from the negligent driver for loss suffered as a result of his crimes? Or suppose hospital authorities discharge a mentally ill person who then commits manslaughter.[86] Should the person be allowed to recover damages from the hospital authorities for loss suffered as a result of his crime?

In this type of case, the question the courts ask is whether 'ordinary people' would be shocked and affronted if damages were awarded, not whether the claimant's conduct was technically illegal. In the suicide case, the action was allowed, but not in the manslaughter case. Damages were awarded to the rapist, but this result was heavily criticised in the manslaughter case. At all events, the cases demonstrate the importance of notions of personal responsibility in traditional tort law. On the other hand, they might also be thought to provide evidence of the role of liability insurance in extending the frontiers of tort liability.[87] It is highly unlikely that any of these actions would have been brought if the defendant in each case had either not been insured or a public authority whose liabilities are underwritten by the taxpayer.

---

84 *Kirkham v. Chief Constable of Manchester* [1990] 2 QB 283 (P of unsound mind); *Reeves v. Commissioner of Police of the Metropolis* [1998] 2 WLR 401 (P of sound mind).
85 *Meah v. McCreamer (No. 1)* [1985] 1 All ER 367. In *Meah v. McCreamer (No. 2)* [1986] 1 All ER 943 the court refused the rapist damages representing compensation he had been ordered to pay his victims, but on the ground that the loss was too remote and not on the ground of illegality.
86 *Clunis v. Camden and Islington Health Authority* [1998] 3 All ER 180.
87 See further 9.8.

3

The Scope of the Tort of Negligence

3.1 The nature of the duty of care

The concept of negligent conduct, which was discussed in chapter 2, together with the notions of causation and remoteness of damage (which are discussed in ch. 5), may be said to constitute the concept of fault as embodied in the tort of negligence. But not all faulty conduct in this sense gives rise to legal liability. The tort of negligence, it is sometimes said, cannot be committed 'in the air'. A person will be liable for negligent conduct only if that person owed the claimant a duty to take care. In the famous case of *Donoghue v Stevenson*[1] Lord Atkin enunciated the equally famous 'neighbour principle' according to which a duty of care is owed to persons whom you ought reasonably to foresee as likely to be injured if you do not take reasonable care. On the basis of this principle it was, for many years, said that the test of duty of care was foreseeability. However, in the 1980s the House of Lords became dissatisfied with this test, especially in relation to cases involving liability for economic loss; and in a series of cases[2] it developed a threefold test for the imposition of a duty of care: first, was it foreseeable that the claimant might suffer damage if the defendant did not take reasonable care? Secondly, was there a sufficient relationship of proximity between the claimant and the defendant? And, thirdly, is it just and reasonable in all the circumstances of the case to impose a duty of care? The House of Lords has also shown unwillingness, in some cases at least, to depart from well-established common law rules denying a duty of care even if these three requirements are satisfied.

We have already examined the concept of foreseeability and come to the conclusion that it signifies little more than that liability will be imposed if the court thinks it fair that the defendant should bear responsibility. Some judges have been prepared to admit that the notion of proximity is also just a means of giving effect to (while at the same time concealing) value judgments about the proper scope of liability for negligently caused injury. This is obviously true of the third criterion of duty: justice and reasonableness. Unwillingness to depart from old rules usually arises out of a desire not to upset settled expectations especially in the business community.

These developments in the law relating to duty of care have mainly affected lia-

---

1 [1932] AC 562.
2 The leading case is *Caparo Industries plc v. Dickman* [1990] 2 AC 605.

bility in the tort of negligence for purely economic loss, that is loss other than injury to person or damage to tangible property, and economic loss consequential on such injury or damage.[3] In the typical case of personal injury (except 'nervous shock') or damage to tangible property, foreseeability is, in practice if not in theory, the sole criterion of the existence of a duty of care. Therefore, the threefold test of duty is not of much importance to the subject matter of this book. It should also be noted that whereas Lord Atkin seems to have put forward the neighbour principle as a way of expanding the scope of liability for negligence, the duty of care concept is most commonly used in modern cases as a means of justifying refusal to impose liability for negligence.

This brief account of the law indicates that the main function of the concept of duty of care is to define the boundaries of liability for damage caused by negligent conduct by reference to what are commonly called 'policy considerations'. So, for example, for fairly obvious reasons, soldiers owe no duty of care to fellow soldiers when engaging the enemy in battle; nor is the army under a duty to provide a 'safe system of work' on the battlefield.[4] Until 2000, barristers owed no duty of care to their lay clients in the conduct of litigation in court, even if such conduct was negligent and caused foreseeable damage to the client, in order (it was said) to avoid creating conflicts between the barrister's duties to the court and to the client.[5] There is no duty to take care not to cause a person economic loss by damaging tangible property belonging to a third party because, it is said, the extent of liability such loss may be 'indeterminate' and, perhaps, uninsurable. And here is a final example: suppose a doctor negligently performs a sterilization operation with the result that a woman conceives and bears a child. Whether healthy or disabled, the child can recover no damages; and, at least if the child is healthy, the only remedy available is an award of £15,000 for interference with the mother's 'reproductive autonomy'.[6] In each of these cases, the denial of liability is based on value judgments about the desirability of imposing liability in the type of case in question. In the last type of case, courts have typically not justified the result by denying the existence of a duty of care to the child, but simply by saying that to allow recovery would be undesirable for various reasons. To say that a person owes a duty of care in a particular situation means (and means only) that the person will be liable for causing damage by negligence in that situation.[7]

---

3 This extremely complex topic is beyond the scope of this book. See generally P. Cane, *Tort Law and Economic Interests*, 2nd edn (Oxford, 1996).
4 *Mulcahy* v. *Ministry of Defence* [1996] QB 737.
5 The rule was reversed in *Arthur JS Hall & Co.* v *Simons* [2002] 1 AC 615.
6 The leading case in this difficult area (for the moment, at least) is *Rees* v. *Darlington Memorial Hospital NHS Trust* [2004] 1 AC 3009.
7 For criticism of this view see N.J. McBride, 'Duties of Care – Do They Exist?' (2004) 24 *OJLS* 417. I agree with McBride that negligence law is at least as concerned with telling people how they ought to behave as with imposing liability for failure to behave as the law prescribes. In this sense, to say that a person owes a duty of care means more than that they can be held liable for negligence. But in practice, the only function of the duty-of-care concept in legal reasoning is to define the scope of liability to pay damages for negligence.

Use of the duty-of-care concept to create immunities from negligence liability has been particularly controversial in relation to the liability of public authorities, such as the police, and education and welfare agencies. Although the reasoning in such cases tends to be very complex, what it boils down to is that a public authority will be immune from liability for negligence in the performance of its statutory functions (i.e. will owe no duty of care to persons injured by its negligence) unless the court thinks that imposing such liability would be compatible with the terms of the relevant statute and would not interfere unduly with the performance of those functions. In *Osman v UK*[8] the European Court of Human Rights (ECtHR) held that this technique for denying liability was inconsistent with the right to a fair hearing under Article 6 of the European Convention on Human Rights (ECHR). The ECtHR objected to the fact that the English court decided the duty issue as a 'preliminary point of law', without giving detailed consideration to all the facts of the case. The House of Lords in *Barrett v Enfield LBC*[9] was influenced by this decision and held, in effect, that the issues of compatibility with the statute, and so on, should be resolved on the basis of a careful consideration of all the relevant facts of individual cases, and not by creating what were called 'blanket immunities' for particular functions (such as taking a child into care or providing protection to potential victims of crime). The ECtHR has since resiled from its approach in *Osman*,[10] but it has left open the possibility that use of the duty-of-care technique might infringe the right to an effective remedy in a national court for breaches of the ECHR (under Article 13 of the ECHR) in a case where the defendant's allegedly negligent conduct also constituted a breach of a Convention right.[11] The argument is that denying liability on the basis of a 'no-duty' immunity might preclude proper investigation of the claimant's allegations and hence deny the claimant an effective remedy.

This chapter contains an examination of certain issues relevant to legal liability for death and personal injury that are usually discussed by lawyers in terms of whether a duty of care is owed. In other words, these are issues relevant to the scope of legal liability for negligently inflicted death and personal injury.

3.2   Specific duty issues

3.2.1   Common situations in which duties of care have been imposed

In practice, the two most important areas of tort liability for death and personal injuries relate to road accidents and industrial accidents. Legal liability for negligence resulting in road accidents has been recognized certainly since the seventeenth

---

8 (2000) 29 EHRR 245.

9 [2001] 2 AC 550.

10 *TP & KM* v. *UK* (2002) 34 EHRR 42; *Z* v. *UK* (2002) 34 EHRR 97; *DP & JC v UK* (2003) 36 EHRR 183.

11 E.g. in *McGlinchey* v. *UK* (2003) 37 EHRR 41 conduct of prison authorities that amounted, in effect, to negligent failure to care adequately for a sick prisoner was held to constitute a breach of the right not to be subjected to inhuman or degrading treatment under Article 3.

century and perhaps earlier. There has never been any doubt that those using the highways are under a duty of care in so doing, and the legal position today is plain: any person using the roads, whether as a motorist, pedestrian or cyclist, will be liable if, by positive action,[12] that person negligently causes physical injury to anybody else. A lawyer would scarcely ever waste time in an ordinary road accident case by inquiring whether the defendant owed a duty of care to the claimant. This would simply be taken for granted. The general principle also holds good for positive, negligent action resulting in industrial accidents.

Another important area of negligence liability is liability for defective products (although the importance of the common law has been considerably reduced by enactment of a regime of 'strict' liability in the Consumer Protection Act 1987, which is discussed in ch. 4). The leading case is *Donoghue v Stevenson*, to which we have already referred. In this case the claimant allegedly suffered gastroenteritis and shock as a result of drinking a bottle of ginger-beer which was said to have contained the remains of a decomposed snail. The bottle of ginger-beer had been bought for the claimant by a friend in a café, but the claimant sued the manufacturer. The question at issue was whether, assuming that the presence of the snail was due to lack of reasonable care on the part of the manufacturer, it would be liable to the claimant. To us, it may seem astonishing that the answer could ever have been in doubt, since there are several good arguments in favour of liability in such circumstances – the desire to compensate the claimant for injuries; the value of providing an incentive for manufacturers of food and drink for public consumption to take precautions against such events; and finally the fact that the manufacturer is better able than the consumer to bear the loss and distribute it by making allowance for it in the price of its products. Nevertheless, despite all this, liability was very much doubted at the time of the case, and it is generally agreed that the majority in the House of Lords, in finding for the claimant, made 'new law' by departing from precedents suggesting that there would be no liability on such facts.

The real importance of *Donoghue v Stevenson* was that it decided that a claimant could recover damages for negligence against a defendant even though there was no contract between them (in other words, even though they were not 'in privity of contract' with one another). Although liability for negligent acts was well established, long before this case, in some areas (such as road accidents) even in the absence of any contractual relationship, there is no doubt that the privity-of-contract principle had become a severe limitation on the extension of the law of negligence, and that it had been used by the courts in the nineteenth century to restrict liability for negligent acts. *Donoghue v Stevenson* removed this restriction on liability for negligence, and this began a movement towards general liability for physical damage caused by positive, negligent conduct that has been going on ever since.

12 Concerning omissions, see 3.2.2.

A significant area of law for our purposes is that relating to the liability of an occupier of premises for personal injury and property damage suffered on the premises by persons who come onto (or 'visit') them ('occupiers' liability'). Loosely speaking, visitors are divided into two classes, namely lawful and unlawful visitors. As a result of the enactment of the Occupiers' Liability Act 1957, the liability of an occupier to lawful visitors has been very largely assimilated to that of ordinary liability in negligence, so that occupiers now owe to their lawful visitors a 'common duty of care', which is for all practical purposes indistinguishable from the ordinary duty-of-care concept used in most common law actions for negligence. Nothing here need detain us because it is plain that occupiers always owe their lawful visitors a duty to take care, and are therefore liable for causing them physical injury by negligence. Indeed liability can be imposed on an occupier either for positive negligence ('misfeasance') or negative negligence ('nonfeasance' or 'omission'). Liability to unlawful visitors (or 'trespassers') is governed by the Occupiers' Liability Act 1984, which imposes on occupiers a duty to take such care as is reasonable considering, in particular, that trespassers by definition force their presence on the occupier without the latter's consent.

Another important statutory source of negligence liability is the Defective Premises Act 1972, s. 4 of which imposes extensive liability on landlords for injury caused, to persons coming onto rented premises, by failure to repair. A number of other statutes have reversed common law rules denying the existence of a duty of care in various circumstances. For example, the Animals Act 1971 largely (though not quite entirely) removes an immunity from liability once enjoyed by owners of animals which cause injury or damage as a result of straying on to a highway. The Highways (Miscellaneous Provisions) Act 1961 imposes liability on highway authorities, for negligently failing to repair a highway; and the Law Reform (Husband and Wife) Act 1962 enables husbands and wives to sue each other for negligence (with a view to obtaining damages from insurance companies). The Congenital Disabilities (Civil Liability) Act 1976 also eliminates any doubts about another possible no-duty situation by making it clear that, in general, legal liability will exist for negligently inflicting injuries on an unborn child.

3.2.2   The distinction between acts and omissions

The paradigm instance of negligence liability arises where bodily injury or property damage results from what we might call 'positive conduct' – where, for instance, two speeding cars collide injuring occupants and vehicles. Lawyers often refer to positive conduct as 'misfeasance', and they contrast this with 'nonfeasance'. This contrast may also be expressed in terms of a distinction between 'acts' and 'omissions' (failures to act).[13] It must be said at the outset that there are many

---

13 See T. Honoré, 'Are Omissions Less Culpable?' in P. Cane and J. Stapleton eds., *Essays for Patrick Atiyah* (Oxford, 1991); H.L.A. Hart and T. Honoré, *Causation in the Law*, 2nd edn (Oxford, 1985); M.S. Shapo, *The Duty to Act* (Austin, Texas and London, 1977).

situations in which it is impossible to draw any clear line between misfeasance and nonfeasance. A solicitor instructed to draft a will allows it to be wrongly witnessed so that it is invalid: this may be seen as misfeasance in preparing the will or as failure to ensure that it was properly witnessed. A person digs a hole on their land and a visitor falls into it: this may be seen as affirmative conduct in digging the hole or as nonfeasance in failing to fence the hole or give a warning. A person turns right across a line of traffic without signalling: this is either positive bad driving or a negative failure to signal.

More generally, whether failure to act is viewed as nonfeasance or misfeasance depends largely on whether the failure is viewed in isolation or as part of a larger activity. Nevertheless, despite the difficulty of the distinction, the law recognizes and acts on it. It is an important aspect of the difference between tort and contract liability: a person is often not bound to take positive action unless they have agreed to do so, and have been paid for doing so; but people are in general bound to abstain from causing damage by negligence whether or not they have agreed to do so, or have been paid for doing so. Tort law embodies a general bias against imposing liability for nonfeasance. However, it is by no means the case that failure to take reasonable steps to prevent another suffering injury or loss is never actionable in tort.

What lies behind the distinction between nonfeasance and misfeasance? How can we regard absent-mindedly driving a motor vehicle through a red light as something more reprehensible than walking by while a child is drowning in a few feet of water? Yet failure to save a drowning stranger is a stock example of a clear case of immunity from liability for negligence (and indeed in the criminal law). Such questions are often posed in terms of a distinction between law and morality: if tort law is based on some concept of moral fault, why does it embody quite a sharp distinction between acts and omissions? There are at least two reasons why we need to be a little wary of thinking about the issue in this way. First, although, according to some views about morality, nonfeasance may be just as reprehensible misfeasance, many people would give at least some moral weight to the distinction between acts and omissions in deciding the right thing to do in various situations and in assessing the behaviour of others. There is no single version of 'morality' that can be easily contrasted with 'the law'. Secondly, it is one thing to say that rendering assistance to someone in danger or distress is (morally) the right thing to do, but quite another to say that a person who fails to do it should be (legally) obliged to pay compensation for harm resulting from the failure to act. A good reason for not turning every moral duty into a legal obligation lies in the nature of legal sanctions and remedies compared with the sorts of disapproval with which breaches of morality are often met. And a person who has reservations about imposing obligations in tort to compensate for harm resulting from nonfeasance would be even less willing to use the criminal law to punish failure to act.

Nevertheless, it is often assumed that the law's approach to nonfeasance is out of step with morality; and so it is worth asking why the law of tort distinguishes between misfeasance and nonfeasance. In seeking explanations it is necessary, first, to remember that in this book we are primarily discussing cases of physical damage and injury. We will not consider cases of nonfeasance that cause only financial loss, as where a person fails to warn another that they face a risk of suffering financial loss, which the former knew about but the latter did not.[14] The question to be answered is how we can justify immunity from liability for nonfeasance causing physical damage or injury.

The first possible consideration is that the imposition of duties to prevent harm (by failure to act) is often more burdensome than the imposition of duties not to cause harm (by acting). In its main spheres of practical operation the law of negligence tends to prescribe not what we are to do, but only how we are to do things we choose to do. Thus I am generally quite free to drive my car when and where I want to on the roads; and it is not particularly onerous to be required to drive it carefully. This obligation does not prevent me going where I want to, when I want to, though it may force me to go a little more slowly than I might have chosen. And even when the law does impose duties to prevent harm, they are frequently of a type that does not involve much expenditure of time and effort.

Requiring someone to render assistance to (or 'rescue') persons in danger may not only be burdensome in time and effort, but may also involve expenditure of significant amounts of money, and involve significant risks to the person(s) providing assistance. If the law were to impose a general obligation to rescue, who would pay the costs of so doing? And if there is an element of risk in rendering assistance, and the risk eventuates, should the rescuer be able to recover compensation for this? Suppose a person dies in the course of rescuing someone who is drowning: who is going to maintain any dependants of the dead person? English law does not recognize any general right to reward or even recompense for rescue. If someone (including the rescued person) created the dangerous situation by negligence, the rescuer may have an action against that person for costs incurred and any injuries suffered in effecting the rescue. It should be noted, however, that in practice, an action against the rescued person would rarely be covered by liability insurance.

A second reason why it may be felt desirable to distinguish between misfeasance and nonfeasance is that in the case of misfeasance, the defendant is normally self-identified by the conduct that results in harm. On the other hand, a person accused of nonfeasance is likely to feel, 'Why pick on me? I didn't do anything.' This sort of reaction may take one of two forms. First, the person may be asserting that they are merely one of hundreds, and that it is unfair to pick on one individual while bypassing all the others. If, for instance, a driver negligently knocks down and injures a pedestrian, it is easy enough to justify fastening liability onto the driver for misfeasance. But if the unfortunate pedestrian is left bleeding in the road and a dozen, or a hundred, other motorists drive by without stopping to render assistance, there would be no clear justification for imposing liability for nonfeasance

---

14 E.g. *Banque Keyser Ullman v Skandia Insurance* [1990] 1 QB 665; *Reid v Rush & Tompkins* [1990] 1 WLR 212.

on any one rather than another. In this type of situation a person is unlikely to deny that they ought to have stopped to render assistance: the complaint is that so ought many others.

The reaction may take a second form, which raises rather different issues. The person accused of nonfeasance may be asserting that it was not up to them to do something, and that the burden of taking the desired precautions really rested on someone else – perhaps on the person in danger or on a third party, but in any case not them. For instance, suppose that a window cleaner sent by an employer to clean the windows at a block of offices is injured in a fall resulting from the use of defective belt-hooks. If the cleaner sues the employer, the complaint will probably be one of nonfeasance; that is, the employee will be complaining that the employer ought to have checked the belt-hooks or ought to have supplied safer means of cleaning windows that did not depend on possibly unsafe belt-hooks. In this situation the employer's reply will probably be: 'It was not my responsibility to check the belt-hooks. The occupiers of the offices should have seen that the belt-hooks were safe; it was their responsibility, not mine.' In some cases the employer might argue that it was the claimant's own responsibility to take the necessary precautions. For instance, suppose an employee's belongings are stolen at their place of work.[15] Whose responsibility is it to take precautions against this possibility: the employee's or the employer's?

A third possible ground for distinguishing between nonfeasance and misfeasance is based on notions of causation. In some cases at least, we would hesitate to say that a person guilty of nonfeasance *caused* injury or damage, and might prefer to say that they *failed to prevent* injury or damage being caused by someone or something else. Assuming that if assistance had been given to a person in danger, it would have prevented the injury or damage occurring, there is, of course, a sense in which a person who negligently failed to render such assistance 'caused' the injury or harm – if they had helped, the injury or harm would not have occurred. But there is a difference between saying that a person caused harm in this ('counterfactual') sense and saying that they should be held responsible for the harm and, perhaps, liable to pay compensation to the victim. According to the 'causal' argument for distinguishing between acts and omissions, we might want to say that although harm would not have occurred but for a person's negligent nonfeasance, nevertheless the person did not 'really' cause it, and so should not be held legally responsible for it.

As grounds for creating immunities from liability for nonfeasance, these arguments are weak. The first point – the possible burdensomeness of affirmative obligations – can easily be met. For one thing, the immunity from liability for nonfeasance does not apply only where it would be unduly burdensome to require affirmative conduct. It applies even, for instance, where all that a person has to do is shout a warning or make a telephone call. A person sees a stranger's house on

---

15 *Deyong v Shenburn* [1946] KB 227 (held that the employer could not be held liable for the theft of the employee's belongings by a third party).

fire: how burdensome would it be to require that person to telephone for the fire brigade? A sighted person can watch a blind stranger walk straight into a hole in the road without liability in tort or any other branch of the law. What burden would it be to require the sighted person to shout a warning? Even if a duty to render assistance would in some cases involve a significant burden, there seems no reason why the burdensomeness of the duty sought to be imposed should not be weighed against the benefit of preventing harm. If the burden seems disproportionate to the benefit, no duty need be imposed. Such an exercise would simply involve applying to cases of nonfeasance the negligence formula used when determining liability for misfeasance. No doubt it would be advisable to move cautiously here so that the standard of what it is reasonable to expect by way of obligations to prevent harm is not pitched too high.

The second argument, that there is difficulty in identifying the person liable for nonfeasance, and that to impose liability would often be to fasten onto the nearest convenient defendant, can be rebutted by observing that the law does this even where misfeasance is in issue. For example, bad road design contributes to many motor vehicle accidents, but road authorities are rarely sued because the negligent driver is a much more convenient target. The fact that the driver may be less or no more culpable than the road designer is not of much importance given that the driver will always be insured and will not pay the damages personally. So the question is not whether there are others more or equally culpable, but whether this defendant was personally at fault.

As for the third (causal) argument, it does often seem easier to justify holding someone responsible for an outcome which that person has 'caused' by affirmative conduct, and we may have doubts about treating nonfeasance as a cause at all. Many people intuitively feel that nonfeasance can be treated as a 'cause' only if there was a duty to act.[16] Take the following example:[17] suppose a passenger on a small pleasure boat falls overboard, through their own carelessness, into ice-cold waters, and eventually drowns. We might well want to say that a fellow passenger who did nothing to help the drowning person could not be held in any way responsible for, and did not 'cause', the death by failing to jump in and attempt a rescue, because they were under no duty to take such action. But we might feel differently if the owner of the boat failed to attempt to manoeuvre it into a position where a lifeline could be thrown to the drowning person. The owner could more easily be said to be a cause of the death because under the circumstances the owner surely had a duty to take advantage of having control over the vessel to help the passenger.

However, this causal argument is open to a strong objection. At first sight, to say that the defendant's nonfeasance did not cause the claimant's loss seems to provide

16 For a review of the literature on this question see A.M. Honoré, *International Encyclopedia of Comparative Law* vol. XI, (1971), ch. 7, ss. 25–8.
17 See *Horsley v MacLaren (The Ogopogo)* [1971] 2 Lloyd's Reports 210 on which this example is based.

a sort of objective justification for not imposing liability. But the way we view the causation issue depends on whether we think that the defendant ought to have done something to help; and if so, whether we think that breach of this duty ought to be translated into a legal liability to pay compensation. These are matters of judgment that cannot be resolved in any 'objective' way. Of course, the question of whether the harm would have been prevented if the defendant had taken action – in other words, whether the defendant's failure to act caused the harm in a counterfactual sense – can, in theory at least, be answered 'objectively' or scientifically, on the basis of facts alone and without having to make value judgments. But the question of whether the defendant's nonfeasance 'really' caused the harm cannot be answered in this way because in this richer sense of the word 'cause', the language of causation provides a way of expressing a judgment about the proper limits of responsibility and liability for negligent failure to act.

While each of these three arguments can be used to explain and rationalize certain cases in which it does not seem fair to impose legal liability for nonfeasance, none justifies a sharp distinction between misfeasance – which may attract legal liability for resulting harm – and nonfeasance – which will not. The distinction between acts and omissions is an important one, but it does not mark the boundary between liability and no liability. In fact, there are various situations in which tort liability for nonfeasance can arise, and these can be conveniently grouped under several headings.

3.2.2.1   Undertakings

A person who contracts to do something may incur liability for not doing it. There is also a somewhat hazy and undeveloped part of the law dealing with voluntary (i.e. non-contractual) undertakings. Suppose a motorist comes upon a car accident in a remote area and tells a person badly injured in the accident that she will call an ambulance from the nearest settlement, but then fails to do so. This would seem a strong case for liability especially if, in reliance on the undertaking, the victim declined help from someone else. Or suppose an altruistic citizen who regularly frequents an isolated beach and is trained as a lifeguard, offers her services as a voluntary lifeguard to those using the beach. This might justify imposition of liability if the self-appointed lifeguard made no attempt to rescue someone who relied on the offer in using the beach. Not unrelated are cases in which a person carries on an especially dangerous activity or creates a physically dangerous situation: here the law might well impose a duty to take reasonable steps to obviate or to warn of the danger.[18] For example, a local authority obliterated road markings when the road was resurfaced but then failed to repaint the road or to warn of the resulting dangerous situation; the council was held liable for injuries suffered by a motorist as a result.[19] Again, for example, a motor manufacturer could probably be held

18 E.g. *Arnold v Teno* (1978) 83 DLR (3d) 609.
19 *Bird v Pearce* [1979] RTR 369.

liable for failure to recall vehicles discovered to suffer from a dangerous defect (this is frequently done voluntarily).

Even contractual undertakings are relevant to the problem of liability for non-feasance in tort, because the person injured may not be the other contracting party.[20] For example: A contracts with B that A will clear the snow off B's doorstep during winter snowfalls. One day A fails to do this and C, a visitor to B's house, slips on the snow and is injured. Is A liable to C in tort for failing to take reasonable care? A has not created the danger, and although A was under a duty towards B to remove it, can C rely on that duty? In this kind of case there is much to be said for imposing liability, and a court would probably do so.[21] Because A owes a contractual obligation (to B) to clear the snow, there is less reason for reluctance to impose tort liability on A in favour of C. Furthermore, in many cases of this kind the undertaking leads other people to rely on it, thus creating dangers which would not have arisen without it. For example, a person takes a car to a garage to have the brakes repaired. The garage omits to do so but the owner (reasonably) thinks that the repair has been done. Here the car owner is induced by reliance on the garage to continue driving the car, thereby creating dangers to third parties on the road. By their undertaking and failure to carry it out, the garage has made a positive contribution to the danger.

3.2.2.2   Duties of physical protection

There are various situations in which the law is prepared to impose duties, to prevent harm, on people who are in a particularly good position to protect or rescue others from physical dangers and who, it might be thought, should offer such protection because of their relationship with the person in danger. So, for example, employers owe their employees legal duties to provide safe tools, a safe workplace and safe working systems; and the basis of such duties is that the individual employee typically has little control over working conditions. Again, doctors and hospitals may be held liable for failure to provide treatment,[22] or for failure to warn patients of risks associated with particular treatments, or for failure to protect a known 'psychiatric and suicide risk' who seriously injures himself by jumping out of a window.[23] More generally, professionals, by virtue of their status as professionals, owe duties to their clients and, to a lesser extent, to third parties, to take positive steps, in the exercise of their professional skills, to protect them from injury, loss or damage and to warn them of impending danger.

---

20 Also because, in general, clients can sue their professional advisers in either contract or tort: *Henderson v Merrett Syndicates Ltd* [1995] 2 AC 145. Not all contractual undertakings are actionable in tort, but a contractual undertaking (whether express or implied) to take all reasonable care and (positively) to do everything reasonably necessary to protect the client from injury, damage or loss, certainly is.

21 But not if the loss suffered was purely economic. For other examples see A.J.E. Jaffey, *The Duty of Care* (Aldershot, 1992), 52–3.

22 *Barnett v Chelsea and Kensington Hospital Management Committee* [1969] 1 QB 428 (but the claim failed on the issue of causation).

23 See *Selfe v Ilford & District Hospital Management Committee*, *The Times*, 26 November 1970.

Adults in charge of children may be required to take positive steps to protect or help them; and prison authorities owe a duty of protection to prisoners.[24] Similarly, a person could probably be held liable for failing to call medical assistance for an occupant or guest in their house who became helpless through disease or accident. There seems little doubt that occupiers of business premises, such as hotels, restaurants, shops and even offices, would be held liable if they failed to take reasonable steps to summon medical help in an emergency arising from sudden illness to a visitor to the premises. In Canada it has been held that a person in charge of a vessel owes a duty to assist a person who falls overboard;[25] that a hotel proprietor may owe a duty of reasonable protection to an intoxicated person turned out of the hotel and who is subsequently run down by a car;[26] and that vehicle owners owe a duty of protection to unlicensed and uninstructed persons whom they allow to use their vehicles. In another case the Supreme Court of Canada held that a ski resort operator owed a duty to take reasonable steps to discourage an intoxicated patron from taking part in a dangerous competition run by the operator.[27]

On the other hand, English courts have held that a taxi driver owes no duty of care to an intoxicated passenger once the passenger has left the taxi;[28] and that the fire service and other emergency services are not liable simply for failing to prevent injury or damage, even with negligence.[29] Liability will arise only if they positively make matters worse. In one case, a local authority was sued for failure to exercise its power to make a road safer by removing an obstruction to sight.[30] The principle underlying the decision that the authority was not liable is that public authorities can only be held liable in tort for failing to perform their public functions, in such a way as to prevent harm occurring, if their conduct was so unreasonable that no reasonable public body could have considered it appropriate.

The basic issue that arises in all of these cases and situations is the extent to which people should take responsibility for their own safety rather than expecting others to protect or rescue them from physical danger – or, at least, rather than expecting to be able to recover damages for harm resulting from another's failure to protect or rescue. To say that the law is sometimes justified in imposing duties of physical protection is probably banal and uncontroversial. Moreover, in imposing duties of

24 *Kirkham v. Chief Constable of Manchester* [1990] 2 QB 283. See also *Metropolitan Police Commissioner v Reeves* [2000] 1 AC 360.
25 *Horsley v MacLaren (The Ogopogo)* [1972] 2 Lloyd's Reports 210.
26 For the position in Australia see *Cole v South Tweed Heads Rugby Football Club Ltd* (2004) 217 CLR 469 (commercial supplier of alcohol owes no duty to intoxicated customer). Concerning the liability of hosts to persons injured by intoxicated guests see J. Horder, 'Tort and the Road to Temperance: A Different Kind of Offensive against the Drinking Driver' (1988) 51 *Modern LR* 735.
27 *Crocker v Sundance Northwest Resorts Ltd* [1988] 1 SCR 1186 (in which the two previous examples also are cited).
28 *Griffiths v Brown, The Times*, 23 October 1998.
29 *Capital & Counties Plc v Hampshire CC* [1997] QB 1004; *OLL Ltd v Secretary of State for Transport* [1997] 3 All ER 897; but contrast *Kent v Griffiths* [2001] QB 36 (ambulance service).
30 *Stovin v Wise* [1996] AC 923.

protection, the law seems to reflect commonly held ethical views by taking account of the nature and closeness of the relationship between the parties, and of the identity of the person who created the dangerous situation – the claimant, the defendant or a third party. The difficult and contentious issue is where the line should be drawn between protection of self and protection of others. For example, consider a case in which a naval airman drank large amounts of alcohol and, as a result, choked to death on his own vomit. While his employer, the Ministry of Defence, was held not liable for allowing him to get himself drunk, it was held liable for failing to look after him even though his colleagues knew that he was incapable of taking care of himself.[31] This decision has been described as 'offensive to normal ideas of justice'[32] – although the judges who held in the claimant's favour would obviously not accept this description of their decision.

There are two important points to bear in mind here. First, while courts may sometimes refuse to impose liability for failure to prevent harm on the basis of a rather abstract statement to the effect that 'the defendant did not owe the claimant a duty of protection', decisions whether or not to impose such liability are more often based on a detailed consideration of whether, in the particular circumstances of the case, the defendant ought to have taken steps to protect the claimant. The court will treat the issue in the case as being whether, on the facts, the defendant was at fault and acted negligently, rather than whether, in the abstract, the defendant owed the claimant a duty of protection. So, for instance, disagreement about the case of the airman, considered in the previous paragraph, centred not on whether, in the abstract, an employer owes a duty of protection to its employees – clearly it should and does. The real issue was whether, in the circumstances of the case, the employer acted negligently in not protecting the employee – in lawyer's jargon, whether the employer breached its duty of care to protect the employee. The second point to note is that even if a court holds that the defendant owed the claimant a duty of protection, and negligently failed to protect the claimant from harm, that may not be the end of the matter. For instance, in the case of the airman, the court held that although the defendant ought to have taken steps to protect the claimant from his own fecklessness, the airmen was also partly responsible for what happened. In fact, the court apportioned the responsibility two-thirds to the claimant and only one-third to the defendant. Both of these points illustrate the distinction between the issue of duty of care and the issue of fault (considered in ch. 2). Duty of care is concerned with whether, in principle, the defendant can be held liable: the scope of liability for negligence, as it was put earlier. This leaves open the issue of fault – whether and to what extent a defendant who owes a duty of care breached that duty and ought to be held responsible ('at fault') for what happened.

---

31 *Barrett v Ministry of Defence* [1995] 1 WLR 1217. See also *Jebson v Ministry of Defence* [2000] 1 WLR 2055.

32 P.S. Atiyah, *The Damages Lottery* (Oxford, 1997), 40–1.

Not only may people disagree about when the law should impose duties of physical protection, but views about this may also change over time. A good illustration is provided by cases where a person suffers injury as a result of diving into shallow water and claims that the defendant ought to have erected a sign warning of the danger. In 1993 the High Court of Australia imposed liability in such a case,[33] and the decision can be seen as part of a general trend in the twentieth century of expansion of the scope of tort liability for personal injury. In the last few years, however, a reaction has set in, and increasing emphasis is now being put in self-reliance and 'personal responsibility'. This change of attitude is reflected in decisions of the courts in personal injury cases.[34] In a recent English case of a young man rendered tetraplegic as a result of diving into shallow water, the House of Lords, by majority, refused to impose liability on the defendant for failing to take steps that would have prevented the tragedy.[35] In a section of his judgment headed 'Free will' Lord Hoffmann stressed that the claimant had acted 'freely and voluntarily', and that the law should not expect occupiers of land 'paternalistically' to prevent visitors from undertaking 'inherently risky activities' on their land in order to protect them from harming themselves. It is worth noting, however, that the Court of Appeal had decided the case in the claimant's favour.

3.2.2.3   Duties to control the conduct of others

A person who has the power to control another may be liable for failure to exercise it. So, for example, parents and school authorities are under a duty to control young children, and prison authorities are under a duty to control inmates.[36] If a child, for instance, is given a gun by a third party, and is known by the parent to have a gun, the parent becomes responsible for seeing that the child is old enough and sensible enough to be allowed to have the gun; for instructing the child in how to use it safely, and so on. If the parent does nothing at all, and if he or she is shown to have been negligent to do nothing, the parent will be liable for injuries caused by the child.[37] Similarly, an employer is under a duty to control employees, although this is not of much practical importance because an employer is vicariously liable for the negligence of employees whether the employer was negligent or not; but there are a few cases in which the employer may be liable for personal nonfeasance though not vicariously liable because, for instance, the servant was not acting in the course of employment.[38]

A person who sees someone being beaten up in the street may walk on without assisting, but a hotel proprietor who saw someone in danger of being attacked by

---

33 *Nagle v Rottnest Island Authority* (1993) 177 CLR 423.
34 E.g. *Wyong Shire Council v Vairy* [2004] NSWCA 247; affirmed *Vairy v Wyong Shire Council* [2005] HCA 62. But contrast *Mulligan v Coffs Harbour City Council* [2005] HCA 63.
35 *Tomlinson v Congleton BC* [2004] 1 AC 46.
36 *Home Office v Dorset Yacht Co. Ltd* [1970] AC 1004.
37 *Newton v Edgerley* [1959] 1 WLR 1031.
38 *Hudson v Ridge Manufacturing Co.* [1957] 2 QB 348.

a guest in the hotel might well be liable for failing to take some reasonable steps to control the attacker. Those in charge of public transport vehicles or vessels would also have some duty to control passengers. The same might also apply to private vehicles; for example, a car driver might be held liable to an injured cyclist if the driver sat and watched a passenger negligently opening the offside door of the car in the way of approaching traffic, at least if the driver was in a position to stop the door being opened.[39]

On the other hand, the police cannot normally be held liable for failure to prevent crime.[40] More generally, regulatory bodies whose function it is to monitor and control potentially dangerous activities are typically not liable for failure to exercise their regulatory powers. The cases which first established this principle dealt with financial loss – where, for example, authorities responsible for regulating banks are sued by depositors and investors who lose their money when the bank collapses.[41] But the principle has also been applied where, for instance, social workers fail to prevent child abuse;[42] and it has even been hinted that a local authority might not be held liable if occupants of a house were injured as a result of bad and illegal construction work which the authority negligently failed to detect when it inspected the house for compliance with building regulations.[43] On the other hand, liability may be imposed where, because of personal dealings between the defendant and the claimant, it would be unreasonable for the defendant not to act for the claimant's benefit. But the mere fact that a public body has powers to control the conduct of others, which it could exercise for the benefit of members of the public, does not open it to tort liability for negligent failure to do so. One reason for this approach is that the courts do not want public funds to be used to compensate individuals when they could be used for the benefit of the public as a whole or sections of it. Another is a fear that if public authorities are vulnerable to tort liability, they may be led to act 'defensively' in performing their functions; that is, in a way designed to avoid potential tort liability regardless of whether such action is in the wider public interest.

It should be noted, however, that in these decisions, English courts demonstrated a much greater unwillingness to impose liability than courts in other major common law jurisdictions, such as Australia, Canada and New Zealand, have displayed. It should also be recalled (as noted in 3.1) that the 'no-duty' technique used in these cases was held by the ECtHR to be incompatible with Article 6 of the ECHR. Subsequently, the House of Lords signalled that it would modify its approach to take more account of the facts of individual cases. Increased willingness to impose

---

39 See e.g. *Brown v Roberts* [1965] 1 QB 1 where the claim was rejected on the ground that the owner of the car was not in fact negligent in failing to prevent the passenger opening the door.
40 *Hill v Chief Constable of West Yorkshire* [1989] AC 53.
41 *Yuen Kun Yeu v Attorney-General of Hong Kong* [1988] AC 175.
42 *X v Bedfordshire County Council* [1995] 2 AC 633; but see now *Barrett v Enfield LBC* [2001] 2 AC 550.
43 *Murphy v Brentwood District Council* [1991] 1 AC 398, 463 (Lord Keith of Kinkel).

liability in such cases can, perhaps, also be detected. For its part, the European Court has drawn back somewhat from its disapproval of the duty-of-care technique by holding that it does not infringe Article 6. However, it has also held that the technique may be incompatible with Article 13 of the ECHR. It remains unclear what impact this jurisprudence of the ECtHR will have on the use of the duty-of-care technique negatively to limit liability for negligence rather than positively, to provide a framework or justification for the imposition of liability.

3.2.2.4   Control over property

Another ground on which liability for nonfeasance may be imposed is that the defendant was in control of some property from which, or by means of which, the damage was done. For example, the duties of occupiers of land to their lawful visitors[44] require them to take positive steps to ensure that visitors are safe either by removing dangers from the premises or by warning of such dangers.[45] Another example of this kind of liability is to be found in the case of *Goldman v Hargrave*[46] in which a tree on the defendant's land was struck by lightning and caught fire. The defendant took some, but (it was found) negligent and ineffectual, steps to put the fire out, and it spread to the claimant's property, causing damage there. The (successful) complaint against the defendant was simply that he had failed to take reasonable steps to put out the fire. He had not started it, nor even created any conditions on his land which could be said to have contributed to the risk of the fire: it was simply a natural hazard.[47] The argument in favour of such liability is that the ownership of land should entail responsibilities as well as rights.

An important argument against such liability, however, is that if people can be held liable for careless attempts to avert danger, they might be discouraged from helping in the first place. The law is keen not to discourage altruism and so, for example, it allows rescuers to recover compensation for injury or loss suffered in the process of rendering assistance from any person negligently responsible for creating the dangerous situation which prompted the 'rescuer' to act.[48] In *Goldman v Hargrave* the Privy Council countered this argument by saying that the defendant, as a landowner, would have been liable even if he had done nothing, provided failure to do anything at all would have been negligent in the circumstances. But suppose a person decides to render assistance to the victim of a road accident and unfortunately does so negligently, thus making matters worse. In the absence of special circumstances, if the helper had done nothing there would, probably, have

---

44 It is unclear to what extent the duty of positive action extends to unlawful visitors.
45 This may include a duty to control other visitors to the premises: *Hosie v Arbroath Football Club Ltd* 1987 SLT 122.
46 [1967] 1 AC 645. See also *Leakey v National Trust* [1980] QB 485 (Trust held liable when a natural mound of earth subsided on to neighbouring land even though the neighbour had been given permission to enter the land and shore up the mound).
47 Related are cases in which damage is caused to a neighbour by the activities of a third party on the defendant's land. For a discussion see Jaffey, *The Duty of Care*, 72–6.
48 E.g. *Chadwick v. British Railways Board* [1967] 1 WLR 912.

been no liability. Should the helper, then, be open to liability for careless intervention? Perhaps liability should be possible if it was clearly unreasonable of the helper
to render aid personally rather than, for example, to call a doctor or ambulance.
Once we have reached this point, however, there seems little reason why we should
not go one step further and allow of the possibility of liability for failure to do anything at all, at least if the burden of doing something to help would not be very
great. In other words, provided the standard of care is pitched low enough, there
may seem little objection to imposing a duty to rescue.

In an attempt to meet this last point, the Privy Council held, contrary to the
normal rule (namely that the personal capabilities of the defendant are irrelevant),
that in deciding what were 'reasonable' steps which an occupier of land must take to
prevent the land being a source of danger to others, account had to be taken of the
resources and capacities of the particular occupier: what is reasonable for the individual landowner may not be reasonable for the large company. This may be a sound
approach in some cases – our road accident example, for instance. But in the great
majority of cases, the cost facing an occupier of land is not really the cost of taking
precautions against the land being a danger to neighbours, but the cost of insuring
against this; and it is perfectly reasonable to regard this insurance cost as an essential part of the cost of using land which the landowner must pay, or vacate the land.
For instance, it may be doubted whether a poor cricket club which fails to erect a
fence around its ground to protect passers-by from being hit by stray cricket balls
should be any better off than a wealthy cricket club. The real effect of imposing liability in such a case would not be to force clubs to build fences but to force them to
buy insurance; and a club which could not afford the insurance premium should not
be in any different position from a club which could not afford to pay rates.

In the particular circumstances of *Goldman v Hargrave*, the Privy Council may
have been wise in restricting the extent of liability. It is very doubtful whether any
good purpose is served by extending liability in tort for damage caused by fire, at
all events in this country; the position in Australia may be affected by special considerations, such as the great danger of bush fires and the importance of providing
every inducement to landowners to take precautions against fire. But the technique
chosen to restrict liability – that is by personalizing the standard of care – is not
desirable. In the wider context of liability for personal injury arising from the use
of land it would be even more unsatisfactory to use a personalized test of standard
of care. Admittedly, the personalized standard of care for nonfeasance may make it
more likely that liability for nonfeasance will be expanded in the future. But not
only is the distinction thus drawn between misfeasance and nonfeasance of doubtful value; also, to consider the wealth of the defendant without regard to whether
they are or ought to be insured, is difficult to justify.

3.3   Nervous shock

There is one other limitation on the scope of liability for negligence which is dealt
with in terms of duty of care principles and which requires discussion here. This

concerns liability for what has traditionally been called 'nervous shock'. This term is often now objected to as having no obvious meaning, and phrases such as 'mental injury' or 'psychiatric damage' are often put in its place. But these do not capture the full range of situations covered by the older label, and so it is used here as an umbrella term. Nervous shock is injury caused by the impact on the mind, through the senses, of external events. Injury caused by the impact on the mind of external events, which is recognized by law, is of three types: physical injury – a pregnant woman may suffer a miscarriage or a person may suffer a heart attack or a stroke; psychological injury such as hysteria, neurosis, depression or any other recognized psychiatric illness; and psychosomatic effects of psychiatric illnesses, such as paralysis.

The history of the law concerning tort liability for nervous shock in the twentieth century was one of gradual expansion of the grounds of recovery as both knowledge of the brain and the mind, and sympathy for those afflicted by mental disturbance, have increased. There is still, however, a bias in the law against allowing recovery for nervous shock. Several arguments have traditionally been put forward to justify this approach. One is that mental injury that has no bodily symptoms, or only psychosomatic symptoms, is relatively difficult to prove; and, moreover, people vary more widely in their susceptibility to mental upset than in their susceptibility to physical injury. The law attempts to deal with this problem by being prepared to compensate for mental injury that is not accompanied by bodily injury to its sufferer only if it amounts to some 'recognizable psychiatric illness'.[49] Thus, expert medical evidence will normally be necessary to establish that a person has suffered nervous shock in this sense. Mere grief, anguish, fear, unhappiness, humiliation, outrage and so on, however distressing they may be, can (with one exception)[50] attract compensation only if they are the result of bodily injury to the person suffering any of these feelings; or, perhaps, of damage to their property[51] or to financial interests which are protected by law.

Even though a judge may, with the aid of expert evidence, not have too much difficulty in distinguishing a real psychiatric illness from less serious mental disturbance, this may not justify drawing a sharp line between the two, because at least some psychiatric disorders (e.g. depression) are just extreme versions of commonplace emotional states. Moreover, it is difficult to assess how big a problem the need to draw this line creates in cases which do not go to court, but are settled out of court simply on the basis of written medical reports and without the benefit of cross-examination of expert witnesses. It may well be that in practice, much more will turn, in settled cases, on the effect of the symptoms on the claimant's lifestyle (e.g. are they confined to bed, unable to work, and so on), rather than on whether the symptoms amount to a recognized psychiatric

---

49 See *Hinz v Berry* [1970] 2 QB 40.
50 Damages for bereavement: 3.4.
51 *Attia v British Gas* [1988] QB 304.

illness,[52] especially in cases where the claim is accompanied by claims for bodily injury by other members of the claimant's family. Furthermore, it is probably the case in practice that damages for mental disturbance are most often paid to a family member who suffers it as a result of injuries to other family members, and that such damages are only relatively rarely paid to persons who are not related to the physically injured person. This is significant because it is well recognized that the closer the relationship between the injured person and the person who suffers mental disturbance, the more serious the mental disturbance is likely to be.

Another reason for the restrictive approach to mental distress is the so-called 'floodgates argument': if recovery for mental distress (like recovery for bodily injury) were allowed simply on the basis that it was foreseeable, there might well be a flood of claims which would clog up the court system and divert too many of society's resources into compensating the victims of nervous shock at the expense of the many who presently receive little or no compensation even for physical injuries suffered as a result of negligent conduct. The force of the floodgates argument is disputed by judges and commentators even in cases where it is relevant to what happened. On the other hand, given the large number of serious accidents each year, and the fact that a person may suffer mental distress even if they are in no personal physical danger, it might be expected that many people would suffer some sort of mental distress as a result of witnessing harrowing events. But it must also be remembered that the narrow definition of nervous shock would probably rule out very many, if not most, of such cases.

Having noted the traditional bias in the law against recovery for nervous shock, it must now be said that the law divides victims of nervous shock into two groups – primary victims and secondary victims; and that the bias against recovery for nervous shock now really only applies to secondary victims. For instance, a person who suffers physical injuries as a result of another's tort (say, in a car accident) may also recover damages for nervous shock resulting from their physical injuries. Moreover, they may, in addition, recover damages for other 'lesser' forms of mental distress such as pain and suffering, awareness of a shortened expectation of life, discomfort and inconvenience arising from confinement to bed or hospital or wheelchair. The extent to which damages for mental injuries may be awarded where physical injury has also been suffered has never been treated as raising a problem involving the duty of care, but merely as involving a problem in the assessment of damages; and this is dealt with fully in chapter 6. Another type of primary victim is a person who suffers nervous shock as a result of being tortiously exposed to a *risk of physical injury* but who actually suffers no physical injury – for instance, a passenger in a car which is involved in a road accident who escapes physically

---

52 In 1991 more than £1 million was paid by insurers under the terms of an out-of-court settlement to fifty-nine families of children who had, it was alleged, been negligently and falsely diagnosed as having been subjected to sexual abuse. The amounts awarded apparently included sums for mental distress short of nervous shock. On the current state of the law, it is by no means clear that the employers of the allegedly negligent doctors were liable for such mental injury.

unscathed. Such a person may recover damages for their nervous shock (but not for lesser forms of mental distress) even if it was an abnormal or extreme reaction to what happened, simply because there was a risk that they would suffer physical injury.[53] A variant of this type of case is where people suffer 'fear for the future'. In 1998, damages were awarded to people who, as a result of having been treated with human growth hormone as children, suffered 'deteriorating psychiatric health' as a result of 'rational fears' of one day succumbing to a ghastly lingering death from CJD.[54] A third type of primary victim is a person who, for instance, suffers psychiatric injury as a result of being exposed to excessively stressful or dangerous working conditions by their employer. Provided their mental injury was not an abnormal or extreme reaction to the situation they were in, they may recover damages for it.[55]

It is in this area, perhaps, that there is greatest pressure to expand the boundaries of tort liability by recognising new types of mental harm as appropriate subjects for compensation. Concepts of illness (especially mental illness) are, to some extent at least, socially constructed; and although the law uses the category of '(medically) recognisable psychiatric illness' as a device to control the expansion of liability, the courts themselves can play a part in causing particular sets of symptoms to be characterised in this way. For this reason, judicial activity in this area is a prime target for those who think that tort law has gone too far in protecting people from life's adversities.

The typical secondary victim of nervous shock is a person who witnesses an accident in which someone known to them is killed or injured, and then sues the person responsible for the injuries or death.[56] Liability for nervous shock suffered by secondary victims is hedged about with limitations. First, the secondary victim's mental injury must have been the result of suffering a 'shock' in the colloquial sense.[57] For instance, a secondary victim could not sue in respect of psychiatric illness resulting from having cared over a long period of time for an injured person. This limitation seems to be an illogical result of calling the injury in such cases 'nervous shock'. It is probably one of the factors that led to judicial recognition of the

---

53 *Page v Smith* [1996] AC 155. The reasoning was that in this day and age, no distinction should be drawn between bodily and mental injury. So if a person could have recovered damages if they had suffered bodily injury as a result of their exposure to risk, they should be allowed to recover for nervous shock suffered as a result of exposure to the same risk. A person who did not face a risk of physical injury but reasonably feared that they did could recover for resulting nervous shock provided it was not an unusual or extreme reaction.
54 For the legal justification for these awards see *Creutzfeldt-Jakob Disease Litigation; Group B Plaintiffs v Medical Research Council* (1997) 41 BMLR 157.
55 *Hatton v Sutherland* [2002] 2 All ER 1. Strictly, this type of victim may not be 'primary' because it was held in *Frost v Chief Constable of South Yorkshire* [1999] 2 AC 455 that by definition, a primary victim is one who was subjected to a risk of physical injury.
56 Recovery may also be allowed where, as a result of another's tort, a person suffers shock arising from reasonable fear for the safety of a third party, even if the fear was, in fact, groundless.
57 What was called a 'sudden sensory perception' by Brennan J in *Jaensch v Coffey* (1983–4) 155 CLR 549. This limitation was expressly adopted by Lord Ackner in *Alcock v Chief Constable of South Yorkshire* [1992] 1 AC 310.

condition called 'post-traumatic stress disorder' (PTSD).[58] Secondly, the secondary victim's mental condition must not have been an abnormal or extreme reaction to the incidents in question. Liability will arise only if a person of 'reasonable fortitude' would have suffered shock. This limitation is based on the perception that different people's susceptibility to mental injury varies much more than their susceptibility to bodily injury. Thirdly, the secondary victim must (as a general rule) have been in a relationship of 'love and affection' with the person injured or killed. Bizarrely, it has been held that some relationships (such as parent and child) are assumed to be relationships of love and affection, but that others (such as aunt and nephew) will only qualify as such if the claimant can prove that there were close ties of love and affection between them and the person injured or killed. How can we justify a rule that requires mentally traumatized people to go to court and prove that they have strong feelings of love and affection towards another? For many years, it was thought that there was an exception to this rule that allowed rescuers to recover for nervous shock even if they were not in a relationship of love and affection with the victims.[59] However, it now seems that a 'rescuer' who suffers nervous shock will recover only if they were subjected to a risk of physical injury (i.e. only if they were a 'primary victim').[60]

Fourthly, a firm line was traditionally drawn between secondary victims who suffer shock merely as a result of being told of events and those who actually witness the events or their aftermath; the former were allowed to recover. Leaving aside the question of whether this distinction has any sound scientific basis, the advent of simultaneous broadcasting of sporting and other events has put severe strain on the law. In the Hillsborough stadium case, some of the claimants claimed damages for shock suffered as a result of seeing the terrible events on television. The House of Lords held that the television pictures in this case were not sufficiently equivalent to being in the stadium itself to warrant recovery, although the judges did not rule out that a media broadcast might be detailed and graphic enough to give rise to a claim. There is no precise definition of 'aftermath', but it is said to require a fairly high degree of temporal and physical proximity to the incident. The longer the gap of time between the accident and the witnessing of its consequences, the less likely is it that recovery for nervous shock will be allowed. For example, one judge in the Hillsborough football stadium case[61] said that shock suffered as a result of seeing the corpse of a dead relative in a morgue 8 hours after the accident which caused the death would not attract compensation.

---

58 For an illuminating discussion of this condition see I. Freckleton, 'Post-Traumatic Stress Disorder: A Challenge for Public and Private Health Law' (1985) 5 *J. of Law and Medicine* 252.

59 *Chadwick v British Railways Board* [1967] 1 WLR 912. Other exceptions have been allowed in cases where the secondary victim is a fellow worker of the person injured or killed (*Dooley v Cammell Laird* [1951] 1 Lloyd's Reports 271; *Mt Isa Mines Ltd v Pusey* (1970) 125 CLR 383) provided they were involved as an actor in the dangerous incident: *Hunter v British Coal Corporation* [1998] 2 All ER 97.

60 *Frost v Chief Constable of South Yorkshire* [1999] 2 AC 455.

61 Lord Ackner in *Alcock v Chief Constable of South Yorkshire* [1992] 1 AC 310, 405.

These limitations on liability to secondary victims of nervous shock (and, indeed, the distinction between primary and secondary victims of shock) involve the drawing of gruesome, invidious and often difficult distinctions that do the law no credit. In fact, many people find the legal regime in this area unsatisfactory and even repugnant. In the late 1990s the Law Commission reviewed the law relating to nervous shock.[62] It made many recommendations, but three stand out as being important. One was that the shock requirement should be abolished.[63] Another was that the distinction between primary and secondary victims should be abandoned. This distinction has been much criticised; but the problem with the Commission's proposal is that their third main recommendation assumes the continued existence of a distinction between people who suffer nervous shock as a result of another being killed, injured or imperilled, and people who suffer nervous shock in other circumstances. This is essentially a distinction between primary and secondary victims. The Commission's third main recommendation is for the abolition of the requirement that a secondary victim of nervous shock may recover damages only if they witnessed the accident or its aftermath personally; and that the only requirement should be that there were close ties of love and affection between the victim of nervous shock and the person killed, injured or imperilled. The Commission further proposed that there should be a fixed list of relationships which are deemed to involve close ties of love and affection, but that people in relationships not on this list should be allowed to prove that they did nevertheless have close ties of love and affection to the person killed, injured or imperilled. While the Commission's proposals would, if adopted, rid the law of some of its more objectionable and complex features, this third recommendation in particular retains some of the more unedifying aspects of the law in this area.

3.4   Family claims

As noted above (3.3 n. 50), there is one exception to the rule that mere grief, anguish or unhappiness cannot attract compensation unless it is a consequence of some other actionable injury. This exception is usually treated as part of the law concerning assessment of damages rather than duty of care,[64] but for ease of comparison, it will be dealt with here. Under the Fatal Accidents Act 1976[65] an award of a fixed sum of £10,000 (called damages for bereavement) may be made to a husband or wife or a civil partner[66] in respect of the death of his or her spouse or civil partner, or to

---

62 Law Com No. 249, *Liability for Psychiatric Illness* (1998).
63 The High Court of Australia has abandoned this requirement: *Tame v. New South Wales* (2002) 211 CLR 317. The court has not adopted the distinction between primary and secondary victims. Australian law on this topic has been contrasted with 'the possibly over-refined state' of English law: R.P. Balkin and J.L.R. Davis, *Law of Torts*, 3rd edn (Sydney, 2004), 253.
64 Partly because the death need not have been caused by negligence but can have been caused by any 'wrongful act, neglect or default'. But negligence is the most common trigger of claims under the Act.
65 Section 1A inserted by the Administration of Justice Act 1982.
66 As a result of the Civil Partnership Act 2004.

parents in respect of the death of an unmarried minor child. These damages are meant as 'solace' (or '*solatium*') for the grief caused by the spouse's or child's death (so they cannot be recovered by the estate of a deceased spouse or parent). This head of damages also constitutes an exception to the principle laid down by the courts that damages under the Fatal Accidents Act 1976 (which, loosely, allows members of the close family of a deceased person to recover damages in respect of that person's death, if it was wrongfully caused) are meant to compensate only for financial loss – basically, loss of financial support formerly provided by the deceased. Damages for bereavement were designed to replace damages for loss of expectation of life (awarded to the deceased's estate), which were abolished in 1982.[67] There is a similar provision for damages for 'loss of society' in Scotland under the Damages (Scotland) Act 1976 but, unlike in England, there is no statutory limit to the award, and the class of eligible claimants is defined more widely.

Naturally the death of a close relative in an accident must give rise to sympathy for the survivors, but damages for bereavement are nevertheless highly objectionable. There are two main objections to all awards by way of *solatium*. One is that the motives of relatives in seeking such awards may be questionable. Much more importantly, it seems arbitrary to select the death of a close relative as the criterion for paying what is still to many people a substantial sum of money. It must be remembered that the relatives of a person who is very severely injured (but not killed) in an accident may well suffer much greater mental suffering than the relatives of someone who is killed. For one thing, the suffering is continuous and may be prolonged in such cases for many years. Even if the victim's injuries were the result of negligent conduct, the suffering of the relatives would not be recoverable as nervous shock either. It does not seem right that, when nothing is awarded in such a case, damages should nevertheless be awarded for the death of a child.

In addition, the fact that the sum to be awarded is fixed by statute means that the same sum would be awarded in a very wide variety of situations, for example, to a mother for the death of a newly born child; to parents of an older child irrespective of whether the child was a comfort or a trial to its parents; and to a spouse or civil partner irrespective of the age, state of health of the other spouse or civil partner, and regardless of whether the spouses or civil partners were the best of friends or had been separated for years and were not on speaking terms. Furthermore, damages for bereavement, unlike damages for financial loss resulting from another's death, are only recoverable by a spouse to a legal marriage or a party to a civil partnership, and not by parties who cohabit without marrying or entering a civil partnership. Apart from all this, there is a further fundamental point that damages by way of *solatium* ought to be a very low priority in any legal system which still denies adequate compensation for loss of income to so many of those injured in accidents or crippled by disabling illness.

---

67 By s. 1 of the Administration of Justice Act 1982. For the history of these provisions see the fourth edition of this book, 76–7.

Besides creating an exception to the rule about liability for mental harm, the Fatal Accidents Act 1976 (the original version of which, known as Lord Campbell's Act, was enacted in 1846) also creates an exception to a basic principle of tort law that damages may not be recovered for financial loss arising out of harm to another person or another person's property. Because this book is primarily concerned with compensation for personal injury and death, we will not discuss this basic principle in any detail. The point to make is that in order to prevent the principle being swamped by the exception, the Fatal Accidents Act 1976 has always contained a list of classes of persons who are entitled to make a claim under the Act. The current list of eligible claimants covers a wide range of *de iure* and *de facto* family relationships. In 1999 the Law Commission recommended that the Act be amended to allow any person who was formerly being 'maintained' by the deceased to make a claim, regardless of the nature of their relationship with the deceased; but this recommendation has not been acted upon.

4

Departures from the fault principle

4.1 Fault liability and strict liability

The fault principle, as embodied in the concept of negligence, is not the only basis of legal liability for personal injuries and death, although it is, in practice at least, by far the most important. In this chapter we will consider modifications to and departures from the fault principle. Such modifications and departures are often said to impose 'strict liability' as opposed to fault liability. Whereas fault liability is based on a judgment that a person should have behaved differently (for instance, by taking certain precautions), strict liability does not involve any judgment that the person should have behaved differently. Putting the same point another way, fault liability is liability for the way a person behaved whereas strict liability is liability for consequences of a person's conduct. Strict liability has often been thought to be morally unjustifiable, even if it has its uses as a legal device – how can it be fair to hold someone liable for the consequences of behaving in a perfectly acceptable way? How can we justify responsibility in the absence of culpability? The best answer to this question appears to be that even in morality (as opposed to law) we sometimes accept responsibility and hold others responsible for things that were not our, or their, fault. For example, if a young child accidentally breaks a neighbour's window while playing ball, its parents might well feel that they ought (morally) to accept responsibility for the broken window and pay to have it replaced, even if they took all reasonable care in supervising their child. Indeed, this example shows that morality might impose strict liability in situations where the law would not – the parents would not be legally liable for the damage done by the child in such a case. So it may be fair to hold someone liable for the consequences of their conduct even if that conduct was not faulty. However, just saying this does not tell us under what circumstances strict liability can be fair. The phrase 'liability without fault' merely eliminates fault as a necessary condition of liability; it does not put anything else in its place. Thus strict liability is not one possible alternative to liability for fault, but a collection of such alternatives. The phrase 'liability for fault' tells us that liability ought to be placed on a faulty party (although it does not tell us on which, if there are more than one). But the term 'strict liability' implies no criterion for deciding on whom liability should rest.[1]

This point is often not appreciated because it is often taken for granted that strict liability is based on the concept of 'legal causation'.[2] For example, it is often assumed that if strict liability were extended to road accidents, a motorist would be held liable under such a regime if, for example, he or she 'caused' an accident by colliding with a pedestrian, even without fault. Similarly, a gas undertaking might be thought to 'cause' accidents arising through leaks from their pipes, and strict liability would simply make the gas undertaking liable for such accidents. But few if any existing forms of strict liability are based on legal causation, at least if we give the word 'cause' its most common meaning. For example, a zoo-keeper whose lion escapes despite all due care is strictly liable for the damage it does, but the zoo owner would not be said to have 'caused' the death of someone killed by the lion. What the zoo owner has done is to create a risky situation by keeping a lion in captivity. Again, as a general rule, employers are strictly (vicariously) liable for torts committed by their employees that injure third parties, even though the employer would not be said to have 'caused' the injuries. In any event, as we shall see later, the notion of causation is a problematic basis for liability because there are considerable difficulties in formulating principles of causation and in justifying legal liability on the basis of such principles.

This is not to say that the concept of 'cause' may not in many cases identify the party who, as a matter of sound policy, ought to be made liable – as in the cases of the road accident or the gas leak mentioned above. But a possible criterion of liability which would cover both of these cases and that of the zoo-keeper, would be to ask which party could more easily bear and distribute the losses caused by the accident, by insurance or other means. Clearly, for example, not only could the driver more easily insure against the risk than the pedestrian, but also it is much easier to enforce compulsory insurance against motorists than it would be against pedestrians. This line of reasoning, however, has important practical implications. It is true, for example, that a scheme imposing strict liability for road accidents caused without fault[3] would entitle more personal injury victims to claim compensation, but only if there was another motorist involved who could be held strictly liable. However, many road accidents involve only one driver, for example, where a car veers off the road and collides with a tree or perhaps another (stationary) car. Motorists as a group are just as able, via insurance, to bear and distribute the costs of such accidents as those of accidents involving more than one driver. It is arguments such as these that have led many reformers towards 'no-fault'

---

1 It does not even tell us that liability ought to be placed on someone who is not at fault. Strict liability is not liability in the absence of fault but liability regardless of the presence or absence of fault.
2 For a detailed explanation of this notion see 5.2.
3 For a limited proposal of this nature see *Compensation for the Injured* (1971), a report of a committee of the Society of Conservative Lawyers, and Professor Atiyah's criticisms in 'Compensation for the Injured' (1971) 34 *Modern LR* 432.

compensation schemes under which entitlement to compensation depends on being injured and not on being able to find someone to sue.

This is not to say that the search for the best 'risk bearer' is the only possible reason for extending strict liability. Another may be that placing the risk on one person rather than another would reduce accidents. Full examination of all these objectives is deferred to chapter 17 of this book. All that needs to be stressed at this stage is that extending 'strict liability' is not a positive programme for reform on its own. We also need to decide on whom strict liability is to be placed or, in other words, what the criterion of liability will be, if it is not to be fault.

4.2 'Procedural' devices

In cases where liability is based on fault, it is the injured party who normally 'bears the burden of proving' that the injurer was at fault. This rule about burden of proof is generally considered to be a corollary of the negative part of the fault principle, namely no liability without (proof of) fault. One way of making it more difficult for a person allegedly guilty of faulty conduct to escape liability for that conduct is to require that person to prove that their conduct was *not* faulty. This device is referred to as 'shifting the burden of proof'. It may be done directly. For example, the EC Commission once issued a draft Directive on liability for services; under the Directive the basis of liability was to be fault, but the burden of proof on the issue of fault was to rest on the provider of the services and not on the person who claims to have been caused injury or loss by the service-provider. The same effect may be achieved more indirectly by the application of a principle referred to by the Latin tag 'res ipsa loquitur' (literally: 'the thing speaks for itself'). This principle applies in cases where harm has been caused by a thing or a process which was under the exclusive control of an identified person; and where the harm-causing incident was of a type which would not, in the ordinary course of things, happen without negligence on the part of that person.[4] In such cases, the harm-doer runs a real risk of being held liable unless they can at least give a plausible explanation of how the harm-causing incident might have occurred without negligence on their part.[5] Because it is, in practice, often much more difficult to establish absence of negligence than to prove negligence, it is sometimes said that application of *res ipsa loquitur* may effectively impose liability without (proof of) fault.

The *res ipsa loquitur* principle is particularly important in product liability cases[6] in which the user of a product has suffered injury as a result of what is often called a 'manufacturing defect' in the product caused by some malfunction in the manufacturing process. If the question is whether the malfunction was the result

4 See generally P.S. Atiyah, 'Res Ipsa Loquitur in England and Australia' (1972) 35 Modern LR 337.
5 Ng Chun Pui v. Lee Chuen Tat [1988] RTR 298. The principle has been abolished in Canada: Fontaine v. Insurance Corporation of British Columbia (1998) 156 DLR 577.
6 It is rarely of much use in a road accident case; but see Widdowson v. Newgate Meat Corporation [1998] PIQR P138.

of negligence on the part of the manufacturer, it will usually be up to the manufacturer to prove that it was not, and it will not be for the injured person to prove that it was. The doctrine gains additional power when used in conjunction with the doctrine of vicarious liability.[7] Suppose a patient goes into hospital for an operation to cure stiffness in a finger, but that something goes wrong and the person leaves hospital with five stiff fingers. On such facts[8] a court would probably be prepared to apply the doctrine of *res ipsa loquitur* and place on the hospital the burden of proof on the question of whether the accident was the result of negligence. Assume that all the medical staff involved in the person's treatment were employees of the hospital. On that assumption, the hospital would be vicariously liable for tortious conduct of any of those medical employees. Even if the injured person could not say which particular member of the medical staff was negligent, the hospital might be held liable for the harm unless the hospital could prove that the harm was not the result of fault on the part of any of these people – which would usually be very difficult indeed.[9]

Although the effect of shifting the burden of proof on the issue of fault may be to impose strict liability, in theory it does not alter the basis of the liability, which remains that the harm-doer should have behaved differently. Therefore, in seeking a justification for shifting the burden of proof we are not looking for a justification of strict liability but rather a justification for relieving the injured person of the normal burden of proof. So far as *res ipsa loquitur* is concerned, the justification is that where a harm is caused by a thing or process under someone's exclusive control, that person is in a much better position than the injured party to know, or to find out, how it happened. In the case of the proposed services Directive, placing the burden on the defendant was essentially a consumer protection measure. In general, disparity of knowledge or resources relevant to resolving the issue of fault is the basic justification for imposing the burden of proof on the issue of fault on the defendant.

4.3   Breach of statutory duty

Whether an action for damages lies for breach of a statutory duty depends in theory on whether Parliament intended to confer a civil remedy when it created the duty. But this is pure theory, because it is only in very recent times that Parliament has ever paused to consider whether it wishes to confer such a remedy. In practice, the action for breach of statutory duty is almost entirely confined to industrial accidents. Factory legislation and mines legislation have long been held to confer a right of action for breach. This dates back to the last years of the nineteenth century when the first Workmen's Compensation Act was passed, and the whole question of industrial

---

7 4.7.
8 The doctrine is unlikely to be very useful in less straightforward cases: M.A. Jones, '*Res Ipsa Loquitur* in Medical Negligence Actions: Enough Said' (1998) 14 *Professional Negligence* 174.
9 See *Cassidy* v. *Ministry of Health* [1951] 2 KB 343.

safety was a prominent subject of discussion.[10] There was little confidence at that time that safety legislation was being adequately enforced, or could adequately be enforced by the government inspectors appointed under the Factories Act; and it may well be that these factors influenced the courts in their decision to impose civil liability for breach of duties of this nature.

Attempts to extend the action for breach of statutory duty to other situations have almost invariably been rebuffed. In particular, in 1923 the Court of Appeal refused to allow an action for breach of statutory duty for breach of Ministry of Transport regulations relating to the construction and use of motor vehicles.[11] If a motorist takes reasonable care to maintain a vehicle – for example, by having it regularly serviced by a reputable garage – and (e. g.) the vehicle's brakes suddenly fail, the motorist will not be guilty of negligence, though they may well be guilty of an offence under statutory regulations. The court refused to impose strict liability for breach of statutory duty on the ostensible ground that Parliament did not 'intend' to confer a civil remedy. Perhaps the court was influenced – consciously or unconsciously – by the fact that in 1923 it was still not compulsory to insure against third party liability, and it may have shrunk from imposing a form of liability without fault on individual motorists, who might not have had the resources to meet a judgment for damages. Had this issue arisen after compulsory insurance was introduced in 1930, the result might have been different.

Liability for breach of a statutory duty can often be imposed even in the absence of proof of fault on the part of the party in breach. But this is by no means always so in practice, and sometimes not even so in theory. Much depends on the wording of the statutory provision imposing the duty. Some prescribe a result to be attained, the most famous and important being s. 14 of the Factories Act 1961 which declares that 'every dangerous part of any machinery . . . shall be securely fenced'. In such a case it is no defence to plead that all reasonable care was taken to fence the machinery; or that the machine would be unusable if securely fenced. Other statutory duties may be stated in terms that do not differ greatly from the usual definitions of the standard of care required by the law of negligence, though the actual requirements of due care will usually be specified in much more detail than at common law. On the other hand, for example, a statute may simply require precautions to be taken 'so far as is reasonably practicable', or words to that effect; although since the burden of proof on the issue of practicable precautions rests on the defendant, such a provision may, in effect, impose liability without proof of fault.[12]

Courts tend to interpret even detailed provisions of industrial legislation in the light of common law notions of fault. For example, 'dangerous machinery' may be held to mean 'machinery which is capable of causing injury if not carefully operated'. Hence a requirement to fence dangerous machinery, though not expressed in

---

10   *Groves* v. *Wimborne* [1898] 2 QB 402; and 13.1.1.
11   *Phillips* v. *Britannia Hygienic Laundry* [1923] 2 KB 832; see also *Tan Chye Choo* v. *Chong Kew Moi* [1970] 1 All ER 266.
12   *Nimmo* v. *Alexander Cowan & Sons Ltd* [1968] AC 107; *Larner* v. *British Steel Plc* [1993] ICR 551.

terms of due care at all, may not in fact impose a burden significantly more onerous than that of taking the due care.[13] Obviously, if machinery is only dangerous when injury from its use can be foreseen, it would not be a breach of the statute to omit to fence machinery which was not a foreseeable source of danger – and this is not very different from the ordinary requirements of the law of negligence. For another thing, contributory negligence and principles of causation and remoteness of damage[14] remain as limitations on liability for breach of statutory duty.

Moreover, many of the requirements imposed by statutes or regulations are in fact no more than what reasonable care would require if only as much was known about accident causation by the reasonable person (or the courts) as by the appropriate government department. Industrial legislation imposing this or that requirement may not always appear to require only what is reasonable care: it may appear unnecessarily solicitous or 'fussy'. This is often because the court or the reasonable person does not know how many accidents are caused by the omission to take the required precautions. Statutory requirements may be drawn up as a direct response to a serious accident rate in this or that area of industry.[15] Sometimes the main purpose of detailed legislation is to give the employer greater guidance as to what is required in the way of reasonable care; clearly in this event, the object is not to impose strict liability.

Much of the time spent by appellate courts in deciding on the proper interpretation of detailed provisions in industrial safety legislation is a waste, because the search for the correct interpretation assumes that small differences in wording between different provisions were intended by the legislator to reflect important considerations of policy, which they rarely, if ever, do.[16] More often they reflect either poor draftsmanship or a desire to cover every possible contingency.[17] Even if courts were to look for policy considerations to guide their decisions as to whether compensation ought to be given in particular cases, it would not be easy to find a rational legislative approach. The problem lies principally in the fact that the primary justification for strict liability for industrial accidents was to a large extent removed by the introduction of the industrial injuries system in 1948.[18] The main justification for strict liability for industrial accidents is (in effect) that this is a form of insurance for the benefit of the worker at the expense of the employer, rather than that the employer is in some way at fault. An excellent case can be made for saying that workers should be insured against industrial accidents, and that this should be wholly or partly paid for by employers; but this is precisely the rationale of the industrial injuries system. It is difficult enough to justify the continued

---

13 See e.g. *Leversley* v. *Thomas Firth* [1953] 1 WLR 1206, 1210.
14 See 5.2.
15 See *Annual Report of the Chief Inspector of Factories* (Cmnd 3745, 1967), 23.
16 See the comments of Lord Reid in *Nimmo* v. *Alexander Cowan & Sons* [1968] AC 107.
17 See e.g. Robens Committee Report, para. 29: 'the attempt to cover contingency after contingency has resulted in a degree of elaboration, detail and complexity that deters even the most determined reader.'
18 See 12.4.

existence of liability based on fault in industrial accidents despite the existence of the industrial injuries system; it is almost impossible to justify the continued existence of strict liability.[19] This is why, in 1946, the Monckton Committee on Alternative Remedies recommended (in effect) that, with the enactment of the Industrial Injuries Act of 1946, liability for breach of statutory duty should cease to be 'strict'.[20] This recommendation was never implemented by Parliament, and in consequence, the courts have had to approach the problem of interpreting industrial legislation against the background of an indefensible policy decision. Small wonder, then, that the courts have failed to evolve any consistent approach to the problem based on a clear and intelligible policy. A statement by Lord Diplock in *Haigh* v. *Ireland*[21] suggests that the courts now appreciate the true situation more clearly. In this case Lord Diplock said that the courts must resist the temptation to stretch the interpretation of industrial legislation in order to ensure the compensation of injured workers. Compensation without fault, as he pointed out, is available under the industrial injuries system to all workers injured in the course of their employment. Statutory provisions should, therefore, be interpreted without any bias in favour of injured workers.

A fresh start in this area was made in the Health and Safety at Work etc. Act 1974. This Act imposes on employers various general duties – such as a duty to ensure the health, safety and welfare of employees. These general duties are all qualified by the phrase 'so far as is reasonably practicable', making them, in theory, duties of reasonable care; but in practice, since the burden of proof of practicability rests on the defendant, the effect may be to impose liability without (proof of) fault. The Act expressly states (s. 47(1)) that the general duties do not give rise to civil liability for damages; and they are enforceable only by criminal prosecution. By contrast, s. 47(2) of the Act provides that breaches of health and safety regulations are actionable in damages unless the contrary is expressly stated – a rare occurrence.[22] As health and safety regulations that existed at the time the 1974 Act was passed are gradually replaced by regulations made under that Act, the importance of the older case-law dealing with the availability of an action for damages, will diminish in this area.

In relation to industrial injuries, the action for breach of statutory duty would appear to be of great importance if judged solely by the number of statutory duties imposed on employers and by the number of reported cases. We have seen that a very large proportion of all litigation is personal injury litigation, and that about 25% of this is industrial in origin (much arising out of breaches of statutory duties). Nevertheless, in practice the great bulk of employees suffering injury still appear to have no legal cause of action; at any rate they do not in fact make tort

---

19 This was one of the reasons why the Pearson Commission (Pearson Report, vol. 1, paras. 918–22) rejected a suggestion that the burden of proof in actions for breach of industrial safety regulations should be reversed.

20 Cmnd 6860; see further 15.4.5.

21 [1974] 1 WLR 43, 54–5.

22 An example is Management of Health and Safety at Work Regulations 1999, reg. 22(1).

claims for damages.[23] It is also noticeable that although there are many 'strict duties' under industrial legislation, and very few under road safety legislation, a much larger proportion of road accident victims than industrial accident victims actually succeeds in recovering some tort damages.

4.4   Contractual duties

The law of contract is primarily concerned with financial losses and not with physical damage or personal injury; but strict liability for such damage or injury may arise from a breach of contract. For example, the liability of a seller to a buyer for injuries caused by dangerous goods does not depend on negligence, but on breach of contractual warranty. A seller of goods is generally held to 'warrant' that the goods sold are neither dangerous nor defective. If they cause injury to the purchaser, he or she can sue the seller without having to establish that the seller was personally negligent. In modern retailing conditions it would often be very difficult to establish that a seller was negligent, because the retailer merely acts as a distributor of goods that cannot be examined because they are packed in sealed containers, such as tins or bottles. In other cases the seller could not hope to do more than ensure the good repute of the maker of goods bought, for they may be products of which the retailer has no skilled or personal knowledge, such as electronic equipment. Even if the retailer was skilled enough to examine the goods, it would often be impossible to do so in practice. Thus the liability imposed on the retailer is in fact a fairly strict one – much stricter than that on the employer under most industrial legislation. If the goods actually cause damage or injury to the buyer, the seller can only escape liability in law by showing that the goods were not defective, or that it was the buyer's 'fault' that the accident occurred. Contributory negligence, as such, probably does not apply here, for it is a tort doctrine; but if the injured person's conduct was sufficiently foolhardy, a court might reject the claim on the ground that the buyer 'caused' the injuries.

Why should a seller of goods be strictly liable to the buyer for defects when, at common law (as opposed to statute),[24] the manufacturer is only liable to the consumer for negligence?[25] At first sight this is an important question because only the actual buyer can sue the seller for breach of warranty; if the injury is caused to a member of the buyer's family or to a friend to whom the buyer has given the goods, no such action can be brought, so that many users may have to sue the manufacturer. However, in practice, the distinction may not be as important as it seems at first sight, because a manufacturer will rarely escape liability for negligence

---

23 See ch. 8.

24 Concerning the position under the Consumer Protection Act 1987, Part I, see 4.8.

25 The manufacturer may be strictly liable in contract, but not to the ultimate consumer who has no contract with the manufacturer. If a retailer is found liable in contract, the retailer can sue in contract the person who supplied the goods to it, whether an intermediate seller or the manufacturer, and that contractual liability will be strict in the same way as the retailer's.

in respect of damage done by a defective product, at any rate if the defect is one in the manufacture rather than the design of the product.[26] Defects are themselves fairly good evidence of negligence, though they may sometimes be explained away, and they may sometimes be due to components purchased from other manufacturers (for which, at common law, the manufacturer would often not be liable).

4.5   Rylands v. Fletcher, nuisance and animals

Considerations of space forbid any attempt at detailed treatment of these parts of tort law. It is enough here to note that liability for damage done by dangerous things escaping from land under the rule in *Rylands* v. *Fletcher* may occasionally be 'strict', in the sense that negligence need not be proved. However, the House of Lords has recently decided that damages for personal injuries cannot be recovered under this rule;[27] and so it is only of marginal relevance to the subject matter of this book. Even in relation to property damage, it is by no means clear whether, in practice, liability under the rule could arise in the absence of negligent conduct. This is not to say, however, that strict liability for the escape of dangerous things might not be socially desirable. Witness the Bhopal disaster in India in 1984. But in Australia, the rule in *Rylands* v. *Fletcher* has been 'subsumed' into the ordinary law of negligence.

Nuisance is of considerable importance as a tort of 'strict' liability, in the sense that interference with the comfort of neighbours may be a nuisance even if all due care is taken to prevent that interference. Even here, however, the defendant may in a sense have been negligent if the concept of negligence is regarded as applying to the whole activity and not merely to the way it is carried out. When a court says that use of a particular piece of machinery, for example, is so noisy as to constitute a nuisance even though every care has been taken to minimize the noise, this is not necessarily an admission that liability in nuisance is 'strict'. Such a decision amounts to holding that the machinery is so noisy that it must not be used at all – that it is unreasonable to use it having regard to the harm it caused to the neighbours, notwithstanding the gain to the person using it. This does not look very different from the ordinary negligence formula. The only difference is that it involves application of that formula to the activity itself, and not to the way it is carried out. As we saw earlier (2.4.9), the law of negligence, though in theory capable of being applied to negligence in the whole conduct of an activity – negligence in design as it were – is usually confined to negligence in operation. The peculiarity of the law of nuisance is that the law is concerned just as much with what is done on land as with how it is done.

Be this as it may, nuisance as a source of liability for damage to person or property is now almost completely coincidental with negligence. The solitary survival of strict liability is the rule that an occupier may be liable for physical damage caused by non-repair of premises even though the occupier neither knew nor had

26 See further 2.4.9.
27 *Transco Plc* v. *Stockport MBC* [2004] 2 AC 1.

means of knowing that they were in disrepair.[28] Even here, liability is rarely likely to be strict in practice; non-repair will normally connote negligence.

As to animals, the common law rules of strict liability were so drawn as to exclude the main forms of damage that animals actually cause, and the Animals Act 1971 has not made much difference in this respect. No doubt the owner of a zoo from which a lion escapes will be liable for the damage it inflicts; and no doubt also, the owner of cattle that trespass on a neighbour's garden or crops will be liable even if no negligence is proved. But many more accidents, resulting in personal injury, are caused by dogs or other domestic animals on the roads[29] than by escaping lions, and here there is no liability without, and often not even with, negligence. And although trespassing cattle may well do a certain amount of damage to crops and such like every year, cattle do not often trespass on another's land without negligence on the part of the owner. There are certainly quite a number of accidents involving bulls, mostly to those employed on farms, but the effect of the Animals Act 1971 on liability for such animals is obscure.[30]

4.6   Joint liability

An instance of liability, which in one sense may be said to be 'strict', and which is certainly of more practical importance than the strict liability of animal keepers, is to be found in the rules relating to 'joint liability'. This is a technical term, but we are using it in a non-technical sense to include all cases in which more than one person is liable for the same damage. There are two main principles. First, all those responsible for committing a tort in concert are liable for all the damage caused by the tort, even though it may be possible to identify the contributions of each to the ultimate damage. Secondly, all those who by their negligence or other fault produce damage in combination (though not acting in concert), will be liable for all the damage unless it is possible to identify the separate contribution of each party.

The first principle applies not only to those actually acting in concert, but also to cases in which one person assists or encourages another to commit the tort. If two people agree to beat up a third, then they are both liable in full for the injuries inflicted, even though it may be possible to identify one assailant as solely responsible for some (or all) of the injuries and the other as responsible for different (or no) injuries. This kind of liability is 'strict' because the defendant is held liable for damage which they may not even have caused, in the sense that the damage may well have occurred even without that person's assistance. Probably no other form of tort liability is as 'strict' as this.

The second principle covers the situation where two (or more) persons combine without design to produce damage; where, for example, two motorists by their

---

28 *Wringe* v. *Cohen* [1940] 1 KB 229.
29 See *Civil Liability for Animals* (Law Com. No. 13, 1967), paras. 36–8.
30 Although the Act abolishes the former principle that an employee could not sue in such cases, the effect of s. 2(2)(b) and s. 6 seems to be to exclude strict liability for injury done by a bull.

negligence cause an accident in which a pedestrian is injured. It may be impossible in this sort of case to quantify the damage done by each of the negligent motorists, and at common law there was no procedure whereby the responsibility could be shared between the motorists.

In both types of case the common law simply provided that both tortfeasors were liable in full to the injured person, but the tort victim could choose to sue one or the other, or both; and likewise, if judgment was given against both, it was left to the injured person to decide whether to enforce the judgment against one or other, or both. The law was changed by statute in 1935 (now replaced by the Civil Liability (Contribution) Act 1978), so that it is now possible for one tortfeasor to claim 'contribution' from another tortfeasor liable for the same damage. The amount of contribution is to be assessed by the court according to the share of the responsibility of the two parties. This change in the law has not affected the tort victim's position in any way. The injured party is still entitled to sue both parties, to obtain judgment in full against both and to enforce judgment against either or both. The only thing not allowed is recovery by the injured person of more in total than the amount of damages assessed by the court.

The law of joint liability has become very controversial in recent years. Complaints have come especially from professional groups, such as auditors and architects, whose job is often to monitor, control or report on potentially dangerous activities of others. The problem is that where two or more people are jointly liable for loss, the harmed person will naturally want to sue the party most likely to be insured against liability for the loss or to have sufficient resources of their own to pay any damages awarded.[31] If such a party is held liable but cannot recover contribution from any other liable person because the latter lacks the resources to pay or is uninsured, the party originally sued may end up bearing the whole of the loss even if their share of the responsibility for it was very small. Various solutions have been suggested for this type of case, but most involve shifting some or all of the risk, that one or more of the liable persons will be unable to pay, on to the tort victim. For this reason, they have been found unacceptable in cases of personal injury. Some people see the problem of joint liability as a symptom of the failure of the tort system. From another point of view, however, it simply illustrates that at times in life, one or another 'innocent' party must lose out, and the only question is, who?

4.7   Vicarious liability

The type of liability we have just mentioned is not essentially dissimilar to vicarious liability – the liability of an employer for the negligence of employees committed in the course of their employment. This is certainly 'strict', in the sense that the employer is liable, however careful it may have been, although the injured person must prove loss or damage suffered as the result of a tort committed by the

---

31 Public authorities are a particularly attractive target from this point of view.

employee in the course of the employment. Vicarious liability is discussed in detail in chapter 9 because it is better understood as a loss distribution device than as a part of the traditional law of torts.

4.8   Products liability

Part I of the Consumer Protection Act 1987 (which implemented an EC Directive) is usually said to have introduced a regime of 'strict' liability for injury or damage caused by defective products. Compensation for personal injury[32] and damage to property (other than the defective product) is recoverable under the Act, but damages for pure economic loss are not. The provisions are complex and we will not consider them in detail in this book.[33] However, a few general comments are in order. First, the Act does impose strict liability to the extent that under it, not only the producer of a defective product can be held liable, but also an 'own-brand' supplier, an importer and even, in certain circumstances, an ordinary distributor of the product, regardless of the fact that none of these persons may have been in any way responsible for the defectiveness of the product. Furthermore, the producer of a product which incorporates components produced by someone else can be held liable for defects in component parts even if the producer of the finished product was in no way at fault, for example, by not doing independent tests on the components to ensure their safety.

Secondly, however, there can be liability under the Act only if the product in question was 'defective'. A product is defective if it is not as safe as people generally are entitled to expect. This test is very little different from the common-law test of negligence because, in essence, it requires the court to conduct a cost-benefit analysis. Indeed, it would seem that the Act has effected little change in the law in this respect. Take, first, a case involving a product which is defective because of an isolated malfunction in the manufacturing process. Such a product would undoubtedly be defective under the Act regardless of whether the malfunction was anyone's fault. A court dealing with such a case under the law of negligence would be very likely to invoke the doctrine of *res ipsa loquitur* which, as we have seen, effectively imposes liability without fault in many cases. So the outcome would probably be the same under either legal regime. Consider, next, a case involving an argument that a product was defectively designed. Under the law of negligence, such allegations are very rarely made and the courts are very wary of them. It may be very difficult indeed for an injured person to convince a court that the costs of a particular product design outweigh its benefits. But things are not likely to be any easier under the Act. This is very obvious in the case, for example, of drugs. All drugs carry risks, but this does not mean that all drugs are defective in the terms of the Act: a

---

32 Strict liability is likely to be of limited value to those who suffer diseases rather than traumatic injuries: J. Stapleton, 'Compensating Victims of Disease' (1985) 5 *Oxford J. Legal Studies* 248, 254.
33 See for further details N.J. McBride and R. Bagshaw, *Tort Law*, 2nd edn (London, 2005), ch. 45.

drug will be defective only if the risks associated with its use make it so unsafe that they outweigh any benefits it may bring. Nor does it seem that an allegation that a product was defective by reason of lack, inadequacy or unclarity of instructions or warnings would be significantly easier to substantiate in an action under the Act than in an ordinary negligence action.

Another important respect in which the Act and the common law are essentially similar concerns the date at which the issue of defectiveness (under the Act) or negligence (at common law) is to be judged: under the Act the relevant date is the date the product left the control of the producer, and at common law it is the date of the alleged act of negligence. This means that liability cannot arise either under the Act or at common law simply because standards of safety have become higher in the meantime.

Thirdly, the Act provides a number of defences, the effect of which is to introduce significant elements of fault into the liability regime: in particular, contributory negligence on the part of the user or the injured person; and the so-called 'state-of-the-art' or 'development risk' defence, which allows a producer to escape liability by proving that the 'state of scientific and technical knowledge' at the time the product left its control 'was not such that a producer of products of the same description as the product in question might be expected to have discovered the defect' if it had existed in the product at the time it was under its control.[34] This latter defence is simply a plea of 'no-negligence' in the designing, development and testing of the product.

These features of the new product liability regime put together mean that it is a regime of strict liability in only a rather weak sense. Two other points should be made. First, the Act only applies to 'goods' (and electricity); it does not apply to services, such as the giving of safety advice. Although this limitation on the scope of the Act is explicable in historical terms, it is very difficult to think of any principled reason why tort liability for defective goods ought to be governed by a different regime of rules from that applicable to substandard services. Even more anomalously, the Act does not draw a clear distinction between goods and services because complaints that goods are defective are usually, at bottom, complaints that someone has performed some service (such as designing the product or supervising the production line) badly.[35]

Secondly, by creating a special regime of liability for product-caused injuries, the Act creates an anomaly between one class of injured persons and other classes (such as those injured by negligent driving). Why do victims of product-caused injuries[36] deserve to be treated differently, and in some respects better than those injured in

34 Consumer Protection Act 1987 s. 4(1)(e).
35 J. Stapleton, 'Three Problems with the New Product Liability' in P. Cane and J. Stapleton eds., *Essays for Patrick Atiyah* (Oxford, 1991), 258–70.
36 The Pearson Commission estimated that between 30,000 and 40,000 persons (about 1% of all victims of accidental injuries) are injured each year in Britain as a result of defects in products (other than drugs) (Pearson Report, vol. 1, para. 1201). It also estimated that some 5% of these

other ways? Once again, there are historical reasons why the law of product liability has been singled out for reform – the Thalidomide tragedy of the 1960s was the major catalyst of reform of personal injuries law in Britain[37] because the litigation which it generated uncovered serious weaknesses in the law of tort, especially regarding proof of fault[38] and causation. But historical explanations are not justifications. It is not easy to think of any good reason why victims of product-caused injuries deserve better treatment than other recipients of tort compensation, let alone the vast majority of injury victims who receive nothing from the tort system.

4.9   Proposals to extend strict liability

4.9.1   Dangerous things and activities

Under the guise of rationalizing and tidying up the present somewhat arbitrary and haphazard law of strict liability, the Pearson Commission made a set of proposals (in ch. 31 of the Report) which, if implemented, would have very greatly extended strict liability. The Commission proposed that there should be two new categories of strict liability introduced. First, the controllers of things or operations which, 'by their unusually hazardous nature require close, careful and skilled supervision' if the risk of personal injury is to be avoided, should be strictly liable. Secondly, the controllers of things or activities which, although normally perfectly safe, are likely 'if they do go wrong, to cause serious and extensive casualties', should also be strictly liable, not merely if there are in fact serious and extensive casualties, but if there is any injury caused which falls within the risk to be guarded against. The first category was designed to cover such things as explosives, inflammable gases and liquids; and the second, such things as large public bridges, dams, major stores and stadiums, and 'other buildings where large numbers of people may congregate'.

Unfortunately, the Commission appears to have paid inadequate attention to the implications of these proposals; nor did it really attempt any serious justification of them in principle. It seems clear that the Commission thought they were of rather minor importance whereas, in practice, their implementation could trigger off a huge amount of litigation. Even so, some of the limitations inherent in the proposals are striking. Why, for instance, did the second category cover only persons injured on 'large' public bridges, dams and so forth? What conceivable difference does the size of the bridge, which collapsed on top of her, or underneath her, make to any rational person? Another difficulty arises from the proposal to cover buildings where large numbers of people may congregate, for this must surely include

may recover some tort compensation (ibid. vol. 1, para. 1202). It appears that the proportion of product liability claims that actually reach the courts is smaller than the equivalent proportion of personal injury claims generally.

37 It was the immediate cause of the setting up of the Pearson Royal Commission.

38 It is ironical, indeed, that the 1987 Act includes a development risk defence, because the existence of such a defence under the ordinary law of negligence cast great doubt on the claims of Thalidomide victims.

many factories and other workplaces. Yet it is clear that the Commission did not intend to introduce any new scheme of strict liability for industrial accidents.

The strongest argument against any attempt to rationalize the law along these lines is the impossibility of providing any workable criterion for deciding what things or activities are 'dangerous'. The problem is that by far the greatest number of accidents are not caused by things normally thought of as 'dangerous' at all, but by everyday things and activities, in particular, motoring. Really 'dangerous' things and activities in fact cause far fewer accidents, no doubt because their use is generally strictly controlled by regulatory statutes and other precautions. It is also exceedingly difficult to provide any general criterion of dangerousness, because it is not possible to measure how dangerous a thing or activity is without agreeing some acceptable accident rate; and it is not easy to compare accident rates for different activities and things. How, for instance, can the dangerousness of (say) bridges be compared with that of motor cars?

The truth is that these proposals of the Commission were ill thought out and will never be implemented.

4.9.2   Railway accidents

The Pearson Commission proposed a modest extension of strict liability for railway accidents. Its proposal was that railway undertakings should be strictly liable in tort for death or personal injury caused wholly or partly by the movement of rolling stock.[39] No justification was given for these proposals other than the statement that certain aspects of the operation of railways can be characterized as inherently hazardous. This argument seems to echo those relating to exceptional risks in general, and it is open to many of the same criticisms. One starts with the paradox that the movement of rolling stock only causes a minority of the accidents; most railway accidents arise from activities not normally thought of as hazardous at all, such as lifting or moving goods and baggage, and slipping or tripping on railway steps.[40] It is impossible to understand why a minority of accident victims should be better treated in the matter of compensation on the ground that they have been injured by 'more hazardous' activities, when in fact it seems that these 'more hazardous' activities actually account for fewer accidents than the 'less hazardous' ones. It is also to be noted that more than half of the injuries occurring on railway lines are suffered by railway staff[41] who are, of course, entitled to the benefit of the industrial injury side of the social security scheme. Why should these workers also be entitled to the protection of a strict liability regime merely because railways are hazardous, when other factory and industrial workers, who also often work with dangerous machinery, are not? On what possible principle can one justify strict liability for railway workers but not (say) for coal miners?

---

39 Pearson Report vol. 1, para. 1186.
40 Ibid., vol. 2, para. 224.
41 Ibid., table 47.

4.10   Ex Gratia compensation schemes

Confronted with claims for compensation based on allegations of fault such as could form the basis of a tort claim, governments sometimes react by establishing schemes the aim of which is to bypass the tort system in favour of an administrative process for assessing and paying compensation. In one sense, such schemes can be seen as an application of the fault principle. But typically, the motivation for such schemes is not an acceptance of responsibility for fault but rather a desire (for reasons such as political expediency, or 'sympathy' for the victims whose plight is particularly heart-rending) to provide compensation regardless of fault. In this sense, such schemes can be understood as involving the acceptance of a form of strict liability. The schemes considered here can be distinguished from special schemes established as adjuncts to the social security system for the benefit of specific classes of people (13.6, nn 104 and 105). The basic aim of such special schemes, as of the social security system generally, is to meet need. By contrast, the schemes considered in this section are usually understood in terms of discharging some sort of responsibility owed by government to the injured.

4.10.1   Vaccine damage

A very small proportion of children suffer severe brain damage as a result of vacci-nation, in particular, vaccination against whooping cough. The Association of Parents of Vaccine Damaged Children told the Pearson Commission that it had reg-istered 356 cases of vaccine-damaged children. The Association pleaded for some form of strict tort liability to be introduced to help such children, mainly on the ground that child vaccination has for many years been recommended by the gov-ernment. Moreover, vaccination is a classic case of the 'free-rider' problem much discussed by economists. The benefit to each individual child of being vaccinated will not be very great provided most other children are vaccinated, thus greatly reducing the risk of infection; yet if the parents of all children reasoned in this way, vaccination would decline and the diseases in question would spread more widely again, with greater risk to all. Unlike the administration of many drugs, vaccination is designed not only to benefit the recipient – although it may do this – but also to benefit other vulnerable members of the population. To this extent, we may think that young children who are vaccinated before they are old enough to understand the issues are being used for the benefit of others.

The imposition of strict liability on drug manufacturers does not meet the problem because it is typically not clear that the vaccine itself is defective. The Pearson Commission therefore proposed the imposition of 'strict liability' in tort on the government or a local authority where a vaccine was given following a recom-mended programme for which the government or local authority was responsible. However, the political pressure on this issue was so great that the government felt forced to announce some concession even before the Commission reported, and it promised a lump sum payment of £10,000 to any child who could be shown to have been 'severely disabled' as a result of a vaccination against various ailments.[42] Effect was given to this promise in the Vaccine Damage Payments Act 1979, though this was treated as an interim measure without prejudice to the possible acceptance of full government liability in tort. Such acknowledgement of liability was never made, and in 1985 the Secretary of State was empowered by legislation to increase the amount of the lump sum payment.[43] It was increased to £30,000 in 1988 and to £100,000 in 2000.[44]

Despite the arguments in favour of compensation for vaccine damage outlined at the beginning of this section, it is not obvious that a small number of children disabled in this particular way should be singled out for especially generous treatment. The OPCS Disability Survey estimated that there were some 136,000 children under 16 in the four most serious disability categories; and the Pearson Commission estimated that 90% of severely disabled children were disabled from birth. Furthermore, it is very difficult to establish a causal connection between vaccination and disability because small children not infrequently develop convulsions for the first time in the first 2 years of life, and only some of these attacks follow routine vaccinations.[45] In fact, however, after an initial wave of applications immediately after the establishment of the scheme, very few awards have been made since 1988, and most applications fail on the causation issue. Moreover, although the scheme is generous to this group of disabled children, £100,000 is only a fraction of what a seriously disabled child could expect to recover as the result of a successful tort claim.[46]

4.10.2   HIV

In 1988 the government established the Macfarlane Trust to administer compensation payments to haemophiliacs infected with the HIV virus as a result of receiving contaminated blood products. The initial amount made available was £10 million; but as a result of continued lobbying by the Haemophilia Society and on the basis of an undertaking to exclude the government from liability, another £14 million was added to the fund in 1990. A further £44 million was added in 1991, and £15 million more between 1993 and 2001. Because the government has never accepted liability for HIV infection resulting from contamination of blood products, and no liability has been established by judgment of a court, this scheme operates effectively as a no-fault compensation scheme.

4.10.3   Hepatitis C

In the 1970s and 1980s several thousand people were chronically infected with Hepatitis C, once again as a result of being treated by the NHS with contaminated

---

42 'Severely disabled' is defined in terms of departure from 'normality' for a child of the relevant age – originally 80% departure, and now 60%.
43 Social Security Act 1985, s. 23.
44 Vaccine Damage Payments Act 1979 Statutory Sum Order 2000.
45 Pearson Report, vol. 1, para. 1389; R. Goldberg, 'Vaccine Damage and Causation – Social and Legal Implications' (1996) 3 *JSSL* 100.
46 S. Pywell, 'The Vaccine Damage Payment Scheme: A Radical Proposal' (2002) 9 *JSSL* 73.

blood products. In 2001 a court held the government liable to pay compensation, ranging from £10,000 to more than £200,000, to a sub-group (but not all) of these people. For some time, the government resisted calls to compensate others, but in 2003 set up the Skipton Fund 'without admission of legal liability' because, it was said, 'on compassionate grounds this was the right thing to do'. Qualified applicants receive a basic payment of £20,000, and applicants who have contracted cirrhosis or liver cancer are entitled to a further payment of £25,000. Applicants who were treated with certain specified products do not have to prove a causal link between their illness and the treatment. Applicants treated with other possibly contaminated products are dealt with 'on a case-by-case basis'. Payments received from other sources (such as tort compensation) do not reduce the sum awarded. The noteworthy thing about this scheme is that it envisages the payment of compensation to people who might have been infected in circumstances that were held not to attract tort liability. Once again, political pressure benefits a group who undoubtedly deserve sympathy but whose plight is no different from that of many other disabled people. Whereas compensation payable to those who were successful in court was, of course, related to the severity of the effects of the contamination on each individual, the Skipton Fund payments only discriminate between victims on the basis of whether or not they have a particular illness.

4.10.4   Variant CJD

In 2001 the government established a trust to compensate victims of variant CJD, the human form of BSE. The Trust Deed states that the government 'wishes to provide funds in such a manner as does not prohibit [sufferers] or their families from taking legal proceedings against the Crown and/or related bodies if so advised but wishes to ensure so far as possible that in the event of such proceedings being brought the sums paid [under the Trust Deed] are taken into account in the computation of damages to be claimed in any such proceedings'. Payments under the scheme are modelled on common law damages; but guidance issued by the vCJD Trust states that the compensation 'is in many respects greater than the payment of damages which would be awarded by a Court'. The assumption seems to be that the government may be liable; and by providing generous compensation, it is obviously hoped that litigation will be averted. The government has pledged more than £67 million to the fund to compensate an anticipated 250 claimants.

5

Causation and remoteness of damage

5.1 Introduction

A person cannot incur tort liability to pay damages for injury or damage suffered by another unless that injury or damage was caused[1] by the former's tortious conduct. This is as true of strict tort liability as it is of fault-based tort liability. Causation of harm is essential to tort liability because tort law is a set of principles of personal responsibility for conduct. Tort law compensates the injured, but only if someone else was responsible for those injuries; and normally a person will not be responsible for injuries unless their conduct caused the harm. In other words, the tort system is a 'cause-based' compensation system.[2] These deceptively straightforward statements raise complex issues which are usually dealt with by considering two questions: first, did the tortious conduct *in fact* cause the damage? Secondly, whatever the answer to the first question, ought the tortfeasor to be held liable for the loss suffered by the injured person? If the answer to the first question is 'no', then the answer to the second will usually, but not invariably, also be negative. But answering the first question affirmatively by no means always leads to the imposition of liability. The reason for this is expressed by the courts in a variety of ways: sometimes by saying that the damage was not foreseeable; sometimes by saying it was too 'remote'; sometimes by saying the damage suffered is not of a kind recognized by the law; sometimes by saying that the defendant's negligence was not the 'real' or 'proximate' cause of the damage. We will consider these different formulations in turn later in the chapter; but, first, we must examine what it means to say that a tort was a 'factual cause' of harm.

---

1 The simplest type of causation is illustrated by a case where a negligent driver hits a pedestrian. Tort law also recognizes other types of causation as being sufficient for liability. Where tort law imposes liability for nonfeasance, the causal connection between the omission and the harm is failure to prevent the harm occurring. An employer may be held vicariously liable for injury resulting from an employee's tort committed in the course of employment even though the employer did not cause the injury but only created the opportunity for the employee to cause it. Yet other forms of causal connection recognized in tort law include inducing or assisting another to cause injury. For the sake of simplicity, the discussion in this chapter for the most part concentrates on causing in the first simple sense.

2 The implications of this statement are explored in more detail in ch. 19.

5.2   Factual causation

5.2.1   Proving causation

Generally speaking a person cannot be held liable in tort unless it can be said that 'but for' that person's tort, the harm complained of would not have occurred; or, in other words, that the tortious conduct was a *necessary condition* of the harm; or, differently again, that the tortious conduct caused or contributed to the harm. We must add the words 'or contributed to' because, of course, a number of actions may combine to cause damage as, for example, in many road accidents where both drivers are at fault.

In the great majority of cases, this requirement of 'but-for' or 'factual' causation gives rise to no practical difficulties. Indeed, in the typical case of personal injury it is easier to determine whether conduct was a factual cause of harm than whether that conduct was negligent. In practice, an injured person who is looking for someone to sue will normally find that person by looking for a factual cause of the harm rather than for negligent conduct. A person who is run over in the road will normally start by blaming the driver of the car that did the damage; the driver was obviously a cause of the accident. Whether the driver was also at fault is a different and often more difficult question. But there are several types of case in which the issue of factual causation may present difficulties.

In the first place, accidents sometimes occur without the cause being immediately apparent. A soft-drink bottle explodes in someone's face, or a person dies while being operated upon, or a baby is born with brain damage; an aircraft falls out of the sky, or a ferry sinks in calm water with the loss of many lives; a fire starts in a crowded football stadium and many are killed or injured in the rush to escape. Much investigation may be required to ascertain the causes of such incidents. In other cases we may know that there has been negligence, but be uncertain at first whether the person guilty of negligence contributed to the damage. A worker, for example, is found dead near some machinery, which has been negligently maintained in a dangerous manner by the employer. The employer is guilty of negligence, but has that negligence caused or contributed to the worker's death?[3] Similarly, we may know that an injured person used a defective product (or took a defective drug) for which its producer is 'strictly liable', but not be confident that the defect caused the injuries. In these types of case, too, a detailed investigation may be required to discover the truth. Such an investigation would obviously be a formidable burden for an injured person to have to arrange, let alone finance. In the case of a large-scale public disaster involving many deaths or injuries, the injured will usually be relieved of such a burden because public inquiries are invariably held under statutory powers to investigate the causes of such accidents. In cases of workplace accidents, the health and safety inspectorate may help to investigate the causes of the accident; but in cases of medical mishap, for example, such publicly funded assistance is unlikely to be available.

---

3 See e.g. *Caswell* v. *Powell Duffryn Collieries* [1940] AC 152.

Sometimes the injured person may be helped by the doctrine of *res ipsa loquitur* which, as we have seen, says that where an accident results from a situation or thing under the exclusive control of X or persons for whom X is responsible; and where, further, the accident is such that, in the ordinary course of events, it would not occur without negligence on X's part, it is for X to explain how it happened and that it was not caused by their tortious conduct.

5.2.2   Causing and increasing the risk of harm

Proving factual causation may be very difficult in many cases involving disabilities, diseases or illnesses as opposed to accidents causing traumatic injuries.[4] Sometimes these problems arise from the fact that medical knowledge about the causation of many conditions is quite limited and because many diseases are the result of a complex combination of factors that interact in unknown ways. In other cases, it may be possible to say that conduct of the allegedly tortious kind is a cause of a particular condition in a certain percentage of cases, but it may not be possible to say whether it caused the condition in *this* case. The first source of difficulty becomes less acute as medical science advances. For example, much more is known today about the causes of heart disease or cancer than was known 40 years ago. But the second source of difficulty may be impossible to eradicate because many conditions can be caused by more than one factor.

Such difficulties of proof are to some extent ameliorated by the fact that the law only requires proof that the injury or damage was 'more probably than not' caused by the negligence: in other words, that more probably than not, the harm would not have occurred but for the tort. In one case[5] the House of Lords appeared to go further by holding that a claimant could recover damages in respect of a skin condition even though it could not be proved on the balance of probabilities that the defendant's negligence caused the condition, but only that it 'increased the risk' (albeit substantially) that the claimant would contract the condition. A major problem with this approach is that a defendant responsible for a harmful process (e.g. one involving the use of some carcinogen) or product may have to pay damages to a large number of people, many of whom contracted their disease from some other source than the defendant's tortious conduct.[6] This may partly explain why the House of Lords later reinterpreted its earlier decision and said that it was in fact

---

4   J. Stapleton, 'Compensating Victims of Disease' (1985) 5 *Oxford J. Legal Studies* 248, 250–2, 267 n. 54; *Disease and the Compensation Debate* (Oxford, 1986), ch. 3.

5   *McGhee* v. *National Coal Board* [1972] 3 All ER 1008.

6   It must be said that this objection also applies, although less strongly, to the 'balance of probabilities' test of causation. Under this test it is theoretically possible for a claimant to recover damages from a defendant whose negligence did not cause the claimant any loss. The justification for the test is that reconstructing the past is a very difficult exercise, and that a high level of certainty is often unattainable. In the criminal law, however, defendants can be convicted only if they are guilty 'beyond reasonable doubt'. As we know only too well, however, it is not unknown for the innocent to be convicted as a result of purported application of this test.

a case in which the court was satisfied that the tortious conduct had more probably than not caused the skin condition.[7]

However, more recently the House of Lords has returned to its earlier approach in a case of major significance involving a disease called mesothelioma.[8] It is known that mesothelioma is caused (only) by exposure to asbestos, and that the risk of contracting the condition increases with increased exposure. Each of the claimants in this case had been tortiously exposed to asbestos in more than one workplace, and it was possible to say that each exposure had increased the risk of mesothelioma. But it was not possible to say, in relation to any of the claimants, which exposure(s) had triggered their illness or even by how much any particular exposure had increased the risk of their contracting the illness. The House of Lords held that all the employers were liable for the harm resulting from the illness because each had 'materially' increased the risk of mesothelioma. This decision clearly establishes that in some cases, it will not be necessary for a tort claimant to prove, more probably than not, that the harm they suffered was caused by the tort. All that need be proved is that the tort 'materially' increased the risk of the harm. Unfortunately, the House of Lords gave very little guidance about the sorts of case in which this exception to the normal balance-of-probabilities rule of causation will be applied. Unless the boundaries of its application are clearly specified, there is a danger that it will eventually swallow up the basic rule. At the very least, uncertainty about the boundaries is likely to generate litigation.

Another possible line of approach to such difficulties (in some cases, anyway) is to argue that the tortious conduct increased the risk, that the victim would contract a particular disease or suffer a particular condition, by a particular amount (say, 25%) and to claim damages proportional to the increase of risk. (In cases where the material-increase-in-risk rule applies, the victim is compensated in full for all the harm attributable to the tortious risk-increasing conduct.) This would mean that if the victim suffered losses valued at, say, £100,000, the claim would be for £25,000. Such an approach might be attractive where, for example, a particular medical procedure has a 25% success rate, but the defendant doctor negligently fails to carry out the procedure in the victim's case, thus depriving the victim of a 25% chance of a positive health outcome. When it first considered this type of claim, the House of Lords rejected it on the basis that damages are payable only if the tortious conduct increased the risk of harm by more than 50%; or, in other words, if the tortious conduct more probably than not *caused the harm*.[9] If it did, the victim would be entitled to damages for all the harm attributable to the tort. But if all the victim could prove is that more probably than not, the tortious conduct *increased the risk of harm by less than 50%*, nothing could be recovered. This means, in effect, that damages for (and proportional to) loss of a chance cannot be recovered in a personal injury tort

7 *Wilsher* v. *Essex AHA* [1988] AC 1074. See generally J. Stapleton, 'The Gist of Negligence, Part II' (1988) 104 *LQR* 389.
8 *Fairchild* v. *Glenhaven Funeral Services Ltd* [2003] 1 AC 32.
9 *Hotson* v. *East Berkshire HA* [1987] AC 750.

claim. The House of Lords has since reaffirmed this approach in a case where delay in diagnosing cancer reduced the claimant's chance, of surviving cancer-free for 10 years, from 42% to 25%.[10]

On the face of things, it is difficult to see how the reasoning in these loss-of-chance cases can be reconciled with the material-increase-in-risk approach. If a person, who can prove (on the balance of probabilities) only that tortious conduct 'materially' increased the risk of harm, can recover damages for that harm, why should a person, who can prove (on the balance of probabilities) that tortious conduct deprived them of a specified (significant) percentage chance of avoiding harm, not recover damages proportional to the increase in risk? As things stand at the moment, it seems that a person who can quantify the increase in risk and asks for damages proportional to that risk is worse off than a person who cannot quantify the increase in risk and asks for damages for the harm. We could also turn the question the other way round: if all the claimant can prove is that the tortious conduct increased the risk of harm by less than 50%, why should damages for the harm – as opposed to damages proportional to the increase in risk – be recoverable? The basic balance-of-probabilities rule strikes a balance between the interests of doers and sufferers of harm: provided the victim can prove that the tortious conduct was more probably than not a factual cause of the harm, damages can be recovered for that harm. But we might think that if the balance-of-probabilities requirement is relaxed (to the victim's benefit) in favour of the material-increase-in-risk requirement, tortfeasors should be given some corresponding concession, such as proportionate liability.[11]

However acceptable proportionate liability may seem in cases where a single tortfeasor materially increases the risk of harm, we might be less happy about it in cases involving more than one tortfeasor (such as the mesothelioma case). Suppose a drug with adverse side-effects is manufactured and marketed by several companies and taken by a large number of people. If victims sue the manufacturers in tort, individuals may not be able to prove which of the several manufacturers made and marketed the particular pills (or whatever) taken by them. One solution would be to impose liability on each manufacturer according to its market share.[12] This would be roughly equivalent to imposing liability proportional to increase in risk. The problem, from the point of view of victims, is that unless they can successfully sue and recover from all the manufacturers, they will not be fully compensated. The rationale of the basic rule of joint liability (see 4.6) is precisely to protect victims from such an eventuality. In some jurisdictions, proportionate liability schemes have been introduced, but typically they do not apply to personal injury cases.

The complexity of the issues of causation that arise in the sorts of cases we have been considering may suggest that we have here reached the limits of the practical utility of tort law as a system of compensating victims of personal injury. However,

---

10 *Gregg* v. *Scott* [2005] 2 WLR 268.

11 At the time of writing, a case raising this issue is before the House of Lords: *Barker* v. *St Gobain Pipelines Plc* [2004] EWCA Civ 545.

12 See J.G. Fleming, *The American Tort Process* (Oxford, 1988), 258–60.

it must be said that such problems of causation are not unique to the tort system – they can arise in any system under which entitlement to compensation depends on tracing a causal connection between some event and the loss suffered. Nor do the problems end here.

5.2.3   Omissions

Suppose that an employer negligently omits to provide safety belts for workers who are working at such dangerous heights that belts should be worn. A worker falls and is killed; if they had been wearing a safety belt the fall would not have occurred. Is the employer's omission to supply the safety belt a factual cause of the worker's death? In order to answer this question we must ask whether, but for the omission, the worker would have died; but we cannot answer that question unless we know (amongst other things) whether the worker would in fact have worn the belt if it had been provided. Because of the hypothetical nature of this latter question (it is not about what happened but about what might have happened), it may in many cases be extremely difficult to answer with confidence. As a result, the outcome of a case that raises such a question may in the end depend on whether the court requires the victim to prove that the precaution would have been taken or the defendant to prove that it would not. In *McWilliams* v. *Sir William Arrol & Co.*[13] the House of Lords held that the normal rule that the claimant bears the burden of proof applies in such a case. In policy terms this approach is arguably unsatisfactory because it gives employers inadequate incentives to perform their duty to provide safety precautions and to see that they are used. This seems to have been appreciated in *Bux* v. *Slough Metals Ltd*[14] where an employer was held liable for the employee's failure to wear safety goggles on the ground that he probably would have worn them if there had been adequate instruction and supervision.

In practice, courts may be prepared (as was Lord Reid in *McWilliams*) to presume, in the absence of some evidence to the contrary, that the victim would have used any safety device which it was generally considered reasonable to use. This approach effectively turns the question: would the victim have used the safety device if it had been provided? into the question: would the reasonable person in the victim's position have used the safety device if it had been provided?[15] The former, we might say, poses the causal question in a 'subjective' way, and the latter in an 'objective' way. The choice between the subjective and the objective approaches is also important in cases where the allegedly tortious conduct is failure to warn: for instance, where doctors fail to notify patients of risks inherent in medical procedures,[16] or product manufacturers fail to warn users of risks inherent in the product.[17] In practice,

13 [1962] 1 All ER 623.
14 [1974] 1 All ER 262.
15 This question is really equivalent to asking: should the victim have used the safety device?
16 E.g. *Chester* v. *Afshar* [2005] 1 AC 134.
17 E.g. *Hollis* v. *Dow Corning Corp.* (1995) 129 DLR (4th) 609 (subjective approach adopted). In *Smith* v. *Arndt* (1997) 148 DLR (4th) 48 the question was whether a woman would have had an abortion if she had known of a risk of injury to her foetus (objective approach adopted).

however, the choice may not be so important as it appears at first sight. This is because evidence given by the victim personally about what they would have done if the tortious conduct had not occurred is likely to be tainted by self-interest and after-the-event rationalization. For this reason, courts are likely to give it little weight and to decide the causation issue mainly on circumstantial evidence, even if the question to be answered is framed subjectively. This approach effectively objectivises the causation test.

5.2.4   Multiple causal factors

The but-for test causes difficulty in cases involving multiple causal factors. Two types of case can be usefully distinguished. A classic example of the first type is that of two fires, independently started by A and B respectively, which unite and spread to C's house which is destroyed.[18] If we ask whether A or B in fact caused the damage, the but-for test would seem to acquit both A and B of liability.[19] The damage would have occurred even without A's conduct and also without B's conduct; but it is generally conceded to be unfair to let both parties escape liability. A similar conundrum is raised by consecutive causal factors, either of which would be sufficient on its own to bring about the result in question. A runs over C, wounding him in the leg; later B shoots at C, inflicting a wound which necessitates immediate amputation of the leg and would have done so even if there had been no earlier wound.[20] Here again we cannot say that but for A's negligence, or B's shot, C would have had an uninjured leg. But again it would be unfair to acquit both A and B of having caused the injury. In this type of case the outcome often depends on whether or not the causal factors operated more or less contemporaneously: if so, both will be held responsible; if not, the first in time will be held liable[21] on the basis that a person cannot be said to have 'caused' an injury which has already been suffered.

A second and slightly different type of case occurs where one of the causal factors is hypothetical. Suppose, for instance, that C is killed in a car accident caused by B's negligence while being driven to an airport to catch a plane. If it had not been for B's conduct C would not have been killed in the car accident: but suppose that the plane which C was to catch subsequently crashes with the loss of all on board. Would we still say that C would not have been killed but for B's conduct? In a US case,[22] a boy fell from a bridge to what was certain death or grave injury below, but in his fall he came into contact with some high tension wires negligently maintained by the defendant, and was electrocuted. Was the defendant's conduct a factual cause of the boy's death? As in cases of the first type, where there is any significant interval of time between the

---

18 See *Kingston* v. *Chicago & NW Railway* (1927) 22 NW 913.
19 A way of overcoming this problem is to adopt the so-called 'NESS' test of factual causation which classifies something as a cause if it was a necessary element of a set of conditions which together were sufficient to cause the outcome in question. In the example in the text, application of this test would result in both A and B counting as factual causes.
20 *Baker* v. *Willoughby* [1970] AC 476.
21 *Performance Cars* v. *Abraham* [1961] 3 All ER 413 (property damage).
22 *Dillon* v. *Twin State Gas & Electric Co.* (1932) 163 A 111.

occurrence of the damage as things actually turned out, and its probable occurrence as things might have turned out, here too the courts are apt to treat causal connection as established. In *Burmah Oil Co.* v. *Lord Advocate*[23] for instance, where British armed forces had destroyed oil installations in Burma to prevent their falling into Japanese hands, it was not questioned that the acts of the armed forces were the 'cause' of the financial losses inflicted on the owner of the installations.

Any feeling of unfairness to the defendant in such cases may be dealt with in assessing damages. Thus, in the US case it was held that the defendant did cause the boy's death, but that the damages awarded must be calculated on the footing that the boy probably had only a few seconds to live, or at best would have been gravely injured. Similarly, in the *Burmah Oil* case, it is probable that any compensation awarded would have taken account of the fact that the installations were about to fall into the hands of an invading enemy army when they were destroyed.[24] In assessing damages for future economic loss the courts regularly speculate about the likely occurrence of events that would increase or reduce that loss, and award damages proportional to the likelihood. In one case, for example, a worker was burnt on the lip as a result of his employer's negligence; the burn triggered off a pre-malignant condition which the worker had before he was burnt, and he contracted cancer. The employer was held liable for the cancer as well as for the burn, but the damages were reduced to take account of the fact that the worker might have contracted cancer even if he had not been burnt.[25]

This assessment-of-damages approach seems a fair way of dealing with relevant hypothetical events. But courts seem willing to apply it only to hypothetical *future* events, not to hypothetical past events.[26] For instance, in a case like *McWilliams* v. *Arroll* (5.2.3), why should the victim not receive damages calculated according to the chance that they would have used the safety belt? Why does the law usually require proof on the balance of probabilities, that the tortious conduct caused the harm complained of, before it will award damages reflecting the chance that the victim would have suffered harm even if the tort had not occurred? One answer may be that the courts wish to discourage litigation in cases where the tortfeasor's contribution to the harm is very hard to assess with any confidence. But even in cases where it is possible to quantify that contribution (as in *Hotson* or *Gregg* v. *Scott* (5.2.2)), there is great resistance to imposing liability proportionate to risk.

In cases (of the type discussed in the first paragraph of this section) involving consecutive causal factors, an approach similar to the assessment-of-damages technique is adopted by applying the so-called 'vicissitudes' principle, which says that where events relevant to the assessment of damages occur before the trial, the court will take those into account. For example, suppose a worker sustains a back injury

23 [1965] AC 75.
24 [1965] AC 75, 112–13, 165.
25 *Smith* v. *Leech Brain* [1962] 2 QB 405.
26 Unless the hypothetical event in question is some act or omission of someone other than the claimant and the defendant: *Allied Maples Group Ltd* v. *Simmons & Simmons* [1995] 1 WLR 1602.

at work through the negligence of the employer and later contracts a condition that would in any event have caused incapacitation at least as great as the injury. In such a case the employer would not be required to pay damages for the period after the onset of the condition.[27]

5.3   Limits on the liability of factual causes

Even where it is clear that the tortfeasor's conduct was a factual cause of the victim's harm, the tortfeasor may be held not liable for damage that has occurred in an unexpected or unusual or unforeseeable way. This limitation on liability covers two somewhat different situations. First, it prevents a person being held liable for the consequences of a tort where these are 'too remote' in time and space from the tortious conduct, and in particular, where some other event intervenes between the tortious conduct and the occurrence of the harm; for example, where A injures B in a road accident and B is injured again in a further accident while being taken to hospital. Once a person has been injured by the negligence of another, they may in time to come suffer further injuries or accidents which might not have occurred at all 'but for' the original negligence; but it is generally felt that it would be unfair to hold the tortfeasor liable for all such consequences. Secondly, this limitation on liability saves a person from liability even for damage which follows tortious conduct closely in time and space, but which occurs in an unusual or freakish way or is of an unexpected kind; for example, where a plank dropped into a ship's hold starts a conflagration which destroys the whole ship.

The policy underlying the denial of liability in cases of this kind is clear enough when the defendant's liability is based on negligence: it is not reasonable to expect a person to take precautions against freakish or unexpected or unusual events. But even in cases where liability for injury or harm is strict, we may think it unfair to hold a person liable for such events: people ought to be in a position to take account of their potential legal liabilities in advance in deciding what activities to engage in and on what scale; and a person cannot reasonably be expected to take account of freakish or unexpected or unusual events. The technical or 'conceptual' shape of this part of the law is a morass. At least three reasons have been given for denying liability for freakish or unexpected outcomes. These are, first, that the tortious conduct was not the 'cause' of the damage; secondly, that the damage was not within the risk required to be guarded against; and, thirdly, that the damage was not foreseeable.

5.3.1   Legal causation

The but-for test is very indiscriminate in that it will identify as causes many factors that are of little interest because they are merely necessary conditions of the harm suffered. In legal terms this is often put by saying that the court is looking for *the* cause of the damage, or the 'real' or 'effective' or 'proximate' cause, or (in legal Latin)

---

27 *Jobling* v. *Associated Dairies Ltd* [1982] AC 794.

the *causa causans* and not just a *causa sine qua non*. In other words, the court must select one or more out of all the factors but for which the damage would not have occurred. All of these factors are causes in fact, but this approach involves selecting one or more of them as a 'cause in law'. Given that there are a very large number of necessary conditions of every event, it might seem a daunting task to have to pick out one (or a few) of them as being 'really' the cause(s) of the event. However, in practice, the job is made very much more straightforward because in a tort action the question is not, 'what really caused the victim's injury?' but rather, 'did the allegedly tortious conduct really cause the victim's injury?'. In fact, it is for this reason that in the majority of tort cases, once it has been established that the defendant committed a tort and that the claimant's injury would not have occurred but for the tort, the tortious conduct will be held also to be the (legal) cause of that injury. It is only in relatively unusual cases that it will be possible to point to some other factual cause as being a stronger candidate than the tort for the title 'legal cause'. In most cases, all the factual causes other than the tortious conduct will simply be the background against which, or the surroundings in which, that conduct occurs and has its effects.

What is actually meant by saying that a person's conduct was *the cause* of this or that event? The first thing to note is that this type of causal inquiry may be made for at least two different reasons: the inquirer may be seeking an explanation of what happened and of how it happened; or they may be asking a question about who ought to be held responsible for what happened. Explanatory inquiries are usually directed either at finding out what has to be done in order to achieve a particular desirable result,[28] or at finding out how to prevent particular undesirable things happening in the future. Different people may have different reasons for seeking causal explanations for one and the same event, and this might lead them to pick out different factual causes of an event as being the causal explanation for it.[29] Take a road accident, for example. The highway authority which is responsible for seeing that road surfaces are not excessively skid-prone may be more interested in one factor; the motor manufacturer who wants to make cars that do not overturn too easily will be more interested in another factor; the driver who wants to learn how to drive without overturning the car, in yet another, and so on.

The legal causation issue in tort law is not concerned with explaining what happened or with preventing injuries in the future[30] but with an 'attributive' question: should we attribute responsibility for this consequence to that cause?[31] If *A* injures *B*

28 Causes as recipes: T. Honoré, 'Necessary and Sufficient Conditions in Tort Law' in D.G. Owen ed., *Philosophical Foundations of Tort Law* (Oxford, 1995), 375.
29 See R.G. Collingwood, 'On the So-Called Idea of Causation' (1937–8) xxviii *Proceedings of the Aristotelian Society* 85, 92–3 for a famous passage making this point.
30 Not everyone would agree with this. Some people say that the whole point of tort law is to reduce accidents and injuries in the future. For such people, the causal issue in tort law would involve a form of explanatory inquiry because in their view, tort liability ought to be imposed on the person best placed to reduce accidents and injuries in the future.
31 For this reason, it has been argued that the word 'cause' should be used only to refer to factual causes, and that issues of legal causation should be thought of in terms of responsibility or scope

and *B* is killed while in an ambulance being driven to hospital, the legal causation question is: should *A* be held responsible for *B*'s death? At first sight, explanatory causal inquiries may appear to be very different from attributive causal inquiries. When we seek explanations, we want to know what happened, not who was responsible for it or who ought to do something about it. When we think about the matter more deeply, however, the two types of inquiry look rather similar. This is because they are both concerned with picking out one or more necessary conditions of an event as being in some sense 'more important' than the mass of such conditions which make up the background of the causal picture. At one level, all necessary conditions are equally important, exactly because they are all, by definition, necessary. For example, where a driver knocks down a pedestrian, the presence of the pedestrian at the site of the accident is just as necessary a condition of the incident as the negligence of the driver. A necessary condition will only assume the foreground if we have some particular purpose in asking the causal question that points to that condition as being more important (for our purpose) than all the other necessary conditions of the incident we are interested in. This is as true of explanatory inquiries as of attributive inquiries. The difference between them is that the purposes that motivate them are different. Whereas the purpose of a highway authority in investigating a road accident in which a pedestrian is injured by a driver may be to discover whether and how improvements in road design (such as the installation of traffic lights) could help to prevent such an accident in the future, the purpose of a court in a tort action arising out of the incident will be to decide whether the driver ought to be required to compensate the pedestrian for injuries suffered in the accident.

Moreover, the law's interest in causation is crucially affected by the fact, noted above, that the question in a tort action is not 'who should be held responsible to pay compensation?' but rather, 'should the defendant be held responsible to pay compensation?'. This question will not be answered 'no' simply because there is some other factual cause which the court thinks ought to share responsibility with the defendant, but only if the court can identify some other factual cause which, in its view, is so 'potent' that it ought to relieve the defendant of any responsibility. The car accident in which Princess Diana died provides a good illustration: it was alleged that the driver of the car was negligent in the legal sense. It was also suggested that occupants of the car might not have died if there had been crash barriers in the underpass in which it occurred. In such a case, if the driver were sued, he could not escape liability simply by pointing to the defect in the design of the road even if, had the road authority been sued, it could have been held liable. More than one person may be legally responsible for an accident, and it is up to the victim to decide which person to sue. Each of the legally responsible parties may be held fully liable to the victim, and they must argue amongst themselves about how responsibility ought to be shared between them (4.6).

of liability for the consequences of factual causes: J. Stapleton, 'Cause in Fact and the Scope of Liability for Consequences' (2003) 119 *LQR* 388.

Explanatory causal inquiries, then, have different purposes from attributive causal inquiries. The criteria we use in deciding whether one thing caused another are directly related to our purpose in making the causal inquiry. What are the criteria that tort law uses to identify the legal cause(s) of injuries for the purpose of deciding whether to impose liability to compensate for those injuries?[32] There are several which can be identified. One is that human conduct tends to be identified as the cause of an event in preference to non-human ('natural') occurrences. So far as the 'natural world' is concerned, the basic approach of tort law is that tortfeasors must take the world as found (i.e. without attempting to offload responsibility onto nature). A natural causal factor will be treated as the cause of an event in preference to tortious human conduct only if it was sufficiently out of the ordinary and improbable that it could be described as 'totally unexpected' or a 'sheer coincidence'.

What does the law say when conduct of someone other than the defendant is amongst the factual causes of the victim's injury? Such conduct may be that of the victim or of some 'third party'. Once again, the law's approach is that only conduct which is out of the ordinary will relieve the defendant of liability. Whereas a 'natural event' will be treated as extraordinary if it was highly improbable, human conduct will be treated as out of the ordinary if it was very unreasonable. For instance, in one case a person was injured by another's negligence and as a result he lost control of his left leg. He fell while descending, unassisted, some steep stairs without a handrail, and broke an ankle. The House of Lords held that the injured persons' conduct, although 'not at all unlikely', was 'quite unreasonable'; and that the tortfeasor was not liable for the broken ankle.[33] Again, suppose that a person is injured in a car accident as a result of a driver's negligence, but then receives further injuries as a result of negligence of a doctor providing treatment for the initial injuries. In such a case, the driver will usually be held responsible for the further injuries;[34] but not,

---

32 By far the most thorough examination of these criteria is that of H.L.A. Hart and T. Honoré, *Causation in the Law* (2nd edn, Oxford, 1985), esp. chs. VI–X. For a very good summary of the authors' views see J. Stapleton, 'Law, Causation and Common Sense' (1988) 8 *Oxford J. Legal Studies* 111. One of the main aims of *Causation in the Law* was to counter the view (which was, at one stage, widely held by scholars in the USA, but never really took hold in the UK) that the only concept of causation used in tort law was factual causation. In my view, the authors entirely succeeded in doing so. (Of course, whether factual causation should be the only concept of causation in the law is a different issue: see n. 31 above.) The discussion of Hart and Honoré's work in the first five editions of this book focused on the authors' assertion that legal notions of causation were derived from 'commonsense usage' of causal language outside the law. The main issue we addressed was whether their account paid sufficient attention to the distinction (which they recognized) between explanatory and attributive causal inquiries and to the role of purpose in choosing amongst factual causes. Our analysis tended to assume (wrongly, as I now believe) that, unlike legal causal inquiries, causal inquiries outside the law are typically concerned with explanation, not attribution, of responsibility. In fact, the purposes of causal inquiries outside the law are extremely various. For this reason, I do not agree with Honoré's view ('Necessary and Sufficient Conditions in Tort Law' in *Philosophical Foundations of Tort Law*, 385) that 'the same concept of cause is used for discovering recipes, for explaining events, and for assigning responsibility for outcomes'. Causation is much more context-specific than this statement seems to allow. It is mainly for this reason that the discussion in this edition concentrates on explaining the criteria of causation used in tort law.
33 *McKew v. Holland and Hannen and Cubitts (Scotland) Ltd* [1969] 3 All ER 1621.
34 But the negligent doctor may also be held liable for them.

according to the High Court of Australia, if the medical treatment was 'grossly negligent'.[35] In that case, the doctor alone will be responsible for the further injuries. There are three possible outcomes in such cases: either the defendant will be held solely responsible for the further as well as for the initial injuries; or the defendant will be held responsible for the initial injuries but not for the further injuries; or the initial tortfeasor will be held jointly responsible with the other person for the further injuries as well as solely responsible for the initial injuries. In the last case, if the other person is the claimant, their damages may be reduced on account of their contributory negligence; and if the other person is a third party, the defendant may be able to recover from them a 'contribution' to the damages payable to the claimant.

Returning to the criteria of legal causation, these examples indicate three more. One is that the agent of harm is more likely to be treated as its cause than the sufferer of harm; another is that tortious conduct is more likely to be treated as the cause of harm than non-tortious conduct; and a third is that more-culpable conduct is more likely to be treated as the cause of harm than less-culpable conduct.[36] Suppose a motorist knocks down and injures a pedestrian. Although both the conduct of the driver and the presence of the pedestrian 'in the wrong place at the wrong time' are necessary conditions of the pedestrian's injuries, the driver is more likely to be treated as their cause if neither the driver nor the pedestrian was negligent. The driver is even more likely to be treated as the cause if the driver was negligent but the pedestrian was not. If both were negligent, the pedestrian's conduct is unlikely to be treated as the sole cause unless that conduct was extremely foolish (as in *McKew* v. *Holland*).

It is clear that these criteria of legal causation are closely related to the idea of personal responsibility for conduct. A basic function of tort law is to allocate responsibility for harm, and the concepts of causation used in the law inevitably reflect this purpose. It is interesting to consider what the relationship is between the responsibility-oriented concepts of causation in tort law and ideas of responsibility adopted in everyday life. Does tort law reflect widely held views about responsibility for harm or is it, by contrast, an ethical system developed by the courts with little or no reference to what ordinary people think? There is a long history of courts saying that issues of legal causation should be resolved on the basis of 'commonsense';[37] but is this the common sense of judges or of non-lawyers? These are difficult questions to answer partly because of the problem of finding out what 'ordinary

---

35 *Mahony* v. *J. Kruschich (Demolitions) Pty Ltd* (1985) 156 CLR 522, 530. Both of these cases are examples of what is called 'intervening causation' where the conduct of the injured person or the third party occurs after the tortious conduct of the defendant and 'intervenes' between the defendant's conduct and some or all of the victim's injuries. Similar principles apply to what might be called 'initial causation' which concerns the allocation of responsibility as between causal factors operating more or less at the same time.

36 This last criterion is the basis of the view of Hart and Honoré (*Causation in the Law*, 42) that '. . . a voluntary human action intended to bring about what in fact happens, and in the manner in which it happens, has a special place in causal inquiries'.

37 Hart and Honoré, *Causation in the Law*, 9. A good example is *Medlin* v. *State Government Insurance Commission* (1995) 182 CLR 1, 6.

people think' about complex issues of responsibility. However, there is empirical research which throws doubt on the idea that legal concepts of responsibility and causation mirror notions which are widely held outside the law.[38] This research suggests that personal injury victims may often sue a person, whom they do not consider responsible for their injuries, simply because they know, or have been told, that suing that person offers the best hope of obtaining compensation. Conversely, a person considered responsible may not be sued because, for example, the victim feels this to be an unjustifiably aggressive act, or judges that the benefits of suing the person would not outweigh the 'anticipated expense, trouble, upset and uncertainties of doing so'.[39] This helps to explain why accidents in the home are so rarely the subject of litigation. People, it seems, often make (or fail to make) tort claims for reasons having little to do with notions of cause and responsibility, and then justify their action by use of such ideas. Furthermore, the decision to sue and, later, the attribution of responsibility, often seem to reflect current legal rules and the pattern of effective tort liability rather than being reflected by the law. In other words, people often sue because they think they have a good chance of success, and they justify this decision in terms of the language and concepts of the law.

It does not follow from these findings that legal attributions of responsibility are not based on morality or on ideas of justice. But the research does suggest that this morality is one worked out by the judges rather than one taken by the law from the reflections of the 'common person' on the sort of situations that may give rise to tort liability. This is, perhaps, not surprising because courts are often confronted with very unusual factual situations and very tricky ethical issues. An interesting example is a case in which A received serious head injuries in a car accident caused by B's negligence. As a result, A suffered a personality change and turned to crime, including rape. A was awarded damages against B, including an amount to compensate him for the effects of being sentenced to life imprisonment for sexual offences, on the ground that this was a compensatable consequence of B's negligence. Two of A's victims then successfully sued him for damages for assault, which led A to sue B again to recover damages representing the amounts awarded to the two victims. This last action failed on the ground that the award of damages to the two victims was too remote a consequence of B's negligence, and that to award A compensation would be 'distasteful' and contrary to public policy.[40] A judge in New South Wales has expressed the view that the decision in the first of these cases was wrong, essentially because the moral responsibility (and, according to the criminal law, the legal responsibility) for A's crimes rested on A, not B, even though A would not have committed them but for B's negligence in injuring him.[41]

38 S. Lloyd-Bostock, 'Fault and Liability for Accidents: the Accident Victim's Perspective' in Harris 1984 Survey, ch. 4.
39 Ibid., 157.
40 *Meah v. McCreamer (No. 1)* [1985] 1 All ER 367; *W v. Meah* [1986] 1 All ER 935; *Meah v. McCreamer (No. 2)* [1986] 1 All ER 943.
41 *State Rail Authority of New South Wales v. Wiegold* (1991) 25 NSWLR 500 (Samuels JA).

Examples such as this show that although legal concepts of causation and responsibility are based on non-legal ideas, they are and need to be much more detailed and complex than their non-legal counterparts. An important reason for this arises out of the point, made earlier, that concepts of cause and responsibility serve a variety of different purposes. An important function of legal concepts (unlike their non-legal counterparts) is to justify the imposition of obligations that can, ultimately, be enforced by the coercive power of the State. Furthermore, tort law is mainly concerned with obligations to pay monetary compensation for personal injury, property damage and economic loss, whereas outside the law the payment of compensation is rarely in issue. Rules and principles on the basis of which people can be forced to pay over large amounts of money to another must be precise, clear and sensitive to the facts of individual cases to a degree not required in non-legal contexts.

A good illustration of the divergence between legal and non-legal concepts is the very use of the word 'cause' itself. Take, for example, the case mentioned above of a person who is negligently injured in a car accident and then further injured by the negligence of a hospital doctor. In everyday parlance, we would probably not say that the negligent driver 'caused' the further injuries – they were 'caused' by the doctor. On the other hand, even in relation to the further injuries, the negligence of the driver could be said to be a more important causal factor than many other of the necessary conditions of the further injuries. The role of the driver in causing the further injuries might be described in terms of 'creating the situation in which the further injuries might be suffered'. In this case, the law is prepared to impose an obligation to pay compensation on the basis of a weaker causal connection than is described by use of the word 'cause'. There are, in fact, many instances of this phenomenon in tort law. Employers can be held vicariously liable for torts of their employees on the basis that the employer provided the opportunity for the employee to commit the tort and cause harm to another. Similarly, under Part I of the Consumer Protection Act 1987, distributors of products may, under certain circumstances, be held liable for personal injuries caused by a defect in a product even though they did not 'cause' the injuries complained of, but, at most, created the situation in which they might occur. Liability for omission provides another example – here it can typically be said that the tortfeasor failed to prevent harm occurring, but not that the tortfeasor 'caused' the harm. A different type of case is where harm results from one person's reaction to the conduct of another person – for instance, where A is induced or persuaded by B to act in a way which causes harm to C, or where A acts in reliance on something said by B with the result that harm is caused to A or C. In such cases we might want to say that the harm was 'caused' by A, even if we want to hold B responsible for their part in producing the harm.

In all these types of case, the law is prepared to impose liability to pay compensation for harm suffered on the basis of a causal connection between that harm and the defendant's conduct which may not be easily described by use of the word 'cause'. And yet in law we say that these 'weaker' forms of causal connection satisfy the *legal* requirement of liability for harm that the harm was 'caused' by the tortfeasor's conduct. The conclusion to be drawn is that although there are obviously connections between notions of causation inside and outside the law, the legal concept of causation is much more complex and detailed than its non-legal counterpart; and that in important respects, the legal concept of causation serves purposes and performs functions which its non-legal counterpart does not.

It is important, however, not to jump from this conclusion to the view that causation in the law is really 'all a matter of policy' and that the language of causation is used merely as a cloak for attributions of responsibility on non-causal grounds. There are certainly concepts in tort law that can be used to relieve people of liability for harm which they can be said to have 'caused'. Such concepts include the ideas of 'scope of the risk' and 'foreseeability', which we will look at a little later in this chapter; and they include the concept of 'duty of care', which we examined in chapter 3. It is also true that the decision to impose liability on the basis of weaker causal connections than are captured by the word 'cause' may be based on non-causal considerations – vicarious liability provides an obvious example. Furthermore, it is important always to bear in mind that the way we answer causal questions will depend on our purpose and interest in asking them. Nevertheless, causal concepts play an independent role in tort law and cannot simply be equated with 'policy'. Two examples may illustrate this point. Suppose a person negligently starts a fire that burns down half a town. We might well say that the negligent person caused all the damage done by the fire. On the other hand, there may be good policy reasons not to hold that person liable for all the damage caused – such as, for instance, that it is much more sensible for the risk of fire damage in crowded urban areas to be dealt with by property owners taking out insurance against fire damage to their own property.[42] Or suppose that a vehicle is left by its owner unlocked and unattended in the street with the keys in the ignition. The car is stolen and the thief injures someone by negligent driving.[43] Causal principles might point to the thief as being (at least primarily) responsible for the harm done, while as a matter of policy there is a good argument for imposing liability on the car owner who is (and indeed must be) insured against such liability, who can be said to have created an opportunity for the harm to occur and who could have reduced the risk of the harm occurring by the simple expedient of locking the vehicle. These examples show that although the questions of whether A caused harm and of whether A ought to be held liable to compensate for that harm are related to one another, they are not one and the same.

5.3.2   Damage not within the risk

One of the ways in which matters of 'policy' can be taken into account in imposing liability for the consequences of tortious conduct may be formulated as follows: liability for breach of a rule only extends to consequences the risk of which that rule

---

42 For further discussion of this example see Hart and Honoré, *Causation in the Law*, 89–90.
43 See e.g. *Topp v. London Country Bus (South West) Ltd* [1993] 1 WLR 976; J.G. Fleming, 'Injury Caused by Stolen Motor Vehicles' (1994) 110 *LQR* 187.

was 'designed' to guard against. This principle is a well-accepted one in English law in connection with actions for breach of statutory duty. In *Gorris* v. *Scott*[44] the defendant shipowners were required by statute to provide pens for all animals carried on board ship. When the claimant's animals were swept overboard in a storm, C sued the defendants on the ground that they had failed to provide pens, which would have prevented this disaster. It was held that they were not liable because (although failure to provide the pens was the cause of the loss of the sheep) the 'purpose' of the statute was not to protect the animals against perils of the sea but against the spread of infection.

Application of the same notion to cases of negligence may be illustrated by reference to the decision in *Doughty* v. *Turner Manufacturing Co.*[45] in which the defendant was a manufacturer who used vats of extremely hot liquid chemicals in its processes. These vats were protected by asbestos covers, and an employee of the defendant replaced one of these covers carelessly so that it fell into the vat. Unknown to anyone, the asbestos was prone, in conjunction with the heated chemicals, to produce a violent explosion; and this in fact occurred and injured the claimant. Since nobody knew of the danger presented by the interaction between the asbestos and the chemicals, C could not argue that D (or the employee in question) should have foreseen the possibility of an explosion; but he contended that the employee should have foreseen the possibility of some of the hot chemicals splashing out and injuring someone; that, accordingly, dropping the asbestos lid into the vat was a negligent act, and that the defendant was vicariously liable for the claimant's injuries. The defendants were held not liable on the ground that the risk of explosion, being unforeseeable, was not a risk which the defendant's employee ought to have taken precautions against when the lid was replaced on the vat.

One way of stating the ground of decision in *Doughty* is to say that the defendant was not negligent in relation to the risk of explosion because that risk was unforeseeable, and it cannot be negligent not to take precautions against an unforeseeable risk. In other words, on the approach currently being considered, a defendant is only liable for consequences the risk of which he or she ought to have taken precautions against. The risks relevant to determining whether the defendant was negligent and, therefore liable at all, are also the risks which define the extent of the liability. Liability only extends as far as the concept of negligence itself.

This 'risk theory' of the extent of negligence liability has several shortcomings. In the first place, as we will see in 5.3.3, there can be liability in negligence for consequences that were not reasonably foreseeable and against which precautions would not be required. Conversely, there are circumstances in which even foreseeable consequences may not fall within the scope of liability even if failure to take precautions against the occurrence of such consequences would be negligent. Secondly, even though the idea of 'harm-within-the-risk' may be able to explain the

44 (1874) LR 9 Ex 125.
45 [1964] 1 QB 518.

results in certain cases, by itself it does not give any guidance as to whether a particular outcome is within a particular risk.

5.3.3   Foreseeability again

In chapter 2 we saw that negligence is failure to take reasonable precautions against foreseeable risks of harm. It cannot be negligent to fail to take precautions against unforeseeable risks of harm. Foreseeability is one (but not the only) component of the legal concept of negligence. Foreseeability is also used in tort law as a criterion to determine the extent of liability for the consequences of negligent conduct. If a consequence is very unusual, or very 'remote' from the tortious conduct, it may be said that the consequence was unforeseeable and that, therefore, the tortfeasor is not liable for it, even if it was caused (in the factual sense: 5.2) by the tort. This course was adopted by the Privy Council in the famous *Wagon Mound (No. 1)* case,[46] which overturned the equally famous Court of Appeal decision in *Re Polemis*.[47] In *Re Polemis* it was held that provided *some* damage was foreseeable, the defendant could be held liable for all the damage which was a *direct consequence* of the negligence. In *The Wagon Mound (No. 1)* the Privy Council rejected this approach and purported to lay down a similar test for the extent of liability as had already been laid down for the existence of liability, namely foreseeability. The justification for doing this was so that the two tests would rest on similar notions of *fault*: if there is to be 'no liability without fault', then that maxim must apply to the extent of liability as much as to the existence of liability. However, the conclusion does not really follow from the premise. If a person ought to have taken certain precautions, it is not obviously unfair to hold them liable for the consequences of their failure to do so whether or not they were all foreseeable.

In any event, as a test of extent of liability ('remoteness of damage', as lawyers call it) foreseeability only requires that the type or kind of damage suffered be foreseeable, not its exact extent or manner of occurrence. For this reason, a tortfeasor can be held liable for consequences of negligence, which are a direct result of foreseeable consequences, but which were not themselves foreseeable. A burn on the lip may lead to cancer and death, and the person responsible for the burn may be liable for the death;[48] an electric shock may stimulate a latent polio virus, and the person responsible for the shock may also have to pay for the effects of the polio;[49] injuries may lead to melancholia and suicide, and the tortfeasor liable for the injuries may also be liable for the death.[50] In this way many injuries or diseases that are in a sense merely 'triggered off' by the original negligently caused accident are brought within the scope of the tort system, and so may be the subject of compensation. Results of

---

46 [1961] AC 388.
47 [1921] 3 KB 560.
48 *Smith* v. *Leech Brain* [1962] 2 QB 405; see also *Warren* v. *Scruttons* [1962] 1 Lloyd's Rep 497.
49 *Sayers* v. *Perrin* [1966] QdR 89.
50 *Pigney* v. *Pointer's Transport Services Ltd* [1957] 1 WLR 1121; see also *Brice* v. *Brown* [1984] 1 All ER 997.

this kind can no doubt be explained by the overriding desire to compensate people for tragic misfortunes,[51] especially in cases where the defendant is insured against liability. But the element of chance or luck is very obvious in such cases. Many people die of cancer every year; many others commit suicide; many contract polio or other crippling diseases. Why should the majority go unaided by the tort system while a handful, who are able to latch their disease on to some negligently caused injury, are so generously treated? In some cases it may seem very unfair to hold the tortfeasor responsible, yet large sums may be awarded. For example, in one case[52] the injured person suffered a minor graze through slipping on steps that had been negligently covered with oil. Unfortunately he suffered a freak reaction to an anti-tetanus injection, with very serious results. He was awarded damages of over £30,000 (in 1974) – yet the only negligence consisted of leaving some oil on a step ladder. Cases of this kind might be seen as involving liability without fault: while initial negligence must be proved, the claimant recovers damages for what most people would regard as nothing but an accident or a coincidence.

Whereas a tortfeasor may, under certain circumstances, be liable for unforesee-able consequences of negligence, there may, conversely, be *no* liability for foresee-able consequences of negligence if they were (partly) the result of the (foreseeable) conduct of a human agent following the tort: 'unreasonable', but foreseeable, conduct by the injured person, perhaps;[53] or criminal conduct by a third party.[54] Such results arise out of the feeling that in most circumstances, one person should not be liable for the conduct of another unless the former is under some sort of moral duty to control or protect the latter. But the law is not consistent in this regard because courts are quite willing, for example, to impose liability, for the results of negligent medical treatment, on the person who caused the injuries that necessitated the treatment.

Another type of case in which there may be no liability for foreseeable conse-quences involves economic loss, not personal injury. Suppose that a person would not have bought a particular property – or any property at all – but for a negligent valuation report to the effect that the property was worth more than its actual value. Suppose, further, that after the purchase, there is a general fall in property values. Is the negligent valuer liable for loss suffered by the purchaser as a result of the fall in property values, or only for the difference between the reported and the actual values of the property? The relevant judicial decisions are difficult to understand and interpret; but the law seems to be that even if the market fall was foreseeable, the valuer will be liable for additional loss flowing from the fall only if the report effectively stated that there would be no such fall. Of course, if the market fall was

51 But the rules may not be so generous when the loss suffered is purely economic; the position in relation to property damage is somewhat unclear.
52 *Robinson* v. *Post Office* [1974] 2 All ER 737. Another extraordinary case is *Versic* v. *Connors* (1969) 90 WN (NSW) (Pt 1) 33.
53 E.g. *McKew* v. *Holland and Hannen and Cubitts (Scotland) Ltd* [1969] 3 All ER 1621.
54 E.g *Lamb* v. *Camden LBC* [1981] QB 625.

foreseeable, it would be negligent of the valuer not to take this into account in valuing the property. But even if the valuer was negligent in this way, the purchaser could not recover damages for the loss resulting from the fall in the market, but only for the difference between the reported value of the property and its actual value at the time of the valuation, taking account of the foreseeable fall in the market. This shows that a particular foreseeable risk might be relevant to deciding whether a person has been negligent even though, if that risk materializes, the person would not be held liable for resulting loss.

An analogous issue might arise in a personal injury case: suppose a person would not have gone mountain climbing but for a doctor's negligent advice that the climber's bad knee would withstand the strain. Suppose, further, that in addition to suffering knee damage, the climber is badly injured in a rock fall. The doctor's liability would probably not extend to the additional injuries despite the foreseeability (or even high probability) of rock falls. Similarly, doctors are required to warn their patients of 'material' risks inherent in medical procedures to be performed by the doctor on the patient. But the mere fact that a risk is foreseeable will not necessarily make it material. Suppose a doctor fails to warn a patient of a material risk, and that the patient would not have consented to the procedure if the warning had been given; but also that the patient suffers harm as a result of the materialization, not of the risk of which warning should have been given, but of a foreseeable but non-material risk. The doctor would not be liable for the harm.

It is clear, therefore, that it is only in a very qualified sense that foreseeability is the test of the scope of liability for the consequences of which negligence is the factual cause. A negligent tortfeasor may be held liable for unforeseeable consequences of the tort, and may escape liability for foreseeable consequences of the tort. To the extent that the 'risk theory' (5.3.2) of the scope of liability rests on the fact that 'foreseeability' is both an element of the legal concept of negligence and also the basic test of liability for consequences, it fails as an explanation of the scope of liability for negligence.

5.4   Conclusion

In tort law, a person cannot be held liable to compensate for harm suffered by another unless there was a causal connection between the harm and that person's conduct. We have seen that the legal concept of 'cause' is a complex and detailed one which, although related to ideas of causation and responsibility utilized in non-legal contexts, has distinctive features which are explicable in terms of the purposes of tort law. It is important to distinguish between the concept of factual causation, which is concerned with the way things happen in the world, and the concepts of legal causation, foreseeability and remoteness of damage, which are concerned with allocating responsibility for life's misfortunes.

6

Damages for personal injury and death

6.1 The lump sum: predicting the future

6.1.1 Personal injury cases

Damages for personal injury and death typically take the form of a lump sum. The award or settlement is made once for all, and there is – except in rare cases – no possibility of increasing it or decreasing it later because of changes in the claimant's situation. In the great majority of instances where the injuries are relatively minor, this raises no real problem because the injured person is likely to be completely recovered long before the damages are assessed, and the whole episode is by then past history.

However, the lump-sum remedy does raise acute problems wherever a person suffers serious injuries, the effects of which may still be felt long after the damages are assessed. The Pearson Commission estimated that about 7.5% of all tort claims (including claims in fatal cases) involved future earnings losses after the trial or settlement of the claim;[1] and this is the type of claim that raises problems with lump sums. In cases of continuing income loss, or where the injured person will have a continuing need for hospital, medical or nursing care, two sets of predictions have to be made at the date of trial or settlement in order to calculate an appropriate sum. First, it is necessary to predict what would have happened to the injured person if they had not been injured, a prediction which obviously cannot be verified or falsified by subsequent events. Secondly, it is necessary to predict what is now likely to happen to the injured person. For example, will they ever make a complete recovery? If so, how long will it take? If not, what residual degree of disability will there be? How will this affect the injured person's earning capacity? Will they suffer further pain and discomfort? Or die sooner than might otherwise have been the case? In the case of certain types of injury there is always a risk of complications in the future; for example, epilepsy is almost always a risk in brain damage cases, and arthritis is a common risk wherever bones are severely fractured. These risks are often low (e.g. the risk of epilepsy following brain damage is often put at one in ten), but lump-sum damage awards must take

1 Pearson Report, vol. 2, paras. 43–4.

account of the risk. This is done by calculating what sum would be appropriate if the risk materialized, and then giving as damages a fraction of this sum proportional to the risk occurring.

Obviously the task of predicting the future is extremely difficult, and mistakes can occur even when best efforts are made. Still, it is highly unsatisfactory that given the extreme difficulty of the task, there is hardly ever any opportunity for making a subsequent correction. If it is predicted that the injured person will make a complete recovery and this does not happen, they will have been awarded less damages than they should have got. Conversely, if a claimant recovers more quickly than predicted, too much compensation will have been awarded. In 'chance' cases (such as those involving a risk of epilepsy) the problem is even worse because the lump-sum award is bound to be wrong. If the risk eventuates, the amount awarded will be too little; if it does not, too much. There is no possibility here of making an inspired guess and hitting the right sum.

These difficulties may be aggravated by the phenomenon of 'compensation neurosis'.[2] This psychological condition – which may be distinguished from conscious 'malingering' – is said to have the effect of prolonging the period of recovery and rehabilitation until after trial or settlement of a tort claim. Anxiety over the likely outcome of the claim may postpone complete recovery. Besides being an undesirable by-product of the once-for-all lump-sum damages system, compensation neurosis can cause problems for assessing damages. If it is assumed that disabilities are permanent whereas they are, in fact, a symptom of compensation neurosis that will disappear once the claim has been resolved, the injured person will have been overcompensated; conversely, if the case is wrongly thought to be one of 'compensation neurosis', the injured person may be under-compensated.

To some extent these difficulties of prediction can be, and are, mitigated by postponing the trial or settlement of the action until a prediction about the ultimate outcome can be made with greater confidence.[3] Indeed, in many cases of serious injury it is essential to do this because no satisfactory predictions can be made at all until many months at least after the injuries were suffered. Although in strict law the assessment of damages in most cases should be related to the time of injury

---

2 This is a very complex and controversial topic. See e.g. T.G. Ison, 'The Therapeutic Significance of Compensation Structures' (1986) 64 *Canadian Bar R*. 605, 610–29; C. Vincent and I.H. Robertson, 'Recovering From a Medical Accident: the Consequences For Patients and Their Families' in C. Vincent, M. Ennis and R.J. Audley eds., *Medical Accidents* (Oxford, 1993), 163; G. Mendelson, ' "Compensation Neurosis" Revisited: Outcome Studies of the Effects of Litigation' (1995) 39 *J. of Psychosomatic Research* 695; P.W. Halligan, C. Bass and D.A. Oakley eds., *Malingering and Illness Deception* (Oxford, 2003), esp. chs. 1, 13, 16, 17 and 18. In suggesting that a person either has or does not have compensation neurosis, the text may be simplistic. There is evidence that injured people who make compensation claims may suffer worse long-term health outcomes than people who do not. The reasons are ill understood, but it appears that the compensation process is only one. See e.g. Royal Australasian College of Physicians, *Compensable Injuries and Health Outcomes* (Sydney, 2001); R. Mayou, 'Psychiatric Outcome Following a Road Traffic Accident' [2004] *JPIL* 61.

3 A variant is to decide the issue of liability first but leave the assessment of damages until later.

because that is when the 'cause of action' vests in the claimant, the courts have always sensibly insisted that what happens between the date of the harm-causing incident and the date of the trial must be taken into account in assessing the damages. Thus, lost earnings suffered between date the harm is suffered and the trial or settlement will be calculated, not guessed; and increases in wage rates during this period will become the basis of the assessment of damages for expected future earnings losses.

On the other hand, postponement of the trial or settlement of cases brings its own evils; indeed, delay in actually securing payment under the tort system is one of the major causes of dissatisfaction with it. It may be possible to reduce these delays, but plainly it would not be in the claimant's interest to require the claim to be determined before the exact nature and extent of the injuries could be predicted. Postponement will not, in any event, solve all the problems that may arise. There are many cases in which, even when a reasonably firm medical prognosis can be given, the effect of a person's injuries on their future working prospects must remain problematical until long after the time at which a claim must be tried or settled.

6.1.2   Fatal cases

There are two quite different types of actions that may be brought in respect of the death of a person as the result of a tortious act. The older type is the dependency[4] action under the Fatal Accidents Act 1976 (a descendant of the original (Lord Campbell's) Act of 1846).[5] This action is primarily designed to provide compensation for the lost income[6] of a person who was formerly maintaining members of their family, normally a spouse or cohabiting partner and children. An action of this kind is brought by the dependants in their own name, in respect of their own loss of financial support resulting from the death. It is still necessary for the dependants to prove that the deceased died as a result of a tort, and any damages awarded will be reduced if the deceased was personally guilty of contributory negligence. The action provides compensation not only for an actual dependant but also for a prospective dependant, so long as the claimant falls within the list of persons entitled to sue under the Act. Thus, a parent may be able to sue in respect of the death (say) of a child of 16 who has not yet contributed anything to the parent's support but who might have been expected to do so in future.

The second type of claim lies under the Law Reform (Miscellaneous Provisions) Act 1934. Under this Act a claim for damages (called a 'survival action') lies on behalf of the estate of a person killed, and such a claim may be brought whether or not the

---

4 The words 'dependency' and 'dependant' are misleading because the Act allows members of a defined class of persons to recover damages for financial loss suffered by them as a result of the death. Such persons will usually be dependants in the ordinary sense, but not always.

5 See generally Law Com. No. 263, *Claims for Wrongful Death* (1999).

6 Including income in the form of social security benefits: *Cox* v. *Hockenhull* [1999] 3 All ER 577.

deceased had any dependants. The only damages recoverable in such an action are for pecuniary and non-pecuniary losses suffered by the deceased between the accident and death, plus funeral expenses. In most cases such an action would be brought concurrently with an action under the Fatal Accidents Act 1976 because a person's dependants are commonly also the beneficiaries under their will.

Assessment of compensation in dependency actions involves the same two sets of predictions as must be made in cases of long-term injuries. It is necessary to start by predicting what would have happened to the deceased if they had not been killed. In particular an assessment must be made of what the deceased's earning prospects were. As Lord Diplock said in *Cookson* v. *Knowles*,[7] the court is required to make assumptions:

> . . . as to the hypothetical degree of likelihood that all sorts of things might happen in an imaginary future in which the deceased lived on and did not die. What in the event would have been the likelihood of his continuing in work until the usual retiring age? Would his earnings have been terminated by death or disability before the usual retiring age or interrupted by unemployment or ill-health? Would they have increased, and if so, when and by how much? To what extent, if any, would he have passed on the benefit of any increases to his wife and dependent children? Would she have gone to work when the children had grown older and made her own contribution to the family expenses in relief of his?

And so on.

The second set of predictions (i.e. about what will now happen in the future) generally causes less difficulty in fatal cases: obviously a lot of predictions required about the prospects of a living claimant are not relevant in a fatal accident claim. But over the years there has been a great deal of difficulty about the problem of remarriage by a widow. Most fatal accident claims are brought by widows, with or without additional claims by dependent children. Prior to 1971 it was the accepted rule that the damages had to be reduced to take account of the remarriage prospects of the widow;[8] and, of course, it followed that they had to be reduced where the widow had actually remarried before the assessment of damages. The application of this rule had a considerable effect on claims by young widows, especially widows without children, but much less effect on the claims of older widows, especially those with several children. The rule was based on the simple idea that damages in a fatal accident case, as in all other tort claims, are designed to compensate for a loss. The damages given to a widow are designed to replace the share of the income of her former husband that was devoted to her maintenance. When the widow remarries she will often make good her loss; and, accordingly, the fact or prospect of remarriage must be taken into account in reducing the damages.

---

7 [1979] AC 556, 568–9.
8 *Goodburn* v. *Thomas Cotton Ltd* [1968] 1 QB 845; the rule was much older than this case, which reaffirmed it.

However, many people found the rule distasteful.[9] It was argued that there was a 'cattle market' element in the valuation of remarriage prospects,[10] and in 1971 a provision was enacted to the effect that the fact or prospects of remarriage of a widow in a fatal accidents claim were to be wholly ignored.[11] This must be one of the most irrational pieces of law 'reform' ever passed by Parliament. It would be as sensible to require a divorced husband to maintain his wife after she has remarried, or for the State to pay pensions to widows after remarriage. An extreme example of the situation thus created occurred in 1974 when a young widow of 25 who had remarried an 'oil man with a five-figure salary' was awarded £65,000 in damages for the death of her first husband 2 years earlier.[12] The real complaint against this provision is that it involves extraordinary generosity to one group of accident victims without regard to the needs of others. In the case just referred to, for example, the deceased was killed in a motor collision with a car driven by a man who was also killed. Since the latter was clearly at fault, his dependants (if any) would have recovered no damages at all, even if they had been in much greater need than the claimant. Another objection to the provision is that it only deals with remarriage and not with the fact or prospects of cohabitation, which are taken into account. This is all the more extraordinary given that a limited class of cohabiting partners can make claims under the Fatal Accidents Act 1976.

The obvious answer to problems raised by changes in the circumstances of claimants, including the remarriage of widows, is to pay compensation in the form of periodical payments rather than a lump sum.[13] Such payments could then be reviewed as circumstances changed, and could be ended if, for example, a widow remarried.[14] But even this would not wholly dispose of the problems arising from the remarriage of widows. Obviously, if widows' compensation took the form of periodical payments which came to an end on remarriage, there would be a temptation for widows to avoid remarriage and enter into less formal relationships. Social security legislation (where analogous problems have to be dealt with) meets this danger by providing that widows' benefits are not payable during periods of cohabitation. The cohabitation rule has been much vilified as involving an intrusion into the private lives of widows, but such an attitude is surely outmoded today

9 See *Buckley* v. *John Allen & Ford Ltd* [1967] 1 QB 637, and the *Report of the Committee on Personal Injuries Litigation* (Cmnd 3691, 1968) (Winn Committee Report), paras. 378–9.

10 Is there not a similar 'cattle-market' element in valuing the loss of marriage prospects of an unmarried woman?

11 See now s. 3(3) of the Fatal Accidents Act 1976. This provision does not apply to men (*Regan* v. *Williamson* [1976] 1 WLR 305); nor to the assessment of damages for a child whose father has been killed (*Thompson* v. *Price* [1973] QB 838). The Law Commission recommended repeal of this provision and its replacement with a much more complex set of provisions.

12 *The Times*, 15 May 1974. This was no doubt an exceptional case, but the fact is that a significant number of widows, especially young widows, do remarry. In 1990 the remarriage rate for widows aged 25–9 was 98 per 1,000, and for those aged 30–4, 86 per 1,000: *Marriage and Divorce Statistics 1990* (OPCS, 1992), table 3.3.c (1990 is the most recent year for which this figure is available).

13 Contrast Law Com. No. 263, 4.30–4.34.

14 But see Pearson Report, vol. 1, paras. 409–17.

when many people openly choose cohabitation as a socially acceptable alternative to marriage, and when legal discrimination against children born out of wedlock has been largely removed. Indeed, under the Fatal Accidents Act 1976 itself, children born to parents who are not married to each other are to be treated as if their parents had been married at the time of the birth.

One of the strangest things about the difficulties encountered by the law in dealing with compensation for widows is that the law is already perfectly well acquainted with the system of periodical payments in the family jurisdiction where amounts payable by way of maintenance can be varied as the situations of the parties change. If a person receiving maintenance remarries or secures a better job or inherits a large fortune, the amount of maintenance payable can be reduced; conversely, if the payer's income goes up, it can be increased. There is no need for the court to guess or make predictions about the future.

Death of her husband may not only make it possible for a woman to remarry but also to go (back) to work. The law requires 'gains' resulting from the death to be set off against losses, but it is not clear in England to what extent actual earnings or the prospect of earnings are in practice set off against the damages awarded. In Australia the courts take the view that the death of a husband does not revive the wife's ability to work since marriage does not prevent a wife working. And if the fact that there were children prevented the wife working, the death of the husband does not alter this. So neither actual nor potential post-death earnings are taken into account in assessing the widow's damages.[15] This approach, too, can clearly be attacked as overly generous, although the disincentive to work that would be generated by the opposite approach might be thought undesirable (even in times of high unemployment).

6.1.3   Variation of awards after trial

In the small proportion of cases which go to trial, it may very occasionally be possible to vary a lump-sum award to take account of changes in circumstances occurring after the trial – at least where they occur soon after the trial. Since, at trial, it is the facts as they are known at that date that are relevant, appellate courts have not shrunk from saying that, in the event of an appeal, it is the facts as they are known at the date of the appeal that are relevant. Notice of appeal must normally be given within 4 weeks; and if the appeal is heard reasonably soon thereafter, there will be little opportunity in the ordinary case for taking new facts into account on appeal. However, the Court of Appeal does have power to extend the time within which an appeal may be entered by granting 'leave to appeal out of time'. This power is discretionary and is not often exercised, but it can be used to increase (or reduce) an award of damages where new facts come to light very soon after the trial. In one case, for example,[16] where damages had been assessed on the assumption that the

---

15 See F.A. Trindade and P. Cane, *Law of Torts in Australia*, 3rd edn (Melbourne, 1999), 544.
16 *Murphy* v. *Stone Wallwork Ltd* [1969] 2 All ER 949.

claimant was still capable of continuing in his former employment, the award was re-opened and increased when he was dismissed as soon as the case was over. In another case[17] the House of Lords allowed evidence to be given that shortly after the trial it became clear that the claimant would have to be maintained in a nursing home, at substantial cost; the assessment of damages at the trial had been made on the assumption that the injured person would remain at home.

Of greater potential importance is a provision in the Supreme Court Act 1981 (s. 32A) designed to deal with the 'chance' cases mentioned above. The provision applies cases in which 'there is proved or admitted to be a chance that at some definite or indefinite time in the future the injured person will . . . develop some disease or suffer some deterioration in his physical or mental condition'. Rules of court have been made enabling damages to be awarded in the first instance on the assumption that the claimant will not develop the disease or suffer the deterioration, and allowing further damages to be awarded at a later date if the disease or deterioration occurs.[18] However, the procedure has been very little used in practice.[19] In *Mitchell* v. *Mulholland*[20] the House of Lords stressed the need for finality in litigation and the undesirability of reopening awards of damages save in very exceptional cases.

It will be noted that this provision only allows awards to be increased, not decreased. This asymmetry in favour of the claimant is usually thought to be required by considerations of fairness, and on the ground that a threat that damages could be reduced if the injured person's condition improved might hinder rehabilitation.[21] In practice, too, it would be very difficult to secure repayment of part of the lump sum if the claimant had spent it or invested it in a fixed asset such as a house or a business; but if repayment were only required if the money had been invested in liquid assets such as shares, claimants would have a strong incentive to deal with their damages in other (and perhaps less prudent) ways. Another limitation of both appeals and the conditional damages procedure is that they do not apply to the vast majority of cases that are settled out of court. In 1997 a health authority paid £700,000 to a 9-year-old who suffered severe injuries at birth for which the authority accepted 75% responsibility. Eight days after the settlement, the child unexpectedly died, and the health authority said that it intended to try to recover the amount of the settlement referable to future care. But there is no clear

17 *Mitchell* v. *Mulholland* [1971] AC 666.
18 It is unclear whether, if the claimant dies before any further claim is made, the dependants can bring an action under the Fatal Accidents Act 1976.
19 According to the Compensation Recovery Unit, it was used in less than 0.03% of cases between 2000 and 2003: DCA, *Variation of Periodical Payment Orders and Settlements in Personal Injury Cases: Partial Regulatory Impact Assessment* (April 2004). It has been held that the provision does not apply to cases of gradual deterioration in the claimant's condition, but only where there is a risk of a 'clear-cut' adverse event: *Willson* v. *Ministry of Defence* [1991] ICR 595. The Criminal Injuries Compensation Authority has power to reconsider and even re-open cases to take account of new evidence and changes in the claimant's condition: see 12.4.4.
20 [1971] AC 666.
21 This is also a problem if the damages are awarded as periodical payments: T.G. Ison, 'The Calculation of Periodic Payments for Permanent Disability' (1984) 22 *Osgoode Hall LJ* 735.

legal basis on which this could have been done. On the whole, insurers want their settlements to be final.

It can be seen, then, that such techniques as the above are of limited value in dealing even with cases of change in the claimant's medical condition; and they do not deal at all with other sources of difficulty in assessing the lump sum.

6.1.4   Suitability of lump sums

As already implied, it is highly questionable whether awarding damages for lost income (whether earnings, in the case of a personal injury action, or support in the case of a fatal accident) or the cost of care in a lump sum is appropriate in cases where the loss will continue after the date when the damages are assessed. Assessing the lump sum involves much speculation and potential inaccuracy. Just as importantly (and perhaps surprisingly) recipients of lump-sum damages awards (except minors[22] and the mentally incapable) are free to use the damages as they choose. A damages award to compensate for future loss to be suffered over a period of years – whether loss of income or cost of care – is, of course, designed to be used progressively to make good those losses as and when they occur, so that at the end of the period of the award (but not before) the damages award will have been completely used up. Lump-sum damages are calculated on the assumptions that they will be invested in 'gilts' – i.e. Index-Linked Government Stocks (ILGS) – a form of investment that is very secure but yields relatively low income, and that the recipient's needs will be met from the combination of the capital invested and the income it generates. In other words, the lump sum awarded takes account of the income that can be earned by investing the damages. But recipients are not required to invest the lump sum in gilts or, indeed, to invest it at all. Nor are recipients required to take investment advice. Indeed this is positively discouraged by the rule that the cost of taking such advice (with a view, perhaps, to making more risky investments that will yield higher income) cannot be recovered from the tortfeasor as an item of damages.[23] There is no legal control over the way damages awards are managed. Nor are recipients required to use the damages for the purposes for which they were given.

The typical recipient of a large lump-sum award of damages is, no doubt, more or less inexperienced in investing and managing such an amount of money. There is a danger that even assuming the amount awarded was adequate to make good the losses suffered over the whole period of the award,[24] it will be invested unwisely or

---

22 In cases under the Fatal Accidents Act 1976 brought on behalf of a widow or dependent children, neither the income nor the capital of damages awarded for the young people will normally be paid out of court except where this is shown to be necessary for the children's own benefit, e.g. to defray school fees, etc. Awards to children are generally paid out to them as soon as they come of age, but in extreme cases the court may press the recipient to agree to settle the money on trust: see e.g. *Warren* v. *King* [1963] 3 All ER 993n, where the CA pressed a woman of 20 to settle an award of £35,000 so that she could not touch the capital until she was 31. It seems that the court has no power to compel a young person to agree to this: *Allen* v. *Distillers Co. (Biochemicals) Ltd* [1974] 2 All ER 365.

23 *Eagle* v. *Chambers (No. 2)* [2004] 1 WLR 3081.

24 See further 6.4.

unsuccessfully, and so be dissipated before the end of the period it was meant to cover. As a result, the injured person (and their family) may be reduced to poverty and made reliant on publicly funded social security payments, and health and welfare services. If, as evidence suggests often happens in more serious cases, the original lump sum was never going to be enough (invested in gilts) to achieve its aims, then even if it is invested wisely and successfully in higher-yield financial products, it may be insufficient to provide an income of the order of that which has been lost or is needed to meet expenses. In this light, the rule that recipients of damages are free to use them as they will, seems very difficult to justify.

There is some evidence as to how wisely or unwisely, successfully or unsuccessfully, large awards of damages are actually used or invested by the recipients. The Pearson Commission found that only about 20% of recipients made any attempt to use their damages for investment, or treated it as capital; most spent the money on current expenses.[25] On the other hand, most of these sums were fairly small (the average was around £250 in 1977 money values) so this would not necessarily have been a profligate use of the damages. Research conducted for the Law Commission in 1992–3[26] found that 60% of those surveyed who received less than £20,000 saved or invested some of their money; that among those who received £20,000–49,999, the figure was 83%; among those who received £50,000–99,999, 90%; and among those who received more than £100,000, 97%. There was a tendency to choose safe investments. A quarter of those who received less than £20,000 and two-thirds of those who received £20,000 or more obtained financial advice; and one in five of those surveyed were unhappy with their investment choices.

As to the adequacy of the amounts received, three in five respondents felt that their damages had been sufficient to cover past losses and expenses. A majority thought that their standard of living had not dropped as a result of the accident, but a significant minority thought it had. About half thought that their standard of living in 10 years' time would be lower than before the accident. A majority also said that they were now less satisfied with the amount they had received than they had been at the time of settlement. The researchers concluded that in many cases, this was because the compensation received for loss of earning capacity turned out to be inadequate. It appears, too, that in a significant number of cases, members of the injured person's household worked shorter hours or gave up work altogether after the accident to care for the injured person; and that this additional income loss was not adequately reflected in the compensation recovered.

Overseas experience of similar problems is not very encouraging. Research conducted in the early 1980s for the New South Wales Law Reform Commission discovered that a significant number of recipients of lump sums have inadequate income from their awards to meet their expenses. In some cases this was the result of mismanagement of the lump sum award by the recipient or unwise investment

---

25 Pearson Report, vol. 2, table 89.
26 *How Much is Enough?*

(e.g. in a house which generated no income, or in low-yield but secure financial products). But in other cases it was due to factors entirely outside the recipient's control, such as inflation or an unexpected deterioration in medical condition. One survey concluded that recipients of high awards who had managed to re-establish themselves in a comfortable and secure fashion had typically benefited from some combination of personal skill and enterprise, good fortune, good advice, and support from family and friends.

No stranger example could be found of the fundamentally inconsistent philosophies which underlie the social security system and the tort system, and which have somehow managed to co-exist for so many years. As long ago as 1944, the government declared that it did 'not regard lump sum payments even if administered under strict control as a satisfactory method of assuring an income';[27] and the payment of benefits periodically has remained one of the basic features of the modern welfare state. This is not to say that the tort system's preference for lump sums is without foundation. The Law Commission survey referred to above found amongst claimants a strong preference for lump sums: '. . . respondents felt that they wanted to make their own decisions [about how to use the compensation] and to be in complete control of their budget.'[28] Those who expressed a preference for instalment payments mainly sought security and protection from their own unsuitable spending patterns and investment decisions. Importantly, the small proportion of respondents who received structured settlements (6.1.5.3) generally thought them preferable to a lump sum, even though most had not requested this form of compensation. Some recipients of structured settlements complained that the lump sum component in the settlement had not been large enough to enable them to make a desired capital investment (e.g. in a new house).

6.1.5   Alternatives to lump sums
6.1.5.1   An argument against abandoning the lump-sum system
The obvious question to which the various problems with the system of lump-sum damages gives rise is whether some system of periodical payments would be preferable. A common argument against periodical payments is that they are inconsistent with the basic principle that the recipient of damages is free to use them as they wish, and is not required to invest them to produce a stream of income to replace what has been lost. But this argument can easily be answered by appealing to the basic function of tort damages, namely to put the injured person back in the position they would have been in had they not been injured. In this light, the most accurate way of replacing a stream of income would be by providing a stream of income, not a lump sum. Of course, damages may also be given to facilitate capital expenditure – for instance, on house modifications. This would suggest that ideal compensation would consist of a mix of lump sum and periodical payments.

27 *Social Insurance*, Part II (Cmnd 6551, 1944), para. 30.
28 *How Much is Enough?*, 181.

While there are certainly pragmatic arguments in favour of allowing recipients to use their damages as they wish – notably, the difficulty of monitoring and enforcing restrictions on the use to which damages are put – it is hard to think of good reasons of principle or fairness to justify such freedom.

6.1.5.2   Early proposals for alternatives

In 1973 the Law Commission reached the conclusion that a system of periodical payments could not be fitted into the existing tort framework.[29] However, a majority of the Pearson Commission recommended that such a system should be introduced for serious personal injury cases and for fatal cases.[30] The Commission proposed that the courts should have power to award damages either as a lump sum or in the form of periodical payments; and that in the latter case, the amounts should be inflation-proofed and variable if the injured person's medical condition subsequently changed. They refrained from insisting that all settlements of fatal and serious personal injury cases should be in this form. Parties would remain free to settle for lump sums (and, hence, free to use the damages however they wished), though the Commission thought that claimants might increasingly become aware of the desirability of settling for periodical payments.

One thing that emerged clearly from the Pearson Report was that very few cases would have been covered by such a change in the law. Of the 215,000 (or so) cases per annum in which (the Commission found) some tort compensation was payable, the Report suggested that only some 2,200 (about 1%) were actually tried in court,[31] though no doubt a substantial proportion of these are fatal and serious personal injury cases. Moreover, the insurance survey carried out for the Commission showed that in November 1973, only about 1% of all tort claimants received more than £10,000 in damages (including damages for non-pecuniary loss) (say, £40,000 in today's money values); and only 2% received more than £5,000 (say, £20,000 in today's money). In other words, only about 2,000 claimants received more than £40,000 in 2006 money. Judging from other figures given in the Pearson Report,[32] we can estimate that only about 20% of these cases (say, 400) might actually have been tried in court. Converting lump-sum damages to periodical payments would only be worthwhile in cases where the lump-sum equivalent was reasonably large. Some idea of how large is given by the fact that, prior to the introduction of periodical payment orders (6.1.5.4), a Supreme Court Practice Direction required the possibility of a structured settlement (equivalent, for present purposes, to a periodical payment arrangement) to be considered by the parties in any case where the amount claimed for future loss[33]

---

29 Law Com. No. 56, *Personal Injury Litigation: Assessment of Damages* (1973), paras. 29–30.
30 Pearson Report, vol. 1, ch. 14.
31 Pearson Report, vol. 2, table 221.
32 Pearson Report, vol. 2, table 128 shows that, of the total number of cases tried in 1974 (2,313), about one-quarter (521) were awarded more than £5,000 (in 1977 currency values).
33 The Pearson Commission recommended that damages for non-pecuniary loss should continue to be awarded in a lump sum: vol. 1, para. 614.

is £500,000 or more. It would seem, therefore, that the Pearson proposals for period-ical payments would have applied, at most, to a couple of hundred cases a year.[34] We know that the number of successful tort claims per annum has increased about three-fold since the 1970s;[35] and on that basis we might conclude that if the Pearson pro-posals were enacted now, they would apply to perhaps 500–600 cases each year.

6.1.5.3   Structured settlements

In early editions of this book the conclusion was that in the light of such calculations, it seemed questionable whether the change proposed by the Pearson Commission would be worth the cost and complexity it would undoubtedly entail. However, development of the so-called 'structured settlement'[36] in the 1990s prompted recon-sideration of this conclusion. Under such a settlement, damages for future losses are calculated as a lump sum; but instead of the lump sum being paid to the claim-ant, the insurer who is responsible for paying it uses it (or part of it)[37] to purchase an annuity to provide the injured person with a continuing inflation-proofed income for as long as this is needed. The annuity may be for a fixed minimum period so that it will continue to be paid to the recipient's estate if the recipient dies sooner than expected. Such an arrangement would provide for dependants.[38] Apart from provid-ing security for the future (the insurer bears the risk of the beneficiary living longer than expected), structured settlements relieve the injured person of the need to make difficult investment decisions or to employ an investment advisor, because the insurer assumes responsibility for investing the lump sum and providing the income. Structured settlements are also attractive by reason of the fact that the income from a structured settlement is not taxable in the hands of the recipient, whereas if the claimant took the lump sum and invested it, the income[39] would be taxable.[40] The major disadvantage of a structured settlement is that once it has been set up, the capital is unavailable to the beneficiary. This disadvantage can be partly neutralized by leaving a lump sum out of 'the structure' or by purchasing a number of 'annuities', one of which provides regular income and another of which provides regular but less frequent lump sums. In short, a structured settlement involves a trade-off between flexibility in the use of damages and security.

Valuable though structured settlements might be, they do not solve all the prob-lems created by the lump-sum system, exactly because they are based on a lump sum

---

34 In 2004–5 the NHS Litigation Authority (which handles medical negligence claims against NHS Trusts) made 49 structured settlements worth about £192 million in total (averaging £3.9 million). These settlements represent about 0.5% of the claims closed in 2004–5, but 38% of the compensation paid in that year.

35 See 8.1.4.

36 See generally R. Lewis, *Structured Settlements: The Law and Practice* (London, 1993).

37 For instance, the parties may agree not to 'structure' damages for non-pecuniary loss.

38 But query whether a Fatal Accidents Act claim could be made after the early death of the beneficiary of a structured settlement under which payments terminated on death.

39 But not the lump sum itself.

40 This also gives a benefit to the defendant's insurer, because the lump sum needed to generate the required annual amount is less than it would be if the amount were subject to tax.

awarded by a court or agreed by the parties. Thus, all the difficulties of calculation and the problems of proof and delay associated with the present system remain.

6.1.5.4   Periodical payments

As the word 'settlement' implies,[41] 'structures' are voluntary. Since 2003, there has been a statutory provision[42] empowering courts to order compensation in the form of 'periodical payments' in certain cases. In cases – but only in cases – where damages for future loss are awarded, such an order (unlike a court order approving a structured settlement) can be made against the wishes of the parties. Moreover, whereas a structured settlement is based on a lump sum,[43] which is then 'structured' to provide periodical payments, the intention is that a periodical payments order might directly specify the amount to be paid periodically without first calculating a lump sum, leaving it entirely to the defendant to decide how to satisfy the order.[44] Before making a periodical payments order, the court must be satisfied that 'continuity of payment under the order is reasonably secure'. There are also provisions about variation of such orders along similar lines to s. 32A of the Supreme Court Act (6.1.3).[45] Like the income from a structured settlement, and unlike the income from investment by the recipient of a lump sum, periodical payments are not taxable. A periodical payments order can provide for payments to continue after the death of the injured person, in order to provide support for dependants. Even if the court decides not to make a periodical payments order, the parties may agree on some form of periodical award (i.e. a structured settlement), and the court may confirm that agreement in a 'consent order'.

The provision empowering the court to make a periodical payments order also requires it to consider whether to make such an order in any case where damages for future loss are awarded. However, in the light of the Practice Direction noted earlier, it is perhaps unlikely that a court would make such an order unless the amount claimed for future loss was at least £500,000 – and such claims are few indeed. Furthermore, it appears that very few insurers sell the sort of financial products needed to secure structured settlements and periodical payments.[46] It is, therefore, unclear how popular or common periodical payment orders will become. It is also very difficult to predict the likely effect of the power to make periodical payment orders on settlement of claims out of court. Relevant factors will be the cost of funding periodical payments relative to that of funding lump sums and structured settlements, and the willingness of the courts to make periodical payment orders.

---

41 A settlement is a contract between the parties.
42 Courts Act 2003, s. 100, amending Damages Act 1996, s. 2. See generally R. Lewis, 'The Politics and Economics of Tort Law: Judicially Imposed Periodical Payments of Damages' (forthcoming, 2006) 69(3) MLR.
43 Sometimes referred to as the 'top-down' method of assessment.
44 Department for Constitutional Affairs, Guidance on Periodical Payments (2005), para. 4. This is sometimes called the 'bottom-up' method of assessment.
45 The details can be found in the Damages (Variation of Periodical Payments) Order 2005.
46 P. Barrie, Personal Injury Law: Liability, Compensation and Procedure (Oxford, 2005), 536.

Periodical payments are an advance on structured settlements in that they do not require the calculation of a lump sum, and are to some extent variable. However, the circumstances in which a variation order may be made are quite restricted; and much of the speculation associated with the lump-sum system will plague the periodical payments regime as well. It must also be said that however desirable structured settlements and periodical payments are compared with lump sums, their effect is to improve even more the position of a very small group of seriously disabled persons who are able to claim tort damages. Furthermore, the tax advantages of structured settlements and periodical payments mean that the additional benefit to these lucky people is paid for, partly at least, by the taxpayer. The original purpose of these tax advantages was to provide incentives for making structured settlements. They seem unnecessary and undesirable in the light of the power to order periodical payments. Why should the injured person's compensation-derived income be taxed if it results from investment by the recipient personally, but tax-free if the necessary investment is made by the defendant? Is it not in the public interest that recipients of lump sums (who are likely to remain the majority of recipients of significant amounts of tort compensation) should be given an incentive to invest their damages as successfully as possible?

6.2   Full compensation

The tort system is the only compensation system that professes to provide 'full compensation'. All pecuniary losses (chiefly medical expenses and loss of income, both past and future) must be compensated for in full.[47] The tort victim must also be compensated for all possible financial ill-effects of the injury; for example, the risk of subsequent medical complications, possible reduction in marriage prospects possible loss of employment prospects and so on. In short, the full compensation principle requires a detailed examination of the particular situation of the individual claimant. From time to time, it has been said that 'full compensation' does not mean 'perfect' or 'absolute' compensation, and that the compensation must only be 'fair' or 'reasonable'. It seems that these remarks have been directed to the assessment of compensation for non-pecuniary losses, where 'full compensation' would be meaningless; they are not intended to suggest any qualification of the principle that the claimant is entitled to full compensation for all pecuniary losses. Indeed, in *Lim Poh Choo* v. *Camden Health Authority*[48] in which (then) record damages of £250,000 were awarded, the majority of the English Court of Appeal and, on appeal, the House of Lords, specifically rejected Lord Denning's argument that it would be unfair and unreasonable to award damages for loss of earnings if the claimant was

---

47 But under statutory schemes of 'strict liability' limits on compensation may be imposed, e.g., there is a threshold for recovery of property damage under Part I of the Consumer Protection Act 1987; and there are limits on the liability of airlines and shipowners for injury to passengers under various international agreements.

48 [1979] QB 196; [1980] AC 174.

in no position to benefit from them (because she was unconscious), had no dependants to support and had been awarded adequate damages to cover the cost of caring for her.

An extreme example of the 'full compensation' principle at work is *Davies* v. *Whiteways Cyder*[49] which was an action under the Fatal Accidents Act 1976. The deceased in this case was a wealthy man who had made gifts of some £40,000 to a child; his death within 7 years of the gift meant that estate duty of some £17,000 became payable. It was held that the duty was recoverable as an additional item of damages. The decision becomes even more remarkable when it is noted that a risk of this nature is commonly insured against by persons who have made substantial capital donations in their lifetime, and that if in this case there had been any insurance to cover the contingency, it would not have been deducted from the damages (by virtue of what is now s. 4 of the Fatal Accidents Act 1976). This is, no doubt, an exceptional case, but the principle for which it stands – that the injured are in general entitled to be fully compensated for their losses – is applied generally throughout the law of tort and contract, and is seen as a corollary of the fault principle.

Because the tort system – alone amongst compensation systems and schemes – professes to provide full compensation, every tort victim who actually succeeds in obtaining damages is – as compared with the great majority of injured and disabled persons – exceptionally well placed in a financial sense. It is against this background that one has to judge the desirability of continuing to adhere to the 'full compensation' principle. And it is also against this background that proposals for the extension of the tort remedy (e.g. by expansion of strict liability) have to be considered. Every extension of the tort system means a small increase in the proportion of personal injury victims obtaining 'full compensation' (estimated at some 6.5% by the Pearson Commission). There will thus be a few more winners in the 'forensic lottery'; but for the losers these extensions of tort liability will, of course, do nothing.

Damages are customarily awarded under two broad heads: 'special damages' and 'general damages'. This distinction is based on the difference between losses that are precisely measurable and quantifiable and those that are not. Special damages are confined to out-of-pocket expenses and loss of earnings incurred before the trial. Damages for expenses and loss of earnings likely to be incurred in the future, plus damages for non-pecuniary losses – whether incurred before or after the trial – such as pain and suffering and loss of amenities, are awarded together as general damages. It used to be customary to award a global figure for general damages, so that it was usually impossible to say how much was intended for future loss of earnings and the cost of care, and how much for pain and suffering and loss of amenities.[50] Now it is usual to itemize damages, particularly in serious cases. The court itemizes the sums it awards under the principal headings recognized by the law, especially as between damages for future loss of earnings and expenses, and damages for non-pecuniary.

49 [1975] QB 262.
50 *Watson* v. *Powles* [1968] 1 QB 596.

But in the most serious cases, it is now quite common for the judges to break the damages down into smaller sub-headings. For example, specific sums may be awarded for estimated losses of future earnings, for estimated losses of pension rights, and for the possible contingency that the claimant may become unemployed and suffer yet further income losses. Moreover, on the expenses side, it has become quite common to itemize the different sub-headings under which the damages are assessed; for instance, so much for nursing care, so much for home adaptations, so much for other extra expenses, and so on.

6.2.1   Interest

The entitlement to full compensation is yet further enhanced by provisions as to interest. Unless there are specific reasons to the contrary, the court is obliged to order the payment of interest[51] on damages in personal injury and fatal cases.[52] Damages for losses and expenses incurred before the trial ('pre-trial damages' or 'damages for past loss') carry interest at half the 'special investment account rate', which is set periodically by the Lord Chancellor.[53] Interest is payable because in theory the entitlement to damages arises at the date of the injuries or, at least, the date the writ is issued. The award of interest compensates the claimant for being 'kept out of their money'.[54] Interest is awarded at half rate because special damages represent sums that have been lost over the whole period between injury and the trial, some closer to the date of injury and some closer to the date of trial. A rough and ready approximation of the amount due is arrived at by awarding half the appropriate interest rate.

Damages for pain and suffering and loss of amenity also attract interest, currently at a rate of 2%.[55] The reason why this figure is so low is that, unlike damages for pre-trial pecuniary loss, damages for pre-trial non-pecuniary losses are calculated in currency values current at the date of judgment. This means that inflation between the date of injury and the date of assessment has been taken into account in the basic award, and the interest rate need not include allowance for inflation, as commercial interest rates do. Nevertheless, the figure of 2% seems a bit low. The discount rate – in other words, the rate of return on the investment of damages for future loss that is assumed in calculating the lump sum – is currently 2.5%.

---

51 Simple, not compound: R. Bowles and C.J. Whelan, 'The Law of Interest: Dawn of a New Era?' (1986) 64 *Canadian Bar R.* 142. The Law Commission has recommended that in cases where the amount on which interest is to be awarded exceeds £15,000, interest should be compound, not simple. This proposal would have the greatest impact on the cases that take longest to resolve, which tend to be medical negligence claims in relation to birth injuries, which also tend to involve very large awards. See Law Com. No. 287, *Pre-Judgment Interest on Debts and Damages* (2004). The Commission estimated that the proposal if implemented would add £20–25 million to the annual cost of medical negligence claims.

52 *Jefford* v. *Gee* [1970] 2 QB 130; *Cookson* v. *Knowles* [1979] AC 556.

53 The Law Commission has recommended that the rate be 1% above Bank of England base rate: Law Com. No. 287.

54 Or, perhaps more realistically in many cases, having to borrow money.

55 *Wright* v. *British Railways Board* [1983] 2 AC 773. The Law Commission has recommended that this rate remain the same, and that interest on it be only simple regardless of the amount awarded for past non-pecuniary loss.

The award of interest acts as a discouragement to delay on the part of defendants, especially in cases which are settled out of court. Damages for loss of future earnings and for future expenses do not carry interest since, by definition, these are designed to compensate for losses that have not yet been incurred. In fatal cases the position is much the same: damages for pre-trial losses carry interest at half the appropriate rate, damages for bereavement would probably carry interest at 2%, and no interest is payable on damages for future pecuniary loss.

6.2.2 Lost earnings and support

We have already seen how many predictions and guesses have to be made in assessing damages for loss of future earnings (in a personal injuries claim) or loss of future support (in a fatal accident claim). The first step in a personal injury or death claim is to assess this probable continuing income loss, i.e. the £X per annum of earnings or support which the claimant would have received but for the accident. This sum (called the 'multiplicand') is then multiplied by a 'multiplier', which is a figure somewhat less than the number of years for which the loss is likely to be suffered. The typical starting point is the number of years for which the loss is likely to continue – i.e. in a personal injury action until the claimant's injuries cease to affect earnings or the injured person dies or retires. This figure is then reduced partly because of 'contingencies' (i.e. that the claimant might not have lived or worked so long or might have lost earnings even if the accident had not occurred), and partly because the claimant is going to receive not an income but a capital sum, which can be invested to produce an income.[56] The multiplier is not the product of precise calculation but of estimation in the light of the facts of the particular case and of other comparable cases. In some cases where the calculation of damages for loss of earnings requires a more than usual amount of speculation (e.g. if the claimant is a young child) the court may not use the 'multiplier method' but may decide directly on a lump sum.

Methods of this kind can produce significant variations in the pattern of awards. The Court of Appeal does what it can to iron out the grosser deviations from the norm, but it will not interfere with awards unless they are much too high or much too low; appeals are often dismissed with the comment that the damages were on the high side or the low side, and that the members of the Court of Appeal would themselves have awarded more or less, but that the award was not so far from the norm that the court should interfere. It may be necessary for the Court of Appeal to take this line, for otherwise there would be an incentive to fight an appeal in every case since there is always room for differences of opinion on matters of this kind. But this does not mean the result is satisfactory to the individual litigants, who are bound to feel aggrieved; nor for the public as a whole, whose faith in the administration of even-handed justice may be shaken by such an appearance of chance in the system.

---

56 Where the parties enter a structured settlement, the lump sum will be further reduced to take account of the tax advantage of a structured settlement to the claimant, and also to compensate the insurer for the costs of setting up and administering the settlement.

Where the action is a dependency action (i.e. it is brought under the Fatal Accidents Act 1976) a similar process is followed, except that it is necessary first to assess the extent of the dependency. In other words, if a person earning £30,000 a year is killed, and they spent £3,000 a year on themselves and the rest on supporting dependants, their dependency would be £27,000 per annum. This is the figure that must then be multiplied by the 'multiplier'. In a fatal case the starting point for calculating the multiplier is the number of years the dependants would have been supported by the deceased. Where there are several dependants – typically, a surviving spouse and children – the damages must be apportioned among the dependants. In practice, the lion's share of the award tends to be given to the spouse and relatively small shares to dependent children. This is because it is assumed that the spouse will maintain the children and may therefore need the income from investment of the lump sum (if not capital) for this purpose. It has, however, been objected that if this is the justification, there is no reason why anything should be given to the children at all.[57] The social security system does not give grants or payments direct to dependent children; the payments are made to the parent or person having the care of the children, in the belief that most parents will spend the money on the children's maintenance.

In fatal cases, as we have seen, two types of action can be brought: a claim by dependants under the Fatal Accidents Act 1976 and a survival action by the beneficiaries of the deceased estate under the Law Reform (Miscellaneous Provisions) Act 1934. In the great majority of cases, the beneficiaries will be the same persons as the dependants. In practice, this means that the surviving dependants can both inherit the deceased's property under the will and any sums paid to the estate as damages under the 1934 Act, and also recover damages for loss of support under the Fatal Accidents Act 1976. In most cases, the damages awarded to the estate will be small – mainly the deceased's out-of-pocket expenses and lost earnings between the accident and the death. The justification for allowing the dependants both to inherit and recover damages for loss of support is that they would have benefited from the inheritance sooner or later even if the deceased had not been tortiously killed.

It is worth noting that damages under the Fatal Accidents Act 1976 can include compensation for the value of the household services of a person killed by tortious conduct, even if those services were performed gratuitously and no money will be expended to replace them. Thus a husband may obtain damages for the value of his wife's lost services;[58] and similarly, a child whose mother is killed may obtain damages for the value of her services.[59] So even though they may not have been in employment, the death of a person who runs a house and cares for children can give rise to quite large claims for damages. It has been held that it is the carer's services which must be valued, excluding any element of emotional or loving support; but

---

57 H. Street, *Principles of Damages* (London, 1962), 152–3.
58 *Regan* v. *Williamson* [1976] 1 WLR 305.
59 *Hay* v. *Hughes* [1975] 1 All ER 257.

on the other hand, account must be taken of the fact that the services of a family member who looks after other family members may be available 24 hours a day to the family.[60]

There has been a certain amount of discussion of how to value such household services.[61] Two possible measures suggest themselves: replacement cost (that is, the cost of hiring someone to perform the services) and opportunity cost (that is, the amount the carer could have earned in paid employment). Neither measure is entirely satisfactory. In some respects a paid domestic helper can never replace a family member. If the person who performed the services has been out of the workforce for a long time, or is unskilled, the opportunity cost measure might not be very useful and will, at all events, only establish a minimum value for the services. The courts appear not to have adopted either measure as an invariable rule, but rather seek to assess the 'reasonable value of the services'. In the absence of any objective price-fixing mechanism, this approach is essentially arbitrary.

If the life expectancy of a tort victim is reduced by the injuries, damages may be recovered for loss of earnings not only up to the date of expected death but also in respect of the years when, but for the injuries, the claimant would have been alive and earning (the 'lost years'). Since, by definition, the claimant will have no personal living expenses in the lost years, these are deducted from the award.[62] The theoretical justification for 'lost years damages' is the full compensation principle, but the main function of the award is to provide support for dependants of the injured person after death. For this reason, the estate of a deceased person cannot recover lost years damages in an action under the 1934 Act – the dependants can recover for loss of support under the Fatal Accidents Act 1976, and any non-dependent beneficiaries of the estate do not need the award (this is sometimes put by saying that such an award would provide a 'windfall' to non-dependent beneficiaries). So if the deceased had no dependants, the damages payable to the estate will be limited to the losses suffered by the deceased between the date of the accident and the death. Here the law recognizes that commitment to the full compensation principle does potentially overcompensate. But this recognition has so far only affected the rules governing fatal cases. The living claimant can still recover substantial lost years damages even if there are no dependants (although in such a case the amount deducted for living expenses will be considerably higher than in the case where there are dependants); and a claimant who has been severely and permanently disabled or even reduced to a persistent vegetative state[63] can recover full damages for loss of earnings for the rest of their life even where there are no dependants, despite the fact that the injured person

---

60 *Regan* v. *Williamson* [1976] 1 WLR 305.
61 K.A. Clarke and A.I. Ogus, 'What is a Wife Worth?' (1978) 5 *British J. of Law and Society* 1; N.K. Komesar, 'Towards a General Theory of Personal Injury Loss' (1974) 3 *J. of Legal Studies* 457; F.J. Pottick, 'Tort Damages for the Injured Homemaker: Opportunity Cost or Replacement Cost?' (1978–9) 50 *U. of Colorado LR* 59.
62 *Pickett* v. *British Rail Engineering Ltd* [1980] AC 136.
63 See further 6.5.3.

can make no use of the award personally (the cost of caring for the victim will constitute a separate head of damages) and the award will eventually accrue as a windfall to the non-dependent beneficiaries of the claimant's estate.[64]

The full compensation principle is seen as a corollary of the basis of tort liability – that the defendant is a 'wrongdoer'. It is not based on any notion of the purposes for which damages are being awarded. By contrast, the idea that an award can constitute a 'windfall' to those who benefit from it is based on the idea that damages serve the purpose of meeting financial needs. Both of these lines of reasoning are present in the law, but the relationship between them is yet to be worked out consistently. It seems undeniable that the purposive approach is much more in line with modern ideas about the role of tort law in a mixed economy. As it is, tort law provides very generous financial benefits to a very few injured and disabled persons who can prove fault. There is no justification for extending those benefits to persons who have suffered no physical or financial loss as a result of the fault.

Finally, another important application of the full compensation principle deserves to be noted here. Only a minority of the population are earners, but many non-earners engage in productive activity (most notably, housework and childcare) and many earners (especially women) combine significant amounts of unpaid work with paid work. As we have seen, compensation for the value of unpaid work may be available under the Fatal Accidents Act 1976 where the unpaid worker is killed. Where a person's ability to engage in unpaid work is impaired by non-fatal tortious injuries, the law's original answer was to give male spouses an action (called the 'actio per quod servitium amisit') against the negligent person; but female spouses could not sue in respect of the unpaid work of a male spouse. This inequality of treatment was based on outmoded ideas of the relationship between men and women, and the action for services was abolished in 1982.[65] Even before this happened the courts had allowed unpaid domestic workers to recover damages for loss of the ability to perform domestic tasks.[66] It does not have to be shown that anything will actually be spent on hiring someone to perform the tasks, probably because it is thought that damages ought to be awarded even if the family decides to cope with the situation by doing more around the house themselves. After all, such damages are in the nature of an award for loss of income, not an award for expenses (to be) incurred. The Australian High Court has recently held, however, that while account can be taken of loss of capacity to perform domestic tasks in assessing 'general damages' (effectively, damages for non-pecuniary loss), such loss of capacity is not a separate head of damages in its own right.[67] The practical effect of this decision will be to reduce significantly the amount likely to be awarded on account of such loss.

---

64 *Lim Poh Choo* v. *Camden AHA* [1980] AC 174.
65 Administration of Justice Act 1982, s. 2. This section also abolished the employer's action for loss of the services of an employee.
66 *Daly* v. *General Steam Navigation Ltd* [1980] 3 All ER 696. Reaffirmed in *Lowe* v. *Guise* [2002] QB 1369.
67 *CSR Ltd* v. *Eddy* [2005] HCA 64.

6.2.3   Medical and other expenses

Since accident and emergency services are only available through the NHS, most victims of personal injury obtain their initial medical treatment free of charge;[68] and no damages can be recovered for medical expenses if no expenses have in fact been incurred. Damages would be recoverable in respect of NHS services (such as dentistry) for which charges may be made. People are, of course, entitled to seek private medical treatment if they wish, and if they incur expense in doing so, the expense is recoverable as an item of damages in a tort action if it was reasonably incurred – and it is provided by statute that it is not unreasonable to 'go private' just because precisely the same treatment is available free in an NHS institution.[69] Before the trial or a settlement is concluded, a claimant cannot normally be sure that the defendant will be liable. If the claimant knew that the defendant's insurers would accept liability, they might be tempted to go private. Otherwise, claimants might be wary of incurring the expense of private treatment unless they had medical insurance. A survey of more than 600 successful tort claimants found that a significant minority had opted for some private medical treatment, but that very few received only private treatment. In a majority of cases, only some of the cost of this treatment was covered by insurance or damages received. Various reasons were given for going private: because the service was quicker, or better than, or not available, through the NHS; or (in more than a third of cases), in order to have an examination necessary for the claim.[70]

In some cases – relatively few in number – a claimant may be so severely disabled or incapacitated that medical and nursing treatment may be required indefinitely, or indeed for the rest of the injured person's life. In these cases the claimant is entitled to damages for private treatment, for example, to employ a private nurse at home, or to enable them to reside permanently in a private nursing home or institution. Even if such facilities are made available by the NHS, the claimant is entitled to go private.[71] Yet once the damages are paid over, there is no obligation to spend them on private care; it is open to the claimant to find a place in a public hospital or institution which levies no charges[72] and use the money for some totally different purpose. The court may reduce the damages if it feels convinced that the claimant will spend substantial periods in a free state institution, for example, where other suitable facilities simply do not exist.

---

68 All ninety of the cases studied in the Harris survey obtained free medical treatment under the NHS: Harris 1984 Survey, 240–2.
69 Law Reform (Personal Injuries) Act 1948, s. 2(4).
70 *How Much is Enough?*, 46–8.
71 The position is different in relation to residential care services provided by local authorities: *Sowden v. Lodge* [2005] 1 WLR 2129.
72 Although local authorities have statutory power to charge for residential care services, tort damages are not available to meet such charges. This means that the cost of such care cannot be recovered in a tort action: *Sowden v. Lodge* [2005] 1 WLR 2129.

It is not at all obvious why, sixty years after the beginning of the NHS, we should continue to subsidize those who seek private treatment in the way that the tort system does. Why should persons with a tort claim enjoy private treatment at the expense of the large proportion of the population who pay or contribute to liability insurance premiums, when others desiring private hospital or nursing care must pay for it themselves by taking out health insurance? It seems difficult to justify the present position, and the Pearson Commission proposed that in future the expenses of private medical treatment should only be recoverable if it was reasonable on medical grounds for the patient to have private treatment.[73] However, given the ever-increasing pressure of demand on the NHS, such a proposal is perhaps unlikely to be attractive to politicians. Indeed, in 1999 the Law Commission recommended against changing the law in this respect.[74] On the other hand, the Chief Medical Officer has recently recommended that the rule not apply to medical negligence claims against the NHS, and that the treatment needs of successful claimants should be met by a 'care package' provided by the NHS.[75]

Other out-of-pocket expenses incurred as a result of an accident are recoverable in the same way as medical expenses; for example, the cost of fares to attend an out-patient department at a hospital, the cost of special medical appliances, or indeed expenses that have nothing to do with medical costs, such as the cost of doing repairs around the house which the claimant is no longer able to do personally, or the cost of alterations to a house necessitated by a permanent disability. The sums awarded for such losses are a significant item in some awards.

Finally, we should note that a claimant may recover damages representing the value of nursing or domestic services provided gratuitously by friends or family members.[76] Normally, tort compensation is given for losses suffered or expenses incurred, but in this case the injured person incurs no expense (indeed, they receive a benefit) because the services are provided for nothing. So the courts say that the compensation is given on account of the fact that the tort has created a *need* for services. In reality, the loss is suffered by the carer, but the law does not allow the carer to sue in their own name. Instead, the claimant holds the damages 'on trust' for the carer which means, in effect, that they must be paid over to the carer. The justification for awarding such damages is that if the injured person chose to employ a professional carer instead of relying on a friend or relative, the cost of doing so could be recovered. Indeed, a common

---

73 Pearson Report, vol. 1, paras. 339–42.
74 Law Com. No. 262, *Damages for Personal Injury: Medical, Nursing and Other Expenses, Collateral Benefits*, 3.1–3.18.
75 Department of Health, *Making Amends: A Consultation Paper Setting out Proposals for Reforming the Approach to Clinical Negligence in the NHS* (2003), 127–8. In November 2005 the NHS Redress Bill was introduced into Parliament. The Bill enables the establishment of a special scheme for dealing with medical negligence claims against the NHS; but it does not directly deal with the issue of damages for private medical treatment. However, a person who accepts an offer of compensation under the scheme will normally not be able to bring a tort claim and so will, effectively, be unable to recover damages for private medical treatment.
76 *Donnelly* v. *Joyce* [1974] QB 454; *Giambrone* v. *JMC Holidays Ltd (No. 2)* [2004] 2 All ER 891.

measure of damages in this context is the reasonable market cost of services equivalent to those provided by the carer; but if the carer has given up paid employment to look after the claimant, the wages foregone may set the amount of the award.

Such damages may not be awarded in cases where the carer is the defendant.[77] There are two somewhat conflicting arguments for this restriction. One is that if D performs the services and then has to pay damages representing their value, D effectively bears the cost of the services twice. The other is that since the claimant holds the damages on trust for D, the odd result is that the tortfeasor receives damages in respect of the tort. The issues that arise here throw light on the relationship between the principles of personal responsibility which underlie the rules of tort liability and the impact on those rules of widespread liability insurance. On the one hand, it seems contrary to the very basis of tort law effectively to compensate a tortfeasor for loss suffered by the tortfeasor as a result of the tort, whether or not D is insured against the loss. On the other hand, if D is insured against liability, D will not personally pay any damages awarded to C; and it may seem hard not to tap into that insurance to recompense D for their generosity. Perhaps the strongest pragmatic reason to allow recovery is so as not to discourage provision of care by family members in preference to professional carers where this is felt to be more appropriate. For such reasons, the Law Commission has recommended legislation allowing damages to be awarded in respect of care gratuitously provided by the defendant.[78]

6.3   Full compensation for lost 'earnings': is it justified?

Apart from the issue of 'windfalls', which was mentioned in the previous section, there are two problems which deserve detailed examination. The first is this: why should accident victims be compensated for the same type of injury on a scale that varies according to their previous level of earnings?[79] If two people suffer identical permanent disabilities, but one was formerly earning £20,000 a year and the other was earning £40,000 a year, what justification is there for compensating the latter at a higher rate than the former? Or, still more striking perhaps, if these two people are killed in similar accidents, what justification is there for compensating their dependants at different rates? This we might call the problem of the earnings-related principle. The second question is whether it is sensible or desirable to attempt to replace every penny of lost income rather than some proportion of it. This we might call the problem of the hundred-per cent principle.

---

77 *Hunt* v. *Severs* [1994] 2 AC 350.
78 Law Com. No. 262, 3.67–3.76.
79 In the case of non-earners the question is slightly different: why should the damages awarded be assessed according to the earnings of a person doing for gain what the injured person was doing gratuitously?

6.3.1   The earnings-related principle

The main advantage of earnings-related benefits over flat-rate benefits is that they enable accident victims to maintain an approximation to their former standard of living. To people who have long-term commitments such as mortgages, hire-purchase instalments and so forth, real hardship can be caused by a sudden and substantial drop in income. Moreover, flat-rate benefits have the disadvantage that a single figure has to be selected for all earners, and it is almost inevitable that a low figure will be inadequate for many to maintain their commitments, while a higher figure will result in over-compensation for lower earners. Nevertheless, there are real problems of equity in supporting the earnings-related principle, and these require some consideration.

The social security system, as we shall see more fully later, is largely based on a flat-rate principle, though there are some earnings-related benefits. But it is important to observe that earnings-related benefits are only payable on a contributory or insurance principle. In general, benefits are the same for all. Whatever obligations may rest on the State to see that its citizens do not want for the necessities of life, or even to see that they have a reasonable standard of living, it is not obvious that the State owes any obligation to maintain disabled persons (or the dependants of deceased persons) for the rest of their lives at the standard of living which they had previously enjoyed – at any rate, it is not obvious that this is equitable regardless of how the compensation is paid for. In a competitive and partly market-oriented society the £40,000 a year person receives, while working, a higher salary than the £20,000 a year person, presumably because the former is thought to provide more valuable services than the latter. Once this person has ceased to work, this justification is no longer open. It is not easy to justify a system under which many taxpayers would have to support a non-working disabled person, or the dependants of a deceased person, at a standard of living higher than their own. The only way in which this could be supported would be by arguing that the higher income taxes paid by the wealthier person while working justify a right to greater compensation when unable to work. This argument proved acceptable in New Zealand;[80] but in Britain it has generally been thought that the mere fact that income taxes are progressive would not justify the payment of earnings-related benefits out of general taxation. For one thing, indirect taxes (which represent a significant proportion of total tax revenues) are not progressive. On the contrary, they may be said to be 'regressive' because they tend to consume a greater proportion of a person's income the lower that income is.

On the other hand, there is no objection to paying some or even full compensation for lost earnings on an insurance principle; that is, in accordance with premiums actually paid. If a person earning £30,000 a year chooses to spend a substantial

80 Where the Accident Compensation Act provides for compensation of 80% of lost earnings up to a maximum set at a high level, while not exacting any earnings-related contributions except from the self-employed.

part of that income on life insurance so that their dependants may enjoy the same standard of living after they die as before, the person is free to do so; and the same is true if that person takes out insurance against the risk of disability or chronic disease. In practice we know that insurance against the risk of serious disease or accident is not very common even among the relatively well-to-do, and is certainly very rare among poorer people. This partly explains the fact that statutory sick pay (a social security benefit) used to be moderately earnings-related; and that there is an earnings-related supplement to long-term incapacity benefit (although this is being phased out).[81] However, such earnings-related social security benefits were never financed out of general taxes, but out of earnings-related National Insurance contributions (according to what might be called 'the contributory principle'). The person who earned more got larger benefits only as a result of paying higher National Insurance contributions. There was no question of the taxpayer paying for earnings-related benefits.

When we turn to the tort system, however, things are very different. Here we find the only systematic method of compensation which pays (what are in effect) earnings-related benefits without earnings-related contributions. How did this come about? The answer is that the tort system operates, in practice, in conjunction with liability insurance and not first-party insurance. A system of liability insurance cannot adjust its premiums according to the income of those to whom compensation will be payable, because at the time the premiums are fixed nobody knows to whom compensation may become payable under the policy. If we look, for instance, at the road accident field we find that the liability insurance premium is adjusted according to the risk presented by the insured, the only person that the insurance company knows anything about. If the insured is a high-risk driver (e.g. a young male), driving a high-risk car (e.g. a sports car), living in a high-risk area (such as London), they pay higher premiums. But the premiums will not be adjusted according to the income of the insured because compensation will never be payable to the insured for loss of income under the policy;[82] indeed, the insured is the one person in the world whose income is irrelevant to the risk undertaken by the insurance company. The person whose income is relevant is the person who may be run over and injured or killed by the insured; and that person is, of course, not identifiable when the insurance is taken out.

On the other hand, since the law does at present provide earnings-related compensation, insurance companies have to consider the likely amounts payable under the policy and adjust the premiums accordingly. In other words, the more compensation that is paid for lost earnings, the higher insurance premiums must go, but the incidence is spread among all insured persons and is not borne rateably according to the incomes of those to whom compensation will eventually be paid. If all motor

81 See 12.4.3.
82 Comprehensive policies often provide for some accident payment to the insured, but this usually takes the form of a flat-rate benefit unrelated to the insured's income.

insurance premiums (for personal injury) are thought of as an insurance pool, it can be seen that higher-income groups draw much more out of the pool, but do not pay correspondingly more into the pool. Our £40,000 a year person and our £20,000 a year person will pay the same premium if they present the same type of accident risk; while if they are the victims of accidents, the former will receive much more compensation in the form of lost earnings than the latter. In addition, of course, a pedestrian stands to gain while not contributing anything at all to the insurance fund. The tort system provides a stark contrast with other compensation systems in this respect. Another consequence of the earnings-related principle is that a spouse or civil partner who was wholly dependent on the other spouse's or partner's earnings is entitled to be maintained for the rest of their life at a standard of living scarcely below that which was enjoyed while the spouse was alive.[83] Even if the surviving spouse or partner is young, childless and well qualified to work, they need not do so; and if they do, this will probably be ignored in assessing damages.[84] There seems no reason why a young person should be maintained for the rest of their life by an award of damages (paid by society in one way or another) simply because their spouse or partner was killed through someone's fault. It is surely not right that the law should reward idleness and discourage gainful activity in this way.

In other areas of the law the position is quite otherwise. For example, a young childless wife separated (or divorced) from her husband cannot obtain maintenance from him without taking account of her own earning capacity, even where he was the 'guilty' party.[85] The National Insurance system generally gives no pension to a bereaved spouse or civil partner with no dependent children unless over 45 at the date of bereavement: if younger, the bereaved person is expected to earn their own living.

A very different criticism of the earnings-related principle (which is, to some extent, at odds with what has been said so far) is that the principle (even if linked with the insurance principle) entrenches existing inequalities in our society. For example, it creates a preference in favour of earners as against non-earners; in favour of higher earners as against lower earners; in favour of men as against women (because on average, women earn less than men); in favour of the ethnic majority as against ethnic minorities (because, on average, members of ethnic minorities earn less than members of the ethnic majority).[86] It might be replied that even if one accepts that such inequalities ought to be eliminated from society,[87] it is not the job of tort law to do this. However, this reply has force only if we assume what we are setting out to

---

83 It is immaterial that the surviving spouse may have a substantial personal fortune, unless it was used to support the spouse: *Shiels v. Cruickshank* [1953] 1 WLR 533.
84 6.1.2.
85 See Domestic Proceedings and Magistrates' Courts Act 1978, s. 3(2). Despite para. (2)(g), conduct is relevant only in exceptional cases: P.M. Bromley and N.V. Lowe, *Bromley's Family Law*, 9th edn (London, 1998), 762.
86 R.L. Abel, '£s of Cure, Ounces of Prevention' (1985) 73 *California LR* 1003.
87 It is clearly accepted, and indeed required by law, that women should be paid the same as men for work of equal value.

prove, namely the validity of the earnings-related principle. This principle is not an intrinsic feature of tort law; its adoption was the result of judicial choice. It is now far too deeply entrenched in the law for *the courts* to remove it, but there is no logical reason why tort compensation has to be earnings-related. We could choose some other principle, if we wished, which better reflected the fact that people with similar disabilities have similar financial needs, and the judgment (if it be accepted) that the law should seek to lessen rather than entrench certain social inequalities.

6.3.2   The hundred-per cent principle

There has never been any question but that tort damages for lost earnings are designed to represent the full amount of the loss. Yet most other compensation systems, especially social security systems (and in other countries, workers' compensation laws) generally reject the hundred-per cent principle. Our own social security system generally pays benefits well below the full amount of lost earnings. Similarly, the New Zealand Accident Compensation Act provides for benefits of 80% of lost earnings; and the Australian Committee of Inquiry recommended benefits equal to 85% of lost earnings.[88] Moreover, in most compensation systems there are minimum loss qualifications. For instance, no social security benefits are payable in this country for the first 3 days' loss of earnings; and the smallest award available under the Criminal Injuries Compensation Scheme is £1,000.

There are two main reasons for rejecting the hundred-per cent principle. One is the cost involved, particularly at the lower end. Large sums can be saved by eliminating entitlement to benefits for the first few days of illness or by refusing compensation for losses below a certain amount. There is no doubt that the hundred-per cent principle, as applied in tort law today, is one of the principal factors leading to over-compensation for minor injuries, and under-compensation for more serious cases.[89] The Pearson Commission proposed that social security benefits should be fully offset against damages for lost earnings;[90] but when a scheme for recovery of social security benefits from tort claimants was introduced in 1989, claims worth less than £2,500 were exempted from its operation. The scheme was amended in 1997 to cover all awards of compensation for personal injuries (but not death).[91] In practice, this reform may discourage tort claims in many minor cases. On the other hand, social security benefits are not set off against damages for non-pecuniary loss, which represent a disproportionately large part of many small awards.

The Pearson Commission also proposed the elimination of claims for non-pecuniary loss suffered in the first 3 months after the accident. If implemented, this proposal would have a very significant effect because it appears that damages for non-pecuniary loss represent a much greater proportion of the damages paid in

88 Australian Committee Report, para. 343.
89 See further 10.6.
90 Pearson Report, vol. 1, paras. 467–76.
91 For details see 15.4.5.

minor cases than in serious cases. Unfortunately, there seems no prospect of this change being implemented in the foreseeable future. By contrast, statutory thresholds (and ceilings) on damages for non-pecuniary loss have been introduced in most Australian jurisdictions in recent years.

The second ground for doubting the wisdom of the hundred-per cent principle is its potentially negative effect on the injured person's incentive to resume work (whether paid or unpaid). In general, it seems desirable that injury victims should be encouraged to become as active as possible as soon as possible. It is true that this problem is not as great in a lump-sum system as it would be under a regime of periodical payments, where resumption of paid employment may lead to a reduction of the compensation payments: once paid, lump-sum damages cannot be taken away. But so long as the claim remains unresolved (either by a court judgment or settlement out of court), the injured person has an incentive to exaggerate their incapacity for work, knowing that if their claim is successful, they will be compensated for lost earnings up to the date the claim is resolved and perhaps into the future. The law attempts to address this problem by requiring the injured person to 'mitigate' the loss (by e.g. returning to work as soon as possible) and by refusing damages for any period during which the claimant ought reasonably to have worked. But this solution depends on being able to distinguish effectively between the 'malingerer' and the person genuinely incapable of work.

Even if the doubtful assertion, that the hundred-per cent principle is a corollary of the fault principle, is accepted, there are good reasons for rejecting it which are given effect to in both the main compensation systems other than tort law. It is difficult to see why (e.g.) tort victims should not forego lost earnings for the first 3 days, as social security beneficiaries are required to do; or why there should not be a lower limit on tort damages of £1,000, as there is on compensation under the Criminal Injuries Compensation Scheme. It is ironical, to say the least, that in an era when personal initiative and individual self-reliance are the common currency of political discourse, the tort system should continue to adhere to a principle which, in other contexts, is seen as inimical to these ideals.

6.4   Full compensation: the commitment in practice

Assuming, for the sake of argument, that the principle of full compensation is a desirable one for tort law to pursue, the question remains of how well that principle is implemented in practice. Forty years ago it was said that 'grave injustice follows from the present practice of the judges in assessing future financial losses'.[92] Two common, related criticisms of the practical operation of the full-compensation principle that have been made over the years deserve attention. First, it has been said that that awards are too greatly reduced to take account of 'contingencies', i.e. the possibility that even if the claimant had not been injured, the income lost

---

92 JUSTICE, *Report on Trial of Motor Accident Cases* (London, 1966), 30.

would not have been earned because of illness, or unemployment or being involved in another accident. Secondly, it has often been argued that too little use is made of actuarial evidence in calculating the multiplier (the assumption being that if they made more use of actuarial evidence, the discount for contingencies would be smaller and, conversely, damages awards would be higher).[93] Actuarial evidence is statistical evidence about matters such as life expectancy, disease, unemployment rates and so on, which takes account of factors such as age, sex, place of residence and occupation. Traditionally, actuarial tables, as such, were inadmissible as evidence because they were 'hearsay'. Actuarial evidence could only be introduced by calling an actuary as an expert witness. Courts were very unwilling to do this for fear of unduly increasing the length and expense of trials. Another objection to the use of actuarial evidence was that, being statistical, it does not take account of the peculiar circumstances of the individual claimant.[94] However, this objection is misplaced. On the one hand, the use of actuarial tables to deal with certain contingencies (such as life expectancy) would not prevent the court also taking account of particular aspects of the claimant's situation in calculating the multiplier. On the other hand, the contrast between statistical evidence and the individual's personal circumstances is misleading because it assumes that when a court speculates on what the future will hold for a particular claimant, it can in a meaningful sense predict that person's future. In reality, the courts' predictions are based on a sort of non-statistical averaging based on the judge's knowledge and experience of what in fact happens to people in general and to persons like the claimant in particular. The difference between speculation based on actuarial evidence and speculation about the claimant in particular is that the former is based on sound scientific methodology whereas the latter is not.

In 1973 the Law Commission recommended the publication of actuarial mortality tables suitable for use in personal injury and fatal accident actions,[95] and these (often referred to as the 'Ogden tables')[96] first appeared in 1984.[97] However, it was not until the enactment of s. 10 of the Civil Evidence Act 1995 that these tables could be used without having to call an actuary as an expert witness to 'prove' them. In 1994 revised Ogden tables were published, dealing with matters such as illness and unemployment as well as mortality. The third edition, published in 1998, incorporated certain other variables not previously taken into account, such as the injured person's place of residence.

Use of the Ogden tables is not mandatory, and even the revised Ogden tables do not cover all of the contingencies that may be relevant in personal injury actions.

---

93 This was on ground on which liability insurers resisted increased use of actuarial evidence. But the claim that awards tend to be higher when such evidence is admitted has not been rigorously tested.

94 E.g. *Hunt* v. *Severs* [1994] AC 350, 365 *per* Lord Bridge.

95 Law Com. No. 56, *Personal Injury Litigation – Assessment of Damages* (1973), para. 230.

96 After Sir Michael Ogden, the chair of the working party that developed the tables.

97 The tables are now in their 5th edition. See P. Barrie, *Personal Injury Law: Liability, Compensation and Procedure*, 2nd edn (Oxford, 2005), ch. 23.

But while it is still open to a court to depart from the tables to take account of matters they do not deal with, failure to apply them in relation to matters they do cover is likely to be overturned on appeal.[98]

Apart from the adjustment for contingencies, another factor critical to the practical operation of the full-compensation principle is the so-called 'discount rate'. The assumption on which lump-sum damages are calculated is that the recipient will invest the damages and meet future losses out of a combination of capital and interest. The discount rate is the rate of interest which, it is assumed, the recipient will be able to earn, after tax, by investing the lump sum. Commercial interest rates have two components: an allowance for expected future inflation and a rate of return on the investment. The discount rate relates to the latter component, called the 'real rate of return' on the investment.[99] So, for instance, if the inflation rate is expected to be 3%, an interest rate of 6% would yield a real return, before tax, of 3%. For many years, the discount rate used in calculating damages was 4–5%. This came to be considered unrealistically high; and in 1998 the House of Lords held that 3% was appropriate.[100] In 2002, the Lord Chancellor exercised a statutory power to set the rate, and reduced it to 2.5%. The reduction reflects a desire to enable recipients of damages to favour security over high income by investing in Index-Linked Government Stock (ILGS), thus protecting the capital from the effect of inflation. It was estimated that this 0.5% reduction of the rate would increase the cost of the personal injury compensation system by around £169 million annually.[101] The discount rate fixed by the Lord Chancellor is not binding on the courts. But it has been held that a court would be justified in adopting a different rate only in rare circumstances not contemplated by the published reasons[102] for the chosen rate.[103]

Despite the increasingly actuarial approach to assessment of damages and reduction of the discount rate, there is some reason to think that judicial practices generally, and use of the Ogden tables in particular, may result in awards of significantly less than full compensation, especially in more serious cases involving long-term future loss of income. Recent research compared assessment methods adopted by English courts with those followed by US courts.[104] It was

---

98 *Wells* v. *Wells* [1999] 1 AC 345, 378–9 *per* Lord Lloyd.
99 *Mallett* v. *McMonagle* [1970] AC 168; *Mitchell* v. *Mulholland* [1971] AC 666; *Cookson* v. *Knowles* [1979] AC 556. For this reason, the common criticism that courts ignored the ravages of inflation in assessing damages was unfounded.
100 *Wells* v. *Wells* [1998] 3 WLR 329.
101 Department for Constitutional Affairs, 'Damages Act 1996: Analysis of the Impact of the Prescribed Discount Rate of 2.5%' (March 2002).
102 Department for Constitutional Affairs, 'Setting the Discount Rate: Lord Chancellor's Reasons' (27 July 2001).
103 *Warriner* v. *Warriner* [2002] 1 WLR 1703. However, it may be that, assuming investment in ILGS and allowing for tax, even 2.5% may be too high.
104 R. Lewis *et al.*, 'Court Awards of Damages for Loss of Future Earnings: An Empirical Study and an Alternative Method of Calculation' (2002) *J. of Law and Society* 406. See also R. Lewis *et al.*, 'Loss of Earnings Following Personal Injury: Do the Courts Adequately Compensate Injured Parties?' (2003) 113 *The Economic Journal* F568.

found that US awards are, on the whole, significantly greater in relative terms than English awards. Two main explanations are given. One is that English courts underestimate the extent to which people's earnings tend to increase over the course of their career. The other is that English courts underestimate the negative impact of disability on people's employment prospects and the amount of time they are likely to be unemployed in the course of their working life. It is worth noting that such problems will arise under the periodical payments regime discussed above as well as under the lump-sum (and associated structured-settlement) system. If, for instance, a court, in making a periodical-payment order in respect of future loss of earnings, underestimates the amount of time the recipient is likely to be unemployed, there will be no way of fixing this later on. It is true that periodical-payment orders may be varied in certain circumstances; but the only ground of variation is a significant change in the recipient's physical or mental condition.

There may also be problems with the adequacy of awards for long-term future medical expenses and the cost of care. A striking example was given in 1974 by the Australian Committee of Inquiry into the National Rehabilitation and Compensation Scheme.[105] In *Thurston* v. *Todd*[106] a young woman of 15 suffered very severe injuries in a motor accident, as a result of which she was rendered a quadriplegic. The accident occurred in 1963. In 1965 she was awarded damages just short of £120,000, which was an exceptionally high award at that time. Over £50,000 of this sum was intended to cover the cost of future nursing services and medical expenses, on the assumption of a weekly cost of some £70. By 1973 the actual cost of these services had risen so much that the income from the entire award of damages (which had all been prudently invested) was inadequate to pay for the nursing expenses alone – despite the mother's unpaid services for some 7 hours each day. Nursing costs alone had nearly doubled in the 9 years since the damages were awarded. Part of the explanation of such outcomes (in Britain, at least) may be that since the end of the Second World War the rate of increase of average earnings has been much greater than the rate of (price) inflation. In other words, the standard of living of those in work has, in general, improved. However, as the research discussed in the previous paragraph suggests, English courts may not make sufficient allowance for improvements in the standard of living; or, putting it another way, for increases in earnings over and above increases in the cost of living. To the extent, therefore, that the income from a damages award has to be used to buy services (usually nursing and medical services), it may well prove inadequate if the cost of these services increases more than the rate of inflation as reflected in market interest rates. This problem is not solved by assuming investment in ILGS because they are linked to increases in the cost of living (as measured by the retail price index),

105 Australian Committee Report, paras. 149–50.
106 (1966–7) 84 WN (NSW) (Pt 1) 231.

not to increases in wages. Furthermore, it has been expressly held that it is not permissible for a court to increase the multiplicand (6.2.2) to make allowance for expected future increases in the cost of care over and above increases in the retail price index.[107]

Another reason why damages awards may turn out to be inadequate is that although the law assumes that the investment of the lump sum will be risk-free and index-linked, the recipient (as we have already noted) is not required to invest in this way but may do what they want with their damages, even if that be investing them in a highly risky way or even squandering them. In fact, research suggests that most recipients of large damages awards typically follow their own self-interest and use the money wisely.[108] Even so, there is a significant public interest that people who suffer long-term disabilities as a result of torts be adequately provided for. In this light, it would surely not be an undue interference with their freedom for the law to lay down guidelines about the investment and management of large lump-sum damages awards designed to provide support and care for the future.

Certainly the fact that lump-sum awards may in some cases turn out to be inadequate to produce as much income as has been lost should not lead us to conclude that it would be right to raise the level of such awards even more. In the first place, in cases where the injured person has suffered large earning losses, substantial awards are also made for pain and suffering and other intangible losses mentioned below. It is possible to take the view that these are as irrational or excessive as awards for lost earnings are inadequate, and that the one therefore helps to balance the other, although the House of Lords has not shown itself sympathetic to such an approach. Nor does the argument apply to dependency actions where (apart from damages for bereavement) no award for pain and suffering and such like will be available to augment the award for lost financial support; and it is possibly in such cases that awards appear most inadequate.[109] But even here, there are often countervailing considerations – for example, the fact that life insurance and other benefits (such as social security) received by the dependants as a result of the death are ignored in the assessment of damages.

Secondly, there is a great deal of 'double compensation'. We shall look into the full extent of this problem later,[110] but here it must be noted that many losses are compensated in full or in part more than once. Fourthly, the question of priorities, which we have stressed so often, must not be forgotten. If more money is to be pumped into the tort system, the effect will be to increase the comparatively generous provision already made for victims of fault-caused injuries who are fortunate enough to collect tort damages while doing nothing for the great mass of the disabled population.

107 *Cooke* v. *United Bristol Healthcare NHS Trust* [2004] 1 WLR 251.
108 See 6.1.4.
109 A.F. Conard and others, *Automobile Accident Costs and Payments* (Ann Arbor, 1964), 179; A.M. Linden, *Report of the Osgoode Hall Study on Compensation for Victims of Automobile Accidents* (Toronto, 1965) (*Osgoode Hall Study*), ch. 4, 25–6.
110 Ch. 15.

6.5   Intangible losses

6.5.1   Assessing intangible losses

So far we have been considering damages for financial loss. In personal injury actions the law also awards damages for certain intangible 'losses'. Damages for pain, suffering, discomfort, humiliation, indignity and embarrassment are awarded under the head of 'pain and suffering'. Damages may also be awarded for loss of the ability to do things and to enjoy life in a way possible before the accident; these are usually referred to as damages for 'loss of amenities' or 'loss of faculty'. These two types of injury may merge as, for instance, where an injured person has suffered a loss of sexual potency, or is so badly injured as to impair the prospect of marriage.[111] The two kinds of damages may both be recoverable since loss of faculty may be accompanied by pain and suffering; but it is possible to have loss of faculty without any pain or mental distress at all, as in the case of someone who is rendered permanently unconscious or is incapable of appreciating their situation. It is also possible to have pain and suffering with no physical or mental disability or loss of faculty. But in most serious cases the two go together. Loss of limbs, paralysis, blindness or deafness, and so on, are unlikely to be inflicted without considerable pain and suffering; and significant pain and suffering is likely to be accompanied by some loss of faculty. Damages for pain, suffering and loss of amenities are usually referred to collectively as damages for 'non-pecuniary loss'.

In fatal cases, until 1981, a small fixed amount could be recovered by the estate of the deceased person to compensate for their 'loss of expectation of life'. Now, an amount of £10,000 is recoverable by the claimants in a claim under the Fatal Accidents Act 1976 to compensate them collectively for their bereavement. As we have seen, they can also recover for loss of support in money and money's worth formerly provided by the deceased. But nothing can be recovered for the loss of the deceased's life as such.

The calculation of damages for non-pecuniary loss has an air of unreality about it. Something that cannot be measured in money is 'lost', and the compensation principle requires some monetary value to be placed on it. There appears to be no objective way of working out any relationship between the value of money – what it will buy – and damages awarded for pain, suffering and loss of amenities. All such damages awards could be multiplied or divided by two overnight and they would be just as defensible or indefensible as they are today.[112]

It is not only lawyers who are concerned with putting monetary values on intangibles. There is a large economic literature dealing with the valuation of 'life'. Economists normally value things by looking for a 'market price'; but there is, of course, no market in human lives. So they need to find alternative indications of

---

111   *Moriarty* v. *McCarthy* [1978] 1 WLR 155.
112   For an analysis of the conceptual basis of such awards see A.I. Ogus, 'Damages for Lost Amenities: For a Foot, a Feeling or a Function?' (1972) 35 *Modern LR* 1.

how much value people put on their lives as such – the 'hedonic' value of life, we might say.[113] The most common method for doing this to gather evidence about how much people are willing to pay to reduce the risk of death from various causes. So, for example, economists look at wage differentials between more and less risky jobs, and at price differentials between more and less safe products. One problem with this approach is that the amount a person is willing to pay will depend to some extent on how much money they have. This is because what economists call 'the marginal utility of money' is greater for a poor person than for a rich person: other things being equal, a rich person is likely to be willing to pay more for any particular commodity than a poor person simply because they have more money to spend. We would not want to conclude from this fact that the life of a rich person is worth more than that of a poor person. It is sometimes suggested that this problem can be solved by asking not how much a person would be willing to pay to avoid a risk of death, but how much they would be willing to accept to incur a risk of death. However, because of the marginal utility of money, a poor person is just as likely to be more prepared to accept less than a rich person as to pay less. However, the impact of ability to pay is not quite as serious as it might at first appear. This is because willingness-to-pay research typically deals with very small risks. The question is not how much a person would be willing to pay to avoid certain (or even a high probability of) death, but how much they would be willing to pay to avoid a small risk of death. So, for example, suppose that 10,000 people are asked how much they would be willing to pay to avoid a one in 10,000 risk of death. If each were willing to pay £300, this would suggest that each valued their life at £3 million. Many more people could afford £300 than £3,000,000, and so the significance of wealth is reduced – but not, of course, eliminated. Moreover, there are many other problems associated with research of this type arising, for instance, from the fact that people vary in their attitude to risk – some people enjoy risk-taking whereas others are very cautious.[114]

This willingness-to-pay approach to valuing life is most commonly used in connection with cost-benefit analyses designed to support decisions about how much to spend, for instance, on road safety measures[115] or on reducing pollution hazards or workplace risks. The other use to which this method might be put is the assessment of compensation. However, we have noted that English law does not provide compensation for loss of life as such. To the extent that a legal value is put on life, the approach used is what economists call the 'human capital' method. This means

113 Or, in other words, the value of life's pleasures.
114 For a quite accessible overview of this sort of research see W.K. Viscusi, 'The Value of Life in Legal Contexts: Survey and Critique' (2000) 2 *American Law and Economics Review* 195.
115 See e.g. R. Elvik, 'Cost-Benefit Analysis of Road Safety Measures: Applicability and Controversies' (2001) 33 *Accident Analysis and Prevention* 9. In Britain, the willingness-to-pay method is the starting point of assessing the 'costs' of road accidents, but other things are also taken into account, such as police costs and lost output: Department for Transport, *Highways Economics Note No. 1, 2003: Valuation of the Benefits of Prevention of Road Accidents and Casualties*. See also M.W. Jones-Lee, 'The Value of Transport Safety' (1990) 6 *Oxford Review of Economic Policy* 39.

that in a fatal accident claim, the deceased's life is valued in terms of the loss inflicted by the death on the deceased's dependants. But the law does not, for instance, take into account loss, resulting from the death, to society generally or to individuals who do not fall within the class of eligible claimants. Some economists think that the willingness-to-pay method of valuing life is appropriate for deciding how much to spend on preventing death, but not for the compensatory purposes of tort law.[116] Other writers, who argue that the function of tort law is not (only) to compensate for harm caused but also to prevent the occurrence of harm, argue that the willingness-to-pay approach has a role to play in tort law.[117]

At all events, this type of research is of relatively little use in assessing damages for non-pecuniary loss because what it values are whole lives, whereas it is (only) for non-fatal injuries that the law provides compensation for intangible loss. Just as there is no market in human lives, so there is no market in pain or lost limbs.[118] In principle, there is no reason why the willingness-to-pay approach should not be applied to non-fatal injuries; but in practice, this has not been done, and the difficulties of conducting the necessary research to generate willingness-to-pay values, for each of the great variety of injuries (and combinations of injuries) that can be caused by tortious behaviour and attract awards of damages for non-pecuniary loss, would be very considerable. The Department for Transport publishes tables, estimating the costs of road accidents, that cover not only fatal accidents but also accidents that result in 'serious' and 'slight' non-fatal injuries. But this classification is, of course, far too crude for compensatory purposes (for which it was not designed). For what it is worth, however, we might note that the 2003 figure for the 'human costs'[119] of a serious injury was £119,550 – only about half the maximum figure that courts award for non-pecuniary loss in the most serious cases of personal injury.

So we have not made much progress in finding a method for calculating damages for non-pecuniary loss. There are, however, two noteworthy and related facts about awards for non-pecuniary loss that may provide a clue: first, that despite the marginal utility of money, the amount awarded takes no account of the wealth of the claimant; and, secondly, that levels of damages for non-pecuniary loss tend to be roughly related to social prosperity. So, they tend to increase as society becomes wealthier; and they tend to be higher in wealthier countries than in poorer ones. These facts suggest that the process of calculating such awards is not entirely lacking in external reference. It is fair to assume that widespread agreement could be achieved on the extreme outer limits of what would be regarded as 'reasonable' compensation for the intangible aspects of personal injury. For example, we might

---

116 E.g. Viscusi, 'The value of Life in Legal Contexts'.
117 E.A. Posner and C.R. Sunstein, 'Dollars and Death' (2005) 72 *U. of Chicago LR* 537.
118 Professional boxing might be thought to get close to a market in injury.
119 Representing pain, grief and suffering to the injured person, relatives and friends: Department for Transport, *Highways Economics Note No. 1, 2003*, para. 5. Damages for non-pecuniary loss in personal injury actions take no account of the effects of the injury on relatives and friends.

confidently speculate that few people would think £100 too much or £1 million too little for the loss of a hand. Perhaps an upper limit of £3 million on compensation for non-pecuniary loss in cases involving the most serious injuries (quadriplegia and the like) would be rejected as too high, partly because such a sum is so far beyond the sort of capital wealth that most people could ever hope to acquire.[120] Equally, £1,000 would be rejected as far too low because to very many people, an extra £1,000 in wealth would be of little moment. Thus it seems that although the selection of particular sums within such wide limits will be a matter of judgment, the limits themselves have some external reference point in that they bear some relationship to the sort of sums that people in general may expect to enjoy as personal wealth.

In 2000 the Court of Appeal laid down guidelines for the assessment of damages for non-pecuniary loss in the process of deciding appeals in eight separate cases.[121] They were that:

- damages for non-pecuniary loss in cases involving the most serious injuries should be increased by one-third (from their level at that time of around £150,000 to around £200,000);
- there should be no increase in cases where the appropriate award for non-pecuniary loss would be less than £10,000; and that there should be 'tapered' increases in cases falling between that threshold and the most serious;
- damages for non-pecuniary loss should be increased regularly in line with increases in the retail price index; and
- new guidelines should be not issued unless there was 'real reason to think that once more the level of awards is significantly out of line with the standards we have identified'.[122]

Unfortunately, the only standard identified by the court for judging the adequacy of awards for non-pecuniary loss was that they should be 'fair, reasonable and just'. In 1996 the Law Commission had recommended that awards of damages for non-pecuniary loss above £3,000 should be increased by between 50 and 100 per cent, and awards of between £2,000 and £3,000 by smaller percentages;[123] but the Court of Appeal criticized this recommendation as being too heavily based on faulty empirical research undertaken for the Commission. In recommending a significant increase in the most serious cases, the court was influenced by the fact that as a result of advances in medical technology, the life-expectancy of many seriously injured people has significantly increased in recent years: the longer an injured person lives, the greater the pain, suffering and loss of amenities they are likely to suffer. On the other hand, it argued that losses that would once have been treated as non-pecuniary – such as the ability to go on an ordinary holiday or to live in an

---

120 It has recently been suggested that at least £3 million is now necessary to sustain the life-style associated with 'millionaire' status.
121 *Heil* v. *Rankin* [2001] QB 272.
122 *Heil* v. *Rankin* [2001] QB 272 at [99].
123 Law Com. No. 257, *Damages for Personal Injury: Non-Pecuniary Loss* (1999).

ordinary home – are now treated as pecuniary losses for which specific amounts can be awarded representing, for instance, the cost of a specially arranged holiday or of home modifications; and this counted against increases on the scale recommended by the Law Commission. Relevant though such considerations might be, they do not explain why an increase of 33% is more 'fair' than one of 50% or even 100%. Some people might think that even £300,000 would be inadequate compensation for non-pecuniary losses associated with catastrophic injuries.

However, the Court of Appeal was also influenced by the likely impact of sudden large percentage increases in awards for non-pecuniary loss on the total amount spent on tort compensation. For example, the court was told that the cost of a 100% increase to the NHS would be £133 million a year in additional compensation payments, and that it would generate additional insurance pay-outs of around £1 billion a year. According to traditional understandings of tort law, such 'social facts' are irrelevant to deciding what is fair and just as between individual 'doers and sufferers of harm'. But the court rightly refused to ignore the fact that in a world of scarcity, choices must inevitably be made between competing calls on society's limited resources. This is one reason why it recommended a threshold of £10,000 before there should be any increase: the large majority of tort claims fall beneath the threshold, and adopting the Law Commission's recommendations for increases in all cases above a £2,000 threshold would have added much more to the total tort compensation bill.

In this respect, it is important to note a difference between judicial law-making (such as laying down 'guidelines' for the assessment of damages)[124] and parliamentary law-making. If the Law Commission's recommendations had been acted upon, this would probably have been done by an Act of Parliament and by regulations made under it. Most likely, such legislation would have been purely prospective in effect – in other words, it would have applied only to claims made after the date the legislation became operative. By contrast, judicial rule-making operates retrospectively – that is, it affects not only the claim in the case before the court, but also, in practice, all unresolved claims that have already been made. Thus the immediate financial impact of (retrospective) judicial increases in levels of damages awards is much greater than that (prospective) legislative increases. This is another reason why the Court of Appeal was unwilling to adopt the Law Commission's recommendations. Indeed, the defendants in the case argued that it was inappropriate for the court (as opposed to Parliament) to increase the level of damages awards in the way it did.

6.5.2   The tariff system

In the case we have been discussing, the Court of Appeal increased the existing levels of damages for non-pecuniary loss. How were those levels arrived at? Until 1934, in cases that went to trial, damages for non-pecuniary loss were assessed by a jury. In

---

124 In strict theory, the guidelines are probably not binding rules of law; but in effect, they are.

the USA, juries still assess such damages. On this side of the Atlantic, however, damages for personal injury are almost invariably assessed by judges.[125] Given the lack of objective relationship between pain, suffering and loss of amenities and damages for non-pecuniary loss, assessment by a jury might seem a suitable way of injecting into the legal process community views about how much compensation particular injuries should attract. On the other hand, because juries were not told about awards by other juries in comparable cases, there was no way of ensuring a desirable degree of consistency in awards. Even if we cannot, in any objective sense, say what a leg or an arm is worth, it should at least be the case that a leg today is worth the same (in real terms) as a leg tomorrow; that an arm must be worth more than a hand; a hand more than a finger; two legs more than one; and so forth. Even here, of course, there is great difficulty. Is an arm worth more than a leg? Is it worse to be totally blind than to lose both legs? Is a hand worth more than a foot? With what can you compare the inability to bear a child? But still, making every allowance for the element of arbitrariness in the whole process of compensating for disabilities, it is possible to have some internal consistency in the process, and such consistency would not be easily attained if the decision were left to a jury.

Consistency in awards for non-pecuniary loss is desirable not merely in the interests of justice, to achieve equal treatment of like cases. It is also important for the smooth running of the tort system because most tort claims are settled by negotiation out of court. Without some consistency in the level of awards, it would be very difficult to predict the outcome of a case and hence to negotiate a settlement. A very small decrease in the proportion of cases settled, and a corresponding increase in the proportion of cases going to trial, could seriously overload the court system.

Judicial assessment greatly facilitated the development of a 'tariff' system of calculating damages for non-pecuniary loss. The group of judges who regularly decide personal injury cases is quite small. Judges may be able to discuss awards with one another, and judicial assessments that deviate too far from the current norm can be corrected by the Court of Appeal. Under the tariff system, particular ranges of awards are established for particular injuries and disabilities. For many years, there was no formal mechanism for fixing these ranges. They simply emerged from reported decisions in individual cases. Indeed, in 1973, the Law Commission came to the conclusion that the fixing of damages for non-pecuniary loss was so arbitrary that no principles could be recommended on which the courts should work. The only question, according to the Law Commission, that needed to be settled was 'who

125 In 1966 the Court of Appeal decided that jury trial would henceforth be permitted only in very special cases: *Ward v. James* [1966] 1 QB 273. An example of such a case might be where the injuries are of so unusual a kind that judicial experience would be of little use: *Hodges v. Harland & Wolff* [1965] 1 WLR 523 (this is the last reported case of trial by jury in a personal injury action); or where exemplary damages are claimed: *H v. Ministry of Defence* [1991] 2 QB 103. The Law Commission's view is that assessment of damages for non-pecuniary loss in personal injury cases should never be left to a jury: Law Com. No. 257, *Damages for Personal Injury: Non-Pecuniary Loss* (1999), paras. 4.1–4.5.

ought to decide'.[126] In 1992 the Judicial Studies Board published a quite detailed set of guidelines, for the assessment of 'general damages'[127] in relation to a long list of injuries, developed by a working party 'to present a snap-shot of the general level of . . . damages [for non-pecuniary loss] reflected by judicial decisions and settlements influenced by them'.[128] The *Guidelines* are 'not intended to promote any views about what the level of damages ought to be'.[129] On the other hand, the working party gives more weight to decided cases than to reported settlements.[130] The figures given (in the form of a lower and upper figure for each injury) are merely guides: 'it is for the courts to set the level of damages and for this book to reflect them'.[131] The *Guidelines* are not sufficiently detailed to be comprehensive, and they have no authority as such. On the other hand, in his Foreword to the third edition, Lord Woolf said that the *Guidelines* should be used as a starting point 'not only because it is convenient to do so' but also because they are 'the most reliable tool . . . as to what is the correct range of damages for common classes of injuries'.[132] They present 'a distillation of the awards of damages that have been and are being awarded by judges in courts up and down the country'.[133]

Another factor that affects awards for non-pecuniary loss in some cases settled out of court is the internationalization of the tort system.[134] In some cases, especially those involving large-scale disasters and large corporate defendants, awards for non-pecuniary loss tend to be higher in the USA than in the UK. If the defendant in a UK action is a multinational corporation with US roots or US relatives, the claimants may seek to bring their action in the USA. Whether or not this will be possible depends not on rules of tort law but on rules of procedure and of the conflict of laws.[135] If there seems a good chance that an action in the USA might be allowed, the defendant and

---

126   Law Com. No. 56, *Personal Injury Litigation: Assessment of Damages*, para. 20.
127   In cases where damages both for pain and suffering and for loss of amenities are awarded, the two are usually combined into a single lump sum called 'general damages' and the individual components are not calculated separately.
128   *Guidelines for the Assessment of Damages in Personal Injury Cases*, 4th edn (London, 1998), vii.
129   Ibid.
130   Ibid., 2.
131   Ibid.
132   Third edition (1996), viii.
133   *Guidelines for the Assessment of Damages in Personal Injury Cases*, 7th edn (Oxford, 2004), vii.
134   The importance of this phenomenon is not limited to awards for non-pecuniary loss. For example, damages recoverable from airline operators by victims of air crashes may be limited by the Warsaw Convention. Before the Convention, injured persons were free to sue under diverse national laws and individual airlines were free to limit their liability by contract with passengers. The Convention was designed to provide a single compensation regime for air accidents. Airlines accepted a form of strict liability in return for limitations on the scope of their liability in terms of compensatable harm (limited to 'bodily injury': *Morris* v. *KLM Royal Dutch Airlines* [2002] 2 AC 628) and amounts of damages. It may be possible to evade such limitations by suing someone other than the airline operator – the aircraft manufacturer, for example.
135   The most famous case in which a US court refused to accept jurisdiction was that which arose out of the Bhopal gas leak: *Re Union Carbide Corporation Gas Plant Disaster at Bhopal in India in December, 1984* (1987) 809 F 2d 195; J. Cassels, 'The Uncertain Promise of Law: Lessons from Bhopal' (1991) 29 *Osgoode Hall LJ* 1, 17–20. Each US jurisdiction has its own rules on this issue. Californian courts have been quite generous to foreign litigants: *Holmes* v. *Syntex Laboratories*

its insurers may be persuaded to settle at what are called 'mid-Atlantic rates', and to pay compensation for non-pecuniary loss at a level somewhere between UK and US norms. This happened, for example, in the *Piper Alpha* oil rig case in 1988.[136]

The question has often been discussed whether there is a case for a legislative tariff to replace the judicial one.[137] At present, the only head of damages fixed by statute is that for bereavement under the Fatal Accidents Act 1976 – the sum awarded is currently £10,000. It is acknowledged that any more extensive statutory tariff would have to be somewhat flexible because experience, both of the tort system and of the industrial injuries system, has shown that very many injuries cannot be neatly labelled and identified in a tariff schedule. Both the Law Commission (in 1973) and the Pearson Commission found little support for the idea of a statutory tariff, and rejected it. There was, however, more support for a legislative maximum on awards for non-pecuniary loss, and the Pearson Commission only rejected this idea by a single vote. It seems unlikely that such a maximum would make a great deal of difference unless it were set well below the current figure. The Pearson Commission discussed the possibility of a maximum of only five times the average industrial wage, i.e. about £110,000,[138] and that certainly is well below the present maximum of about £220,000. In its 1995 Consultation Paper the Law Commission adopted an agnostic position in relation to all forms of legislative tariff. By contrast statutory limits on this and other heads of damages have, in recent years, been adopted in all Australian jurisdictions.

The Pearson Commission accepted the general basis of most of the present law, though they made one important proposal, namely that no damages for non-pecuniary loss should be recoverable for non-pecuniary loss suffered during the first three months after the date of injury.[139] As about 95% of those injured in accidents are sufficiently recovered to return to work within 3 months,[140] this would have a

---

Inc. (1984) 202 Cal Rptr 773; *Corrigan* v. *Bjork Shiley Corp.* (1986) 227 Cal Rptr 247. But attempts to sue engine and aircraft manufacturers in Louisiana following the M1 air crash in 1989 (partly in order to evade limits on compensation imposed by international Conventions) failed; as did attempts to bring actions in Indiana on behalf of claimants suing in respect of a drug called Opren (see C. Hodges, *Multi-Party Actions* (Oxford, 2001), 329). English courts have the power to issue an injunction to prevent a person bringing an action in a foreign court, but will do so only in extreme cases: *Dicey and Morris on the Conflict of Laws*, 13th edn (London, 2000), 12-057–12-069. English courts can also 'stay' (i.e. stop) claims that are brought in England when another 'forum' could be more suitable. Various factors are relevant to deciding which is the most suitable 'forum' for a case to be heard in. One is the availability of funding for the claim: *Connelly* v. *RTZ Corporation Plc* [1998] AC 854; *Lubbe* v. *Cape Plc* [2000] 1 WLR 1545. See also P. Muchlinski, 'Corporations in International Litigation: Problems of Jurisdiction and the United Kingdom Asbestos Cases' (2001) 50 *IC LQ* 1.

136 Occidental Oil, the rig operators, paid out over £100 million in compensation and then sued contractors working on the rig for an indemnity. The action took more than 4 years to reach judgment: 'Judgment in the United Kingdom's longest civil hearing' [1997] *New LJ* 1302.

137 Law Com. No. 56 (1973), paras. 31–6; Pearson Report, vol. 1, paras. 377–9; Law Com. Consultation Paper No. 140 (1995), paras. 4.53–67.

138 The 'average industrial wage' is no longer used in government statistics. Instead I have used median annual earnings for full-time employees, which were £22,060 in the 2002–3 tax year.

139 Pearson Report, vol. 1, paras. 382–9.

140 Ibid., table 2.

very dramatic effect on eliminating claims for pain and suffering and loss of amenity in minor cases. Moreover, the total saving would be very substantial. The insurance survey conducted for the Pearson Commission showed that some two-thirds of damages paid out by insurers was for non-pecuniary loss, and that the proportion was highest in small cases.[141] In its 1995 Consultation Paper the Law Commission rejected the Pearson Commission's proposal on a number of grounds including that pain is often at its most intense in the early stages after injury.[142] Indeed, the Law Commission is against any form of threshold for recovery for non-pecuniary loss.

6.5.3   Subjective factors

The tariff approach is largely a result of the demise of juries in personal injury actions, which has led judges and appeal courts to stress the value of consistency in assessing damages for non-pecuniary loss. However, the courts still profess to compensate the injured person for the effects of the injuries on them as a unique individual. Clearly, there is potential inconsistency between this personalized approach[143] and a tariff system; but as already noted, the tariff for particular injuries consists of a range of possible awards (i.e. an upper and lower figure) rather than a single sum. This allows the individual circumstances of particular victims to be taken into account. Thus, a claimant with a hand injury may recover more if he or she was an amateur pianist who took much pleasure in the hobby; a woman with a leg injury may recover more if she was formerly keen on dancing and is now unable to dance at all. Here again, we find a fundamental inconsistency between the tort system and the social security system. In the latter, only the industrial injuries scheme recognizes loss of faculty or disability as a ground for compensation under the scheme, and the assessment is entirely objective: no personal factors (other than age and sex) are taken into account. Indeed, a committee reviewing the assessment of disabilities in the industrial injuries scheme thought that it would be 'inequitable' to do so, as the Pearson Commission apparently did despite its acceptance of the common law system.[144] This is doubtless based on the view that everyone places an equal value on, for example, their hand (leaving out of account loss of earnings, which are separately compensated). The case for equality of treatment in this respect seems very strong.

One problem which has caused much trouble is that of assessing the damages awardable to a victim who has been reduced to a 'persistent vegetative state'.[145] Medical science can now keep people with the most devastating injuries alive

---

141 Ibid., vol. 2, table 107.
142 Law Com. Consultation Paper No. 140, paras. 423–6.
143 The most extreme version of the personalized approach is that of Diplock LJ (dissenting) in *Wise* v. *Kaye* [1962] 1 QB 638, who would have assessed the effect of injuries on each individual victim's happiness.
144 Pearson Report, vol. 1, para. 823; see also paras. 379–81.
145 It is lawful in certain circumstances to withdraw life support from a person in such a state: *Airedale NHS Trust* v. *Bland* [1993] AC 789. This possibility should, in theory, be taken into account in assessing tort damages both for financial and for non-pecuniary loss. The cost of maintaining people in such a state is very high, and has been the cause of much controversy.

in a state of complete coma for many months, or even years, with no hope of recovery. In a case of this nature it is hard to see what purpose there can be in awarding lump-sum damages for disabilities or loss of amenities, or even for lost earnings if there are no dependants. There is no question of providing substitute pleasures for those forgone, because the injured party is unable to enjoy any pleasures; nor is there any question of providing a solace for pain, suffering or mental distress, because the victim feels none. Yet, the courts have held that although damages for pain and suffering cannot be awarded, none the less, damages for loss of 'amenities' or 'faculties' must be awarded; and these damages run into many thousands of pounds. In *West v. Shephard*[146] a majority of the House of Lords, following the majority of the Court of Appeal in *Wise v. Kaye*,[147] decided that compensation is awarded for the objective fact of 'loss' in cases of this nature. A person who 'loses' a leg gets compensation for the fact of losing the leg, and a person who is deprived of all the pleasures of life gets compensation for the fact of that deprivation. Lack of consciousness of the deprivation, said the House of Lords, cannot reduce the objective fact of the 'loss'; though consciousness of the deprivation can increase the damages by reason of the mental distress that this would involve.

The result of this approach is that the law draws a very sharp distinction between death and permanent unconsciousness. If a person dies as a result of personal injuries, no damages for loss of amenities will be recoverable in respect of the period after death, even if the deceased has dependants; but if a person is reduced to a state of permanent unconsciousness, substantial damages under this head will be awarded even if that person has no dependants and the damages will eventually accrue as a windfall to the beneficiaries of the estate. The Pearson Commission recommended that damages for non-pecuniary loss should cease to be recoverable in cases of permanent unconsciousness.[148]

6.5.4   Should damages be payable for intangible losses?

As we have seen, damages for non-pecuniary loss may be awarded to victims of personal injury, but otherwise they will only be awarded for the death of a spouse, civil partner or unmarried minor child under the Fatal Accidents Act 1976. In other circumstances, no damages can be awarded for non-pecuniary loss. This rules out, for instance, any damages for the distress and anguish of parents whose child suffers crippling brain damage and whose life may thereby be shattered. Similarly, nothing is recoverable for the death of someone other than under the Fatal Accidents Act 1976. So no damages will be awarded for the death of an adult child or of a non-marital or 'non-civil' partner; and a husband or wife cannot recover anything for the effects on themselves of a serious accident to their spouse. All this is not to suggest

146 [1964] AC 326.
147 [1962] 1 QB 638.
148 Pearson Report, vol. 1, paras. 393–8. The Law Commission reached the opposite conclusion: Law
     Com. No. 257, 2.8–2.24.

that there should be payment of damages for non-pecuniary loss in these situations, but to stress the difficulty of justifying such damages in the cases where they are presently awarded. As we have seen previously, the Pearson Commission discovered that something of the order of two-thirds of all tort payments are attributable to non-pecuniary loss; and much of this sum is paid in relatively trivial cases where a complete recovery is made by the victim within a short time. The majority of the Pearson Commission found it 'hard to justify payments for minor or transient non-pecuniary losses', and they went on to say: 'The emphasis in compensation for non-pecuniary loss should in our view be on serious and continuing losses, especially loss of faculty.'[149]

It is, once again, necessary to remember the remarkable disparity in treatment between tort victims who obtain full compensation for their pecuniary losses and damages for non-pecuniary losses as well, and most other classes of victims of accidents and disease who rarely obtain full compensation even for pecuniary losses, let alone anything extra for non-pecuniary losses. The truth would appear to be that there is a penal or punitive element underlying damages for non-pecuniary loss,[150] especially damages for bereavement. This is particularly obvious in cases against corporate defendants arising out of mass disasters such as railway accidents and fires. Indeed, in recent years there has been considerable public pressure, largely generated by such disasters, for increases in the size of awards for non-pecuniary loss, especially to relatives[151] and to survivors of such incidents who may have suffered little by way of physical injury but who, nevertheless, have endured much mental suffering, including the condition called 'post-traumatic stress disorder'. Calls for increases in awards of damages for non-pecuniary loss in personal injury cases also arose as a response to a number of widely reported defamation awards which were far greater than the largest awards for non-pecuniary loss given to victims of personal injuries.[152] Such awards supposedly compensate the claimant for (non-pecuniary) loss of reputation, and there was a common feeling that if injury to reputation warrants high damages, mental injury resulting from personal

149 Pearson Report, vol. 1, para. 384.
150 See also A. Unger, 'Pain and Anger' [1992] New LJ 394.
151 I.e. damages for bereavement under the Fatal Accidents Act 1976. It is also suggested that the class of entitled claimants should be extended beyond the present married spouses and civil partners (it is anomalous that some cohabitees can recover damages for financial loss under the Act but not for bereavement) and parents of unmarried minor children. Under the Damages (Scotland) Act 1976, damages for bereavement are subject to no monetary limit and are available to a wider class of relatives than in England.
152 The size of such awards starkly illustrates the undesirability of allowing juries to assess damages. The larger defamation awards were also quite out of proportion to awards in e.g. false imprisonment cases. For instance, a child who received 129 days of 'treatment' under the notorious 'pin-down regime' imposed in local authority homes in Staffordshire reportedly received only £42,000: The Times, 29 May 1991. Considerable controversy was generated in the early 1990s by the size of awards for wrongful dismissal made to women forced to leave the armed forces when they became pregnant, as compared with damages for personal injuries recovered by service personnel and civilians injured in the course of action: see e.g. Independent, 29 March 1994; 6 April 1994.

injury, whether to oneself or to others, deserves more. Steps have now been taken to bring defamation awards more into line with damages for non-pecuniary loss in personal injury cases, and this particular cause for dissatisfaction has thus been removed.

Despite all this, however, punitive damages are wholly inappropriate when damages are normally paid by insurers and not by tortfeasors. It is perhaps only in the most serious cases of long-term pain and loss of faculty resulting from major physical injuries that there is a good case for damages for non-pecuniary loss.[153]

6.6   Overall maxima[154]

While damages for non-pecuniary loss are subject to an informal upper limit, the operation of the hundred-per cent principle means that there is no upper limit on damages for pecuniary loss. The result is that awards in cases of serious and long-term injuries causing severe disablement are very great indeed. The largest reported lump sum recovered in a personal injuries action to date is in the region of £9 million.[155] Awards of this size are worth very much more than the social security benefits payable even to the most seriously handicapped people. On the other hand, there is no reason to think that the element of such awards which represents financial losses is excessive given the cost of living.[156] It is, nevertheless true that recipients of tort awards are a *very* privileged class of the disabled, and their position has, if anything, improved over the last 20 years relative to that of other disabled persons.

6.7   Punitive damages

It was argued earlier that damages for non-pecuniary loss may often have a punitive element even though, in theory, they 'compensate' the injured person. We must also make some mention of what are called 'punitive' or 'exemplary' damages. Such damages are expressly designed to express the court's disapproval of what the wrongdoer has done and have no compensatory component or function but are

---

153 Contrast the view of the Law Commission: Law Com. No. 257, 2.25–2.28.
154 Damages awards vary widely from one jurisdiction to another within the EC: D. McIntosh and M. Holmes, *Personal Injury Awards in EU and EFTA Countries*, 3rd edn (London, 2003). This may encourage forum-shopping within the Community. So, too, may different rules affecting the recoverability of damages awards: A. Geddes, 'Difficulties Relating to Directives Affecting the Recoverability of Damages for Personal Injury' (1992) 17 *European LR* 408.
155 *Biesheuvel* v. *Birrell* [1999] PIQR Q40.
156 Long-term care costs represent a significant proportion of damages in serious cases and may be the largest single item. In aggregate, such costs have no doubt accounted for a significant proportion of increases in the cost of tort compensation over the past 30 years as advances in medical technology have made it possible to keep alive seriously injured people who would formerly have died. This is one reason why road-accident fatalities have fallen dramatically in the past 40 years. The relatively small number of serious cases account for a very significant proportion of total tort compensation. As increasing numbers of seriously injured people are kept alive, the cost of compensation may go on increasing in real terms even if the total number of claims remains constant or even falls.

additional to compensatory damages. They are available only in a limited range of circumstances. For our purposes the only situation of importance in which punitive damages might be available is where a tortfeasor has acted with deliberate disregard for the safety or health of the claimant in order, for example, to save money. Such damages may be available against corporate defendants in mass disaster cases resulting from disregard of safety laws.

It is commonly believed that an award of punitive damages could not be made in an ordinary negligence action because negligent conduct is, by definition, not calculated, and because the purpose of a negligence action is solely to compensate the injured person.[157] The first of these reasons is groundless because the essence of negligent conduct is failure to take reasonable precautions against foreseeable risks, and this may be done in a deliberate and indeed callous way. As for the second argument, there is no reason why the tort of negligence should not be used to punish as well as to compensate, if this is thought a good idea. Punitive damages are more common in personal injury cases in the USA, especially where people are injured by defective products. The best justification for such damages is that they may deter the defendant and others similarly placed from taking deliberate risks with health and safety in the future by stripping them of any financial gain that may have been made and perhaps by imposing a penalty over and above any financial benefit derived. Punitive damages are, however, objectionable, in personal injury cases at least, because they over-compensate the injured person and encourage vindictive gold-digging. It would be better to find ways of forcing enterprises to invest their 'ill-gotten gains' in safety than to divert such resources to tort claimants who have already been fully compensated.

---

157 See *Kralj* v. *McGrath* [1986] 1 All ER 54. The terms used in this case was 'aggravated damages', but these are essentially the same as punitive damages. The law is different in Australia: *Lamb* v. *Cotogno* (1987) 164 CLR 1. There is Privy Council authority for awarding exemplary damages for 'gross' or 'outrageous' or 'flagrant', although non-deliberate, departure from the standard of care (*Bottrill* v. *A* [2003] 1 AC 449), but this decision is hard to reconcile with the House of Lords case of *Rookes* v. *Barnard* [1964] AC 1129. Decisions of the House of Lords are binding on English courts, but decisions of the Privy Council are not. However, the decision in *Bottrill* might indicate that the House of Lords would modify the restrictive approach in *Rookes* if it got the chance.

7

An appraisal of the fault principle

The fault principle has traditionally been understood as a principle of morality, which can justify not only the imposition of liability for death and personal injury but also the assessment of compensation according to the full compensation and hundred-per cent principles. Grosser fault may even be seen as justifying the award of exemplary or punitive damages. But in moral terms, the fault principle might be thought to suffer from serious defects. It can also be attacked on social and practical grounds. In this chapter we consider various arguments that might be made against the fault principle as a basis for the payment of compensation to victims of personal injuries by those who inflict them.

7.1 The compensation payable bears no relation to the degree of fault

Under the fault principle, being required to pay compensation is a sort of penalty for bad conduct. In the criminal law, it is seen as a basic requirement of justice that 'the punishment fit the crime' in terms of the seriousness of both the offender's conduct and the consequences of that conduct. In tort law, on the other hand, there is no such idea that the compensation payable should be proportional to the tortfeasor's fault. Fault is like a magic talisman; once it is established, all shall be given to the injured party. It is generally immaterial whether the fault was gross or trivial[1] or whether the consequences of the fault were catastrophic or minor. A degree of fault on the part of someone justifies compensating the injured person for all the losses suffered, provided the claimant was in no way personally at fault. Yet the seriousness of the consequences of a negligent action often bear no relation to the degree of fault which gave rise to it. A piece of momentary thoughtlessness on the road may cost someone their life and cause great loss to their family; but similar acts of thoughtlessness may be committed by scores of others every day with only

---

1 There are some exceptions. For example, people are expected to take more care for the safety of others than for their own safety, and adults are expected to take more care than children. In some cases, too, a defendant will be held liable for negligence only if their conduct was so unreasonable that no reasonable person in their position would have engaged in it: see P. Cane, *The Anatomy of Tort Law* (Oxford, 1997), 41–2.

minor or even no adverse consequences. It has been estimated that for every accident on the roads there are 122 near misses,[2] and a US study found in a test under normal driving conditions in Washington, DC that even 'good' drivers committed an average of nine driving errors of four different types in every five minutes.[3] Yet in this country, in 2004 only about two car drivers in every 1,000 were injured in road accidents,[4] and most road accidents cause only minor property damage. Thus, it seems that whether an act of negligence ends up in the accident statistics or as a near miss, and whether it causes much, little or no harm, are largely matters of chance, outside the control of the person at fault. They would certainly appear to have little correlation with the defendant's culpability.

On the other hand, in applying the fault principle courts do sometimes explicitly recognize a distinction between negligence, on the one hand, and error or mistake, on the other.[5] Not every mistake constitutes fault, because even reasonable people can make mistakes. For instance, when dealing with allegations of medical negligence, and in the context of contributory negligence, courts are apt to insist that not every mistake should be treated as grounds for imposing liability or reducing the claimant's damages, as the case may be. But in other cases courts often appear to assume that the reasonable person never makes a mistake. On the road, for instance, almost any driving error is apt to be treated as negligence without argument, despite the evidence that the typical driver commits driving errors every few minutes. And in other situations it often happens that acts of casual or momentary carelessness can be treated as negligence, even though most of us regularly commit such acts without thinking ourselves to be guilty of fault or blameworthy conduct.

It is true that there is some evidence for asserting that in road accident cases there is some correlation between accident involvement and driving ability. Transport and Road Research Laboratory (TRRL) Reports show, for instance, that there were significant differences between the driving ability of two groups of fifty drivers, the members of one group all having been convicted of careless or dangerous driving.[6] Consequently, it is going too far to say that accident involvement is entirely a question of bad luck; careless drivers are more likely to have accidents than careful drivers. Moreover, it may well be that many road accidents, and perhaps the more serious accidents, are the result of acts of carelessness which are seriously and undeniably

---

2 M. Austin, *Accident Black Spot* (Harmondsworth, 1966), 33.
3 *Driver Behaviour and Accident Involvement: Implications for Tort Liability* (Automobile Insurance and Compensation Study: US government Printer, Washington, 1970), 176–80. In a British survey of 300 drivers in 1996, the respondents admitted to making an average of 50 serious errors a week and to being careless at least once on 98% of their journeys. More than half the motorists said they had had an accident; only 4% said their crashes were genuine accidents with no human error involved: *The Times*, 2 December 1996.
4 Department for Transport, *Road Casualties in Great Britain 2004*, table 30.
5 A. Tunc 'Fault: A Common Name for Different Misdeeds' (1975) 49 *Tulane LR* 279.
6 Laboratory Report (LR) 70 (1967) and LR 146 (1968); see also LR 395 (1971) and LR 449 (1972). More recent research stresses the relationship between individual accident risk and psychological and social factors (such as social deviance): Research Report 306 (1991); Contractor Report 309 (1992).

culpable, such as driving while intoxicated or speeding. There is also evidence to suggest that drivers who commit many 'violations' (i.e. deliberately unsafe driving behaviour) – as opposed to 'errors' (such as misjudgments and failures of observation) – are more likely to be involved in accidents.[7] Nevertheless, it is a matter of everyday observation and experience that extreme carelessness, and even deliberate violations, are very frequently committed with no, or only minor, ill consequences.

Tort law's lack of concern with the relationship between culpability and liability for consequences is a reflection of the fact that tort law is much more concerned with victims than is criminal law. Although the idea of personal responsibility might seem to require that attention be paid to the relative culpability of the tortfeasor's conduct, tort law has an equally strong concern with compensating for harm suffered. The basic idea is that as between a tortfeasor and a totally innocent victim, it is only fair that the harm suffered be borne by the former rather than being shared between them. However, even as between the victim and the tortfeasor, doubts are often felt about the justice of imposing liability on the latter for the most catastrophic consequences of a negligent act. We have already seen how various attempts are made to limit liability in extreme cases by invoking causal or risk principles, or by denying liability for unforeseeable consequences. But even if justice between victim and tortfeasor demands that liability be imposed on the latter however extreme the consequences, and however trifling the negligence, it may nevertheless be felt unjust that tortfeasors should be left to bear this bill as between themselves and society. Since the tortfeasor may be no more culpable than many others, and may only have done what others are constantly doing, it may seem inequitable that the few whose negligence results in injury or loss to others should be required to bear this burden while the majority of negligent people go free. From this perspective, liability insurance, which spreads the burden of compensation amongst a pool of potential tortfeasors, may be seen not only as a means of ensuring that victims are compensated, but also as a way of reducing the injustice of the law's lack of attention to degrees of fault.

7.2   The compensation bears no relation to the means of the tortfeasor

In tort law, the tortfeasor's wealth or financial means are usually irrelevant to liability.[8] The fact that a tortfeasor is rich is no ground for imposing liability, and the fact that they are poor is no ground for not imposing liability. Most people would probably accept as morally right this principle of equality before the law regardless of wealth, which is implicit in the fault principle. But when we take into account the fact that once liability is imposed, the compensation payable will bear

7 Driver Behaviour Research Group, University of Manchester, *Influencing Driver Behaviour and Attitudes (No. 17)* (undated).
8 But, as we have seen (3.2.2.4), in some circumstances the wealth of the defendant can affect the standard of care required.

no relationship to the means of the tortfeasor, we may begin to doubt whether it really is fair to ignore their financial position. So, for example, a parent might feel morally obliged to pay a neighbour a few pounds for a window broken by their child; but it is doubtful whether parents would feel morally obliged to sell up house and home and impoverish themselves and their family if the child were to blind a neighbour's child with an airgun and were held liable for damages of tens or hundreds of thousands of pounds. A person who loses a book borrowed from a friend would not hesitate to pay for the book even if its loss was not the borrower's fault; but a person who borrows a friend's car may be very reluctant to pay out the whole value of the car if it was completely wrecked in an accident while they were driving it, and it turned out to be uninsured.

No criminal court would think of imposing a fine for culpable conduct of the amounts that civil courts award as damages every day, without serious inquiry into the ability of the defendant to pay.[9] The fact that tort law ignores the wrongdoer's means is justified by saying that the 'purpose' of the civil law is to compensate and not to punish. But the 'purpose' of the law is irrelevant to the tortfeasor who is made to pay the damages – what matters to them is the effect of the law, not its 'purpose'. So far as the wrongdoer is concerned, deprivation of money by the court is precisely as painful whether the 'purpose' is to punish the wrongdoer or to compensate the victim.

There are strong social grounds for not placing crushing legal liabilities on people of modest means. Most people would experience the utmost difficulty in paying a damages award of any appreciable size. The only asset of any real value that very many people own is the house in which they live – or, more accurately in most cases, the value of the house over and above the value of any mortgage secured by it. To impose a liability on a person which would require that person to dispose of their house (or to borrow large amounts of money using it as security) would plainly cause them and their family a great deal of dislocation and misery. Of course, the victim must not be forgotten, and as between a needy victim and a tortfeasor of limited means, justice may seem to favour the former. But it hardly seems fair or socially desirable to strip a person of everything because of what may have been a venial act of negligence. It is exactly for this reason that the law allows liability insurance, and without it the tort system could not operate effectively as a compensation mechanism. However, liability insurance conflicts with the rationale of the fault principle in that it relieves the faulty person of the burden of paying damages. Moreover, like tort damages themselves, liability insurance premiums are unrelated to the means of the insured.

Suppose the tortfeasor is not insured against the liability; if there is no way of compensating the victim except at the expense of someone who has caused the

9 In criminal law, the idea that monetary punishments should reflect the means of the offender is called 'the principle of equal impact'. It was embodied in the Criminal Justice Act 1991, ss. 18–21, but these provisions have since been repealed. See A. Ashworth, *Sentencing and Criminal Justice*, 3rd edn (London, 2000), 210–11.

injuries, we may well feel that justice is on the side of the victim even if the tortfea-sor has to sell up house and home to pay for the damages. Even in this situation, however, a case could be made for dropping damages for non-pecuniary loss. If the victim's economic losses are made good it would arguably be more harmful to society to require the tortfeasor personally to pay substantial damages for intangi-ble losses than it would be for the victim to forgo them.

7.3   A harm-doer may be held legally liable without being morally culpable and vice versa

As we will see later, the fault principle cannot be justified on practical grounds, such as convenience, efficiency, speed or cheapness of operation. The traditional justi-fication is that the legal concept of liability for fault embodies a moral principle to the effect that if a person, by blameworthy conduct, causes damage or loss to an innocent person, the former should compensate the latter for that damage or loss. But there are at least two grounds on which people have questioned whether tort law actually does embody such a moral principle. In the first place, it is said, if tort law was based on fault would it not prohibit liability insurance, vicarious liability and other loss distribution devices by which the burden of paying compensation can be shifted from a party at fault to another party not at fault?

7.3.1   Collective liability

Consider collective liability in this regard. As a moral concept, the idea of fault applies most straightforwardly to conduct of individuals. When it is argued that a company, or a local authority or some other organization or group was at fault, the moral content of the allegation may seem rather more attenuated. Suppose a claim is brought against a corporation for negligent failure to appreciate and guard against a danger in the workplace. Often, the real complaint is not that some particular indi-vidual was at fault, but that as a result of some failure of organization in the company, no individual had responsibility for anticipating and preventing the acci-dent that occurred. We might be perfectly happy to hold the company responsible even though we cannot point to any individual who was personally to blame. In *Carmarthenshire County Council* v. *Lewis*[10] a young child wandered out of a nursery school maintained by the council, down a lane, through a gate and on to a busy road, where a lorry driver, trying to avoid the child, crashed into a tree and was killed. The Court of Appeal held that the child's teacher was negligent in failing to keep a sufficient eye on him, but the House of Lords exonerated the teacher from the charge of negligence while still holding the defendants liable. 'They' (that is, the County Council) were negligent; 'they' should not have allowed an unlocked gate at the end of a lane near a nursery school bordering a busy road. But who actually was 'at fault'? Was it every councillor who ought to have proposed a resolution at a meeting of the

10   [1955] AC 549.

Council for the appointment of someone whose duty it was to prevent such accidents? Or the town clerk? Or the head-teacher of the school? And why hold the Council liable rather than the person(s) who ought to have taken precautions to prevent the accident?

If our purpose in asking such questions were to prevent similar occurrences in the future, we would have a strong incentive to try to find a responsible individual so that we could repair the defect in the organization's risk-management system. Similarly, if our purpose were to discipline or punish someone for what had happened, we would want to be able to identify the individual who should have taken steps to prevent the accident. But the main aim of a negligence action is to compensate injured persons; and so long as we are satisfied that appropriate precautions ought to have been taken within the organization to prevent the harm, there is no good reason not to impose liability to pay compensation on the organization, even though there is an obvious sense in which the (moral) fault must have lain with individuals within the organization rather than the organization as such.[11] Traditionally, the law has been much less willing to impose criminal liability on organizations than to impose civil liability, partly at least because organizations were thought incapable of the sort of (morally) culpable conduct that justifies criminal punishment. But when it comes to civil liability to compensate for harm, the law has, for centuries, had no qualms about organizational liability. In this respect, it reflects attitudes and values held widely in the community at large. For this reason, to say that tort law sometimes imposes liability in the absence of fault is not a criticism but only an observation.

7.3.2   The objective definition of fault

A second ground on which tort law's adherence to a moral principle of responsibility for fault has been questioned is this: if the law really reflected morality, it would not adopt an objective definition of fault which, on the whole, ignores the personal qualities of the persons involved and which does not require that the harm-doer should have had any consciousness of moral wrongdoing, or even of the risk they were creating or of the dangerousness of their conduct.[12]

Negligence, as we have seen, is defined as the failure to take reasonable care; that is, the care which the reasonable person would have taken to avoid risks which the reasonable person would have guarded against. It does not matter that the injurer is not a 'reasonable person' but is clumsy or stupid or forgetful or has bad judgment. It does not matter that the injurer is inexperienced or young or old or (probably)

---

11 See also *Cassidy* v. *Ministry of Health* [1951] 2 KB 343.

12 As explained in the sixth edn, my views on this topic have developed and changed. However, because I still agree with the basic thrust of what follows, and because to take matters further would launch the discussion into deep philosophical waters, I have decided again to leave this section largely untouched. My current views can be found in 'Retribution, Proportionality and Moral Luck in Tort Law' in P. Cane and J. Stapleton eds., *The Law of Obligations: Essays in Celebration of John Fleming* (Oxford, 1998); *The Anatomy of Tort Law* (Oxford, 1997), ch. 7; and *Responsibility in Law and Morality* (Oxford, 2002), ch. 3.

even that they are handicapped or disabled. It does not generally matter that the injurer could not personally have foreseen the risk or avoided the accident. Even those who have wholeheartedly supported the principle of 'no liability without fault' have also subscribed wholeheartedly to the objective definition of fault. A reason often given for this approach is that the injury inflicted is the same whether the injurer could or could not personally have avoided the accident. So, for instance, Mr Justice Holmes declared, in a celebrated passage:[13]

> If for instance, a man is born hasty and awkward, is always having accidents and hurting himself or his neighbours, no doubt his congenital defects will be allowed for in the courts of Heaven, but his slips are no less troublesome to his neighbours than if they sprang from guilty neglect. His neighbours accordingly require him, at his proper peril, to come up to their standard, and the courts which they establish decline to take his personal equation into account.

This is a weak argument because it does not go far enough: the damage or injury is the same whether or not there has been fault at all, even as objectively defined by the law. If the reason for adopting an objective standard of fault is that when damage is done the victim has been hurt and deserves to be compensated whether or not there has been subjective fault, it is hard to see why it does not also follow that an injured person should be compensated whether or not there is fault at all, whether objectively or subjectively judged.

A different approach would be to argue that the law's objective definition of fault is not actually out of line with morality at all. Morality does not always acquit a person of blame for acts traceable to defects of personality or capacity. If an adult[14] behaves badly as a result of stupidity or forgetfulness or bad judgment, we would not necessarily hold that person morally blameless. We might say that they should try harder next time or that they should not put themselves in situations in which their personality faults are likely to produce adverse outcomes. If a person suffers from some physical disability about which nothing can be done, we would not normally[15] blame them for accidents resulting from that disability, but we might well blame them for putting themselves in situations where their disability might cause accidents.[16] A blind person is not to be blamed for being blind, but could be blamed for attempting to drive a car on a public road and for any accident resulting from the attempt. On the other hand, if a person is suddenly and unexpectedly overtaken by a physical disability (e.g. if a person has a heart attack while driving) and as a result

---

13 *The Common Law,* Holmes's most famous extra-judicial writing, was originally published in 1881. This passage can be found at pp. 86–7 of the edition edited by M. DeW. Howe (Boston, 1963).

14 Children must be given time to develop physical skills and a sense of moral responsibility before being subjected to the full rigours of our moral code. The law, too, treats young children more leniently than adolescents and adults: *McHale* v. *Watson* (1964) 111 CLR 384.

15 But it would be different if the disability was self-inflicted as a result e.g. of consumption of alcohol or drugs.

16 See *Jones* v. *Dennison* [1971] RTR 174.

causes an accident, we would not call that person morally blameworthy; nor would he or she be legally liable for negligence.[17]

It would appear, therefore, that a dichotomy between objective legal fault and subjective moral fault is too simple.[18] The gap between law and morality is not as great as might at first appear. However, there are some areas in which the gulf seems quite wide. The most obvious is the way the law deals with lack of skill resulting from inexperience. In general, the inexperienced driver, for instance, is held to the same standard of care as the experienced, even though it is clear that inexperienced drivers *as a group* cause more accidents than experienced drivers.[19] But drivers must learn to drive somewhere, and they must acquire experience of driving on the roads amidst traffic; to expect inexperienced drivers as a group to display the same skill and judgment as experienced drivers does seem morally unfair. The courts have, in several cases, also taken a harsh approach to accidents caused by mental impairment that the injurer could do nothing about.[20]

But even if the law is out of step with morality, it does not follow that this is a bad thing. If we think of the law as designed to regulate the conduct of people to whom it is addressed, it does indeed seem unreasonable to treat as negligence something which a person could not avoid. On the other hand, if we think that the main purpose of the law is to compensate injured persons, there is no reason why moral fault should be the criterion of liability to pay compensation. Indeed, if this is our aim, the criterion of whether a person is entitled to compensation ought to be whether they have been injured, regardless of how they were injured. From this point of view, the chief shortcoming of the tort system is not that it sometimes compensates people whose injuries were not the result of moral fault, but that it fails to compensate very many other people who have suffered injuries in circumstances that do not fall within the tort system at all.

7.3.3   Moral culpability without legal liability

So far we have been discussing cases of legal liability that may not involve moral culpability. The converse – where a person may be morally blameworthy without having committed a legal wrong – is less likely; but there is one sort of case which does raise the possibility, namely where a person has been guilty of an omission. We have already discussed liability for omissions (3.2.2), and it remains only to notice

---

17 *Waugh v. James Allan Ltd* [1964] 2 Lloyd's Reports 1.
18 The main point can be put starkly by saying that ability to comply with morality, as much ability to comply with the law, may be a matter of luck.
19 One survey showed that 6.8% of drivers with over 5 years' experience were involved in single-vehicle accidents (i.e. those least likely to be the result of the fault of anybody else), while 19.4% of drivers with less than 6 months' experience were involved in such accidents: Ministry of Transport, *How Fast?* (HMSO, 1968), para. 77. See also TRRL Laboratory Report 567 (1973). It has been estimated that motor cyclists have twice as many accidents in their first 6 months as drivers as they cause in their second 6 months: Austin, *Accident-Black Spot*, 60.
20 E.g. *Adamson v. Motor Vehicle Insurance Trust* (1957) 58 WALR 56; *Roberts v. Ramsbottom* [1980] 1 WLR 823.

here that this is one further difficulty in the way of equating legal liability with moral fault.

7.3.4   The fault principle and popular morality

Criticisms of tort law based on its divergence from moral principles assume that there is a clear distinction between law and morality, and that morality provides the proper standard for judging the law. However, there is a certain amount of empirical evidence that casts doubt on these assumptions. Research[21] has shown that personal injury victims do not always think that being responsible for an accident entails moral culpability, or that either of these entails an obligation to pay compensation; nor, conversely, that absence of moral responsibility entails absence of an obligation to pay damages. It seems that whether an injured person thinks that someone else should pay depends much more on what he or she knows (or is told) of what the law says about when compensation is payable than on independent ideas of morality and fault. So, for example, in the industrial context where employers have for a long time been subject to liability in certain circumstances regardless of fault, injured workers are quite likely to think that their employer ought to pay, without basing that judgment on an attribution of fault.

In relation to accidents in the home, it seems that injured persons are very unlikely to attribute fault and even less likely to think that they ought to be compensated. It is arguable that this has little to do with morality and more to do with a desire not to disrupt harmonious domestic relations by the aggressive act of litigating; and perhaps with a realization that since the party responsible will rarely be insured, litigation would be pointless. In brief, it may well be that for many victims of personal injury, thinking that someone is (morally) responsible for injuries is neither a sufficient nor a necessary condition for thinking that the person ought to pay compensation for the injuries.

It does not follow from this that the fault principle is not defensible as a principle, but only that it may not be defensible on the ground that it is based on popular conceptions of who ought to pay.

7.4   The fault principle pays little attention to the conduct or needs of the victim

If no-one can be identified as being to some extent at fault for the victim's injury or loss, no compensation will be available under the fault principle. In this event, it is immaterial whether the claimant was injured while in a drunken stupor; was driving a car with a slight degree of negligence; was indulging in some perfectly

---

21 S. Lloyd-Bostock, 'Fault and Liability for Accidents: the Accident Victim's Perspective' in Harris 1984 Survey. See also by the same author, 'Propensity to Sue in England and the United States of America: The Role of Attribution Processes' (1991) 18 *J. of Law and Society* 428 in answer to H.M. Kritzer, 'Propensity to Sue in England and the United States of America: Blaming and Claiming in Tort Cases', ibid., 400.

ordinary activity with all due care; or was engaged in an heroic attempt at rescuing someone in great peril, at risk to their own life. On the other hand, where, for instance, a person has been killed in an heroic attempt to rescue another, judges will make every effort to find someone at fault if they possibly can. Conversely, a person injured as a result of a piece of utter folly on their own part would find a judge somewhat unreceptive to the argument that another person was partly responsible for their injuries.[22] But when courts take account of the victim's conduct in this way, they often do so in spite of the fault principle and not because of it.

It is also true, of course, that where a negligent party can be found, the law does pay some attention to fault on the part of the injured person. We have seen before how the treatment of contributory negligence as a relative doctrine requires comparison of the injured person's degree of fault with the injurer's; and how this leads to results which, however justifiable as between injured and injurer, appear indefensible in a wider context. Though it may be justifiable in terms of the fault principle to refuse compensation to a wholly innocent victim because they were injured without fault on the part of anyone else, while giving part compensation to another victim, who may have been 80% to blame for their own injuries, because someone else was partly to blame, it seems quite inequitable in light of the fact that in most cases of fault it is not the injurer who will pay but an insurer and, ultimately, the public at large. Why should fault on the part of the injurer be a precondition of an award of compensation when it is not the injurer who will pay the compensation?

Popular sentiment is much more sensitive than the law to the perceived merits of victims of injury or disability. We are generous to rescuers regardless of whether the rescue was precipitated by someone's fault. We are much more prepared to help people who suffer injury through no fault of their own than people who bring misfortune upon themselves, regardless of whether anyone else was to blame. It would, in theory, be possible to construct a compensation system based on the fault of the injured person alone, if that were felt to be desirable. A claim against a compensation fund could be admitted wherever a person was injured without fault on their part, even if no other person at fault could be found; and reduced compensation could be given to an injured person who was partly to blame, if that was felt to be just. This would also be a 'fault' system, and perhaps a more fair system (though it would be open to similar objections as the present doctrine of contributory negligence).[23] But it is not the fault system we have now.

In addition to paying little attention to the injured person's conduct, the fault principle largely ignores the injured person's needs – just as it ignores the injurer's capacity to pay. Here again, this may be just as between injured and injurer, although even this is open to doubt in some cases. For example, it is by no means obvious that justice requires a working person to provide an annuity for a young, healthy and

22 E.g. *ICI* v. *Shatwell* [1965] AC 656.
23 2.5.1.

childless widow whose husband they have killed (say) by negligent driving.[24] But even if this is thought to be just, our opinion might change if it was not the injurer personally who was to pay the damages. As between the widow and the public, it seems difficult to say that justice requires compensation for the death of the husband without considering the widow's needs.

7.5   Justice may require payment of compensation without fault

Neither in law nor in morality is fault the only ground on which a person may be required to compensate another. For example, where a person has been overpaid by mistake, both morality and the law (of restitution, not tort) say that the over-payment should be returned. No question of fault arises in this sort of case, but we require repayment because otherwise the recipient would be 'unjustly enriched' at the expense of the payer. This sort of argument for liability without fault may at first sight appear to have little place in the field of accidental damage to person or property, because in such circumstances there is rarely any 'gain' in an obvious or tangible sense to the harm-doer. But this depends on what we mean by 'gain'. Let us look for a moment at a leading US case in the law of torts, *Vincent* v. *Lake Erie Transportation Co.*,[25] which illustrates the struggle between the principle of no-liability-without-fault and other grounds for requiring compensation to be paid.

In this case the claimants were the owners of a dock in which the defendant shipowner's vessel was anchored. A storm was threatening and both parties were anxious for the safety of their property. The defendant was requested to remove the ship, but the shipowner declined to do so for fear that damage would be done to it in the storm. The result was that the vessel remained at anchor, and in the ensuing storm it was repeatedly hurled against the dock, and the dock was damaged. The question was whether the claimants were entitled to compensation for the damage. The court conceded that perhaps the shipowner would not be considered morally culpable or blameworthy. A person whose property is in jeopardy may not be thought of as acting wrongly by trying save it, even at the expense of creating a risk of loss to someone else. However, the court said in *Vincent*, even though we might not morally blame a person who chooses to save their own property at the expense of risk to someone else's property, we might nevertheless think the former ought to pay for the privilege thereby enjoyed. Even if life and not just property had been at stake, would fairness not require compensation to be paid?

The idea that compensation ought to be paid even though the person paying it is not morally culpable is well established in public law contexts. For example, if a government authority compulsorily acquires private land in order to build a road or a school, few would regard this as in any way morally reprehensible (assuming, for the sake of the argument, that the power to acquire has been exercised wisely and

24 6.1.2.
25 (1910) 124 NW 221.

reasonably), but most people would think it only fair that the deprived landowner should be paid compensation for loss of the land. The payment of such compensation is usually provided for by statute. The idea that it can be fair to require compensation to be paid even in the absence of wrongful conduct plays very little part in private law. Even the principle of *Vincent* would probably not be applied in England.[26] But why should it not be applied?

Admittedly, in cases of negligence we cannot usually say that the injurer has been unjustly enriched at the expense of the injured.[27] But we may be able to say, as in *Vincent*, that the injurer has 'gained', or furthered their own ends, by taking a risk at the expense of the injured person. For example, in *Bolton* v. *Stone*[28] the House of Lords held that the cricket club had not acted unreasonably in not building a higher fence around their ground, because the risk of a ball escaping and injuring someone was very remote. Thus the club benefited by not having to spend money on a higher fence, but at the cost of a risk of injury to the claimant and others. In such circumstances one might think that it would be fair for the club to pay compensation to the person injured by the escaping ball, even though their actions were not negligent. Or take the case of the installation by British Railways of automatic half-barrier level crossings, which was the subject of investigation at the Public Inquiry into the Hixon crossing rail crash.[29] The inquiry found that these half barriers were not as safe as the supervised gates they replaced.[30] The reason for installing the new barriers, despite this finding, was that they saved time and money. British Railways estimated that they would save £2 million a year by installing automatic barriers at all level crossings; and such barriers were much quicker in their operation than the old ones, thus reducing delays to people using the crossings. So, the installation of the barriers benefited certain people but created risks of injury for others. If the benefits are thought to outweigh the disadvantages, it seems only fair that those who benefit should compensate those who are injured, regardless of whether installation of the barriers was in some sense negligent or blameworthy.

The point becomes even clearer when the impact of insurance is taken into account. In a situation such as that in *Bolton* v. *Stone*, for example, the law would not require the club to build a fence even if it was held liable for escaping balls. It would be open to the club simply to insure against the risk of liability and, except in cases where the risk of balls escaping was quite high,[31] this course would usually be cheaper than building a new fence. Once the issue is reduced to terms of who should insure against a particular risk, it seems clear that it might be fair for a person to do so even if that person was not at fault in creating the risk.

---

26 See further P. Cane, *Tort Law and Economic Interests*, 2nd edn (Oxford, 1996), 224–7.

27 But see ibid., 324.

28 [1951] AC 850.

29 Cmnd 3706 (1968). See also 2.4.2.

30 Later research found otherwise: *Level Crossing Protection* (HMSO, 1978), para. 10.10. See also *Railway Safety 1983* (HMSO, 1984), para. 50; *Railway Safety 1991/2* (HMSO), table 6.

31 As, perhaps, in *Miller* v. *Jackson* [1977] QB 966.

7.6   It is often difficult to adjudicate allegations of fault

So far we have considered suggested ethical objections to the fault principle. Its value can also be doubted on the basis of the practical difficulties to which adjudication on fault gives rise. There are three distinguishable problems. The first arises out of the nature of the legal test of fault; the second out of problems of proof; and the third from concentrating too much on one specific cause to the exclusion of statistical and other evidence about accidents of the kind in question.

Looking at the first problem, the essence of the legal concept of fault is unreasonable failure to take precautions. This concept is both abstract and fact-dependent. As a result, it may be difficult for a person to determine what they must do in order to meet the standard of reasonableness. This has serious implications for the utility of the concept of fault as a guide to conduct.[32] The nature of the negligence test may also affect the settlement of tort claims. There is, for instance, evidence in relation to medical injuries that claims may succeed in the absence of negligence and fail despite its presence.[33]

Turning to the second problem, in the case of many accidents, the events that cause the injury occur in a very brief period of time, often in a fraction of a second. Adjudication on the fault issue requires witnesses to be able accurately to recall what occurred in that fraction of a second if we are to have any confidence that the findings of fact made by a court correspond with what actually happened. Similarly, if a case is settled by negotiation, the parties' advisers need to be able to assess with reasonable confidence the likelihood that a court will find fault on the basis of the evidence of the witnesses. The unreliability of observations of eyewitnesses (even highly trained and experienced ones) has often been demonstrated by experiment. To the inaccuracies of observation must be added the difficulties of recall produced by the considerable period that often elapses between the time of the accident and the time when witnesses are asked to give an account of what happened; and also the fact that people do not always tell the truth. If, as a result of such defects, the version of some witnesses conflicts with that of others, what chance does the court have of reaching a correct conclusion? In addition to all this, we must not forget that in a not-insubstantial number of cases, suitable evidence is simply unavailable at all, and 'real' evidence (i.e. objects) may disappear.[34] Different, but equally difficult, problems may arise in proving fault in cases of illness or disease as opposed to traumatic accident.[35]

Other serious problems arise out of the need to prove that the injurer's fault caused the victim's loss. This may be difficult in the case of accidents that happen

---

32 See further 17.7.1.1.

33 M.M. Mello and T.A. Brennan, 'Deterrence of Medical Errors: Theory and Evidence for Malpractice Reform' (2002) 80 *Texas LR* 1595, 1618–20.

34 The courts can make orders to facilitate the preservation of evidence (see Civil Procedure Act 1997, s. 7), but the time taken to obtain such an order may deprive the power of much practical use in many cases.

35 J. Stapleton, *Disease and the Compensation Debate* (Oxford, 1986), ch. 4.

in a moment, for all the reasons we have just mentioned. Problems of proving causation also arise acutely in cases of medical negligence, for instance, and in cases where it is alleged that a person has become ill or contracted some disease as a result of exposure to some chemical or the taking of some drug.[36] Our knowledge of the way many diseases and illnesses come about is inadequate, and this fact may present an impenetrable barrier to much tort litigation. Of course, this problem is not unique to the fault-based tort system, but is shared by any compensation system in which entitlement depends on proving the cause of loss. But all of these problems of proof do suggest that fault, at least, is not a satisfactory criterion of entitlement to compensation. And if this is true of cases tried by a court, how much more is it likely to be true of cases settled by negotiation. Insurance companies frequently have only the witnesses' statements to go by, and one experienced senior barrister once said that 'more often than not' the evidence a witness gives in court differs substantially from that in pre-trial statements.[37] Moreover, such difficulties of proof mean that the process of deciding what caused an accident and who was at fault is extremely expensive and time-consuming in many cases. Several surveys have found that difficulties of proof are one of the major reasons why people either abandon tort claims or do not make them in the first place.[38]

Concerning the third problem, it may be true, despite the above difficulties, that if we concentrate exclusively on the behaviour of the principal parties involved in an accident, we can, in a reasonable proportion of cases, arrive at a workable conclusion on fault and causation. However, this exercise may often be misleading because it omits to take account of factors that would not always, or indeed often, be thought to be responsible for accidents. Statistical investigation of the causes of accidents generally, as opposed to legal investigation of the causes of individual accidents, often throws an entirely different light on matters. The point is well put in the following extract from a volume on road safety published in 1963:[39]

> The statistician does not think so much of the individual accident and its causes, but of the probability of accidents and whatever may affect this probability. Now such things as the width of a street, its curvature or gradient, the quality of its surface, the flow of traffic and its speed, all influence the probability of an accident in a street. Such things, since they influence the probability of accidents and therefore the number of accidents, should appear in the statistical picture of factors important in accident causation . . .

36 Ibid., ch. 3.
37 C.P. Harvey, *The Advocate's Devil* (London, 1958), 67.
38 E.g. Harris 1984 Survey, tables 2.12, 3.12; S.B. Burman, H.G. Genn and J. Lyons, 'The Use of Legal Services by Victims of Accidents in the Home: A Pilot Study' (1977) 40 *Modern LR* 47, 57.
39 *Research on Road Safety* (HMSO, 1963), 3–4; see also J.J. Leeming, *Road Accidents: Prevent or Punish?* (London, 1969); J. Reason, *Human Error* (Cambridge, 1990), ch. 7; J. Mosedale, A. Purdy and E. Clarkson, *Contributory Factors to Road Accidents* (Department of Transport, 2004). An interesting example of this phenomenon is the road accident in which Princess Diana died. At first, this was attributed to the conduct of the driver of the car and of certain paparazzi. However, it was later pointed out that a major factor contributing to the seriousness of the accident was the fact that the central columns in the tunnel were unprotected by any sort of guard rail.

When individual accidents are studied and 'causes' sought it is not, in general, these factors that will be cited. Then only the unusual or abnormal are usually noticed: not the width of the road but only whether it narrows suddenly, not the visibility allowed by the size and shape of the car's windows but only the obstruction caused by pennants or a dangling doll. Ignoring the normal gives rise to a tendency to ascribe most accidents to human factors such as error or carelessness, since it is usually possible to believe that there would have been no such accident if someone had acted differently.

This is not to say that driver 'error' is never the cause of road accidents. Indeed, the Pearson Commission noted research which suggested that as many as 65% of road accidents were the result of human error alone.[40] Nor do statistics by themselves prove what caused any particular accident. On the other hand, statistical information about the causes of particular types of accidents may alert us to factors, other than the conduct of those involved in the accident, which might have caused or contributed to it. The more we appreciate the significance of factors other than driver behaviour in the cause of road accidents, the less does the almost exclusive concentration of the tort system on driver conduct make sense.

For example, as a result of research it is now known that skidding accidents can be greatly reduced by altering the surface of the roads. One survey compared fifty-five skidding accident sites with an average length of a quarter of a mile before and after the sites were treated with a non-skid surface.[41] The treatment produced a dramatic reduction in the number of accidents at those sites. Who, then, was primarily to blame for the accidents that occurred before the sites were treated?[42] And suppose that lack of funds had held up treatment of other sites and skidding accidents had continued to occur there, who would be to blame for them? Suppose that a local authority prefers to spend its income on building a new school rather than treating skid-prone sites, who would be to blame for the accidents that would inevitably occur? Or indeed, suppose that it is simply not appreciated that the road surface is contributing to accidents so substantially. Consider also the case of the motorist who tries to reduce speed on approaching a roundabout, skids and crashes into a bollard in the centre of the road. If this case ever came into court the motorist would almost certainly be found entirely responsible for causing the accident by negligence. Yet this sort of accident is so common at some roundabouts that it has been found cheaper to treat the road with a non-skid surface than to replace the bollards every time they are damaged. If this is not done, who is more at fault, the motorist or the highway authority?

40 Pearson Report, vol. 2, table 42. Similarly, it has been said that driver behaviour (as opposed to barrier design) is an important cause of level-crossing accidents: Health and Safety Executive, *Railway Safety 1991/2* (HMSO, 1992). See also Robens Committee Report, paras. 30–1.
41 *Research on Road Safety* (HMSO, 1963), 498.
42 Leeming, *Road Accidents: Prevent or Punish?*, argues that the law was itself a factor in preventing earlier recognition by highway engineers of the importance of surface type in skidding accidents, because it encouraged highway authorities to think that skidding accidents were simply the fault of drivers and to ignore the need for accident prevention measures not directed at motorists.

Many other illustrations could be given. A motorist crashes into the car in front while driving at night, although that car has its lights on. Who is to blame? Evidently the driver of the rear car. But suppose we discover that cars as old as the front vehicle are six times as likely as other cars to be involved in accidents of this kind because their lights are less satisfactory: would we still so confidently say that the driver of the rear car was to blame? A motorist fails to see, or understand the meaning of a road sign, and an accident ensues. Who is to blame? Obviously the motorist. But is it still so obvious when we know that many motorists, even when under observation and consciously trying to be at their most attentive, still fail to observe some road signs?[43] Or when we know that only a small fraction of motorists know what some signs mean?[44]

There are still wider considerations that emerge from statistics. A child, playing ball with another child in the street, is run over and killed. Whose fault is it? Plainly the child's own fault. But when we know that children who come from poor homes and have nowhere to play are more likely to be involved in road accidents than other children, are we still so confident of our conclusion?[45] Do we not begin to think that the organization of society may have some responsibility in the matter?

Research into the causes of road accidents shows that some accidents (and some injuries) can be prevented more easily by improved road engineering and improved vehicle design[46] than by punishing or deterring bad drivers or exhorting them to drive more safely.[47] If society chooses to spend its money on other things

---

43 See Austin, *Accident Black Spot*, 138. Leeming, *Road Accident: Prevent or Punish?*, 64–8 gives an example of a road junction which was the scene of many accidents. More than one hundred motorists were prosecuted and fined for failing to stop etc., before it was realized that the layout of the junction was such that motorists were unable to see the 'Stop' line in the road until it was too late.

44 TRRL Laboratory Report 91.

45 *Research on Road Safety* (1963), 57; N. Christie, 'Social, economic and environmental factors in child pedestrian accidents: a research review' Transport Research Laboratory (TRL), Project Report 116 (1995) (this report also reviews empirical research which supports the imposition of lower standards of care on children on the basis of developmental limitations); N. Christie, 'The high risk child pedestrian: socio-economic and environmental factors in their accidents' TRL Project Report 117 (1995).

46 The obvious example is the introduction of seat belts: TRRL Report RR 239 (1989). One writer claims that in the USA, where product liability claims by road accident victims against vehicle manufacturers are quite common, only one out of every 320 victims of disabling injuries on the road makes a serious claim against a vehicle manufacturer: G.T. Schwartz, 'The Beginning and the Possible End of the Rise of Modern American Tort Law' (1992) 26 *Georgia LR* 601, 633. On the other hand, a very significant proportion of product liability claims in the USA are made by employees injured at work who, under workers' compensation laws, are not allowed to sue their employers in negligence. This contrast tells us nothing about the causal relevance of product defects in the two contexts; it only tells us that in the road context, there is no great incentive to sue a manufacturer because motorists make much easier targets.

47 It has also been suggested that product and environmental design is a more efficient way of reducing the frequency of home and leisure accidents. Despite the fact that personal and social factors (such as illness or a stressful family environment) play a very important part in the causation of many such accidents, it is thought that education and publicity are less effective than safe product and environment design at avoiding accidents: Department of Trade and Industry, *Personal Factors in Domestic Accidents: Prevention through Product and Environmental Design* (1983).

than improved roads, is the 'negligent' motorist, rather than society as a whole, really responsible for accidents? So far as vehicle design is concerned, the motor manufacturer bears the primary responsibility; but society as a whole cannot escape all responsibility. Safer cars are, typically, more expensive cars, and for this reason alone manufacturers are unlikely to be willing to produce safer cars unless car buyers are willing to pay more for them.

The fact that in the road accident field the fault system has hitherto been directed almost exclusively at motorists does not mean that it may not in the future be used against motor manufacturers – and highway authorities as well: the Highways (Miscellaneous Provisions) Act 1961, which abolished the immunity of highway authorities from liability for nonfeasance, removed a major legal obstacle in the way of suing them for negligence in respect of road accidents (although this has not resulted in much litigation).

But all this makes little difference to the central point. Certainly, the fault system could be a lot less crude; certainly, we could start bringing negligent design within its scope; and in the result we might even succeed in shifting (at least in the first instance) quite a lot of the cost of road accidents to motor manufacturers and highway authorities. But the central point we have been making is that the fault principle leads us to seize on a limited number of relatively obvious accident-causing factors, and to blame the party responsible for these as having been 'negligent'. This whole process looks a lot less rational when we move away from the particular accident in question and survey the whole field. From this new vantage point, many accident victims who go uncompensated because there does not appear to have been any responsible negligent individual, may be thought to have a good claim against society. And even if we cannot say that society is in any meaningful sense 'at fault', we might still want to say that since road accidents are a cost of living in a mobile society, that cost ought to be borne by society at large and not by the individuals who suffer on the roads. Furthermore, the issues raised in this section become much more acute when we turn our attention to illness and disease. In this context, we are much more alive to the possibility that personal injury may have a number of concurrent causes; that none, one or some of these causes may be faulty human conduct; and that we know very little about the causation of many diseases. As a result, we more easily recognize that the fault-based tort system is an extremely poor mechanism for deciding which victims of illness and disease deserve compensation.

More generally, the fact that many accidents and diseases are not the result of the fault of any identifiable individual does not mean that the victims of such accidents and diseases do not deserve compensation; and the fact that many accidents and diseases are not, in any meaningful sense, anyone's fault but are the result of perfectly legitimate choices between conflicting goals, does not mean that the victims of such accidents and diseases do not deserve compensation. Even if we accept that fault is a suitable criterion of entitlement to compensation, we may not accept that it is the only suitable criterion.

7.7   The fault principle contributes to a culture of blaming and discourages people from taking responsibility for their own lives

Finally, let us consider a criticism of the fault principle from a social point of view. Some people disparagingly say that we now live in a 'blame culture'[48] or a 'compensation culture'.[49] By this they seem to mean that when things go wrong, people tend to look for someone else to blame rather than entertaining the thought that they themselves ought to take responsibility for what happened to them or just accepting the misfortune as 'one of those things'. Increasingly, too, so it is said, people go beyond blaming to complaining to some official or body, or even claiming in tort or on some other legal basis. In Britain, at least, the development of the 'blame culture' may be associated with major shifts in economic and social policy that have occurred in the last 30 years. In the heyday of the Welfare State in the 1960s and 1970s, people spoke of the 'dependency culture'. The idea was that being able and even encouraged to look to the state to deal with misfortunes made people dependent and sapped their personal initiative. New emphasis in the 1980s and 1990s on the individual was designed in part to wean people off dependence on the state and on to self-reliance. But things have gone rather wrong. For many, so the argument might run, individualism has come to mean not self-reliance in the face of adversity, but the assumption that some other individual must be to blame for one's misfortunes. The focus is not on the individual's *responsibility* for themselves but on the individual's *rights* against others. Atiyah argues that the courts have contributed to this regrettable development by 'stretching the law' in various ways in favour of the injured[50] to the point where it is possible to recover large awards of compensation for injuries from people who are not, in any real sense, to blame for those injuries.

In evaluating the validity of such concerns in relation to liability for personal injuries and death in particular, we need to distinguish between growth in the number of tort claims, and growth in the amounts paid out in tort compensation. Consider, first, the number of tort claims for personal injury and death. As we will see (8.1.4), the Pearson Commission estimated that there were about 250,000 tort claims a year in the early to mid-1970s, of which perhaps 215,000 resulted in the payment of some compensation. A review in the late 1980s estimated that the annual number of tort claims had increased to about 340,000. Reliable statistics show that there are now some 750,000 successful tort claims each year. So even if we assume that the earlier figures were under-estimates, we can say with some confidence that the number of successful tort claims has increased about threefold in the past 30 years

---

48 A major statement of this position is P.S. Atiyah, *The Damages Lottery* (Oxford, 1997). The argument was pithily put by Lord Templeman when he said, 'People now look for someone to blame, anybody but themselves, whereas many accidents are purely bad luck': *The Times*, 20 June 1995.

49 See e.g. F. Furedi, *Courting Mistrust: The Hidden Growth of a Culture of Litigation in Britain* (London, 1999); Institute of Actuaries, *The Cost of Compensation Culture* (London, 2002); Aon Ltd, *Compensation and Blame Culture: Reality or Myth?* (London, 2004).

50 Atiyah, *The Damages Lottery*, chs. 2 and 3.

or so. But this ball-park figure masks some significant details. For instance, it appears that the number of medical negligence claims has increased about seventeen times since the 1970s, while the number of public liability (occupier's liability) claims may have increased eight times. However, these figures are apt to mislead unless attention is also paid to the relative numbers of claims of various types. According to the Pearson Commission, the largest single group of claims (about 47%) arose out of workplace injuries and diseases. Road-accident claims came second at about 41%. Public liability claims represented only about 5% of the total, and medical negligence claims considerably less than 1%. The latest figures present a rather different picture. More than half of all successful tort claims today arise out of road accidents. Workplace claims now represent only about 30% of claims, while public liability claims come in at around 12%. Despite large growth in the absolute numbers of medical negligence claims, they still represent only about 1% of the total. Although certain types of claims – for instance, those arising out of the side-effects of drugs – often attract a great deal of media attention and potentially, at least, test the limits of tort liability, they represent a vanishingly small proportion of successful tort claims.

In my opinion, even if it is true that courts have 'stretched' the rules of tort liability in the past 30 years in favour of claimants, this cannot explain the greatly increased volume and changed pattern of tort claiming over that period. This is not to say that there have been no significant pro-claimant changes in tort law in recent years. The decision of the House of Lords in the mesothelioma case of *Fairchild* (5.2.2) is an obvious example of such a development – although its impact on the total number of tort claims is likely to be relatively small. However, the basic rules of tort law, as they apply to the vast bulk of road accident, employer's liability, occupier's liability and medical negligence claims, have not changed significantly since the 1970s. It may be that courts have become more 'pro-claimant' in the way they apply the rules, and that this has affected settlement practice; but it seems highly unlikely that such a change in the practice of courts and insurance companies could have played more than a minor role in generating a threefold increase in successful tort claims in three decades.[51] Moreover, the fact that the relative number of employer's liability claims has fallen significantly should alert us to the possible relevance of non-legal factors in explaining changing patterns of tort claiming – in this case, perhaps, the rapid decline of high-risk manufacturing industry (such as coal-mining) and growth in the service sector (where rates of injury and illness are much lower), as well as improved safety standards and practices in the workplace.

So how might we explain the tripling of tort claiming since the 1970s? Probably significant have been changes in the legal services market. In the 1970s qualified lawyers were, effectively, the only providers of what are now called 'claims management services'. There were few, if any, specialist personal injury lawyers,

---

51 The 'stretching the law' argument seems to imply that some types of negligence claims that would certainly have failed in the 1970s can succeed in 2006. This may be true, but it seems unlikely that a significant proportion of the main categories of successful tort claims are of such types.

certainly amongst solicitors; and lawyers did not advertise their services. Specialist personal injury law firms representing claimants began to emerge in the 1980s, and some are now very large. The Association of Personal Injury Lawyers represents and promotes the interests of personal injury lawyers (who, in the USA, are called 'plaintiff's lawyers'), and even publishes its own journal – the *Journal of Personal Injury Law*. Today, qualified lawyers are not the only providers of claims management services. It is estimated that there are some 400 claims management companies (CMCs) (10.2) handling around 500,000 claims (including tort claims) each year. Claims management services are now widely advertised, especially on TV. Such advertising, and increased media coverage of the tort system, have probably raised significantly public awareness of the possibility of claiming damages for personal injury as well as expectations about the chances of success of such claims.[52]

More speculatively, increased claiming is perhaps one aspect of a larger social development that might be described as 'the rights culture', reflected most obviously in the Human Rights Act 1998 (HRA 1998), which gives force in English law to the European Convention on Human Rights (ECHR). The enactment of the HRA 1998 was the culmination of a political process that began in the late 1980s. In the 1990s the Conservative government's Citizens' Charter also played an important part in creating a social environment in which complaining and claiming was encouraged and became accepted as an appropriate response to individuals' grievances. The rights culture is built on a strong concept of individual entitlement. Courts and legal processes play a central role in vindicating such entitlements; and in 3.1 we saw that the ECtHR has already had an impact on negligence law, causing English courts to modify their techniques for limiting the scope of liability. In such circumstances it should not, perhaps, surprise us that people have had increasing recourse to tort law and the tort system.

My tentative conclusion, therefore, is that factors other than 'stretching' of the rules of tort liability provide the best explanations of increased tort claiming, especially in the past 20 years.

Turning to growth in the amounts paid out in tort compensation, the Pearson Commission estimated that annually some £202 million was paid out in tort compensation at an administrative cost of some £175 million. Making allowance for inflation, these amounts would respectively be around £800 million and £700 million in today's money. On the basis of a threefold increase in claims, we might estimate that the cost of the tort system today would be in the region of £4.5 billion per annum. However, various contemporary estimates (or guesstimates) are considerably higher than this, ranging from £7.2 billion[53] to as high as

---

52 For recent research about the link between advertising and perceptions of the tort system see Department for Constitutional Affairs, *Effects of Advertising in Respect of Compensation Claims for Personal Injuries* (March 2006).

53 Compensation Bill Final Regulatory Impact Assessment (2005), para. 21. This figure relates to 2004.

£14 billion. Let us suppose for the sake of argument that the cost of the tort system has almost doubled in real terms (i.e. over and above what would be expected given inflation and the increase in the number of successful claims) since the 1970s. How might we account for such an increase? Advances in medical technology have probably played an important part. Although the most serious tort claims represent a very small proportion of the total number of claims, they account for a very significant proportion of total tort compensation. As a result of advances in medical technology in the past 30 years, seriously injured people can be kept alive for much longer and with a better quality of life than formerly, although at very considerable expense. As a result, compensation for loss of income and for medical expenses in such cases may be very much higher than it would have been in the 1970s. Moreover, the cost of medical and nursing care and services appears to have increased at a rate considerably above the general rate of inflation. But in relation to the size of tort claims as opposed to their number, it is also more plausible to attribute at least some of the increase in the total cost of claims to changes in the law. Important developments have included changes relating to interest payable on damages awards; the introduction of damages for loss of earnings in the 'lost years', for the value of gratuitous care and for loss of ability to perform unpaid domestic services; increased itemization of damages for financial loss (6.2); increases in the tariff of awards for non-pecuniary loss; reduction of the discount rate; and the introduction of a scheme for recoupment from liability insurers of social security benefits paid to victims.[54] The cost of tort compensation will increase even more when the scheme for requiring tortfeasors to pay a significant proportion of the cost to the NHS of treating victims is fully operational (probably sometime in 2006). Furthermore, some people argue that changes in procedural rules in recent years have meant that the legal costs of settling claims, especially smaller claims (which greatly outnumber large and serious claims), have increased considerably. Finally, the new power to make periodical payment orders (6.1.5.4) may put upward pressure on the cost of compensation in serious cases.

So while it seems unlikely that changes in the law have played much role in the increase in the number of tort claims, it seems plausible that they are responsible for a significant real increase in the cost of tort compensation. Whatever the real cause, the rhetoric of individual responsibility and the blame culture, and the supporting idea that the tort system is out of control, has had a potent effect on legal policymaking in countries such as the USA and Australia. Over the past 20 years, 'tort reform legislation', designed to reduce the incidence of tort claiming and the aggregate amounts paid out in tort compensation, has been passed in many US jurisdictions. Much of this legislative activity has been provoked by political lobbying and

---

54 See 15.4.5. This scheme did not increase the total amount of compensation paid but did transfer some of the cost from the public purse to private (liability) insurance.

media campaigns based on false or misleading assertions about the volume of tort claims and levels of tort compensation payable in individual cases.[55] In Australia in 2001–2 premiums for certain classes of liability insurance – notably medical indemnity and public liability insurance – rose sharply, with actual or potential adverse effects (or so it was alleged) on the availability of certain types of medical services in certain areas of the country, and on community activities such as fetes and sporting fixtures. A resulting sense that there was an 'insurance crisis', combined with a suggestion that the tort law was 'the last outpost of the welfare state',[56] provoked a spate of tort reform legislation designed partly to make it harder for tort claims to succeed, and partly to reduce compensation levels and payments.[57]

One of the assumptions underlying these reforms was that increases in the volume of tort litigation and in the aggregate amount of compensation had been a significant trigger of increases in premiums. However, such evidence as was available revealed no increases in tort claims or recoveries such as could explain the size and suddenness of the premium increases. Probably the most important precipitating factors were the recent collapse of a major medical indemnity insurer and a major public liability insurer. Another contributory factor may have been sharp increases in the cost of reinsurance[58] as a result of the events of 11 September 2001.[59] These company failures suddenly and significantly reduced capacity in both the affected sectors of the insurance market; and reduced availability of a product without any decrease in demand tends to push prices up. Moreover, government inquiries found that both failed insurers had been badly managed: during the 1990s they had competed aggressively for market share by setting premiums at uneconomically low levels, thus forcing other insurers to do the same; and as a result, inadequate provision had been made for future claims. When the aggressive competitors fell out of the market, the remaining insurers were then able to take the necessary and overdue step of raising premiums to make up for past losses and increase provision for future liabilities. Such increases were necessarily large.

In Britain, too, there has been liability insurance 'crisis' in recent years, involving sudden, large premium increases and reduced availability; but it has mainly affected

---

55 W. Haltom and M. McCann, *Distorting the Law: Politics, Media and the Litigation Crisis* (Chicago and London, 2004); S. Daniels and J. Martin, 'Persistence is not Always a Virtue: Tort Reform, Civil Liability for Health Care and the Lack of Empirical Evidence' (1997) 15 *Behavioural Sciences and the Law* 3.

56 J.J. Spigelman, 'Negligence: The Last Outpost of the Welfare State' (2002) 76 *Australian LJ* 432. This article was particularly influential not only because of its timing but also because its author is Chief Justice of New South Wales.

57 For background see P. Cane, 'Reforming Tort Law in Australia: A Personal Perspective' (2003) 27 *Melbourne ULR* 649. Various other measures were taken at the taxpayer's expense to reduce the burden of medical indemnity insurance premiums on doctors in the private sector.

58 Reinsurance is wholesale insurance purchased by retail insurers to cover their exposure to their policy-holders.

59 But the Association of British Insurers told the Office of Fair Trading that any increase in the cost of liability insurance as a result of increases in the cost of reinsurance was 'negligible': OFT, *The UK Liability Insurance Market: Summary of Key Findings* (2003), para. 4.19.

employers' liability insurance.[60] It is no coincidence that 2001 saw the collapse of an insurer (Independent Insurance) specializing in this line of insurance, which had engaged in aggressive competition and premium discounting in the 1990s.[61] But since this company held only about 7% of the market, the effect of its collapse would not have been as great as the effect of the collapses in Australia of companies with a much larger share of the relevant market. Nevertheless, the main cause of sudden increases in the cost of employers' liability insurance appears to have been the need to catch up after a long period of unrealistically low premiums in the 1990s.[62] There have been no consequential calls or moves to change tort law. Instead, 'initiatives' have been taken by the government, insurers and employers' organizations to reduce the legal costs of low-value claims by employees and to reward employers, who can demonstrate that they have devoted increased resources to improved safety, with reduced premiums. The latter development, at least, appears to have had little impact on premiums. This would not be surprising if the main cause of insurance crises were (as all the evidence suggests) features of the operation of the insurance market rather than changing patterns of tort claims and compensation. The basic point is that even if the volume of tort claims and the cost of compensation are on an inexorably upward trend, this cannot easily explain sudden large 'spikes' in the cost of insurance which earn the name of insurance 'crises'.

Is a three-fold increase in the number of tort claims and a doubling of tort compensation payouts in 30-odd years cause for either concern or celebration? Much will depend on the perspective taken. Those who think well of the tort system will see these developments as cause for satisfaction, while those who (like Atiyah and Cane) think that it is a socially undesirable and economically inefficient way of compensating victims of personal injury will bemoan the fact that it now consumes relatively much more of society's resources than it did in the 1970s. An important criticism of the tort system is that for various reasons, a significant proportion of injured people who might in theory be entitled to tort compensation do not actually receive it. We have also noted the criticism (6.4) that the tort system does not fulfil in practice its theoretical commitment to the full compensation principle. To the extent that the increase in the number of tort claims and in the

---

60 Employers are required by statute to take out liability insurance in respect of injuries to their employees; but it has been suggested that one result of the insurance crisis was an increase in the numbers of employers failing to insure. (Whereas failure to take out compulsory motor vehicle liability insurance is a criminal offence, failure to take out compulsory employers' liability insurance is not.) See generally Department for Work and Pensions, *Review of Employers' Liability Compulsory Insurance: First Stage* Report (June 2003); *Second Stage Report* (December 2003). For a more recent survey of the liability insurance market generally see Office of Fair Trading, *The UK Liability Insurance Market: a Follow-up to the OFT's 2003 Market Study* (June 2005). There is also some evidence of problems in the public liability sector: e.g. D. Bamber, 'School Trips and Charities Hit by Soaring Insurance Costs', *Telegraph*, 29 August 2004.
61 Office of Fair Trading, *The UK Liability Insurance Market: Summary of Key Findings* (June 2003), paras. 4.24–5, 4.32.
62 Coupled with falls in insurers' investment income: insurers have two main sources of income – premiums and returns on investment of reserves. See DWP, *Review of Employers' Liability Compulsory Insurance: First Stage Report*, 35–42.

total compensation payout represents an increase in the effective coverage of the tort system and achieves a closer approximation to the ideal of full compensation, they can be seen as desirable developments. However, they might be viewed differently by those who consider unjustified the favoured position of those disabled people fortunate enough to secure tort compensation.

There is no simple answer to the question of how much society should spend on compensating the injured, or on what basis such compensation ought to be distributed. Independently of the cost of insurance, it might be thought that litigation is an undesirable way of solving personal and social problems and ought to be discouraged, especially in cases of minor injury; or that excessive tort litigation threatens to stifle innovation. On the other hand, it may be argued that the possibility of legal liability for personal injuries provides useful incentives to potential injurers to take more care than they otherwise might; that increasing recourse to tort law can only improve safety and reduce the social toll of accidents and injury; and that being able to sue empowers the injured and provides 'access to justice'. Even if we had the facts necessary to assess properly arguments such as these – which, on the whole, we do not – people could still reasonably disagree about how much 'blaming and claiming' is too much or too little.

One thing seems clear: the language of 'crisis' and the 'compensation culture' has a powerful effect on the way people view the tort system, however firmly or insecurely rooted in reality such ideas might be.[63] Perceptions may be just as important as facts, and it may be very difficult to align the two.

63 See, for instance, Better Regulation Task Force, *Better Routes to Redress* (May 2004); *Tackling the 'Compensation Culture'. Government Response to the Better Regulation Task Force Report: 'Better Routes to Redress'* (November 2004). Recent research found a strong and widespread belief that the number of people making successful personal injury claims and false personal injury claims has risen greatly since 2000, and that there is a culture of false claiming: DCA, *Effects of Advertising in Respect of Compensation Claims for Personal Injuries* (March 2006).

Part 3

The tort system in operation

8

Claims and claimants

8.1 Accident victims and tort claimants

Who actually makes tort claims and gets tort damages? How are these claims resolved? What proportion of people who could in theory make tort claims actually do so? In this chapter we investigate such important issues.

8.1.1 Cases reaching trial

According to the Pearson Commission, in 1974 some 2,203 cases of personal injury and death (less than 1% of the estimated number of tort claims) were actually tried in the courts of the whole of the UK. In England and Wales alone, the figure was 1,870. Of this figure of 1,870 cases reaching trial and receiving a full hearing, 1,169 were tried in the High Court, and 701 cases in the county courts.[1] At the time these figures were compiled, personal injury and fatal accident cases constituted the overwhelming bulk of the work of the Queen's Bench Division. Indeed, the Pearson Commission estimated that nearly 80% of the work of this Division consisted of such actions.[2] By contrast, personal injury actions formed a much smaller proportion of the business of county courts. This was still true in 1986 when, according to the Civil Justice Review,[3] the number of personal injury trials completed was 1,400 in the High Court and 3,500 in county courts. As a result of subsequent reforms, the great majority of personal injury actions that reach court are now tried in county courts by circuit (senior) or district (junior) judges.[4] Thus in 2004, 290 medical negligence and 400 other personal injury actions were set down for trial in the High Court, whereas about 10,000 personal injury claims were set down for

---

1 Pearson Report, vol. 2, table 124.
2 Ibid., para. 83.
3 Cm 394 (1988), para. 393.
4 This change was effected by the High Court and County Courts Jurisdiction Order 1991. Cases involving claims for less than £50,000 must be commenced in the county court, and if such a claim reaches trial, the trial will usually take place in the county court. However, cases can be transferred to the High Court if this is thought advantageous. For instance, this was done in relation to a large number of claims arising out of the use of the drug Benzodiazepine, so that the claims could be managed as a group rather than being dealt with individually by circuit judges.

Table 5. *Court waiting times in personal injury actions*

Court and Location	Average time between issue of claim and setting down	Average time between setting down and start of trial (or date of disposal)	Average time between issue of claim and start of trial (or date of disposal)
High Court, London	16 weeks	67 weeks	85 weeks
High Court outside London	85 weeks	54 weeks	139 weeks
County court, London	28 weeks	31 weeks	60 weeks
County court outside London	23 weeks	29 weeks	53 weeks

trial in the county court.[5] Judgment was given in only 40 of the medical negligence and 130 of the other personal injury cases in the High Court. The rest were settled either before or during the hearing, withdrawn or struck out. In the county court, judgment was given in about 6,800 of the 10,000 cases that were set down for trial.

The main aim of this jurisdictional change was to reduce delays; but at the time there were serious delays in the county court itself. Table 5 shows waiting times in 2004. Judging by these statistics, the reform seems to have had a positive effect, at least in relative terms. It needs to be borne in mind, however, that waiting times are determined not solely or even primarily by the availability of judicial time, but by the pace at which the parties progress the case. Furthermore, the cases now heard in the High Court are likely to be the most serious and so likely to take the most time to prepare and try. Even so, the difference between waiting times in the High Court in London and elsewhere is striking.

The jurisdictional change was criticized on the ground that because High Court judges are of higher calibre and occupy a more important constitutional position than circuit judges, it was wrong to remove from the High Court exactly the type of action which is most commonly brought by individual citizens as opposed to corporations or public bodies.[6] High quality justice, it was argued, should not be the preserve of the rich and powerful.

The Pearson Commission did not give any details of personal injury cases that received a full hearing. Some further information is available from a study conducted by Professor Zander in 1973–4.[7] Zander examined some 660 cases of personal injury claims in the Queen's Bench Division in four large cities in 1973. The

5 *Judicial Statistics 2004*. In the county court, a claim likely to be worth no more than £1,000 will be dealt with by the small-claims procedure (10.4). About 15% of personal-injury claims in the county court are dealt with in this way. In 2000 the average time between issue of proceedings and the start of a small-claims trial was 29 weeks: N. Madge, 'Small Claims in the County Court' (2004) 23 *CJQ*, 201, 204.

6 J. Malins, 'A signal failure' [1988] *New LJ* 419.

7 *Guardian Gazette*, 25 June 1975, 679.

vast majority (92%) of these claims arose out of accidents on the road and at work. Only 124 of these claims actually reached trial,[8] and they were overwhelmingly (91%) industrial injury cases. In the Civil Justice Review sample of 796 tried cases, 42% arose out of work accidents and 32% out of road accidents.

Although road and work accident cases together constitute by far the largest proportion of personal injury actions which receive a full trial, it is clear that some other categories of case may be more common now than in 1973. For example, in Zander's sample of 660 claims there were only five claims arising out of medical treatment. It is known that there was a significant increase in the number of such claims in the 1980s[9] and the 1990s,[10] and it is unlikely that this increase in claims was not also accompanied by an increase in trials. There has also been a great increase in recent years in the number of tort claims based on major disasters (such as fires and rail crashes) and on the suffering of illness and disease as a result of exposure to toxic substances (such as asbestos) and the use of drugs (such as Opren and Vioxx) and other products (such as intra-uterine devices and silicone breast implants). Although the vast majority of such claims that result in the payment of compensation are settled out of court, a significant increase in claims will inevitably produce some increase in trials in the form, for instance, of 'lead cases'.

8.1.2   Cases set down for trial

As already noted, very many cases set down for trial never actually receive a full hearing. In 2004, 290 medical negligence and 400 other personal injury cases were set down for trial in the High Court;[11] but of these, only 40 and 130 respectively received a full trial. In the county court in the same year, about 10,000 personal injury cases were set down for trial, of which about 6,800 received a full hearing. The pressures to settle are great, even after a case is set down, and a significant number of cases are settled, more or less literally, at the door of the court just before the trial is due to begin. A significant number are even settled during the course of the trial.

8.1.3   Actions commenced

According to the Civil Justice Review, of an estimated total of 340,000 personal injury claims made in 1986, court proceedings were started in some 51,000. By contrast, in 2004 only 384 medical negligence actions and 749 other personal injury actions were commenced in the High Court. There are no equivalent

---

8 In the Harris 1984 Survey only five out of the 1,177 cases in the survey were fully tried; court proceedings were commenced in just under 40% of the cases in which out-of-court settlement was finally reached (112).

9 P. Fenn and C. Whelan, 'Medical litigation: trends, causes, consequences' in R. Dingwall ed., *Sociolegal Aspects of Medical Practice* (London, 1989).

10 P. Fenn *et al.*, 'Current Cost of Medical Negligence in NHS Hospitals: Analysis of Claims Database' (2000) 320 *British Medical Journal* 1567.

11 *Judicial Statistics 2004.*

statistics for the county court, where the majority of personal injury actions are commenced.[12]

A significant proportion of cases in which proceedings are commenced are settled before being set down for trial: [13]

> Formal legal proceedings may be used to indicate the plaintiff's resolve in the face of an apparently intransigent defendant; to prevent a claim becoming time barred; or because a proposed settlement involves a child and this requires the approval of the court.

The Pearson Commission estimated that 86% of claims are disposed of without commencement of legal proceedings,[14] and that a further 11% are settled after proceedings commence but before being set down for trial.[15] According to the Civil Justice Review, 960 High Court actions and 500 county court actions were settled at this stage in 1986 (compared with 1,400 completed High Court trials and 3,500 completed county court trials). A survey of 759 medical negligence claims made in 1989 found that 33% were resolved without the issue of formal proceedings; but also that the larger the claim, the more likely that court proceedings would be started. Indeed, this happened in all cases in which the amount recovered was more than £50,000.[16] Research conducted in the late 1990s found that proceedings were commenced in only about 10% of medical negligence claims.[17]

8.1.4   All tort claims

The Pearson Commission for the first time offered, as being reasonably precise, some estimates of the total numbers of tort claims for personal injury and death, whether settled or tried. The Commission estimated that every year there were approximately 250,000 such claims; in about 215,000 cases the claimant received some payment whether as a result of a settlement or a trial. In 1988 the Civil Justice Review estimated annual personal injury tort claims to number about 340,000.[18] According to figures published by the DWP, in 2004–5 more than 755,000 'cases' were 'registered', and more than 845,000 'settlements' were 'recorded', with the Compensation Recovery Unit (CRU) for the purposes of the schemes for recouping social security payments and NHS costs from tortfeasors (15.3, 15.4.5). Note

---

12 Since the introduction of the Woolf reforms the total number of actions (of all types) commenced in English county courts has dropped by almost 30%: J. Peysner and M. Seneviratne, *The Management of Civil Cases: the Courts and the Post-Woolf Landscape* (DCA Research Series 9/05, November 2005), p. 8.

13 P. Hoyte, 'Unsound Practice: The Epidemiology of Medical Negligence' [1995] *Medical LR* 53, 55.

14 As a result of the Woolf procedural reforms (see generally ch. 10), this percentage may have been increased: R. Lewis, 'Insurance and the Tort System' (2005) 25 *LS* 85, 88 n. 18.

15 Pearson Report, vol. 2, table 12.

16 Hoyte, *Unsound Practice*, p. 55.

17 L. Mulcahy, 'Threatening Behaviour? The Challenge Posed by Medical Negligence Claims' (2000) 3 *Current Legal Issues* 81, 90.

18 Cm 394, para. 391.

that the higher Pearson figure and the Civil Justice Review figure represent all tort claims, successful and unsuccessful, whereas the CRU figures represent successful claims.[19] It appears, therefore, that the total number of personal injury claims has increased some threefold since the 1970s, and has more or less doubled since the late 1980s. The CRU figures are likely to be more accurate than earlier estimates, and the apparently huge increase in tort claims in the past 30 years or so may suggest that the earlier figures were too low.

According to CRU figures, more than half (by number) of all tort compensation payments are made in road accident cases, more than a quarter in cases of work-related injury and illness, around 12% in cases involving accidents in public places and on privately owned land ('public liability' cases), and less than 2% in all other types of case, including medical negligence and product liability. There is no reason to think that these proportions of the various types of successful tort claims do not roughly reflect the proportions of the various types of tort claims, both successful and unsuccessful. Comparing these figures with equivalents given by the Pearson Commission[20] we can see that over the past 30 years or so there has been a significant fall (from around 47% to around 30%) in the proportion of work claims and a large increase (from about 5% to around 12%) in the proportion of what Pearson called 'occupiers' liability claims' – these are roughly equivalent to public liability claims in the CRU figures. The former difference is explicable by reference to improvements in workplace safety, and to decline in high-risk manufacturing industry and growth in the service sector. There is no obvious explanation for the latter difference, although some would probably see it as evidence of the growth of the 'compensation culture' (7.7).

It is worth noting that public liability has been the only area of major relative growth in tort claiming since the 1970s. It is true that the number of medical negligence claims has grown greatly in the past 20 years (8.3.3), but such claims still represent only around 1% of tort claims. It is also worth noting that the largest absolute increase has been in road accident claims, which have increased in relative terms (from around 41% to around 53%) and so have increased in absolute numbers by at least three times since the 1970s.

In 2000 it was estimated by a claims management company that there were 11.2 million personal injury accidents in the UK each year, and that 2 million injured people blamed someone else. On the basis that 350,000 tort claims are made each year, the company estimated a potential untapped market of more than 1.5 million tort claims per annum.[21] But in the light of the CRU

---

19 To be absolutely precise, 2,538 (0.3%) of the registered cases and 931 (0.1%) of the recorded settlements resulted in 'no liability'. The reason why the figure for recorded settlements is higher than that for cases recorded appears to be that the latter is inflated by double-counting as a result of the recording of both interim and final settlements in some cases. Note too that cases not caught by the recoupment schemes do not appear in the CRU figures.

20 Pearson Report, vol. 2, table 11.

21 Department for Constitutional Affairs, *The Report of the Lord Chancellor's Committee to Investigate the Activities of Non-Legally Qualified Claims Assessors and Employment Advisers* (2000), para. 68.

figures, if the estimate of 2 million potential tort claims a year is anywhere near correct, the untapped market is considerably smaller than this. Perhaps the estimate of potential tort claims should be much higher. But there is really no way of knowing.

8.2   Why do people (not) make tort claims?

8.2.1   Some research findings

In newspaper reports of tort litigation, tort claimants are often quoted as saying things like, 'I didn't really do it for the money, although that will obviously help'. But what do we actually know about why people make personal injury tort claims? In the 1990s and early 2000s several British research projects focused on medical negligence claims.[22] This is interesting in its own right. It is, perhaps, a reflection of the fact that many people would see the use of the tort system as more problematic in this context than in other areas such as road and work accidents. Suing a doctor may be seen as a 'betrayal' of the relationship of trust that ideally exists between medical practitioner and patient. It may also be seen as an attack on that most sacred of British institutions, the NHS. There have also been two more general British studies of legal claiming.[23] A striking result of such research is that for very many claimants, obtaining compensation is not the primary reason to make a claim.[24] Other important motivations in the context of medical negligence are: to prevent the same thing happening to other people; to obtain an explanation of what went wrong or an apology; and to force an individual or organisation to take responsibility and be held accountable for what happened. Whether the tort system is an effective or efficient way of achieving such goals is another matter, which is considered in more detail in chapter 17. Nevertheless, explanation and accountability are recurrent themes in lay attitudes to tort litigation and often appear, for instance, in anecdotal accounts of why actions against the police have increased greatly in recent years. However, it is perhaps unlikely that such motiva-

---

22 C. Vincent, M. Young and A. Phillips, 'Why Do People Sue Doctors? A Study of Patients and Relatives Taking Legal Action' (1994) 343 *The Lancet* 1609; H. Genn, 'Access to Just Settlements: the Case of Medical Negligence' in A.A.S. Zuckerman and R. Cranston eds., *Reform of Civil Procedure: Essays on 'Access to Justice'* (Oxford, 1995); S. Lloyd Bostock, 'Calling Doctors and Hospitals to Account: Complaining and Claiming as Social Processes' in M.M. Rosenthal, L. Mulcahy and S. Lloyd-Bostock eds., *Medical Mishaps: Pieces of the Puzzle* (Buckingham, 1999); Department of Health, *Making Amends: A Report by the Chief Medical Officer* (2003), 75.

23 National Consumer Council, *Seeking Civil Justice* (1995); H. Genn, *Paths to Justice: What People Do and Think about Going to Law* (Oxford, 1999).

24 A 2003 follow-up to the Genn, *Paths to Justice* survey showed that 76% of respondents experiencing an injury/work-related ill-health problem who did something to resolve it gave a money-related objective as the reason. The equivalent figure for those with medical-negligence problems was 3%: P. Pleasence *et al.*, 'Causes of Action: First Findings of the LSRC. Periodic Survey' (2003) *J. of Law and Society* 11, 26–7. The survey reported in Department of Health, *Making Amends* revealed that only 15% of even the most seriously injured claimants said that financial compensation was the most appropriate remedy.

tions play as great a role in the great bulk of straightforward road and work accident cases.[25]

Equally important is why people who, in theory at least, could make a tort claim do not do so. We know, for instance, that only a small proportion of cases of medical negligence result in a tort claim. In the *Paths to Justice* study[26] more than one third of respondents who experienced a 'justiciable' injury or work-related ill-health problem[27] serious enough to require a visit to a hospital, doctor or dentist, did nothing to try to 'solve the problem'.[28] Amongst those who took some step, 39% sought advice, 28% talked to 'the other side', 14% threatened legal action, 8% 'went to court' or started a court action and 1% went to mediation or conciliation.[29] The main reasons given for doing nothing were that there was 'no dispute' or 'no-one was to blame' (57%), the problem was not thought very important (17%) and the sufferer thought that nothing could be done about it (10%). Only 1% of respondents said that they did nothing because they were too scared, or because it would cost too much, or because it would damage their relationship with the other side.

8.2.2   Alternative remedies

If the tort liability system worked as, in theory, it should (that is, if people suffering personal injury or property damage generally recovered damages where the loss suffered was the fault of someone else), we would expect to find claims for damage to property as a result of road accidents far exceeding claims for personal injuries. Although no precise figures are available, it has been estimated that road accidents causing only property damage are probably six times as frequent as those causing personal injuries, however slight. And the figure for accidents involving only private cars is estimated to be even higher – some 7.7 times as many as personal injury accidents.[30] Property damage amounting to many millions of pounds each year is

---

25 In the Genn, *Paths to Justice* survey, no respondent who experienced accidental injury cited 'obtaining an apology' as a reason to claim. About 6% referred to the desire to prevent the same thing happening again to someone else. Genn comments: 'This may reflect the high number of work accidents and work-related illnesses in the sample' (185).

26 For a theoretical/anecdotal discussion of this issue see S.L. Brodsky *et al.*, 'Why People Don't Sue: A Conceptual and Applied Exploration of Decisions Not to Pursue Litigation' (2004) 32 *J. of Psychiatry and Law* 273.

27 'Justiciable' problems were defined as those raising legal issues.

28 In a follow-up study, 40% of respondents with injury/work-related ill-health problems did nothing. Of these, around 50% said that the problem was not regarded as involving a dispute, or was not thought to be very serious: Pleasence *et al.*, 'Causes of Action', 25.

29 Genn, *Paths to Justice*, 52.

30 Road Research Laboratory (RRL), LR 79 (1967). In 2002 the official statistics as to the costs of road accidents were calculated on the basis that there were about 6.7 damage-only accidents for every injury accident: Highway Economics Note No. 1 (2002), para. 19. It has been estimated that 55% of motorcycle accidents involve injury to the rider: Transport and Road Research Laboratory (TRRL) Report CR 146 (1990). It is also estimated that one in five injury accidents are not reported to the police; but nothing is known about what proportion of damage-only accidents are reported.

also caused by fires. In fact, however, except in the road accident context, tort claims for property damage alone are rare.

Even if we confine our attention to personal injury accidents, there are large numbers which scarcely ever figure in the tort scene at all. In particular there are accidents in the home. Home accidents cause at least as many deaths as road accidents, and it has been estimated that about 3 million people injured each year in British homes require medical treatment – many more than in the case of people injured on the roads.[31] The personal injury survey conducted for the Pearson Commission found that 27% of all injuries occurred within the home.[32] Nobody can be sure what proportion of accidents in the home is due to fault,[33] or whether this proportion is anything like the proportion of road and industrial accidents due to fault. No doubt it is probable that more home accidents are due to the fault of the victim,[34] in which case there could be no tort liability. But such evidence as there is suggests that a considerable proportion of home accidents are due to 'fault' at least in the sense that they could have been prevented by due care on the part of someone other than the victim, or by better buildings or design etc. For example, between 1981 and 1984 there were between 3,300 and 3,600 fires started in upholstered furniture; about 150 people died and 1,000 were injured each year in such fires. The design of furniture is crucial to fire-resistance; but also about half the fires were started by cigarettes and so could, in many instances, probably have been prevented by the exercise of more care.[35] One survey estimated that one-third of accidents to young children at home could have been prevented by greater care.[36] In this light, the Pearson Commission's estimate that rather under a fifth of home accidents could have been due to fault on the part of someone other than the victim seems somewhat low, but it still amounts to about 8% of all accidental injuries.[37]

A US survey (the Harvard Medical Practice Study)[38] produced revealing statistics about medical misadventure. It was estimated that about 27% of injuries to

31 Department of Trade and Industry, *Home Accident Surveillance System, 20th Annual Report* (1996). In 1996, 33% of all injuries requiring medical treatment were the result of accidents in the home; 25% are the result of work accidents; and only 11% of road accidents. In 1990, about 700 people died as a result of fires attended by fire brigades, and 12,000 were injured. Of these, some 500 fatalities and 8,500 non-fatal injuries were the result of fires in the home: National Audit Office, *Fire Prevention in England and Wales* (HC 318, 1992–3). See also 1.4.1 nn. 23 and 24 and text.
32 Pearson Report, vol. 2, para. 326.
33 One recent estimate is 0.5%: R. Lewis, 'Insurance and the Tort System' (2005) 25 *LS* 85, 91 n. 30.
34 E.g. with knives, ladders and so on.
35 *Hansard* written answer (Michael Howard) HC Debs, vol. 100, cols. *467–8* (1 July 1986).
36 *Accidents in the Home* (London, 1964), 8.
37 Pearson Report, vol. 2, para. 326. In another survey, 17.6% of home accidents were blamed by the victim on someone else: S.B. Burman, H.G. Genn and J. Lyons, 'The Use of Legal Services by Victims of Accidents in the Home: A Pilot Study' (1977) 40 *Modern LR* 47, 51–5.
38 The results of this study are summarized and discussed by D.R. Harris, 'Evaluating the Goals of Personal Injury Law: Some Empirical Evidence' in P. Cane and J. Stapleton eds., *Essays for Patrick Atiyah* (Oxford, 1991), 289ff.

hospital patients resulting from medical intervention were due to negligence; but also that only one in eight of the victims of such injuries made a tort claim, and that only one in sixteen received any damages.

It is clear from the figures alone that the incidence of actual claims for tort damages is affected by factors other than the existence of theoretical liability, including the existence of other and more satisfactory forms of compensation, such as personal property or fire insurance. Nobody is likely to bring an action for damage caused by fire when an easily settled claim can be made against an insurance company.[39] Even in personal injury cases, the fact that (emergency) medical care is typically obtained free of charge under the NHS, that many employers will pay wages or salary for a reasonable period of absence due to sickness or injury, and that social security benefits are often available to injured persons, probably means that very many minor cases are never made the subject of a tort claim.

The incidence of tort claims is also profoundly affected by the possibility of actually enforcing a judgment against the defendant. Unless the defendant is insured, or is a substantial corporation, no tort claim is likely to be made in practice. This, no doubt, places a large majority of home accidents beyond the pale of tort law. The problem is not that the person at fault is likely to be a member of the same family as the person injured; the law does not prevent a person suing a member of their own family in tort. Rather, the problem is that the person at fault in the home may well not be insured against liability to other members of the family.

In the Pearson survey, although about 42% of tort payments were made in respect of work injuries, such injuries accounted for less than 25% of all injuries. Similarly, road accident victims obtained about 45% of all tort payments, but accounted for less than 10% of all accidents. On the other hand, 27% of all the injuries occurred at home, but those in this category received less than 1% of all tort payments. These figures show that it is wrong to think of the tort system as being in practice a fault system; it is really a fault-cum-insurance system, because the chances of obtaining damages depend on the availability of insurance just as much as on the existence of fault.

8.2.3   Claims consciousness

Another important but ill-understood factor affecting the incidence of tort claims is that generally known as 'claims consciousness'. Some people are more 'claims conscious' than others, and so they are more likely to think of making a claim than others. A national survey in Britain found that only one in three of road accident victims, one in four of work accident victims, and one in fifty of other accidents, consulted a solicitor.[40] It was also found that women are less likely to consider

---

39 In theory, the insurance company could sue the person, if any, whose fault caused the fire to recover amounts paid out to the policy-holder under the doctrine of subrogation, but in practice such actions are rarely brought: 15.3.
40 Harris 1984 Survey, 65.

making a claim,[41] or to seek legal advice, than men; that children and the elderly are less likely than those in other age groups to do so; and that those in higher socio-economic groups are less likely to do so than those in lower groups.[42] The Pearson personal-injury survey showed that only 11% of those injured took any steps at all towards making a claim for damages.[43] It also found that 19% of those who thought that someone might be held responsible for their injuries made no claim because they did not know how to claim or even that they could claim.[44] A large US survey[45] produced comparable results despite the fact that the USA is widely regarded as a highly litigious society.[46] The Harvard Medical Practice Study found that only one in eight victims of medical negligence in New York State hospitals made a tort claim, which is a surprisingly low figure for a group of victims who might be expected to have a high level of claims consciousness.[47]

At the most general level, claims consciousness is related to cultural attitudes to law and the legal system. One writer has said that 'the American links adversity with recompense while the Englishman or woman accepts adversity as a routine part of life'.[48] Many people would argue that Britain is a more litigious society today then ever before; but there is no reliable evidence on the basis of which such a claim can be assessed. For instance, although we know that the number of medical negligence claims has risen steadily over the past 25 years or so, there is no way of knowing to what extent the increase is the result of increased claims consciousness and to what extent it can be explained by other factors, such as changes in the law, increased medical activity, and advances in medical technology that enable seriously disabled people to be kept alive. Interestingly, one study found that justiciable problems relating to injury and medical negligence are amongst those about which people are most likely to do nothing at all.[49] On the other hand, it seems intuitively plausible to think, given the obsession of the popular media with legal matters, that

---

41 Harris 1984 Survey concludes that the group of victims who give no thought to claiming is 'very large': 71; see also 49, 61.

42 Ibid., 53, 63, 68. This somewhat surprising result is perhaps explained by the fact that people in higher groups are more likely have to a greater proportion of their financial losses met from other sources, and so do not need to make a tort claim to recover such losses.

43 Pearson Report, vol. 2, para. 389. In the Genn, *Paths to Justice* survey, 14% of respondents with injury/work-related ill-health problems threatened legal action and 8% 'went to court or started a court case' (fig. 2.18).

44 Pearson Report, vol. 2, table 84. In the Genn, *Paths to Justice* survey, 10% of respondents with injury/work-related ill-health problems took no action to try to solve the problem because 'they did not think anything could be done' (fig. 2.19).

45 For details see Harris 1984 Survey, 296–8.

46 For an exploration of litigiousness in the UK, the USA and Germany see B.S. Markesinis, 'Litigation Mania in England, Germany and the USA: Are We So Very Different?' [1990] *Cambridge LJ* 233. See also P.S. Atiyah, 'Tort Law and the Alternatives: Some Anglo-American Comparisons' [1987] *Duke LJ* 1002; H.M. Kritzer, 'Propensity to Sue in England and the United States of America: Blaming and Claiming in Tort Cases' [1991] 18 *Law and Society* 400; S. Lloyd-Bostock, 'Propensity to Sue in England and the United States of America: The Role of Attribution Processes. A Comment on Kritzer' [1991] 18 *Law and Society* 428.

47 Harris, 1884 Survey, 300–1.

48 Kritzer, 'Propensity to Sue', 422. See also ibid., 420–1.

49 Genn, *Paths to Justice*, 250.

people generally are more aware of law and legal processes, and put more faith in them as solutions to social problems, that they did 30 or even 20 years ago.

At the same time, ignorance of the law is probably an important factor in many cases in explaining why many injured people never think of making a claim.[50] No doubt many people's image of the law (if they have one) is as something meted out by magistrates; some are probably unaware of the existence of the civil law (except, perhaps, the law of defamation) as opposed to the criminal law. For example, a survey by the Consumer Council in 1968 estimated that only 22% of people knew that a retailer is legally liable to the buyer (in contract) for damage or injury caused by defective goods sold by it.[51] It may be, too, that some people are unaware of the role of liability insurance in meeting claims arising, for example, out of road accidents. A person who thinks that the defendant personally will pay any damages awarded is perhaps unlikely to think of suing if the negligent person was a member of their own family, or a friend, or perhaps even a long-term professional adviser such as a GP. Also, to many people suing another would seem an aggressive act out of place in close relationships.[52] The Pearson Commission found that 10% of people who thought that someone else might be responsible for their injuries did not make a claim because it would have been against a family member or friend.[53]

Furthermore, some types of accidents (e.g. road and work accidents) are more likely to lead to claims being made than others (e.g. leisure and domestic accidents) partly because people probably associate 'the law' more with some types of accidents than with others.[54] For example, few people injured in a private house would think of suing the occupant for negligence, even though this kind of liability may well be covered by a householder's comprehensive insurance policy. A study of home accidents in Bristol in 1976 confirmed the great reluctance of the victims of such accidents to make claims. Although there were a number of serious injuries, only one person in this study of 905 cases had actually taken steps to claim compensation; only two sought legal advice; and only seven even considered making a claim.[55] Claims consciousness may also be greater in relation to accidents that occur in public (and are, therefore, more likely to be witnessed and reported) than in relation to domestic accidents, for example.[56] This may help to explain why about 12% of personal injury claims fall within the broad description of 'public liability': many such claims will arise out of accidents in public places as a result, for instance, of tripping and falling on uneven pavements. On the other hand, claims consciousness

---

50 'A clear message that emerges from the study is . . . the pervasive lack of the most rudimentary knowledge about legal rights and procedures for enforcing or defending rights': Genn, *Paths to Justice*, 255.
51 See A.L. Diamond, 'Codification of the Law of Contract' (1968) 31 *Modern LR* 361, 372.
52 But in the Genn, *Paths to Justice* survey, only 1% of respondents with injury/work-related illness problems said that the reason the did nothing at all about the problem was the risk of damaging their relationship with the 'other side'.
53 Pearson Report, vol. 2, table 84.
54 Harris 1984 Survey, 69–70.
55 Burman, Genn and Lyons, 'The Use of Legal Services by Victims of Accidents in the Home'.
56 See Harris 1984 Survey, 67

in respect of diseases is likely to be lower than in respect of traumatic injuries, if only because the tort system compensates relatively very few disease victims.[57] Important in overcoming ignorance about the possibility of legal claims are the activities of bodies, such as trade unions and Citizens' Advice Bureaux,[58] which can provide injury victims with advice soon after an accident.

Claims consciousness is likely to be higher in relation to accidents in which many people are killed or injured ('mass torts', such as a rail or air crash or a fire in a public place), or in respect of products (especially drugs) the use of which has had adverse effects on large numbers of people.[59] The number of claims made and the amounts paid out in such cases ('group claims') can be very large indeed. For example, there were more than 250,000 claimants world-wide in the Dalkon Shield contraceptive litigation. Over £100 million was paid out in compensation following the *Piper Alpha* oil-rig disaster and it has been suggested that claims against Pan Am's insurers in respect of the Lockerbie bombing in 1988 might finally total more than £500 million. The world-wide Dow-Corning settlement package for women who had silicone breast implants amounts to more than US$3 billion. A UK government-funded compensation scheme for miners suffering from work-related lung disease was set up in 1999 worth at least £1.5 billion. It is anticipated that the total bill for compensating victims of asbestos-related diseases in the UK may be in the region of £8 billion – and perhaps much more.

Mass torts have a number of features that will tend to heighten claims consciousness. First, the incidents which give rise to them typically attract a great deal of attention from the media, and the media may be used to advertise for claimants. More generally (as already suggested), the media has played an important part in recent years in raising the general level of personal injury claims consciousness in the community, even in respect of torts affecting only one person. It is probably true that many more people today would consider the possibility of making a tort claim if they suffered personal injury or illness than would have done so 30 or even 20 years ago. Secondly (although this is probably less true now than it was 10 or 20 years ago), whereas personal injury actions brought by single claimants may be handled by solicitors with limited expertise in or experience of personal injury litigation, multi-claimant actions will almost certainly be handled by personal injury specialists who are able to identify victims and to suggest the possibility of making a claim. Thirdly, large-scale accidents are usually followed by some sort of public inquiry to investigate what happened.

Another factor influencing claims consciousness may be that many people do not appreciate that a tort claim can be made and settled by negotiation. The public

---

57 J. Stapleton, *Disease and the Compensation Debate* (Oxford, 1986), 101–4.
58 But for a recent negative assessment of the role of CABx see Genn, *Paths to Justice*, 256.
59 But it has also been claimed that there is a significant pool of cases of work-related, asbestos-induced diseases that are not pursued at law: W.L.F. Felstiner and R. Dingwall, *Asbestos Litigation in the United Kingdom* (Oxford, 1988). The passage of 20 years since this research was done may have changed the situation somewhat. Asbestos-related diseases probably account for a significant proportion of disease-related tort claiming.

image of the 'law' seems to be confined to what happens in courts – and this is not surprising since the public tends to think of the law mainly as the criminal law, and criminal cases cannot be 'settled' in the way that civil claims are.[60] Even in the case of defamation actions, some of which receive considerable publicity, the distinction between settling a claim and trying it may not be easy for the non-lawyer to discern. If people assume that a tort claim necessarily involves a judicial hearing, fear of the cost of such a hearing, as well as of the burden of giving evidence, may deter them from making a claim.[61] In industrial cases there is often a real fear of causing trouble to workmates by requiring them to give evidence against their employer.[62]

Finally, many people are reluctant to consult solicitors; and contrary to what might at first be expected, this reluctance appears, at least in relation to obtaining compensation for personal injuries, not to be confined to (or even more common amongst) lower socio-economic groups.[63] In the *Paths to Justice Survey*, only 32% of respondents with an injury/work-related illness problem who sought advice went in the first instance to a solicitor; but another 50% went to a solicitor as their second source of advice.[64] In the Pearson Commission personal injury survey, a substantial proportion of those injured who sought no legal advice or redress said that this was because they did not want to make a fuss, or that it was too much trouble.[65] The Royal Commission on Legal Services found that a third of those surveyed who had a problem about which they felt at some stage that a solicitor's help or advice might have been useful did not consult a lawyer because of concern about costs.[66]

In cases where some consideration is given to making a claim, factors such as perceived difficulties in obtaining evidence and fear of legal expenses have found to be important in explaining why claims are not made in the first place or are abandoned once made.[67] Fear of legal expenses might itself, to some extent, be a product of ignorance. A survey in 1992–3 of 650 accident victims who recovered compensation found that in three out of every four cases the claimant did not have to pay any legal costs – the bill was met by legal aid, the defendant('s insurer) or a trade union.[68] Yet the Harris 1984 Survey found that even amongst those who consulted a solicitor, only one in four knew of the legal advice scheme and less than one half

---

60 Although, of course, the police can decide not to prosecute; and plea bargaining is not totally dissimilar to settlement of civil cases out of court. But plea bargaining is very controversial in a way that settlement out of court is not, and this fact supports the statement in the text.

61 'There is a widespread perception that legal proceedings involve uncertainty, expense and potential long-term disturbance and that only the most serious matters could justify enduring those conditions': Genn, *Paths to Justice*, 254.

62 E.A. Webb, *Industrial Injuries: A New Approach* (Evidence of the PO Engineering Union to the Pearson Royal Commission, London, 1974), 8.

63 Harris 1984 Survey, 53, 63, 68.

64 Genn, *Paths to Justice*, 128. Other first sources of advice were trades unions (18%), insurance companies (15%), police (15%) and CABx (5%).

65 Pearson Report, vol. 2, table 84.

66 Cmnd 7648–1 (1979), vol. 2, table 8.56.

67 Harris 1984 Survey, tables 2.12, 3.12; Genn, 'Access to Just Settlements', 401–2.

68 Law Com. No. 225, *How Much is Enough?* (1994), 149.

knew of the legal aid scheme.[69] On the other hand, a Consumers' Association survey in 1997 found that 73% of their (inevitably middle-class) members said that they had heard of conditional fees.[70] Since then, legal aid has been abolished for most personal injury claims, the bulk of which are now funded by some form of insurance or by lawyers operating on a no-win, no-fee basis. There is some recent evidence that fear of costs is not a major barrier to claiming.[71]

Although the evidence on claims consciousness is slight and difficult to interpret, there is a sufficient core of established fact to make it certain that the presence and strength of claims consciousness is an important factor in determining the number of potential tort claims which are, in practice, pursued. A survey conducted in 1981 examined a scheme under which leaflets were distributed and posters displayed in hospitals, doctors' surgeries and so on offering a free interview with a solicitor. It was found that as a result of the scheme, many accident victims who would not otherwise have thought of making a tort claim or who would not have consulted a solicitor, sought legal advice. The largest group using the scheme were victims of accidents suffered otherwise than on the road or at work, and 42% of users said that they had not thought of making a claim before they saw a leaflet or poster advertising the scheme. Furthermore, 80% of free interviews resulted in some action being taken by the solicitor to obtain compensation.[72]

These facts are not of merely academic interest, for if one of the main purposes of the tort system is to compensate those suffering injury from another's fault, then the system does not work well to the extent that people who have good tort claims do not in fact make them. It must, of course, be admitted that this criticism is not confined to the tort system. The social security system does not in practice reach all those who are entitled to social security benefits, particularly income-support benefits on which many of the very poorest in society depend.

8.3   Particular types of claims

8.3.1 Road accidents

According to figures published by the CRU, in 2003–4 and 2004–5 there were more than 400,000 successful tort claims for personal injury and death arising out of road accidents.[73] The Pearson Commission estimated that tort compensation is recovered in respect of only about one-quarter of injuries and deaths resulting from road

---

69 Ibid., 67; many of those who have heard of legal aid are very vague about how to obtain it: see B. Abel-Smith, M. Zander and R. Brooke, *Legal Problems and the Citizen* (London, 1973), 194–5.
70 About conditional fees see 10.2.
71 DCA, Effects of Advertising in Respect of Compensation Claims for Personal Injuries (March 2006), para. 2.4.9.
72 H. Genn, *Meeting Legal Needs? An Evaluation of a Scheme for Personal Injury Victims* (Oxford, 1982).
73 As we noted in 1.4.1, only about 280,000 people were recorded as having suffered death or injury in road accidents in 2004. The difference between this and the CRU figures suggests that the road accident statistics give a very misleading picture.

accidents. It is very probable that the proportion of those who obtain damages is higher in cases where the injuries are more serious. According to the Commission, in fatal cases damages are recovered in about one case in two; and in some 96% of cases where a tort claim is made, some payment ensues.[74] If these Pearson estimates are correct, they would suggest that each year around 2 million people may suffer personal injury or death in road accidents, and that between 400,000 and 500,000 road accident tort claims are made each year. On the other hand, the facts that the number of successful tort claims has increased threefold since the 1970s and that road accident claims now represent a larger proportion of successful claims than they did in the 1970s might support the conclusion that a much higher percentage of road accident victims now recover tort compensation than did 30 years ago.

Even so, there are at least two reasons why we might expect that a significant proportion of those injured and killed on the roads would not recover tort compensation: first, the requirement of proof of fault; and, secondly, the fact that the insurance system is far from being comprehensive. If we take the fault factor first, we cannot tell from looking at the figures what proportion of accidents was caused by someone's fault, but we can make some reasonable guesses about some types of accident. In 2004 out of a total of 207,410 recorded road accidents involving personal injury, almost 62,000 involved only one vehicle; and of these accidents, more than 1,300 resulted in fatalities and about 12,000 resulted in serious injury.[75] These figures include accidents in which one or more pedestrians were injured; but in accidents involving no pedestrian, about 40,000 vehicle users were injured (some 6,600 seriously) and 820 were killed.[76] About half the motorcycle accidents in 1987–8 involved no vehicle or object other than the cycle. One in ten involved a roadside object.[77] Some of these accidents may have been due to the fault of a third party who was not directly involved in a collision; and in addition to pedestrians injured in single-vehicle accidents, some of the victims would have been passengers who might have recovered tort damages against their drivers. But single vehicle accidents must account for a substantial proportion of those killed and injured in road accidents in respect of which no tort compensation is recovered. It is perhaps significant in this context that about 21% of drivers and motorcycle riders who die in road accidents have blood alcohol levels above the legal limit;[78] it would be surprising if most of these were not at least partly to blame for the accidents in which they died.[79]

Then there are accidents caused by sudden vehicle defect, such as tyre blow-outs, sudden brake or steering failure, or the like. There has been much controversy

74 Pearson Report, vol. 2, paras. 199–201. See also Harris 1984 Survey, figs. 2.8, 2.9.
75 Department for Transport, *Road Casualties in Great Britain 2004*, table 19.
76 Ibid., table 23.
77 TRRL CR 146 (1990).
78 TRRL Report RR 266 (1990).
79 A high proportion of pedestrians killed and injured on the roads are intoxicated: *The Times*, 7 December 1992 (reporting findings of the RRL).

about the extent to which vehicle defects cause or contribute to road accidents; but such data as we have suggests that less than 10% of road accidents are primarily the result of vehicle defects.[80] One problem from our point of view is that vehicle defects are often attributable to the fault of the owner of the car in not maintaining it properly. In this event there could be tort liability, and although the negligence would not be in driving but in maintaining the vehicle, it is covered by compulsory insurance. On the other hand, proving negligence in such a case might be very difficult. Accidents due to sudden illness or death of the driver, which would also fall outside the tort system unless the driver had reason to know there was a likelihood of such attacks, are not common, but have been estimated to account for between 0.1% and 2% of all road accidents.[81]

In addition to accidents that occur without fault on anyone's part, it must also be remembered that there may be many accidents which, though caused by someone's fault, cannot be proved to have been so caused. The particular problem of the hit-and-run driver is now largely taken care of by the Motor Insurers' Bureau,[82] but proof that someone was to blame for the accident is still required. If, there are no witnesses of the accident, and the physical facts (such as the position of the vehicles etc.) do not themselves amount to evidence of negligence, the claimant will fail. In practice, this simple lack of evidence is a very common problem.

The second factor mentioned above was insurance. We shall look at the insurance system in detail later, but there are many road accidents which are the fault of persons who are not required to be – and usually are not – insured against tort liabilities, such as pedestrians and cyclists. Then there are accidents caused by animals on the roads. One estimate is that dogs are involved in some 500–700 personal injury accidents per year.[83] Another estimate is a good deal higher, and suggests that about 2,400 road injuries a year are caused by accidents involving dogs.[84] How many of such accidents are the fault of the dog owner is unknown. Dog owners are sometimes comprehensively insured, and such insurance covers third-party liability, but it is thought that not many owners would be so covered.

8.3.2   Industrial injuries and illnesses

Although many industrial accidents are required by law to be reported, it is well known that the statistics are patchy and not always very reliable.[85] The

80 See TRRL Report LR 498 (1972), para. 196 (2–3%); *Road Accidents Great Britain 1975* (HMSO, 1977), xiv (8%).
81 *Medical Factors and Road Accidents* RRL Report LR 143 (HMSO, 1967). See also *Medical Aspects of Fitness to Drive* (1968, published by the Medical Commission on Accident Prevention); L.G. Norman *Road Traffic Accidents, Epidemiology, Control and Prevention* (Geneva, 1962).
82 9.8.
83 Law Com. No. 13, *Civil Liability for Animals* (1967), paras. 36–8.
84 Pearson Report, vol. 2, para. 294.
85 The Health and Safety Commission once estimated that about a third of reportable non-fatal injuries are in fact reported: *Annual Report 1991–2*. See also S. Dawson *et al.*, *Safety at Work: The Limits of Self-Regulation* (Cambridge, 1988), ch. 2.

number of people killed at work has fallen dramatically in the last 30 years or so, mainly as a result of changes in patterns of employment away from high-risk industries.[86] In 1961, 1,228 people were killed at work while in 2004–5 the corresponding figure was 220.[87] The number of non-fatal injuries has apparently not fallen as much. The Pearson Commission estimated that about 680,000 employees and 40,000 self-employed people were injured at work each year;[88] whereas there were about 151,000 reported non-fatal work injuries to employees in 2004–5.[89] According to the Labour Force Survey, there were about 363,000 reportable injuries in 2003–4. There are no reliable figures in respect of occupational disease, but one estimate is that around 5,600 deaths a year result from workplace exposure to carcinogens;[90] and more recent estimates put asbestos-related deaths in Britain (most of which result from workplace exposure) at around 3,500 a year. The 1990 Labour Force Survey found that about 6% of adults who have ever worked suffer from illness which they believe to have been caused or made worse by their work (including past work); about half believe their illness to have been caused directly by work. The Health and Safety Commission estimates that in 2004–5, about 2 million people suffered from ill-health that they thought was work-related.

According to the CRU, there are about 250,000 successful workplace personal-injury and disease claims each year.[91] The Pearson Commission estimated that about 10.5% of those injured at work obtain some tort compensation.[92] There is, however, a widespread view that the proportion is much higher in serious injury cases[93] and this is to some degree confirmed by the Pearson Report[94] and more clearly by the Harris 1984 Survey.[95] It seems clear that the proportion of successful claims is a great deal lower than it is in the case of road accidents.[96] On the face of it, this is rather surprising. There are a various factors that might lead to the assumption that an industrial injury victim has a greater chance of success in a tort claim; for instance, employers are often 'strictly liable'; industrial accidents are probably less likely to occur unwitnessed; trade union advice and assistance is more likely to help the industrial accident victim. The Harris 1984 Survey also found that although about the same proportion of road and work accident victims consider

---

86 The most dangerous industry now is the construction industry.
87 Health and Safety Commission, *Health and Safety Statistics 2004/5.*
88 Pearson Report, vol. 2, table 29.
89 Reportable injuries are those resulting in an absence of at least 3 days from work.
90 J. Stapleton, *Disease and the Compensation Debate* (Oxford, 1986), 8. The Health and Safety Commission puts the figure at between 3,000 and 12,000: *Health and Safety Statistics 2004/5.*
91 The Pearson Commission's estimate was 90,000 successful accident claims and about 1,700 successful illness/disease claims: Pearson Report, vol. 2, paras. 168 and 180 respectively.
92 Pearson Report, vol. 2, table 14.
93 Evidence of the TUC to the Pearson Commission, para. 97.
94 Vol. 2, paras. 77–8.
95 Harris 1984 Survey, table 2.8.
96 Ibid.: 19% as against 29% for road accidents; and, according to Pearson, about one in eight as against one in four for road accidents.

making a claim, a smaller proportion of the latter actually seek legal advice.[97] One might have expected fewer road accident victims either to consider making a claim or to consult a solicitor, if only because many road victims are young children or elderly persons in retirement who would not suffer lost earnings, whereas an industrial accident victim is by definition a wage or salary earner. It seems that these factors must be outweighed by a number of other factors, for example, reluctance of employees to make claims against their employers; the road accident victim, by contrast, is less likely to feel reluctant to sue a motorist whom is thought to have been 'at fault'. Possibly, the fact that in road accidents the injured person may also have suffered damage to a vehicle makes a claim seem more worthwhile. Such evidence as there is, however, suggests (rather surprisingly) that whether or not the injured person received sick pay has little effect on the propensity of employees to claim damages;[98] and that 'road accidents in general appear to result in fewer permanent injuries than either work or other accidents do'.[99]

The Pearson Commission estimated that about one in four road accident victims obtain some tort compensation. If the correct equivalent figure for workplace injury and disease victims is (as the Commission suggested) considerably less, say one in eight, then on the basis of the CRU figure of 250,000 successful claims against employers each year, we might speculate that around 2 million people suffer occupational injury, disease or ill-health each year.

There seems little doubt that a considerable proportion of industrial accidents that do not lead to any claim are nevertheless due to negligence on the part of someone.[100] The annual Reports of the Chief Inspector of Factories used to contain an analysis of the cause of all fatal accidents. The proportion of cases in which some responsibility was attributed to the employer went as high as 61%.[101] Some unions have gone so far as to assert that in industries covered by statutory safety codes, compensation could be recovered in as many as 50% of the cases, though often at a very unsatisfactory level.[102] No doubt there are very many quite trivial industrial accidents in which the victim is only away from work for a few days, and it is not thought worthwhile to make a tort claim – particularly if some wages are still being paid. But it must not be assumed that people do not in fact claim relatively small amounts in tort actions – we shall see later that the actual amounts paid over in tort settlements are usually quite small. So far as industrial diseases are concerned, it is impossible to estimate what proportion could form the basis of a successful tort action.

97 Ibid., fig. 2.2.
98 Ibid.
99 Ibid., 57.
100 Contrast the conclusion of an HSE-commissioned report in 2002 that most compensatable work injuries enter the tort system: *Changing Business Behaviour: Would Bearing the True Cost of Poor Health and Safety Performance Make a Difference?*, Research Report 436/2002.
101 *Manufacturing and Service Industries*, Report of HM Factory Inspectorate 1977 (HMSO, 1978), table F.
102 Society of Labour Lawyers, *Accidents at Work: Compensation for All* (Evidence to the Pearson Commission, 1974), 7.

8.3.3   Public liability claims

According to the CRU, public liability claims – which are roughly equivalent to occupier's liability claims arising out of injuries resulting from the use of land – make up about 12% of all successful personal injury claims. As noted in 8.1.4, this represents more than a twofold relative increase since the 1970s and a very much larger increase an absolute numbers. There is little reliable information about such claims. Most are probably made against local authorities and other public bodies who are responsible for the maintenance of roads, pavements and other public spaces. A certain proportion are made against organizers and providers of sporting and recreational facilities. There is some evidence that the increase in such claims has resulted in reduced availability and increased price of public liability insurance in recent years.

8.3.4   Medical injuries

The Pearson Commission found that in England and Wales between 1973 and 1975 there were an average each year of 2,819 deaths from adverse effects of drugs and 77 deaths from 'complications' of medical or surgical care. It was estimated that in the UK there were 24,000 injuries per year caused by the adverse effects of drugs, and 13,000 resulting from medical or surgical complications. Research conducted in various countries in recent years suggests that perhaps one in ten patients in acute-care hospitals suffer 'avoidable' mishaps as a result of their treatment and care. It is notoriously difficult to identify the causes of many medical mishaps, but the Pearson Commission thought that only a minority of the cases of 'complications' would be attributable to negligence.[103] The Harvard Medical Practice Study, by contrast, estimated that about 27% of those in the study who suffered injuries as a result of medical intervention were the victims of negligence. Extrapolating the results of this study to the UK, it has been suggested that 'about 200,000 adverse events per annum occur in English hospitals, with around 50,000 being due to negligence'.[104]

So far as drug-related injuries are concerned, leaving aside mistakes in administration, liability for negligent 'design' of drugs or for negligent failure to warn of possible adverse side-effects is extremely difficult to establish in most cases, not only because of difficulties in proving causation but also because of the existence, both at common law and under the Consumer Protection Act 1987, of a development risk defence; and as a result of the rule that fault is to be judged at the time of the alleged act of negligence and not in the light of later developments in knowledge. Despite a number of much-publicised attempts, tort actions against drug companies in the UK have been spectacularly unsuccessful. The most notorious example is the so-called 'tranquilliser' or 'benzodiazepine' group litigation, on

103 Pearson Report, vol. 2, paras. 233–5.
104 M. Ennis and C. Vincent, 'Effects of Medical Accidents and Litigation on Doctors and Patients' (1994) 16 *Law and Policy* 97, 99. See also 1.4.1, n. 25.

which £40 million of legal aid funds were spent for preliminary work before legal aid was withdrawn and the claims abandoned.[105] At the time of writing, a potentially very large number of tort claims are brewing, arising out of use of the arthritis drug Vioxx, after a US jury made a large award to the widow of a Vioxx user for failure by the manufacturer to warn about known, adverse side-effects of the drug while at the same time engaging in a vigorous marketing campaign.

The Pearson Commission estimated that each year about 500 medical negligence claims (that is, claims based on alleged negligence by dentists and doctors) were referred to legal advisers; but 305 of these were subsequently abandoned. In 175 cases (35%) some compensation was paid, in all but five by way of an out-of-court settlement. The Commission also found that a relatively high proportion of medical negligence claims were actually tried or set down for trial. However, unlike other categories of claim studied, only a minority of the medical negligence claims that reached trial resulted in the payment of compensation.[106] The situation today is dramatically different from that in the 1970s. Medical negligence claims against NHS Trusts are now handled by the NHS Litigation Authority (NHSLA). It received more than 6,000 new claims in 2004–5.[107] On average, only 2.5% of the cases handled by the NHSLA go to court, and this figure includes settlements made on behalf of minors, which must be approved by a court. Research conducted in the 1990s suggests that more than half of medical negligence claims are abandoned at an early stage, 25% are settled and 3% go to trial. Of those that go to trial, about four in five succeed.[108]

The Pearson Commission estimated the amount of compensation paid by the three medical defence societies (who, at that time, provided insurance for medical and dental practitioners) to medical negligence claimants annually to be in the region of £1 million (in 1977 currency values). In 1988 the largest of these societies (the Medical Defence Union) alone paid out nearly £26 million. An estimate made in 1989 of the total annual cost of such claims was £75 million. The authors of this estimate suggest that it reflected an eightfold increase since the mid-1970s in the likelihood that a victim of a medical mishap will make a negligence claim, and a doubling in real terms of the average amount paid in compensation.[109] In 1996, the

---

105 C. Hodges, *Multi-Party Actions* (Oxford, 2001), ch. 22.
106 Pearson Report, vol. 2, paras. 237–9. A more recent UK estimate is that some payment is received in 20–25% of medical negligence claims: R. Dingwall, 'Litigation and the Threat of Medicine' in J. Gabe, D. Kellaher and G. Williams eds., *Challenging Medicine* (London, 1994), 50. The Harvard Medical Practice Study found that about half of medical negligence claimants recovered some compensation.
107 National Health Service Litigation Authority, *Report and Accounts 2005*.
108 H. Genn, 'Access to Just Settlements: The Case of Medical Negligence' in A.A.S. Zuckerman and R. Cranston eds., *Reform of Civil Procedure: Essays on 'Access to Justice'* (Oxford, 1995), 401. Other research found that less than 20% of medical negligence claims ended in a payment of compensation: Mulcahy, 'Threatening Behaviour?', 97.
109 Ibid. For attempts to explain the increase see M.J. Trebilcock, D.N. Dewees and D.G. Duff, 'The Medical Malpractice Explosion: An Empirical Assessment of Trends, Determinants and Impacts' (1990) 17 *Melbourne ULR* 539.

NHS was reported to have paid out £150 million to meet medical negligence claims.[110] In 2004–5 the NHSLA paid out more than £500 million in compensation in settlement of about 8,400 claims. This represents a seventeen-fold increase in claims and (making allowance for inflation) a 125-fold increase in compensation since 1977. No other area of tort litigation has grown to anything like this extent in the past 30 years. Nevertheless, medical-negligence claims represent only about 1% of all successful personal injury claims.

8.3.5   Group claims

Most road, work and medical negligence claims are made by individuals. Much less common are claims by groups of individuals – called 'group' or 'multi-party' claims. In the UK, such actions date back to the 1980s. Group personal injury claims have arisen out of large transport accidents, the use of pharmaceutical products and medical devices, and work-related illnesses and diseases.[111] Although uncommon, such claims tend to attract a lot of media attention, and may involve very large numbers of claimants and amounts of compensation. Because of the multi-national nature of the pharmaceutical and medical devices industries, group claiming has become a world-scale phenomenon; and the largest claims involve hundreds of thousands of claimants. Perhaps the largest group action so far anywhere in the world has been that against government-owned British Coal on behalf of former employees who suffered respiratory disease and vibration-related conditions as a result of working in the defendant's mines. Liability was established in 1996, and compensation schemes were established by the government. Applications to these schemes have now closed. More than 746,000 claimants have registered, and it is estimated that the total compensation bill will top £7.5 billion.

Although group claims are atypical, because of their size, value and high public profile, they have become a sort of lightning rod for fears and accusations that the tort system is out of control. At the same time, others see group claims as a symbol of the tort system at its best, empowering the injured and ill victims of corporate negligence, greed and deceit. Either way, group claims are the shop window of the tort system.

110 P. Toynbee, 'Legal leeches are bleeding the NHS' *Independent*, 28 February 1996, 13.
111 For accounts of some of the leading claims see Hodges, *Multi-Party Actions*, Part V.

9

Tortfeasors and insurers

9.1 Defendants

In legal theory, the victim of personal injury who wishes to make a tort claim can sue either the person whose negligence actually caused the accident; or, where that person was acting in the course of employment at the time the tort was committed, the victim may sue the employer who is vicariously liable for the employee's tort; or both may be sued. As a matter of law, the tort victim (except in limited circumstances: 9.3) cannot sue the insurance company that has agreed to indemnify the tortfeasor or the employer against the tort liability. The insurer has committed no tort, and the only person with legal rights against the insurer is the insured. But if we look at the matter from a more practical and realistic viewpoint, we can see certain similarities between employers who are vicariously liable and liability insurers. Both may be legally liable for tort damages in the ultimate result; neither of them is (usually) in any way personally to blame for the victim's loss; both of them can act as 'loss distributors' in the sense that they can pass the cost of paying damages on to others, namely premium payers (in the case of insurers) and customers, employees and shareholders (in the case of employers). From this perspective, the fact that the employer can be sued by the tort victim while the other cannot is a technicality. But even technicalities can have practical consequences, and there are some circumstances, as we shall see, in which there is an important distinction between the liability of an employer and that of an insurance company. Moreover, although the liability of employers is regarded as a part of the law of torts, the liability of insurance companies is regarded as something standing outside the tort system.

9.2 Individuals as tort defendants

Most tort claims for death or personal injury are made against insured individuals or against corporations or bodies which, if they do not carry liability insurance, have sufficient resources to pay a substantial award of damages. Most individuals could not afford to pay a substantial damages award out of their own resources, and in 7.2 we examined the argument that the fault principle is unjust to the extent that it takes no account of the means of the defendant. But there is no reason in theory why a claim should not be made against an individual who is backed neither by insurance nor a financially substantial employer. For example, a driver injured in an accident through the negligence of an uninsured pedestrian or cyclist may sue the latter for damages. What would actually happen if the victim tried to bring such an action and enforce recovery against the negligent defendant personally?

The first matter the claimant must consider is how to finance the claim. The first thing to say here is that since the sixth edition of this book was published, the financing of personal injury claims has been transformed by the abolition of publicly funded legal aid for most such claims and the introduction of conditional fee agreements (CFAs), more colloquially (but inaccurately) known as 'no-win, no-fee' arrangements. Under a CFA a qualified lawyer can agree to handle a claim for a client on the basis that if the claim fails, the lawyer will receive no fee for services; but also that if it succeeds the lawyer will be entitled to a fee 'uplift' (i.e. an additional payment) consisting of a certain percentage of the fee that could be charged for the services rendered if the claim were not being handled under a CFA. Because the basic rule of English law (as opposed to US law) is that a claimant whose claim fails is required to pay reasonable legal costs incurred by the defendant in defending the claim, CFAs can be supplemented by 'after-the-event' (ATE) insurance against potential liability for the other side's costs if the claim fails. If the claim succeeds, the defendant will normally be liable to pay not only compensation to the claimant but also the claimant's legal costs, plus the premium for the ATE insurance and the uplift provided for in the CFA between the claimant and their lawyer. Another method for financing personal injury claims is 'legal expenses insurance', also known as 'before-the-event' (BTE) insurance. This can be understood as a private form of legal aid: the insurance policy covers the reasonable costs of making the claim, and the defendant's reasonable costs of defending the claim if the claim fails. Legal aid was not abolished for medical negligence claims because they are considered to be so complex, difficult and risky that lawyers are likely to be very unwilling to handle them on a conditional fee basis.[1] In the present context, we can ignore medical negligence claims, because such a claim will always be made against in insured defendant or the NHS.

The first thing to note is that if the injured person has BTE insurance, it will ultimately be the BTE insurer, not a lawyer, who decides whether to pursue a claim against an uninsured defendant.[2] Unless the insurer is reasonably confident that the defendant will be able to pay the claimant's costs if the claim succeeds, it is unlikely to be willing to back the claim. Assuming that the injured person does not have BTE

---

1 See the discussion in H. Genn, 'Access to Just Settlements: The Case of Medical Negligence' in A.A.S. Zuckerman and R. Cranston eds., *Reform of Civil Procedure: Essays on 'Access to Justice'* (Oxford, 1995), 399–406.

2 Trades unions also support personal injury claims financially. Typically, these will be work-injury claims against insured defendants. But although employers' liability insurance is compulsory, it is not universal. A trades union may be asked to fund a claim against an uninsured defendant and might be more willing to do so than a BTE insurer.

insurance, the question that must be addressed is whether the fact that the defendant is an uninsured individual is likely to affect the willingness of a lawyer to handle the claim. In practice, unless the lawyer is willing to act on a conditional-fee basis, the typical personal injury claimant will probably not hire a lawyer to pursue the claim. Most tort claims for personal injuries are settled out of court, and in the typical case where the defendant is insured against liability, the insurer will normally pay the claimant's solicitor's costs (including the uplift) and the ATE insurance premium as part of the settlement. If the claim fails, the ATE insurer will pay the defendant's costs, and the claimant will only have to find any amounts not covered by the CFA plus (perhaps) the ATE insurance premium.[3] By contrast, if the defendant is an uninsured individual, there is a serious risk that if the claim succeeds, the claimant's lawyer will not get paid for their services. For this reason, it is unlikely that a lawyer would be prepared to take on a personal injury claim against an uninsured defendant on a conditional-fee basis unless, perhaps, the defendant were a large, self-insuring corporation or a very wealthy individual.

Does the claimant have any other options? Besides CFAs, there are two other avenues for financing personal injury claims: through a claims management company (CMC), (sometimes disparagingly called a 'claims farmer') and through a claims assessor.[4] CMCs are essentially legal services intermediaries who organize for an injured client the range of services and service-providers (legal, medical and so on) needed to make a personal injury claim. They typically operate on a no-win, no-fee basis. But because they are not qualified lawyers, they cannot make CFAs with their clients or charge an uplift. They may, however, require the client to buy ATE insurance. There is no obvious reason why a CMC would be any more likely than a lawyer to take on a claim against an uninsured defendant. Claims assessors, like CMCs, are not qualified lawyers, and so cannot represent clients in legal proceedings. Claims assessors, it seems, typically operate on a no-win, no-fee basis and contract for a share of any compensation recovered.[5] The service they offer is the negotiation of settlements. But because they cannot initiate and conduct court proceedings on behalf of clients, they are unable to use a direct 'threat' of legal action to give the defendant an incentive to settle.[6] For the same reason, they might not be in a good position to negotiate a settlement that made allowance for the assessor's entitlement, as against the client, to a share of the compensation. Once again, there is no obvious reason why a claims assessor would be prepared to handle a claim against an uninsured defendant unless the defendant were a substantial self-

---

3 ATE insurance may be expensive, and poorer claimants may have to borrow to pay for it in the first instance.

4 See generally Department for Constitutional Affairs, *The Report of the Lord Chancellor's Committee to Investigate the Activities of Non-Legally Qualified Claims Assessors and Employment Advisers* (2000).

5 In US parlance, this would be called a 'contingent-fee' arrangement as opposed to a conditional-fee arrangement. In the UK it is illegal for practising lawyers to enter contingent-fee arrangements.

6 All they can do is point out that the claimant may end up going to a lawyer if the defendant does not make a reasonable offer.

insured corporation or a very wealthy individual. Finally, an injured person might attempt to negotiate directly with the person thought responsible; but without being able to wield the threat of legal action, this strategy is unlikely to be successful, especially if the other person hires a lawyer.

Even if a claimant manages to overcome the funding difficulty and recovers judgment against, or negotiates a settlement with, an uninsured defendant, the next problem will be to enforce the judgment. For a defendant who has no substantial assets at all and only a modest income, the most effective and simplest (although perhaps not the most attractive) way of escaping liabilities is to file a petition for their own bankruptcy. The cost of doing this is relatively low, and once the petition is granted, the claimant will get no money and will have incurred much trouble and expense. If the defendant owns a house or has other assets such as a life insurance policy with a cash surrender value, or a car with some secondhand value, the claimant may be in a slightly better position. Bankruptcy of the defendant will enable C to lay hands on some of the bankrupt's property. But even so C will be faced with difficulties if, as is likely, the house is mortgaged, for in this event the mortgagee has first claim on the proceeds. Moreover, C will have to get D out of the house before it can be sold; this will take time, and if D is recalcitrant, further legal proceedings will be necessary to obtain an order for possession. When all this has been done the mortgagee may insist on making a quick sale (at a price sufficient to cover the mortgage) even though C may think a better price could be obtained by waiting.

A bankrupt can be made to pay damages in weekly or monthly instalments out of income rather than in the form of a lump sum. But in practice this procedure is very hard to use satisfactorily. An undischarged bankrupt is entitled to retain enough of their income to maintain self and family, and most people likely to find themselves in this position (i.e. those with no capital assets) are unlikely to have anything much to spare out of their income once they have taken what they need for their maintenance. In any case, even if this procedure worked smoothly, the bankrupt would be entitled to ask for discharge in due course – long before the debt would be paid off. If the bankrupt could show the indebtedness arose from some momentary piece of negligence, and if they had co-operated satisfactorily with the official receiver, the court would probably grant a discharge within a year or 18 months. Thus, if the judgment were for a substantial sum, the bankrupt would probably escape paying more than a relatively small part of it.

If the defendant does not choose the bankruptcy option, there are several routes by which, in theory anyway, the claimant might secure payment. Court orders for the sale of goods or real property may be obtained and 'executed'. If the defendant has a bank or building society account, it may be possible to obtain an order, called a 'third party debt order', requiring the bank or building society to freeze the defendant's account(s) and to pay a specified sum to the claimant out of the defendant's account.[7] There are provisions to deal with cases in which the freezing of the

7 Civil Procedure Rules (CPR), Part 72.

account causes hardship to the defendant or their family. An 'attachment of earnings order' requires the debtor's employer to deduct a specified sum from wages each week and remit the money to the court office. These orders first became generally available for the enforcement of judgment debts under the Administration of Justice Act 1970, which abolished imprisonment for debt.[8] They had not been an unqualified success in matrimonial cases, where they had been available since 1958; but some members of the Payne Committee (on whose recommendations the 1971 legislation was based) thought that they would be much more effective for short-term liabilities of a commercial character.[9] There are many problems in enforcing attachment of earnings orders against a really recalcitrant debtor. Frequent moves and changes of employment may be made. The debtor may simply disappear, and the creditor may have no means of tracing them. The police will not help because this is a civil matter, though it would be different if the debtor were first made bankrupt.

But even if all these difficulties are overcome and the defendant complies with the order, the procedure may not be a very effective way of compensating the claimant. In one case[10] the claimant's husband had been killed while a passenger in the defendant's car. The claimant recovered judgment for £7,100 against the defendant, who was uninsured, and the court ordered payment at the rate of £10 per month. If regularly paid, this sum would doubtless be better than nothing. But the payment of £10 per month never actually gave the claimant what she was held entitled to, since it represented a payment of interest alone of under 2%, while a judgment debt at that date carried statutory interest at 4%.[11] Thus the defendant's indebtedness would have been increasing all the time, despite the payments. In this light, it is not in the least surprising that few claims are brought against uninsured individuals. The difficulties in the way of enforcing a judgment by periodical payments are in practice enormous. On the whole this seems no bad thing. It is questionable whether justice is served by requiring a defendant to shoulder the burden of paying a certain amount a week out of income for the indefinite future.

It may be said that we have underestimated the chances of enforcing a judgment for a capital sum against an individual defendant. No doubt many people have some capital – for instance, a life insurance policy with a surrender value, or savings in a building society or bank. And a tiny percentage of people own really

---

8 See now the Attachment of Earnings Act 1971. In 2004, more than 40,000 attachment orders were made to secure payment of a judgment debt. Also in 2004, more than 300,000 'warrants of execution against goods' were issued; and about 6,400 third party debt orders. But we do not know how many, if any, of these various orders were issued in personal-injury cases.

9 *Report of the Committee on the Enforcement of Judgment Debts* (Cmnd 3909, 1969), para. 602.

10 *Jones v. Lloyd*, The Times, 22 March 1967. Insurance for this type of case was not compulsory until 1971.

11 There is some doubt as to whether statutory interest is due where the judgment is made payable by instalments, but this is usually an academic question. Surprisingly, it does not appear to have been settled by the Attachment of Earnings Act 1971.

significant capital investments. Furthermore it would be a mistake to think that all or most tort claims are for huge sums. As we shall see later, a very large proportion of tort claims are in practice settled for modest amounts up to a few thousand pounds, and there must be many people who could raise such a sum without bankruptcy or even serious financial strain.[12] Yet despite this, it seems that claims are rarely made against or paid by individual defendants out of their own resources, except in one type of case. Where a modest amount of damage is done in a road accident and the claim is no more than a few hundred pounds – which usually means that the claim is for property damage only – the defendant may prefer to pay personally rather than ask the insurance company to pay. If the insured is required to pay an excess of £100 or more under the policy and has a valuable no-claims bonus, then it may seem preferable to pay a claim of such an amount rather than make a claim. But where personal injury has been suffered, there seem to be few cases in which individual defendants are asked to pay tort claims out of their own resources, even where these are of amounts that many could afford to pay.

Several factors may contribute to this perhaps surprising result. First, people who do have capital (and so are able to pay) are probably more likely to be insured against less obvious risks of personal injury – for example, to have a comprehensive householder's policy covering risks to visitors, or a comprehensive liability policy covering liability for damage done by a dog or a child. Secondly, the most serious injuries tend to be caused by machines; and the most common kind of machine is the motor vehicle, which is required to be insured. Other kinds of machines, and also injury-causing processes, are likely to be owned or operated by employers or corporations. There are, of course, many household accidents, but claims are rarely made in such cases even if the accident is covered by a householder's comprehensive policy. Thirdly, if the defendant is neither insured nor backed by an employer, the claimant's solicitor (if one is consulted) will very probably advise that it is pointless to proceed.

Whatever the reason, the fact remains that very few individual tortfeasors pay tort damages out of their own resources. One survey found that fewer than 3% of the claimants received any tort payment from individual tortfeasors.[13] The Pearson Commission was unable to provide any estimate of the number or proportion of tort claims which are made against individuals,[14] but it must be very small indeed, probably only a fraction of 1%. The fact that the vast majority of tort payments are made by insurers or corporations is of fundamental importance to a proper understanding of the tort system and of the way in which it could best be reformed.

12 The Criminal Injuries Compensation Board found that only a minute fraction of offenders would normally be worth suing (*CICB Third Report* (Cmnd 3427, 1967), para. 21; *CICB Seventh Report* (Cmnd 4812, 1971), para. 17), but there must be a certain proportion of negligent tortfeasors with some assets.
13 A.F. Conard and others, *Authomobile Accident Costs and Payment* (Ann Arbor, 1964), 221.
14 Pearson Report, vol. 2, para. 61.

9.3   Employers and corporations as tort defendants

Unless a private individual carries liability insurance, it will usually be a waste of time and money to sue them. Not so if the tortfeasor is a financially substantial body such as a corporation or other business enterprise, a local authority, an NHS health authority or a government department. Anyway, even when not required to do so by law,[15] many such bodies protect themselves from the risk of tort liability by purchasing liability insurance from a commercial insurer (that is, an insurer who aims to make a profit). Some, particularly professionals, may belong to what is called an 'insurance mutual', that is an organization which, because it does not aim to make a profit, can provide insurance cover more cheaply than a commercial insurer. Also, mutuals are often formed in the hope that they will be able to settle claims more cheaply than a commercial insurer in terms of administrative costs. A very large body may act as a 'self-insurer', which means that it does not buy insurance from a commercial insurance company nor does it belong to a mutual insurer. Such a body calculates that over a period of years the cost of dealing with any tort claims made against it, plus the cost of paying compensation, will be less than the cost of buying appropriate liability insurance. Self-insurance only makes sense if the likely amount of any tort claim is small relative to the total resources (either actual or potential) of the entity that will have to pay it, so that paying it will not produce undue financial dislocation or lead to liquidation.[16] An entity which can borrow significant amounts of money easily (such as a large multi-national corporation) or which has access to public funds (such as a government department) may find it attractive not to buy insurance against legal liabilities, or indeed against other losses (such as losses to their property). So far as personal injuries are concerned, the Pearson Commission estimated that defendants who self-insured met about 12% of all tort claims, and paid about 6% of total tort payments in 1973.[17]

An alternative to self-insurance for a large organization that is a prime target for litigation is to set up a 'captive insurer', that is, an insurance company owned by the insured itself. London Transport did this in 1995 because it was dissatisfied with the

15 Since 1969 all employers (subject to a few exceptions) who carry on a business or who are incorporated or unincorporated bodies, have been required to insure against tort liability to their own employees (but not to others): Employers' Liability (Compulsory Insurance) Act 1969. The insurance must cover claims up to a total of £5 million arising out of any one occurrence. It is not compulsory to insure against illness and injury suffered by employees while they are working abroad; and the employer is under no common law (or statutory) obligation to arrange or to advise the employee of the desirability of procuring such insurance: *Reid v. Rush & Tompkins* [1990] 1 WLR 212. It is a criminal offence not to comply with the compulsory road-accident liability insurance legislation, but failure to comply with the compulsory employers' liability insurance legislation is not.

16 The principles underlying self-insurance can be illustrated by a choice between a lower and a higher 'excess' on an ordinary motor insurance policy. An excess provision, under which the insured bears the first £X of any claim, is essentially a form of self-insurance. People are prepared to accept such provisions if they calculate that they will save money by agreeing to pay the excess in the event of a claim in return for a reduced premium; and because the amount of the excess is usually small relative to the wealth of the insured.

17 Pearson Report, vol. 2, table 119.

high level of premiums being charged by its commercial insurers. Unlike a mutual insurer, a captive aims to make a profit, but the insured is able to take the profit.

So far as the law of torts is concerned, the liability of an employer (whether a corporation or an individual, and whether to employees or others) is said to be of two distinct kinds. First, it may be vicarious liability, that is to say, liability imposed on the employer simply because the damage was the result of a tort committed by an employee acting in the course of employment.[18] Secondly, the liability may be 'personal' in the sense that the employer or corporation is itself responsible, regardless of whether any identifiable employee was responsible. The distinction, however, appears to have little practical importance; and it may well be that cases tend to be classified as vicarious or personal according to whether the damage was done by misfeasance or nonfeasance. In the former case, there is usually no difficulty in identifying a particular employee as responsible; in the case of nonfeasance, however, it may be that no one person is responsible. Indeed, the gist of the complaint may be that the corporation has not nominated anybody as the person responsible for taking the precautions that were neglected on the occasion in question. We may therefore commit the solecism of speaking of 'vicarious liability' as covering both these species of legal liability.

Ever since the doctrine of vicarious liability came into the law in around 1700 it has been steadily expanded by the courts in two principal directions: the categories of persons for whose torts such liability is recognized has been enlarged;[19] and the kinds of act for which vicarious liability can be imposed have been extended.[20] There can be no doubt that in doing this the courts have been profoundly influenced by the fact that imposing vicarious liability was a satisfactory way of securing the payment of compensation to injured claimants, without imposing crushing liabilities on a negligent tortfeasors. Thus, whereas the doctrine of vicarious liability was originally only used to render an employer liable for the acts of menial servants under the employer's direct 'control', it came in course of time to cover all skilled and professional employees, however attenuated the control possessed by the employer. Moreover, there has been a steady increase in the number of situations in which an employer can be held liable for the torts of an 'independent contractor'.

Originally, there was no vicarious liability for the torts of independent contractors. This was because the main reason why the courts imposed vicarious liability – the fact that the employer of labour was usually an organization better able to bear the risk of loss or damage than the injured person – did not necessarily apply

---

18 Suppose an employee intentionally inflicts personal injury on another. In certain circumstances, such conduct may be in the course of employment, and the employer may be vicariously liable for it. The victim may also be able to claim under the Criminal Injuries Compensation Scheme. The relationship between this scheme and the tort system is considered in ch. 15.

19 See P.S. Atiyah, *Vicarious Liability in the Law of Torts* (London, 1967), Parts II, III and VII. For more recent developments see e.g. N.J. McBride and R. Bagshaw, *Tort Law*, 2nd edn (Harlow, 2005), ch. 35.

20 Atiyah, *Vicarious Liability in the Law of Torts*, Part V.

to the employer of an independent contractor. In one sense, the 'employer' of an independent contractor included every individual who engaged a company to perform some service: the individual client who engaged a builder to build a house; the individual who hired a vehicle and driver; even perhaps the traveller who purchased a railway ticket and travelled by train. On the other hand, the person who engages the services of an independent contractor is often a substantial corporation. Instead of being a large building contractor employed by an individual client, the independent contractor might be a small business employed by a local authority; instead of being a large concern renting vehicles with drivers to individuals, the independent contractor might be a single individual lorry owner who hires the lorry with their services as driver to a large company; instead of being a railway company which carries the public, the independent contractor might be a one-person, car-hire firm renting cars to a substantial company. In cases of this kind, the independent contractor might well be an inadequate risk bearer, at least in cases where the contractor has no liability insurance beyond what the law requires. For this reason, the courts have been willing over the years to extend vicarious liability to cover the torts of independent contractors in certain circumstances.

It may be objected that there is a danger that in our anxiety to compensate the injured we will create a rule which works well where the contractor is a small business and the employer a large enterprise, but badly when the contractor is a large enterprise and the employer a small business or private individual. In fact this danger has not been realized, and the explanation is probably that claimants offered two potential defendants, one of whom can easily bear the liability and one who cannot, will choose the former. In other words, if both employer and contractor are liable, and one is a large organization and the other is not, the injured person will sue the former whether that party is the employer or the contractor. If both are small organizations and neither is able to bear the liability, the chances are that the injured person will go uncompensated. If both are large organizations, then the law may have to decide which is the more appropriate body to bear the loss; but in this case there will at least be no difficulty in the injured person obtaining compensation from someone.

From the claimant's point of view, multiplication of possible defendants is obviously a good thing because it increases the chance that someone will be able to pay compensation or will be insured. But there are disadvantages; in particular, if, as will often be the case, it is unclear which of a number of possible defendants will ultimately bear a loss in the end, they may all take out insurance against the same potential liability, which is economically wasteful. Furthermore, any arguments about who should ultimately bear the claimant's loss may well take place between insurance companies at great expense but without any real gain to society as a whole.

Employers and corporations are more likely than individual defendants to have assets out of which to meet a tort claim and are more likely to be adequately insured. But a business might be forced into bankruptcy by a tort claim of significant size; and even large corporations can be plunged into serious financial difficulties by large or multi-party tort claims. Perhaps the most significant example is provided by asbestos litigation which, in the USA in particular, has led many corporations, large and small, into liquidation. The social impact of the liquidation of large corporations can be enormous, and in both the USA and the UK it is possible for corporations to implement reorganization plans as an alternative to liquidation in cases where the corporation's liabilities exceed its assets (where, in other words, the corporation is insolvent). The basic aim of such plans is to secure compensation for tort victims while at the same time enabling the tortfeasor to continue its business.[21] However, the reality is much less attractive than the theory. In the USA, corporations have been able to enter 'Chapter 11 bankruptcy' (as the procedure for corporate reorganization is colloquially called) even though not insolvent, and in this way to limit the funds available for compensation of tort claimants to an amount set aside for the purpose.[22] The result may be that the fund is exhausted before all present and future claimants are compensated. In Australia, the corporation which had been the largest manufacturer of asbestos products over many years attempted to protect itself by channelling its tort liabilities into a newly created and custom-designed offshore subsidiary, and by creating a fund to meet all its existing and future asbestos liabilities. The object was to provide financial protection for the operations of the main trading corporation in Australia. The fund proved inadequate after only a couple of years of operation. Negative publicity, government and union pressure, and a public inquiry forced the corporation to pump large additional funds into the trust.

Such techniques for controlling corporate exposure to tort liabilities are particularly objectionable in cases where, as with asbestos, it seems quite clear that corporations deliberately concealed known risks of the products they were producing and marketing. The story is similar in the case of tobacco products, the crucial difference being that cigarette manufacturers, unlike asbestos manufacturers and users, have been largely successful in defending themselves against tort liability. Such glaring examples of successful concealment of health risks raise serious questions about the idea that the risk of tort liability provides incentives to take precautions against such risks.

Quite apart from the fact that vicarious liability may help to provide the injured person with a defendant who can afford to pay compensation, it also has certain other advantages. The most important of these is that it may enable the claimant to get compensation even where the identity of the person responsible for the damage is unknown. A person is run over by a van bearing the name 'Bloggs Bakery'; the claimant can make a claim against Bloggs Bakery even though they cannot identify the driver or the registration number of the van. A person who is injured while unconscious on the operating table of a hospital may have no idea

21 See J.G. Fleming, *The American Tort Process* (Oxford, 1988), 250–1.
22 P. Spender, 'Blue Asbestos and Golden Eggs: Evaluating Bankruptcy and Class Actions as Just Responses to mass Tort Liability' (2003) 25 *Sydney LR* 223.

who was responsible for the injury; but if all those who might have been responsible are employees of the same hospital authority, the patient can sue the authority, and it is immaterial that they cannot identify any particular tortfeasor.[23] A person is injured in a factory by the negligence of a workmate who cannot be identified; again vicarious liability can be imposed. This advantage of vicarious liability may be particularly valuable where the claimant's argument is that some (unidentified) person in the defendant's organization ought to have taken precautions against the harm suffered, but no-one did. It is, of course, a requirement of the imposition of vicarious liability that *some* employee of the defendant committed a tort against the claimant. This means that a claimant who seeks to obtain compensation from an employer must establish two things: first, that a tort was committed by an employee of the defendant; and, secondly, that the defendant is vicariously liable for that person. The process is thus a double-barrelled one, similar to that involved in liability insurance (is the insured liable and does the insurance policy cover the liability?), and different from that involved, for example, in the case of first-party insurance (where the only question is whether the insurance policy covers the victim's loss).

There are important respects in which vicarious liability differs from liability insurance. First, the obligations of a liability insurer under the policy are owed to the insured, not to the claimant. As a general rule, this means that the claimant cannot sue the insurer; but if the insured goes bankrupt or into liquidation, the Third Parties (Rights Against Insurers) Act 1930 entitles the claimant to claim directly against the insurer instead of having to claim as a creditor of the defendant.[24] The fact that the insurer's obligation is normally to the insured also explains s. 153 of the Road Traffic Act 1988, which is designed to prevent the proceeds of a compulsory liability insurance policy being intercepted by creditors of a bankrupt insured rather than being paid in full to the claimant. By contrast, a person who is vicariously liable is under a legal obligation owed directly to the injured person.

Secondly, a liability insurer cannot recover the amounts paid out under the policy from the insured. By contrast, an employer held vicariously liable for the tort of another is legally entitled to seek to recover the amount of the liability from the tortfeasor, whether employee or independent contractor. Indeed the tortfeasor is legally liable to 'indemnify' the employer.[25] In practice, however, an employee (as opposed to an independent contractor) is not likely to be called on to indemnify an employer.[26] This point is pursued later when we look at the issue of subrogation and its attendant problems.[27]

---

23 *Cassidy* v. *Ministry of Health* [1951] 2 KB 343.
24 The third party's claim is subject to any defences the insurer may have against the insured: *Lefevre* v. *White* [1990] 1 Lloyd's Rep 569, 577.
25 *Lister* v. *Romford Ice & Cold Storage Co. Ltd* [1957] AC 555 (employee; the same rule applies to independent contractors).
26 Atiyah, *Vicarious Liability in the Law of Torts*, 426–7.
27 See 15.3.

9.4   Insurers

The vast majority of personal injury claims arise out of circumstances in which liability insurance is compulsory by law, and the Pearson Commission estimated that in personal injury cases, 88% of claims were handled, and 94% of compensation payments were made, by liability insurers.[28] Moreover, most other personal-injury cases involve as defendants large corporations or public authorities who act effectively as self-insurers[29] and can, for most practical purposes, be treated as though they were insurers as well as tortfeasors. The effect of this is that in most situations only an insurer has a real stake in a tort claim, and most tort claims are handled throughout by an insurance company rather than by the tortfeasor.

In practice, the great majority of tort claims are settled by agreement between the claimant (with or without legal advice) and the insurance company concerned, and only a tiny handful ever see the inside of a court. Of this tiny handful, only a very small fraction ever get to an appellate court where issues of 'law', as opposed to issues of 'fact', are likely to be discussed. This does not mean that the decisions of appellate courts concerning liability for personal injuries are irrelevant to the settlement of cases out of court, any more than statutory rules about liability for personal injuries are irrelevant to that process. Cases are settled 'in the shadow of the law' as it were; settlements are more or less influenced by what the parties think would happen if their case was tried by a court. On the other hand, the dynamics of the settlement process are very different from the dynamics of the court room, and it is wrong to assume that the result reached by an out-of-court settlement between a claimant and an insurer will accurately reflect what a court would have decided in that case. We will examine the settlement process in more detail in chapter 10.

Sometimes liability for personal injuries will be met by an insurer which has not provided insurance against the risk of liability for personal injuries. This happens most commonly where an injured person sues a firm of solicitors as a result of whose negligence (commonly in neglecting to start proceedings in time)[30] they have failed to recover damages for personal injury. A claim of this kind will be handled by the solicitor's liability insurers,[31] and if the negligence is clear enough, the claim will come to be treated very much as though it were an ordinary personal injury action.[32] Similar claims may occasionally be made, for example, against an insurance broker through whose negligence a policy has expired; here too, the broker's insurer may take over the claim.[33]

---

28 Pearson Report, vol. 2, para. 509.
29 Self-insurers in respect of road accidents are required to lodge a security deposit of £500,000 with the Accountant General of the High Court: Road Traffic Act 1988, s. 144.
30 The courts have a discretion to extend the period within which a personal injury claim must be made, and the fact that the claimant can sue their (insured) solicitor is a factor the court can take into account in deciding whether to exercise the discretion in the claimant's favour: *Hartley* v. *Birmingham CC* [1992] 1 WLR 968.
31 Solicitors are required to insure against liability up to a specified amount.
32 *Paterson* v. *Chadwick* [1974] 2 All ER 772.
33 See *McNealy* v. *Pennine Insurance Co.* [1978] RTR 285.

9.5   The nature of liability insurance

Looked at from the point of view of the insured and the insurer, liability insurance does not differ greatly from most other forms of insurance. Like other forms of insurance, it is an agreement whereby, in return for a premium, the insurer agrees to indemnify the insured against a loss – in this case, certain types of legal liability. On the face of it, the purpose of this type of insurance – as of all others – is to protect the insured against some contingency. It is the insured who pays the cost of the insurance because it is the insured who gets the benefit of it; the injured party has no direct claim against the insurer. Nor is there any question of the insurance company paying damages under the policy for the benefit of a claimant who cannot establish a claim in law against the insured. Since the policy is purchased by the insured and is an ordinary contract between the insured and the insurer, it is governed by the ordinary principles of the law of contract. So, for instance, if the insured has obtained the policy by fraud or misrepresentation or has failed to comply with the conditions of the policy, the insurance company should not be liable even though the real sufferer in such circumstances may be the claimant, not the insured.

From the insured's point of view, then, liability insurance is a protective device. From the claimant's point of view, it is a vital means of ensuring that people injured by others' torts obtain compensation; and in the context of personal injuries, this is how liability insurance is now viewed.[34] Indeed, insurance against liability to third parties in respect of personal injury is compulsory under the Road Traffic Act 1988[35] and under the Employers' Liability (Compulsory Insurance) Act 1969; and this is not for the protection of drivers and employers but for the protection of injured road users and employees.[36] It is misleading to think of tort law as being the primary vehicle for ensuring payment of compensation to accident victims, with liability insurance as an ancillary device to protect the insured. It is more accurate to view insurance as the primary medium for the payment of compensation, and tort law as a subsidiary part of the process. As we have previously seen, one of the chief reasons why the great mass of personal injury

---

34   For a thorough analysis of the relationship between tort liability insurance and the goals of tort law see G.T. Schwartz, 'The Ethics and Economics of Tort Liability Insurance' (1990) 75 *Cornell LR* 313.

35   Under this Act it is also compulsory to insure against third-party property damage up to a total of € 1 million.

36   There are significant differences between the compulsory motor and compulsory employers' liability insurance schemes. For instance, motor insurance has to be for an unlimited amount of liability, whereas employers' liability insurance only has to provide £5 million of cover for liability 'arising from any one occurrence'. In the case of motor, but not employers' liability, insurance the insurer's right not to pay if the policy was obtained by fraud or misrepresentation is limited. In the case of both types of insurance, insurers are prohibited from inserting certain types of clauses in the policy; but there are more prohibited clauses in the case of motor than in the case of employers' liability insurance. Failure to take out motor insurance is actionable in tort as breach of statutory duty, but failure to take out employers' liability insurance is not. See generally C. Parsons, 'Employers' Liability Insurance – How Secure is the System?' (1999) 28 *Industrial LJ* 109.

claims arises out of road accidents and industrial injuries is that insurance is nearly always available in these cases.

If this is the right way to view the relationship between tort liability and liability insurance, certain difficulties at once become apparent. First, why should the protection of insurance cover be restricted to those cases in which the victim's injuries are the result of actions of someone liable in law? Secondly, as a compensation mechanism, a system of tort liability coupled with liability insurance in which everybody is effectively insuring for the protection of everybody else, is vastly more complicated and expensive than would be a system of insurance (which in this book has been called 'first-party' insurance) in which everybody insured against their own losses without the interposition of tort liability.

It may help to appreciate the significance of these considerations if we pause for a moment to compare liability insurance with first-party (or 'loss') insurance. The risks covered by tort liability insurance could also be, and to a certain extent in fact are, covered by first-party insurance. For example, a person who has a comprehensive insurance policy on a car is insuring not only against the risk of incurring legal liability but also against the risk of any damage to the car arising from any of the events specified in the policy. Since one of these events will be the car being damaged in an accident caused by the negligence of another driver, this risk may be covered twice over: the owner of the car may claim either under their own insurance policy or may make a tort claim against the other driver which will be met by that driver's insurance company. If both drivers carry comprehensive insurance policies, the risk of damage to either car by the negligence of the driver of the other is covered twice.

The protection afforded by the tort claim and the tortfeasor's liability insurance is much less extensive than the protection afforded by first-party insurance. Liability insurance can only protect where there is legal liability, and this, as we saw in Part Two, generally means that the insured must have been at fault. Of course the more 'strict' tort liability is, the nearer liability insurance approaches to first-party insurance, until it eventually reaches the point at which it is, in effect, loss insurance purchased by one person for the benefit of others.[37] This is the basic position with regard to liability arising from nuclear hazards. Tort liability here is (by statute) so strict that in effect, the owner of a nuclear installation is simply required to provide first-party insurance for everybody else.

However strict the liability, it is still the case that the insured must be found, and must (if the insurer insists) be proved to have been liable. But a person's property may be damaged or destroyed in ways other than by the liability-attracting behaviour of someone else who carries liability insurance. For example, a car may be damaged without anyone's fault, or solely by the fault of the owner of the property, or by the fault of someone who carries no liability insurance, such as a pedestrian or a cyclist. The average motorist who has invested many thousands of

---

37 S. Jorgensen, 'Towards Strict Liability in Tort' in F. Schmidt ed., *Scandinavian Studies in Law 1963* (Stockholm, 1963), 25, 33.

pounds in a car is clearly unwilling to run these risks and is willing to buy insurance against them. On the other hand, although the motorist's first-party ('comprehensive') insurance covers many more risks than liability insurance, a motorist will generally be better off by claiming against another person and, through that person, against a liability insurer, than by claiming against their own loss insurer.

In practice, there is a very important difference between personal injury and damage to a car or other property, namely that people do not generally insure themselves against the risk of personal injury. Although a person's most valuable asset is typically their own earning power, very few people insure against loss of, or damage to, this asset. In the case of people of modest means, this is understandable because they are already (in effect) insured under the social security system, which gives them a significant degree of protection. But even people whose standard of living is a good deal higher than could be enjoyed on social security benefits rarely insure themselves against injury; and if they are injured, tort law and liability insurance may be their only method of obtaining really substantial compensation. It is not simply a question of preferring to claim against the other party to save a no-claims bonus: it is a choice between tort liability and liability insurance or no compensation at all other than social security payments, occupational sick pay or such benefits as may be available under a superannuation scheme if the victim retires early as a result of the injuries. If personal income-loss and disability insurance were as common as comprehensive insurance for cars, tort claims for personal injury would probably decline enormously in number and importance;[38] moreover, people would be compensated for personal injury even if it occurred without anybody's fault, just as they are at present compensated under comprehensive insurance policies for damage to their cars even though caused without anybody's fault.

If first-party loss insurance became the normal method of financing compensation for personal injuries, the premium would be related to the value of what is at stake (i.e. the earning capacity of the insured). Thus, just as the person with the more expensive car pays more for comprehensive insurance (though not for third-party liability insurance, because a more expensive car, as such, is no more likely to damage another than a less valuable car), so the person with higher earning capacity would have to pay more to insure against diminution or loss of that capacity.

Another difference between liability insurance and first-party insurance concerns the extent of the insurance cover. The likely monetary size of legal liability may be very difficult to predict in advance, but the insured may well want (or be required by law to have) insurance to cover the liability no matter how great it turns out to be. On the other hand, if the potential liability is unpredictable but could be

---

38 Although under present law, a tort claimant who received insurance benefits would also be entitled to recover tort damages and so, in effect, benefit twice over: see further 15.4.3.

very large, insurers may not be prepared to grant unlimited cover.[39] Where a person takes out loss insurance, however, this problem does not normally arise because the insured is much more likely to be able to predict the size of any possible loss, and the insurer can agree in advance with the insured a ceiling on the insurer's liability under the policy.

A major difference between liability insurance and first-party insurance is that a liability insurance system is affected by the law relating to contributory negligence. Since contributory negligence reduces the liability of the tortfeasor, and the insurance company is only bound to indemnify the tortfeasor against the insured's legal liability, it follows that the money actually payable by the insurance company under a liability policy will be reduced by the contributory negligence of the injured party. Most forms of first-party insurance do not work in this way because people wish to protect themselves against the risk of their own negligence as well as against the risk of other people's negligence; and also the risk of pure accident. When people insure houses against the risk of fire or cars against 'all risks', they do not expect the insurance payout to be reduced if they are themselves partly or even wholly to blame for any resultant loss. It is true that some insurance policies may require the insured to take 'all reasonable care' or all 'reasonable precautions' against the occurrence of the risk, but it is usually only in extreme cases that conditions of this kind prevent an insured person from recovering compensation under a first-party policy.[40] On the other hand, a policy may also specify particular precautions which the insured must take, and if these are not taken, the insurer may refuse to meet a claim under the policy.

Where both liability and first-party insurance cover the same risks, as in the case of a comprehensive motor policy, the effect of contributory negligence can, in theory, be extremely complicated. For instance, suppose that A and B are involved in a collision for which both are partly to blame, and that both cars, which are comprehensively insured, are damaged. In law A can recover from B and through B, from B's insurers, for the damage to A's car to the extent that B is to blame for the accident; and from A's own insurer in respect of the balance of the loss (less any excess which A is required to pay under the policy). Similarly B can recover part of

39 Large potential liabilities are often insured by several insurers, each of whom insures a certain part of the potential loss. Another common practice is for insurers to protect themselves by 'reinsuring', that is by finding another insurer who will insure part of the first insurer's potential liability to the insured. Reinsurers may do the same thing by purchasing 'retrocession' insurance. Certain syndicates at Lloyds suffered very large losses in the early 1990s by accepting highly risky reinsurance business in respect of liability for asbestos-related diseases and for environmental pollution in the USA.

40 A motorist who damages their own car by careless driving can normally recover under a comprehensive policy unless e.g. the driver had crammed eight people into a small car and as a result lost control of it: *Clark* v. *National Insurance Corporation* [1963] 3 All ER 375. See also *Stephen* v. *Scottish Boatowners Mutual Insurance Association* [1989] 1 Lloyd's Reports 535. The issue of reasonable care often arises in connection with claims for loss of property under holiday insurance policies; and in this context, too, the courts are indulgent to the policy-holder. In *Morley* v. *United Friendly Insurance Plc* [1993] 1 WLR 996 the phrase 'wilful exposure to needless peril' in a personal accident policy was interpreted generously to the insured.

the compensation from their own insurer and part from A's insurer. This appears to be a wasteful and complex procedure, and for many years insurers preferred to bypass it, if they could, by 'knock-for-knock' agreements. Under such arrangements, insurers agreed, in effect, to convert comprehensive insurance policies, so far as they related to damage to vehicles, from liability-*cum*-loss insurance into loss insurance alone. Thus A's insurer paid A for the damage to A's car, and B's insurer paid B for the damage to B's car; this saved much trouble and expense. In any particular case, the effect of the knock-for-knock agreement may have been less advantageous to one insurer than the other; for example, if A was largely to blame for the accident and the damage to B's car was more serious than the damage to A's car, then the effect of the knock-for-knock agreement was that A' s insurer got off much more lightly than if the agreement had not existed, while B's insurer came off much worse. But insurers calculated that in the long run these advantages and disadvantages were likely to iron themselves out as between large insurers, and that if they stuck to the letter of the law they themselves (and hence their customers) would bear the cost of adjusting the compensation according to the degree of fault of the parties.[41]

However, an insurer has an incentive to enter knock-for-knock agreements only if it sells both liability-only and comprehensive policies. The effect of a knock-for-knock agreement is that holders of liability-only policies are subsidised at the expense of holders of comprehensive policies. In recent years, insurers selling both types of policy have come under competitive pressure from insurers selling only or mostly comprehensive policies, who were able to offer lower premiums. As a result, most knock-for-knock agreements have now collapsed. The complexity and cost which such agreements were designed to avoid have been mitigated by the adoption between insurers of agreed formulaic approaches to the apportioning of blame between the parties involved in various types of accidents.

We can see, then, that liability insurance is a much more cumbersome form of insurance than personal insurance. It involves three parties (the victim, the insured and the insurer) rather than two (the insured and the insurer), and it involves two legal issues (the insured's liability to the victim and the validity and extent of coverage of the policy) rather than one (validity and extent of coverage of the policy). Moreover, in practice, the issue of legal liability of an insured is much more likely to raise difficult problems of proof and adjudication than the issue of coverage under a policy. The latter may sometimes be an issue, but in the great majority of cases of first-party insurance, no problem at all arises about whether the risk falls within the cover granted by the policy. On the other hand, it is only too common that difficult questions arise about the liability of an insurer under a liability policy.

41 A major factor in the failure in 1972 of the V & G Insurance Company was that it thought it could operate more efficiently without a knock-for-knock agreement: *Report of the Tribunal of Inquiry* (HMSO, 1972).

9.6   Some problems of liability insurance

These features of liability insurance make it particularly problematic for insurers. In principle, liability insurance premiums are based on an estimate of the likely number and size of claims, plus the administrative costs of selling insurance, collecting premiums and processing claims,[42] plus an allowance for the insurer's profit; on the other side, allowance is made for income which the insurer expects to earn on investments. The calculation of the likely cost of claims can be particularly difficult. The cost of claims is a function of three main variables, namely the number of successful claims against policy holders, the amount of harm suffered by claimants and the levels of damages awards. In the case of road and industrial accidents, the first two variables do not present great problems. Given previous experience from which the insurer can judge trends in accident numbers and severity of injuries, an insurance company can make reasonably sound estimates for the future. Of course, insurers can be caught out by sudden, unexpected changes in trends; but large fluctuations in these variables, in the case of road and industrial accidents, are rare. Estimating these variables – particularly the number of claims – can, however, present much greater problems in the case of liability for diseases.[43] An employer, for example, may be held liable to pay damages to employees who contract diseases as a result of exposure to dangerous working conditions. Many diseases take time to develop,[44] and in some cases symptoms may not be noticeable for 20 or 30 years after exposure. Employers and insurers generally may not be alerted to the risk of claims until after the first successful claims are made. Even if they do become aware sooner, and insurers start charging premiums to cover such liability, it may be extremely difficult for them to fix premiums at adequate rates because of lack of past experience. In such circumstances, insurers may be faced with a large number of claims over a short period of time in respect of which no, or only inadequate, premiums have been collected.[45]

The third variable – the amount of damages awards – can also cause considerable difficulties in two ways. First, the size of awards is partly a function of the rules governing assessment of damages. If the rules are changed without warning in such a way as to increase considerably the level of awards, this can upset insurers' calculations significantly. This problem is exacerbated by the fact that changes in common law rules operate retrospectively; that is, they apply to all trials and settlements after the date of the change, including those relating to events that occurred before the change, even though the relevant insurance premiums, which fund the compensation, were calculated several years previously when the law was different. Examples are the introduction in 1974 of damages for gratuitous nursing

---

42 The cost of reinsurance is also relevant.
43 J. Stapleton, *Disease and the Compensation Debate* (Oxford, 1986), 130–3.
44 As it is put: they have a 'long latency period'.
45 This assumes that what triggers the insurer's liability under the policy is the making of a claim. If the trigger is the incident which gives rise to the liability the insurer may have even greater problems.

services; in 1979 of damages for loss of earnings in the 'lost years'; in 1980 of damages for loss of ability to provide domestic care; and in 2000 of substantially increased awards for non-pecuniary loss. Another example was the reduction of the discount rate for the calculation of lump sum awards. Statutory changes in the law are not, in strict theory, retrospective; but they may be so in effect. For example, when s. 4 of the Law Reform (Miscellaneous Provisions) Act 1971 greatly increased the entitlement to damages of widows in Fatal Accident Act 1976 claims, the Act came into force one month after it was passed. Similarly, when the law relating to interest on awards of damages for personal injuries was changed in 1969, the effect was a substantial increase in the aggregate amounts which insurance companies had to pay. These increases took effect long before insurers were able to allow for them by increases in premium rates.

The general problem that insurers may be confronted with claims under liability insurance policies based on events that occurred years before the claim is made and years after the premium for the relevant policy was calculated, is referred to in terms of 'long-tail liability'. Suppose, for instance, that a claim is made in 2006 in respect of events that occurred in 1976. The premiums charged in 1976 might have taken no account of the risk of such liability, and would certainly not have taken account of changes in the law since 1976. Liability for traumatic accidents is 'short-tail' because typically the harm occurs and the claim is made at the time of or relatively soon after the harm-causing events. So far as personal injuries are concerned, the most important forms of long-tail liability arise out of workplace illness and disease, certain forms of medical negligence and liability for certain products, notably drugs.

The long-tail problem arises under liability insurance policies that provide cover on an 'occurrence' basis. This means that the policy covers liability based on events that occur during the period of the policy regardless of when liability arises and the claim on the policy is made. For instance, an occurrence-based policy current in 1976 will cover liability arising out of events that occur in 1976, whenever the liability arises. An insurer might seek to overcome the long-tail problem by selling insurance on a 'claims-made' basis, covering only liability arising out of claims made during the period of the policy. This would mean, for instance, that a policy for the year 1976 would cover only claims made in that year, and a policy for the year 2006 would cover only claims made in that year. This reduces greatly the risk of legal and other changes (such as improvements in medical technology) that might affect the number and size of claims between the date when the premium is calculated and the date of the claim because that period will probably only be a year or so. So claims-made cover is good for insurers but bad for potential defendants and claimants.

Suppose a potential defendant buys a claims-made policy in 2006, then retires or goes out of business in 2007. Suppose further that a negligence claim is made against the insured in 2016 arising out of events that occurred in 2006. Unless the insured has purchased 'run-off cover' in respect of claims for events in 2006, whenever made, the insured may have to meet the claim personally or the claimant may be unable to enforce the liability in whole or in part if the defendant lacks the necessary resources. For this reason, claims-made cover might be thought socially undesirable. The private insurance industry is not capable of resolving these difficulties; and suggestions are sometimes made for tax-funded compensation schemes to deal with long-tail personal injury liability. The social importance of this issue cannot be overestimated. Witness the current financial ramifications of liability for long-past exposure to asbestos. Asbestos-related diseases have latency periods of up to 30 years. It is anticipated that deaths and illness from past exposure will not peak until 2020; and that the total compensation bill for asbestos-related liability will top £8 billion.

Another source of difficulty in estimating the third variable is inflation. This affects most components in damages awards – compensation for loss of earnings and for costs (such as medical and hospital expenses) resulting from the injuries are affected quite directly; and damages for non-pecuniary loss are now increased more or less in line with inflation. Inflation causes most difficulty when the rates of increase of wages and prices vary erratically from year to year, for this makes predicting the size of future awards almost impossible. But even when, as in recent years, the pattern of inflation has become much more regular, predicting future rates is always a risky activity. And yet it is essential when, say in Autumn 2006, an insurer is calculating premiums for 2007, to calculate them in the light of expected damages in 2007. The position is even worse than this because of the length of time it takes to settle many personal injury claims. The premiums collected in 2007 must be adequate to pay all claims based on liabilities arising in 2007, even though a substantial proportion of these claims will not be settled for 2, 3 or 4 years, and a small number (probably of the larger claims) will still be outstanding in 5, 6 or 7 years. When the claims are finally paid, they will be paid in the light of wages and prices at that time, just as a court assesses damages in the light of wages and prices at the date of judgment. So an insurer, to be safe, may have to estimate inflation rates up to 8 years into the future. Even in times of relatively stable currency values, this is a daunting task. And because liability insurance is a competitive business, it is not easy for the insurer to play safe and fix premiums on the assumption of larger than expected increases in earnings rates and costs over the next 3 or 4 years. If it does this, it may be undercut by other companies which assume a lower rate of inflation. If, on the other hand, the insurer underestimates the rate of inflation, it can expect large losses.

Accurate prediction of the future will be particularly important in cases where a court makes a periodical payment order (PPO) (6.1.5.4). When damages are assessed as a lump sum, the insurer is able to close its books on the claim once the damages have been paid. From that point, the risk of future inflation and other adverse financial developments shifts from the insurer to the claimant. Similarly, when a liability insurer makes a structured settlement (6.1.5.3) based on a lump-sum assessment, the liability insurer will typically fund the settlement by using part or all of the lump sum to purchase one or more 'annuities' from a life insurer, thus shifting (part of) the financial risk onto the life insurer. Any remaining risk will pass to the claimant. Once again, the liability insurer can close its books on the claim. By contrast, an insurer against whose policy-holder a PPO is made will remain liable, under the policy, to meet the order for as long as, and however long, the order remains active. Even if the liability insurer chooses to meet (some of) its liabilities under the PPO by purchasing annuities, the risk that the arrangements it has made will not be adequate to meet its policy-holder's obligations under the order will remain with the liability insurer, which cannot close its books on the claim until the PPO expires.

The problems for liability insurers of accurately predicting future liabilities are aggravated by the fact that accounting principles require private insurance companies to balance their books from year to year. This means that in any particular year the company must (in theory, at least) have sufficient resources to meet all claims under the policies current in that year, even claims that may be made in future years and claims for losses that will be suffered in future years. In other words, the premiums charged in any particular year must be sufficient to enable the insurer to build up 'reserves' to meet future liabilities under policies current in that year. If an insurer significantly underestimates its future liabilities it may find itself without sufficient reserves to meet all its liabilities to policy-holders. If other insurers have made better predictions it may, in practice, be impossible for the under-resourced insurer to build its reserves by raising its premiums because it will be undercut by its competitors. In that case, the under-resourced insurer may be in a position where it is unable or, at least, likely at some future date to be unable, to satisfy claims against it and, for that reason, to be insolvent.

This simple picture of a properly functioning, competitive insurance market in which a well-run insurance company underestimates its future liabilities is complicated by a phenomenon which has become known as the 'insurance crisis'. The main symptoms of this phenomenon are sudden, unusually (and sometimes very) large increases in premiums for various lines of liability insurance. In Australia, such an event occurred in 2002 affecting mainly medical indemnity and public liability[46] insurance. Various measures were taken by governments to deal with the crisis, including a raft of reforms to the rules of tort liability, most notably those affecting assessment of damages. In Britain, the early twenty-first-century crisis has primarily affected employers' liability insurance.[47] The largest expense facing liability insurers is the cost of claims. But it is unlikely that increases in the cost of claims are a major part of the explanation of the typical insurance crisis because the cost of claims does usually not increase sufficiently far or sufficiently fast to explain the speed and magnitude of the increase in premiums that characterizes

---

46 Effectively, insurance against occupiers' liability.
47 Department for Work and Pensions, *Review of Employers' Liability Compulsory Insurance*, First Stage Report (June, 2003); Second Stage Report (December, 2003).

insurance crises. An important part of the explanation is what analysts call 'the cyclical nature of the insurance market'. The liability insurance market has been shown to experience successively 'hard' and 'soft' phases. For various reasons, what economists call 'barriers to entry to and exit from' the liability insurance market are relatively low. This means that it is relatively easy for new insurers to set up in business when it seems that easy profits can be made, and for existing insurers to leave the market when conditions are not so good. In periods when there is a lot of capacity in the market (that is, when there are plenty of insurers offering cover), competition may become very fierce, and this may force down premiums. If premiums drop to uneconomic levels (in the sense that the income of the insurer is insufficient to cover its expenses, including the cost of claims), and if this goes on for any length of time, there will sooner or later come a point at which an adjustment has to be made to the level of premiums to restore profitability, and that adjustment may need to be sudden and large. If, as a result of excessive competition forcing premiums down, a smaller or less well-managed insurance company collapses, this may aggravate the problem because like any market, the liability insurance market is sensitive to changes in the balance of supply and demand. If the demand for liability insurance remains constant, but the supply suddenly drops as a result of a company failure, insurers remaining in the market may take the opportunity presented by the change in market conditions to increase premiums to make up for past losses and uneconomically low premiums.[48]

Liability insurance crises are particularly problematic for activities in relation to which liability insurance is either actually or effectively compulsory. Without adequate insurance cover, such activities are either illegal or extremely unattractive. But even in other areas, sudden increases in the cost of, or sudden decreases in the availability of, liability insurance may affect people's willingness to engage in socially desirable activities. The fact appears to be that because of the significant role played by the tort system and liability insurance, many people have come to think of such insurance as a sort of 'essential service' rather like public utilities such as gas and electricity. However, an important difference between liability insurance and these public utilities is that the price and supply of the latter is more heavily regulated by the state those of the former. In both the USA and Australia, 'tort reform' legislation, designed to limit tort claims and levels of tort compensation, has proved a politically popular response to insurance crises, despite serious uncertainty about the role of liability law in causing such crises.

If, as a result either of bad luck, bad management or the outworking of the insurance cycle, a liability insurer becomes insolvent and is unable to meet its liabilities, the potentially disastrous effects for its policy-holders will largely be forestalled by the operation of the Financial Services Compensation Scheme (FSCS), established

---

48 For a more detailed discussion of the insurance cycle see P. Cane, 'Reforming Tort Law in Australia: A Personal Perspective' (2003) 27 *Melbourne ULR* 649, 658–63.

under Part XV of the Financial Services and Markets Act 2000 and administered by the Financial Services Authority (FSA). The FSCS is funded by levies on firms authorized by the FSA to carry on business. In the cases of compulsory (motor and employer's liability) insurance, the FSCS pays 100% of any claim against the failed insurer. In the case of non-compulsory liability insurance, it pays 100% of the first £2,000 of any claim, and 90% of the remainder. So far this has not happened in the UK; but neither have governments been prepared to regulate the insurance market with a view to mitigating the effects of its cyclical nature.

9.7   First-party insurance for the benefit of others

There is one important species of insurance which is a sort of cross between first-party and liability insurance. If a person, for instance, a warehouse owner, a carrier, a repairer or the like – a 'bailee' in legal terms – has possession of valuable goods belonging to other persons, it is quite possible that the parties will wish to take out some insurance beyond that provided by property and liability insurance. Liability insurance would not normally satisfy the bailor because it would only provide protection if the goods were lost or damaged in circumstances in which the bailee was liable in tort; and the latter would only be liable if at fault in some way. So if the goods are stolen despite all precautions, or if they are struck by lightning or burnt despite all fire precautions, there will be no tort liability and therefore, no insurance compensation. On the other hand, the bailee would not be protected by the normal form of property insurance taken out by the bailor, because this kind of insurance does not prevent the bailor from suing the bailee in tort (although it does prevent the bailor from recovering both types of compensation).[49] How is this situation to be dealt with? One possibility is for the bailee to exclude the bailee's normal tort liability by contract, i.e. to persuade the bailor to agree that the bailee is not to be liable for loss or damage to the goods. But although possible, this is a dangerous course because in practice the courts frown on this kind of exclusion and try to interpret such provisions favourably to the bailor. There is also the possibility of such a clause being ineffective under the provisions of the Unfair Contract Terms Act 1977 designed to prevent the use of unreasonable exclusion clauses in certain classes of contract.

The second way of meeting the problem is for the bailee to take out property insurance for the full value of the goods, partly to protect its own interest in the goods and partly to protect the interest of (or, in other words, in trust for) the owner of the goods.[50] Under this form of insurance, either bailor or bailee may claim against the insurance company, and tort liability once again drops out of the picture. Nothing corresponding to this type of insurance exists in the case of injury to the person. In fact the law places great obstacles in the way of taking out insurance against bodily injury directly for the benefit of another person, as opposed to

---

49 The insurance company is subrogated to the claim of the bailor; see 15.3 concerning subrogation.
50 E.g. *Hepburn* v. *Tomlinson* [1966] AC 451.

taking out much more cumbersome liability insurance. In practice, few people would wish to insure other persons directly against such risks, but an employer may well wish to insure its employees. However, the doctrine of privity of contract places serious difficulties in the way of such insurance being legally enforceable by the employee against the insurance company.[51] Thus, if an employer takes out an insurance policy designed to protect its employees against risks of bodily injury, including those for which legal liability would not arise, the policy may be unenforceable by the employee, unless the requirements of the Contracts (Rights of Third Parties) Act 1999 are met. Moreover, if an employer does take out such a policy and the insurance company (as may be anticipated) does not take any technical point about privity of contract but pays under the policy, the payment may be disregarded in any subsequent action against the employer. This will certainly be the case where the employee is killed and the employee's dependants receive the insurance money, for it is explicitly provided by statute that benefits to the dependants resulting from the deceased's death (and this includes insurance policies on the deceased's life) are to be disregarded in an action under the Fatal Accidents Act 1976.[52] It is perhaps not clear whether the result would be the same if the worker were only injured and not killed, but it seems probable that it would. If the employer attempts to meet the absurdity of this position by inviting its employees to give up their common law rights of action in return for better rights under some insurance scheme which would cover them even for injury or death not caused by fault, it will be found that this course is actually prohibited by law.[53]

The result of all this is that in the one area in which direct insurance against bodily injury and death by one person for the benefit of another might have been expected, the law has discouraged the possibility so strongly that, in practice, no real alternative usually exists to liability insurance, on the one hand, and first-party insurance, on the other. However, there are some cases in which such insurance may be found despite these difficulties, for example, an athletic club may insure its members against the risk of personal accident.

9.8   The impact of liability insurance on the law

The widespread availability of liability insurance has had a profound effect on tort law as a mechanism for compensating for death and personal injuries.

9.8.1   Statutory provisions

The most obvious way in which this has happened is through the enactment of statutory provisions. The Law Reform (Miscellaneous Provisions) Act 1934, for instance, which enabled proceedings to be brought against the estate of a deceased

---

51 *Green* v. *Russell* [1959] 2 QB 226.
52 Fatal Accidents Act 1976, s. 4.
53 Law Reform (Personal Injuries) Act 1948, s. 1(3); *Smith* v. *BEA* [1951] 2 KB 893.

tortfeasor, was a direct consequence of the system of compulsory road accident liability insurance introduced in 1930. The Law Reform (Contributory Negligence) Act 1945 also owed much to the fact that, with the spread of liability insurance, it no longer seemed reasonable to deprive a claimant of all right to damages merely because they had been negligent. The abolition of the doctrine of common employment by the Law Reform (Personal Injuries) Act 1948 was at least partly due to the complete change, which the practice of employers' liability insurance had produced, in the legal treatment of industrial accidents. The Law Reform (Husband and Wife) Act 1962, which enabled husbands and wives to sue each other in tort, was largely due to the feeling that it was unfair that a spouse was the one person who could not claim damages from an insurance company in the event of injury in a road accident through the negligence of the other spouse. Similarly, although the Congenital Disabilities (Civil Liability) Act 1976 provides that a child who suffers pre-natal injury may not sue its mother for negligence, there is an exception where the child's injuries were the result of a motor accident for which the mother was responsible.

Above all, the introduction by statute of compulsory liability insurance, first for road accidents and later for industrial accidents, has changed the whole focus of the law of torts from penalizing tortfeasors to compensating their victims. The system of compulsory road accident liability insurance under what is now the Road Traffic Act 1988 recognizes over and over again the fact that liability insurance is a method of compensating accident victims, and cannot be treated as though it were merely a device for protecting a tortfeasor against legal liability. One of the principal concerns of the Road Traffic Act 1988 is that matters arising under the contract of insurance between the insured and the insurer should not be allowed to defeat the claim of the accident victim as against the insured. Thus, for instance, if the insured obtains a policy by fraud or misrepresentation, the insurer's normal legal right to avoid the contract is severely restricted. If the insured breaks some condition in the policy relating, for example, to the condition of the vehicle or the driver (e.g. that the vehicle must not be driven in an unroadworthy condition, or that the driver must not drive while drunk) this does not affect the rights of the accident victim; although the insured may be under a liability to indemnify the insurer against the damages which the insurer has to pay. Similarly, a failure by the insured to comply with a condition of the policy as to anything occurring after an accident, for example, that the insured must give notice to the insurers within a stipulated time, does not affect a third-party accident victim. In fact, as we shall see shortly, the provisions of the Road Traffic Act 1988 are in practice supplemented by the extra-legal liability of the Motor Insurers' Bureau, which renders even less effective many stipulations in insurance policies so far as concerns the accident victim. In addition, since 2002 it has been possible for the accident victim to claim directly against the insurer without first claiming against the insured driver.[54]

---

54 European Communities (Rights Against Insurers) Regulations 2002. However, the accident victim stands in the shoes of the insured; and so the insurer is entitled to avoid paying by pleading against the victim defences that would have been available against the insured but which would have been of no avail if the insured had been sued instead of the insurer.

Employees, however, have no analogous right under the Employers' Liability (Compulsory Insurance) Act 1969.

Section 153 of the Road Traffic Act 1988, and the Third Parties (Rights against Insurers) Act 1930,[55] deal with the possibility that the defendant might become bankrupt. Normally it is not permissible to take legal proceedings against a person who has been adjudicated bankrupt or against a company in process of liquidation; such claims must be made to the trustee in bankruptcy or the liquidator, who will pay a dividend out of the bankrupt's assets. But if there is an insurance company standing behind the bankrupt, this process can be by-passed under s. 153 of the Road Traffic Act 1988, and the claimant can recover from the insurer in the normal way. However, this provision did not solve all the potential problems. If the claimant sued the tortfeasor to judgment and the tortfeasor was unable to pay the damages personally, the claimant could originally do nothing to prevent the tortfeasor going bankrupt after the judgment.[56] As a result, the insurance money would have been claimed by the tortfeasor's trustee in bankruptcy or the liquidator, and the accident victim (whose injuries were the sole reason for the payment of the insurance money) would have had to submit a proof for the claim and rest content with a share of the insurance money along with all the other creditors. This was changed by the Act of 1930, so that if a tortfeasor becomes bankrupt, the tortfeasor's rights against the insurance company pass to the accident victim, who can sue the insurers direct. This once again recognizes that the purpose of liability insurance is to protect the accident victim and not the insured.

A couple of important gaps in the provisions of the Road Traffic Act 1988 deserve mention. The compulsory policy need only cover the use of a vehicle by drivers specified in the policy; it is not necessary to cover use of the vehicle by anyone. If an insured owner allows a person not specified in the policy to use the car, the owner is guilty of an offence and may also be sued for damages for breach of statutory duty in respect of death, injury and property damage resulting from negligence of the uninsured driver.[57] But this right of action will not be of much use unless the owner is wealthy enough to pay the damages. In practice, however, the damages in such a case will usually be paid by the Motor Insurers' Bureau, which we will discuss later. Another gap results from the fact that the requirement to insure relates only to the use of a vehicle on a road. If the accident occurs in a car park, for instance, an injured person may be without redress if the driver is uninsured or the policy does not cover what occurred.[58]

---

55 This latter Act is not limited in its operation to road accident cases.
56 The Law Commission has proposed that under the 1930 Act, the claimant should be able to sue the insurer in the same proceedings: Law Com. No. 272, *Third Parties – Rights Against Insurers* (2001).
57 *Monk* v. *Warbey* [1935] 1 KB 75; but the principle is not applicable to pure economic loss: *Bretton* v. *Hancock* [2005] EWCA Civ 404.
58 E.g. *Charlton* v. *Fisher* [2002] QB 578; *Cutter* v. *Eagle Star Insurance Co. Ltd* [1998] 4 All ER 417.

Parliament again recognized the crucial role of liability insurance when it established the Legal Aid Scheme in the 1940s, under the terms of which an insured tortfeasor was normally unable to secure legal aid as a defendant.[59] The practice of insurers conducting the insured tortfeasor's defence was already established when the scheme started, and it was thought undesirable to throw these costs on to the taxpayer and thereby relieve the insurance companies. Yet, remarkably enough, Parliament did just this when it created the NHS only one year before the Legal Aid Scheme. Medical costs arising from road accidents are by and large borne by the taxpayer and not by insurance companies and their premium payers. However, from 2006 a scheme to recoup a proportion of NHS costs from tortfeasors will be in operation.[60]

Another notable example of Parliament ignoring insurance considerations is the provision contained in the Occupiers' Liability Act 1957 to the effect that an occupier of land will be liable for the negligence of an independent contractor only if the occupier was in some way at fault, for example, in selecting an incompetent contractor or in failing to supervise the contractor adequately.[61] Recognition that the occupier is the person best placed to insure against personal injuries occurring on the premises, and that contractors may be impecunious or may become impossible to trace or identify, might have led to a different result, at least in the case of business as opposed to private premises. Much the same criticism could be levelled against the Animals Act 1971, which pays insufficient attention to possible extensions of liability insurance. On the other hand, it is interesting and encouraging to note that the Unfair Contract Terms Act 1977 requires the courts to have regard to the availability of insurance (among other factors) in deciding whether certain types of exclusion clauses are reasonable.[62]

9.8.2   The impact of insurance on the common law

What impact, if any, has the prevalence of liability insurance and, indeed, the fact that it is compulsory in the great majority of cases in which tort claims are made, had on the reasoning of courts in personal injury cases? This not an easy question to answer, and it will help if we disentangle a number of separate issues. In the first place, there is the question whether the fact that the defendant in any particular case is or is not insured against liability is likely to affect the outcome in that case. The second question is whether the prevalence of insurance against certain types of legal liability has affected the rules of law or procedure in cases of those types.

---

59 Legal aid is no longer available for most personal injury claims.
60 15.3.
61 In *Gwilliam* v. *West Hertfordshire Hospitals NHS Trust* [2003] QB 443 it was held (over a strong dissent by Sedley LJ) that the occupier of premises may be liable to a visitor for failure to ascertain whether an independent contractor engaged to do work on the premises has liability insurance.
62 See s. 11(4) of the Act.

9.8.2.1   Effect of insurance in the particular case

With regard to the first question, it seems reasonably clear that the presence or absence of liability insurance in any given case is not a material factor in deciding whether the claimant or the defendant is entitled to judgment. In the days when personal injury cases were commonly tried by juries, it was a firm rule that the jury was not to be informed that the defendant was insured. This rule probably does not apply to trial of an action before a judge alone,[63] but judges can be assumed to be aware of the law and practice of liability insurance (e.g. that it is compulsory under the Road Traffic Act 1988). It has been vigorously asserted that the judge must disregard the possibility that the defendant is insured. In *Davie* v. *New Merton Board Mills*, an action by a worker against his employer, Viscount Simonds said that it was 'not the function of a court of law to fasten on the fortuitous circumstances of insurance to impose a greater burden on the employer than would otherwise lie on him'.[64] It seems unlikely that decisions in particular cases by judges, either on issues of liability or assessment of damages, would be affected by whether or not the defendant had insurance against liability, if only because judges probably assume in the normal case that the defendant is insured.[65]

It has been suggested that the best reason for rejecting as irrelevant the fact that the defendant is or is not covered by insurance in any given case is that any other rule would make it impossible to fix premium rates for liability insurance.[66] However, liability insurance rates are fixed by insurers in the light of past experience as to the number of incidents covered by the policy for which legal liability is likely to be incurred. If liability itself turned on whether insurance existed, the extent of such insurance would merely be one more matter relevant to the assessment of the risk. Of course, confining liability to cases in which liability insurance existed would greatly discourage this form of insurance, for many people would not willingly pay premiums to cover a risk for which they would not be liable if they did not insure.

Just as whether or not the defendant has liability insurance is ignored, so also, whether or not the claimant has first-party insurance is irrelevant.[67] In a personal injury case, the established rule is that the claimant is permitted to keep insurance proceeds and recover damages in addition.[68] In a property damage case (where

---

63 *Harman* v. *Crilly* [1943] 1 KB 68.

64 [1959] AC 604, 627.

65 There is some empirical evidence from the USA which suggests that a jury is likely to award higher damages against an insured defendant than against one who is uninsured and is likely to award less than full compensation against an uninsured defendant: H. Kalven, 'The Jury, the Law and the Personal Injury Damage Award' (1958) 19 *Ohio State LJ* 158, 171. Jury trials are extremely rare in personal injury actions in the UK.

66 Jorgensen, 'Towards Strict Liability in Tort', 29.

67 'In determining the rights *inter se* of A and B, the fact that one of them is insured is to be disregarded': *Lister* v. *Romford Ice* [1957] AC 555, 576–7 *per* Viscount Simonds.

68 15.4.3.

first-party insurance is more common), the insurance company takes over the claimant's tort rights by subrogation.[69]

9.8.2.2   Possible influence of practice of insurance on the common law

When we turn to consider the effect of the practice of insurance on the development of common (judge-made) law as opposed to the result in individual cases, it seems very likely that it has been influenced by the growing availability and use of liability (and other) insurance.[70] It is not easy to prove this proposition rigorously, but it is surely the case that the steady expansion of liability for negligence during the past hundred years or so is partly due to the fact that insurance enables judges to give effect to their desire to compensate claimants without imposing undue hardship on defendants. It has been said that the standard of care required in the law of negligence has been tightened up over the years partly as a response to the prevalence of liability insurance.[71] The tendency to 'objectivize' the standard of care, and to ignore the personal characteristics of the defendant may also have been influenced by insurance considerations.[72] The fact that more subjective considerations are taken into account in deciding questions of contributory negligence than in deciding questions of negligence[73] seems to support the general proposition; as does the fact that the courts nearly always 'bend' the law in favour of the claimant in cases in which a trivial act of negligence has resulted fortuitously in serious personal injury.[74]

Judges do occasionally discuss the relationship between liability rules and liability (and other) insurance. For instance, in one case, in which an injured rugby player sued an amateur referee for negligent failure to enforce the rules of the game, both the trial judge and the Court of Appeal thought it weighed in favour of recognizing a duty of care in such circumstances that a large rugby organization, which was vicariously liable for the negligence of the referee, was able to insure against liability.[75] On the other hand, the possibility that players might purchase personal accident insurance was also mentioned. By contrast, in a case in which an injured boxer sued the boxing regulatory body for failure to require adequate ringside medical facilities, a duty of care was recognized in express disregard of any financial or insurance difficulties this might have caused the defendant.[76] It has been held that an occupier of land owes a duty to visitors to the land to check that

---

69 In this type of case, the insured cannot keep both the insurance monies and the tort damages: if the insurer pays out and the claimant recovers tort damages, the insured must pay the damages over to the insurer.

70 But see J. Stapleton, 'Tort, Insurance and Ideology' (1995) 58 *Modern LR* 820, 824–8.

71 See e.g. Jorgensen, 'Towards Strict Liability in Tort', 53 ff.

72 Lord Denning, perhaps the greatest English judge of the twentieth century, was certainly influenced by insurance considerations: *Nettleship* v. *Weston* [1971] 2 QB 691, 699–700.

73 2.5.1.

74 5.3.3.

75 *Vowles* v. *Evans* [2003] 1 WLR 1607 at [12].

76 *Watson* v. *British Boxing Board of Control* [2001] QB 1134 at [89].

an independent contractor employed to do work on the land has public liability insurance cover.[77] However, the duty was held not to extend to checking that the policy was current or that it provided adequate coverage. Moreover, it has been held that a school owes no legal duty to advise parents to insure their children against personal injury suffered while playing sport;[78] and that an employer owes its employees no duty to advise them to take out personal accident insurance when working abroad for the employer.[79]

Of course, although it seems very likely that the prevalence of liability insurance has influenced the development of the law, it does not follow, even in cases such as road accident cases, where liability insurance is compulsory, that the claimant will always recover. For example, problems of proving fault are still significant, and the tort system is very far from being one of strict liability backed up by liability insurance.[80] On the other hand, defences – especially contributory negligence – the effect of which is to deprive an uninsured claimant of compensation which would be paid by an insured defendant, remain an important aspect of negligence law. In fact, tort law is, at bottom, a system of rules and principles of personal responsibility for conduct and its consequences; and although tort law could not operate as effectively as it does as a compensation system, and would probably not have developed as it has, without widespread liability insurance, the basis of tort liability is personal responsibility, not the availability of insurance. The fact that liability insurance was available only tells us that the defendant *could pay* any damages awarded, not that D *should be held liable* to pay compensation.

At the same time, however, it is surely the case that the size of damages awards in personal injury cases is explicable only on the basis that judges are influenced by the widespread presence of insurance. It can hardly be supposed that judges would habitually award thousands or tens of thousands of pounds in damages without a thought for the effect of such awards on the defendant, if they did not appreciate that the damages would not be paid by the defendants themselves.[81] The fact that tort damages are usually paid by insurance companies does not necessarily make the size of damages awards a matter of no concern. First, and at the most general level, it can be argued that whoever pays tort damages, compensating people uses

77 *Gwilliam* v. *West Hertfordshire NHS Trust* [2003] QB 443. But contrast *Naylor v Payling* [2004] EWCA 560, discussed in R. Lewis, 'Insurance and the Tort System' (2005) 25 *LS* 85, 108.

78 *Van Oppen* v. *Clerk to the Bedford Charity Trustees* [1990] 1 WLR 235.

79 *Reid* v. *Rush & Tompkins Group Plc* [1990] 1 WLR 212.

80 Lewis, 'Insurance and the Tort System', 103–5. One US survey found that in 68% of the serious cases in which no tort compensation was received, the reason was that there was no party at fault, or that fault could not be proved, or that the claimant was guilty of contributory negligence (which at the time was a complete bar to recovery in many US jurisdictions): Conard, *Automobile Accident Costs and Payments* table 6.2, 210. The Harris 1984 Survey found that problems in obtaining evidence and attribution of the injury to the claimant's own fault were the two most frequently cited reasons for abandoning claims (table 3.12), and the second and fourth most frequently cited reasons (respectively) for not claiming at all (table 2.12).

81 See *Morris* v. *Ford Motor Co.* [1973] QB 792, 798 *per* Lord Denning MR.

up resources which could be used for other, and perhaps more pressing, purposes. Society's resources are not unlimited, and money used for one purpose is unavailable for other purposes. Secondly, it has occasionally been argued that very high damages awards might result in the failure of insurance companies.[82] This, however, is a weak argument: properly regulated insurance companies should not go bankrupt because damage awards are high. Premiums are fixed partly by reference to the level of awards made by the courts; if awards go up, then premiums must go up too. Unless awards are suddenly doubled overnight without warning, no insurance company should be in trouble merely as a result of the high level of awards. When insurance companies get into financial difficulties, it is usually a result of a sudden and unpredicted increase in the numbers of claims, or of bad management, or of excessive competition in the insurance market leading to the setting of premiums at unrealistically low levels.

Thirdly, it is sometimes argued that if liability insurance premiums rise too high as a result of wide liability rules or generous damages awards, manufacturers of goods and providers of services might not be able easily to afford them, and might go out of business, thus making their goods and services unavailable to consumers. There are several problems with such arguments. First, while it is true, for example, that there were large increases in the liability insurance premiums paid by many professional groups, such as doctors and lawyers, in the 1980s, it seems that these were the result of the dynamics of the insurance market rather than of changes in the rules governing tort liability or the assessment of tort damages.[83] Secondly, while it is often alleged, for example, that rising insurance costs and increased risk of being sued has affected recruitment into and retirement from high-risk medical specialties such as obstetrics, there is inadequate evidence of such a causal relationship.[84] Thirdly, insurance premiums form a very small part of the costs of most businesses, and injury costs would have to reach astronomical proportions before premium rates caused serious financial trouble to most businesses. Fourthly, there is an argument for saying, at least in some contexts, that if an industry cannot afford to pay adequate compensation for injuries it inflicts, it should go out of business.

This last argument has to be treated with some care. In one case Lord Denning took the view that no damages for future loss of income should be awarded to accident victims who are reduced to a state of permanent unconsciousness and have no dependants.[85] The defendant in the case was an NHS hospital. Obviously, the resources available to NHS trusts are limited, and the more they have to spend on meeting damages awards, the less there is available for their core functions. For

---

82 *Fletcher* v. *Autocar Ltd* [1968] 2 QB 322, 335 *per* Lord Denning MR.
83 P. Cane, 'Liability Rules and the Cost of Professional Indemnity Insurance' (1989) 14 *Geneva Papers on Risk and Insurance* 347; R. Dingwall, P. Fenn and L. Quam, *Medical Negligence: A Review and Bibliography* (Oxford, 1991), 13–18 (on the position in the USA). See also J.G. Fleming, 'The Insurance Crisis' (1990) 24 *U. of British Columbia LR* 1.
84 Dingwall, Fenn and Quam, *Medical Negligence*, 51–5.
85 *Lim Poh Choo* v. *Camden AHA* [1971] 2 QB 691.

example, a ward may have to be closed to finance a judgment.[86] It does not follow that victims of medical mishaps should not be awarded tort compensation, but the case does reinforce the point that when resources are limited, tort compensation may only be payable at the cost of some other desirable end. This general insight, as we said earlier, is valid whoever bears the immediate cost of the tort award. However, Lord Denning was alone in the view he took, and the House of Lords reaffirmed the decision of the majority awarding compensation for future loss of income, effectively on the ground that since income loss had been suffered, it should be compensated for.[87]

9.8.2.3   Limited effect of practice of insurance

Despite the influence of widespread liability insurance on the common law of torts, it must be said that there has been no really deep-seated change such as might have been expected if judges or law reformers had wished to rebuild the law on the foundations of the liability insurance system. Had it been openly acknowledged that tort damages are usually paid by liability insurers, that this system has come to stay and that it is a good system on which to base a system of compensation for personal injuries, one might have expected the basic criterion of liability for personal injuries to change from fault to something like ability to insure cheaply and easily. Such a shift would probably lead to the imposition of much stricter liability; and to the extension of vicarious liability so that, for example, the owner of a car could be held liable for the negligence of a passenger in opening a car door in the path of an incoming cyclist;[88] so that parents could be held liable for torts of their children; and so that the organizer of a sporting events could be held liable for injuries caused by participants in the event. Under the present law the car owner, the parent or the sports organizer can only be held liable if they were personally at fault in some way; but each is in a good position to insure against liability.

There are many areas of law and procedure in which the realities of insurance and the tort system are ignored. First, and most obviously, the claimant must still find and, if necessary, sue a defendant who is legally liable even in cases in which the case will be handled throughout by an insurance company on the tortfeasor's behalf. Except in road accident cases, the claimant cannot claim directly against the insurer. If the claim cannot be settled without the commencement of court proceedings, a claim form must be served on the defendant or on a party authorized by the defendant to accept service. If this cannot be done, and the court does not waive the requirement for service,[89] the claim may not proceed.

---

86 Dingwall, Fenn and Quam, *Medical Negligence*, 55–6.
87 [1980] AC 174.
88 The obligation to insure under the Road Traffic Act does not extend to a passenger in a car but not using it: *Brown* v. *Roberts* [1965] 1 QB 1; comprehensive motor policies usually cover such accidents, but the insurer has no obligation to indemnify a passenger who is not a party to the policy.
89 A.A.S. Zuckerman, *Civil Procedure* (London, 2003), 4.51–2.

Until quite recently, great difficulty could arise where the defendant was a company that had become defunct and had been removed from the Companies Register before the action was commenced.[90] If the action was commenced within 2 years of the company's removal from the Register, an application could be made to have the company restored to the Register for the purpose of being sued. But after that, any action would fail for lack of a defendant, even if the company's insurer was still in existence.[91] Fortunately, however, there is now no time limit on making an application for revival of a company for the purposes of suing it for personal injuries or under the Fatal Accidents Act 1976.[92]

A problem may arise where one spouse is injured in a road accident due to the negligence of the other spouse, who is killed in the same accident. If the surviving spouse wishes to claim damages against the insurance company, the nominal defendant must be the representative (that is, the executor or administrator) of the other's estate. This will often be the surviving spouse; but serious legal difficulties would arise if the surviving spouse were both claimant and nominal defendant, and it is therefore necessary to obtain a special grant of representation in such circumstances by which a third party is appointed administrator for the sole purpose of being defendant in the proceedings which the spouse wishes to bring.[93]

Another kind of difficulty arising from unwillingness to recognize the effect of liability insurance is to be found in the decision of *Lister* v. *Romford Ice and Cold Storage.*[94] In this case the House of Lords decided that an employee who negligently injures another employee in the course of the former's employment, and who thereby renders the employer vicariously liable to compensate the injured employee, is personally liable to indemnify the employer against this liability. The employee's liability arises from the fact that the employee has been guilty of a breach of contract in negligently injuring the other employee. On the face of it the decision seems sensible; but when it is appreciated that the employer was insured against the liability, that the damages were paid by the insurance company, and that the proceedings in the name of the employer and against the negligent employee were effectively brought by and for the benefit of the insurance company, the whole process begins to look grotesque. But – and this is typical of the way the English legal system tries to come to terms with liability insurance – the decision has proved of little practical importance, because insurers have generally agreed that they will not take proceedings of this nature without the consent of the employer.[95] And in a case not falling

---

90 A particularly farcical example was *Re Harvest Lane Motor Bodies* [1969] 1 ch. 457.

91 *Bradley* v. *Eagle Star Insurance Co. Ltd* [1989] AC 957.

92 Companies Act 1989, s. 141. Of course, revival will be allowed only if the ordinary limitation period for the action has not expired. The Law Commission has proposed that in such a situation, the claimant should be able to sue the insurer alone without having to apply for revival of the company: Law Com. No. 272, *Third Parties – Rights Against Insurers* (2001).

93 *Re Newsham* [1966] 3 All ER 681.

94 [1957] AC 555.

95 See Atiyah, *Vicarious Liability in the Law of Torts*, 426–7.

within the terms of this agreement, the Court of Appeal has come very close to refusing to follow the *Lister* case.[96]

Finally, two cases which illustrate strange effects of the law's refusal to pay attention to liability insurance. First, *Chaplin* v. *Boys*:[97] the claimant was injured in a road accident in Malta; Maltese law did not recognize claims for pain and suffering, and the claim was brought in England. The question was whether damages could be awarded for pain and suffering according to English law, and the House of Lords ultimately held that they could. Nowhere in the lengthy judgments was the question of insurance raised; but perhaps the strongest argument against allowing such a claim is that in all probability the defendant's third-party insurance was taken out in Malta, and the premium fixed according to Maltese law. It seems difficult to justify a decision that can result in an insurance company being held liable to pay damages much higher than those on the basis of which the premium is fixed.

Secondly, consider the case of *Hunt* v. *Severs*:[98] the claimant was very seriously injured in a motorcycle accident caused by the negligence of her partner, the defendant (whom she later married). The claimant needed continuing care, and the defendant was involved in providing it. The question was whether the claimant was entitled to damages representing the value of the defendant's services (6.2.3). The House of Lords held that she was not, on the ground that if damages had been awarded, the defendant would have paid twice over: once by providing the services, and a second time by paying damages representing their value. This argument ignores the fact that the damages would not have been paid by the defendant but by his insurer; and, more importantly, that by denying damages the court was in fact depriving both claimant and defendant of a certain amount of financial support. It might also be argued that since, as Lord Bridge said, the purpose of awarding damages for gratuitous care is to compensate the carer,[99] the odd effect of making an award in respect of services rendered by the defendant would be that the tortfeasor would receive damages in respect of the tort.[100] Perhaps the strongest pragmatic reason to allow recovery is so as not to discourage provision of care by family members in preference to professional carers where this is felt to be more appropriate.[101]

96 *Morris* v. *Ford Motor Co. Ltd* [1973] 1 QB 792.
97 [1971] AC 356.
98 [1994] 2 AC 350. See also *Hayden* v. *Hayden* [1992] 1 WLR 986. The High Court of Australia has decided otherwise: *Kars* v. *Kars* (1996) 187 CLR 354.
99 The House of Lords also held that damages representing the value of gratuitous services rendered to the claimant are held on trust by the claimant and must be paid over to the carer.
100 But note that one effect of the Law Reform (Husband and Wife) Act 1962, which reversed the rule that one spouse could not be held liable in tort to the other, was to enable spouse-tortfeasors to benefit indirectly from damages recovered by the claimant spouse. Such indirect benefit will accrue in any case where claimant and defendant are part of the same domestic economic unit.
101 The social security system also recognizes the importance of providing support for family members who care for disabled relatives: 12.4.3.2.

9.9   The Motor Insurers' Bureau

The Motor Insurers' Bureau (MIB) was set up by the insurance industry in 1946 under pressure from the then Ministry of Transport.[102] It is a limited liability company the members of which are insurance companies engaged in road traffic insurance in the UK. It was established to provide redress, through a Guarantee Fund, for people injured in road accidents by the negligence of uninsured[103] and untraced ('hit and run') defendants.[104] All authorized insurers are required to become members of the Bureau, and the Guarantee Fund is financed by levies on the members of the MIB. Ultimately, the cost of the MIB's activities is borne by insured motorists generally. In 2004, the MIB received more than 63,500 new claims, and settled more than 82,000 claims, paying out around £275.5 million in compensation.

Most of the obligations of the MIB are contractual in origin, not statutory.[105] There are two agreements between the MIB and the government: the Uninsured Drivers Agreement and the Untraced Drivers Agreement. The former requires the MIB to meet unsatisfied judgments, in respect of death, injury and property damage,[106] against identified motorists who should have been, but were not, insured under the Road Traffic Act 1988. In this type of case, the MIB acts like an ordinary insurance company. Certain conditions must be fulfilled by the claimant,[107] including that of informing the MIB of the proceedings in question within 14 days of their commencement. In practice, the MIB does not normally require the case to be fought to judgment but negotiates in the normal way with the claimant or the claimant's solicitor over the claim. If no settlement is reached, the MIB will defend the proceedings on behalf of, and by agreement with, the uninsured defendant. But note that a claim can be made to the MIB only after court proceedings have been commenced. By contrast, the vast majority of tort claims are settled without this step having been taken. The MIB provides claimants with free legal expenses insurance.

Under the Untraced Drivers Agreement, the MIB is required to consider applications for compensation from victims of hit-and-run accidents. Initially, the MIB

---

102 R. Merkin ed., *Colinvaux's Law of Insurance*, 7th edn (London, 1997), 433–46.

103 It is estimated that at least 5% of motorists are uninsured. In 2001, there were almost 267,000 convictions for driving without insurance: Department for Transport, *Uninsured Driving in the United Kingdom* (2004).

104 The MIB also operates the Motor Insurers' Information Centre, which holds information about vehicles and insurance in order to facilitate claims in relation to road accidents.

105 But see Motor Vehicles (Compulsory Insurance) (Information and Compensation Body) Regulations 2003, regs. 11 and 13.

106 Compulsory insurance against third-party property damage was introduced in 1987 as a result of an EU Directive. It must cover damage up to a value of € 1 million (about £670,000). Originally, liability for the first £175 (later £300) worth of damage did not have to be insured, but this concession was removed by a later EU Directive.

107 These conditions have been described as 'very onerous' and 'excessive'; and the MIB has a reputation for enforcing them quite strictly: P. Barrie, *Personal Injury Law: Liability, Compensation and Procedure* (Oxford, 2005), para. 8.02.

was very reluctant to deal with this type of case on the ground that in the absence of a defendant, and therefore of the possibility of a trial, the MIB could not contest the claimant's allegations on the issue of negligence or the amount of the damages claimed. Yet in one way, the argument for holding the MIB liable is stronger in this type of case. In the case of uninsured driving, the MIB pays out despite the fact that no premium has been paid in respect of the liability-attracting conduct; but if the 'hit and run' driver was insured with a member of the MIB, a premium would have been paid. In response to considerable pressure over a long period from several sources, the MIB finally agreed in 1968 to accept claims where no defendant could be traced.[108] Originally, compensation for property damage was not recoverable in this type of case, so as to guard against the risk of car owners deliberately damaging their own cars and then claiming that the damage was done by a hit-and-run driver. But since 2003, the MIB considers claims for property damage provided the offending vehicle has been identified (even though the driver remains untraced).

Under the current procedure[109] the MIB will investigate claims in such cases and will, if satisfied that the claimant was injured in circumstances in which insurance is compulsory under the Road Traffic Act 1988, offer compensation assessed on normal common law principles. If the claimant refuses to accept the MIB's decision, they may appeal to an arbitrator appointed by the MIB from a panel of Queen's Counsel maintained for this purpose. The arbitrator's fee is normally paid by the MIB, but the arbitrator can order the claimant to reimburse the MIB for part or all of the fee if the arbitrator thinks there were no reasonable grounds for the appeal. Not everyone is satisfied with this procedure, and attempts to circumvent it and bring proceedings in court have been made, though without success.[110] There is something to be said for the view that a claimant should be able to have their claim tried in the ordinary courts like the victims of all other road accidents. On the other hand, why should a claimant be entitled to a judicial hearing when (e.g.) criminal injury claimants who pursue their claims against the Criminal Injuries Compensation Authority have no right to a judicial hearing?

In cases where the MIB accepts liability even though no defendant can be identified, the issue of compensating the claimant is, of course, adjudicated upon without the defendant being a party to the proceedings, or present. The purpose of the insurance in this situation is simply and unequivocally the compensation of the claimant, and not the protection of an insured tortfeasor. Nevertheless, the claimant must still show that the injuries were the result of a tort committed by the unidentified driver.

The MIB is only liable where insurance is required under the Road Traffic Act 1988. For instance, the MIB is not liable in respect of personal injury arising from an accident not caused on a public road;[111] nor for injuries to a person driving an

108 *Hansard*, 5th series, HC Debs, vol. 770, col. 93.
109 Which resembles that under the criminal injuries compensation scheme: 12.4.4.
110 *Persson* v. *London Country Buses* [1974] 1 All ER 1251; *Clarke* v. *Vedel* [1979] RTR 26.
111 *Randall* v. *MIB* [1968] 1 WLR 1900.

uninsured vehicle at the time of the accident, even if the driver was not the owner
and the injuries were attributable to the negligence of the owner (e.g. in failing to
warn the driver that the vehicle's brakes were faulty) and even if the driver is driving
the vehicle at the request and for the benefit of the owner.[112]

The statutory obligation to insure a vehicle extends to passengers in the vehicle
as well as to other road users. However, there are provisions in the MIB Agreements
designed to deny compensation to a person who voluntarily[113] travels in a vehicle
that they knew or ought to have known was stolen, uninsured or being used for a
criminal purpose. In order to make these provisions consistent with EU law, the
words 'ought to have known' have been held not to extend to mere negligence.[114]
Moreover, it is clear that the statutory obligation to insure extends to *non-
passengers* who are injured as a result of deliberately, as opposed to negligently,
wrongful use of a vehicle.[115] In other words, the mere fact that the vehicle is being
used for a criminal purpose does not put that use outside the scope of the insurance requirement. While it is clear that the driver of a car may owe no duty of care
to a passenger who, at the time of the accident, is involved with the driver in a criminal activity,[116] the provisions of the MIB Agreements go much further than this in
denying passengers compensation. Their purpose, it seems, is to restrict compensation to 'deserving' passengers.[117] To the extent that these provisions deny compensation in circumstances in which tort law would impose liability that falls
within the requirement to insure, they may be of no effect.

The MIB is, in many respects, an anomalous institution, which operates partly
within and partly outside the legal system. In the first place, most of the obligations of the MIB are not statutory but arise under a contract with the Secretary of
State, and this contract cannot be enforced by the accident victim because of the
doctrine of privity of contract; although in practice courts do award declarations
of entitlement to recover from the MIB. In theory, no doubt, if the MIB broke its
agreement, the government might be able to get an order of specific performance
requiring the MIB to comply with the agreement.[118] In practice, however, it is
almost unthinkable that the MIB would violate the agreement, and if it did so
there is not much doubt that the whole scheme – or some alternative – would be
put on to a statutory footing. The result is that the MIB simply does not take the

---

112 *Cooper* v. *MIB* [1985] QB 575.
113 E.g. *Pickett* v. *Motor Insurers' Bureau* [2004] 1 WLR 2450. Contrary to what Chadwick LJ said in
     this case, the issue is not whether the passenger voluntarily accepted the risk of being injured,
     because there is a provision in the Road Traffic Act 1988 (s. 149(3)) which prevents reliance on
     the defence of assumption of risk by a negligent driver against the passenger.
114 *White* v. *MIB* [2001] 1 WLR 481. There are analogous but narrower provisions in the Road
     Traffic Act 1988, s. 151(4).
115 *Gardner* v. *Moore* [1984] AC 548.
116 *Ashton* v. *Turner* [1981] QB 137 (the claimant and the defendant had committed a burglary and
     the accident occurred during their getaway); *Pitts* v. *Hunt* [1991] 2 QB 24.
117 In much the same way that the Criminal Injuries Compensation Scheme is designed to help
     'deserving' victims of crime: 12.4.3.2.
118 *Beswick* v. *Beswick* [1968] AC 58; *Gurtner* v. *Circuit* [1968] 2 QB 587.

privity of contract point and behaves as though it were legally liable to accident victims.

Like liability insurance itself, the existence of the MIB may cast a shadow over proceedings in court, but is rarely taken account of in the legal process except where the MIB is directly involved. For instance, the offence of driving a motor vehicle while uninsured is still treated by the courts in precisely the same way as when it was first created in 1930. Yet the existence of the MIB has changed the character of the offence altogether; instead of being an offence which involves the risk of depriving accident victims of compensation, it is now an offence more in the nature of tax evasion. Similarly, in *Corfield* v. *Groves*[119] it was held that the action under *Monk* v. *Warbey* for permitting an uninsured person to drive in breach of the Road Traffic Act was unaffected by the fact that the MIB would meet any judgment against the uninsured driver.

On the other hand, courts do sometimes take a more realistic approach to the existence of the MIB. In *Gurtner* v. *Circuit*[120] the MIB applied to be made a party to an action brought by a road accident victim. The claimant had been injured in an accident by a motorist who was insured, but the insurance company was never discovered and the driver had gone abroad and could not be traced. In such circumstances, it is possible for the claimant to obtain permission to dispense with service of the claim form and then to obtain judgment by default against the defendant for damages to be assessed. The difficulty is that, unless the MIB is then made a party to the case, there is nobody in a position to appear and contest the claimant's claim when the damages come to be assessed. The Court of Appeal decided in these circumstances that the MIB should be made party to the case. The court made an attempt to bring the MIB within the law, as it were, by stressing that the MIB did have a legal obligation – albeit an obligation only enforceable by the government – to meet any judgment awarded to the claimant, and accordingly that the MIB had sufficient 'interest' in the case to be made party thereto. On the other hand, in *Albert* v. *MIB*[121] Lord Dilhorne protested at the anomalous situation in which the courts, who are the judges of legal rights and duties, are required to give judgment against a person who is not liable in law.

Finally, it should be noted that there is no equivalent to the MIB to accept liability in cases where an employer fails to take out compulsory insurance under the Employers' Liability (Compulsory Insurance) Act 1969.

119 [1950] 1 All ER 488.
120 [1968] 2 QB 587.
121 [1972] AC 301.

10

Trials and settlements

Settlement is so pervasive that is has been argued that in civil litigation those cases that result in contested hearings are to be considered as deviant . . . The conduct of negotiations and the path to settlement are largely dictated by court procedures. There is no separate settlement procedure. Settlement is achieved by preparing for trial – going through the ritualistic procedures determined appropriate for adversarial contest in open court. Parties who want peace and want it on good terms have no alternative . . . but to prepare for war.[1]

10.1   The importance of settlements

The vast majority of tort claims are settled by negotiation and agreement between the claimant and the defendant's liability insurer, or, occasionally, the defendant personally, usually through the agency of solicitors on both sides.[2] This process has been memorably called 'litigotiation'.[3] The Pearson Commission estimated from its various surveys that 86% of cases are settled without the commencement of legal proceedings (i.e. a claim form); 11% are settled after the commencement of proceedings but before the case is set down for trial; 2% are settled after setting down; and 1% are settled at the door of the court or during the trial, or are actually disposed of by trial.[4] Many other surveys and studies confirm the general pattern of these figures.[5]

On the basis of these facts, the tort system could be regarded as an administrative process handled by insurance adjustors and solicitors incorporating a 'right of appeal' to a court of law. Looked at from this point of view the system may be said to resemble the social security system more closely than might be thought at first sight. This latter system is run by an administrative process in which there is a right

---

1 H. Genn, 'Access to Just Settlements: The Case of Medical Negligence' in A.A.S. Zuckerman and R. Cranston eds., *Reform of Civil Procedure: Essays on 'Access to Justice'* (Oxford, 1995), 406 (footnote omitted).
2 D.R. Harris, D. Campbell and R. Halson, *Remedies in Contract and Tort*, 2nd edn (London, 2002), ch. 24.
3 M. Galanter, 'Worlds of Deals: Using Negotiation to Teach About Legal Process' (1984) 34 *Journal of Legal Education* 268, 268
4 Pearson Report, vol. 2, table 124.
5 Winn Committee Report, paras. 116–18, 123 and Appendix 8; T.G. Ison, *The Forensic Lottery* (London, 1967), Appendix C, table 11; Harris 1984 Survey, 112.

of appeal to tribunals established under statute. But there are important differences apart from the obvious one that the 'appellate' tribunals for the tort system are the ordinary courts, while for the social security system they are statutory tribunals. In particular, social security administration is in the hands of the State and is handled by civil servants; on the other hand, the tort administrative machine is privately run. One consequence of this is that the object of the administrators who run the social security system is (or, at any rate, should be) to see that every claimant gets what they are legally entitled to receive; and the purpose of the appeal procedure is to put right mistakes. In the tort system, by contrast, the administrators are not concerned to see that the claimant gets what is legally due: insurers are primarily concerned to settle cases for the lowest figure they can induce the claimant to accept.

In this light, the right of 'appeal' to the courts should be seen not so much as a mechanism to put right the mistakes of the adjudicators, but as a weapon to induce the administrators to behave reasonably. This is why such a large proportion of cases in which proceedings are commenced, or even in which preparations are made for trial, are never tried; and this is why a former Chief Justice of Ontario once said that 'the judicial process is . . . used for other than judicial purposes . . . as a threat to bring about an adjustment rather than as a means of adjudication'.[6]

10.2   Obtaining legal assistance and financing tort claims

There is nothing to prevent an individual claimant attempting to negotiate a settlement personally, and a certain number of claimants do so.[7] In this event the negotiations will probably be conducted by experts on one side and a complete novice on the other; and less reputable insurance companies may take advantage of an unrepresented claimant.[8] In such cases, any settlement reached may be seriously inadequate, and it has been suggested that there should be a power to review such settlements within, say, 12 months.[9] Settlements made on behalf of children (even by qualified lawyers) require the approval of the court in any event, and very few people have the necessary skill or expertise to bring a case before the court for approval without legal advice; it is also unlikely that such approval would be given, unless the court was satisfied that the amount had been regarded as satisfactory by an experienced solicitor or barrister.

How might a person who wishes to make a tort claim go about finding suitable assistance to do so? A trade union member might in the first instance approach his or her union.[10] Large numbers of claims for damages arising out of industrial

6 J.C. Mc Ruer, 'The Motor Car and the Law' in A. Linden ed., *Studies in Canadian Tort Law* (Toronto, 1968), 312.
7 The Harris 1984 Survey found that 8% of personal injury claimants recovered damages without the help of a lawyer: 81–2.
8 JUSTICE, *Report on the Trial of Motor Accident Cases* (London, 1966), 2; Harris 1984 Survey, 82.
9 JUSTICE, ibid., 3.
10 Assistance in making and defending claims is also offered by the motoring organizations (the AA and the RAC) and, sometimes, by employers as a fringe benefit for senior employees.

accidents are handled by trade unions. Many of the larger unions do not confine their assistance to workplace injury and ill-health. Some assist with road accidents occurring while travelling to and from work; others assist with all road accidents; some decide whether to assist in each case individually. There are also variations in the practice of unions as regards the securing of legal assistance. Some unions simply pass the case on to solicitors; others handle the case in the first instance themselves, but pass it on to solicitors if litigation becomes necessary, or if the case raises particular difficulty. Some make preliminary investigations into the facts, and send the case on to solicitors only if they think there is any prospect of success in a common law claim. In all cases, the expense is borne by the union.

For people who have no union to turn to, there are various options apart from approaching a solicitor directly. Possible first points of contact include a Citizens Advice Bureau or a legal referral service, such as Accident Line, which is endorsed by the Law Society (the solicitors' professional association). Of major significance are claims management companies (CMCs). The CMC sector of the legal services industry is largely a product of abolition of legal aid for most personal injury claims in 2000. It has recently been estimated that there are some 400 CMCs handling about 500,000 claims (including personal-injury claims) a year.[11] CMCs are legal services brokers who often operate on a no-win, no-fee basis to arrange for the claimant the various services – of solicitors, medical experts, litigation insurers and so on – needed to achieve settlement of the claim. Yet another possible source of assistance in making a claim is a claims assessor (CA). Unlike CMCs, CAs conduct negotiations on behalf of claimants. They typically operate on a no-win, no-fee contingency basis – i.e. on the basis that if the claim succeeds they will be entitled to a percentage of the amount recovered.[12] That percentage is not regulated by law. Because they are not legally qualified, CAs are unable to issue legal proceedings on behalf of a claimant or to represent the claimant in such proceedings. We will discuss later the likely impact of this on the dynamics and course of settlement negotiations.

Despite the existence of these various alternative avenues of assistance in making claims, it is probably still the case that most personal-injury claims, and especially the largest and most serious and complex, end up in the hands of qualified lawyers.

The first issue to be decided in relation to any claim is whether it is worth pur-

---

11 Compensation Bill Final Regulatory Impact Assessment (2005), para. 2.9. See generally Department for Constitutional Affairs, *The Report of the Lord Chancellor's Committee to Investigate the Activities of Non-Legally Qualified Claims Assessors and Employment Advisers* (2000). 'CMC' is an umbrella term covering various types of operator: Boleat Consulting, *The Claims Standards Council* (December 2005), paras. 1.8–1.24. Marketing practices and other activities of CMCs have generated considerable publicity and unease. Two of the leading CMCs collapsed, one in 2002 and the other in 2003. In November 2005 the Compensation Bill was introduced into Parliament to enable the creation of a regime to regulate providers of claims-management services (solicitors, of course, are already quite heavily regulated).

12 It is illegal for qualified lawyers to operate on a contingent as opposed to a conditional fee basis. But expert witnesses and forensic accountants, for instance, may do so: *R (Factortame)* v. *Secretary of State for Transport, Local government and the Regions (No. 8)* [2003] QB 381.

suing at all. Most personal injury claims are funded on a no-win, no-fee basis. In practice, this means that if the solicitor thinks that the claim is hopeless, the client will probably pay nothing for an initial assessment of the claimant's case. Solicitors who belong to the Accident Line referral scheme offer a free exploratory consultation. Legal aid may be available for a medical negligence claim, but only if the claimant meets the statutory means test. In that case, the cost of assessing the strength of a medical negligence claim may be met in the form of Investigative Help. Investigative Help may be initially refused if the Legal Services Commission (LSC) concludes that it would be more appropriate for the applicant first to use the NHS Complaints Scheme. Since the Complaints Scheme does not handle negligence claims, Investigative Help is likely to be refused on this ground only in relatively minor cases where it is unclear what went wrong, or if the applicant is not seeking compensation, but only wants an explanation or an apology, for instance.

If the solicitor decides that the client has a claim worth pursuing, the next issue is how to fund the claim. In practice, there are three main possibilities.[13] The client may have a legal expenses insurance policy (also called 'before-the-event' (BTE) insurance) that covers the claim.[14] Secondly, if the claim is one for medical negligence, the claimant may (depending on their income and capital wealth) qualify for legal aid (technically, 'community legal service funding'). But only solicitors who have a contract with the LSC can provide publicly funded legal services; and in practice, this means firms that specialize in medical negligence work. Thirdly, the solicitor may handle the claim on a no-win, no-fee basis, and in that case will probably make a conditional fee agreement (CFA) with the client.[15] The basic rules about the costs of litigation is that the loser must pay the winner's legal costs as well as their own. Typically a CFA will stipulate that if the claim fails, the client will pay nothing to their lawyer except, perhaps, some out-of-pocket expenses ('disbursements'); but in the event of success, that the solicitor will be entitled to remuneration calculated on a fee-for-service (typically hourly) basis, plus an additional amount – called an 'uplift' or 'success fee' – calculated as a percentage of that remuneration. To cover

13 We can safely ignore the possibility that a personal-injury claimant will finance the claim out of their own pocket. This is possible, of course, but must be extremely rare. There is, generally, no reason why a benefactor should not agree to finance a claim out of charity or generosity, provided their motivation is to help the claimant pursue what the funder perceives to be a genuine case. If the claim fails, the funder will not be liable for the defendant's costs (although the claimant will be): *Hamilton* v. *Al Fayed (No. 2)* [2003] QB 1175.

14 Since about half of all tort claims arise out of road accidents, it is significant that BTE insurance is commonly provided as a component of comprehensive motor insurance. It is also commonly available as a component of household contents insurance policies. 'Free-standing' legal expenses policies are available, but they are expensive, partly because free-standing BTE insurance suffers from a serious problem of 'adverse selection', which means that many people who want to buy it are people likely to make a claim on the policy in the near future because they take out the insurance in anticipation of legal trouble. This problem can be ameliorated to some extent if the insurance is sold to groups through a trade union, employer or trade association, rather than directly to individuals. Like legal aid, legal expenses insurance may cover the cost of defending claims.

15 Unions which handle a large number of claims on behalf of members may make a 'global CFA' with a lawyer under the Collective Conditional Fee Regulations 2000.

the risk of having to pay the defendant's costs in the event of failure of the claim, the claimant may purchase 'after-the-event' (ATE) insurance. If the claim actually succeeds, in addition to compensation, the claimant will recover from the defendant('s insurer) not only their solicitor's remuneration, but also disbursements, the success fee and the ATE insurance premium.[16] In the event of failure, the ATE insurer pays the defendant's costs, and the ATE insurance premium may be reimbursed or waived. Normally, a client with BTE cover should be referred to the BTE insurer before being offered a CFA with ATE insurance.[17]

As a means of funding personal injury claims, BTE insurance bears certain similarities to public funding, in that the insurer, like the LSC, will decide whether the claim is worth pursuing (according to criteria laid down in the BTE insurance policy or the Funding Code, respectively), and will exercise a certain degree of control over the conduct of the proceedings. The major difference between BTE insurance and public funding is that if the claim succeeds, the recipient of legal aid, but not the BTE policy holder, may have to reimburse the funder: the LSC has what is called a 'statutory charge' over the compensation awarded to the claimant. If the defendant('s insurer) pays all the claimant's solicitor's fees and disbursements in addition to compensation, the claimant will be in effectively the same position as a BTE insurance policy holder. Otherwise, the lawyer must deduct from the compensation such of the costs as are not paid by the defendant, and repay these to the LSC. A legally aided claimant may also be required to make a contribution to the cost of the case while it is in progress; such contribution is set off against the statutory charge. In this respect, the recipient of legal aid is also worse off than the claimant who enters a CFA with their lawyer and takes out ATE insurance. In that case, if the claim succeeds, the defendant('s insurer) will pay all the claimant's legal costs, including the lawyer's success fee and the ATE insurance premium.

The option of funding claims by CFAs was first introduced in 1995. Before that, lawyers were allowed to handle cases on a no-win, no-fee 'speculative' basis, but they were not allowed to charge a success fee. The main reason for introducing conditional fees was to improve 'access to justice' – i.e. to facilitate the funding of claims made by the increasing proportion of the population who did not satisfy the means test for legal aid eligibility, but who were not affluent enough to fund the claim out of their own pockets and were without BTE insurance. Once CFAs were up and running, legal aid was withdrawn for most personal injury claims[18] in 2000, chiefly to reduce legal aid expenditure[19] and to transfer the cost of funding such claims from the taxpayer to liability insurance premium

---

16 But claimed costs can be challenged in costs proceedings on the basis that they are unreasonable, and in this way courts can regulate success fees and ATE insurance premiums.

17 *Sarwar* v. *Alam* [2002] 1 WLR 125.

18 Except medical negligence claims; certain other types of personal injury claim, such as those based on allegations of sexual assault or child abuse, or serious wrongdoing by public officials and bodies; and complex multi-party cases of public importance.

19 Although only a relatively small proportion of the total was spent on personal injury claims.

payers.[20] In fact, this move meant not only a transfer of the cost of funding claims, but also an overall increase in cost resulting from the addition of success fees and ATE insurance premiums to the costs bill.[21]

The market for ATE insurance really only started to develop in 2000 when the premium, along with the success fee, was made recoverable from an unsuccessful defendant. It seems that ATE insurance is available, at least at a reasonable cost, only in relation to claims that have a significantly better than even chance of success. The Office of Fair Trading has said that a significant number of claims are made without the benefit of ATE insurance. In that case, the lawyer bears the risk of having to pay the defendant's costs in case the claim fails and the client is unable to pay. In theory, the new system of funding personal injury litigation should make it easier for people who would not have been eligible for legal aid to make claims. However, one qualification should be made. Whether or not a claim will be publicly funded depends partly on its chance of success, but also partly on its value and importance to the claimant and to the public more generally. By contrast, the lawyer's decision whether or not to handle a case on a no-win, no-fee basis (with or without a CFA), and an ATE insurer's (or, for that matter, a BTE insurer's) decision whether or not to underwrite the claim, is likely to depend solely, or at least primarily, on its chance of success. For the lawyer or private insurer, the decision whether to invest in a claim is a commercial one based on their own financial interests. As a result, it may be more difficult for a seriously injured claimant of modest means[22] to find funding for a relatively high-risk claim under the new regime than it was under the old. Generally, the new regime is more likely to facilitate straightforward accident claims than difficult and speculative illness and disease claims.[23]

How is the success fee calculated? By statute, the success fee cannot be more than 100% of the 'basic fee'.[24] For road accident and work accident (but not illness)

---

20 The abolition of legal aid for most personal-injury negligence claims was a hotly contested policy. On behalf of potential claimants it was said that the poorest in society, who would qualify for legal aid, would not be able to afford the up-front premium for ATE insurance. On behalf of potential defendants, it was said that conditional fees, in conjunction with costs insurance and the liability of losing defendants to pay the claimant's lawyer's success fee, would take too much of the risk out of litigating and would put claimants in too strong a bargaining position, analogous to that described under the former system as 'legal aid blackmail'. It was also pointed out that CFAs could not replace legal aid for defendants; although this was not a big issue in the personal-injury area, where almost all claims are made against insured parties or parties who would not qualify for legal aid.

21 Recent years have also witnessed growth in car-hire arrangements under which payment of the hiring charges is deferred until damages are recovered. The House of Lords has held that the cost of the credit thus extended (as opposed to the hire charges) is not recoverable as damages from a tortfeasor: *Dimond* v. *Lovell* [2002] 1 AC 384.

22 A seriously injured person who could no longer work might well, for that very reason, have qualified for legal aid.

23 According to recent research, in around 80% of CFA cases (other than clinical negligence claims) there is no (significant) dispute about liability; and in around 85% no (significant) dispute about the causation: P. Fenn *et al.*, *The Funding of Personal Injury Litigation: Comparisons Over Time and Across Jurisdictions* (DCA Research Series 2/06, February 2006), para. 5.1.

24 Courts and Legal Services Act 1990, s. 58(4)(c).

cases (except small claims)[25] there are fixed success fees.[26] If the claim is settled after the trial has started or is concluded by judgment, the success fee is 100%. In cases settled earlier than this the fixed success fee is much less – 12.5% in motor accident cases. These figures no doubt reflect the fact that the success rate of road and work accident claims is high, and that only the most difficult go to trial. For other types of case, the level of success fees is not regulated. The concept of the basic fee is itself a bit problematic, because lawyers' fees are not tightly controlled,[27] and there is not much price competition amongst solicitors. The success fee is, of course, designed to compensate the lawyer for cases that fail, for which no remuneration is received. Because the overall success rate of personal injury claims is high, the success fee charged in any particular case by a lawyer who handles a significant number of personal injury claims should be relatively low, reflecting the relatively low risk of failure of such claims as a class. But lawyers, especially those who handle relatively few personal injury claims, might calculate the success fee for any particular claim according to their estimate of the likely success of *that* claim, especially if it is considered to have a less-than-average chance of success. Because of the complexity of the economics and dynamics of CFAs, it may be quite difficult for the average client to assess the reasonableness of the terms being offered by the lawyer under a CFA.

It can be seen, then, that the market in personal injury claims is characterized by a diversity of service-providers and of funding arrangements. Competition amongst providers has increased considerably in the past 10 years, and policy-makers have become increasingly concerned about consumer protection in this environment. There is a common view that for every tort claim made, another two or three could be made. There is also a view (but little hard evidence) that recent developments have not only made it easier to make a tort claim than it was before the introduction of conditional fees and the abolition of legal aid for most personal injury claims, but have also increased the amount of tort claiming. Whether significant increases in tort claims are a good idea must be a matter for personal opinion. But if we stand back and survey the scene in a wider perspective, we can at least say that government policy in the past decade has been to shift financial costs of disability from the public purse to private pockets. Measures have been introduced not only to expand 'access to justice' for the disabled via the tort system, but also to increase levels of tort compensation (e.g. reduction of the discount rate: 6.2.1), and to reduce the amount spent on social security payments and NHS services provided to tort victims (15.3). In the 1970s it seemed possible that public policy might be nudged in the direction of placing less and less reliance on the tort system to provide support for the disabled. At the beginning of the twenty-first century it seems clear not only that the tort system is here to

---

25 I.e. claims worth less than £1,000.
26 CPR Part 45.III and IV.
27 Except that costs are fixed for road accident claims where the agreed damages do not exceed £10,000: CPR Part 45.II. There are also fixed costs for some trials under CPR Part 46.

stay, but that it will become an increasingly important part of society's provision for the disabled.

We have noted that the abolition of legal aid did not apply to medical negligence claims. This is because such claims may be very complex and expensive to prepare;[28] and the chance of success may be difficult to calculate.[29] Medical negligence claims may, of course, be handled under a CFA without legal aid, even if the claimant qualifies for legal aid.[30] But whereas the possibility of CFA funding is normally taken into account in deciding whether to grant legal aid, it is ignored in medical negligence cases, except multi-party (or 'group') actions. Most multi-party actions are personal injury claims, arising, for instance, out of major transport accidents, or from the adverse effects of the use of drugs or other products. Unless such an action relates to medical negligence it will not, as such, qualify for legal aid. However, legal aid can be granted if a multi-party claim raises significant issues of wider public interest – and most such claims have the potential to do so. It is likely that not all of the parties to a group claim will be financially eligible for legal aid. But so long as some of them are, the criterion for funding is whether it is reasonable for the issues raised by the litigation to be pursued with the support of public funding.[31] However, the LSC can, and normally will, require a contribution to the cost of funding a multi-party action not only from the parties who are financially eligible for legal aid but also from those who are not.

The fact that some of the parties to a group action may be publicly funded and others not may cause serious funding problems. In the Opren litigation,[32] which concerned the alleged side-effects of a drug for the treatment of arthritis, about one-third of the 1,500 or so claimants did not qualify for legal aid. A fully legally aided claimant was chosen to launch a 'lead action', which was designed to decide issues relevant to the settlement of a large number of the other claims. The judge in charge of the proceedings decided that the costs of the lead action should be borne rateably by all of the affected claimants, even those who did not qualify for legal aid. The Court of Appeal held that this order was within the judge's jurisdiction.[33] One result of the order was that many of the claimants who did not qualify for legal aid could

---

28 According to the National Audit Office, in 65% of medical negligence claims settled for £50,000 or less, costs exceed compensation: *Handling Clinical Negligence Claims in England* (2001), Executive Summary, para. 14, paras. 2.20–21.

29 In 2003–4, almost 50% of legally aided medical-negligence claims went no further than initial investigation. Of the balance, 64% were successful.

30 Although CFAs are relatively rare in medical negligence cases: Department of Health, *Making Amends: A Report by the Chief Medical Officer* (2003), 71; Fenn *et al.*, *The Funding of Personal Injury Litigation*, para. 5.2. By contrast, about 90% of non-medical personal injury claims are funded by CFAs: ibid., para. 5.1.

31 The LSC has power to waive eligibility limits, but this may not result in an increase in overall funding.

32 See generally National Consumer Council, *Group Actions: Learning from Opren* (1988); M. Mildred and R. Pannone in M.J. Powers and N.H. Harris eds., *Medical Negligence*, 2nd edn (London, 1994), ch. 14.

33 *Davies* v. *Eli Lilley & Co.* [1987] 1 WLR 1136.

not afford to continue their actions. Another was to discourage even legally aided claimants: in the majority of the Opren claims, the compensation payable was likely to be so small that a very large proportion of the amount recovered would have been repayable to the Legal Aid Board.[34] The Opren claimants were, in the end, bailed out by a private benefactor who agreed to pay their costs.[35] This was, of course, before the days of conditional fees; and now, it is possible that non-funded group members may have BTE insurance, or may be able to make conditional fee arrangements. Indeed, the LSC's overall aim in multi-party actions is to achieve a mix of public and private funding, the private funding being provided by CFAs with ATE insurance or by some other insurance-based arrangement.

Because they are typically very costly[36] and legally complex, and may be highly speculative, multi-party claims are likely to be handled only by qualified lawyers. CMCs and CAs operate primarily in the road accident, and to a lesser extent in the work accident, sectors of the personal injury claims market. In practice, therefore, the only practical options for funding multi-party actions are legal aid or CFAs. But it is only very large law firms with the capacity to raise significant amounts of capital and which specialize in such litigation that are likely to be willing to handle multi-party claims,[37] especially since ATE insurance may be difficult to obtain, and very expensive if it is available. On the other hand, a feature of multi-party claims that may make CFAs possible is that typically several or many firms of lawyers are involved, and they can share the cost of preparation among themselves.

10.3   The course of negotiations

Settlement negotiations lie at the heart of the tort system.[38] How well such negotiations are handled will obviously depend partly on the skill and experience of the

---

34 Legal Aid Act 1988, s. 16(6). Under the so-called 'statutory charge' over damages recovered, a successful assisted party must repay to the Legal Aid Board any required contribution which remains unpaid, plus any costs not recovered from the other party (see n. 21). If a legally aided litigant loses, they may be ordered to pay an amount on account of costs to the Legal Aid Board (Legal Aid Act 1988, s. 17). Orders for costs can be made against the Board itself only in narrowly defined circumstances (s. 13).

35 Only one of the Opren lead actions (in respect of 338 claims) was successful. In that case the defendant was ordered to pay all the claimant's costs and not just a rateable proportion: 'Successful Lead Action Plaintiff Costs in Group Litigation' (1993) 12 *Civil Justice Q* 4.

36 An extreme example of the cost of drug-related claims is the litigation surrounding the use of a group of tranquilliser drugs called 'benzodiazepines'. This was funded by legal aid in the 1990s, and about £40 million was spent on preliminary research and development before legal aid was withdrawn on the ground that the claims were unlikely to succeed.

37 For a negative assessment (prompted by withdrawal of public funding for a claim arising out of use of the MMR vaccine) of the possible role of CFAs in any but the strongest multi-party claims see M. Day and J. Kelleher, 'Lessons from MMR and the Future of Group Litigation Funding' [2005] *JPIL* 98.

38 For sociological studies of the settlement process see H.L. Ross, *Settled Out of Court: The Social Process of Insurance Claims Adjustment*, 2nd edn (Chicago, 1980); H. Genn, *Hard Bargaining* (Oxford, 1987). These studies need to be read with care because they relate to a system with very different funding arrangements than are currently in place in Britain.

negotiator, who may be a solicitor, a claims assessor, some other representative of the claimant or (exceptionally) the claimant personally. Most solicitors do not handle many personal injury claims on behalf of claimants. On the other hand, there are firms that specialize in this type of work. They can join a Law Society panel of personal-injury specialists; and only specialist firms have contracts with the LSC for legally aided personal-injury work. Larger specialist personal injury firms usually play a leading role in handling group claims. There is an Association of Personal Injury Lawyers (APIL), which is an interest group and lobbying organization.[39] On the defendant's side, personal injury claims are almost always dealt with by a lawyer or an insurance company employee with a great deal of specialized experience in handling such claims. There is a body called the Forum of Insurance Lawyers (FOIL), a counterpart to APIL.

In an extremely influential article published in 1974,[40] US scholar Marc Galanter distinguished between participants in legal processes on the basis of whether they were 'one-shotters' or 'repeat-players'. In terms of this distinction, the typical personal injury claimant is a one-shotter, while the typical defendant – in the guise of a liability insurer – is a repeat-player. Galanter's basic argument was that repeat-player defendants have various (unfair) advantages over one-shotter claimants in the litigation process. Galanter's analysis has provided the conceptual framework for academic studies of the tort settlement process over the past 30 years, which, in their authors' opinions anyway, have tended to confirm Galanter's thesis. By contrast, those who argue that we now live in a 'blame' or 'compensation' culture maintain that developments over that period have turned the tables, and that the advantage now lies with claimants to an extent that threatens economic prosperity and the value of personal responsibility. Where the 'truth' lies is partly a matter of perspective and interpretation; and the opposing sides of the debate predictably argue for very different 'reforms' of the tort system. What follows is an attempt to give an account of the settlement process on the basis of what we know about its operation.

10.3.1   Individual claims

In the typical case involving a single personal injury claimant and a single defendant, the first step is for the 'claimant' (meaning, in the normal case, the claimant's representative) to write to the potential defendant or the defendant's insurers asking whether the defendant admits liability. Few, if any, insurers would admit liability at this stage, whatever the circumstances. The most common practice would be for the insurer to write a standard letter denying liability, but asking on what ground it is suggested that the defendant was negligent.[41] At this stage, if not before, the claimant's representative will probably start collecting evidence in the form of

39 Barristers have their own Personal Injury Bar Association.
40 'Why the "Haves" Come Out Ahead: Speculations on the Limits of Legal Change' (1974) 9 *Law and Society Review* 95.
41 JUSTICE, *Report on the Trial of Motor Accident Cases*, 5.

witness statements, photographs, medical reports and so on. Litigation procedures (embodied in the CPR supplemented by 'Pre-Action Protocols') have recently been changed to encourage as many cases as possible to be settled without the commencement of court proceedings. This puts a premium on early collection of evidence to establish the strength and value of the claim. It is widely believed that the consequent need to collect evidence earlier than used to be the case has increased the average cost of settling personal injury claims by a process of what is called 'front-loading'. Under the old regime, parties were likely not to start collecting evidence assiduously until it was clear that no satisfactory settlement was likely to be reached. Now, evidence collection is seen as part of the process of achieving early settlement rather than as the first step in preparation for trial in case settlement negotiations break down.

An important aspect of the tactics of settlement is the selective disclosure to the other side of evidence that indicates the strength of the discloser's case. Parties are not entirely free to decide what to disclose and when. Pre-action protocols impose disclosure obligations, and these may be backed up by court orders for pre-action disclosure. In complying with disclosure obligations, each party will do their best to maximize the chance of a settlement favourable to their interests by discovering as much as possible about the other's case while revealing as little as possible about their own.[42] Information is power, and effective negotiating involves a certain amount of bluff and counter-bluff. Each party will want some evidence up its sleeve, which can be used as a bargaining chip at a later stage if negotiations drag on.[43]

Sometimes, the course of negotiations, especially in road accident cases, may be affected by criminal proceedings taken in a magistrate's court; or in fatal accident cases, by a coroner's inquest.[44] Although in legal theory the outcome of a civil case is largely unaffected by what may have been decided by magistrates or a coroner, in practice, such proceedings may be of the greatest importance. It is not merely the result of the proceedings that matters, but the evidence which emerges, the witnesses who appear and the way in which they give their evidence. In a simple road accident case, for instance, in which the only question is which of two motorists was responsible for a collision, the prosecution of one of the motorists for careless or dangerous driving may provide something like a dress rehearsal of a civil action. Naturally, therefore, insurers usually wish to represent a defendant who is prosecuted for an offence as a result of the accident from which the claim arises; and insurance policies usually provide that the insurer will secure proper legal representation for the conduct of the defence in any such proceedings.

In some cases the defendant will accept full or partial liability and any dispute will be largely, if not entirely, about the amount of damages. In such a case it is sometimes necessary to wait and see how the claimant's injuries develop so that medical prognosis may become more certain. This tends to contribute to the delay

---

42 JUSTICE, *Report on the Trial of Motor Accident Cases*, 9–10; Genn, *Hard Bargaining*, ch. 7.
43 Winn Committee Report, para. 131 ff.
44 Winn Committee Report, 209.

of negotiating settlements. Where (as happens in a significant proportion of cases) there is a possibility of a finding of contributory negligence if the case goes to trial, much of the negotiations may involve trying to agree on some percentage deduction to be made from the figure agreed upon for damages.[45]

It will be recalled that the burden of proof in a tort action normally rests on the claimant. The Harris 1984 Survey found that the most commonly given reason for abandoning tort claims after making them was difficulty in obtaining evidence.[46] There may have been no witnesses to the accident, or the witnesses may have disappeared; or they may be reluctant to make statements especially if they fear that this may lead to being called to give evidence at a trial. Although it is possible to subpoena a witness to compel them to appear and give evidence in court, few lawyers would be willing to take the risk of calling a witness 'blind', that is, without the person having previously made a statement which gives some idea of what they may be expected to say in evidence.

Problems with witnesses are not the only difficulties a claimant may face. Physical evidence (such as allegedly defective tools or equipment) may 'disappear' after an accident and the scene of the accident (such as a roadway or a building site) may change rapidly, making it very difficult to ascertain the conditions prevailing at the time of the accident. In some cases, difficulties of proof are inherent in the very nature of the claim. This is particularly so in relation to claims which arise not out of traumatic accidents but out of the contraction over a period of time of a disease or illness as a result, for example, of exposure to some process or substance or of taking some drug. Problems of proof increase with the passage of time, and the symptoms of illnesses and diseases often do not appear until years after the events that started the process leading to the symptoms.[47] The aetiology of many diseases and illnesses is imperfectly understood, and there is often more than one possible cause. In cases such as this, obtaining evidence may be an extremely time-consuming and costly exercise with an inconclusive outcome.

The settlement process involves, in economic terms, a 'bilateral monopoly' because the claimant can 'sell' their claim to only one potential buyer – the insurer – and the insurer can 'buy' the claim from only one potential seller – the claimant. Thus the claimant cannot, as it were, 'shop around' to get good value for the claim. How long the bargaining process goes on depends on a number of factors: the efficiency, skill and experience of the claimant's representative; the time needed to collect evidence; whether it is necessary to wait and see how the claimant's medical condition will develop; the number of issues in dispute; and whether the parties and their representatives take a confrontational or a co-operative approach to the settlement process.[48] On the whole, defendants and insurers have less to lose by delay than claimants. One of the incentives given to defendants to settle sooner rather than later

45 Harris 1984 Survey, 91–2; Genn, *Hard Bargaining*, 120–1.
46 Harris 1984 Survey, table 3.12.
47 J. Stapleton, *Disease and the Compensation Debate* (Oxford, 1986), 29–30.
48 On these differing approaches see Genn, *Hard Bargaining*, 38–52.

is the fact that pre-trial interest is payable on damages awards; although it is not clear what impact this has on the settlement of cases which do not go to trial.

The type of representative the claimant has may also affect the course of the negotiations. For instance, because claims assessors are not qualified lawyers and cannot initiate or conduct court proceedings on their clients' behalf, it may be argued that they will be less able to take a robust approach to negotiation and will be more likely to settle earlier and for lower amounts than a qualified lawyer would. But this argument has been said to ignore several facts.[49] One is that a claims assessor has an incentive to hold out for a higher offer because their remuneration is typically calculated as a percentage of the compensation recovered. Another is that insurers know that if the claims assessor does not achieve a settlement acceptable to the client, the claim might be handed on to a lawyer, thus increasing the insurers' costs. Finally, it is said, claims assessors may have an advantage over qualified lawyers for clients who are prepared to trade off the size of the settlement payment against speed of resolution. In the absence of empirical evidence, it is impossible to assess the validity of these various arguments.

However, an important issue raised by such arguments concerns whether the claimant and their representative have the same aims and motivations or whether, on the contrary, conflicts of interest may arise between them. The aim of the defendant and the defendant's insurer in the settlement process is usually the same: to minimize the amount paid out to the claimant.[50] For this reason, insurers tend to exploit to their own advantage any inexperience or ineptitude on the part of the claimant's representative, any weaknesses in the claimant's case and any uncertainties in the law. By contrast, the interests of the claimant and their representative may be in conflict: the best move for the representative may be to settle quickly,[51] while

---

49 Department for Constitutional Affairs, *The Report of the Lord Chancellor's Committee to Investigate the Activities of Non-Legally Qualified Claims Assessors and Employment Advisers* (2000), para. 80.

50 Genn, *Hard Bargaining*, 50–2. But insurer and insured may not agree on the best strategy to achieve this aim. For instance, in product liability and medical negligence cases the insurer may want to settle early, and thereby minimize expenditure on legal services and experts' reports; while the insured may wish to spend money on having the claim properly investigated and rigorously resisted so as to minimize any damages paid in the hope of protecting their commercial or professional reputation. (I owe this point to a private communication from Chris Hodges.) For a specific example of this phenomenon, see 'Compensating the Bullied' [1996] *New LJ* 1787. But for the contrary suggestion that the insured may wish to settle quickly while the insurer may wish to hold out see J. Lowry and P. Rawlings, *Insurance Law: Doctrine and Principles*, 2nd edn (Oxford, 2005), 338.

51 J. Peysner, 'Finding Predictable Costs' (2003) 22 *CJQ* 349, 368. Under a CFA the lawyer has an interest in the success of the claim but not in the amount of the settlement. This is because the success fee is related to the amount of work the lawyer does, not the amount of compensation. It is said that conditional fees reward inefficient lawyers and those who deliberately do unnecessary work. By contrast, an efficient, honest lawyer may have no incentive to hold out for a higher settlement unless this will require more work; but a lawyer with a tight cash-flow may not be able to afford to do extra work. Some people think that contingent fees are preferable to conditional fees precisely because they tend better to align the interests of lawyer and client – provided the lawyer cannot take too great a proportion of the compensation. See R. O'Dair, 'Legal Ethics and Legal Aid: The Great Divide' (1999) 52 *Current Legal Problems* 419; M. Zander, 'Where are We Heading with the Funding of Civil Litigation?' [20xx] *CJQ* 23. See also Better Regulation Task Force, *Better*

the client's best interest may lie in pressing the claim and possibly commencing proceedings to put pressure on the defendant. Rejection of an insurer's offer commonly leads to a second increased offer being made,[52] and in some cases the process can be repeated several times.[53] However, the Harris 1984 Survey found that the first offer was accepted in about two-thirds of cases where an out-of-court settlement was reached.[54] The difficulty and uncertainties of litigation and fear of lengthy further negotiations are, no doubt, potent factors in explaining the high level of acceptance of first offers.[55] Many personal-injury claimants will have had no previous experience of making a legal claim, and may find the whole process bewildering or even frightening. The emotional stress generated by having been injured, and then by having to engage in disagreeable haggling, often produces a desire to settle as quickly as possible, even if at an unreasonably low figure. The insurer, who is experienced in the process and not emotionally involved, can afford to 'sit it out'.[56]

The imbalance of bargaining power which seems to affect the settlement of many personal injury claims may be overcome by interposing a third party between the two negotiating parties. One way of doing this is, of course, to have the claim adjudicated by a court, but the expense and difficulties associated with this course mean that it is very rarely pursued except in cases that raise complex and disputed issues of fact or law, or in which much is at stake financially. Another avenue for facilitating (fair) settlements without recourse to courts is 'alternative dispute resolution' (ADR) – arbitration, conciliation and particularly mediation.[57] ADR techniques are, by and large, only available in the private sector[58] and only in the context of family disputes can legal aid be obtained for mediation.[59] If a successful party in

---

Routes to Redress (2004), 4.5; *Tackling the 'Compensation Culture': government Response to the Better Regulation Task Force Report*, *'Better Routes to Redress'* (2004), response to recommendation 5. Significantly, perhaps, fixed costs for motor-accident claims under CPR Part 45.II contain an element calculated as a percentage of the damages recovered. It has been suggested that fixing costs in cases where damages are agreed may discourage settlement by claimants' lawyers: Peysner, ibid., 368–9.

52 Pearson Report, vol. 2, para. 402.

53 See Harris 1984 Survey, 101–4 for some information about the relative amounts of first, second and third offers.

54 Ibid., 104.

55 See generally ibid., 93–112. See also J. Macfarlane, 'Why do People Settle?' (2001) 46 *McGill LJ* 663, who suggests three main factors affecting propensity to settle: (1) the expectations the parties bring to the process; (2) whether the dispute is understood to be about principle or resources; and (3) how fair the parties think the settlement process is.

56 Genn, *Hard Bargaining*, 121–3. But for criticism that Genn treats defendants as a group as more homogeneous than they actually are see R. Dingwall *et al.*, 'Firm Handling: the Litigation Strategies of Defence Lawyers in Personal Injury Cases' (2000) 20 *LS* 1.

57 For a brief account of such techniques see P. Cane, *Tort Law and Economic Interests*, 2nd edn (Oxford, 1996), 358–66. See also H. Genn, *Mediation in Action: Resolving Court Disputes Without Trial* (London, 1999).

58 R. Williams, 'Should the State Provide Alternative Dispute Resolution Mechanisms' (1987) 6 *Civil Justice Q.* 142.

59 The legislation authorising CFAs does not apply to private arbitrations; but it has been held that a CFA for an arbitration which is consistent with the statutory rules governing CFAs for court proceedings is perfectly legitimate: *Bevan Ashford (a firm)* v. *Geoff Yeandle (Contractors) Ltd (in liq.)* [1998] 3 All ER 238.

a personal-injury claim unreasonably refused to take part in an ADR process, they may be penalized by having an order to pay costs made against them.[60] However, it seems that use of ADR in the personal injury context is very rare.[61] A court may encourage parties to resort to ADR, but cannot force them to do so.

The hallmark of arbitration is that the parties agree to be bound by the decision of the arbitrator, but the procedure followed by the arbitrator tends to be less formal than court procedure and more in the control of the parties. Arbitration is most suitable for more difficult or complex cases, and for this reason offers relatively little advantage in terms of cost or delay over adjudication by a court, because such cases require much the same amount of preparation whether they are heard by a judge or an arbitrator.[62] Mediation and conciliation are non-binding procedures designed to facilitate agreement between the parties. Such techniques are probably most suitable for straightforward, low-value claims and would probably not be very attractive to either party to a personal injury claim which was even moderately difficult or in which the amount at stake was more than a few hundred pounds.[63] But simple, low-value claims are the most easily settled anyway. Another serious source of worry about the suitability of such consensual techniques of dispute resolution in personal injury cases is that they may not work well unless the two parties are of roughly equal bargaining strength[64] – which may often not be the case in personal injury cases.

10.3.2   Group claims

Individual claims are the bread-and-butter of the tort system. Group (or 'multi-party') claims are rare; but because of their high public profile and special characteristics, they deserve separate discussion. Group claims tend to be complex both because of the numbers involved,[65] and especially if they raise difficult issues of fact

60 *Halsey* v. *Milton Keynes General NHS Trust* [2004] 1 WLR 3002; *Dunnett* v. *Railtrack Plc* [2002] 1 WLR 2434.
61 In 2003–4 neither side proposed ADR in 96% of publicly funded medical negligence cases: Department of Constitutional Affairs, *A New Focus for Legal Aid: Encouraging Early Resolution, Discouraging Unnecessary Litigation* (2004), para. 4.20.
62 S. Hirst and A. Morrish, 'Arbitrary justice' [1991] *New LJ* 1696.
63 This conclusion is supported by the results of a mediation pilot scheme set up at the Central London County Court: see H. Genn, *The Central London County Court Pilot Mediation Scheme: Evaluation Report* (Lord Chancellor's Department, 1998). A sample of parties litigating in the court were offered the alternative of mediation. In 91% of the personal injury cases in which an offer of mediation was made, both parties rejected it, as opposed to 80% for all types of case. Reasons for rejection included that complex evidence was involved in the case, that there were difficult disputes over fact and/or law, and that the case would be likely to settle anyway (this last reason is reflected in evidence in the report showing a very high rate of settlement of personal injury cases in which mediation was rejected – higher than in cases which were mediated). The median settlement figure in mediated cases was significantly lower than in non-mediated cases. In most mediated cases, the claimant ended up paying his or her own legal costs.
64 See Genn, ibid., para. 7.7.5.
65 The largest group claims are very large indeed: there were over 250,000 claimants world-wide in the Dalkon Shield litigation. In the British benzodiazepine litigation there were some 15,000 claimants (of whom 5,500 commenced court process), 6 'lead firms' and 1,553 'feeder firms': C. Hodges, *Multi-Party Actions* (Oxford, 2001), ch. 22. For some examples of medical-negligence group claims see Department of Health, *Making Amends: A Report by the Chief Medical Officer* (2003), 61.

or law (as in cases concerning the side-effects of drugs); and so they demand a higher level of organizational skill and efficiency than do individual claims. Often many firms of solicitors are involved; but it is now common for a small number of specialist personal injury firms ('lead firms') to form a steering committee to negotiate with the defendant(s) on behalf of all the claimants and their solicitors, and to handle matters common to the group as a whole. The other firms ('feeder firms') deal with matters relating to their own clients personally.[66] Legal aid funding arrangements reflect this division of labour, and although it can produce conflicts between the steering committee and the firms not represented on it,[67] this way of proceeding gives the claimants as a group a bargaining strength which a firm acting for an individual claimant could probably never achieve.[68] Group claims often attract considerable media attention, and use of the media by both claimants and defendants to attract public support and to influence the course of settlement negotiations has become a standard feature of group claims.[69] The media may also be used to advertize for potential claimants. This can be advantageous to defendants as well as to claimants because it increases the chance that all potential claims can be dealt with in one set of negotiations. On the other hand, it may unrealistically raise the expectations of potential claimants and, it is argued, have various other undesirable consequences.[70]

So far as collecting evidence is concerned, group claimants may be assisted by the fact that disasters in which many people are killed or injured are frequently followed by a public inquiry which will investigate how the accident was caused and who was to blame.[71] The findings of such inquiries can profoundly affect the course of negotiations. But they can also be a source of frustration and delay, especially if a number of different inquiries take place: public inquiry, police inquiry, inquest and so on. The *Marchioness* pleasure boat case prompted calls for a simplified inquiry process involving just one inquiry,[72] possibly with adjudicative powers.[73] It should be noted, too, that the sorts of group claims which tend to raise the most difficult factual issues – namely those involving defective products or drugs – normally do not trigger any sort of public inquiry.[74]

---

66 W. McBryde and C. Barker, 'Solicitors' groups in mass disaster claims' [1991] *New LJ* 484. Cases involving groups of defendants also lend themselves to this approach on the defendants' side.

67 See 'Herald tragedy victims unhappy with lawyers' [1988] *New LJ* 656.

68 The claimants may also be assisted by the formation of a support group which can help maintain the morale of the claimants and can interact with the professional steering committee.

69 D. McIntosh, 'Defending trial by media' [1990] *New LJ* 1224; P. Allen, 'Plaintiffs and the media' [1990] *New LJ* 1530. In the tobacco litigation, an attempt by the defendants to prevent the claimants' lawyers talking to the media was unsuccessful: *Hodgson* v. *Imperial Tobacco* [1998] 2 All ER 672.

70 For a generally negative assessment see Hodges, *Multi-Party Actions*, ch. 6. The accusation that advertising for claims may raise unrealistic expectations has also been made in relation to CMCs.

71 On disasters generally see C. Wells, *Negotiating Tragedy: Law and Disasters* (London, 1995).

72 P. Allen, 'The New Marchioness Enquiry' [1992] *New LJ* 44.

73 S. Sedley, 'Public Inquiries: A Cure or a Disease' (1989) 52 *Modern LR* 469, 477.

74 This is an aspect of the all-pervading preference in the law (and in other social contexts?) for assisting victims of traumatic accidents as opposed to victims of disease and illness.

Efficient solicitors can achieve positive results for groups of claimants in a relatively short time. For example, the *Piper Alpha* oil rig settlement (£100 million) was reached in less than 2 years. Speedy results depend crucially on co-operation by the defendant(s) and on whether there are disputed issues of law or fact. Victims of large-scale accidents are often cushioned from the worst financial effects of delay by receiving payments from charitable funds established in the wake of the disaster.[75] Such payments are not set off against tort damages, and so represent a real advantage to claimants in such cases, which is not enjoyed by the typical personal-injury claimant. Defendants facing group claims may also be prepared to make very prompt interim payments, and this is another respect in which group claimants may be better off than individual claimants.

Solicitors representing groups have made creative use of the courts in assisting the settlement process. Until quite recently, the only formal mechanism for dealing with group actions was the 'representative action', in which one party sues as representative for a group.[76] In such an action, the court's decision binds all the represented parties even though there is no mechanism for ensuring that all those parties are notified of the action or wish to be represented in it. The representative action is of limited use because the court can only decide issues common to the claims of all the represented parties. English courts have taken the view that because the assessment of tort damages is a highly individualized matter, it will not normally be possible to make a single assessment in relation to all the claimants; and so it is not possible for group personal-injury claims to take the form of a representative action. One way around this would be for a court to award a global sum of damages, which could then be divided up amongst the claimants, according to the facts of each particular claim, by an arbitrator, for example. But English courts have no power to do this. The US 'class action' is more flexible than the representative action, but it has been relatively little used in personal injury actions even in the USA.[77]

The representative action has now been supplemented by the mechanism of the 'group litigation order' (GLO) under CPR Part 19.III. A GLO can be made in relation to claims that give rise to 'common or related' issues. Once the order is made, a register of claims is established. Judgments and orders of the court in relation to 'group issues' are binding on all parties to claims on the register. In this respect, the GLO regime differs from both the representative action and what, in other jurisdictions, is called the 'class action' – under those regimes, court decisions can bind

---

75 After the *Piper Alpha* oil rig explosion, e.g., over £45 million was raised; and more than £10 million was given after the Hillsborough stadium disaster. The Red Cross publishes a manual to assist in the launching of appeal funds after disasters ('Disaster appeal scheme' [1991] *New LJ* 1215).

76 See generally R. Mulheron, *The Class Action in Common Law Systems: A Comparative Perspective* (Oxford, 2004), ch. 4.

77 J.G. Fleming, *The American Tort Process* (Oxford, 1988), 240–4; 'Mass Torts' (1994) 42 *American J. of Comparative Law* 507, 516–8; C. Harlow and R. Rawlings, *Pressure Through Law* (London, 1992), 124–32; American Law Institute, *Enterprise Responsibility for Personal Injury* (Philadelphia, 1991), vol. II, ch. 13; D.R. Hensler *et al.*, *Class Action Dilemmas: Pursuing Public Goals for Private Gain* (Santa Monica, CA, 2000).

members of the represented group or the defined class who have not 'opted in' to the claim.

Before the introduction of the GLO procedure, English lawyers developed strategies to deal with group claims. These included choosing one or more cases from the group as 'lead' or 'test' cases for submission to trial in order to have disputed issues resolved with a view to using the result as a basis for settling other similar cases. This technique is still possible under the GLO regime. The judge assigned to such GLO litigation plays an active managerial role in getting cases ready for trial, for example by imposing a cut-off date beyond which claims may not be added to the register. The GLO technique is most suitable for resolving issues such as duty of care and causation, but less so for dealing with disputes about assessment of damages. A course sometimes followed is for the defendant(s) to make a settlement offer to the group as a whole and for a judge to be asked to act as an arbitrator to divide it up amongst the claimants. Alternatively, a formula may be adopted and a judge asked to arbitrate individual cases in which the claimant challenges the application of the formula to their case.[78]

This type of approach to group claims has clear advantages for claimants. But it does rely heavily on the co-operation of the defendant(s), as well as on a high degree of cohesion within the claimant group. Also, each claimant sacrifices a degree of flexibility in achieving a settlement tailored to their own particular needs; and some claimants may find this sacrifice unacceptable. On the other hand, the risks for an individual making a claim alongside a group claim are bound to be great, at least in cases where there is any dispute as to liability.

So far we have viewed group claims in terms of their advantages to claimants. Grouping of claims may also be good for defendants (despite the power which claimants derive from concerted action) because it enables them to deal with a large number of claimants in one exercise with the hope of bringing the whole matter to a close rather than having to fight many individual claims over a long period. On the other hand, there is some reason to believe that the phenomenon of group litigation may create a situation where product manufacturers (in particular), faced with large, well-organized groups of claimants and the prospect of extremely expensive and lengthy legal battles with attendant bad publicity and loss of customer goodwill, may calculate that it makes commercial sense to settle even quite doubtful claims at relatively generous compensation levels.[79] For instance, although more than US$3 billion

---

78 By far the largest group claim in Britain to date was brought against British Coal in respect of respiratory diseases and vibration-related conditions contracted by miners. Once liability had been established by court judgment, a Claims Handling Agreement was established (and approved by the court) to deal with hundreds of thousands of claims and distribute billions of pounds of compensation. The Agreement set up an internal disputes procedure, but otherwise there was no right of appeal. The only judicial involvement was by way of approving the broad design of the Agreement.

79 In a case where the costs are likely to be very high and any damages awarded very modest, the court may prevent the action proceeding if the defendant so requests: AB v. John Wyeth & Brother Ltd [1994] PIQR P109. But normally the defendant is left to fend for itself and settle for the best terms it can negotiate with the claimants.

is being paid in the world-wide silicone breast implant litigation, the evidence of causal link, between implants and the more serious symptoms complained of, was very weak. Closer to home, in 1996 Lincolnshire Health Authority agreed to pay about £500,000 to families of victims of the child murderer, Beverly Allitt, for post-traumatic stress disorder despite significant legal doubt as to its liability.[80] It is surely a bizarre development of the tort system that generous compensation payments may be made in response to very weak claims when it seems that, for a variety of reasons, many individuals with strong tort claims receive nothing from the tort system, and when disabled people who cannot make even a weak argument that they should receive tort compensation must content themselves with much less generous forms of support through the social security system and so on.

In the USA, the tobacco industry has agreed to pay about US$360 billion over 25 years to public health authorities to cover the costs of treating smoking-related illnesses, despite the lack of any clear basis for legal claims against cigarette manu-facturers and the general lack of success of claims by smokers in the US courts. In the UK, the industry resisted a similar settlement with the NHS on the ground that because cigarettes are much more heavily taxed in the UK, smoking 'pays its way' in terms of health-care costs.

Where, for whatever reason, a defendant is prepared to accept responsibility to compensate for widespread illness or disability, it may be possible and commer-cially sensible to establish a 'domestic' administrative compensation scheme along the lines of the industrial injuries scheme, which is examined in chapter 13. For instance, British Nuclear Fuels Ltd has long run a compensation scheme for its employees who contract certain radiation-related illnesses.[81] Such arrangements avoid costly litigation and promote good industrial relations.

10.4   When negotiations break down

If the parties cannot reach a settlement, what happens next is considerably influenced by the operation of rules about legal costs.[82] If a case goes to trial, the basic rule is that the unsuccessful party pays the costs of both parties. For a claimant backed by a union, a BTE or ATE legal-expenses insurer or some other financial benefactor, this rule presents no disincentive to litigation. For a legally aided claimant, the rule may not be too intimidating: if the claimant loses, their liability for costs will be limited to any contribution required under the legal aid regulations,

---

80 *The Times*, 28 November 1996.
81 B. Leigh, 'The Radiation Worker Compensation Scheme: Managing the Risk of Civil Liability through Voluntary Arrangements' in R. Baldwin ed., *Law and Uncertainty: Risks and Legal Processes* (London, 1997), ch. 11.
82 The discussion in this and the following sections is primarily relevant to individual claims. In group claims, trials are better understood as an integral part of the settlement process rather than as a last resort. So far as concerns the time taken to resolve group claims and the amounts recov-ered, there are too few such claims and they are too diverse to make generalization possible or desirable.

plus the amount of any order for costs made by the court against the claimant.[83] If the claimant wins, such of the costs incurred by the LSC as are not recovered from the other party will be a first charge on the damages recovered.[84] Since costs will normally be awarded to a successful claimant against an unsuccessful insured party, costs should not prove a serious disincentive to a publicly funded party.

So far as insurers are concerned, the court does have power to order the LSC to pay the costs of a successful, unaided party who has been sued by a publicly funded claimant, and this power can be exercised for the benefit of an insurer.[85] But since such an order can be made only if the court is satisfied that otherwise the successful party will suffer severe financial hardship, it is highly unlikely that the power would be exercised in favour of an insured party. Trade unions sometimes pay the costs of a successful defendant where they have acted for the claimant, but they have no obligation to do so (the obligation rests on the claimant), and sometimes do not.[86] The MIB never claims costs.[87] An order for costs may be made against an unsuccessful self-financed claimant for the benefit of an insurer, but such an order may well prove unenforceable unless the case was brought under a CFA and the claimant has ATE insurance. So whether it wins or loses, an insurer may end up paying its own costs. For the insurer, the question is whether the chance of winning and the value to it of a decision in its favour outweigh the risk of losing and having to pay the claimant's costs as well as its own.

The balance of these considerations can be altered by the making of what is called a 'Part 36 offer' or, in other words, a formal offer to settle. Until 2000, only a defendant could make such offers, the chief rationale of which was to enable defendants to limit their potential costs liability in cases where the only real dispute concerned the amount of damages payable.[88] Now, either party can make a Part 36 offer.[89] The

---

83 An order for costs can be made against a legally aided party, but only for such amount as is reasonable having regard, amongst other things, to the resources of all the parties to the action. A legally aided party who sues an insured defendant is unlikely to be ordered to pay much, if anything at all.

84 For more on costs see A.A.S. Zuckerman, *Civil Procedure* (London, 2003), ch. 26. One might intuitively expect that the smaller the damages recovered, the greater would the costs be as a proportion of the damages. But the amount of work entailed in any particular tort claim bears no necessary relationship to the likely compensation, and data contained in the Harris 1984 Survey (128–30) reveals no consistent relationship between costs and the amount of compensation. However, a solicitor should, especially at this reasonably late stage in the process, be able to give a claimant some idea of the total costs likely to be incurred if the case goes to trial so as to help the claimant assess what their ultimate liability for costs will be.

85 *Davies* v. *Taylor (No. 2)* [1973] 1 All ER 959.

86 Ison, *The Forensic Lottery*, Appendix C19; KU, 'Liability of Trade Unions for Costs in Personal Injury Actions' (1986) 5 *Civil Justice Q* 30.

87 JUSTICE, *Report on the Trial of Motor Accident Cases*, 59.

88 Zuckerman, *Civil Procedure*, 827–8. Research suggested that under that regime, offers to settle did not increase the chance of settlement but did reduce the amount of the settlement: B.G.M. Main and A. Park, 'The Impact of Defendant Offers into Court on Negotiation in the Shadow of the Law: Experimental Evidence' (2002) 22 *International Review of Law and Economics* 177.

89 But not in relation to a claim made in the small claims jurisdiction of the county court (see n. 96). Offers analogous to Part 36 offers can be made in cases that do not fall within CPR Part 36, but the consequences of making such an offer are for the court to decide.

chief rationale for allowing claimants to make Part 36 offers (and an additional reason for allowing defendants to do so) is to promote early settlement: by making a Part 36 offer, one party can put considerable pressure on the other to accept the offer and settle the claim before the trial begins.[90] Suppose the defendant makes a Part 36 offer to settle for £X (and makes a 'payment into court' of that amount),[91] but the claimant does not accept the offer. If judgment is given for the claimant at trial, but for less than £X, the claimant will be liable for their own and the defendant's costs as from the latest date on which the offer could have been accepted.[92] Conversely, suppose that the claimant makes an offer to settle for £Y, but the defendant does not accept the offer. If judgment is given for the claimant at trial for more than £Y, the claimant will normally be entitled to additional interest on the whole amount of the judgment as well as an enhanced award of costs.

In the rare case in which the claimant or the defendant will, for some reason, end up paying their own costs personally (i.e. where they are not backed by legal aid, costs insurance or some other source of funding), the making of a Part 36 offer by the other party dramatically raises the stakes. Although the costs and interest sanctions may seem a reasonable way to encourage settlement and discourage trials, the underlying assumption that a party – especially a claimant – who disagrees with the other side's assessment of value of the claim, was unreasonable to continue the case after the offer was made, may not be justified. In many cases damages are extremely difficult to assess, and even experienced counsel may be unable to advise precisely about the amount likely to be awarded at trial.[93] Nevertheless, the costs and interest sanctions will normally be applied, and need to be if the system is to achieve its functions of saving costs and encouraging early settlement. But the court has a discretion not to apply the appropriate sanction if doing so would be unjust in the light of the respective behaviour of the parties in conducting the litigation.[94]

Assumptions underlying the CPR Part 36 regime are that settlement is preferable to trial and that earlier settlement is preferable to later settlement. From some points of view, these assumptions are undoubtedly valid. Other things being equal, the administrative costs of resolving a claim are likely to be less if it is settled out of court than if it goes to trial; and the earlier it is settled, the lower the costs are likely to be. Furthermore, if the proportion of tort claims going to trial increased by only a few per cent, the court system would be put under great strain.

---

90 For the position once the trial has started see *Gaskins* v. *British Aluminium* [1976] QB 524.

91 Once money has been paid into court, it is available to satisfy the claim even if the defendant subsequently goes bankrupt. The government has proposed (inter alia) that the requirement of payment into court be removed in most cases: DCA, *Part 36 of the Civil Procedure Rules: Offers to Settle and Payments into Court* (Consultation Paper 02/06, January 2006).

92 *Finlay* v. *Railway Executive* [1950] 2 All ER 1969. The claimant, having lost, will also have to bear the whole of their own costs. In calculating how much C has been awarded, social security benefits which have to be paid over to the Compensation Recovery Unit (15.3) are ignored: *McCafferey* v. *Datta* [1997] 1 WLR 870.

93 JUSTICE, *Report on the Trial of Motor Accident Cases*, 31.

94 Zuckerman, *Civil Procedure*, 846–58.

On the other hand, it may be thought undesirable to establish formal mechanisms and procedures specifically designed to put pressure on parties to settle for amounts that may diverge significantly from those that would be awarded by a court after trial.

Nor is it necessarily the case that early settlements save on administrative costs. There is evidence that procedural changes in recent years have encouraged earlier settlement of claims; but also that they have done this by requiring more to be spent on investigating and preparing the claim at an earlier stage than hitherto ('front-loading' of costs, it is called). The obvious question this raises is whether earlier settlement is worth the cost. The answer must depend in part on who benefits from earlier settlement and who, if anyone, loses out. For instance, if it turned out that earlier settlements disadvantaged claimants at the expense of their lawyers, we might doubt the wisdom of spending more to encourage it. In fact we lack the information that would be necessary to resolve such issues.

Most personal injury actions that end up in court go to the county court rather than the High Court. A claim likely to be worth less than £50,000 cannot be started in the High Court; and, in practice, 'it would be unusual for a claim worth less than £250,000 to begin in the High Court unless it [had] some special features of difficulty'.[95] Claims begun in either court can be transferred to the other in appropriate circumstances. Claims with a likely value of £1,000 or less will normally be dealt with by 'small claims' procedure.[96] Effectively, this is a form of ADR, more akin to arbitration than to traditional court proceedings. Procedure is relatively informal, and less adversarial than normal court procedure. Parties rarely have legal representation (except in road-accident cases, which represent about a fifth of all small claims, including non-personal injury claims); and normally the successful party can recover only very limited costs. On the other hand, small claims are resolved on the basis of the relevant legal rules, and there is a right of appeal from the small claims ('district') judge to a circuit judge (i.e. a senior county court judge). Research suggests that those who use the small claims procedure are generally happy with it; but that like all court proceedings, it presents a forbidding prospect to the average person.[97]

10.5   The time taken to achieve a settlement

Preparing for and conducting the trial of a personal injury claim can often be a lengthy business; but the process of negotiation can take considerable time even in

---

95 P. Barrie, *Personal Injury Law: Liability, Compensation and Procedure*, 2nd edn (Oxford, 2005), para. 37.05.
96 The lower limit for most types of case is £5,000. Because of the much lower limit for personal injury claims, only about 15% of personal injury claims that get to trial in the county court are dealt with as small claims. The reason given for the low limit is the complexity and difficulty of personal injury claims. The House of Commons Constitutional Affairs Committee has recently recommended that the limit be raised to £2,000–2,500: First Report, 2005–6, para. 53. On small claims generally see J. Baldwin, *Small Claims in the County Court in England and Wales: The*

cases that are settled.[98] From the outset, it is important not to assume that time spent on negotiating and litigating is necessarily time wasted, or automatically to equate the passage of time with 'delay'. These processes necessarily take time, and in the absence of accepted and reasonably precise criteria, it is hard to define how long is too long.

The Pearson Report provided a good deal of information about the time taken to resolve claims, both in cases which are dealt with by the courts and in cases which are settled.[99] As to the former group, the Commission found that in 1974 the average time between the date of the injury and the date of disposal of the claim was 36 months.[100] However, cases took much longer in the High Court (where all serious claims were then heard) than in the county courts. In the High Court, the average time between injury and disposal of the claim was 43 months in London and 41 months in the provinces; in the county courts the figure was 21 months. A survey conducted for the Civil Justice Review,[101] which sampled cases started in 1980–2 or tried in 1984, found that the average time from the incident giving rise to the action to the trial was more than 5 years in the High Court and almost 3 years in the county court. In 65% of cases studied, proceedings had not started within a year of the incident, and in 19% of cases they were started more than 2½ years after the incident. Solicitors interviewed for the survey identified the main causes of 'delay' as waiting for the claimant's medical condition to stabilize, waiting for medical reports and waiting for trial.[102] The figures, however, conceal the wide variations between the shortest and the longest delays. The Cantley Working Party found that among cases in which a High Court writ was issued in 1977, the average time from injury to disposal was 45 months, and no fewer than 122 cases (out of a total number of 5,701) were still outstanding 8 years after the injury.[103]

As for settled cases, according to the insurance survey conducted for the Pearson Commission, nearly half of all claims were disposed of within 12 months, though it is plain that these must have been the less serious cases because they only account for under a quarter of the total payments. By the end of 2 years from the injury over 80% of claims had been settled; but nearly 5% took up to 4 years, and nearly 1% (some 2,000 cases a year) were still unsettled after 5 years.[104] These findings generally confirm the pattern found by other less comprehensive studies.[105]

    Bargain Basement of Civil Justice? (Oxford, 1997).
97 J. Baldwin, 'Litigants' Experiences of Adjudication in the County Courts' (1999) 18 *CJQ* 12.
  98 Genn, *Hard Bargaining*, 100–8.
  99 The distinction between litigated cases and settled cases is blurred in those cases in which the settlement process itself involves the initiation of proceedings.
100 Pearson Report, vol. 2, table 129.
101 Cm 394, 1988.
102 The average waiting time from setting-down for trial until trial was 65 weeks in the High Court in London, 54 weeks outside London and 2 months in the county court: Civil Justice Review, para. 433.
103 *Report of the Personal Injuries Litigation Procedure Working Party* (Cmnd 7476, 1979) (the *Cantley Committee Report*), Appendix E. See also Civil Justice Review, para. 414(ii).
104 Pearson Report, vol. 2, table 17.

Furthermore, the larger the settlement, the longer it takes to negotiate. The Pearson Commission's insurance survey found that 96% of payments under £500 were made within 2 years, but only 42% of payments over £10,000 were made within this time.[106] And in the most serious cases of all, where payments over £25,000 were ultimately made, only 27% were settled within 2 years. In exceptional circumstances, settlements may take many years. One of the causes which led to the establishment of the Pearson Royal Commission was the realization that many of the Thalidomide cases were still unsettled after 10 years.

Delay in settling claims may be the result of inefficiency on either side or of deliberate procrastination by insurers, who generally have less to lose by delay than do claimants. An insurer has little incentive to keep the settlement process moving[107] except that which derives from the rule that interest is payable on damages awards[108] and from a desire to close files. The only way the typical claimant can put pressure on a dilatory insurer is to issue proceedings,[109] the various stages of which are subject to formal time limits (which may, however, be extendable by the court).

The settlement process is also inherently time-consuming because of the complex nature of the issues that arise in personal-injury actions and the difficulties that often attend the gathering of evidence.[110] In cases of more serious injury, a longer time must generally elapse before a firm medical prognosis as to the effects of the injuries can be given; because tort settlements are normally in the form of a once-for-all lump sum (even if the settlement is then structured), it is often in the interests of both claimants and defendants to postpone final agreement until the claimant's medical condition has stabilized. Moreover, the larger the claim the more prolonged and vigorous the haggling is inclined to be.[111] The aim of the insurer in the settlement process is to pay not what the claimant is legally entitled to, but as little as possible. The smaller the claim, the more likely it is that the cost of prolonged negotiation will outweigh the value of the claim, and this results in small claims being paid more promptly. It is a sombre thought, and no credit to the tort system, that the more serious a person's injuries, the longer it takes for the claim to be settled. If it were not for the social security system, which provides

---

105 See Winn Committee Report, Section IX and Appendix 13; 'A New Breed of Settlor?' [1967] *New LJ* 198; Ison, *The Forensic Lottery*, Appendix C, 178–80; Harris 1984 Survey, 105–10.
106 Pearson Report, vol. 2, table 115; see also Ison, *The Forensic Lottery*, 179 and Law Com. No. 225, *How Much is Enough?*, 70–1. The Harris 1984 Survey found a more direct correlation between length of time and degree of residual disability than between time and size of award as such.
107 And, indeed, has reason to slow it down: T. Swanson, 'A Review of the Civil Justice Review: Economic Theories Behind the Delays in Tort Litigation' [1990] *Current Legal Problems* 185, 196–201.
108 Supreme Court Act 1981, s. 32A; but see Law Com. No. 56, para. 271.
109 Group actions are different. In such cases, lawyers have become very skilled at using media publicity and other forms of pressure to encourage defendants and their insurers to make timely and acceptable settlement offers.
110 R. Dingwall, T. Durkin and W.L.F. Felstiner, 'Delay in Tort Cases' (1990) 9 *Civil Justice Q.* 353; R. James, 'The Causes and Effects of Delay in Personal Injury Claims' (1985) 36 *Northern Ireland Legal Q.* 222.

many claimants with benefits during the settlement process, the tort system would probably have collapsed long ago. Compensation for lost earnings and for medical expenses is needed when the earnings are lost or the expenses incurred, not 3 years later. The effects of delay on tort claimants are vividly portrayed in the following passage:[112]

> During the litigation process the victim and the victim's family face a long period of financial difficulty during which debts accumulate, savings are reduced and legal costs increase. These lengthy periods of financial hardship, in addition to physical distress, affect the degree of satisfaction with damages and attitudes to adequacy. The stress of litigation and apprehension about the future may impede recovery, which has an impact on the probability that accident victims will eventually return to the workforce. Delay in receiving damages also influences decisions about the use of money as accident victims seek to make up for the material comforts that they lacked in the years while waiting for the case to be settled.

One of the main aims of the Woolf reforms was to encourage earlier settlement by requiring lawyers to investigate and prepare claims at an earlier stage than formerly. One result appears to have been an increase in the average cost of settling claims. That earlier settlement is worth the cost is assumed rather than demonstrated.

10.6   The amount of compensation

In Part Two we devoted a good deal of space to the rules of legal liability and the principles on which damages for personal injuries are assessed by the courts. Now that we have seen how settlements are arrived at in practice, it will be appreciated that in cases which are settled, the legal principles laid down by the courts do not by themselves determine how much, if anything, will be recovered. Naturally, the law relating both to liability and the assessment of damages plays an important part in influencing the parties to a settlement. But the actual result is arrived at in a very different way: the object of a settlement is not to arrive at the result which a judge would probably arrive at according to the established legal principles.

In the first place, when a case is tried in court, the judge actually decides the issues of liability and assessment of damages that are in dispute between the parties. By contrast, when a case is settled by negotiation these things are never finally determined. There is merely a greater or lesser probability that, if the case were litigated, the judge would decide in this or in that way. Accordingly, in practice the damages are usually discounted to a greater or lesser extent according to the parties' estimates of the probabilities. If the claimant's case is extremely strong, it may be settled on the basis of full compensation; but where there is any doubt about the facts, or where the relevant legal rules are uncertain or of uncertain application, the damages which the parties estimate that a court would award if

111 Swanson thinks that the main problem in many cases is a lack of bargaining: 'A Review of the

the claimant succeeded at trial are likely to be discounted by some percentage. A settlement is a business bargain in which the claimant sells a claim to an insurer for the best price on offer, which will be as little as the insurer can get away with. The claimant will often be (reluctantly) willing to sacrifice some part of even a good claim in order to reduce the risk (which can never be wholly eliminated) that the action may fail wholly or in part.[113] Furthermore, a settlement may be further discounted if the claimant receives the money significantly sooner than if the case had gone to trial.

Where the claim is less strong, or where there is the possibility of an adverse finding on contributory negligence, the probable damages may be discounted quite heavily. The settlement arrived at in the Thalidomide cases illustrates this procedure very well: because of doubts about proving negligence against the defendants and also about the validity of the claim as a matter of law,[114] the claimants were advised by their counsel to accept a settlement of 40% of 'full compensation', and this was approved as a fair and reasonable settlement by the court. According to Pearson Commission findings, over a quarter of cases settled with insurers are disposed of on the basis of partial liability only, that is, on the basis that the claimant must have been guilty of contributory negligence.[115] In serious cases, in particular, the effect of this process of discounting may be that the compensation paid is inadequate to replace income lost, and to meet extra expenses incurred, as a result of the injuries suffered. Typically, nothing can subsequently be done about this. The inadequacy of the compensation is the price paid by the claimant for being relieved of the risk of receiving even less or nothing at all if the case went to trial. In the case of Thalidomide, however, both the government and the drug manufacturer subsequently (in 1996) gave additional funds (£7 million and £37 million respectively) to the victims.

There are some grounds for believing that claimants tend to recover a larger proportion of what they have 'lost' in cases of minor injury.[116] The Pearson Report does not provide statistics directly relevant to this issue, but it points in the same direction. For instance, it is clear from the Pearson findings that the proportion of the settlement attributable to non-pecuniary loss is much higher in small claims. Indeed, for claims of up to £5,000 (in 1973) over two-thirds, and in many minor cases over 70%, was for non-pecuniary loss. For larger claims, the proportion

Civil Justice Review', 190–1.

112 Law Com. No. 225, *How Much is Enough?*, xxi.

113 Research suggests that the most common reason why claimants accept offers which they feel, or come to feel, are inadequate is because they are advised to accept: Law Com. No. 225, *How Much is Enough?*, 86. Other reasons are the amount of time already taken pursuing the claim, fear of the costs of carrying on, and the effect on their health.

114 At the time these cases were being settled there was doubt as to whether a duty of care could be owed in respect of injuries suffered by an unborn child in the womb.

115 Pearson Report, vol. 2, table 117.

116 Conard, *Automobile Accident Costs and Payments*, table 6–14, 197; table 5–13, 179; fig. 5–11, 177. The *Osgoode Hall Study* does not show such dramatic differences between more and less serious cases, though it shows serious under-compensation in fatal cases (ch. IV, table IV-6). The Harris

attributable to non-pecuniary loss drops to around 50%.[117] Since the maximum amount normally awarded by a court for non-pecuniary loss is in the region of £220,000 (in 2005), the proportion of the largest awards and settlements attributable to non-pecuniary loss may be much lower even than these figures suggest. Sums paid in settlements for non-pecuniary loss may help compensate for the discounts made on account of the risks of litigation and contributory negligence. The Pearson figures suggest that this happens to a greater extent in less serious cases.

Intuitively, one would expect small claims to be contested less vigorously by insurers, both as to liability and as to quantum, than large ones because the smaller the claim, the greater its nuisance value; or, in other words, the greater the likelihood that the cost of contesting it will be greater than the amount of the claim. There is no necessary relationship between the size of a claim and how difficult and complex it is in legal terms. Large claims may be very simple and small claims very complex. But the smaller the claim, the more likely that resisting it will not be financially worthwhile. Insurers do not like large claims and will investigate and resist them with vigour.[118] On the other hand, however weak the claimant's case, it may still pay the defendant to settle a small claim rather than to fight. For reasons of cost and administrative efficiency, insurers typically settle low-value claims on the basis of rules-of-thumb – such as that rear-end accidents are always the fault of the following driver – rather than a thorough investigation of the issue of fault.[119] Such rules-of-thumb are not only simpler and cheaper to apply than the legal concept of fault, but they also tend to be more favourable to claimants than strict rules of law. If the claimant's solicitor appreciates this, the claimant's bargaining position is improved. In practice, few claims are totally worthless so long as there is at least some room for argument about fault. Because there are many more small claims than large ones, the tort system has an inherent bias in favour of those with low-value claims at the expense of the more seriously injured.

Group claims, once again, deserve special attention. In such cases solicitors may, by making realistic threats of instituting proceedings in the USA, secure settlements at mid-Atlantic rates. Even in cases with no US element, solicitors may secure for group claimants sums in respect of non-pecuniary loss higher than prevailing rates and even, in fatal cases, higher than the statutory maximum of £10,000 for bereavement; or compensation beyond the limits laid down by international Conventions dealing with air and sea disasters. In the case of very large group claims (such as the claim against British Coal mentioned in n. 77) a non-judicial administrative process may be established to assess compensation in individual cases. In a discussion of the British Coal scheme in later related litigation[120] the judge noted that although compensation under the scheme was calculated according to common law principles, the scheme was constructed in such a way that some awards would

1984 Survey found that there was no clear correlation between likelihood of obtaining damages at all and degree of residual disability or amount of time off work: 56–8.
117 Pearson Report, vol. 2, table 108.
118 Genn, *Hard Bargaining*, 69.

exceed and others would fall below what a court would award in individual cases. Nevertheless, the scheme received judicial approval because the level of inaccuracy in individual cases was more than offset by savings in administrative costs and in court time. In fact, there were so many claims (more than 740,000) that it would have been impossible for the court system to deal with even a small proportion of them.

The result of all this is that in cases which are disposed of by settlement – and this probably means about 99% of all claims – the principles of law laid down by the courts do not alone determine whether and how much compensation will be paid. It is highly likely that the settlement process often leads to awards of compensation higher (especially in low-value claims) or lower (especially in high-value claims) than would be awarded in the courts. As Professor Conard and his colleagues at Michigan put it many years ago: 'The statistics confirm what every lawyer and adjustor knows – the questions about negligence, proof, the defendant's ability to pay, and the client's desire for an end of litigation, lead to compromises of claims at levels which correspond to no theory of legal right.'[121]

These criticisms of the settlement process usually stimulate demands for reform of that process, so as to improve the position of the claimant.[122] But it must always be borne in mind that the claimant with a tort claim is already in a very privileged position compared with the great majority of the injured and the disabled. Thus, it is possible to make criticisms of the settlement process not with a view to its improvement but with a view to the abolition of the tort system of which it is a major part.

119 R. Lewis, 'Insurance and the Tort System' (2005) 25 *LS* 85, 89.
120 *AB* v. *British Coal Corporation* [2004] EWHC 1372 at [325]–[328].
121 Conard, *Automobile Accident Costs and Payments*, 199.
122 E.g. Genn, *Hard Bargaining*, 169.

Part 4

Other compensation systems

11

First-party insurance

11.1 Types of first-party insurance

Under a 'third-party' or 'liability' insurance policy one person (the 'first party' we might say) is insured by the insurer (the 'second party') against the risk of being held legally liable to another (the 'third party'). Under a 'first-party' or 'loss' insurance policy the policy holder (the first party) is insured against the risk of suffering loss specified in the policy by causes defined therein. Nearly all accident risks can be covered by first-party insurance of one kind or another. Life insurance, which usually covers death from any cause except (in some cases) sane suicide, is by far the most common form of first-party insurance against risks to the person (i.e. death from personal injury and other causes). In 1996–7, 61% of UK households were paying for some life insurance.[1] A significant proportion of life insurance is mortgage-related – that is, it provides security against the death of the mortgagor. Total UK premium income in 1997 for life insurance was about £28 billion.[2] The popularity of life insurance is partly attributable to the fact that it is used as a form of investment, not merely as a protection against risks; but also partly to the fact that premiums for this type of insurance are low relative to the benefits provided. One reason for this is that the administrative costs of life insurance are low: '. . . the characteristics of death facilitate the administration of life assurance on a voluntary and individual basis, for death is inevitable, non-recurring, readily ascertainable when it occurs, is something which the assured is generally anxious to avoid as long as possible, and is a matter of public record and inquiry.'[3] There is little scope for fraud or abuse[4] on the part of those claiming life insurance benefits.

Property insurance is very common in the form, for example, of household contents and all risks cover. In 1996–7, 74% of UK households had some contents insurance. Total UK premiums for property damage insurance in 1997 amounted to almost £8.3 billion.[5] Motor insurance is also very big business. Gross

---

1 Association of British Insurers, *Insurance: Facts, Figures and Trends 1998* (London, 1992), 9.
2 Ibid., 10.
3 Ison, *The Forensic Lottery*, 43.
4 Insurers call this 'moral hazard'. Suicide is the only common form of abuse, but this is relatively very rare.
5 *Insurance: Facts, Figures and Trends 1998*, 20.

motor insurance premium income in the UK in 1997 amounted to some £7.6 billion.[6]

Insurance against injury and illness takes a number of forms. Personal accident insurance (PAI) is designed to cover short-term loss of earnings.[7] Benefits under PAI policies are in the form of lump sums and sometimes periodical payments for a fixed period. Critical illness insurance protects against the risk of conditions such as cancer, heart attacks and stroke; benefits are usually in the form of a lump-sum payment. Income protection insurance (IPI) (formerly known as permanent[8] health insurance) is designed to insure an income where the insured suffers long-term sickness or disability. Private medical insurance (PMI) covers the cost of non-NHS medical treatment (primarily hospital treatment and surgery). Both IPI and PMI policies are taken out by individuals and by employers on behalf of employees through group policies. Long-term care insurance is designed to cover the cost of care in the insured's own home or in a nursing home made necessary by permanent illness or disability. It is marketed as a private supplement to care-related social security benefits and local authority care services.

Compared with that for life insurance, the market for insurance against injury and ill-health is small. In 1997, UK premium income from IPI was around £389 million (representing some 1.3 million individual policies)[9] and around £400 million from group policies. In 1997, UK premium income from PAI, IPI and PMI together was around £3.3 billion. In 2001 only 15.4% of adults were covered by PMI.[10] Relatively few people insure themselves in the private market against disability which prevents them earning a living for weeks, months or even longer;[11] nor against partial disability, which may deprive a person of some of the pleasures of life, such as the ability to drive or dance or play sports, or which may inflict chronic pain and discomfort.[12] People whose whole living depends on some par-

6 Ibid.
7 Research conducted for the Law Commission in 1992–3 found that only one in ten recipients of tort damages surveyed had received any payments under personal accident insurance policies: Law Com. No. 225, *How Much is Enough?*, 155.
8 In the sense that 'once an insurer has accepted a proposal, the terms of the policy are that renewal cannot be refused until some pre-arranged expiry date, usually the retirement of the insured': P. Corfield, 'Private Insurance' in Harris 1984 Survey, 222.
9 T. Burchardt and J. Hills, *Private Welfare Insurance and Social Security* (York, 1997), 13.
10 Office for National Statistics, *The Demand for Private Medical Insurance* (2004). About equal numbers of PMI policies are paid for by individuals and by employers respectively. Individuals with high incomes are much more likely to be covered than individuals with low incomes; and individuals in the top income percentile are very much more likely to be covered by employer-purchased PMI than any other group. People in professional, managerial and technical occupations are more likely to be covered by PMI than people in unskilled occupations.
11 For a discussion, in the US context, of why insurance against disability is relatively rare see K.S. Abraham and L. Liebman, 'Private Insurance. Social Insurance and Tort Reform: Towards a New Vision of Compensation for Illness and Injury' (1993) 93 *Columbia LR* 75, 101–5.
12 Life insurance is much more common than disability insurance despite the fact that 'at most ages the risk of premature death is small by comparison with risks of illness or injury . . . The explanation is perhaps to be sought in some peculiarity in attitudes to risk or more probably in imperfections in the private market for personal insurances against illness, injury and death': Corfield, 'Private Insurance', 224; see also 230–3.

ticular ability sometimes have substantial personal accident insurance; for instance, a musician may insure their hands, a footballer their legs, a film star their facial appearance. Egon Ronay (the famous food critic) reportedly insured his taste buds! Many comprehensive motor insurance policies contain an element of such insurance, but the benefits provided are usually very low.[13] Similar cover is sometimes included in other special *ad hoc* types of insurance, such as holiday insurance. Personal accident insurance is often of short duration, being taken out to cover only a particular event or risk; and many policies cover only a particular risk such as being injured while playing sport.[14] Accident insurance is an unattractive way of insuring against income loss because the risk of accident is very low compared with that of illness. What most people need is some form of life insurance to provide benefits on death plus some form of insurance against income loss, from whatever cause, while they are alive.

The relative unpopularity of income protection insurance to provide cover against income loss is due partly to the fact that it is quite expensive; partly to the fact that benefits under such policies are usually only payable for a relatively short fixed period;[15] and partly to the fact that the risk of long-term income loss as a result of ill-health is sufficiently small that most people fail to appreciate it or are prepared to run it. More importantly, perhaps, there are other sources of compensation for income loss. The social security system provides benefits for both short-term and long-term incapacity for work. These benefits are low, and many employees, especially the higher-paid, would be in serious financial difficulties if social security were the sole source of income replacement. Very many employed workers (as opposed to self-employed workers) are covered by occupational sick pay schemes. The Pearson Commission concluded that about half of those injured by accidents who suffer some loss of pay receive some sick pay from their employers, and that, in aggregate, these sums totalled about £125 million per annum (in 1977 currency values).[16] In 1981 it was estimated that some 90% of employees participate in some form of voluntary (or 'occupational') sick pay scheme.[17] According to a 1985 survey by the Social Security Policy Inspectorate,[18] public employees and office and managerial staff are more likely to receive occupational sick pay than those working in industrial, construction or transport fields; larger firms are more likely to have a scheme than smaller firms; and lower-paid employees are less likely to receive occupational sick pay than well-paid ones.

---

13 Ibid., 224–5.
14 In *Van Oppen* v. *Bedford Charity Trustees* [1990] 1 WLR 235 it was held that a school has no duty to take out insurance to cover children playing sport for the school or to advise parents of the wisdom of purchasing such insurance. A specialized variant of accident insurance is insurance against the risk of giving birth to a handicapped child.
15 The same is true of related forms of insurance such as mortgage protection insurance, which provides cover against the risk of not being able to keep up mortgage payments as a result of an unexpected reduction of income.
16 Pearson Report, vol. 1, paras. 137–41; see also Corfield, 'Private Insurance'.
17 See HC Debs, 6th Series, vol. 13, cols. 642–3 (23 November 1981).
18 *Inquiry into Statutory Sick Pay* (HMSO, 1985).

There are wide variations in the conditions of entitlement and the amounts payable under sick pay schemes, and there are also wide variations between different industries. In some cases, full pay is granted; in others half pay; and in yet others a flat-rate payment is made. Sick pay may be reduced to take account of social security benefits received by the employee. The 1985 Social Security Policy Inspectorate survey found no employer which paid statutory sick pay[19] in addition to occupational sick pay when the latter was equivalent to the normal rate of pay. Often a waiting period of a few days is prescribed before entitlement accrues. A qualifying period of service with the employer is also often required. There are also wide variations in the length of time for which sick pay is payable. Research done for the Law Commission in 1992–3 found that fewer than one in five of the victims surveyed received full pay for the entire time they were off work as a result of their injuries, and a small proportion received nothing.[20] By contrast, in 67% of the fatal cases surveyed, relatives received insurance money, thus confirming the popularity of life insurance.[21]

A person who is so severely injured or disabled or sick that they are forced to retire prematurely from employment may be entitled to a pension under an occupational pension (or 'superannuation') scheme or may have a personal pension. Some 55% of full-time male employees and some 56% of full-time female employees are members of an occupational pension scheme.[22] Membership is more likely the longer an employee has worked for the current employer, the higher the employee's wages, the larger the employer's establishment and if the employee's job is non-manual.[23] In both the public and the private sector, accrued pension rights are normally unaffected by premature retirement for sickness or ill-health, and are payable as of right. Indeed, a large proportion of those who are members of such schemes would get enhanced pension rights if they had to retire on grounds of ill-health. In the public sector, 5 years' service usually qualifies the employee for such benefits, and most private schemes are at least as generous. Some schemes provide benefits that vary with the degree of incapacity, higher benefits being payable in cases of serious disability. Some schemes also provide benefits for spouses of employees who die in service. In addition to employees who belong to an occupational pension scheme, some 23% of men and 16% of women in full-time employment have a personal pension. Overall, some 68% of men and 65% of women in full-time employment have some form of pension.

The main gap in private provision for insurance against income loss occurs where entitlement under a sick pay scheme runs out before entitlement under a pension scheme arises. It is here that income protection insurance might be

19 This is a social security benefit payable in the first instance by the employer, who may be able to recover some of the amounts paid from the DWP: see 13.4.3.1.
20 Law Com. No. 225, *How Much is Enough?*, 134–5.
21 Ibid., 242.
22 *Social Trends 35*, table 8.6 (2003–4).
23 M. Lunnon, 'New Earnings Survey data on occupational pension provision' [1998] *Labour Market Trends* 499.

thought to have a role to play, but it has not really caught on even in this context; although some employers do take out this form of insurance for their employees to cover the gap.[24]

Not every risk protected against by the tort system is insurable in practice. For instance, it is hardly possible to protect oneself by insurance against bereavement as such. It is true that a person may insure their life for an amount which is much greater than their income would warrant, so that if the person dies prematurely their spouse or partner and children may to some extent be compensated in money for the loss of the person as well as for loss of income; but few people are likely to take such considerations into account in deciding how much life insurance to buy. Moreover, the Industrial Assurance and Friendly Societies Act 1948 prohibits insurance of the life of a child under the age of 10 which provides for any benefit other than the return of the premiums. This Act is a reminder of the grisly fact that in some circumstances life insurance on the life of a young child might be a temptation to homicide or at least neglect.

War risks are excluded from most insurance policies as a matter of course. Today it has become customary for the State itself to take on the business of providing war-damage insurance and of compensating those who suffer personal injury, and the dependants of those killed, as a result of enemy action. Other uninsurable risks are also taken care of by special means. For instance, personal injury caused by rioting would probably fall within the Criminal Injuries Compensation Scheme; in the case of damage to property, compensation may be payable under the Riot (Damages) Act 1886. Damage done by nuclear installations is the subject of a set of legal rules and insurance practices designed to spread the cost of such risks as widely as possible while retaining the compensation process in private hands.

11.2   First-party insurance compared with tort liability

First-party insurance differs from tort compensation in many important ways. First, it is almost entirely optional. There are no legal requirements to insure one's life, person, earning capacity or property with a private insurer. Moreover, a person who buys first-party insurance can choose the amount of coverage desired. It may be thought that some degree of compulsion would be a good thing, even in the area of damage to property. Insurance against fire damage to houses is, in many cases, compulsory in practice because building societies and other mortgagees require the property to be insured against such risks to protect their security. But mortgages are eventually paid off, and insurance policies may then be allowed to lapse. Grave hardship would obviously be caused to most people if their houses were destroyed or seriously damaged by fire and they had no insurance cover. But the case for compulsion is much less strong in relation to other property such as cars. Nobody who runs a motor vehicle can be unaware of the requirement of compulsory third-party

24 Pearson Report, vol. 2, para. 144.

liability insurance, and this means that the motorist is very likely to be made aware of the choice between comprehensive cover and liability cover alone.

So far as insurance against lost income is concerned, there is an element of compulsion in the sense that social security benefits for income loss are funded out of compulsory taxes and National Insurance contributions. Moreover, many employees are required by their employers to belong to sick pay and pension schemes as a term of their employment. But the State imposes no legal compulsion on individuals to insure privately against income loss, and relatively few people do so.

A second major contrast between first-party insurance and the tort system is the fact that in the case of first-party insurance the form of compensation normally depends on what has been lost. Thus, loss of a capital asset (e.g. destruction of a house or car) will be met by payment of a lump sum; whereas loss of income will normally be met by periodical payments if the loss continues long enough to make this desirable. There is, moreover, more scope for correcting mistakes in the case of personal insurance than under the tort system. We have seen how tort damages must be assessed once-and-for-all, and how this may lead to over- or undercompensation if things do not turn out as anticipated. Because an insurance policy is a contract, it can contain provision for the reduction, for example, of compensation for loss of earnings if the insured's earning capacity unexpectedly improves. Again, if a person insures a valuable piece of jewellery against loss or theft and payment is made under the policy, this usually has the effect of transferring the legal title to the jewellery from the owners to the insurers. If, therefore, it turns up again later, the insurance company can claim it and the former owner cannot keep both the insurance money and the article insured. In most cases, the article will be offered back to the owner on condition that the policy money is repaid.

A third point of difference between tort compensation and first-party insurance is that the latter often does not provide 'full compensation'. The amount of coverage is usually optional, but there are many types of insurance in which the standard policy requires the insured to bear part of the loss either by imposing an upper limit (or ceiling) on the benefits payable or by requiring the insured to pay the first slice of any claim (called an 'excess' or 'deductible'). Such provisions are a very common feature of comprehensive motor insurance policies, but they are also found, for example, in householder's policies (at least for some risks) and income protection policies (which do not usually cover the first month or 3 or 6 months of lost income, and normally limit the income loss insured against to three-quarters of the insured's normal earnings). Ceilings and deductibles are designed to reduce the risk of fraudulent claims; to encourage the insured to take precautions against the occurrence of the insured loss; and to reduce the cost of the insurance. The way ceilings achieve this third aim is obvious. The basis of deductibles is that small claims are very much more common than large ones, and the cost of processing them is high relative to their value, so that by excluding them from the cover the cost of the insurance can be significantly reduced. Under the tort system, the principle of full compensation rules out ceilings or thresholds;[25] but this is not necessarily in the public interest. Money spent on tort compensation is money not available for other purposes, and however fair the full compensation principle may seem as between individual claimants and defendants, it may seem less desirable when viewed in a wider social context.

A fourth major difference between tort liability and first-party insurance, as we have seen,[26] is the fact that negligence on the part of the insured will often not affect a first-party insurance claim. However, an insurance policy may exclude from coverage losses arising from specified events akin to contributory negligence – for example, driving while drunk in the case of a comprehensive motor policy. Deliberate acts that bring about the event insured against are not normally covered because claims based on such conduct are usually fraudulent. Where there is no fraud – as often in the case of suicide under life policies – liability is usually accepted. Moreover, suicide is a cause of death reflected in the mortality tables on which premiums are based.

Despite these differences, there are certain similarities between tort liability and first-party insurance. A first-party insurance policy will give cover only against certain defined risks. Cover may be limited to events occurring in specified places or at specified times or in specified ways. Such limitations may give rise to disputes between insurer and insured as to whether the event on which a claim is based fell within the risk or occurred in the circumstances defined in the policy. Disputes of this sort may turn on questions of interpretation of the words of the policy (exactly what risks does it cover?) but they may also raise issues very similar to issues of causation which arise in tort cases (how did the loss occur?).

In theory, there is no reason why non-pecuniary loss should not be recoverable under a first-party insurance policy as it is under the tort system. But, with the exception of life assurance, which may be for a sum much greater than the assured's earning capacity would warrant, non-pecuniary loss insurance is very uncommon. Accident insurance policies, such as travel insurance and household insurance, may provide limited cover for personal disabilities, but the sums offered are usually small and fixed in amount and can, anyway, be seen as designed to meet expenses rather than to compensate for intangible loss. It is reasonable to suggest that there is little public demand for insurance against pain and suffering or loss of amenity as such.[27] This is really not very surprising: monetary compensation is not a great

---

25 Liability insurance (even if compulsory) may impose a ceiling. For example, the sum insured under the Employers' Liability (Compulsory Insurance) Act 1969 must be £5 million per incident. Any excess may be insured separately, perhaps with several insurers in layers; or it may be borne by the insured. Similarly, a (compulsory) liability insurance policy may provide for an excess or deductible. E.g., under the Road Traffic Act 1988 the first £300 of third-party property damage liability does not have to be insured against, and the MIB will not pay the first £300 of any claim (but the EU 5th Motor Insurance Directive of 2005 requires abolition of this deductible). In some jurisdictions in the USA and Australia, lower and upper limits on various heads of damages have been imposed by statute in an attempt to limit the cost of the tort system.

26 9.5.

27 But see S.P. Croley and J.D. Hanson, 'The Non-Pecuniary Costs of Accidents: Pain and Suffering Damages in Tort Law' (1995) 108 *Harvard LR* 1785.

deal of consolation for loss of amenity.[28] Yet the tort system, backed up by liability insurance, in practice compels people to buy this kind of insurance for each other even though, given the choice, few buy it for themselves. This casts doubt on the desirability of retaining damages for non-pecuniary loss in the tort system.

This line of argument could be extended. The system of tort liability with (compulsory) liability insurance requires people to pay indirectly for benefits (or levels of benefits) which they might not choose to buy under a system of (optional) first-party insurance. Furthermore, these benefits are only available if the relevant losses are caused by tortious conduct of another, whereas benefits under first-party insurance policies are, with minor exceptions, usually payable regardless of how the relevant loss was caused. In this way, the tort system infringes people's freedom of choice. Extending the argument in this way perhaps shows that it proves too much: few people buy income-protection insurance and the sort of cover which is freely available is limited; yet this provides no good argument for not compensating people, via the tort system, for permanent loss of income, and no reason not to require people by law to insure others against the risk of income loss by taking out third-party liability insurance.[29]

Indeed, the wider argument has force only if we compare the tort system with optional first-party insurance. But, of course, the National Insurance system is a form of compulsory first-party insurance which gives people no choice whether to insure or about the level of benefits. There are some losses which we feel justified in requiring people to insure against. On the other hand, levels of social security benefits are quite low, and we do not force people to buy greater cover in the private market. In this light, the questions we must ask ourselves are, which losses are we justified in requiring people to insure against, and what is the most efficient way of securing such insurance? It may be that the tort system requires people to insure, in effect, against losses which they should not be required to cover; and it is certainly a very inefficient form of insurance. But the mere fact that some, or even many, people would not voluntarily insure against a particular loss does not make compulsory insurance against that loss necessarily undesirable.

Insurance policies in respect of property only provide compensation for the financial value of the property, although this might be defined as the cost of replacing the property rather than its sale value at the time it was lost, damaged or destroyed. Although such 'new-for-old' cover increases the risk of fraudulent claims, it is now very commonly available to private individuals under household contents policies. Compensation for property damage in the tort system is also basically calculated according to the market value of the property at the time of the loss or destruction; but in practice, the sum awarded is often the cost of repairing or replacing the property. Normally cost of repair or replacement will not be awarded if this is greater than the value of the property at the time of the tort; but

---

28 See also S.A. Rea, 'Economic Analysis of Fault and No-Fault Liability Systems' (1986–7) 12 *Canadian Business LJ* 444, 451–2.

29 See J. Stapleton, 'Tort, Insurance and Ideology' (1995) 58 *Modern LR* 820, 833–7.

in exceptional cases the claimant may be awarded more than the market value of the property.[30]

Compensation for lost profits arising from damage to or destruction of profit-earning property is also available under both the tort system and via first-party insurance, and the assessment of compensation would follow similar lines in the two cases.

One final point by way of summary: the tort system is much more important as a source of compensation for personal injury, illness and death than as a source of compensation for damage to or destruction of property. This is because damage to or destruction of valuable property, about which it would be worth litigating, whether caused by a tort or not, is very likely to be the subject of a first-party insurance policy. On the other hand, although people commonly insure against the risk of death, and although private insurance against the risk of personal injury or illness is available, many people have little or no private insurance cover against many of the losses for which the tort system provides compensation.

30 See further P. Cane, *Tort Law and Economic Interests*, 2nd edn (Oxford, 1996), 92–3.

12

Compensation for criminal injuries

12.1   Tort claims

Victims of criminal offences causing personal injury can claim in tort against
the criminal, but in the great majority of cases the criminal would not be worth
suing.[1] In its *Third Report*, the Criminal Injuries Compensation Board (CICB)
(now the Criminal Injuries Compensation Authority (CICA)) reported that it had
found the number of cases in which offenders would be worth suing to be seventeen, i.e. 0.7% of the cases which had by then come before the Board.[2] By the time
of the *Seventh Report* the number had dropped to 6 out of nearly 6,000 cases, i.e.
about 0.1%.[3] Just occasionally, tort liability may be established against someone
other than the offender personally. For instance, the offender's employer may be
vicariously liable in cases of fraud. In cases of personal injury, such liability will not
often be established because criminal assaults and similarly violent conduct will not
often be regarded as within the course of the offender's employment (so as to
render the employer vicariously liable), but it may be in some cases.[4] Personal tort
liability may occasionally be imposed on the victim's employer, for example, where
it is alleged that the employer had exposed the victim to unnecessary risk of
criminal attack, for example, by sending a young woman to the bank to collect

1   A bizarre exception was a case in which two victims of sexual assaults brought a successful tort
action against their attacker (*W* v. *Meah* [1986] 1 All ER 935) who had himself been awarded tort
damages on the basis that his criminal activities were a result of his having been negligently
injured in a car accident (*Meah* v. *McCreamer (No. 1)* [1985] 1 All ER 367); the assailant then
unsuccessfully sued the driver to recover the amounts awarded to the two victims (*Meah* v.
McCreamer (No. 2) [1986] 1 All ER 943). Recourse to tort law by victims of violent crimes has
apparently increased in recent years. Most controversial are cases in which the person sued has
been prosecuted and acquitted, or where the prosecuting authorities have decided not to proceed
because of lack of evidence. The most notorious example is that of O.J. Simpson; but there have
been several successful tort claims in such circumstances in the UK. Critics argue that allowing
tort claims in such cases deprives the alleged offender of the protections of the criminal law,
notably the higher burden of proof ('beyond reasonable doubt', not 'on the balance of probabilities', as in civil law). The force of the argument lies in the fact that as a result of the victim's success
in the civil action, the defendant may be 'branded as a criminal' in the public mind (see e.g. 'Man
Branded as a Killer in Civil Ruling', *The Times*, 25 March 1998).
2   Para. 21; *CICB Fifth Report* (Cmnd 4179, 1969), para. 11.
3   Para. 17; see also *CICB Seventeenth Report* (Cmnd 8401, 1981), paras. 53–4.
4   P.S. Atiyah, *Vicarious Liability in the Law of Torts* (London, 1967), esp. 262ff; F.A. Trindade and
P. Cane, *The Law of Torts in Australia*, 3rd edn (Melbourne, 1999), 736–9.

wages for a company's employees.[5] As a general rule, the police cannot be sued by victims for allegedly negligent failure to apprehend criminals or to prevent crime.[6] On the other hand, prison authorities who negligently allow a criminal to escape may incur liability for injury or loss resulting from crimes committed by the escapee.[7]

From its inception until 1994, awards under the Criminal Injuries Compensation Scheme (CICS) were assessed according to principles similar to the rules for assessing damages for personal injury in tort cases.[8] Now, however (as we will see later), the CICS is what has been called an 'enhanced tariff' Scheme. For a number of reasons, awards under this 'new' enhanced-tariff Scheme may, in certain cases, be less than could be obtained by suing in tort.[9] This may encourage tort claims in some situations where, hitherto, such action may not have been worthwhile.

12.2   Compensation orders

Under the Powers of Criminal Courts Act 2000[10] a magistrates' court may award up to £5,000 compensation for any personal injury, loss or damage resulting from an offence,[11] and other criminal courts may award an unlimited sum.[12] Compensation orders are designed to be a summary remedy for use in simple cases. It has been stressed that the victim of a criminal assault has a tort remedy by way of civil proceedings,[13] and should be left to pursue that remedy in serious or complicated

5 *Williams* v. *Grimshaw* (1967) 3 KIR 610; *Houghton* v. *Hackney BC* (1961) 3 KIR 615; *Charlton* v. *Forest Printing Ink Co.* [1978] IRLR 559.
6 *Hill* v. *Chief Constable of West Yorkshire* [1989] AC 53.
7 *Home Office* v. *Dorset Yacht Co.* [1970] AC 1004.
8 As at October 2004, 425 claims made under the 'old scheme' were outstanding: Criminal Injuries Compensation Appeals Panel, *Annual Report, 2003–4*, 9.
9 The maximum award under the new CICS is £500,000. In 2001 an almost completely paralysed youth was awarded £4.75 million under the old Scheme. Earlier in 2001 an award of about £50,000 under the new Scheme to a young teacher, Sarah Potts, who was very seriously injured while protecting students from an attacker, caused considerable controversy: 'Why the rules on compensation should be changed', *The Times*, 20 February 2001.
10 Ss. 130–4. For discussion of the relationship between 'reparation' and punishment in the criminal justice system see L. Zedner, 'Reparation and Retribution: Are they Reconcilable?' (1994) 57 *Modern LR* 228; T. Campbell, 'Compensation as Punishment' (1984) 7 *U. of New South Wales LR* 338.
11 Orders can be made in favour of persons other than the direct victim of the crime.
12 See generally D. Miers, *Compensation for Criminal Injuries* (London, 1990), chs. 8–11; D. Moxon, J.M. Corkery and C. Hedderman, *Developments in the Use of Compensation Orders in Magistrates Courts since 1988*, Home Office Research Study No. 126 (London, 1992); D. Tucker 'Victims' rights? – wrong' [1991] *New LJ* 192; C. Flood-Page and A. Mackie, *Sentencing Practice: An Examination of Decisions in Magistrates' Courts and the Crown Court in the Mid-1990's*, Home Office Research Study 180 (1998). There is no lower limit on compensation orders, whereas there is a lower limit on payments under the CICS.
13 Somewhat controversially, civil liability is not a precondition of the making of a compensation order: Miers, *Compensation for Criminal Injuries*, 200–5; M. Wasik, 'Compensation Orders and Civil Liability' (1985) 48 *Modern LR* 707. If the victim brings a civil action against the offender after a compensation order has been made, and the civil court holds that the injury, loss or damage resulting from the offence was less than the criminal court took it to be, the compensation order may be discharged or the amount payable under it reduced.

cases.[14] Long-term orders for compensation, which may take years to pay off, are generally discouraged.[15]

In 1988–9 over 100,000 orders were made by magistrates' courts, and in 1989 more than 11,000 orders were made by Crown Courts. Orders were made by magistrates' courts in 39% of cases in which an order could have been made;[16] and in 17% of cases by Crown Courts. Looking just at offences against the person, orders were made in 46% of cases by magistrates' courts and 28% of cases by Crown Courts. The use of compensation orders has declined considerably since 1990. In 1990, 29% of defendants sentenced for an indictable offence in a magistrates' court were ordered to pay compensation, but in 1996 the corresponding figure was 19% and in 2003, 15%. In 1990, 21% of those convicted of a violent offence in the Crown Court were ordered to pay compensation, but in 1996 only 12%, and in 2003 only about 7%.[17] Even when an order is made, enforcing it can be difficult. This is a reason why compensation orders are rarely awarded in conjunction with a custodial sentence.[18] According to the Home Office, only 1% of offenders sentenced to immediate custody are ordered to pay compensation.[19] Compensation orders are not commonly made in conjunction with a fine because, it is said, 'crimes where there is likely to be a direct victim are far more likely to be punished with a community sentence than a fine'.[20]

The court is required to give reasons for *not* making a compensation order (although in practice, this requirement is very often not complied with). The main reasons that have been given are that the offender lacked the means to pay compensation,[21] that the court lacked relevant information,[22] that compensation was not sought and that the relationship between the victim and the offender made an

---

14 *R* v. *Daly* [1974] 1 All ER 290.
15 Ibid. Compensation orders for large sums may be made in exceptional cases. In 1996 an order for some £160,000 was made against a thief who stole rare books from Oxford college libraries. The court was told that the defendant had liquid assets of nearly £200,000: *The Times*, 17 February 1996.
16 Orders cannot be made in cases in which compensation would be available under an insurance policy required by the Road Traffic Act 1988 or from the MIB.
17 It is not clear why the use of compensation orders has declined so much. It may be that fewer offenders are being convicted, and of those who are being convicted, a greater proportion is impecunious. (I owe these points to Professor Andrew Ashworth.)
18 M. Ogden, 'Compensation Orders in Cases of Violence' [1985] *Criminal LR* 500. Another reason may be that to impose a custodial sentence and a compensation order may be thought unduly severe: Home Office Consultation Paper, *Compensation and Support for Victims of Crime* (2004), 12. In 2003, compensation orders were made in some 120,000 cases of indictable and summary offences (not counting summary motoring offences). The compensation order was the sole or main penalty in about only 8,000 of these.
19 Home Office Consultation Paper, *Compensation and Support for Victims of Crime* (2004), 11.
20 Ibid., 12.
21 There is a statutory obligation to take account of the means of the offender; whereas in the law of tort, of course, this is irrelevant. The court is required by statute to give priority to a compensation order over a fine, and a compensation order can be made on its own. But it appears not uncommon for compensation to be reduced because of lack of means at the same time as a fine is imposed in addition.
22 Ss. 95 and 96 of the Courts Act 2003 (obligation to provide information about resources) may help to overcome this problem.

order inappropriate because, for example, they were members of the same family.[23] In relation to personal injuries, another important reason is lack of information about the nature of the injuries[24] and difficulties in assessing appropriate amounts of damages. There are also considerable problems in enforcing compensation orders and collecting fines.[25]

Both financial and non-pecuniary loss may be the subject of compensation. In addition to compensation for the injuries themselves, compensation for distress and anxiety arising from the offence can be awarded.[26] In practice, however, compensation orders are less likely to be made in cases where the victim was not physically hurt. It seems that in many cases, orders in respect of personal injury fall far short of full compensation. In 2003, the average amount of compensation ordered by the Crown Court in cases of violence against the person was £608. Of 2,604 orders made in such cases, only 267 were for more than £1,000. In magistrates' courts, the average compensation in cases of violence against the person was £245; and of 7,748 orders made in such cases, only 190 were for more than £1,000.[27]

Awards under the CICS are reduced to take account of the proceeds of any compensation order, damages award or settlement (2001 Scheme, para. 48);[28] and recipients of awards are required to repay to the CICA any such amounts received after the CICS award is made (2001 Scheme, para. 49). In 2002–3 the CICA recovered £209,000 from the proceeds of civil actions and £522,000 from the proceeds of compensation orders in respect of awards made under the new (enhanced tariff) Scheme, which in that year totalled £160.3 million. Thus, criminals provided less than 0.5% of the compensation paid out under the CICS in that year. In an attempt to increase this figure, in 2004, the Criminal Injuries Compensation Act 1995 was amended to give the CICA the power to recover directly from convicted criminals compensation paid to victims under the CICS.[29]

12.3   Other sources of compensation

Victims of crime may obtain compensation from other compensation systems. Victims of personal injuries may benefit from the social security system, or occasionally from personal accident insurance; in fatal cases a spouse or partner may

---

23 In 2002, a Crown Court judge reportedly made but then, in the face of public protest, withdrew, a compensation order in favour of an alleged drug dealer who had been assaulted by the father of one of his supposed clients: *The Times*, 17 May 2002.
24 See *R* v. *Horsham Justices, ex parte Richards* [1985] 2 All ER 1114.
25 Home Office Consultation Paper, *Compensation and Support for Victims of Crime*, 12–13; *Compensation and Support for Victims of Crime: Summary of Responses to Home Office Consultation Paper* (2004), 6–8.
26 *Bond* v. *Chief Constable of Kent* [1983] 1 All ER 456. Compensation for bereavement can be awarded to persons entitled to such damages under the Fatal Accidents Act 1976 for an amount up to the statutory maximum (currently £10,000).
27 These figures come from *Criminal Statistics for England and Wales 2003*.
28 See 12.4.1 for the history of the CICS.
29 Ss. 7A–D, inserted by Domestic Violence, Crime and Victims Act 2004, s. 59.

receive the proceeds of a life insurance policy or bereavement benefits under social security. Loss of property from criminal activity is quite likely to be covered by private insurance. Occasionally, in cases of fraud, the government may provide compensation, as after the collapse of the Barlow Clowes investment bank following a recommendation of the Parliamentary Commissioner for Administration (the Parliamentary Ombudsman).

12.4   Criminal injuries compensation scheme

12.4.1   Justifications for the Scheme

Until the Criminal Injuries Compensation Scheme[30] was set up in 1964,[31] most victims of violent criminal attack received little financial support other than through the social security system. Many regarded this as inadequate, partly because of public sympathy for the occasional victim of an especially vicious crime, and partly because the social security system offers no compensation for disability as such, except to those injured at work. Nevertheless, the idea of selecting yet another group of injured and disabled people for special treatment is not easily defensible, and it is hard to believe that the government would have regarded the Scheme with much favour if it had not been of relatively small quantitative significance, and therefore cheap compared with most other claims for compensation which are made on the State.[32]

The discussions which led up to the Scheme reveal an extraordinary intellectual confusion. The Home Office Working Party which first looked into the matter, for instance, rejected the idea that the State should assume the burden of compensating victims of criminal violence because it had a duty to protect citizens; this was a 'fallacious and dangerous doctrine', because the State could not possibly protect its citizens from attack at all times and all places, and because, in any event, if there was such a duty it would be impossible to confine it to personal injury as opposed to damage to property.[33] The Committee went on to say that they could find no 'constitutional or social principle on which State compensation could be justified', but they nevertheless thought that compensation could be based on the more 'practical' ground that 'although the welfare state helps the victims of many kinds of misfortune, it does nothing for the victims of crimes of violence, as such'.[34] Accordingly, although there was no 'bounden duty' to compensate these victims, such compensation could be justified.

---

30 See generally D. Miers, *State Compensation for Criminal Injuries* (London, 1997).
31 The Scheme was last revised in 2001. It is worth noting that there have been six major reviews of the scheme – in 1973, 1983, 1991, 1999, 2004 and 2005. This is a good indication of its problematic nature. Concerning the 2005 review, see the postscript to this chapter (p. 327).
32 P. Rock, *Helping Victims of Crime* (Oxford, 1990), 78, 84–5.
33 Cmnd 1406, 1961, para. 17. In 1985 it was said that 'in present economic circumstances a central fund to make public provision for victims of property crime is not practicable': *First Report of the Home Affairs Committee on Compensation and Support for Victims of Crime*, HC 43 (1984–5); and government Reply (Cmnd 9457, 1985), para. 19.
34 Ibid., para. 18.

The Committee never really came to grips with the crucial issue, which is not whether victims of criminal violence ought to be compensated by the State, but whether there are any grounds for giving such victims financial support over and above social security benefits available to others. The Committee did point out that the Welfare State did nothing for the victims of crimes of violence 'as such'. But why this should matter, provided it does something for them? The working party perhaps thought that social security benefits were too low. If this is so, the right solution is to increase benefits across the board, not to provide extra benefits for particular groups of needy people at the expense of the generality.

A number of arguments for special treatment for victims of violent crime were listed by a JUSTICE Report in 1962.[35]

- First, criminal injuries are analogous to war injuries, and the State has always accepted some obligation to provide for those injured in war and their dependants.[36] But there is an obvious difference between people who are requested or required by the government to risk life and limb in war and ordinary victims of crime. At all events, benefits payable in respect of injury, illness of death attributable to military service are much more generous than those available under the CICS in its current form.[37]
- Secondly, the State discourages citizens from carrying weapons for self-protection. But this ignores the fact that citizens gain more than they lose from living in a generally weapon-less society.
- Thirdly, citizens are under a moral duty to assist the State, for example, by going to the assistance of a police officer effecting an arrest or suppressing violence, and they may be deterred by the absence of compensation for injury suffered while doing so. But why should altruism be any more rewarded when it takes this form rather than, for example, that of trying to rescue a child from a burning house or a climber trapped on a mountain?
- Fourthly, neglect of the interests of victims of crime makes it more difficult to adopt enlightened penal policies because every demand for better treatment for criminals is met by complaints that society is looking after the criminal better than the victim.[38] This argument is based on political expediency, not on principle. On the other hand, it may be said that while greater use of non-custodial sentences, for example, can be justified in the interests of society as a whole as well as of offenders, it does involve risks; and that those who suffer as a result should be compensated by society. The general principle underlying this approach, namely that individuals who suffer extraordinary loss as a result of the execution of government policy should be compensated, is highly

---

35 JUSTICE, *Report on Compensation for Victims of Crimes of Violence* (London, 1962).
36 An analogy was also drawn with riot damage which is, in some cases, the subject of State compensation under the Riot (Damages) Act 1886.
37 The compensation scheme for members of the armed forces who suffer injury, illness and death attributable to military service has recently been overhauled: Ministry of Defence, *A Framework Document for the Armed Services Compensation Scheme for Injury, Illness and Death Due to Service*, (March 2004). For background and an account of the scheme that has been replaced see N.J. Wikeley, *Wikeley, Ogus and Barendt's The Law of Social Security*, 5th edn (London, 2002), ch. 21.
38 This was an important strand in the thinking of early proponents of victim compensation: Rock, *Helping Victims of Crime*, ch. II.

controversial and could only be accepted in this context if it could be shown that victims of penal policy were particularly deserving.

- Fifthly, since the State prohibits the victim from 'taking the law into their own hands to obtain redress', it should provide some effective alternative. This argument proves too much because 'taking the law into one's own hands' is, with few exceptions, prohibited generally and not just to victims of crime. The State accepts no general obligation to make good the lack of a defendant worth suing. Perhaps a more convincing argument is that the risk of injury from criminal attack is so remote that it would be impractical to insure against that risk and no other. There may be, therefore, something to be said for the view that the whole population should be regarded as insured by the State, and the compensation paid for by taxation.[39] But this still fails to explain why this kind of injury should be singled out for special treatment by the State: it is true of very many victims of personal injury that they are not insured.

- Sixthly, offenders are often imprisoned for long periods, thus depriving the victim of any chance of effective redress. This argument is misleading. In 2003, for example, of some 38,000 persons convicted of indictable offences against the person in England and Wales, some 11,500 received an immediate custodial sentence, while some 4,000 were fined and another 4,000 received an absolute or conditional discharge. Some 10,300 persons convicted of offences of violence against the person were made subject to a compensation order in favour of their victim.[40]

Another line of argument seeks to set victim compensation in a wider context: the offender, it is said, owes a public duty to the State to submit to punishment and a private duty to the victim to pay compensation.[41] This private duty may give rise to liability in tort, for instance, or to the making of a compensation order. However, for various reasons, many victims have no realistic prospect of being properly compensated by the offender, and the State owes a residual obligation to victims to fill this compensation gap. This obligation of the State 'forms part of the State's general duties of enforcing the criminal law and protecting individual rights'.[42] In answer,

39 A.M. Linden, *Report of the Osgoode Hall Study on Compensation for Victims of Crime* (Toronto, 1968), 3. This approach led some to advocate that the State should simply meet judgments obtained by victims of crimes of violence against offenders, but the working party pointed out some formidable objections to this: Cmnd 1406, paras. 136–40.

40 These figures are derived from *Criminal Statistics for England and Wales 2003*. Ironically, however, the argument is more firmly based now than in the past because of increased use of custodial sentences (in 1990, e.g., of nearly 52,600 persons convicted of indictable offences against the person, only about 5,800 received an immediate custodial sentence, and over 19,000 were fined: *Criminal Statistics: England and Wales 1990* (Cm 1935, 1992), table 7.2) and a sharp decline in the use of compensation orders (from 27,000 in 1990).

41 For a view that payments to the victims of crime should not be seen as compensation but as a recognition that wrong has been done and that crime causes its victims mental suffering, see J. Shapland, 'Victims, the Criminal Justice System and Compensation' (1984) 24 *British J. of Criminology* 131. Under this approach, the compensation function would be left to tort law and the social security system. Shapland would not limit this approach to crimes of violence (135) or to intentional crimes (145), and it is not clear why it should be restricted to criminal wrongs, since victims of non-criminal tortious wrongs (especially those who suffer serious injuries) no doubt often also suffer the sort of mental suffering experienced by victims of crime.

42 A. Ashworth, 'Punishment and Compensation: Victims, Offenders and the State' (1986) 6 *Oxford J. Legal Studies* 86.

it might be argued that the State has analogous duties at least to people injured by non-criminal but still unlawful conduct (such as tortious negligence), and that victims of crime deserve no better treatment than these others.

In the parliamentary debates which preceded the establishment of the Scheme Lord Shawcross did not feel it necessary or useful to attempt to justify the case for compensation 'by an elaborate theoretical or philosophical speculation as to why the State should intervene in a matter of this kind'.[43] It was enough to rely on the 'public instinct'. Lord Dilhorne, speaking on behalf of the government, rejected the notion that the State was 'liable', but regarded the Scheme as an extension of our 'welfare system'.[44] Since nobody suggested that the State was legally liable, this was tantamount to asserting that the State was not morally liable; but nevertheless Lord Dilhorne thought that the 'welfare system' should be extended to cover it. Others justified the Scheme by asserting that society was 'responsible' for much crime because of the laxity of its moral code and the failure to bring up its young as good citizens rather than criminals.[45] Only Lady Wootton protested that the attempt to assess people's needs by reference to fault was 'illogical and uncivilized'.[46] The debate in the Commons followed much the same lines though with even less attempt to justify the Scheme, and with universal self-congratulation on a good job well done.

One particular piece of sophistry which this intellectual confusion produced was the suggestion that the compensation should be awarded *ex gratia*, not as of right; and this suggestion was eventually incorporated in the Scheme propounded by the government.[47] Although, in a technical sense, payments under the Scheme were *ex gratia* because the Scheme was not authorized by or embodied in a statute, in reality the CICB had no discretion to refuse claims which fell within the terms of the Scheme; and the payment of compensation – though not legally enforceable – followed automatically once the Board had determined that it should be awarded.[48] So it was held, soon after the establishment of the Scheme, that decisions of the Board could be challenged in judicial review proceedings on the ground that they did not comply with the terms of the Scheme.[49] The new Scheme has a statutory basis in the Criminal Injuries Compensation Act 1995.

In 1978 a Working Party[50] appointed to review the operation of the CICS reiterated the views of the Working Party of 1964 that the public feels a sense of responsibility for, and sympathy with, the innocent victim, and 'it is right' that this feeling should find practical expression in the provision of compensation by the

---

43 HL Debs, 5th series, vol. 245, col. 263.
44 Ibid., vol. 257, col. 1353.
45 Ibid., vol. 245, cols. 267, 269.
46 Ibid., vol. 257, col. 1381.
47 See para. 4 of the 1990 version of the Scheme (which we will call 'the old Scheme') (Miers, *State Compensation for Criminal Injuries*, 243).
48 *Review of the Criminal Injuries Compensation Scheme: Report of an Interdepartmental Working Party* (HMSO, 1978), para. 5.1.
49 *R v. CICB, ex parte Lain* [1967] 2 QB 864.
50 See n. 48.

community. The Pearson Commission, after referring to some of the above criticisms,[51] simply asserted that compensation for criminal injuries was 'morally justified as in some measure salving the nation's conscience at its inability to preserve law and order', and insisted that 'it is right that there should be reasonable provision for the victims of crime'.[52] At that time, awards under the CICS were calculated in much the same way as tort damages; but the Pearson Commission made no attempt to explain why 'reasonable provision' should mean provision according to scales of tort damages. It could be argued with some justification that levels of tort damages are not 'reasonable provision' but exceptionally generous provision. And it is odd that the Pearson Commission should have used the argument that compensation for the victims of crime 'salves the nation's conscience at its inability to preserve law and order', for this argument had always been repudiated by governments and previous working parties. The Commission's only recommendation was that the Scheme should be looked at again in light of the proposals on damages in tort.

The upshot of all this is that the Scheme was in fact based on little more than feelings of sympathy for innocent victims of crime who are unable to obtain redress from the offender.[53] As one writer has said: [54]

> Society is seen to recognise and sympathise with the innocent victim's suffering and this serves to reaffirm that the victim's faith, and that of the general public, in society and its institutions has not been misplaced . . . [the] role [of the CICS] is to symbolize social solidarity with the victim of violence.

In 1984 the government appointed another working party to make recommendations for putting the Scheme on a statutory footing.[55] Appropriate provisions were included in the Criminal Justice Act 1988,[56] but they were never brought into operation.[57] However, in 1994 the government, worried by the ever-increasing cost to the public purse of criminal injuries compensation and by the time taken to process

---

51 As made in the second edition of this book.
52 Pearson Report, vol. 1, paras. 1588, 1591.
53 In 2001 the CICA was reported to have 'agreed to consider' claims from relatives who saw the events of 11 September on television and received farewell phone calls from victims. Criticising the authority, Libby Purves (*The Times*, 20 November 2001) described the authority's remit as being 'to compensate victims for the failure of the authorities to protect them from violent crime'. In reply, the Chief Executive of the CICA (*The Times*, 21 November 2001) described its job as being 'to provide a tangible token of public sympathy to people in Great Britain who have suffered clear injury as a result of a crime of violence' even if the crime took place on the other side of the Atlantic. (Under the CICS, the injury must have been suffered in Great Britain, but the crime need not have occurred there.) 'Successive governments have recognized that the public feel . . . sympathy with the innocent victim of a crime of violence': Home Office, *Compensation for Victims of Violent Crime: Possible Changes to the Criminal Injuries Compensation Scheme* (1999), para. 11.
54 P. Duff, 'Criminal Injuries Compensation: the Symbolic Dimension' [1995] *Juridical Review* 102.
55 Report of an Interdepartmental Working Party, *Criminal Injuries Compensation: a Statutory Scheme* (HMSO, 1986).
56 P. Duff, 'Criminal Injuries Compensation: The Scope of the New Scheme' (1989) 52 *Modern LR* 518.
57 HC Debs, 6th series, vol. 163, col. 410.

applications for compensation, altered the basis for calculation of CICS awards.[58] Instead of being analogous to tort damages, awards were now to be made according to a tariff of listed injuries. In more serious cases, at least, the level of awards under the tariff was considerably lower than under the tort basis of assessment. This change was greeted by loud protests and, when challenged in the courts, was held to be illegal by the House of Lords.[59] As a result, applications dealt with under the illegal scheme had to be reassessed according to the rules of the old CICS. In response to the House of Lords' decision, the government secured the passage of the Criminal Injuries Compensation Act 1995, and under its provisions the old CICS was replaced by a new tariff scheme. The 1996 CICS (called by the government an 'enhanced tariff scheme') was more generous than the 1994 tariff scheme; but as we will see, it departs from principles of tort damages in some important respects. The 1996 version of the CICS was replaced by a new version in 2001 (which we will call the '2001 Scheme'), which increased the levels of awards generally and for multiple injuries in particular, and extended eligibility for awards in fatal cases to same-sex partners. So far as the rules of entitlement to compensation are concerned, the new Scheme differs from the old in only minor respects. The discussion which follows focuses on the new CICS, as there are now relatively few outstanding claims made under the old Scheme.

12.4.2   The scope of the Scheme

The Scheme provides for the payment of compensation to persons who have sustained:[60]

> One or more personal injuries[61] directly attributable to (a) a crime of violence (including arson, fire-raising or an act of poisoning); or (b) an offence of trespass on the railway; or (c) the apprehension or attempted apprehension of an offender or suspected offender, the prevention or attempted prevention of an offence, or the giving of help to any constable who is engaged in any such activity.

The Scheme also provides for payments to the dependants of those killed in the same fashion. Whereas a compensation order can be made only against a convicted

---

58 The changes were set out in a Home Office White Paper, *Compensation Victims of Violent Crime: Changes to the Criminal Injuries Compensation Scheme* (Cm 2434, 1993).

59 *R* v. *Secretary of State for the Home Department, ex parte Fire Brigades' Union* [1995] AC 513.

60 2001 Scheme, para. 8. The text of CICS and the *Guide to the Criminal Injuries Compensation Scheme* (hereafter referred to as the 'Guide') are available on the CICA website.

61 '... personal injury includes physical injury (including fatal injury), mental injury (that is, temporary mental anxiety, medically verified, or a disabling mental illness confirmed by psychiatric diagnosis) and disease (that is, a medically recognized illness or condition': 2001 Scheme, para. 9. Being conceived and born with a congenital defect as a result of an act of incestuous sexual intercourse is not a personal injury within the meaning of the CICS: *P's Curator Bonis* v. *Criminal Injuries Compensation Board* (1996) (available on the website of the Criminal Injuries Compensation Appeal Panel (CICAP): www.cica.gov.uk). (Being born is not actionable damage at common law, either.) However, where a woman becomes pregnant as a result of rape and an award is made to her in respect of non-consensual vaginal intercourse, an additional amount is also payable to her in respect of each child born alive which she intends to keep: 2001 Scheme, para. 27.

offender, compensation can be given under the CICS even if the offender is never convicted.[62] Indeed, compensation may be paid even in cases where the offender is acquitted because the burden of proof of guilt applicable under the CICS is the civil burden 'on the balance of probabilities', not the criminal burden 'beyond reasonable doubt' (2001 Scheme, para. 20).

12.4.2.1   Crime of violence

Confused thinking about the justification for the Scheme has, not surprisingly, generated difficulty in defining its scope. Originally, the Scheme did not use the words 'crime of violence'. It was believed that it would be sufficient to refer to injuries 'directly attributable to' an offence, on the assumption that unless the offence was one of violence, it would not lead to personal injury. Of course, this is not so, as the express extension of the Scheme to arson and poisoning shows. For instance, offences under industrial safety or food and drug safety legislation can easily lead to personal injuries, but these kinds of offences were not meant to fall within the Scheme. Therefore, both the Board[63] and a Divisional Court of the Queen's Bench Division[64] have held them to fall outside the Scheme. The term 'crime of violence' is nowhere defined. There is, for instance, no exhaustive list of crimes that qualify as crimes of violence for the purposes of the CICS. On the other hand, the Scheme itself classifies arson, fire-raising and poisoning as crimes of violence; and while most of the items in the tariff of awards available under the Scheme are cast in terms of injuries, a few (relating to physical and sexual abuse) refer to specific criminal conduct. But in general, whether conduct amounts to a crime of violence is to be decided on a case-by-case basis by reference to the purposes of the CICS (whatever they may be).

Conduct will count as a crime of violence only if the relevant injuries were inflicted intentionally or recklessly (in the technical sense in which these words are used in the criminal law). Behaviour which is merely careless, even if grossly so, does not constitute a crime of violence. For example, in one case, a man was injured by flying glass when a snowball was thrown at his kitchen window.[65] The application for compensation was rejected on the basis that there was no evidence that the snowball had been thrown with the intention of causing damage. In fact, it appeared that children were in the habit of playing near the house, and it was likely that the snowball had been thrown in the course of a game.

Particular difficulty has arisen in relation to suicide. In *R v. Criminal Injuries Compensation Board, ex parte Clowes*,[66] a policeman was injured by a gas explosion in a house where he had been investigating a gas leak. The occupier of the house

---

62 2001 Scheme, para. 10.
63 *CICB First Report* (Cmnd 2782, 1965), para. 14(3).
64 *R v. CICB, ex parte Webb* [1986] QB 184.
65 *CICB Sixteenth Report* (Cmnd 8081, 1980), para. 17. See also e.g. *Twenty-First Report* (Cmnd 9684, 1985), para. 20; *Twenty-Fifth Report* (Cm 900, 1989), paras. 16.3–4.
66 [1977] 1 WLR 1353.

had committed suicide by breaking off the end of the gas pipe and allowing gas to escape. A Divisional Court (by majority) held that the offence of unlawfully damaging the property of another[67] was not a crime of violence because it was concerned with damage to property, not with violence to the person. But the court also held that the offence of unlawfully damaging property with the intention thereby of endangering life, or recklessly as to whether life would thereby be endangered,[68] could constitute a crime of violence because although violence to the person was not part of the definition of the offence, it could have personal injury as one of its consequences. However, when the Board reconsidered the case, it came to the conclusion that the deceased had not acted intentionally or recklessly to cause injury to another, and that the only thing present in his mind was a desire to take his own life.

A significant number of applications to the Board are made by train drivers who suffer anxiety and depression after their trains strike people who have deliberately gone onto the tracks, often to commit suicide. This constitutes the offence of unlawfully endangering the safety of railway passengers.[69] In *R v. Criminal Injuries Compensation Board, ex parte Webb*,[70] the Court of Appeal held that this was not a crime of violence; that it was for the Board to decide whether particular crimes were crimes of violence; and that the words 'crime of violence' ought to be given the meaning the reasonable and literate person would give them. The fact that the commission of a crime carries with it the danger of violent injury to another (in such a case as this, e.g. by derailment of the train) does not make it a crime of violence. Although most crimes of violence involve the infliction or threat of force, some might not. It is the nature of a crime, not its consequences, which determines whether it is a 'crime of violence'. Although *Clowes* was not overruled or even disapproved in *Webb*, it is perhaps unlikely that the offence held to be a crime of violence in *Clowes* would be so classified following to the approach in *Webb*. It has been said that *Webb* reduces the scope of the Scheme 'to something closer to what was envisaged by its creators'[71] by concentrating on crimes which involve as one of their ingredients the intentional or reckless infliction of violence to the person.

As a result of pressure exerted by the train drivers' unions, the CICS was amended to include such cases. Why should train drivers benefit more than other innocent objects of public sympathy such as the victims of train crashes or fires in public places? This extension of the Scheme is as unprincipled as the whole idea of compensating the victims of violent crime.[72] Moreover, despite the fact that the

67 Criminal Damage Act 1971, s. 1(1).
68 Ibid., s. 1(2).
69 Offences Against the Person Act 1861, s. 34. In 2002–3 trespass and suicide on railway tracks caused 256 deaths and 137 cases of injury.
70 [1987] QB 74 (CA).
71 P. Duff, 'Criminal Injuries Compensation and "Violent" Crime' [1987] *Criminal LR* 219, 228.
72 A proposal by the government to remove railway suicides from the Scheme was abandoned in the face of opposition from the railway industry and unions: Home Office, '*Compensation and Support for Victims of Crime*': *Summary of Responses to a Home Office Consultation Paper* (2004), 18.

extension was primarily motivated by the problem of railway suicides, it is framed in terms of the offence of 'trespass on a railway'. Thus it is apt to cover cases where, for instance, people deliberately go onto the tracks but with no intention of taking their own life. Even more anomalously, it could cover a case where a person places a plank of wood on the track in order to derail a train.[73] The formulation was chosen in preference to the offence of unlawfully endangering the safety of railway passengers because the latter offence can be committed by merely negligent conduct,[74] whereas the offence of trespass can, perhaps, only be committed intentionally or recklessly.[75]

An indication of the anomalous lack of principle involved in including such cases in the CICS is that the extension was prompted primarily by cases in which the train driver suffers only mental injury. Under the 2001 Scheme (para. 9), compensation for mental injury standing alone is not payable unless the applicant 'was put in reasonable fear of immediate physical harm to his own person', or had a 'close relationship of love and affection' with a person who suffered physical injury or death, or was 'the non-consenting victim of a sexual offence', or was a railway employee who 'either witnessed and was present on the occasion when another person sustained physical (including fatal) injury directly attributable to the offence of trespass on a railway, or was closely involved in its immediate aftermath'. It will be noted that taken alone, the first two categories cover a narrower area than the common law rules of tort liability for mental injury. At common law, people directly involved in accidents and disasters, either as participants or rescuers, may recover in their own right for mental injury standing alone; but under the CICS, this is true only in relation to injury resulting from trespass to the railway. Moreover, whereas a person who 'accidentally' suffers injury while engaged in an activity 'directed to containing, limiting or remedying the consequences of crime' may recover compensation under the CICS only if they were 'taking an exceptional risk which was justified in all the circumstances',[76] this limitation does not apply to cases of trespass to the railway.

In one of its reports the Board said that the job of defining the term 'crime of violence' would tax 'the ingenuity of the participants in a moot'.[77] This is partly, no doubt, because the restriction of the Scheme to crimes of violence is impossible to explain even in terms of its avowed 'justifications': it is not only victims of violent crime who may attract public sympathy. For instance, victims of large-scale frauds, such as those that gave rise to the Barlow Clowes and BCCI bank collapses, may also arouse such feelings. Nevertheless, the European Convention on the Compensation of Victims of Violent Crimes and the EU Directive on compensation to crime victims are also limited to crimes of violence.[78] There is constant pressure for the

---

73 Miers, *State Compensation for Criminal Injuries*, 92.
74 Ibid., 91.
75 But the tort of trespass to land can be committed negligently and, indeed, purely innocently.
76 2001 Scheme, para. 12.
77 *CICB Twentieth Report* (Cmnd 9399, 1984), para. 17.
78 Council of Europe, European Treaty Series, No. 116; EU Council Directive 2004/80/EC respectively.

recognition of particular crimes as falling within the Scheme. For example, it has held that child abduction can be a crime of violence even if the child is not physically hurt.[79] On the other hand, it has been held that bigamy is not a crime of violence, even if it involves procurement of sexual intercourse by deception and inflicts mental harm.[80] It has also been held that consent of the victim may (but will not necessarily) prevent conduct being a crime of violence even if the criminal could not have pleaded consent as a defence to a criminal prosecution in respect of the conduct.[81] Such an ad hoc approach is hardly a satisfactory way of defining the limits of a compensation scheme.

Injuries caused by children and mentally unstable persons cause considerable difficulty. Unsoundness of mind can excuse a person from criminal responsibility; and in England children under 10 (8 in Scotland) are treated as incapable of committing crimes. In such cases it cannot easily be said that the victim's injuries were attributable to a crime. The Scheme provides that compensation can be paid even though the offender could not be convicted of the relevant offence because of age or insanity.[82] According to the Guide to the old Scheme, this provision requires the Authority to decide whether, if the offender had not been immune from conviction on one of the stated grounds, the conduct in question would 'as a matter of fact . . . have amounted to a crime of violence if committed by' a person not labouring under the relevant disability.[83] The trouble is that this question will usually be impossible to answer. Conduct will amount to a crime of violence only if the perpetrator had the requisite criminal intent. Some children below the age of criminal responsibility may be capable of forming such an intent, but the very reason why the immunity exists is because many young children are not so capable; and even if a particular child could form the requisite intent, it may be very difficult to prove that they had done so.[84] In the case of insanity, if a person is legally insane, they are, by definition, incapable of forming the requisite intent. Nevertheless, the Court of Appeal has said that the CICS 'would be a most defective scheme if anyone injured by a mentally unbalanced person could not be paid compensation'.[85] It is the lack of a reasoned justification for the Scheme that has generated this problem. Why should compensation be paid to a person intentionally injured, but not to a person accidentally (that is, neither intentionally nor recklessly) injured, by a young child when the child is not criminally responsible in either case? Either both should be compensated, or neither.

---

79 *Independent*, 8 March 1993.
80 *Gray* v. *Criminal Injuries Compensation Board* (1998) (available on the CICAP website).
81 *R* v. *Criminal Injuries Compensation Appeals Panel, ex parte Wade* (2000) (available on the CICAP website).
82 'or diplomatic immunity': 2001 Scheme, para. 10. 'Insanity' is a legal term with a technical meaning.
83 Guide to the old Scheme, para. 7.
84 The Guide to the old Scheme dealt separately with cases of children playing dangerous games, as does the Guide to the 2001 Scheme, 26.
85 *R* v. *Criminal Injuries Compensation Board, ex parte Webb* [1987] QB 74, 80.

12.4.2.2   Accidental injuries

Despite all that has just been said, it is possible in certain cases to recover compensation under the CICS for accidental injuries (that is, injuries not caused intentionally or recklessly). Accidental injuries suffered while engaged in law enforcement activities (arresting or attempting to arrest an offender or suspected offender, preventing or attempting to prevent an offence, or assisting a constable) are covered; as are injuries suffered in the course of 'any other activity directed to containing, limiting or remedying the consequences of a crime'; provided, in both cases, that at the time the injuries were suffered, the victim was taking 'an exceptional risk which was justified in all the circumstances'.[86] It does not matter what the immediate cause of the injuries was, provided the Authority is prepared to treat them as directly attributable to the law-enforcement activity. But innocent bystanders injured in the course of law-enforcement activities are not entitled to compensation.[87]

The Guide to the 1996 Scheme attempted to define 'exceptional risk' by giving examples of risks that cannot be so defined.[88] Compensation would not normally be awarded, for example, to a police officer who trips over while running after an offender, or is injured while climbing over a fence.[89] An act which would not be regarded as presenting an exceptional risk if done in daylight might be so regarded if done at night. Civilians are more likely to be treated as taking an exceptional risk than a police officer or fire-fighter. Police officers injured in traffic accidents during car chases are unlikely to be compensated in the absence of an exceptionally risky factor such as extreme adverse weather conditions.[90]

Despite the 'exceptional risk' limitation, it is difficult to appreciate the justification for the inclusion of such cases in the Scheme, given that if the victim is a police officer,[91] they will be covered by the industrial injuries scheme (by virtue of being an employed worker); and if the victim is an ordinary citizen, they will be entitled in the normal way to social security benefits. The rationale for awarding compensation in such cases must be very different from the original aim of the Scheme which was, essentially, to compensate the victims of intentional violence. One of the problems is that the relationship between the CICS and other compensation schemes has never been properly thought out. Although social security benefits, tort damages and compensation received under compensation orders are

---

86 2001 Scheme, para. 12. As we saw earlier, the proviso does not apply to the crime of trespass on a railway. A government proposal to remove such cases from the CICS was abandoned in the face of opposition from twelve respondents to a Home Office consultation paper: Home Office, 'Compensation and Support for Victims of Crime' Summary of Responses to a Home Office Consultation Paper (2004), 17.
87 K. Williams, 'Compensation for Accidental Shootings by Police' [1991] New LJ 231.
88 Paras. 7.16–17.
89 Unless doing so was essential and the victim did not or could not see what was on the other side.
90 Contrast the decision at common law in which a police officer injured during a car chase was awarded £286,000 damages for injuries attributable to negligent driving by the person being chased: The Times, 16 January 1997.
91 In 2002–3 awards were made to 1,700 police officers injured on duty (4% of resolved cases).

all set off against awards under the Scheme, no systematic attempt has ever been made to justify awarding compensation under the CICS (which may be greater than that available from other sources) when alternative sources of compensation exist.

A related issue arose in a case in which a man deliberately drove his car at another man, seriously injuring him.[92] The defendant was not insured against liability, and the House of Lords held that the MIB was liable to pay damages. Although the CICS does not, in general, cover injuries attributable to traffic offences,[93] it does include cases of deliberate injury resulting from the use of motor vehicles. The MIB argued that the claimant ought to have brought his claim under the CICS and not against the MIB. The House held that he had a choice between the two schemes, and was entitled to choose the MIB alternative, which the House considered to be more advantageous to him than the CICS. The House seems to have ignored the fact that the CICB did not make awards in such cases where compensation was available from the MIB or under an insurance policy. This sort of issue is bound to arise so long as there exists a variety of compensation schemes with overlapping rules of entitlement. The only way of eliminating such problems is to adopt a unified compensation scheme based on the claimant's need rather than on the cause of injuries.

12.4.2.3 Exclusions

As we have just seen, the CICS does not cover injuries resulting from traffic offences, except where the injuries are due to a deliberate attempt to run the victim down, or where they are directly attributable to law-enforcement activities. The reason for this exclusion is that there are usually other means of ensuring that adequate compensation is paid in these cases.

Another important restriction relates to violence within the family. In 1963, F.H. McClintock found that as many as 30.8% of criminal assaults were 'domestic', although he included within this category quarrels between neighbours, not merely assaults on members of the same family.[94] Subsequent research suggests that perhaps 15% of indictable crimes of violence occur within families.[95] Where the victim and the person responsible for the injuries were living in the same household as members of the same family at the time the injuries were inflicted, several conditions have to be satisfied before compensation is payable.[96] These conditions are mainly designed to exclude cases of collusion between victim and offender; so, normally, the offender must have been prosecuted. If offender and victim are both adults, they must be no longer living together at the time of the application. Furthermore, the Authority will not award compensation where it appears that the

---

92 *Gardner* v. *Moore* [1984] AC 548.
93 2001 Scheme, para. 11; Guide, 22.
94 *Crimes of Violence* (London, 1963), 32.
95 *Review of the Criminal Injuries Compensation Scheme: Report of an Interdepartmental Working Party*, 89.
96 2001 Scheme, para. 17.

offender might benefit from it.[97] Where the claimant is under 18 years of age, compensation will not be awarded unless the Authority is satisfied that this will not be against the claimant's interests.[98] Awarding a child compensation in respect of an act of an adult member of the same family may only have the effect of making relations between the adult and the child even more strained, especially if they continue to live as a family. A violent adult may well try to extract the compensation from the child.

Although one naturally feels sympathy for children who suffer as a result of criminal violence and abuse, the Scheme does create considerable anomalies. Suppose a man is convicted of murdering his spouse or partner and is sent to gaol. His children will be entitled to substantial compensation from the Scheme for loss of their mother's services and income. Is there a rational justification for awarding such compensation when nothing is awarded to a child who is, say, orphaned through the death of both parents without anyone's fault? If fault is the essential element, is it evident that death or injury of one spouse in an accident in the home caused by the negligence of the other (for which, in practice, a child is highly unlikely to receive any tort compensation) is less worthy of sympathy and compensation?

12.4.3   Comparison between the CICS and tort liability
12.4.3.1   Mental distress and nervous shock

In tort law, personal injury includes mental as well as bodily injury. Similarly, 'personal injury' for the purposes of the CICS includes 'mental injury'. In tort law, compensatable mental injury is limited to psychiatric illnesses and conditions, whereas under the 2001 Scheme it is defined more widely to include 'temporary mental anxiety, medically verified, or a disabling mental illness confirmed by psychiatric diagnosis'.[99] The tariff of CICS compensation payments elaborates this definition by listing various psychological and physical symptoms. As in tort law, mental injury may attract compensation under the CICS whether or not it is accompanied by physical injury. The basic rules of recovery under the Scheme for mental injury standing alone are similar to, but somewhat narrower than, their common law counterparts; and there are special provisions relating to sexual offences and the offence of trespass on a railway. Unlike the common law,[100] the Scheme does not cover shock attributable to loss of possessions because (with the minor exception of physical aids) loss of or damage to property is not covered by the CICS.

---

97 Ibid., para. 16(a). This condition applies to all applications, not just those arising out of domestic violence. The tort system does not normally object to compensation being given even though the tortfeasor might benefit from it (but see 6.2.3). Indeed, the Law Reform (Husband and Wife) Act 1962 was enacted to enable a spouse to obtain damages from the other spouse('s insurers) in the case of injuries in road accidents, though there is clearly a difference between paying compensation to a spouse in such a case, and paying it where the other spouse has been guilty of a criminal assault on their partner.
98 2001 Scheme, para. 16(b).
99 2001 Scheme, para. 9.
100 *Attia* v. *British Gas Plc* [1988] QB 304.

Mental injury, like all other injury, qualifies for compensation under the CICS only if it was 'directly attributable' to a crime of violence. In one case, the mother and stepfather of a child suffered reactive depression as a result of learning that their child had been the victim of serious indecent assaults by the stepfather's father over a period of time.[101] The judge held that on the facts, the Board had been entitled to deny compensation. However, he also said that if the claimants had suffered mental injury as a result of being given a graphic description of one of the assaults by their child, almost immediately after it had occurred, at a time when the child was obviously very upset about the incident, the mental injury could properly be said to be directly attributable to the crime. By contrast, under English common law it seems that there can be no recovery for psychiatric injury suffered as a result of being told of the death of or injury to another.

12.4.3.2   Conduct of the claimant

Paragraphs 13(d) and (e) of the 2001 Scheme give the CICA a wide discretion to reduce an award or to make no award at all because of the conduct of the claimant[102] (before, during or after the offence), or of their character as shown by criminal convictions or by other evidence. These provisions have some affinity with the common law concept of contributory negligence[103] in that they involve looking at the conduct of the victim; they also cover ground which might be covered by the defences of illegality and *volenti non fit injuria* (assumption of risk) and the notion of intervening cause. However, they are much wider than any of these because they allow account to be taken of the victim's character as well as their actions, and because there need be no causal relationship at all between the relevant conduct of the victim and the injuries.[104] Consider the following claims under the Scheme: a man is having an affair with a married woman, and is assaulted or beaten up by the woman's husband;[105] a claimant was drinking in a low-grade public house, flashing

---

101 R v. *Criminal Injuries Compensation Board, ex parte Kent and Milne* [1998] PIQR Q98.
102 Where the victim is killed and the claim is made by dependants, both the claimants' and the victim's conduct and character are relevant: 2001 Scheme, para. 15.
103 In R v. *CICB, ex parte Ince* [1973] 3 All ER 808 the Court of Appeal said that this provision should not be thought of in terms of the doctrine of contributory negligence. This is partly because the CICA can take into account a much wider range of factors than are included within the concept of contributory negligence; and also because, both at common law and under the Scheme, mere negligence, when weighed against a violent intentional assault, may rightly be disregarded as immaterial. It is not clear why it is wrong to think in terms of contributory negligence at least in relation to accidental injuries which fall within the Scheme. Such injuries tend to occur in 'emergency' situations, such as fire-fighting or law enforcement, and in such cases the common law tends to take a rather lenient attitude towards mere negligence on the part of the claimant.
104 Past criminal convictions may be relevant even if they are totally unconnected with the incident if the applicant was injured. Guide, 26–9 sets out a points system for calculating the possible percentage reduction of the award; Miers, *State Compensation for Criminal Injuries*, 159–60. Use of these provisions to justify low awards in rape cases (e.g. *CICB Twenty-Seventh Report* (Cm 1782, 1991), para. 24.5) has been particularly controversial: *Independent on Sunday*, 20 December 1992, 6; F. Bawdon, 'Putting a Price on Rape: Increasing Compensation Awards' [1993] *New LJ* 371.
105 *CICB Fourth Report* (Cmnd 3814, 1968), para. 11(4)(d).

money around, and is subsequently robbed while in a drunken condition;[106] a man is solicited by a prostitute and then beaten up by her associates.[107] Cases of this sort at first caused much disagreement amongst CICB members, but it is now clear[108] that even the most tenuous connection between the applicant's conduct or character and the injuries can bar compensation. By contrast, consider the tort case of *Revill* v. *Newbery*[109] in which a burglar was awarded damages (reduced on account of contributory negligence) for injuries suffered when the property owner negligently shot at him. To deny liability, Evans LJ said, 'would mean . . . that the trespasser who was also a criminal was effectively an outlaw'.[110]

The aim of the provision dealing with the claimant's conduct and character seems to be to restrict the Scheme to 'deserving' victims and to exclude 'delinquent' victims from its benefits.[111] Indeed, the CICA's professed aim is to support 'blameless' victims of violent crime.[112] An applicant can be denied compensation simply because the CICA considers that they are 'not the sort of person' to whom taxpayer-funded compensation ought to be given. The only analogous principle at common law is that damages will not be awarded under the Fatal Accidents Act 1976 to the extent that the deceased maintained dependants out of the proceeds of crime;[113] nor will an injured person be compensated for loss of actual or potential 'income' from crime. The significance of claimant conduct as a basis for refusing to make an award can be gauged by the fact that in 2002–3, of the 38,884 claims that were disallowed (as compared with 42,283 awards made), 7,253 were rejected because of the claimant's conduct or criminal record.[114]

The Guide contains detailed provisions about fights. Compensation will not normally be awarded if the victim voluntarily participated in the fight (even if it turns out to be much more serious than expected); or, without reasonable cause, struck the first blow (regardless of the severity of the retaliation); or provoked the attack; or was taking revenge. Nor will an award be made if the fight was part of a pattern of violence between the victim and the assailant; or if the victim was intoxicated.[115] The CICB has said that a 'realistic attitude' to fights is appropriate so as to avoid just compensating the loser or the one with the more serious injuries.[116] It seems that similar results might be reached at common law as a result of the

106 Ibid., para. 11(4)(e).
107 Ibid.
108 *R* v. *CICB, ex parte Thompstone* [1984] 1 WLR 1234.
109 [1996] QB 567. But note Tony Weir's outrage: 'Swag for the Injured Burglar' [1996] *Cambridge LJ* 182.
110 [1996] QB 567, 579.
111 Miers, *State Compensation for Criminal Injuries*, 156–9. The Guide to the old Scheme made it clear that members of violent gangs were very unlikely ever to receive compensation however their injuries occurred; and that terrorists would never be compensated: para. 33.
112 E.g. CICA *Annual Report 2002–3*, 4.
113 *Burns* v. *Edman* [1970] 2 QB 541.
114 Another 9,500 or so were rejected because of the claimant's failure to report the crime in a timely fashion or to co-operate with the police in bringing the assailant to justice.
115 Guide, 25–6.
116 *CICB Nineteenth Report* (Cmnd 9193, 1983), para. 29.

decision in *Murphy v. Culhane*,[117] in which it was held that if a person initiates a serious assault on another, and then gets more than they bargained for, any claim in tort by the initiator may be met by pleas of *volenti non fit injuria*, illegality or, in an appropriate case, contributory negligence. But at common law, unlike under the CICS, a trivial assault which is met by savage retaliation may still entitle the victim to full damages.[118] This difference in result may, once again, be justified on the basis that the CICS is funded by the State, not by offenders. Tort law does not distinguish between an action in which the damages will be paid by the tortfeasor and one in which they will be paid by someone else, for example, an employer. Insurers would rarely be responsible for payment of damages in this sort of case because few liability policies would cover criminal assault.[119]

Normally, no award will be made unless the applicant has reported the crime to the police, though in some cases a report to some other authority (such as a school in the case of violence amongst students) may suffice. This is partly a protection against fraud,[120] and partly an aspect of the concept of the blameless victim. But it does raise issues of equity and fairness in the Scheme's operation. For example, unemployed people are less likely to report crime than people in work; and crimes of which women are the main victims – rape and domestic violence, for instance – are seriously under-reported. Moreover, awards are not made in cases of domestic violence unless the offender has been prosecuted or, in the case of violence between adults, the applicant has separated from the assailant (2001 Scheme, para. 17).

12.4.3.3   Assessment of compensation

It is in relation to the assessment of compensation that the new Scheme differs most from the old Scheme. Under the old Scheme, compensation was, in general, assessed according to the same rules (including statutory rules) as govern the award of damages by the courts in claims for personal injury and death; but there were certain important exceptions to this principle. In the first place, in the interests of economy, awards were made only in cases where the amount of compensation payable was not less than £1,000 after deduction of social security benefits, but ignoring other deductions required under the Scheme (so, in practice, awards of less than £1,000 could be made).[121] In 1985 the Home Affairs Committee[122] thought that the threshold was too high when it stood at £400, but it no doubt had the

---

117 [1977] QB 94.
118 *Lane v. Holloway* [1968] 1 QB 379.
119 It would be 'contrary to public policy' for an insured person to enforce payment under a liability policy for their own benefit where they have been guilty of criminal conduct, but this does not prevent the policy being enforced for the benefit of a third party: *Hardy v. MIB* [1964] 2 QB 745; see also *Gray v. Barr* [1970] 2 QB 626.
120 See also National Audit Office, *Compensating Victims of Violent Crime* (2000), paras. 3.23–6.
121 This threshold produces a compensation gap because criminals are rarely worth suing in tort, and many victims of crime do not benefit from compensation orders, which are, anyway, typically for an amount less than £1,000.
122 Report, HC 43 (1984–5), para. 50.

advantage of discouraging a large number of small claims. As we saw earlier, all the evidence suggests that trivial injuries and losses are vastly more common than more serious injuries and losses.[123]

There was also an upper limit on awards for net loss of earnings, namely one-and-a-half times 'gross average industrial earnings' at the date of assessment. So far as compensation for non-pecuniary loss was concerned, the Board issued guidelines for the award of compensation for non-pecuniary loss in particular types of case.[124] The figures[125] included £20,000 for the loss of an eye, £11,500 for loss of hearing in one ear and £1,750 for the loss of two upper front teeth. A large facial scar rated £6,000 for a male and £9,000 for a female. Each case was considered on its own facts in the light of these guidelines.

In fatal cases under the old Scheme, dependants, as defined in the Fatal Accidents Act 1976, could make a claim and the compensation was assessed along the same lines as in proceedings under that Act (with the same limit as above on compensation for loss of income). An award for bereavement could be made. No compensation (other than for funeral expenses) was payable for the benefit of the deceased's estate.[126]

The majority of awards under the old CICS were for relatively small sums. In 1996–7, 2.7% were for sums under £1,000 and 83.1% for sums under £5,000; only 14.2% of awards exceeded £5,000, and only fourteen applicants received more than £500,000 (the largest award in 1996–7 was about £1.1 million).[127]

As far as assessment of compensation is concerned, the new 'enhanced tariff' scheme is a cross between a tariff-based, social security-type scheme and the common law. The tariff element – called the 'standard amount of compensation' – is determined by reference to the nature of the injury suffered by the claimant. Under the tariff there are twenty-five levels of compensation and more than four hundred separately listed injuries. Compensation at level 1 is £1,000,[128] and at level 25, £250,000. For instance, quadriplegia attracts compensation at level 25, while deafness lasting 6–13 weeks attracts compensation at level 1. A perforated ear drum attracts compensation at level 4 (£1,750), permanent moderately blurred vision at level 12 (£8,200), severe multiple injuries resulting from child abuse at level 14 (£13,500), loss of an arm at level 20 (£44,000) and so on. Compensation

---

123 This is also borne out by the *Osgoode Hall Study (Victims of Crime)*, 35, table VIII which showed over 28% of victims of crimes of violence with out-of-pocket losses less than $100 and (since 44% had no out-of-pocket losses at all) an equal percentage with losses exceeding this figure. Of course, this does not take into account pain and suffering and loss of amenities; but, on the other hand, in many cases it includes an item for medical expenses – which would not normally arise in this country.

124 Punitive damages cannot be awarded under the CICS.

125 See *CICB Thirty-Third Report*, Appendix G.

126 Old Scheme, para. 15. See 2001 Scheme, para. 37.

127 *CICB Thirty-Third Report*, para. 3.15.

128 In 2002–3, 10,670 applications were rejected because the injuries suffered were found not to be serious enough to justify an award of £1,000.

for mental injury ranges from level 1 to level 18, and sexual assault from level 1 to level 19.[129] In the words of Baroness Blatch:[130]

> Under the enhanced tariff scheme we do not try to make a finely judged assessment of compensation, in the sense of attempting to put the individual back into the position in which he or she would have been had the attack not occurred. What we aim to do is to make a generous payment in recognition of society's concern for the blameless victim of violent crime.

The tariff approach has been widely criticized for being inflexible and unfair because it does not take account of the individual claimant's circumstances.[131] It was argued that, as at common law, the tariff should consist of compensation bands rather than fixed amounts for itemized injuries (of which more than 400 are listed in the 2001 Scheme). But the government resisted this argument on the basis that the use of bands would defeat the whole point of the tariff scheme, which was to provide quicker, simpler and more transparent decision-making.

At the time the new Scheme was first introduced in 1996, the highest standard amount of compensation – £250,000 at level 25 – was very much higher than the highest awards for non-pecuniary loss at common law (then about £130,000). The explanation for this lies in the way the standard amounts were arrived at. Under the first tariff scheme introduced by the government (which was subsequently held illegal), the standard amounts were the only compensation available – there were no additional amounts for loss of earnings or for expenses. The standard amounts were arrived at by calculating the median of past awards for various types of injuries under the old Scheme. Such awards included compensation for loss of earnings and expenses as well as for non-pecuniary loss. The standard amounts, therefore, included a component for pecuniary loss. When the current enhanced tariff scheme was introduced in 1996, the same standard amounts were used, even though (as we shall see) 'additional amounts' for loss of earnings and for expenses are available under the new Scheme. On the other hand, such additional amounts are not payable in respect of the first 28 weeks of loss of earnings (although expenses can attract compensation from the date of the injury). Moreover, compensation 'in respect of the same injury' under the new Scheme is capped at £500,000;[132] and where a claimant has suffered multiple injuries as a result of a crime, the tariff award will consist of the standard amount for the highest rated injury plus 30% of the standard amount for the second highest-rated injury and

---

129 'The Tariff includes an element of compensation for the degree of shock which an applicant in normal circumstances would experience as a result of an incident resulting in the injury': 1996 Guide, para. 4.9. It is only more serious shock which attracts compensation in its own right.

130 HL Debates, vol. 566, col. 637 (16 October 1995).

131 For other criticisms of tariffs see 13.4.3.2.

132 2001 Scheme, para. 24. Suppose that if there was no upper limit on compensation, an applicant's standard amount of compensation plus compensation for loss of earnings and expenses would be £1 million. Still, the maximum award is £500,000, and that before any deduction, e.g. to take account of the applicant's contribution to the injury-causing incident. So if the applicant's contribution were assessed at 20%, only £400,000 would be awarded.

15% of the standard amount for the third highest-rated injury. As under the old Scheme, £1,000 (the standard amount at level 1) is the minimum award available under the CICS. The net result of these various rules is that in more serious cases, in particular, awards under the CICS may be much lower than at common law for equivalent injuries and losses.

As has been noted, as well as the standard amount of compensation, the Authority may award 'additional amounts' for 'loss or earnings or earning capacity' and for 'special expenses', provided the applicant has lost earnings or earning capacity for longer than 28 weeks as a direct consequence of the criminal injury suffered. No compensation for lost earnings can be awarded for the first 28 weeks of loss. The 28-week period coincides with the period for which statutory sick pay (and the lower rate of short-term incapacity benefit)[133] is payable. In cases where compensation for expenses is available, it is calculated from the date of injury. As at common law, the multiplier method is used in relation to continuing future expenses and loss of income. The basis for arriving at the multiplicand is the figure for 'net loss of earnings' (as defined in para. 32 of the 2001 Scheme). The maximum amount of *net* loss of earnings that can be taken into account is set at one-an-a-half times 'gross average industrial earnings' at the time of assessment. (In 2002 average weekly earnings of full-time male employees in manufacturing industries[134] were about £480, and of female employees about £349.) Net earnings above this figure are ignored. This maximum is probably not aimed at keeping costs down: the number of potential applicants whose net earnings are more than £480 must be very small indeed. The real reason for the limitation is that it was thought to be inequitable to have widely varying awards for similar injuries because of wide variations in earnings, given that the CICS is financed by the taxpayer and not according to an insurance principle under which those earning more pay higher contributions. The ethical problems involved in the earnings-related principle have already been discussed.[135]

In fatal cases under the new Scheme,[136] the compensation payable includes a standard amount – at level 13 (£11,000) if there is only one qualifying claimant, and at level 10 (£5,500) for each qualifying claimant, if more than one. Where the deceased died as a direct consequence of the criminal injury, additional compensation may be payable where a claimant was financially dependent on the deceased. Such compensation is calculated as from the date of death and in basically the same way as in a fatal accident claim at common law. A dependent claimant under 18 may recover in addition an annual payment for loss of the parental services of a deceased parent (at level 5 (£2,000)). Where the deceased's death is not a direct consequence of the criminal injury, but the deceased, had they lived, could have recovered addi-

133 See 13.4.3.1.
134 The term 'average industrial earnings' has no technical meaning. The figure given is the nearest equivalent in published statistics.
135 6.3.
136 2001 Scheme, paras. 37–44.

tional compensation for loss of earnings of expenses, supplementary compensation may be awarded to dependants calculated in accordance with the rules for assessing additional damages for lost earnings and expenses. There are two respects in which compensation in fatal cases is more generous under the new Scheme than at common law. First, the amounts of standard compensation payable under the Scheme are higher than damages for bereavement under the Fatal Accidents Act 1976 (currently £10,000 to be divided amongst all claimants), and they are payable to a larger class of claimants than under the Act. Secondly, compensation for loss of parental services is not, as such, available at common law.

As noted above, the maximum award under the new Scheme is £500,000, which is considerably less than the highest awards under the old Scheme, and very much less than the highest awards at common law. Awards usually take the form of a lump sum, but the CICA can make a structured settlement.

The general pattern of awards under the new Scheme is similar to that under the old Scheme. About 86% of applicants received tariff awards of £5,000 or less. Only 46 of more than 42,000 awards were for £30,000 or more. The maximum tariff award of £250,000 was made in three cases, and the maximum award of £500,000 in four cases.

One very important distinction between the assessment of damages in tort and compensation paid under the CICS is that under the Scheme, many more deductions are made from compensation to take account of the existence of alternative forms of compensation.[137] The difference between awards under the CICS and tort damages in this regard is particularly pronounced in relation to compensation awards under the Fatal Accidents Act 1976 which, as we will see, are very favourably treated in terms of deductions. Under the old Scheme, the deductions were made from the total award of compensation. Under the new Scheme, certain amounts are deducted from the total CICS award (2001 Scheme, paras. 48, 49)[138] while others are set only against compensation for loss of income or expenses (2001 Scheme, paras. 45–7).

It has been pointed out that when the establishment of the CICS was being debated in the early 1960s, no clear explanation or justification was given for the adoption of common law damages as the model for compensation under the Scheme.[139] The introduction of the first tariff scheme in 1994 seems to have been prompted primarily by a desire to reduce, or at least contain, the cost of the CICS; and the enhanced tariff scheme, introduced in 1996, was designed to assuage criticism of the 1994 Scheme. In 2001, the level of most tariff awards was increased by 10%, but the level of awards for sexual offences and child abuse was increased more than this, suggesting a concern to mark the perceived seriousness of certain

---

137 15.4.
138 It follows that although no award can be made unless the injuries were serious enough to justify a tariff award of £1,000, the actual payment may be less than £1,000.
139 P. Duff, 'The Measure of Criminal Injuries Compensation: Political Pragmatism or Dog's Dinner?' (1998) 18 *OJLS* 105.

offences. Thus the rules for assessment of CICS compensation rest on a mix of ideas. Tariff awards address the seriousness of the injury suffered and, to a lesser extent, the seriousness of the offence, while payments for loss of income and for expenses promote the common law's traditional goal of compensation for harm.

12.4.4   Administration

When we turn to the administrative machinery of the Scheme we find major departures from the processes of the common law. Under the new Scheme, applications for compensation are determined by claims officers on the basis of written material without an oral hearing. A decision of a claims officer may be reconsidered in the light of new evidence or changed circumstances at any time before 'actual payment of a final award' (2001 Scheme, para. 53). Moreover, an award may be re opened (normally no more than 2 years after the date of the final decision):[140]

> . . . where there has been such a material change in the victim's medical condition that injustice would occur if the original assessment of compensation were allowed to stand, or where he has since died in consequence of the injury.

The claimant may seek a review of a decision of a claims officer, and the review will be conducted by a more senior claims officer. A claimant who is dissatisfied with the outcome of a review may appeal within 90 days of the review decision. Appeals are heard by adjudicators who are members of the Criminal Injuries Compensation Appeals Panel (CICAP). Where the appeal is against a decision to make, withhold or seek repayment of an award, there may be an oral hearing (normally in private) before at least two adjudicators. The claimant may be represented by a legal or non-legal adviser at an oral hearing, but must bear the cost. If the appellant fails to attend the hearing without giving a reasonable excuse, it may take place in their absence; but such an appellant may apply to have the appeal reheard. This elaborate mixture of administrative and quasi-judicial modes of decision-making is perhaps a reflection of the mixed nature of the new Scheme, having, as it does, tariff and non-tariff (tort-like) elements, the latter requiring much more attention to individual circumstances than the latter.

The cost of administering the Scheme in 1996–7 was 8.8% of total expenditure; and in 2002–3, 13.5% of total expenditure. These figures compare favourably with the cost of administering the social security system, and are very much lower than the cost of administering the tort system, as we shall see later.[141] However, it is surprising that the administrative cost of the new, and supposedly simpler and less resource-intensive, Scheme is significantly greater than that of the old Scheme.

One of the besetting problems of the old Scheme was the time taken to process applications and the size of the backlog of claims waiting to be dealt with; and one of the main justifications for the new Scheme given by the government was that

140   2001 Scheme, para. 56.
141   16.1.

claims could be dealt with more quickly. Under the old Scheme, in 1993–4, 30% of claims took more than 12 months to resolve; in 1996–7 this figure had jumped to 52%. As at 31 March 1997 there was a backlog of about 44,167 unresolved applications despite the fact that no new applications under the old Scheme were received after 1 April 1996. As for cases that went to a hearing under the old Scheme, in 1996–7, only 37% were resolved within 12 months of the request for a hearing being made. As at 31 March 1997 there was a backlog of more than 25,400 unresolved hearings. Because figures were not given for how long it took to resolve the large number of cases that were still active after 12 months, it was difficult to compare the old Scheme with the tort system in this respect. However, it was clear from the figures available that the CICS (like the tort system) could not be seen as a source of immediate financial help.[142]

Under the new Scheme, of the cases resolved in 2002–3, about 24% took more than 12 months; and as at 31 March 2003 there was a backlog of more than 91,000 cases, despite the fact that there were fewer new applications in 2002–3 (73,928) than in recent previous years. The drop in the backlog (5,300) was less than the drop in new applications. On the other hand, as at 31 March 2004 the backlog of cases on appeal was only about 5,000. It is hard to resist the conclusion that, overall, the Scheme is significantly under-resourced.

Advice and assistance ('legal help') is available under the publicly funded legal aid scheme for applications to the CICA, but legal representation is not; and the CICA cannot pay for representation.[143] However, it seems that many solicitors would be willing to act for a claimant on a no-win, no-fee basis; and claims management companies operate in the criminal injuries compensation area. In 1980, the last year for which statistics were kept, 34% of applicants were represented by solicitors in respect of initial decisions, while 19% were represented by a trade union representative. A small survey by the National Audit Office in 2000 found that almost two-thirds of applicants sought assistance in making their claim.[144] The rest acted on their own behalf. In the typical appeal, where there is an oral hearing, about half of applicants are advised or represented by a lawyer, a non-legal adviser or a friend/relative.[145] The CICAP describes the quality of representation at appeals as 'variable', but observes that represented appellants 'generally appear to feel more comfortable' whatever

---

142 Shapland, 'Victims, the Criminal Justice System and Compensation', 144–7.
143 Moreover, there is no 'defendant' against whom an order for costs could be made. In evidence to the Home Affairs Committee (*Compensating Victims Quickly: the Administration of the Criminal Injuries Compensation Board* (HC 92, 1989–90)), Victim Support, the Law Society and the TUC all supported giving the Board power to pay applicants' costs of investigating claims. Under the new Scheme, the adjudicators who hear an appeal can direct the CICA to 'meet reasonable costs [other than costs of representation] incurred by the appellant and any person who attends to give evidence at the hearing': 2001 Scheme, para. 74.
144 *Compensating Victims of Violent Crime* (2000), para. 2.8. In a small sample, the NAO found little difference between the success rate of represented and unrepresented applicants; but also that represented applicants were twice as likely to appeal as the unrepresented.
145 Criminal Injuries Compensation Appeal Panel, *Annual Report 2003–4*, 10. In 2003–4 about 46% of appeals (1,876) were successful.

the quality of representation. Because the hearing process is not adversarial, representation is, perhaps, less critical than in proceedings before an ordinary court. In 1978, the success rate of those who are represented at hearings was estimated to be much higher than the success rate of those who are not.[146] This is consistent with other research into the effectiveness of representation before tribunals. However, in 2000 the National Audit Office found that the difference between the success rates of represented and unrepresented appellants was less than 2%.[147]

Although there is no further right of appeal from decisions of the CICAP, the Panel's decisions can be challenged by application for judicial review in the Administrative Court. In 2002–3, fourteen such applications were made, and fifteen were decided by the court, all in the CICAP's favour.[148]

12.4.5   Claims consciousness

Since the CICS was started in 1964, the Board has been conscious that the level of claims has been a good deal lower than might have been expected merely by looking at the figures for crimes of violence against the person. Typically, the number of applications received in any one year under the old Scheme was only about a fifth of the notifiable crimes of violence recorded by the police in that year. One of the reasons for introducing the new tariff scheme was to make it 'more accessible to, and better understood by, members of the public'.[149] However, the number of applications has remained more or less the same in recent years, and actually fell in 2002–3. The British Crime Survey estimated that there were about 2.4 million violent incidents against adults in England and Wales in 2004, of which about half might have resulted in personal injury. However, in many of those cases, the victim would have suffered only minor injuries that would not qualify for CICS compensation.[150] In addition, the domestic violence exclusion (2001 Scheme, para. 17) no doubt cuts out a large number of potential claimants.

However, there is still reason to think that a significant number of potential claimants remain unaware of their rights under the Scheme and fail to claim.[151] One researcher found that over half of the victims surveyed 'did not know of any means to obtain compensation, although between 57 and 64% would have wished it'; and, moreover, that there was no evidence that the majority who did not apply to the Scheme were less likely to qualify for compensation than the minority who did.[152]

---

146 70–85% as against 43% according to the *Review of the Criminal Injuries Compensation Scheme: Report of an Interdepartmental Working Party*, 75.
147 *Compensating Victims of Violent Crime*, para. 2.9.
148 Summaries and transcripts of judicial review applications are available on the CICAP's website.
149 *CICA Annual Report 1995/6*, 7.
150 According to F.H. McClintock's findings, at least 75% of victims of violent crime were back at work within a week, about 12% were off work for 10 days, and less than 2% suffered permanent disability: *Crimes of Violence*, 54.
151 For unknown reasons, the rates of applications by victims of violent crime varies greatly around the country: National Audit Office, *Compensating Victims of Violent Crime* (2000), paras. 2.14–16.
152 Shapland, 'Victims, the Criminal Justice System and Compensation', 144.

In 1990 the House of Commons Home Affairs Committee, in its report on the CICS, expressed itself to be sure that many who are entitled do not claim, and suggested that special attention should be given to the possibility of claims for compensation by child victims of crime and abuse.[153] The CICA is aware of the need to make the Scheme more widely know to potential applicants and in 2002–3, for instance, launched a poster and leaflet campaign in police stations, doctors' surgeries and Victim Support offices which, it is said, generated a significant increase in traffic to the Authority's call centre. Whether such steps will be reflected in increased numbers of applications remains to be seen.

Postscript: *Rebuilding Lives: Supporting Victims of Crime* (December 2005) announced proposals to reduce the amount spent on criminal injuries compensation and to spend the savings on other forms of support for victims. The plan (except in relation to fatal cases and sexual offences) is to limit the CICS to 'serious' injuries; to abolish additional payments for loss of earnings and care costs; to increase tariff payments for injuries remaining within the Scheme and to raise the £500,000 cap. These proposals are designed not only to reduce the cost of the CICS but also to reduce the time taken to handle claims. The CICA would be given power to make interim awards. A further proposal to reduce the cost of the Scheme is to remove from it injuries suffered 'at work'.

---

153 Home Affairs Committee Second Report, *Compensating Victims Quickly* (HC 92, 1989–90), paras. 44, 45. See J. Plotnikoff, 'Conference on Criminal Injuries Compensation for Children' (1991) 10 *Civil Justice Q.* 30. In 1989–90 there were 4,825 applications to the Board in respect of child abuse; in 1994–5 there were 13,162 such applications, and in 1995–6 there were 11,969.

13

The social security system*

13.1 Foundations of the social security system

13.1.1 Workers' compensation

Although the origins of the modern social security system have been traced to the poor law of the Elizabethan age,[1] it is sufficient for our purposes (since we are concerned primarily with disability) to look no further back than 1897 when the first Workmen's Compensation Act was passed. In the nineteenth century the tort system rarely provided any compensation to the victim of an industrial injury because of the three defences which the courts had evolved for the protection of employers – namely common employment, denying liability for the negligence of a fellow worker; contributory negligence, denying liability where the worker was partly responsible for their own injuries; and *volenti non fit injuria* (assumption of risk) which (as then interpreted) denied liability for injuries occurring from a known and obvious risk. However, in 1880 Parliament passed the Employers' Liability Act, which restricted the scope of the doctrine of common employment;[2] and in 1891 the House of Lords limited the availability of the defence of *volenti*.[3] Furthermore, between 1878 and 1901 a stream of new factory legislation emerged dealing with the health and safety of workers, and the common law responded with the creation of the action for breach of statutory duty.[4]

But these developments were dwarfed in significance by the enactment in 1897 of the Workmen's Compensation Act, which broke away entirely from the common law principle that liability must be based on fault, and conferred on a worker (or

---

* I am deeply indebted to Professor Nick Wikeley for his detailed comments on a draft of this chapter. Of all the matters dealt with in this book, social security law is undoubtedly the most difficult for the non-specialist to penetrate and understand. I know of no-one more knowledgeable in this area than Nick. His help saved me from many errors. Of course, he bears no responsibility for this version.
1 R. Cranston, *Legal Foundations of the Welfare State* (London, 1985), ch. 2.
2 The doctrine was not entirely abolished until 1948: Law Reform (Personal Injuries) Act 1948, s. 1(1); W.R. Cornish and G. de N. Clark, *Law and Society in England 1750–1950* (London, 1989), 522–8, 537–8.
3 *Smith* v. *Baker & Sons* [1891] AC 325.
4 The action for breach of statutory duty was firmly established in *Groves* v. *Wimborne* [1898] 2 QB 402; but the development had begun in the 1850s: Cornish and Clark, *Law and Society in England* 518–20.

the worker's dependants) a right to compensation for any accident 'arising out of and in the course of employment'. In effect, this Act treated workers as insured against such risks, although employers were not compelled to insure against their new statutory liability. In practice, however, most employers did insure against this liability; indeed, the new and fast-growing liability insurance industry obtained a tremendous boost from this species of liability.[5] The Act did not follow the common law in providing 'full compensation'; it was based on the idea that industrial risks should be shared between employers and employees. Compensation was to be assessed on the basis that the employee was to bear half the loss, and the employer the other half. Over the years, legislation gradually ate into this principle, and by 1940 it was possible for compensation to be as much as seven-eighths of lost earnings in some cases.[6]

Although in these two ways workers' compensation broke away from common law principles, in other important respects the new remedy was cast in the traditional mould. For example, something very like contributory negligence remained a defence to the employer under the Act: compensation was denied if the accident was due to the worker's 'serious and wilful default'. In 1906 this defence was excluded by statute in cases of serious and permanent disablement and in fatal cases, but it was still possible in some circumstances to deny compensation for an accident caused by the worker's fault (even though not serious and wilful) on the ground that the worker's conduct was beyond the 'sphere of employment', so that the resulting accident was held not to arise 'out of and in the course of employment'.

The administrative process of workers' compensation law was also almost identical to that of the tort system. Disputed cases typically went to a county court, and many cases were taken on appeal to the Court of Appeal and even the House of Lords.[7] The out-of-court settlement process was similar to that which is a feature of tort claims today. The pressure on injured workers to settle was even greater than it is now, partly because trade unions were not so willing and able as they are today to give moral and financial support to litigation by their members; and partly because (with no other social security payments to fall back on) an injured person, or that person's dependants, could not afford to wait while a case meandered through the legal process. Parties were free to settle the claim by the award of a lump sum. Although the Act did envisage and provide for the award of compensation by periodical, weekly payments to take the place of lost wages, insurance companies preferred to dispose of claims in lump sums and often put pressure on accident

---

5 W.A. Dinsdale, *History of Accident Insurance in Great Britain* (London, 1954), 152; H.E. Raynes, *A History of British Insurance*, 2nd edn (London, 1964). Insurers soon became skilled at contesting claims and at securing settlements which were quite disadvantageous to the injured worker: Cornish and Clark, *Law and Society in England*, 531–2; see also 513–14, 524.

6 Sir William Beveridge, *Social Insurances and Allied Services* (Cmnd 6404, 1942) (Beveridge Report), para. 99 and 216–17, 233. For a detailed account of the legal developments of the nineteenth century see P.W.J. Bartrip and S. Burman, *The Wounded Soldiers of Industry* (Oxford, 1983); also Cornish and Clark, *Law and Society in England*, ch. 7.

7 Cornish and Clark, *Law and Society in England*, 533–6.

victims to accept them.[8] Like tort law, the workers' compensation system dealt with partial incapacity as well as total incapacity.

The stipulation in the 1897 Act that the injury must have arisen 'out of and in the course of the employment' meant that the employment must have been not only a cause-in-fact of the injury, but also that there must have been some relationship between the employment and the injury similar to that embodied in the common law notion of legal cause (5.3.1). This gave rise to difficulty in respect of diseases. Knowledge about the causes of many diseases was even more rudimentary than it is now, and this generally made it impossible to require proof of causation in individual cases. The solution eventually adopted was to include only those industrial diseases that were known to be caused by certain types of work (e.g. pneumoconiosis).[9]

The workers' compensation system was, like the modern tort-cum-liability-insurance system, one under which the worker was insured by the employer. No contributions or premiums were exacted from employees, although in practice some of the costs of the system were probably passed on to employees in the form of lower wages.

13.1.2   National insurance

The second major contribution to the foundations of the modern social security system was Lloyd George's National Insurance Act of 1911. While the Workmen's Compensation Act 1897 was concerned to fill in gaps left by the common law, this Act dealt with matters with which the common law did not concern itself at all; that is, with earnings loss arising from sickness unrelated to employment, and with unemployment.[10] So far as insurance against sickness is concerned, the Act represented a major departure in many ways. First, it was a national insurance system established by the government and administered by 'approved societies',[11] in effect as agents of the State.[12] Administration of the system was not based on the adversarial model; those responsible for administering the system were required to ensure that applicants received the benefits to which they were entitled as a matter of law. Secondly, the cost of the benefits was paid for partly by the employee, partly by the employer and partly by the taxpayer. Thirdly, the insurance was compulsory, and the premiums were flat-rate contributions which generally did not depend on the nature of the risk covered.[13] The benefits payable were not earnings related; the national insurance system was not concerned with replacing what had been lost – not with 'compensation' – but with the meeting of basic financial needs.

8 See further Beveridge Report, para. 77ff.
9 J. Stapleton, *Disease and the Compensation Debate* (Oxford, 1986), 21–3.
10 Concerning unemployment see J. Creedy and R. Disney, *Social Insurance in Transition* (Oxford, 1985), 28–32.
11 These were friendly societies and commercial insurers.
12 Creedy and Disney, *Social Insurance in Transition*, 32–3.
13 It thus entailed subsidization of more risky by less risky industries.

The National Insurance Act 1911 was not intended to provide sufficient to maintain those who were dependent on it; the object of the Act was rather to assist the industrious and thrifty working person who had a regular occupation by supplementing the claimant's own savings and the proceeds of private insurance schemes operated by commercial insurers, trade unions and friendly societies.

13.2   The Beveridge report and the 1946 Acts

In course of time these two pillars of the social security system became exceedingly complex.[14] At the same time, other forms of national insurance (principally against unemployment and medical expenses) and pension schemes for the retired and for widows grew in importance and complexity. The Great Depression, which started in 1929, went a long way towards destroying the national unemployment insurance system because it became impossible to maintain 2 million unemployed out of the contributions the system generated. Then persistent inflation brought by the Second World War so reduced the value of other national insurance and workers' compensation benefits which were related to contributions made years earlier, that the State was forced to provide various supplements during the war. This was the background to the Beveridge Report, which was published in 1942.[15]

Beveridge proposed a new streamlined national (i.e. public) insurance system based on six fundamental principles. These were: flat-rate subsistence benefits; flat-rate contributions; the unification of administrative responsibility; adequacy of benefits; comprehensiveness; and classification (by which Beveridge meant the provision of different treatment according to the different needs of various classes of people).[16] The system of national insurance against sickness established in 1911 remained in essence undisturbed. When Beveridge turned his attention to workers' compensation, he found a system which was becoming increasingly unpopular with employees and trade unions.[17]

> It allows claims to be settled by bargaining between unequal parties, permits payment of socially wasteful lump sums instead of pensions in cases of serious incapacity . . . and over part of the field, large in the numbers covered, though not in the proportion of total compensation paid, it relies on expensive private insurance.[18]

He therefore had no hesitation in proposing the integration of the workers' compensation system with the national insurance system. Beveridge was then faced with question of whether workers' compensation should be shorn completely of its tort-like characteristics or whether it should retain certain special features

---

14 Re workers' compensation see P.W.J. Bartrip, *Workmen's Compensation in Twentieth-Century Britain* (Aldershot, 1987).

15 A.W. Dilnot, J.A. Kay and C.N. Morris, *The Reform of Social Security* (Oxford, 1984), 9–23.

16 Beveridge Report, paras. 17 and 303–9; Dilnot, Kay and Morris, *The Reform of Social Security*, 31–2.

17 Beveridge Report, paras. 93–6.

18 Ibid., para. 80.

despite its merger with national insurance. He recognized that in principle there was a good deal to be said for a complete unification of the two systems:[19]

> . . . it might well be argued that the general principle of a flat rate of compensation for interruption of earnings adopted for all other forms of interruption, should be applied also . . . to the results of industrial accident and disease . . . If a workman loses his leg in an accident, his needs are the same whether the accident occurred in a factory or in the street; if he is killed, the needs of his widow and other dependants are the same, however the death occurred . . . adoption of a flat rate of compensation for disability, however caused, would avoid the anomaly of treating equal needs differently and the administrative and legal difficulties of defining just what injuries were to be treated as arising out of and in the course of employment . . . whatever words are chosen difficulties and anomalies are bound to arise. A complete solution is to be found only in a completely unified scheme for disability without demarcation by the cause of disability.

Despite these arguments, Beveridge decided to retain a separate and more favourable scheme for industrial injuries, and gave three main reasons for this course.[20] First, some work is especially dangerous, and it is desirable that people should not be discouraged from doing such work by the risks involved; secondly, a person injured while at work is injured 'whilst working under orders'; and, thirdly, only if special provision was made for industrial injury would it be possible, as Beveridge wanted, to limit the employer's liability at common law to actions for which the employer was 'morally and in fact' responsible. None of these arguments is very convincing.[21] First, the fact that work is more dangerous than other activities[22] may be a reason to pay people more for doing it but not for compensating injuries caused by it more generously.[23] Secondly, the fact that a person injured at work was 'under orders' is merely an indication that the worker did not, in some sense, voluntarily choose to incur the risk; but this is also true of the sick and disabled generally. The fate of Beveridge's third argument is somewhat ironical because the introduction of the industrial injuries national insurance scheme was followed by a decision to widen the scope of liability for common law damages,[24] and not as a ground for confining common law actions within narrow limits. It is estimated that by 1996, total payments of compensation for work-related injury and illness under the tort system were greater than those under the social security system.[25]

---

19 Ibid.
20 Ibid., para. 81; see also Pearson Report, vol. 1, paras. 93–108; S. Jones, 'Social Security and Industrial Injury' in N. Harris ed., *Social Security Law in Context* (Oxford, 2000), 470. But the real reason was union pressure: Bartrip, *Workmen's Compensation*, 184.
21 *Report of the Royal Commission of Inquiry on Compensation for Personal Injuries in New Zealand* (New Zealand, 1967) (Woodhouse Report), paras. 52–4; Report of the Committee on Local Authority and Allied Personal Social Services (Cmnd 3703, 1968) (Seebohm Report), para. 327; V. George, *Social Security: Beveridge and After* (London, 1968), 184.
22 Itself a questionable assumption: Bartrip, *Workmen's Compensation*, 183.
23 See also Creedy and Disney, *Social Insurance in Transition*, 129–30.
24 See 15.4.5.
25 C. Parsons, 'Employers' Liability Insurance – How Secure is the System? (1999) 28 *Industrial LJ* 109, 113–14.

The Pearson Commission adopted a somewhat peculiar stance on the issue. On the one hand, it appeared to condemn the industrial preference as unjustified; but, on the other hand, it recommended (in effect) that the industrial injuries scheme should be extended, with modifications, to road accident victims. As we shall see in chapter 18, the problem of reform is much affected by the extent to which preferences of this nature are treated as 'vested rights' which cannot be abrogated. Yet, in reality, the rights are only vested for those who have already become entitled to benefits, and certainly no reform is likely to remove or whittle away rights which are vested in that sense. The present extent of the industrial preference will be made clear later in this chapter.

Despite Beveridge's decision to recommend special treatment for the industrially injured, workers' compensation was to become part of the National Insurance system. The private insurance companies and the adversary process of settlement and litigation were to go; the system was to be financed by contributions from employer, employee and State in the same way as National Insurance, and payments were to be weekly and not by way of lump sums. On the other hand, Beveridge wanted earnings-related pensions for victims of long-term disablement;[26] but this was rejected by the government, which was even more wedded than Beveridge himself to the flat-rate philosophy.[27] Beveridge also wanted to impose a 'special levy' on industries with particularly bad accident records;[28] but this, too, was rejected by the government,[29] principally because of opposition from the trades unions. Beveridge had intended that only those who were off work for more than 13 weeks should receive preferential treatment, but the government extended it to all those injured at work.[30] Instead of earnings-related pensions for the long-term disabled, the government decided on disability pensions and gratuities for the disability 'as such', irrespective of lost earnings. These payments resemble tort compensation for 'loss of faculty'. One of the main reasons for reverting to this tort idea was that great resentment had been caused by the fact that payments for partial incapacity under the workers' compensation system were liable to be reduced if the worker recovered and began to earn substantially more again.[31] The government agreed with Beveridge that compensation for lost income should not take the form of lump sums, though payment of lump sums for disabilities in minor cases was adopted.[32]

13.3   Developments since 1946

The social security system has undergone many changes since Beveridge's day, some of them of major significance. The main pieces of legislation for our purposes are

26 Beveridge Report, para. 85.
27 Government White Paper, *Social Insurance*, Part II (Cmnd 6551, 1944), para. 28.
28 Beveridge Report, paras. 86–9.
29 Cmnd 6551, para. 31.
30 Ibid., para. 26.
31 Ibid., para. 29(3).
32 Ibid., para. 30.

the Social Security (Contributions and Benefits) Act 1992 (SSCBA) and the Social Security Administration Act 1992 (SSAA), which are consolidating Acts; and the Social Security Act 1998. It is beyond the scope of this book to chart the many twists and turns in the social security system since it was set up, and the main aim in what follows will be to give an account of the present position of disabled people within the system. But a few general comments are needed.

First, concerning the level of social security benefits, between 1948 and 1977 prices increased by about five times and earnings by about ten times, but social security benefits about twelve times. This was particularly important for the long-term disabled and the chronically sick. In 1974 the Labour government enacted a commitment to review the levels of National Insurance benefits annually, and to increase them sufficiently to keep pace with the general level of earnings; but in 1979 the Conservative government altered this to a commitment to increase benefits (other than earnings-related benefits and some others) in line with prices. This was part of a policy of reducing the cost of social security provision.[33]

Secondly, a number of major changes in the social security system after Beveridge's day deserve mention. One was the introduction of earnings-related elements. Earnings-related benefits were first introduced in 1961 in connection with retirement pensions; in 1966 they were extended on a limited scale to sickness and unemployment benefits, as well as to industrial injury benefits. In 1975 National Insurance contributions became earnings-related, subject to upper and lower limits. Under the Social Security Act 1975, a new long-term earnings-related retirement pension scheme (called SERPS) was introduced. Although this change was grafted onto the existing system with a minimum of structural alteration, it represented an enormous shift in the philosophy of the National Insurance system as a whole. Beveridge was opposed to earnings-related additions: he thought that the State had done its duty when it had provided a subsistence income for all its citizens who were unable to provide their own; protection above this level on a compulsory basis was an unjustifiable interference with the freedom of the individual to spend money as they chose.[34] If individuals wanted more than basic benefits, they could provide them for themselves by means of private insurance. Adoption of the earnings-related principle was partly a product of increased affluence, and partly of a popular desire to reflect wage differentials in benefits, especially since many poorer people would not be able to afford to buy earnings-related additions in the private market.

In the 1980s the Conservative government, as part of its philosophy of 'rolling back the frontiers of the State' and encouraging private arrangements, eschewed the earnings-related principle. Earnings-related additions to short-term benefits were

---

33 *Wikeley, Ogus and Barendt's The Law of Social Security,* 265–7.
34 Beveridge Report, para. 304. In this respect, there is a fundamental contrast between the British and European models of social security: House of Commons Social Security Select Committee Report, *The Contributory Principle* (Fifth Report, 1999–2000), para. 19.

abolished as from 1982. When statutory sick pay was introduced in 1983 it was payable at three different rates depending on earnings; but in 1987 the rates were reduced to two, and in 1994 to one. There are still some earnings-related, long-term benefits, but these are being phased out. In the mid-1980s the Conservative government wanted to abolish SERPS because of its anticipated cost, but in the face of widespread protest it legislated in 1986 just to reduce benefits under the scheme.[35] The extent to which social security benefits are earnings-related has important ramifications for the tort system which is, of course, fully earnings-related. Complete abolition of tort as a means of compensating for personal injuries is unlikely to be politically attractive so long as social security benefits for disabled people are flat-rate.

Another important change in the social security system since Beveridge has been improvement of provision for the disabled, and especially the long-term disabled. In the last 35 years or so the Disability Income Group and the Disability Alliance have been very active pressure groups and have secured many legislative improvements in the position of the disabled, such as the introduction of attendance and mobility benefits and benefits for carers in addition to income-replacement benefits. After pensions, spending on the sick and disabled is the second largest component of the social security budget; and more is spent on the disabled than on any other group of working-age people.[36] In the 1980s the Conservative government conducted a major review of the social security system (the Fowler review) which led to radical changes made by the Social Security Act 1986. Benefits for the disabled were specifically excluded from this review pending the outcome of a major survey of the extent and nature of disability in the population by the Office of Population Censuses and Statistics (OPCS). The results of this survey were referred to in chapter 1. In 1988 the Social Security Advisory Committee published proposals about benefits for the disabled; and the government's response to this, *Benefits for Disabled People: The Way Ahead*,[37] identified four objectives: first, to improve the position of those unable to work, especially those disabled from birth or early life; secondly, to improve assistance in meeting the extra costs of disablement for people of working age and below; thirdly, to help those who want to work by making it easier for them to enter and remain in the workforce; and, fourthly, to avoid duplication of assistance from various sources. Major changes designed to meet these objectives were enacted in the Social Security Act 1990 and the Disability Living Allowance and Disability Working Allowance Act 1992.[38] What the review did not achieve was any overall rationalization of the disability benefits system; in particular, the distinction between those disabled at work and other disabled

---

35 It has not been possible to acquire new rights under the SERPS scheme since April 2002 following the introduction of the State Second Pension (S2P).
36 N. Wikeley, 'Social Security and Disability' in N. Harris ed., *Social Security Law in Context* (Oxford, 2000), 363.
37 Cm 917; T. Buck, 'The Way Ahead: Benefits for the Disabled (Cm 917)' (1990) 19 *Industrial LJ* 125.
38 Now consolidated in the SSCBA 1992.

people is still significant. Nor is there any single benefit that 'can be identified as providing an adequate basic income by itself'.[39]

In the 1980s and early 1990s, the numbers of people claiming, and expenditure on, the main long-term sickness and disability benefit – invalidity benefit – increased enormously. This benefit became the target of the government's cost-cutting agenda, and the Social Security (Incapacity for Work) Act 1994 replaced invalidity benefit with a less generous incapacity benefit and made it harder to obtain. The New Labour government continued this policy in the Welfare Reform and Pensions Act 1999, which tightened up eligibility criteria and imposed new contribution conditions.[40] Notably, receipt of a private or occupational pension is now taken into account in determining the amount of incapacity benefit payable. One result of the many piecemeal adjustments to social security provision for the disabled over the years is that the system is extremely complex and by no means free of anomalies.

A third important change in the social security system since Beveridge's day has been a weakening of the contributory (or 'insurance') principle. Beveridge had envisaged that entitlement to benefits would be conditional on the claimant having paid a certain number of weekly contributions. Now, many benefits are wholly non-contributory (which means that even a person who has never paid National Insurance contributions may be eligible for them); in particular, there are no contribution conditions for the receipt of most benefits for the disabled.[41] Indeed, National Insurance contributions are, in effect, a tax, not an insurance premium. There is no National Insurance fund, except in a book-keeping sense, and contributory benefits are funded on an annual basis and not out of accumulated revenue.[42] There is a good case for abolishing National Insurance contributions entirely; among other things, this would save considerable administrative expense. A step in this direction was taken in 1999 with the transfer of the work of the Contributions Agency (which collects National Insurance contributions) to Her Majesty's Revenue and Customs (formerly the Inland Revenue).

When Beveridge first put forward his proposals in 1942 he intended that the levels of benefit payable under the National Insurance system should not be less

---

39 P. Larkin, 'Social security provision for disability: a case for change?' (1998) 5 *J. of Social Security L* 9, 11.

40 D. Bonner, 'The Incapacity and Disability Provisions in the Welfare Reform and Pensions Act: Work for Those Who Can and Security for Those Who Cannot?' (2000) 7 *JSSL* 208.

41 Statutory sick pay and industrial injury benefits, for example, are contributory in the sense that they are only available to employed earners, but there are no contribution conditions for their receipt – a person may be eligible for them even if the sickness or injury is suffered on the first day at work. The only benefits relevant to our discussion which have contribution conditions attached are short-term incapacity benefit (the counterpart of statutory sick pay for the self-employed) and bereavement benefits. The contribution conditions for incapacity benefit were made more restrictive by the Welfare Reform and Pensions Act 1999 (see Bonner, 'Work for Those Who Can and Security for Those Who Cannot?').

42 That is, on a 'pay-as-you-go', not on a 'fully-funded', basis. For more explanation of these terms see 18.2.5. For a general consideration of the role and future of the contributory principle in the social security system see Social Security Select Committee Report, *The Contributory Principle.*

than was thought necessary for subsistence. It was also appreciated that national assistance (as it was first called; we will refer to it as 'income support') would still be needed in some cases where there was no entitlement to the benefits payable under the National Insurance Act 1911 (because the required contributions had not been paid). But Beveridge was determined to maintain the insurance element in National Insurance – the idea that people were paying for their benefits – and he therefore felt it necessary that national assistance should be made 'less desirable'[43] than National Insurance. He proposed to achieve this by making it subject to a means test. Beveridge clearly thought national assistance would become a fringe area of social security dealing with a small number of special cases.

As things have developed, matters have taken a very different course from that envisaged by Beveridge. Income-support benefits have never been conceived by any government as merely filling in the gaps for those who fail to qualify for the other benefits, but as an addition to the other benefits to bring them up to subsistence level and to accommodate housing costs that Beveridge's contributory benefits failed to cover. Ordinary sickness benefits were in fact from the very beginning below the rates required for subsistence. Furthermore, an insurance-based system assumes that most people are either in work or dependent on someone who works; it makes no allowance for those who, because of disability, for example, have never been able to work or who have worked only intermittently, or for the long-term unemployed or for those (such as single parents engaged in full-time child-care) who, for some other reason, do not participate in the labour market. One of the most important changes since Beveridge's day has been an enormous increase in the number of people dependent on non-contributory benefits and on means-tested, income-support benefits.[44]

A policy of keeping contributory benefits for specific groups (such as the unemployed and the disabled) relatively low and supplementing them with income-support benefits reflects a social welfare philosophy quite different from Beveridge's insurance principle. It means that that those who are better off not only pay more of the costs of the system through contributions (which are earnings-related) and through the tax system; also they receive less in benefits from the system because they are less likely, even when they are in receipt of contributory benefits, to qualify for income-support benefits. In this respect, the social security system differs greatly from the system of tort liability with liability insurance. Under this system, the better off the claimant, the greater the compensation; at the same time, liability insurance premiums are unrelated to income and so bear more heavily on those who are less well off.

43 Beveridge Report, para. 369.
44 The long-term unemployed are more heavily dependent on income-support benefits than the long-term disabled because contribution-based jobseeker's allowance (the successor to unemployment benefit) is payable only for a limited period. Old age is also a major cause of poverty.

13.4   The industrial injuries system

13.4.1 The scope of the system

The Industrial Injuries Scheme (IIS)[45] covers, as workers' compensation did before it, all accidental injuries arising 'out of and in the course of employment'. The first requirement of the Scheme is that the victim should have been an 'employed earner' which, in the vast majority of cases, means employed under a contract of service; the system does not extend to the self-employed.[46] Apart from cost considerations, two justifications are offered for this limitation: lack of demand from the self-employed and potential problems in defining the scope of an expanded scheme.[47] This second reason is perhaps supplemented by a fear of abuse or fraud. For instance, a small shopkeeper might be tempted to allege that they fell and broke a leg in the shop instead of in the living quarters above the shop, and it would be impossible to detect the fraud since there would be no employer present to verify the allegation. But employed workers no doubt also have opportunities to make fraudulent claims. Moreover, if a self-employed person converts their business into a limited company, there is nothing in law to prevent the person being employed by the company,[48] in which case that person will then fall within the IIS. The Pearson Committee[49] and the Industrial Injuries Advisory Council have both recommended that the Scheme should be extended to cover the self-employed. Given that there are no contribution conditions for industrial injury benefits, and that extending the scheme to the unemployed would not greatly increase its cost, reluctance to do so seems petty.

The phrase 'arising out of and in the course of employment' is an extremely difficult one. The difficulty is inherent in the concept of insurance against 'employment risks' because there is no clear and sound policy reason for distinguishing between employment risks and non-employment risks; and so it is almost impossible to construct a satisfactory criterion for distinguishing injury within the Scheme from injury outside the Scheme. This generates many borderline cases. Despite universal dissatisfaction with the formula in the workers' compensation system, it was retained in the National Insurance (Industrial Injuries) Act 1946 subject to reversal of a number of specific decisions under the old scheme, which were felt to be particularly hard. For instance, the Act reversed a decision of the House of Lords[50] that a worker travelling to a coalmine in a train provided by his employers was not in the course of his employment unless he was required to travel on the train, even though there was no other practical way of getting to work.[51] But even the present law

---

45 *Wikeley, Ogus and Barendt's The Law of Social Security*, ch. 20. The term 'industrial injury scheme' (or 'system') is used here even though there is no longer a separate Act or a separate fund. Industrial injury benefits are simply a part of the social security system provided for in the SSCBA 1992 and the SSAA 1992.
46 Who represent about 8% of the workforce.
47 *Wikeley, Ogus and Barendt's The Law of Social Security*, 721.
48 *Lee v. Lee's Air Farming Ltd* [1961] AC 12.
49 Pearson Report, vol. 1, paras. 851–7.
50 *St Helen's Colliery Ltd v. Hewitson* [1924] AC 59.
51 SSCBA 1992, s. 99.

distinguishes between an injury occurring to a person travelling in a bus or train provided by or by arrangement with the employer and injury occurring to a person travelling by public transport or their own transport. It has been a persistent source of complaint by the trades unions that injuries incurred while travelling to and from work are not covered by the industrial injuries system. By a single vote, the Pearson Commission recommended that the IIS should be extended to cover commuting accidents,[52] but in the debate in the House of Commons on 17 November 1979, Patrick Jenkin described this as an eccentric proposal that few would support.[53] The fact is that although the way travel accidents are classified affects the benefits to which the injured person is entitled, there is no obvious way of deciding whether they should be treated as work accidents or as ordinary transport accidents.

The requirement that the accident should arise 'in the course of' employment normally indicates that the claimant must have been doing the employer's work when injured; while the requirement that the accident should arise 'out of the employment' indicates that the injury must have arisen out of a risk peculiar to the employment. For instance, a person working at a workshop bench is in the course of employment; but if the injury is the result of an assault by an escaped prisoner who has wandered into the factory, the injury will not have arisen 'out of' the employment – unless the employment in some way added to the risk of such injury, as, for example, if the factory was part of the prison. However, where a person is injured in the course of employment, the injury is presumed, in the absence of contrary evidence, to have arisen out of the employment.[54] In addition, under s. 101 of the SSCBA 1992 certain types of accident are treated as having arisen 'out of' the employment if they occurred in the course of employment. This provision was introduced in 1961 to deal with certain types of situation in which claimants had previously been denied benefit, but it is hard to see that there is any intelligible policy behind these extensions of the scheme, unless it is merely the feeling that the place where accidents occur is a more important criterion for compensation than the way in which they occur. Certainly we appear to have got very close to a point where an accident arising in the course of the employment will almost inevitably fall within the system, and be treated as having arisen 'out of' the employment. This makes it difficult to justify having a special scheme for work-caused accidents. But at least these provisions have had a good practical effect: in 1976 the then Chief National Insurance Commissioner commented that the 'out of' requirement now gives little trouble.[55]

It is possible, though not very common, for injuries to arise 'out of' the employment, but to a person who is not 'in the course' of employment. A person who, while taking a prolonged and unauthorized break to drink tea or smoke a cigarette, is

52 Pearson Report, vol. 1, paras. 858–68.
53 *Hansard*, 5th series, HC, vol. 958, col. 795. However, most other EU social security schemes cover commuting accidents: *Wikeley, Ogus and Barendt's The Law of Social Security*, 734.
54 SSCBA 1992, s. 94(3).
55 R.G. Micklethwait, *The National Insurance Commissioners* (London, 1976), 82–3.

injured by a risk arising 'out of' the employment, may be held not to have been in the course of employment.[56] In this kind of situation, the 'course of employment' formula performs a function not very different from that of the common law defence of 'contributory negligence', even though 'fault' as such plays no part in the industrial injuries scheme. There are certain other situations in which the conduct of the claimant is relevant. Under s. 10(1)(b) of the SSAA 1992, for instance, a claimant may be disqualified from receiving benefit for up to 6 weeks on account of wilful obstruction or other misconduct in respect of any medical examination or treatment to which they are required to submit. Again, there is a proviso to the operation of s. 101 of the SSCBA 1992 (which was mentioned above) relating to the conduct of the claimant. The fault idea, although out of place in a social security system, dies hard. Perceived administrative difficulties may have been as important as theoretical objections in preventing the wider introduction of fault ideas into the scheme.[57]

13.4.2 Accidents and diseases

The term 'accident' as used in the IIS means something like 'separate incident' as opposed to 'continuous process'.[58] It does not mean an event which was 'accidental' in the everyday sense. Thus, injuries inflicted deliberately in an assault may be accidental in the relevant sense.[59] Basically the distinction is between 'accidental injury' and 'disease', and the main reason for drawing such a distinction is the difficulty of deciding, especially in relation to diseases common in the population at large – such as cancer and heart failure – whether, in any particular case, the disease was contracted as a result of the employment. Under the IIS all accidental injuries arising out of, and in the course of, employment, are insured against; but diseases are not insured against unless they are 'prescribed' by the Minister.[60] When it becomes possible to assert with some confidence that there is a causal connection between a certain disease and a certain type of employment, the Minister can provide by regulation that the disease is a 'prescribed' disease under the Act. Any person employed in the relevant occupation who then contracts the disease is treated in the same way – subject to certain exceptions – as a person suffering accidental injury in the course of employment.[61]

---

56 R v. Industrial Injuries Commissioner, ex parte Amalgamated Engineering Union (No. 2) [1966] 2 QB 31.
57 When the CICS was under consideration it was thought administratively impossible to combine an industrial injury-type scheme and weekly payments etc. with a provision for reducing benefits on the ground of 'provocation': Cmnd 1406, para. 92.
58 Wikeley, Ogus and Barendt's The Law of Social Security, 722–6.
59 In such cases there is a complete overlap between the IIS and the criminal injuries scheme, though double compensation is not generally permitted. Since the cost of the two systems falls on different parties, it is necessary to ask which is the more appropriate body to pay for such injuries: see generally 15.2.
60 There are more than 60 prescribed diseases.
61 In 1981 the Industrial Injuries Advisory Council recommended a new system (to supplement that of prescribing diseases) under which, except in relation to certain diseases such as lung cancer and coronary conditions, the causes of which are much disputed and which are common in the population at large, it would be open to a worker to claim benefit in relation to any disease which could

Although most diseases do not fall within the IIS unless they are prescribed diseases, the accident part of the scheme does cover diseases caused by a single event or series of separate incidents (as opposed to a continuous process). For instance, a worker may suffer a heart attack while trying to lift a heavy object.[62] Inclusion of such cases in the scheme seems to be the result of sympathy more than logic. The anomaly in such a case is that the incident may have acted merely as a trigger; the worker may have been prone to a heart attack at any moment from any cause, and only if it happens while the person is at work and working is the result treated as within the system. The only difference, between this sort of case and the case of a disease which falls firmly outside the scheme unless prescribed, is that in this type of case it is possible to point to some specific event or series of events which produced the disease. In some cases, where disease is contracted as a result of a special risk arising from the employment, the result seems less anomalous; as, for instance, where a nurse catches a disease from a patient. Another problem is that the distinction between a series of separate incidents and a continuous process is very difficult to draw, and it produces some hard cases, such as that of injury to a hand by constant use of a pneumatic drill which is held not to have been caused by an accident but is not a prescribed disease either.[63]

In recent years, claims arising out of stress-related illnesses have caused trouble. One result of the dramatic decline of manufacturing industries in the UK in the latter part of the twentieth century and their replacement by service industries has been a corresponding change in the pattern of work-related illness. Work-related mental illness has become a much more prevalent, or at least a much more recognized, phenomenon than it was 30 or 40 years ago. But, for instance, post-traumatic stress disorder (PTSD) is not a prescribed disease; and in 2004, the Industrial Injuries Advisory Council (IIAC) concluded that work-related stress as not suitable for inclusion in the list of prescribed diseases.[64] This means that if such conditions are to come within the scope of the IIS, they must qualify as injury by accident. In one case a prison officer, who suffered PTSD after a confrontation with a prisoner, made a successful claim for benefit. By contrast, the claim of a fire-fighter who suffered stress as a result of attendance at a series of horrific accidents, was refused because there was insufficient evidence linking the claimant's condition to any particular incident(s).[65] The result that a person who suffers a stress-related illness as

be proved to have been contracted as a result of employment. But when it considered the matter again in 1995, it declined to recommend any change.

62 For a much more difficult example concerning passive smoking see J. Meltzer, 'Smoking at Work' [1991] New LJ 596.

63 Micklethwait, *The National Insurance Commissioners*, 82. But note that since 1996 carpal tunnel syndrome (A12) has been a prescribed disease for those working with 'hand-held power tools'. See also Jones in Harris, *Social Security Law in Context*, 476.

64 IIAC Position Paper 13. Perhaps the main reason was that diagnosing stress-related illness and linking it to work would require a degree of investigation of individual cases which, although characteristic of the common law, was impractical in a high-volume social security system. This suggests a general limit on the potential coverage of disability-related social security systems.

65 *Chief Adjudication Officer v Faulds* [2002] 2 All ER 961.

a result of one incident should be able to claim, but that a person who becomes ill as a result of repeated exposure to stressful conditions cannot, does not easily admit of a convincing explanation. For instance, all that the IIAC says, apparently by way of supporting the House of Lords' decision about the fire-fighter, is that claims from the emergency services are problematic because their work is intrinsically stressful.[66] Nevertheless, the IIAC has said that stress-related illness (in the form of PTSD) will fall within the accident part of the IIS only if it results from a single event that is 'quite outside the realms of normal human experience'; is, or could readily be perceived to be, life-threatening or extremely dangerous to the claimant or others; and would be sufficient to cause severe distress to almost anyone.[67]

In numerical terms, the accident part of the scheme is very much more import-ant than the disease part. For example, in 2002 some 278,000 disablement benefit pensions were being paid, of which some 217,000 resulted from accidents.[68] The reason for this disparity is not that industrial diseases are a less frequent source of incapacity than industrial accidents; the converse is undoubtedly the case. But many diseases which may result from working conditions are not prescribed; and even in relation to prescribed diseases, it is probably the case that many workers do not claim because they are less likely to attribute a disease to their working condi-tions than an accident. One reason for this is that we tend to see diseases as being the result of 'natural causes', perhaps because they are often partly the result of indi-vidual predisposition, or of voluntary action (such as smoking) by the sufferer, or of environmental factors to which everyone is subject. A second reason is that much remains unknown about the causation of diseases.

13.4.3 Benefits

The law relating to the benefits provided under the IIS[69] is every bit as complicated as the law relating to the assessment of damages at common law, though it is a much more precise and rigid system in which specific sums are laid down as the appro-priate payments for particular cases. We may for convenience divide the benefits into three main classes, namely short-term benefits, long-term benefits and benefits for the bereaved. However, this classification cuts across another important dis-tinction, namely that between benefits for income loss, benefits for disabilities as such and benefits for the extra expenses incurred as a result of being disabled. There are no 'contribution conditions' for benefits under the IIS. A person injured on the first day at work is entitled to benefits. Moreover, provided a person is an 'employed

---

66 Position Paper 13, para. 44. So far as tort liability is concerned, the traditional rule is that mental harm will attract compensation only if it is the result of a 'shock' as opposed, e.g. to a long period of anxiety about the fate of a missing loved one. Australian law has now abandoned this limita-tion because, it is said, the 'shock' rule (which is similar to the criteria adopted by the IIAC) is not supported by medical knowledge.

67 Ibid., para. 46.

68 *Work and Pensions Statistics 2005*, tables IIDB 1.3 and 1.4.

69 The following account aims only to explain the basic principles underlying the relevant law. For more detail the reader should consult *Wikeley, Ogus, Barendt's The Law of Social Security* or other works on social security.

earner', that person is covered by the scheme whether or not they are liable to make National Insurance contributions.

13.4.3.1   Short-term incapacity

The main short-term benefit is statutory sick pay (SSP). This is an earnings-replacement benefit payable in respect of periods of incapacity for work. As is generally the case in relation to social security benefits, nothing is payable for the first 3 days of incapacity. This rule performs a function similar to that of the 'excess' in first party insurance, and eliminates a large number of very small claims, which would cost a great deal in aggregate and would generate disproportionate administrative expense. SSP is not limited to those whose sickness falls within the IIS, and to this extent the victim of industrial injury is no better treated than other sick workers. But the industrial victim is better off in that entitlement to long-term disablement benefit under the IIS arises after 15 weeks, whereas entitlement to long-term incapacity benefit for other workers arises only after 52 weeks of incapacity for work. SSP is administered[70] and payable by the employer.[71]

If one considers SSP in isolation, it seems that very few, if any, persons injured at work would be better off (or even as well off) on benefits as at work; and the great majority of workers would be much worse off receiving SSP rather than their ordinary wages. A large proportion of employees[72] enjoy a contractual right to receive sick pay from their employers, and such 'occupational sick pay' will often represent a higher proportion of ordinary earnings than SSP does (and commonly 100% for higher-paid workers).[73]

SSP is available for the first 28 weeks of incapacity. For the period between 29 and 52 weeks of incapacity, the relevant benefit is called 'short-term incapacity benefit', which is paid at the same rate as SSP.[74]

SSP and short-term incapacity benefit are payable in respect of total incapacity to earn. The social security system, unlike the tort system, provides no short-term benefits for partial earnings loss. The common law, of course, in theory aims to

---

70 Sickness benefits payable under the National Insurance Act 1911 were also administered by the private sector. After 1946 administration of all sickness benefits was taken over by the State; but in 1983, administration of short-term sickness benefit was returned to the private sector in order to cut costs. A more radical step would be to privatize the provision as well as the administration of short-term sickness benefits, by requiring employers to set up minimum occupational sick pay schemes underwritten by private insurers: Creedy and Disney, *Social Insurance in Transition*, 215–18.

71 Until 1994 employers were reimbursed by the government for most or all of the cost of SSP. In 1994 reimbursement was abolished except for 'small employers'. The system was changed again in 1995 so that now all employers are reimbursed but only for expenditure above a certain (high) level.

72 Estimated to be about 90% in 1981: *Wikeley, Ogus, Barendt's The Law of Social Security*, 160. See also Creedy and Disney, *Social Insurance in Transition*, 133.

73 Concerning the extent to which the coverage of occupational sick pay schemes is correlated with the risk of sickness in particular industries see Creedy and Disney, *Social Insurance in Transition*, 134–8.

74 There is a lower rate of short-term incapacity benefit payable for the first 28 weeks of incapacity to people who do not qualify for SSP.

replace net loss of earnings precisely, and for short periods of incapacity this aim can be achieved without too much difficulty. The main advantage which social security benefits have over tort damages is that the former are paid more or less immediately, and periodically, whereas tort damages will usually be paid in a lump sum, and many months or even years after the injury is suffered. Tort also provides damages for short-term non-pecuniary loss, and such damages tend to be a larger proportion of the total award in less serious than in more serious cases. By contrast, industrial injury benefits for loss of faculty do not become payable until 15 weeks after the injury.

13.4.3.2   Long-term incapacity

Long-term incapacity arising from industrial injury is treated in a very complex way. It is in this area that the industrially injured are privileged when compared with those suffering from non-industrial injuries and diseases or congenital disability chiefly because they are entitled to benefits referable to non-pecuniary loss (a 'disablement pension' or, as it is more commonly known, 'disablement benefit') as well as to benefits to cover the extra financial costs of disability.[75] Entitlement to industrial disablement benefit can add very considerably to a person's total entitlement to social security benefits.[76]

We will consider disablement benefit first. Incapacity is assessed for each individual claimant under the IIS in terms of percentages of total (i.e. 100%) disablement according to guidelines laid down in the SSCBA 1992 and with the assistance of a 'tariff' for specified types of disability laid down in regulations made under the Act.[77] Degrees of disablement of less than 14% do not, in most cases, qualify for benefit.[78] Degrees between 14% and 19% are rounded up to 20%. Other degrees are rounded up or down to the nearest 10%. Disablement benefit is paid in the form of a pension, which bears the same relation to the maximum pension as does the individual claimant's degree of disability to 100% disablement.

The basic principle for assessing degree of disablement is that the assessment must be based on all disabilities 'to which the claimant may be expected, having regard to his physical and mental condition at the date of the assessment, to be subject . . . as compared with a person of the same age and sex whose physical and mental condition is normal'.[79] The assessment is almost wholly objective and ignores the personal characteristics of the claimant – the particular pleasures they may have lost, the particular hobbies they may no longer be able to pursue and so

---

75 Some existing recipients are also entitled to reduced earnings allowance (REA, formerly special hardship allowance) which was abolished for new claims in 1990.

76 The maximum rate of disablement benefit payable to a claimant over 18 is higher than the basic incapacity benefit payable to a couple. Incapacity benefit is the main income-replacement benefit payable to the disabled generally. A person disabled at work may be entitled to both disablement benefit and incapacity benefit.

77 Social Security (General Benefit) Regulations 1982, Sch. 2.

78 Lump sum gratuities for minor disablement were abolished in 1986.

79 SSCBA 1992, Sch. 6, para. 1(a).

forth. 'The assessment shall be made without reference to the particular circumstances of the claimant other than age, sex and physical and mental condition.'[80] This contrasts with the common law approach, which is partly subjective.[81] A departmental committee, which examined the principles of assessment of disablement benefit in 1965, rejected the introduction of subjective factors which (it thought) 'apart from being impossible to quantify, would clearly have no place in the determination of equitable and consistent assessments'.[82] It has been argued that too little attention is paid to the functional effect of the disablement – what actually does the disability prevent the person from doing?[83] More importantly, perhaps, disablement benefit tends to be regressive because it focuses on physical disabilities, and these typically affect the earning power of lower-paid (typically manual) workers more than they affect the earning power of higher-paid (typically non-manual) workers. For example, the loss of a leg would have no effect on the earning power of a judge, but a great effect on that of a construction worker.

The 'tariff' is not, and is not intended to be, exhaustive; nor, in fact, is it rigidly binding in any given case. It merely prescribes the percentage assessment appropriate to certain kinds of disability (such as loss of a hand or loss of sight), where no special features present themselves. Schedules of this kind are in widespread use throughout the world,[84] but they have given rise to much dissatisfaction. This is partly because they often appear arbitrary, and partly because the main difficulties in the assessment of disabilities are associated with less readily identifiable handicaps. Low back injuries, for example, are very common and notoriously difficult to assess. No schedule is likely to help much in such cases.[85] Moreover, the assessment of disabilities in percentages gives a misleading impression that it is possible to make comparisons across the whole field of disability in precise terms. Attempts have been made to work out more objective methods of measuring disabilities, by allocating points to a simple series of tests to be done by the subject.

The pension is payable for the expected period of the disability. Many disabilities are only temporary. In fact, according to the Pearson Commission, about 70% of disablement pensions last for less than 5 years, and 30% last for only 6 months.[86] Determination of the claimant's entitlement to benefit may be 'provisional' or 'final'. At the termination of the period of a provisional assessment, a new assessment (either provisional or final) will be made. Once a final assessment has been made, the pension cannot be reduced, although it can be increased if there is an unforeseen aggravation at a later date.

80 Ibid., para. 1(c).
81 6.5.3.
82 Cmnd 1847, 1965, para. 14.
83 *Wikeley, Ogus and Barendt's The Law of Social Security*, 753.
84 It has been suggested that the common law should adopt one: N.J. Mullany, 'A New Approach to Compensation for Non-Pecuniary Loss in Australia' (1990) 17 *Melbourne ULR* 714, 727–32.
85 A Report of the IIAC on Occupational Deafness gives some idea of how difficult it is in practice, even in relation to a single disability, to measure disablement in percentage terms: Cmnd 7266, 1978.
86 Pearson Report, vol. 2, table 7.

So far as the rates of disablement benefit are concerned, the more severely disabled seem, in relative terms, to be treated less well than the less severely disabled. It is dubious whether one can really say that a 100% disablement should only be worth five times the compensation awardable for a 20% disablement. Once a person is assessed as more than 70% disabled (or thereabouts) it is likely that the incapacity will have serious effects on the whole life of the disabled person, and also of their family. It may also be noted that there are very few cases of disablement at the 100% rate, so that it would cost relatively little to increase the proportion payable at the top end of the scale. In 1981 the government proposed a re-alignment under which, for example, a 30% assessment would attract a 25% pension and an 80% assessment would attract an 85% pension.[87] This proposal was not put into operation.

It is by no means easy to compare the value of disablement benefit with its common law equivalent, namely damages for non-pecuniary loss (disablement benefit is not intended to replace lost earnings and is payable even if the claimant has suffered no loss of income as a result of the injury). A meaningful comparison can only be attempted in relation to permanent disability. The fact that disablement benefit takes the form of a pension means that the total value of the benefit will depend crucially on the age of the claimant at the time of the injury, whereas at common law, the age of the claimant is likely to have a substantial effect on the amount awarded for non-pecuniary loss only in cases of extreme youth or old-age. Comparison is also rendered difficult by the fact that the concept of 'disablement' under the IIS is quite different from the concepts of 'pain and suffering' and 'loss of amenities' at common law: the latter are much more concerned than the former with the effects of particular disabilities on the injured person's capacity to lead a full life. To take a stark example, total deafness and loss of speech might attract damages of between £60,000 and £77,000 at common law[88] which represents about 30 or 35% of the largest awards for non-pecuniary loss; but 'absolute' deafness qualifies as 100% disablement under the IIS tariff. Even more extreme is the case of severe facial disfigurement, which the IIS tariff assesses at 100% but which, at common law, would attract damages of between £16,000 and £53,000 (depending partly on the sex of the claimant).[89] On the other hand, the common law is prepared to award extra damages for the psychiatric effects of injury and, to a limited extent, to take account of personal characteristics of the claimant; whereas such factors are ignored under the IIS. Probably the only worthwhile generalization is that young claimants under the IIS are likely to do much better than older claimants; and at the extremes, the young IIS claimant will probably do better than a similarly placed tort claimant, while an older IIS claimant will fare worse than their tort equivalent.

87 A.I. Ogus and N.J. Wikeley, *Ogus Barendt and Wikeley's The Law of Social Security*, 4th edn (London, 1995), 339–40.
88 Judicial Studies Board, *Guidelines for the Assessment of General Damages in Personal Injury Cases*, 7th edn (2004), 16.
89 Ibid., 59.

In addition to disablement benefit, other allowances are payable to claimants who suffer income loss. Since entitlement to disablement benefit arises 15 weeks after injury, while SSP is payable for the first 28 weeks of incapacity and short-term incapacity benefit for weeks 29–52, there is an overlap between disablement benefit and the latter two benefits. If the injuries are so serious that the claimant has been incapable of work for a period of 52 weeks,[90] they will normally be entitled to the non-industrial incapacity benefit[91] and an age-related allowance at one of two rates depending on how old the claimant was at the time of disablement (the higher rate for those incapacitated before the age of 35 and the lower rate for those incapacitated between the ages of 35 and 45). Increases for dependants are payable in some cases. An earnings-related addition to incapacity benefit, which was introduced in 1975, has been abolished for new claimants and has been frozen in cash terms for existing claimants. Where a recipient of incapacity benefit is in receipt of an occupational or private pension worth more than a certain amount a week, their incapacity benefit is (since 1999) reduced by 50 pence for every pound over the specified amount.[92] This change introduced an important element of means-testing into provision for the disabled. Incapacity benefit is not payable to people over retirement age (65).

Until 1990 the industrially disabled who were incapable of following their regular occupation or similar employment were also entitled to an income-replacement benefit called reduced earnings allowance (REA). REA, unlike incapacity benefit (and its predecessor, invalidity benefit), was payable to those who were able to work but had reduced earnings as well as to those who were incapable of work.[93] REA was abolished in 1990 on the ground that it overlapped with invalidity benefit. But this was true only in relation to recipients who were wholly incapable of work, and not in cases of partial incapacity. However, there is a benefit for people – including disabled people – who are able to work, called working tax credit (WTC), which was introduced in 2003 as an 'integrated' successor to two benefits – disabled person's tax credit (DPTC) and working families' tax credit (WFTC). DPTC was, in turn, introduced in 1999 as a successor to disability working allowance (DWA). DWA was a means-tested[94] income-support benefit designed to encourage and enable partially disabled people to return to work. For the first time with the introduction of DWA, the British social security system contained a

---

90 There are two tests of incapacity for work, namely the less stringent 'own occupation' test and the more stringent 'personal capability' test. For those who have been in remunerative work, the own occupation test applies for the first 28 weeks, and the personal capability test applies for the period from 29–52 weeks. The personal capability test applies to other claimants except those in exempt categories, who are subject to a less stringent test analogous to the own occupation test. The personal capability test is based on controversial 'objective' assessments of incapacity for work.

91 Concerning proposed changes to this benefit see 'Editorial' (2005) 12 *JSSL* 49.

92 See Bonner, 'Work for Those Who Can and Security for Those Who Cannot?', 220–1.

93 Disablement benefit is a benefit for partial (as well as total) incapacity but it is not, in theory, an income-replacement benefit.

94 At the time, this was the only benefit specifically for the disabled that was means-tested. However, as already noted, the Welfare Reform and Pensions Act 1999 introduced an abatement of incapacity benefit for those with occupational pensions or private health insurance.

general benefit for partial incapacity. When DWA was introduced, it was anticipated that about 50,000 people would claim it; but by 1999, only some 18,000 had
done so. Most claimants were in work: the benefit helped very few people to find
work.[95] DPTC was more generous than DWA and, like WFTC (and now WTC), was
administered by the Inland Revenue (now Her Majesty's Revenue and Customs).
The tax credit system is designed to reinforce the link between the receipt of benefit
and participation in the labour market.[96] Thus, a disabled person has to work for
at least 16 hours a week in order to qualify for WTC. But despite its name, WTC is
not a form of tax-break but a means-tested social security benefit.

Finally, we must mention social security benefits designed to meet the extra expenditure which people disabled at work may incur because of their disablement.[97]
Constant attendance allowance is payable in cases of 100% disablement where the
injured person requires continuous attendance;[98] and there is a further 'exceptionally
severe disablement allowance' for the worst cases in which constant attendance is permanently required.[99] These benefits are technically additions to a disablement
pension. Very few people receive these allowances.[100] People injured at work may also
be entitled to disability living allowance (DLA), which was introduced as from 1992.
DLA replaced and extended the scope of both attendance allowance[101] (which was the
non-industrial equivalent of constant attendance allowance and exceptionally severe
disablement allowance) and mobility allowance, and has two components: a care
component (which is payable at three rates) and a mobility component (which is
payable at two rates). A person's entitlement to DLA may consist of either component
or both. A person in receipt of constant attendance allowance, with or without exceptionally severe disablement allowance, would not be entitled to the care component.

As under the tort system, the recipient of social security benefits designed to
meet specific needs is under no legal obligation to use the amount received to meet
that need. On the other hand, the social security system, unlike the tort system,
caters for only two needs associated with disability, namely the need for care and the
need for mobility. These are by no means the only needs generated by disability.[102]

95 Social Security Advisory Committee, *Social Security Provision for Disability: A Case for Change?*
(TSO, 1997), 21; K. Rowlingson and R. Berthoud, 'Social Security and Disincentives to Work:
The Case of Disability Working Allowance' (1997) *Industrial LJ* 198.
96 Between 2000 and 2003 the number of people classed as unemployed fell by 15% (156,000) and
the number claiming benefits for sickness and incapacity rose by 5% (137,000).
97 For detailed analysis of the 'costs of disability' see R. Berthoud, 'Meeting the Costs of Disability'
in G. Dalley ed., *Disability and Social Policy* (London, 1991), ch. 4; M. Tibble, *Review of the
Existing Research on the Extra Costs of Disability* (DNP Working Paper 21, 2005). See also P. Large,
'Paying for the Additional Costs of Disability', ibid., ch. 5. As in the case of tort damages, recipients of social security benefits to meet extra costs of disability are not required to use the benefits for their intended purpose.
98 *Wikeley, Ogus and Barendt's The Law of Social Security*, 760–1.
99 Ibid., 761.
100 In 1994–5 (the last year for which figures are available), 1,000 people were receiving exceptionally severe disablement allowance, and 2,000 were receiving constant attendance allowance:
Social Security Statistics 1996, table F2.07.
101 Which is, however, retained for those over 65.
102 Berthoud 'Meeting the Cost of Disability' in Dalley, *Disability and Social Policy*, 92–3.

The social security equivalent of damages for gratuitous nursing and domestic services is carer's allowance, which is payable to a person over 16 who spends at least 35 hours a week caring for a disabled person who is in receipt of one of various benefits, including constant attendance allowance. Tort damages under this head are likely to be more generous in many cases than the equivalent social security benefits; tort damages represent the 'reasonable value' of the services actually provided, whereas carer's allowance is a low fixed amount which takes account neither of the nature nor the market value of the care provided nor of the earning power of the carer.[103] It is assumed that the carer will be a close relative or a friend who is prepared to forego substantial paid employment.

Just as under the tort system there are rules designed to prevent 'overlap' between different heads of damages,[104] so too under the social security system there are regulations designed to ensure that claimants do not receive more than one benefit in respect of one and the same need.[105] For example, someone who is looking after a disabled person could not claim both carer's allowance and jobseeker's allowance, since both are income-replacement benefits. As in the case of tort compensation, the proceeds of private insurance are not set off against social security benefits. On the other hand (as we noted earlier) there is a partial set-off of the proceeds of occupational and private pension benefits against entitlement to incapacity benefit.

For several reasons, it is very difficult in general terms to compare the value of all these social security benefits for pecuniary and non-pecuniary loss with tort damages. First, tort damages are fully earnings-related whereas those long-term social security benefits for the disabled that are intended to replace lost earnings are not. This means that high earners are, in principle, likely to do better out of tort damages than under the IIS. Secondly, most social security benefits are periodical and index-linked whereas at common law, only structured settlements and periodical payments have these characteristics. Thirdly, whereas tort damages for loss of earnings are only payable up to the end of the claimant's expected working life, long-term income-replacement social security benefits for the disabled are payable so long as the person remains disabled. Fourthly, the impact of taxation complicates the comparison. Lump-sum tort damage awards are not taxable, but income from the investment of such an award is subject to tax unless it has been put into a structured settlement. Some social security benefits (such as SSP and incapacity benefit) are taxable, while others (such as disablement benefit[106]) are not. Fifthly, the amount received by tort claimants in cases settled out of court may well be significantly less than would be required by a strict application of the rules governing assessment of tort damages; whereas social security claimants can normally expect to receive their

103 The recipient is allowed to earn a small amount per week. By contrast, constant attendance allowance and the care component of DLA are payable without reference to the earning capacity of the carer.

104 E.g. Administration of Justice Act 1982, s. 5.

105 *Wikeley, Ogus and Barendt's The Law of Social Security*, 259–65.

106 Including constant attendance allowance and exceptionally severe disablement allowance.

full legal entitlement. Despite the difficulties, however, the comparison is an important one because of the operation of the provisions, for recovery of social security benefits, examined later (15.4.5). There is little point in bringing a tort claim unless the damages are likely to exceed by a significant amount the total sum of the social security benefits that will be deducted from the award – although this is only a relevant consideration in cases where the only compensation awarded is for past loss.

13.4.3.3   Benefits for bereavement

Until 1986, the widow of a person who had died as a result of injury sustained at work was entitled to benefits under the IIS different from (and originally substantially greater than) those payable to 'non-industrial' widows. This aspect of the 'industrial preference' in the social security system became unpopular, and the differential between industrial and non-industrial widows' benefits was gradually eroded. The Pearson Commission recommended that industrial death benefits should be abolished on the ground that financial provision for dependants should not vary according to the cause of death.[107] This was done in 1986.

Until 1999, death benefits were payable only to a woman who was married to a man at the time of his death. Now, a bereavement payment of £2,000 is available[108] both to widows and widowers and, since 2004, to bereaved 'civil partners' – i.e. partners in a formal same-sex relationship, called a civil partnership. This is not an income-replacement benefit but can be seen either as compensation for bereavement as such (i.e. for non-pecuniary loss) or as providing financial assistance to meet special needs arising from the death.[109] For qualified persons with dependent children the relevant benefit is widowed parent's allowance (WPA),[110] which is payable from the date of the spouse or civil partner's death. WPA is based on the assumption that the parent will not be working; but, inconsistently with this, there is no limit to the amount the recipient can earn while receiving it. WPA consists of a basic pension and an additional amount for each dependent child. If there are no dependent children, a bereaved spouse or civil partner will receive a bereavement allowance (BA), but only if they were over 45 at the date of the spouse or partner's death or upon ceasing to be entitled to WPA. The full rate of BA is payable only to qualified persons aged 55 or over at that date. Refusal to pay bereavement benefits regardless of age and need goes back to Beveridge himself. He took the view that a young childless widow[111] should not expect to be maintained by the State. 'If she is able to work, she should work.'[112] This principle was reinforced in 1999 by introduction of the rule that BA is available for only 52 weeks. After that, bereaved spouses and civil partners are expected to become self-supporting or to transfer to another benefit.

107 Pearson Report, vol. 1, paras. 835–44.
108 Subject to an easily satisfied contribution condition.
109 *Wikeley, Ogus and Barendt's The Law of Social Security*, 575.
110 For the contribution conditions for WPA and for BA see *Wikeley, Ogus and Barendt's The Law of Social Security*, 576–7.
111 Until 1999, bereavement benefits were payable only to widows.
112 Beveridge Report, para. 153.

In relation to bereavement, the tort system[113] is generous by comparison with the social security system. First, a widow can receive substantial damages under the Fatal Accidents Act 1976 for the loss of her husband despite the fact that she is young, childless and able-bodied.[114] Moreover, the amount awarded in respect of a widow's loss of support[115] under the tort system is not affected by the fact, or her prospects, of remarriage. By contrast, WPA and BA cease to be payable if the recipient enters a new marriage or civil partnership, and are not payable during any period of hetero-sexual or same-sex cohabitation (as the case may be).[116] Secondly, although tort benefits for dependants are not directly related to the income of the deceased, they are indirectly related in that the more the deceased earned, the more the dependants are likely to have lost in financial support. Social security benefits, by contrast, are modest and only limited earnings-related benefits are available. Thirdly, under the Fatal Accidents Act 1976[117] the value of social security benefits is not set off against tort damages.[118] So far as concerns earnings by the bereaved spouse or partner, these are ignored by the social security system; and they are not directly relevant to tort compensation either, although they may have an indirect effect on compensation if the fact that the bereaved spouse or partner was earning at the time of the death or was likely to enter paid employment meant that they were receiving or could expect to receive less by way of support from their spouse or partner.

The result of these differences in approach is that it is not easy to make mean-ingful general comparisons between the value of the social security benefits for a bereaved spouse or civil partner and damages awarded to a spouse or civil partner under the Fatal Accidents Act 1976. What can be said, however, is that both the social security system and tort law treat bereaved spouses and partners more favourably than any other class of claimant.

13.4.4   Administration[119]

A claim for an industrial injury or other social security benefit must be submitted in writing on an official application form to an office of the DWP (Jobcentre Plus). Applications are initially assessed entirely on the basis of the documents submitted.

---

113 And the Criminal Injuries Compensation Scheme.
114 An equivalently placed female cohabitee is much less likely to receive a substantial award: she will not recover damages for bereavement, her prospects of marriage will be taken into account, and the operation of s. 3(4) may work against her.
115 But the amount awarded in respect of dependent children may be affected.
116 The so-called 'cohabitation rule' is much disliked because of the intrusions into privacy which it may involve. The basis of the rule is that it would be inequitable to treat a person who marries or enters a civil partnership less favourably than a person who cohabits without doing so. Short of paying bereavement pensions without regard to remarriage/entering a new civil part-nership, there seems no other solution to this problem. The lump sum payment is not lost on remarriage/entering a new civil partnership, but it is not payable if the claimant was cohabiting at the time of the spouse's/partner's death.
117 But not under the CICS.
118 Fatal Accidents Act 1976 s. 4; Social Security (Recovery of Benefits) Regulations 1997, reg. 2(2)(a).
119 *Wikeley, Ogus and Barendt's The Law of Social Security*, chs. 5 and 6; J. Baldwin, N. Wikeley and R. Young, *Judging Social Security* (Oxford, 1992). The main statute is the Social Security

However, since 1999 applicants for certain benefits, including bereavement benefits and certain benefits for the disabled (but not industrial injury benefits) must attend a 'work-focused' interview. This is one manifestation of a more general policy of seeking to get people off welfare and into the paid workforce. In cases where the claimant's medical condition is relevant to entitlement (as in the case of benefits for sickness and incapacity), a certificate from a medical practitioner may be required.

Simplifying a little, a claimant who is dissatisfied with the initial decision on a claim has a month in which to apply for it to be reviewed. If the claimant is dissatisfied with the outcome of the review process, he or she has a further month in which to appeal to an appeal tribunal.[120] Such a tribunal may consist of one, two or three members (depending on the issue at stake), of which at least one must be legally qualified. The members of individual tribunals are chosen from a panel formally appointed by the Lord Chancellor.[121] At the apex of the social security tribunal system are the Social Security Commissioners who hear appeals on points of law from appeal tribunals.[122] There is a right of appeal (with leave) on points of law from a Social Security Commissioner to the Court of Appeal,[123] and from thence to the House of Lords. Appeals to the courts are very rare indeed.

In 2004 there were some 174,000 appeals to social security tribunals, but this represents a tiny proportion of all claims for social security benefits.[124] Moreover, in the quarter ending March 2005, of more than 41,000 tribunal hearings, only 2,310 concerned claims for industrial disablement benefit. On the other hand, more than 10,000 concerned claims for incapacity benefit and more than 18,000 claims for disability living allowance. The power to revise decisions, which was mentioned above, is designed to prevent cases entering the appeals system unnecessarily.

The social security decision-making process generally operates rather faster than the tort system. Appeals are lodged with the DWP, and may take 10 weeks to make their way to the Appeals Service.[125] In 2004–5 the average waiting time from receipt of an appeal by the Appeals Service to hearing by an appeal tribunal was about 10 weeks.[126] Of course, if a case is appealed to the Social Security Com-

---

Administration Act 1992 (SSAA) as amended by the Social Security Act 1998. For a brief overview of the 1998 Act see N. Wikeley, 'Decision Making and Appeals under the Social Security Act 1998' (1998) 5 *J. of Social Security Law* 104.

120 However, applying for a review is not a statutory precondition of exercising the right of appeal.

121 In the case of panel members who are medical practitioners, the Lord Chancellor must consult the Chief Medical Officer before appointment.

122 Micklethwait, *The National Insurance Commissioners*; D. Bonner, 'From Whence the Social Security Commissioners?' (2002) 9 *JSSL* 11. The relative importance of the Commissioners in cases of disability can be gauged by the fact that in 1999, 74% of all determinations by the Commissioners concerned disability benefits (mainly incapacity benefit). The average success rate in such appeals was about 75%: D. Bonner, T. Buck and R. Sainsbury, 'Researching the Role and Work of the Social Security and Child Support Commissioners' (2001) 8 *J. of Social Security Law* 9, 20–1.

123 The Court of Session in Scotland.

124 *Work and Pensions Statistics 2005*, Appeals 1.

125 *Report of the President of Appeals Tribunals 2004–5*, 9.

126 *Appeals Service Annual Report 2004/5*, 8.

missioners (or even further) it is bound to take longer. An appeal can be made only with the leave of an appeal tribunal or a Commissioner. In 2004–5 the average time taken by the Commissioners to decide applications for leave to appeal was about 9 weeks; and the average time taken for an appeal to the Commissioners to be resolved was around 20 weeks.[127] The Commissioners may return a claim to an appeal tribunal for re-hearing; in 2004–5 the average waiting time for re-hearing was about 8 weeks. In the extreme case, therefore, the waiting time from lodgment of an appeal with the DWP to rehearing by an appeal tribunal could be 60 weeks or more. Given that social security claimants may be in extreme financial need, such waiting times may cause considerable hardship.

Social security tribunals differ considerably from the ordinary courts.[128] There is an oral hearing only if the claimant requests one; otherwise, the appeal will be decided on the basis of written submissions. For instance, in the quarter ending March 2005 about 73% of appeals to appeal tribunals received an oral hearing.[129] The success rate of claimants in appeals heard orally was much higher (52.2%) than in cases decided on written submissions (22.5%).[130] Overall, rather more than 40% of appeals are decided in the claimant's favour.

Procedure tends to be relatively informal and the person chairing the tribunal tends to take a more active part in the proceedings than do judges in civil courts, especially when the appellant attends the hearing unrepresented. Presenting officers, who sometimes represent the DWP at tribunal hearings, do not see it as their role (nor, indeed, is it their role) to argue the Department's case in an adversarial way;[131] they tend to play a passive or reactive role. Where the appellant is represented by someone with experience of tribunal hearings, the proceedings tend to become more formal and the tribunal less active. But a majority of appellants who attend tribunal hearings are unrepresented, and by no means all representatives have relevant experience or expertise. Furthermore, legal aid is not available for representation before social security tribunals. The official view is that representation is not necessary because tribunal members, by taking an active part in the proceedings, can make up for the lack of representation. But most appellants, like most tort claimants, have had little experience of dealing with the law, and empirical evidence has shown that represented appellants are significantly more likely to be successful than unrepresented ones.[132] It is widely accepted outside government circles that appellants before social security tribunals should have access to experienced representatives.

127 The Office of the Social Security and Child Support Commissioners of Great Britain, *Annual Report 2004–5*, 13.
128 Baldwin, Wikeley and Young, *Judging Social Security*, ch. 4. Concerning plans to overhaul the system of tribunals, including social security tribunals see 'Editorial' (2004) 11 *JSSL* 179.
129 *Social Security Statistics 2005*, The Appeals Service, table 3. The figure for industrial injuries disablement benefit was 76.6% and for incapacity benefit 76.2%.
130 The corresponding figures for industrial injuries disablement benefit were 41.5% and 21.3% respectively; and for incapacity benefit 56.7% and 16.8% respectively.
131 Baldwin, Wikeley and Young, *Judging Social Security*, ch. 7.
132 H. Genn and Y. Genn, *The Effectiveness of Representation at Tribunals* (Lord Chancellor's Department, 1989); Baldwin, Wikeley and Young, *ibid.*, 109–14.

An important consideration is that much of the law of social security (including the law governing entitlement to industrial injury benefits) is very complex and not easily understood by many appellants; a significant number of appellants even have difficulty in understanding the appeal documentation,[133] let alone in presenting a coherent and relevant case at the hearing.

Hearings before social security tribunals are typically quite short; indeed, researchers found that only 36% of cases in which the appellant was not present took more than 10 minutes, compared with 86% of cases in which the appellant was present.[134] The length of the hearing is also affected by the ability of the person chairing the tribunal to control the flow of the proceedings[135] and the complexity of the issues involved. Hearings at which the appellant is unrepresented are likely to take longer than those at which a representative is present.[136] Nevertheless, it is undoubtedly true that hearings before tribunals are very much shorter than trials in the ordinary courts. This is partly because witnesses are unlikely to be called at such hearings, and because time is not spent in expounding the relevant law for the benefit of the tribunal.

The decision of the tribunal is usually communicated to the parties immediately it has been arrived at on the day of the hearing. If requested within one month, a full statement of the decision with reasons and findings of fact will be sent to the parties with notification of the right of appeal to a Commissioner. Leave to appeal to a Commissioner must be sought within one month of the notification of the decision of the appeal tribunal. If leave is granted, the respondent to the appeal is informed and has a further month in which to make written submissions. Most appeals are resolved without an oral hearing.[137] In 2004–5 the Commissioners decided 2,219 appeals.

Oral proceedings before a Commissioner are more formal than before a tribunal;[138] but as in the case of appeal tribunals, it is basically for the Commissioner to decide the procedure to be followed, subject only to the rules of natural justice. Nothing like the Rules that regulate High Court and county court procedure governs the procedure before a Commissioner.[139] The Commissioners have power to summon a person to attend as a witness to answer questions or produce documents. Strict rules of evidence do not apply, and the Commissioners have no power to award costs.[140]

There are eighteen full-time Commissioners and a Chief Commissioner (all of whom are qualified barristers or solicitors of at least 10 years' standing), and in cases of special difficulty they may sit as a tribunal of three. Legal representation by

133 Genn and Genn, *The Effectiveness of Representation at Tribunals*, 157–8.
134 Baldwin, Wikeley and Young, *Judging Social Security*, 107.
135 Ibid., 114–123.
136 Ibid., 109.
137 *Wikeley, Ogus and Barendt's The Law of Social Security*, 203.
138 See generally Micklethwait, *The National Insurance Commissioners*.
139 Contrast the CPR and the Social Security Commissioners (Procedure) Regulations 1999.
140 *Wikeley, Ogus, Barendt's The Law of Social Security*, 203.

the Department before a Commissioner or a tribunal of three Commissioners is not uncommon; and a full reasoned judgment is typically given by the Commissioner(s). Some of the decisions of the Commissioners are reported by the DWP.[141]

13.4.5   The tort system and the IIS compared

By way of summary, we can say that the IIS has a number of advantages as compared with the tort system. First, the decision-making process under the IIS is generally faster than that under the tort system, and it is designed to determine the legal entitlement of the claimant to benefit, rather than to produce a compromise figure determined as much by the bargaining strengths of the parties as by their legal entitlements and obligations. Secondly, all industrial injury benefits, except the initial lump sum for bereavement, are payable periodically. Thirdly, as under the tort system, it is for the IIS claimant to prove entitlement to payment; but the claimant is assisted in doing this by a regulation which imposes on the employer obligations to investigate and to report to the DWP on the circumstances of industrial accidents.[142] The adverse effects of the passage of time on the proof of claims are also mitigated by a provision which allows the question of whether an accident arose out of and in the course of the claimant's employment to be decided at an early stage of the claim process.[143] The procedure for determination of medical questions under the IIS also seems more satisfactory than what happens in a tort claim where the claimant will often shop around to find the doctor whose report will justify the highest possible damages award. Fourthly, the IIS system solves some of the problems of the tort system caused by the need to speculate on the future. Provisional assessments may be made which are open to review; disability assessments may be increased even after a final assessment if there is any unforeseeable aggravation; bereavement payments terminate when the recipient remarries or enters a new civil partnership, and are suspended during cohabitation.

But in some respects, the tort system is superior. The commitment of the tort system to full compensation and to earnings-related compensation makes it, in principle at least, much more generous than the social security system, which aims only to meet certain minimum needs. The tort system also deals with partial incapacity in a much more satisfactory way than the social security system. The disablement tariff under the IIS is unsatisfactory in a number of respects. The IIS embodies a preference in favour of the industrially injured which is simply indefensible.

13.5   Non-work-related disablement

People injured at work, together with those injured on the road, are very much more likely to obtain tort compensation than any other group of disabled people.

141 Ibid., 204–5.
142 Social Security (Claims and Payments) Regulations 1979, reg. 25.
143 Social Security Act 1998, s. 29.

Those injured at work are also better treated by the social security system than any other group of disabled people in terms of the benefits available. But those injured at work represent only a small proportion of the disabled.[144] Many more suffer sickness and disability as a result of non-industrial accidents or of natural causes. With the exception of road-accident victims, such people are unlikely to obtain anything from the tort system; and unless they are covered by private insurance or an occupational sickness scheme, the social security system will provide the main source of financial support for those disabled people who find it difficult or impossible to obtain well-paid work. The most disadvantaged group of the disabled are those who have never been able to work, because they are not eligible for contributory benefits and they will be unable to satisfy any contribution conditions attached to particular benefits.

As we have seen, short-term benefits for those who suffer periods of incapacity for work do not vary according to the cause of the incapacity. Long-term benefits under the IIS are more generous than those under the general social security system: no disablement benefits are payable to those whose disability is not work-related. Victims of workplace injury receive these in addition to the incapacity benefits available to disabled generally. The provisions governing basic incapacity pension and allowances are the same for all disabled workers, and there is a special qualifying route for WTC for disabled workers on low earnings. But the care benefits available to those whose disability is work-related (constant attendance allowance and exceptionally severe disablement allowance) are more generous than the care component of disability living allowance, which is available to the disabled generally. The mobility component of DLA is the same for both groups; and the provisions for carer's allowance apply to the disabled generally. Disabled people who did not qualify for incapacity benefits (because they have never been in paid employment) used to be entitled to severe disablement allowance (SDA) (plus an age-related supplement), but the basic rate of SDA was lower than that of incapacity benefit. SDA was abolished (except for existing recipients) in 1999, and there is now no non-contributory incapacity benefit for those incapacitated in later life.[145] The only income-replacement benefit to which such people have access is income support, a means-tested benefit of last resort. Since 1986, bereavement benefits have been the same regardless of the cause of death.

13.6   Preferences within state provision for the disabled

It can be seen, therefore, that the social security system embodies two important preferences: a preference in favour of those disabled as the result of an accident at

144 Expenditure on the IIS is a small fraction of total social security expenditure on sickness and disability.
145 Those incapacitated in youth may qualify for incapacity benefit despite not having satisfied the contribution conditions.

work or of a prescribed work-related disease;[146] and a preference in favour of disabled people who were in paid employment at the time they became disabled. These preferences ignore the fact that people in different groups but suffering from similar disabilities have similar needs for financial support. In the 1980s the Conservative government espoused the idea that provision for the disabled should depend on need, and so earnings-related additions to benefits for the disabled were phased out and means-testing was extended. This commitment to the need principle could have been carried much further and used as a basis for undermining these two preferences and for making even more benefits subject to a means test.

There are yet other preferences in social provision for particular groups of the disabled which have resulted from the creation by government of ad hoc compensation schemes in response to political pressure exerted by interest groups. The most notable of these is the Criminal Injuries Compensation Scheme. Others include the vaccine damage payments scheme[147] and a scheme for compensating former slate-quarry workers suffering from certain lung diseases.[148] The Family Fund (administered by the Joseph Rowntree Memorial Trust) provides financial support for severely handicapped children under the age of 15;[149] and haemophiliacs who contracted the HIV virus as a result of being transfused with infected blood products have benefited from a special compensation scheme (administered by the Macfarlane Trust).[150] Such responses to lobbying on behalf of particular groups of the disabled are hard to justify when viewed in terms of need. It is always easy to make an impassioned emotional plea for special treatment of one group for this or that reason; but all the disabled are entitled to equal sympathy and equal support from the State, and ad hoc treatment of special

---

146 For an estimate of the financial value of this preference see Jones, 'Social Security and Industrial Injury' in Harris, *Social Security Law in Context*, 468–9.

147 4.10.1.

148 The workers were entitled to industrial injury benefits, but they could not sue their former employers in tort because they had gone out of business before the symptoms of lung disease became apparent. Their claim to special treatment was considered and rejected by the Pearson Commission (Pearson Report, vol. 1, paras. 88–92) on the ground that any decision in their favour would have to be applied to anyone in a comparable position, which it thought unjustifiable. But the government of the day sought to obtain the support of the independent Welsh Nationalist Members of Parliament in a vote of confidence by offering special treatment for the quarrymen. In due course the pledge was redeemed by the passing of the Pneumoconiosis etc. (Workers' Compensation) Act 1979 providing for lump-sum payments to the quarry workers. In 1974 the government provided £100 million to assist the National Coal Board to arrive at an agreement with the trades unions for a special compensation scheme covering a number of miners suffering from pneumoconiosis: Pearson Report, vol. 1, paras. 788–91; Coal Industry Act 1975.

149 The fund was set up as a response to the Thalidomide tragedy. Another incident arising out of this tragedy is worth mentioning. When the terms of the settlement were negotiated between the parents and the Distillers Company, the parents were apparently unaware that income from the trust fund into which the money was put, when paid to the children, would be subject to income tax. When the parents discovered this they appealed to the government, which decided to waive the tax liability. Subsequently, it was found that this would produce too many anomalies, and the government therefore made a once-for-all grant to the charity in lieu of waiving the children's tax liability.

150 4.10.2.

groups can only lead to the abandonment of rationality in policy. Ad-hockery of this sort benefits only those disabled whose supporters are well organized and have loud voices.

One laudable preference within the social security system is that benefits for long-term disablement are more generous than those for short-term disablement. Entitlement to disablement benefit does not arise until 15 weeks of incapacity for work has elapsed; the rates of long-term incapacity benefit are higher than the rate of SSP and short-term incapacity benefit; and there is a 3-month waiting period for DLA. By contrast, the principle of full compensation under the tort system does not, in theory, distinguish between injured people in this way. However, in practice, the tort system tends to treat the long-term disabled less well than those with short-term injuries because if the amount claimed is small, the damages received are likely to represent a greater proportion of the total loss suffered than if the amount claimed is large. This is partly a result of the fact that small claims are disproportionately expensive for insurers to contest; also, seriously injured claimants may be under much more pressure than claimants with minor injuries to settle quickly for an inadequate sum.[151]

13.7   Income-support benefits

13.7.1   Benefits

Income-support benefits are designed to provide people with a minimum level of income necessary for subsistence. They are, therefore, means-tested (or 'income-related'). The only means-tested benefit specifically for the disabled is the variant of WTC for low-paid disabled workers.[152] The main income-support benefits are WTC and income support (IS). Broadly stated, WTC is paid to families which contain a disabled or low-paid earner, while IS is paid to individuals and families without an income from employment. Assistance with paying rent is also available on an income-related basis, but this is administered by local authorities, not by central government. IS was introduced as from 1988 to replace supplementary benefit (SB). SB performed two functions: to provide a regular weekly income calculated in the same way for all claimants, and to provide lump-sum payments to meet the special needs of individual recipients of SB. This latter function is now performed by the Social Fund (SF) which has two parts: the non-discretionary part covers maternity, funeral, cold-weather and winter fuel payments; and the discretionary part covers other special needs. Payments from the discretionary part can be in the form either of a grant or a loan, but grants are made only to meet a few specified needs. The discretionary part of the SF has an overall annual budget and each social security office has an SF budget.

---

151 10.6.
152 Tax Credits Act 2002, s. 10 and Working Tax Credit (Entitlement and Maximum Rate) Regulations 2002, reg. 4(1). This was formerly disability working allowance (DWA) and disabled person's tax credit (DPTC).

The disabled receive preferential treatment in this part of the social security system. First, additional amounts (called 'premiums') are payable to disabled recipients of IS.[153] Disability premium, severe disability premium, enhanced disability premium and disabled child premium are designed to cover extra expenses incurred by disabled people. A premium is also payable to recipients of IS who receive carer's allowance. Secondly, in calculating the income of the claimant for IS, the amount of income which is disregarded is greater in the case of disabled than of non-disabled claimants (but disablement benefit is taken into account). Thirdly, in calculating the income of claimants of both IS and WTC, amounts received, *inter alia*, by way of DLA or from the Macfarlane Trust are disregarded. Fourthly, in calculating the capital of claimants of both IS and WTC, payments from the Macfarlane Trust or from any trust fund set up to compensate for personal injury (but not from the CICS or by way of tort damages)[154] are disregarded.

In 2004 about 2.2 million people under 60 years of age were receiving IS; and 2.3 million people over 60 were receiving the equivalent benefit for older people. Of the recipients of IS, 51% were disabled. In 2004, 1.5 million people were receiving incapacity benefit, and about 342,000 were receiving disablement benefit. These figures show that disability is a major cause of poverty: the disabled are disproportionately represented amongst recipients of income-related benefits.[155] The poorest group amongst the disabled are those who become disabled during the course of their adult working life but do not qualify for National Insurance benefits because of failure to satisfy the contribution conditions and who are, therefore, at best eligible for IS.

Widespread reliance on income-related benefits, which are funded out of general taxation, has transformed the social security system since it was first established from a predominantly insurance-based system to one which effects very significant income redistribution.

---

153 *Wikeley, Ogus and Barendt's The Law of Social Security*, 297–302. In 1988 the government set up a fund (the Independent Living Fund), outside the social security system, to provide financial assistance for severely disabled people who wanted to live 'in the community' rather than in institutional care, to pay for personal or domestic care provided by a personal assistant or care agency. It was initially designed to help people who would suffer a reduction of benefit as a result of the changeover from SB to IS. The fund was wound up in December 1992 (at which time about 18,000 people were receiving an average of £105 per week from the fund), but people who were being assisted are now helped by the ILF (Extension) Fund. A new (less generous) Independent Living (1993) Fund was set up in April 1993 to deal with new cases. In 2003–4 the Independent Living Funds paid out more than £189 million in grants to more than 16,000 people, at an administrative cost of about 2.9% of total expenditure: *Independent Living Funds Annual Report 2003/4*. Extension fund grants can be up to £715 a week, and 1993 Fund grants up to £420 a week. In 2003–4 the average award under both funds was less than £250 a week.

154 Even though IS is set off against tort damages under the Social Security Act (Recovery of Benefits) Act 1997; and against compensation under the CICS.

155 N. Wikeley, 'Social Security and Disability' in N. Harris *et al.*, *Social Security Law in Context* (Oxford, 2000), 389.

13.7.2   Administration

We have already considered the system for administering the social security system in some detail. This system covers all the benefits for the non-industrially disabled as well as IS benefits, with the exception of the discretionary part of the SF. Claims for discretionary SF payments are handled in accordance with the Social Fund Manual which contains binding directions and non-binding guidance issued by the Secretary of State. There is no appeal from a discretionary SF decision to an external body but only the possibility of an internal review by an 'appropriate officer' (which is the term used in the Social Security Act 1998) and a further review by a Social Fund Inspector. The extent of the Secretary of State's control over discretionary SF decisions, coupled with the lack of external review and the fact that the SF is subject to a budget, have been the cause of much criticism.

13.8   Fraud and abuse

It may be worth concluding this chapter by discussing the effectiveness of tort law and social security in guarding against fraudulent claims for compensation and benefits.[156] Discussion about and attitudes to abuse of the social security system is often affected by political opinions about the Welfare State. Despite continuing concern about fraud and a constant stream of legislative and other measure to tackle fraud,[157] it seems that the level of fraudulent claims and fraud-induced overpayment is relatively low. In 2000 the Department of Social Security (now the DWP) estimated that across the social security system as a whole around £4 billion (or 4% of total expenditure) is lost each year through fraudulent claims and overpayments. A DWP press release of 15 June 2004 had reduced this figure to £2 billion;[158] but even so asserted that 'people think it's more important to stamp out benefit fraud than litter, graffiti or tax evasion'.[159] An investigation in 2001 by the DWP estimated that the amount of overpayment of incapacity benefit attributable to fraud was in the region of £19 million, or less than 0.5% of expenditure

---

156 The converse problem is failure to claim benefits to which a person is entitled. In relation to tort compensation, claim rates were discussed in ch. 8. Low take-up of social security benefits is mainly associated with means-tested (income-related) benefits. It is estimated that IS is claimed by between 86% and 95% of those eligible (representing 91–98% of the total entitlement in money terms), and that the total unclaimed is between £220 million and £880 million: DWP, *Income Related Benefits – Estimates of Take-up 2001/2002* (DWP, 2004). A report in 1993 said that family credit (the predecessor but one of WTC) was claimed by only 64% of people entitled to it: Policy Studies Institute, *Families, Work and Benefits* (London). When DWA was introduced in April 1992, the estimated take-up was 50,000, but by 1999 there were only about 18,000 current awards.

157 See e.g. G. McKeever, 'Tackling Benefit Fraud' (2003) 32 *Industrial LJ* 326.

158 By 2005 the estimate had fallen further to £900 million: National Audit Office, *Dealing with the Complexity of the Benefits System* (2005), para. 17.

159 One report concluded that the general public see benefit fraud as much less serious than crimes against the person or property, such as burglary, but more serious than prostitution or petty shop-lifting, and much more serious than TV licence or fare evasion: K. Rowlingson *et al.*, *Social Security Fraud: The Role of Penalties* (DSS, Research Report No. 64, 1997).

on incapacity benefit. In 2004 the DWP estimated the overpayment rate for DLA at 9.1%, but also that most of this was the result neither of fraud nor error but of changes in the circumstances of recipients, which were not reported to the Department.

In 1973, the Fisher Committee[160] identified six principal types of abuse of social security benefits: failure to disclose earnings where means-tested benefits are claimed; misrepresentations relating to incapacity for work and the cause of such incapacity;[161] voluntary unemployment; cohabitation and 'fictitious desertions'; itinerant frauds; and failure to report changes in the maintenance of dependants where dependants' allowances are being paid. Misrepresentations relating to capacity for work are an ongoing problem.[162] Medical certification by GPs plays a central gate-keeping role in the process of determining entitlement to sickness and incapacity benefits. The doctor's task may be problematic, especially in relation to symptoms and conditions that are difficult to measure objectively, such as back pain or anxiety. Research has shown that doctors vary considerably in their attitudes to and the way they perform the certification function. Factors other than the patient's medical condition – such as the relationship between doctor and patient, and the patient's domestic circumstances – may influence the doctor's decision whether or not to provide a certificate and for what period.[163] Medical examinations for incapacity benefit are held at DWP offices. Failure to attend for medical examination is certainly not unknown, and the effort required to attend may inhibit at least some baseless claims. On the other hand, there is reason to believe that some people find the medical examinations, required for entitlement to care benefits (in particular), humiliating and intrusive; and for this reason they may not apply for the relevant benefit, or having done so may not attend the medical examination.[164]

In addition to the sort of relatively small-scale fraud by individuals identified by the Fisher Committee, there is also a certain amount of large-scale 'organized' social security fraud, involving the theft and counterfeiting of and trafficking in identity documents and benefit books. This sort of fraud affects sectors such as jobseeker's allowance and housing benefit in particular, but appears not to be prevalent in the disability area.

The Criminal Injuries Compensation Board once said that it identified only a small number of fraudulent applications.[165] So far as the tort system is concerned, there is really no data on the question of abuse,[166] though some generalizations can

---

160 *The Abuse of Social Security Benefits* (Cmnd 5228, 1973) (Fisher Committee Report), para. 129.
161 So e.g. a person may fraudulently claim to have been injured at work in order to qualify for benefits available only to the industrially disabled.
162 Fisher Committee Report, paras. 185–90.
163 J. Hiscock and J. Ritchie, *The Role of GPs in Sickness Certification* (DWP, 2001).
164 Berthoud, 'Meeting the Cost of Disability' in Dalley, *Disability and Social Policy*, 87–8, 90, 92.
165 CICB *Thirty-Third Report* (Cm 3921, 1998), para. 8.1.
166 It was estimated that an undercover anti-fraud unit within the London Fire Service (which was disbanded in 1990) had saved the Fire Service £2.2 million in 3 years by uncovering 'bogus and inflated injury compensation claims': *The Times,* 22 October 1990. But many of these claims may have been for sick pay.

probably be safely made. The tort system shares with the social security system the problem of assessing the validity of claims of unfitness for work when the alleged symptoms are not easily verifiable. In most serious cases, the adversary procedures of the tort system probably operate as a very effective control over fraud and abuse. When every claim is scrutinized with a jaundiced eye by the insurer who is going to pay the claim or by a court, it is reasonable to suppose that few serious cases of abuse escape undetected. On the other hand, this is not true of minor claims. As we have already seen, because of the disproportionate cost of contesting minor claims, insurers often agree to pay without serious examination of the claimant's case. On the other hand, it is possible for anti-abuse measures to be too vigorous. Because of the claimant's need to prove fault on the part of the defendant in a tort case, some fraudulent claims may be prevented; but a great many more perfectly genuine claims fail too. Furthermore, the dynamics of the settlement process probably result in a certain proportion of deserving claimants never receiving compensation. On the other hand, there are some respects in which tort law may be liable to encourage the malingerer. In particular, the fact that loss of earnings can be recovered in full in claims for damages is thought by many to be a serious disincentive to a prompt return to work by a person who may think that he or she has a good claim. This is one reason why social security systems normally do not provide full replacement of lost earnings. The willingness of the tort system to compensate for mental distress and pain and suffering also lays it open to claims which may, at least, be difficult to verify.

Whatever the fact of the matter, recent research suggests a widespread belief that fraudulent tort claims are more common than fraudulent social security claims.[167]

---

167 DCA, *Effects of Advertising in Respect of Compensation Claims for Personal Injuries* (March 2006), para. 1.2.4.

14

Other forms of assistance

So far we have considered the main sources of what might loosely be called 'compensation' for personal injury, and physical and mental disability; or, in other words, monetary payments designed to give financial support to the injured and sick on account of their disabilities. There are some other forms of assistance, not in the form of money payments, which also deserve to be considered briefly.

To provide some context for the discussion, we can note a recent estimate that there are 11 million disabled people[1] aged 16 or over in Britain. Of these, 45% (compared with 15% of non-disabled people) are over State pension age (SPA). The majority of disabled people over SPA become disabled later in life. Amongst disabled people under 45, around 20% were disabled from birth and another 20% from childhood. Disabled people tend to be less qualified than non-disabled, and are more likely to be in skilled or unskilled, as opposed to professional, jobs. Overall, 44% of disabled people (as opposed to 79% of non-disabled people) are economically active. About a quarter of disabled people surveyed said they could work and expect to do so in the future. Only 13% of disabled working people have special working arrangements because of their disability.[2]

14.1 The taxation system

The tax system as a whole is, of course, designed to raise revenue. But, by exempting some people from tax liability to which they would otherwise be liable, financial assistance of a negative sort can be provided to victims of accidents, disease and disability. So far as social security benefits are concerned, SSP and carer's allowance are taxable, as is incapacity benefit (except for the first 28 weeks). Industrial

---

1 According to the definition of disability in the Disability Discrimination Act 1995.
2 I. Grewel *et al.*, *Disabled for Life? Attitudes Towards, and Experiences of Disability in Britain* (DSS Research Report No. 72, 2002). According to another survey, two-fifths of disabled adults aged under 50 were in work, but fewer than a quarter aged between 50 and retiring age were in work: E. Grundy *et al.*, *Disability in Great Britain: Results form the 1996/7 Disability Follow-Up to the Family Resources Survey* (DSS Research Report No. 94, 1999). It was also found that the percentage of disabled people permanently unable to work had increased greatly since 1985 consistently with 'a deterioration in the labour market prospects of disabled workers and with increasing availability and attractiveness of disability payments'; and that very few disabled people were engaged in full-time education or training schemes: ibid., 78.

disablement benefit is not taxed; nor, for instance, is income support, severe disablement allowance, disability living allowance or attendance allowance. The policy of paying benefits (other than income-related benefits) free of tax is arguably undesirable because it benefits the better-off (who pay higher taxes) disproportionately. So far as tort damages are concerned, lump-sum awards are not taxable, but income from the investment of a lump sum is subject to tax unless it is derived from a structured settlement. The (non-) taxability of tort compensation is taken into account in calculating the amount of the compensation.

The link between the tax and social security systems is being strengthened. In 2000, the collection of National Insurance contributions was transferred from the Contributions Agency (a part of what is now the DWP) to the Inland Revenue (now Her Majesty's Customs and Revenue, HMCR); and in 1999, disability working allowance was replaced by disabled persons tax credit (now working tax credit), and family credit was replaced by working families tax credit (now working tax credit). Both credits are administered by HMCR; although they are effectively social security benefits rather than tax concessions – i.e. they are payments by the State rather than reliefs from liability to make payments to the State. These changes are part of a larger 'welfare to work' policy designed to maximize the participation of the disabled in the labour market.

There are a number of (true) tax reliefs for the disabled. For example, a registered blind person receives an allowance to set against taxable income, as does a person who maintains a disabled relative.[3] Disabled people are also eligible for some relief from liability to pay tax in respect of a car provided by an employer and in respect of travel expenses met by an employer. A disabled person's vehicle maintenance grant is not taxable.[4] Tax concessions are hard to defend as part of a rational system of compensating the disabled and sick. For one thing, they tend to be available only to selected groups of the disabled. The blind are particularly favoured. Secondly, income tax reliefs benefit only the better-off – they do not help those whose earnings are too low to attract significant tax liability. Another objection to tax concessions is that they make no allowance for the fact that other compensation methods may exist. A person disabled in circumstances in which a tort claim lies may get substantial compensation but will still be entitled to tax concessions.

There are also a large number of other reliefs available to the disabled, such as free dog licences (for the blind), public transport concessions, free medicines, free dental and optical treatment, free milk for disabled children and so on.

Taxation, or rather the absence of it, is also indirectly relevant to compensation for injuries in that the income of many charities deriving their funds from subscriptions, donations and legacies is exempt from income tax. In one sense, this form of tax relief makes little difference to the ultimate burden which falls on the

3 Income and Corporation Taxes Act 1988, ss. 265 and 263 respectively.
4 Income and Corporation Taxes Act 1988, s. 327.

public, since if charities were taxed and were therefore able to do less themselves to help the disabled, the sick and the injured, a correspondingly heavier burden would fall on the taxpayer. Thus, what the taxpayer surrenders in the form of tax reliefs may be saved in social welfare expenditure. But it does mean that rather more is devoted to relief and assistance of a kind which might not be possible under the Welfare State; and it also means that the large amount of voluntary work which is done is not completely starved of funds. To the extent that tax reliefs encourage voluntary work which might otherwise not be forthcoming, the taxpayer gets a good deal by granting these reliefs. But since some groups of the disabled attract more charity than others, the question does arise whether it is equitable to enlarge this differential by tax reliefs. On the one hand, it could be said that the differential should be narrowed, and that if charities had to pay tax, the tax paid by the wealthier charities could then be partly devoted to the relief of less popular charitable causes. On the other hand, it might be argued that this would be essentially an undemocratic procedure, since it would mean overriding the deliberate choice of members of the public to favour, by their free donations and subscriptions, some charities over others.

14.2   Social services

Britain has an elaborate system of social welfare services[5] in connection with employment, education, housing, health and so on. Most of these services are provided by local authorities in pursuance of statutory powers and duties under Part III of the National Assistance Act 1948, the Local Authority Social Services Act 1970, the Chronically Sick and Disabled Persons Act 1970 and the Housing (Homeless Persons) Act 1977. Few involve the payment of cash benefits. In 2002–3, local authorities spent a total of £15.2 billion on personal social services, of which about 27% was spent on people with disabilities and mental health needs. It is sometimes said that benefits in kind are preferable to cash payments because they cannot be wasted. On the other hand, such a belief might be thought to smack of paternalism and class prejudice, and to deny freedom of choice to those in need of welfare benefits and services. Whether it is better to provide services for disabled people or to give them money with which to purchase services (whether from public or private providers) is partly a question of political ideology, but also partly a question about how goals of assisting the disabled can be most efficiently achieved. At all events, no comprehensive inquiry into provision for the disabled can ignore social services because they perform some of the same functions as monetary compensation.[6]

The social service which is, perhaps, of most obvious importance to the sick and disabled is the National Health Service. Despite a growth in the private sector of

5 OPCS Disability Survey, Reports 4 and 6.
6 Beveridge Report, Appendix 13, para. 15.

health care in recent years, it is only of marginal importance, especially to the chronically sick or disabled, who still look predominantly to NHS general practitioners and hospitals for medical services. The Harris 1984 Survey found that road accident victims were more likely to require hospitalization than work accident victims, while the latter are more likely to use outpatient and general practitioner services; but accident victims are much less likely to use any of these services than the ill.[7] The NHS is also a major provider of residential care for disabled people. But there are other social services of considerable importance to the disabled.

14.2.1   Employment

Compensation for lost income is obviously vital for many sick and disabled people. But for those with long-term disabilities, cash benefits for lost income may be very much a second best. Both from a personal and an economic point of view, it is at least as important to focus on what a person can do and to assist them to enter or re-enter the ordinary workforce.[8] If this is not possible, an alternative may lie in providing the disabled with employment in special ('sheltered') conditions, which take account of their disabilities. These objectives may be met to some extent by payments of money to disabled people, but facilities provided by the State or by private charities can also play an important part. Provision was first made to assist in the rehabilitation and employment of the disabled during the First World War, and these services, which were increased during the Second World War, continue as a component of social service provision.

Payment of social security benefits on account of disability rests on a 'medical model' of disability in which people are seen as disadvantaged by their impairment. In the late 1980s and the early 1990s the number of people receiving long-term incapacity benefits increased enormously. One official reaction to this development was to make such benefits less attractive by tightening eligibility criteria and reducing the amounts payable. The underlying assumption was that a certain proportion of claimants were in some sense 'choosing' incapacity in preference to economic activity in the workforce. Many people saw this assumption as one of the darker aspects of a broad policy of 'welfare to work', which came to prominence at this time. Another response, launched by the New Labour government in late 1990s, was the so-called 'New Deal for Disabled People' (NDDP). This initiative can be understood in terms of a 'social model' of disability in which the problem to be overcome is society's failure to accommodate the disabled so that they can function as full members of society.[9] According to the official website, the New Deal for Disabled People is 'a voluntary programme delivered through a network of Job Brokers who have been chosen by Jobcentre Plus because of their

7 Harris 1984 Survey, 240–3.
8 M. Floyd, 'Overcoming barriers to employment' in G. Dalley ed., *Disability and Social Policy* (London, 1991), ch. 11.
9 Social Security Advisory Committee, *Social Security Provision for Disability: A Case for Change?* (TSO, 1997), 6.

experience working with people with health conditions or disabilities'. The basic aim of the NDDP is to assist disabled people to find jobs and to provide some support once work is found. According to DWP figures, as at March 2005, 174,390 people had taken part in the New Deal programme, and some 76,000 had found jobs. A recent assessment of the NDDP concluded that: 'Job Broker interventions [have] clearly had a significant impact at the level of individual customers, particularly in terms of . . . confidence and access to post-recruitment support . . . Some of the appointments would not have been made without the support of the Job Broker.'[10]

Besides NDDP, Jobcentre Plus runs various programmes to assist disabled people into work. These include the provision of Disability Employment Advisers and Access to Work Advisers; employment assessment interviews, work preparation courses and a job introduction scheme, which provides short-term financial subsidies to employers who take on disabled workers. The background to all this activity is the problematic relationship between disability and employability. Successive governments have been keen to reduce the numbers of people claiming long-term incapacity benefits and to move them on to less attractive unemployment benefits (jobseeker's allowance) or income-related benefits. Because incapacity is partly a social as well as a medical concept, whether people are disabled depends partly on how they are viewed by themselves and others. There is a cohort of people, described in the literature as 'movers',[11] who rotate around part-time or full-time work, jobseeker's allowance and incapacity benefits even in the absence of substantial change in their medical condition. The best question to ask in relation to such people is not whether they qualify for incapacity benefits at any particular point of time, but rather how they can best be helped to maximize the quality of their lives.

For many years there was a register of disabled persons[12] maintained for employment purposes under the Disabled Persons (Employment) Act 1944. However, because a high proportion of people who were entitled to register did not do so,[13] it was very difficult to ascertain the rate of unemployment[14] amongst disabled people. Most estimates are that it is at least twice the rate of unemployment in the

10 J. Aston et al., Employers and the New Deal for Disabled People: Qualitative Research, Wave 2 (DWP Research Report 231, 2005), 3.
11 A. Hedges and W. Sykes, Moving Between Sickness and Work (DWP Research Report 151, 2001); K. Ashworth et al., Well Enough to Work? (DWP Research Report 145, 2001).`
12 The term 'disabled' was not precisely defined in this context; to register, people had to show that they had a substantial handicap (resulting from impairment) in obtaining or keeping employment which was likely to last at least 12 months.
13 The OPCS Disability Survey found that only 20% of men and 8% of women under pension age were registered; this represents about 300,000 people. Department of Employment statistics for 1992 put the figure near 370,000. The OPCS Disability Survey also found that registration rates increased with severity of disability. A survey in 1971 found that only 16% of those registered under the 1944 Act thought that being registered had helped them to find employment: Handicapped and Impaired in Great Britain (HMSO, 1971), Part II, para. 8.5.
14 I.e. of those willing and able to work. There is still no evidence on the point: Social Security Advisory Committee, Social Security Provision for Disability, 22.

population as a whole. The 1944 Act imposed an obligation on an employer[15] of more than twenty people to recruit at least 3% of its labour force from persons on the disabled persons' register; but permits dispensing from the obligation to employ a disabled worker were readily available (although some employers did not bother to obtain such permits even though this put them in breach of the scheme). There were only ten prosecutions for failure to meet the quota during the time the system operated. In 1981 the Manpower Services Commission estimated that disabled people represented only 1.5% of the workforce,[16] and it is thought that subsequently, this figure fell to below 1% in both the public and the private sector. In 1987 a report by the National Audit Office called the quota scheme 'ineffective, unenforceable and incapable of achieving its aim'.[17] The proportion of employers meeting the quota dropped from 53% in 1965 to 27% in 1986.[18]

The register and the quota scheme were abolished by the Disability Discrimination Act 1995. Under the Act, a disabled person is one who 'has a physical or mental impairment which has a substantial and long-term adverse effect on his ability to carry out normal day-to-day activities' (s. 1(1)). The Act makes it unlawful to discriminate against disabled people in matters of recruitment and terms of employment. Discrimination consists in treating a disabled person less favourably than the able-bodied without justification, or failing (without justification) to 'make reasonable adjustments' to arrangements or physical features of premises which place a disabled person at a substantial disadvantage in comparison with the able-bodied. Justification consists of a relevant and substantial reason for the discrimination. Victims of discrimination can complain to an industrial tribunal, which has power to award compensation for pecuniary and non-pecuniary loss resulting from unlawful discrimination. The Act also makes it unlawful to discriminate against the disabled in the provision of certain goods and services, including (since 2002) education.

Potentially, at least, the Act considerably improved the lot of the disabled in the labour market. However, it had several important shortcomings. First, like the quota scheme before it, the Act did not apply to employers with fewer than twenty employees.[19] Secondly, it seemed that it would be easier to justify discrimination against the disabled than it was to justify discrimination on grounds of race under the Race Relations Act 1976 or on grounds of sex under the Sex Discrimina-

---

15 Except government departments, other government bodies and the NHS; but public sector employers voluntarily accepted the quota target. See generally *The Employment of People with Disabilities* (Employment Department Research Paper No. 77, 1990).
16 *Review of the Quota System for the Employment of Disabled People* (MSC, 1981), 6–7.
17 *Employment and Assistance to Disabled People* (HC 367).
18 This was partly a result of the fact that compliance was assessed in terms of registered disabled people, and the number of people registered in the 1980s was less than half what it was in 1956.
19 It was estimated that about 85% of employers fell into this category, but that in total they employed only about 22% of the workforce: J. Bryant, 'Disability Discrimination Act 1995 – An Estimate of the Number of Employers and Employees Affected' [1997] *JPIL* 251. In 1998 the exemption threshold was reduced from twenty to fifteen.

tion Act 1975.[20] Thirdly, whereas there is an enforcement agency to deal with sex discrimination (the Equal Opportunities Commission) and race discrimination (the Commission for Racial Equality), the 1995 Act did not establish such a body to investigate allegations of systemic discrimination against the disabled or to assist disabled people to bring discrimination claims. The last defect was remedied by the establishment in 2000 of the Disability Rights Commission, which operates along the same lines as the other anti-discrimination Commissions. As for the first shortcoming, from 2004 the operation of the Act has been extended to cover all employers.

The 1944 Act enabled the Minister to designate certain types of employment as specially suitable for the disabled, and it was illegal for an employer to employ a non-disabled person in such a capacity unless no disabled person was available. Only two types of job were ever designated under the Act, namely lift attendant and car park attendant. The power to reserve jobs for the disabled was abolished by the 1995 Act. On the other hand, provisions of the 1944 Act under which assistance is available to persons who are so severely handicapped that they could not find employment in open competition in the labour market have been retained. The government makes grants to local authority and private undertakings which provide employment in sheltered factories and workshops. By far the largest provider of sheltered employment is Remploy Ltd, which is a non-profit-making, publicly owned company employing some 5,700 disabled people in eighty-three business locations. In 2004, it helped 3,500 disabled people find jobs with other employers. It also supports about 2,800 people through the WORKSTEP programme (of which it is the largest provider), which is designed to make it easier for more seriously disabled people to get mainstream employment by providing support and advice to both the employer and the employee. Remploy is funded partly by its commercial activities and partly by a government grant (£111 million in 2005–6). Workers in sheltered employment are paid at union-agreed rates of about 70% of the rate in the open market, reflecting the lower productivity of disabled people.

The importance of these employment opportunities for disabled people must not be exaggerated. Although estimates vary, on its website Remploy says that 2.5 million disabled people are 'out of work'. The proportion of disabled people with no work qualifications is significantly higher than the proportion of unqualified but non-disabled people. Disabled people are twice as likely to be unemployed as non-disabled people. It remains to be seen whether the Disability Discrimination Act 1995 will change this situation significantly.

14.2.2 Mobility

Besides mobility-related social security benefits, there is an independent non-profit organisation, called Motability, which provides subsidised hiring and hire-purchase

---

20 On this point see K. Monaghan, *Blackstone's Guide to the Disability Discrimination Act* (Oxford, 2005), 21–4.

facilities on cars, scooters and electric wheelchairs to disabled people in receipt of mobility allowance. Lack of mobility is a problem that cannot be entirely overcome by aid to the disabled themselves. Buildings and public transport need to be designed so as to facilitate movement and access by the disabled. Public expenditure to improve mobility for disabled people generally is surely a higher priority than, for example, disablement benefits for the industrially injured.

Important progress was made in this respect by the Disability Discrimination Act 1995. Failure to provide suitable access to premises for disabled people can amount to unlawful discrimination under the Act, of which complaint can be made to an Industrial Tribunal (in employment cases) or to a county court (in non-employment cases). Part V of the Act gave the Secretary of State power to make regulations prescribing minimum access requirements for taxis, public service vehicles and rail vehicles. Failure to comply with such regulations constitutes a criminal offence but (unlike unlawful discrimination in employment or the provision of goods and services) is not actionable at the suit of individuals. The Disability Discrimination Act 2005 contains new measures relevant to mobility. The 1995 Act did not apply to transport services. This exemption has been narrowed so that it now applies only to transport vehicles themselves; and there are new provisions dealing with accessibility of rail vehicles.

14.2.3   Housing and residential accommodation

The provisions of the Disability Discrimination Act 1995 dealing with the provision of goods and services will apply in certain cases to housing and residential accommodation. Local authorities have power under the National Assistance Act 1948 to make grants to disabled persons to cover the cost of conversions or adaptations to a house, necessitated by the disability; and s. 2 of the Chronically Sick and Disabled Persons Act 1970 requires them to make such grants where they are satisfied that they are necessary. A survey conducted in the late 1960s found that half of those severely disabled had benefited from this facility, but that there was still scope for a 'massive expansion of activity here'.[21] The OPCS Disability Survey found that 24% of all disabled adults had a home adaptation of some sort; that 41% of these people had paid for the adaptations entirely out of their own resources and that 41% had had them provided by the health or social services, a housing department or a voluntary organization. It also found that 35% of those with locomotor disabilities and 42% of those with personal care disabilities thought they might be helped by an adaptation they did not have.[22] Another survey in the early 1970s found evidence that about half of severely handicapped people needed to be re-housed because of inaccessibility of toilets or because they were unable to get upstairs and had to sleep in their sitting-rooms.[23]

---

21 P. Townsend, *The Disabled in Society* (London, 1967), 10.
22 Report 4, Martin, White and Meltzer, *Disabled Adults*, 59.
23 *Handicapped and Impaired in Great Britain* (HMSO, 1971), Part II, table 117.

Local authorities also have a duty to provide residential accommodation for persons who by reason of age or infirmity or other circumstances are in need of care and attention not otherwise available, as well as urgently needed temporary accommodation arising from unforeseeable circumstances.[24] The provision of such accommodation accounts for one-third of the total expenditure of local authorities on personal social services, and half of the expenditure on residential care is for elderly people.[25] The OPCS Disability Survey found that of all disabled residents of communal establishments, 80% were aged 65 or over, and 67% were aged 75 or over. In 1986 there were over 14,700 younger disabled persons being looked after in such institutions.[26] About 12% of residential accommodation is run by voluntary organizations with the assistance of grants from local authorities; and about 22% of such accommodation (much of it for the old) is provided by the private commercial sector. The rest is run by local authorities and the NHS.

During the 1980s the Conservative government adopted a policy of encouraging people to leave institutions and to live in the community,[27] and of shifting expenditure from the provision of residential care to helping people to live outside institutions. One manifestation of this policy is the availability from the Social Fund of community care grants.[28]

14.2.4   Other social services

There are many other social services which lie on the extreme fringe of the subject matter of this book, and which it is impossible to discuss fully here. Some mention should be made of the more important of these because their very existence is a continual reminder of the need to strike a balance between cash benefits and services. For example, home-helps are provided by local authorities (often at a charge) mostly for the benefit of the elderly and the chronically sick, but also for the disabled and handicapped.[29] Day-centres (mostly run by local authorities) provide some social, recreational and also health and educational facilities for the old and the disabled.[30] Some also provide employment services.[31] Teachers visit blind

24 National Assistance Act 1948, ss. 21–8, as amended by Health Services and Public Health Act 1968 and National Health Service and Community Care Act 1990 Part III. See H. Qureshi, 'Social Care Services for Disabled People' in Dalley, *Disability and Social Policy*, 125–37.
25 Qureshi, 'Social Care Services for Disabled People', 122.
26 Ibid., 131–2.
27 The meaning of the term 'live in the community' is complex: Ibid., 133.
28 *Wikely, Ogus and Barendt's The Law of Social Security*, 608–13.
29 The 1989 OPCS disability survey found that 30% of people over 75 and 8% of people aged 16–49 who were in the two categories of most severe disablement received the services of a home-help. But most home care for disabled people is provided by family, friends or neighbours: Department of Health White Paper on Community Care *Caring for People* (1989), para. 2.3. See generally S. Baldwin and G. Parker, 'Support for Informal Carers – the Role of Social Security' in Dalley, *Disability and Social Policy*, ch. 8.
30 In 1989 there were 8,471 day-centre places for younger disabled people (16.6% fewer than in 1979) but more than 24,000 for old people and more than 54,000 for the mentally handicapped: Qureshi in Dalley, *Dsiability and Social Services Policy*, 137–40.
31 S. Beyer *et al.*, *Working Lives: The Role of Day Centres in Supporting People with Learning Disabilities into Employment* (DWP Research Report 203, 2004).

people in their homes and teach them to read Braille. There are provisions for a home-laundry service in some areas,[32] and for the 'meals on wheels' services, primarily for the old but also for the disabled. There are special schools for the physically and mentally disabled, although current thinking favours integrating such children into normal schools.[33] All of these personal social services are important in improving the quality of life of the disabled.[34]

Not-for-profit organizations play an important part in providing, or supplementing public provision of, personal social services to the disabled. For example, special holiday houses for the disabled are almost all provided by voluntary agencies. In recent years, the role of voluntary organizations has become more and more important as a result of government pressure on local authorities to reduce spending, and also because of an ideological belief in encouraging the voluntary sector, and that social welfare provision should be a matter for partnership between the public and private sectors.[35] There are statutory provisions under which grants can be made by local authorities and health authorities to voluntary agencies for the provision of relevant services. Local authorities can also make cash payments directly to disabled people in need of services, leaving the person to procure and pay for the services. Research suggests that this is cost-effective and popular with the disabled. But in the view of the Social Security Advisory Committee, it is unclear how widely such arrangements could be fairly and effectively applied to the disabled.[36]

14.3   Conclusion

The most important point to emerge from this very brief consideration of social services available to the disabled (amongst others) is that cash compensation and benefits are not the only way of helping the disabled to cope with their disabilities and live decent and fulfilling lives. The provision of facilities for rehabilitation and for enabling disabled people to engage in remunerative work is of very great importance, especially for those with long-term disabilities; and such facilities are unlikely to be provided by the private sector, at least without public encouragement

---

32 The Harris 1984 Survey found that 'for every local authority and community health service used, illness victims as a group made nearly three times as much use of these services as did accident victims': 243–4.

33 86% of disabled children attend mainstream schools, mostly without special provision for disabled students. A recent survey found that the majority of these has positive educational experiences. Non-disabled people are twice as likely as disabled people to engage in higher education: Grewel et al., Disabled for Life?.

34 See Handicapped and Impaired in Great Britain (HMSO, 1971), Part I, tables 38, 39 and 40.

35 See generally M. Brenton, The Voluntary Sector in the British Social Services (London, 1985); also D. Morris, 'Charities in the Contract Culture: Survival of the Largest?' (2000) 20 LS 409. One source of funding for such bodies is the National Lottery. For instance, more than £2 million was awarded by the Millennium Commission in 1998 for projects to help disabled people. The National Lottery Charities Board also makes grants to voluntary organizations for the disabled.

36 SSAC, Social Security Provision for Disability, 29–30.

and financial support. But monetary compensation is the only help which the tort system provides. It should not be assumed that compensating injured people for all their losses and providing individuals with enough money to meet all the needs arising from their injuries is socially the best course of action. It may be that some needs are better met and some losses (such as non-pecuniary losses) better dealt with by the provision of services to which all disabled people, whatever the cause of their disabilities, have access.

Finally, it should not be forgotten that one of the most important sources of assistance for all disabled people are family, friends and neighbours.[37] Some of these may receive carer's allowance, but many receive no payment at all.[38]

37 According to Grundy, *Disability in Great Britain*, 'nearly two-fifths of people needing some regular care relied on their partners for at least one task (one sixth of all with disability) and a similar percentage relied on informal care within the household': 112.
38 Harris 1984 Survey, 244–8; *How Much is Enough?*, 160.

Part 5

The overall picture

15

A plethora of systems

15.1   The concept of over-compensation

The question we must now ask is how the various systems for providing compensation and monetary benefits to disabled people fit together. Where a person is entitled to payments from two different sources (or 'compensation systems'),[1] three principal alternatives present themselves. First, the person may be allowed to receive and keep money from both systems so that in the result they receive more than either system alone allows. This is sometimes called 'cumulation'.[2] Secondly, the person may be allowed to receive compensation from one source only, and in this case it will be necessary to decide which that source will be. Thirdly, the person may be entitled to receive a particular amount (perhaps the larger of the two amounts on offer) partly from one source and partly from the other.

Where a person receives money payments from more than one source, they may receive more than is necessary to achieve the purpose that either of the payments is designed to serve. For example, if both payments are designed to replace lost income, a person who receives a payment from both sources may receive more in compensation than has been lost in earnings. Such over-compensation, as we might call it, appears, *prima facie*, to be a wasteful use of resources. Although there are some circumstances – discussed below – in which over-compensation may appear unobjectionable, it seems a reasonable starting point to assume that money spent on over-compensating people could be better spent on other things. This general approach was endorsed by the Pearson Commission.[3]

Compensation systems usually try to avoid over-compensation within their own confines. For example, the tort system will not give damages for the same injury more than once. Thus, if a person is injured in an accident caused by the negligence of two or more tortfeasors, that person may recover any damages awarded from the various tortfeasors in any proportions possible, but is not allowed to recover in total more than the amount of the award. Again, where a tort claimant is awarded damages both for lost earnings and for the cost of care in a

---

1 Even more complicated issues might arise where more than two sources were available.
2 E.g. R. Lewis, 'Deducting Collateral Benefits from Damages: Principle and Policy' (1998) 18 *LS* 15.
3 Pearson Report, vol. 1, ch. 13.

residential institution, the former will be reduced to take account of savings in living expenses as a result of living in the institution. As we have seen,[4] the social security system also sets its face against overcompensation within its own confines. A person can claim both incapacity benefit and disablement benefit, but this is because the former is designed to replace lost income while the latter is compensation for the disability as such and is not intended to be for lost income.

First-party insurance which is designed to replace something with measurable financial value – 'indemnity insurance' – only provides cover for the loss actually suffered, whatever that may be. For instance, a person may be covered by two separate policies, each covering the full loss, but the insured may only recover once. *Prima facie* each insurer will have to bear half the loss.[5] However, the position is different in the case of insurance against losses which cannot be measured in money terms. For instance, a person who buys more than one life insurance policy, or more than one policy of personal accident insurance against disability alone, can recover under both because it is not really possible to say, in respect of a loss which cannot be measured in money terms, that receiving £2X rather than £X is overcompensation. By contrast, tort law does not allow a claimant to recover full damages for non-pecuniary loss from several tortfeasors merely because the loss is non-pecuniary. This is partly because the courts pretend that there is a 'proper' sum to award as damages for disabilities. Perhaps a better reason for distinguishing between first-party insurance and tort liability in this respect is that tort damages are not paid for by the claimant, whereas first-party insurance is paid for by the insured: if a person chooses to buy more than one policy to cover the same loss, there is no good reason why the insured should not be allowed to keep all the insurance benefits paid for.

Our main concern in this chapter is with the way in which different compensation systems fit together, rather than the way in which each system treats the problem of over-compensation within its own confines.

15.2   The choice of compensation system

Because the compensation systems we have discussed have developed in a haphazard way, there is no coherent set of rules or principles governing the relationships between them. Many social security benefits are payable regardless of whether the claimant has access to other sources of compensation. For example, statutory sick pay is payable even if the employee is entitled to occupational sick pay, and it is for the employer to decide whether to reduce the latter to take account of the former. Again, social security benefits are payable to recipients of criminal injuries compensation or tort damages; it is the criminal injuries compensation or tort damages which are reduced to take account of social security payments and not vice

4 12.4.3.2.
5 *Gale* v. *Motor Union Insurance Co. Ltd* [1928] 1 KB 359.

versa.[6] On the other hand, in assessing entitlement to means-tested social security benefits, account is taken of criminal injuries and tort compensation, for instance.

It is probably the case that most employers deduct statutory sick pay from occupational sick pay. It is, however, less usual to take account of tort damages when sick pay is granted. This is partly because it will usually be months or years before any tort damages are received. Also, a claim for tort damages is probably not a sufficiently common event to make it worthwhile to insert special provisions dealing with it in sick-pay schemes. But it is apparently permissible to make provision for the employer to 'advance' wages as a 'loan' to a person injured in an accident giving rise to a tort claim, the injured person having an obligation to repay the employer if and when the employee recovers damages for lost earnings.[7] This is a device to place the cost of wages for an injured employee onto the tortfeasor (and hence liability insurers) rather than the employer. The main issue here is whether employers or motorists should pay for lost wages arising from road accidents. In general the cost is borne by motorists to the extent that fault can be proved, and it might therefore be thought that there was no reason why an employer who organizes a sick-pay scheme should not be entitled to insist that wages lost through negligent driving should be borne by motorists rather than by the employer. But it is doubtful if this is sound policy because the advantage to the employer must be small: it can only be in a small proportion of cases that sick pay can be recouped in this way, while the administrative cost of recoupment is likely to be high, because it involves reliance on the tort system.

First-party insurers are free to try to shift their losses onto other compensation systems by the terms of their insurance policies. For example, a personal accident policy could stipulate that there is to be no liability if compensation is obtained from other sources. In fact insurance companies do not generally attempt to do this. They are mainly concerned with preventing the insured recovering for the same loss under more than one policy. First-party insurers also have various subrogation rights, which we will examine shortly.

The lack of clear rules of priority between compensation systems may create difficulties where one system refuses to meet a claim on the basis that another will do so. For example, in one case[8] the MIB sought to argue that a claimant, injured by a defendant who deliberately used his car (which was uninsured) to run him down, ought to have sought compensation from the CICB rather than from the MIB, even though the latter was, as the House of Lords held, liable under its agreement with the government in cases of deliberate running down. In this type of case, the CICB does not normally award compensation precisely because the MIB agreement covers it. The House of Lords, without adverting to this fact, held that the CICS and the MIB scheme were not mutually exclusive, and that the claimant could

---

6 As we will see later, in some cases the value of social security benefits paid to a recipient of tort damages is recoverable by the Compensation Recovery Unit from the tortfeasor.

7 *IRC v. Hambrook* [1956] 2 QB 641, 656–7.

8 *Gardner v. Moore* [1984] AC 548.

choose to proceed under whichever scheme was more favourable to him. Thus stalemate was avoided, but the basic issue of which compensation scheme ought to have borne the loss was not tackled. Like the CICA, the MIB sets off sums received from other sources against the claimant's compensation.

Less satisfactory is a case in which the claimant's leg was rendered stiff as a result of a car accident due to the fault of D; he was later shot in the same leg by X and had to have it amputated.[9] The House of Lords held that D was liable for all the claimant's loss except that caused by the amputation of the leg. In a later case,[10] doubt was cast on this result and it was suggested that D ought to have been liable only for loss suffered up until the time the claimant was shot, partly on the ground that C could have made a claim to the CICB in respect of the shooting. This criticism of the earlier decision ignores the fact that, in general, the CICB will only give compensation for losses that are compensatable according to common law principles.

The mere fact of having different systems generates the need to spend time deciding which is the appropriate system to bear the loss. For example, entitlement to damages requires proof of negligence; entitlement to industrial injury benefits requires proof that the accident arose 'out of and in the course of employment'; entitlement to criminal injuries compensation requires (with a few exceptions) proof that a crime of violence has been committed. Each of these (and other) criteria of entitlement tend to produce troublesome borderline cases; and the allocation of such cases to the 'appropriate' compensation system absorbs a disproportionate amount of administrative effort and cost. The more systems there are, the more borderline cases there will be; and the more demarcation disputes will have to be solved. Such disputes appear even more futile when it is remembered that the burden of most compensation systems is ultimately borne by (large sections of) the public. One of the undoubted attractions of an integrated approach to the question of compensation is that it would eliminate many of these demarcation disputes.

15.3   Subrogation and recoupment

Where two persons are legally liable to compensate a third party for some loss, and as between these two, one is under a 'primary' liability and the other is only 'secondarily' liable, the latter is normally entitled, on paying the compensation, to be 'subrogated' to the rights of the third party against the person primarily liable. In the tort system, tort liability is still treated as primary liability while insurance is still treated as an ancillary or secondary feature of the system. Therefore, a tortfeasor can sometimes be sued by an insurer who has indemnified the victim against the loss. For example, if a person insures a house against fire and the house is burned down as a result of the negligence of a tortfeasor, the owner of the house will prob-

---

9 *Baker* v. *Willoughby* [1970] AC 467.
10 *Jobling* v. *Associated Dairies Ltd* [1982] AC 794.

ably claim from the insurer who is then subrogated to the owner's claim against the tortfeasor. In practice, it would be worthwhile for an insurer to make a claim in this sort of situation only if the tortfeasor was insured against the liability, as in the familiar case of two motorists, both comprehensively insured, who collide as a result of their combined negligence. Here each motorist can claim against their own insurer for the damage to the vehicle; each insurer is then subrogated to the claims of its insured against the other driver and is entitled to pass on to the other insurer the cost of the claim by its own insured.[11]

Another instance of subrogation is to be found in the case of an employee whose negligent conduct has caused the employer to be held vicariously liable to a third party; if the employer was insured, the 'primary' liability is treated as resting on the employee and the insurer is subrogated to the employer's claim against the servant.[12]

The government has statutory rights analogous to subrogation rights under the Social Security (Recovery of Benefits) Act 1997, which is discussed further later in the chapter (15.4.5). Under this Act, a person paying compensation to another as a consequence of injuries or disease suffered by that other person for which the payer is, or is alleged to be, liable[13] is required to deduct from the compensation paid to the injured person the amount of specified social security benefits received by that person in respect of the injuries resulting from the tort in the period of 5 years from the date of the injuries, or in the period from the date of the injury to the date of the compensation payment, if this is less than 5 years. The sum thus deducted is to be paid to the DWP. These provisions do not apply to payments made by the CICA under the CICS; to payments made under criminal compensation orders; to damages or settlements under the Fatal Accidents Act 1976;[14] or to government-funded compensation payments made under the Vaccine Damage Payments Act 1979, or to haemophiliacs suffering from AIDS, or under the 1974 scheme for compensating miners suffering from pneumoconiosis,[15] or to occupational sick pay. But they do apply to payments by the MIB. The MIB does not have subrogation rights because it is not under a legal obligation to claimants to make the payments it does.[16]

---

11 If a person is covered by two liability policies issued by different insurers and covering the same liability, neither insurer has subrogation rights against the other, but either or both can claim contribution: *Austin* v. *Zurich Insurance Co.* [1945] KB 250.
12 *Lister* v. *Romford Ice and Cold Storage Co. Ltd* [1957] AC 555; but see *Morris* v. *Ford Motor Co.* [1973] 1 QB 792 and 9.8.2.3.
13 The Act does not apply to payments under first-party insurance policies.
14 The Law Commission is of the view that the rules about collateral benefits in fatal accident cases should be consistent with those in personal injury cases: Law Com. No. 263, *Claims for Wrongful Death* (1999), para. 5.39.
15 See 4.10 and 13.6.
16 This also used to be true of the CICB; but now payments under the CICS have a statutory basis in the Criminal Injuries Compensation Act 1995. In relation to the old scheme, the CICB once expressed the view that there were very few cases in which it could usefully have sued the criminal even if it had had the power to do so: *CICB Eighth Report* (Cmnd 5127, 1972), para. 18. But in 2004 the 1995 Act was amended to give the CICA power to recover directly from criminals compensation paid to victims under the CICS (12.2).

The NHS has statutory rights analogous to subrogation rights under the Road Traffic (NHS Charges) Act 1999. Under the Act, where a person, who has died or been injured as the result of a road accident and has received treatment in an NHS hospital, receives compensation, the person who pays the compensation is liable to pay to the government an amount in respect of that treatment, at a flat rate (in 2005) of £483 for treatment without admission and at a daily rate (in 2005) of £593 for treatment with admission, up to a maximum in any one case of £35,500. Under Part 3 of the Health and Social Care (Community Health and Standards) Act 2003 this recoupment scheme has been extended to all cases where a person legally liable or alleged to be legally liable pays compensation for personal injury, regardless of cause; and to ambulance services as well as hospital treatment. This extension will have its greatest impact in relation to work accidents which, after road accidents, are the main cause of tort claims. Because of recent concern about the state of the employers' liability insurance market (7.7), the new scheme will not be introduced until October 2006. When it comes into effect, it will supersede the 1999 scheme. Certain compensation payments, including payments made pursuant to a criminal compensation order or as a result of a fatal accident claim, are not subject to the 2003 recoupment scheme.[17] A noteworthy limit on the scheme arises from the fact that 'personal injury' does not include any disease. The explanation given by the Department of Health for this limitation is that 'it would be difficult to quantify the cost of diseases . . . to the NHS due to the complexity of the treatment path and the period of time over which a person with a . . . disease would need treatment'.[18]

From time to time suggestions have been made for a wider use of subrogation in the compensation process. For example, the Law Reform Committee once proposed that an employer who pays wages to a person injured as a result of a tort should be subrogated to the injured person's rights against the tortfeasor.[19] Again, when the CICS was under consideration, it was suggested that the State should have subrogation rights against the criminal;[20] but it was not until 2004 that such a proposal was adopted (12.2). The Winn Committee on personal injury litigation put forward for consideration a scheme under which the State would pay some, or all, of the damages which a road accident victim might be able to recover in subsequent litigation, and would then recoup itself by taking proceedings against the tortfeasor.[21] And the Society of Labour Lawyers (in evidence to the Pearson Commission) once advocated a similar scheme for industrial injuries.

17 See Sch. 10 to the 2003 Act. Also not included in the scheme are payments made under s. 158 of the Road Traffic Act 1988 by users of motor vehicles to medical practitioners who give emergency care.

18 *The Recovery of National Health Service Costs in Cases Involving Personal Injury Compensation: A Consultation* (2002), para. 4.3.

19 *Eleventh Report* (Loss of Services, etc.) (Cmnd 2017, 1963), para. 5. The Law Commission rejected the idea (Law Com. No. 56, paras. 146–50) as did the Pearson Commission (Pearson Report, vol. 1, para. 446). The employer's own right to sue for loss of an employee's services was abolished by s. 2 of the Administration of Justice Act 1982.

20 JUSTICE, *Report on Compensation for Victims of Crimes of Violence* (London, 1962), 20.

21 *Winn Committee Report*, paras. 107–10 and Appendix 7.

The main argument in favour of subrogation rights is to ensure that the cost of compensation ultimately rests on the party legally responsible for the harm which the compensation redresses.[22] However, various arguments can be made against subrogation. Two types of subrogation claim require consideration: first, a claim by the State against a tortfeasor with private liability insurance, or by a private (loss) insurer against a tortfeasor with private liability insurance; and, secondly, a claim by the State or an insurer against an individual tortfeasor who has no liability insurance. In the first type of case, the main objection to subrogation is that it ought not to be allowed if the party claiming subrogation is the most appropriate party to bear the loss; and if this is not the case, the law should perhaps be changed so that the cost is placed on the most appropriate party in the first instance. However, this objection may be too simplistic. For example, even if we accept that tortfeasors ought, *prima facie*, to bear the costs of their torts, we may still approve of the provisions of the Social Security (Recovery of Benefits) Act 1997 discussed above on the ground that tort victims may need financial assistance in the short term, and in reality the social security system is much more likely to provide assistance quickly than the tort system. Delays inherent in the tort system may justify the scheme contained in the 1997 Act. On the other hand, we might say that what the 1997 Act really shows is the need to replace the whole tort system with a more efficient personal injury compensation system, which could deliver compensation as quickly as the social security system.[23]

Where subrogation rights are asserted against an individual who is neither insured nor an effective self-insurer, the principal objection is the same as the objection against making individuals pay tort damages, namely that it is not practicable nor, in the majority of cases, is it just or in the public interest. If we accept that one of the principal aims of any compensation system should be to spread losses widely so that the cost does not fall too heavily on any individual, it follows that a loss which has fallen on a party able to spread it (such as an insurer) ought not to be shifted again to a party unable to spread it effectively. In the case of the CICA, an argument used against giving it subrogation rights against a criminal who had already been or was likely to be successfully prosecuted was that in pursuing the criminal, the CICA might appear to be seeking a second punishment, even though this would not technically be the case.[24] By 2004, a desire to limit the cost of the CICS was felt to justify giving the CICA power to recover directly from convicted criminals amounts paid out under the Scheme.

---

22 A similar case could be made against rights of contribution. For a fuller discussion in a different context see P. Cane, *Tort Law and Economic Interests*, 2nd edn (Oxford, 1996), 435–43.

23 'The recovery of NHS costs is but a symptom of a New Labour desire to make the public services more efficient in terms that a Thatcherite would approve, but which would dishearten many welfarists': R. Lewis, 'Recovery of NHS Accident Costs: Tort as a Vehicle for Raising Public Funds' (1999) 62 *MLR* 903, 911.

24 JUSTICE, *Report on Compensation for Victims of Crimes of Violence*, 20; *Hansard*, 5th series, HC, vol. 694, col. 1159.

Another objection to subrogation is that shifting losses around is costly.[25] The initial allocation of liability is expensive[26] and subrogation adds further to the cost by shifting it again. Even if we thought that subrogation was in principle a good idea in certain circumstances (e.g. under the Social Security (Recovery of Benefits) Act 1997), we might want to reconsider the matter if it turned out that the cost of enforcing rights of subrogation was very high relative to the amounts recovered. It was probably for this reason that when the scheme for recovery of social security benefits was first introduced in 1989, compensation payments of £2,500 or less were excluded from its scope. The 1997 Act removed this exclusion, but allows regulations to be made in the future to exclude 'small payments' from the recoupment scheme. In fact, the administrative costs of the social security and NHS recoupment schemes seem to be very modest. In 1997–8 £177 million was recovered under the social security scheme at a cost of less than £4 million; and in 2002–3 just over £98 million was recovered under the NHS scheme at a cost of around £1 million, to which must be added the (relatively small) additional costs to insurers of making the payments.[27]

There is no doubt that the schemes for recoupment of social security payments and NHS costs out of tort compensation payments are financially justifiable in the sense that they generate a substantial net benefit for the public purse. Moreover, they do this at the expense of the activities which, in legal terms, caused the harm that attracted the compensation, thus furthering goals of the tort system, such as deterrence (17.7) and corrective justice (17.5). On the other hand, given that most of the costs of tort compensation are widely spread across society as a whole through insurance and the cost of goods and services, we might seriously question the value of spending any money to transfer a proportion of such costs (in the form of social security benefits and NHS services) from the public in the guise of 'the taxpayer' to the public in the guise of consumers of insurance, goods and services. No doubt, this process of transferring costs from the public to the private ledger is symbolically and politically important; but whether it makes any economic sense is more doubtful. However, the main objection to the social security and NHS recoupment schemes is not their cost, but that they entrench and impliedly endorse the tort system as a mechanism for compensating disabled people.

Insurance companies, which are potentially the main beneficiaries of the doctrine of subrogation, realize that it may not always be very useful.[28] So-called

---

25 This was the main reason given by the Monckton Committee for rejecting subrogation in favour of the National Insurance Fund: *Final Report on the Committee on Alternative Remedies* (Cmnd 6860, 1946).

26 Remember that the Pearson Commission found that it cost 85p to deliver every £1 of tort compensation.

27 The cost of the payments themselves fall, of course, on premium payers. It has been estimated that extension of the NHS scheme to all compensation payments in 2006 will add about 5% to premiums for relevant lines of insurance: Department of Health, *The Recovery of National Health Service Costs in Cases Involving Personal Injury Compensation: A Consultation* (2002), para. 4.16.

28 R. Lewis, 'Deducting Collateral Benefits from Damages: Principles and Policy' (1998) 18 *LS* 15, 33–4.

'knock-for-knock agreements' (9.5) represented an abandonment of subrogation rights – although only in relation to property damage. In cases where an employee renders the employer vicariously liable and is in law liable to recoup the employer's insurers, the insurance industry has voluntarily abandoned the right of sub-rogation by agreement even in relation to personal injuries.[29] In some countries subrogation is severely limited by law; for example, in Denmark, a person who has insured property against accidental damage has no tort action against a person who damages it, and hence the insurers have no subrogation rights.[30] Other Scandinavian countries permit a tort action, but the insurance proceeds are deducted from tort damages and once again there are no subrogation rights.[31] Insurers say that without subrogation rights, premiums would have to be higher; but others deny that subrogation rights are of much economic value overall, given the cost of enforcing them.

15.4   Tort damages and other compensation

15.4.1   General principles

Two questions are addressed in this section. First, to what extent does tort law tol-erate over-compensation by allowing a claimant to recover tort damages in respect of any particular loss in addition to compensation from some other source in respect of that same loss? Conversely, to what extent does tort law pursue a policy of 'reduction' by setting off against tort damages compensation received from some other source? Secondly, to the extent that tort law does allow over-compensation, how, if at all, can this be justified?

We will consider the second question first by looking at three traditional answers to it. The first answer is that compensation from other sources should be ignored if it is 'collateral' or comes from a 'collateral source'. Taken literally, this might be thought to mean that benefits deriving other than from the tortfeasor will be ignored, while benefits coming from the tortfeasor (other than the tort compensa-tion itself) will be taken into account. However, such a straightforward approach has never been accepted by the courts: some benefits provided by tortfeasors are set off, but not all; and some benefits received from third parties can be kept, but not all. As a result, the word 'collateral' does not provide an independent criterion for the decision whether to set off or not to set off, but merely expresses a conclusion based on a value-judgment about whether the injured person should or should not be allowed to keep the benefit. The second answer is that compensation from other sources should only affect the tort compensation if the injury occasioned by the tort was the *causa causans* (the 'effective' or 'proximate' cause) of the receipt of the non-tort compensation and not merely a *causa sine qua non* (or 'the occasion') of its

29 P.S. Atiyah, *Vicarious Liability in the Law of Torts* (London, 1967), 426–7.
30 J. Hellner, 'Tort Liability and Liability Insurance' in F. Schmidt ed., *Scandinavian Studies in Law 1962* (Stockholm, 1962), 140–1.
31 Ibid.

receipt. But as we saw earlier (5.2), the answer to the question of whether one thing is merely a necessary condition of another or its 'real cause' depends on why the question is being asked. Whether the tort 'caused' the receipt of the benefit boils down to whether the recipient ought to be allowed to keep it or not.

The third answer is based on the assumption that tortfeasors actually pay tort damages, and that therefore the reduction of tort damages because of compensation received from another source will 'benefit' the tortfeasor. Why, it is asked, should this outside source of compensation 'benefit' the tortfeasor rather than the victim? But once it is appreciated that only in a very small proportion of cases in practice does the tortfeasor personally pay any damages at all, the argument collapses. On the whole, this argument tends to receive short shrift in the courts, not so much on the ground that tortfeasors do not pay damages but because it is essentially an argument in favour of penal damages. If the claimant is already adequately compensated, then obliging a defendant to pay money to the claimant for the same loss on the ground that the defendant should not get the 'benefit' of the other compensation, is merely to penalize the defendant. And on the whole this is now unfashionable.

The principal considerations relevant to answering the set-off question are these.[32] First, in so far as the tort and the non-tort compensation are paid for by essentially the same people, over-compensation should be avoided. This is particularly important when the source from which the compensation comes is the State. Public money should not be wasted by over-compensating some personal injury victims, particularly when so many other deserving cases (such as victims of disease) receive much less. In modern conditions, 'public money' is not just money actually collected by the State in the form of taxes or social security contributions. Tort damages too are, for all practical purposes, paid out of public money, since they are mostly financed by road traffic and employers' liability insurance premiums, which are paid (or paid for) by a very large proportion of the public, and are required by law to be paid.

A second consideration is the purpose of the compensation. If it replaces something (such as lost income) with a measurable financial value, then there can be little justification for paying compensation more than once from more than one source. If, on the other hand, the compensation is for something with no measurable financial value such as pain and suffering, the argument against paying compensation from more than one source may seem less strong. Because nobody can say what value we should put on pain and suffering, it cannot be said that a person has been over-compensated by receiving money from more than one source. This argument also appealed to the dissenting minority on the Monckton Committee, who thought that full tort damages and social security payments should be payable to accident victims because compensation for disabilities could never be

---

32 See also R. Lewis, 'Deducting Collateral Benefits From Damages: Principle and Policy' (1998) 18 *LS* 15; Law Com. Consultation Paper 147, *Damages for Personal Injury: Collateral Benefits* (1997).

excessive.[33] However, this argument is undermined by the fact that compensation for non-pecuniary loss is calculated and paid by each compensation system on the assumption that this sum will be the only compensation payable on this account.

A third consideration is whether the people financing one or other of the sources of compensation want the recipient to have compensation twice over. This is particularly relevant to charitable donations: donors sometimes intend the beneficiaries to receive some benefit in addition to their legal claims, and this may be a good reason for refusing to deduct the value of such donations from tort damages. On the other hand, most charitable donors probably give no thought to the question of whether the beneficiaries have legal compensation rights.

A fourth, and more difficult, argument which has played an important role in some cases is that double compensation is less objectionable if the recipient has in some sense 'paid for' the compensation. In *Parry* v. *Cleaver*[34] Lord Reid said that the real justification for allowing an accident victim to receive tort damages unaffected by the amount of any personal accident insurance payments was that the victim had paid for the accident insurance and should therefore receive the benefits of the premiums. This is a tricky argument. On the one hand, there is no reason why a person should not buy several life insurance policies, for example, and recover under them all. However, the reason for this is not simply that the insured has paid for all the policies. There are circumstances in which allowing a person to recover from two sources may provide serious temptation for fraud. For example, a person is not generally allowed to recover the value of damaged property twice over, even if it has been insured twice over and the insurance has been paid for with two lots of premiums. Furthermore, where a person receives payment under a first-party insurance policy and is also awarded tort damages, that person will have paid for the insurance but will not have 'paid for' the tort damages in the same sense.

A fifth policy consideration concerns the administrative cost of avoiding over-compensation. If the amount it would cost to avoid over-compensation would likely be as much as or more than the value of any excess compensation, this would be a good reason for not seeking to avoid over-compensation. This may be why statutory sick pay (SSP) is payable to those who receive occupational sick pay, and why employers may not always deduct the value of SSP from occupational sick pay.

Let us now consider how the law actually deals with cases of potential over-compensation.

15.4.2 Tort damages and sick pay

First, if the employer is bound by contract or statute to pay the employee wages while away from work through sickness, the employee has not 'lost' any income and cannot recover it in damages.[35] Secondly, if the employer is not so bound but pays none the less, it is not clear whether this should be treated as a 'charitable' payment

---

33 Cmnd 6860, 53.
34 [1970] AC 1.
35 *Parry* v. *Cleaver* [1970] AC 1.

which is not to be deducted from the damages even if the employer is also the defendant,[36] or as deductible because, even though voluntary, it is in the nature of sick pay.[37] Thirdly, if the employer, while not bound to pay the wages, pays them in the form of a 'loan' subject to an undertaking to repay them out of any tort damages that may be recovered, then again there will be no deduction.

15.4.3   Tort damages and personal insurance

In respect of property damage the owner cannot recover both tort damages and private insurance. Once the insurer has paid out under the policy it is subrogated to the owner's tort claim: the property owner cannot, after collecting the insurance money, sue in tort for their own benefit; any damages recovered by the owner must be paid over to the insurer. By contrast, a victim of personal injury can recover under a first-party insurance policy in respect of the injury and can also sue in tort for damages on his or her own behalf. The insurer is not subrogated to the insured's right of action because personal injury insurance is not 'indemnity' insurance; and so the insured is not required to hand any tort damages recovered over to the insurer. Furthermore, the proceeds of personal injury insurance policies are not set off against tort damages.[38] The most commonly given reason why the proceeds of such policies are not set off is that they are benefits which the insured has bought and paid for personally; but, of course, this is also true of property insurance.

This rule has caused great difficulty in the case of payments made by employers to injured workers. If the payments are essentially sick pay, then the tort damages are reduced by their value even if they are funded by an insurance policy taken out by the employer.[39] Similarly, payments under a group personal accident policy taken out by an employer for the benefit of employees will be set off unless the payee actually paid or contributed to the premiums.[40] If a person injured at work is made redundant or accepts redundancy, any redundancy payments received will be set off against tort damages in respect of the injury, provided the worker would probably not have been made redundant if they had not been injured.[41] But if the payments are in the form of a pension payable to an employee who is no longer able to work because of disabilities, they will not be set off against tort damages.[42] This is so whether the pension scheme is voluntary or compulsory and (apparently) whether

---

36 This view is indirectly supported by *McCamley* v. *Cammell Laird Shipbuilders Ltd* [1990] 1 WLR 963. See 15.4.4 concerning charitable payments.
37 This view is indirectly supported by *Parry* v. *Cleaver* [1970] AC 1 in which the non-deductibility of an occupational pension was unaffected by whether the pension scheme was voluntary or not.
38 *Bradburn* v. *Great Western Railway* (1874) LR 10 Ex 1.
39 *Hussain* v. *New Taplow Paper Mills* [1988] AC 514.
40 *Gaca* v. *Pirelli General Plc* [2004] 1 WLR 2683.
41 *Colledge* v. *Bass Mitchells & Butlers Ltd* [1988] 1 All ER 536.
42 *Parry* v. *Cleaver* [1970] AC 1. However, in respect of the period after the date on which the employee would normally have retired, the proceeds of a disablement pension are set off against any retirement pension the employee would have received if the employee had worked to normal retiring age when assessing damages for loss of pension rights: *Longden* v. *British Coal Corporation* [1998] AC 653.

the employee makes contributions or not;[43] and even if the employer is also defendant and provider of the pension (that is, even if the scheme is not funded by an insurance policy taken out by the employer).[44]

The confusion here results from the fact that different criteria are in use: the basis on which sick pay is set off is its nature – sick pay is a form of wages, and an employee who receives sick pay suffers, to that extent, no loss of wages. The basis on which redundancy payments are set off is not that they are a form of wages (which they are not), but that if the redundancy was a result of the injury, the redundancy payment is a benefit accruing from the injury and must, as a matter of general principle, be set off against loss resulting from the injury. The basis on which occupational pensions are not set off is different again, namely that they are in the nature of insurance proceeds paid for, either directly or indirectly, by the employee. The trouble is that these different criteria may conflict. For example, an occupational pension paid to a disabled worker who retires early as a result of the disability does provide a substitute for wages even if it is also the proceeds of an insurance policy. Even more problematically, whereas payments from an employer's non-contributory pension scheme will not be set off because they are in the nature of insurance proceeds, payments from an employer's group personal accident insurance policy will be set off unless the employee paid or contributed to the premiums; and an employee will not be treated as having contributed to the cost of such a policy merely by reason of the fact that the employer bought the policy for the benefit of its employees.[45] In fact, it seems that the law is in a transitional state, and its ultimate destination may be a rule that all payments made by the tortfeasor to the victim will be set off.

15.4.4   Tort damages and charitable payments

Payments made to the injury victim by a person who is under no legal obligation to make them – i.e. payments in the nature of charitable donations or made out of 'benevolence' – are ignored unless made by the tortfeasor.[46] Similarly, no deduction from damages is made for the value of services gratuitously rendered to an injured person by relatives or friends (other than the tortfeasor); furthermore, the damages will include a sum to enable the victim to pay for the services.[47] Nor is the value of free public health care deducted (individuals pay for this through taxation), except that if the injured person saves living expenses by being looked after

---

43 On the basis that even if the employee does not contribute directly, he or she will have paid for the pension indirectly in the form e.g. of lower wages. But this is also true of occupational sick pay. The difference between sick pay and an occupational pension is said to be that the former is, but the latter is not, a form of wages.

44 *Smoker* v. *London Fire and Civil Defence Authority* [1991] 2 AC 502.

45 *Gaca* v. *Pirelli General Plc* [2004] 1 WLR 2682.

46 *Gaca* v. *Pirelli General Plc* [2004] 1 WLR 2682; *Williams* v. *BOC Gases Ltd* [2000] ICR 1181.

47 *Hunt* v. *Severs* [1994] 2 AC 350. In Australia, damages under this head can be awarded even if the carer is the tortfeasor; and the Law Commission has recommended that this should be the law in England, too: Law Com. No. 262, *Damages for Personal Injury: Medical, Nursing and Other Expenses; Collateral Benefits* (1999), 3.67–76.

in a public institution, the value of such savings is deducted from damages for loss of earnings.[48]

15.4.5   Tort damages and social security benefits

Under the workers' compensation system the injured worker was required to elect between suing the employer in tort at common law and claiming workers' compensation. Beveridge apparently favoured the abolition of the employee's tort action: one of the justifications he gave for treating victims of industrial injuries preferentially in the social security system was the argument that only if this were done would it be possible to restrict liability at common law in industrial injury cases. However, Beveridge did not consider this question fully but recommended that a special committee should be set up to inquire into the question of 'alternative remedies'.

A committee (consisting principally of lawyers) was set up under the chairmanship of Sir Walter Monckton.[49] The committee recommended that the tort action should be retained and that the rule of election should be abolished. It also decided that entitlement to National Insurance benefits should be unaffected by the possibility that tort damages would be recovered in the future, if only because it is necessary to pay such benefits at once and not to wait and see whether any damages may be recovered. The committee was then faced with the question whether the amount awarded in tort damages should be affected by the receipt of National Insurance benefits. The committee thought that there was a fundamental difference in principle between voluntary insurance and compulsory national insurance, which is more like a tax.[50] The committee recommended that social security benefits should be deducted in full from tort damages on the ground (unjustified, as things have turned out) that this would discourage tort actions. The strongest argument against duplication is that tort damages and social security benefits (whether contributory or not) are paid for by much the same group of people (that is, a significant section of the public), and there is no justification for paying double compensation for the same loss at expense of the same group.

The trades unions opposed the off-setting of benefits, and the political compromise finally enacted in s. 2 of the Law Reform (Personal Injuries) Act 1948 was far more favourable to injury victims (and especially industrial injury victims) than

---

48 Administration of Justice Act 1982, s. 5.

49 The committee issued three reports: Cmnd 6580, 1944; Cmnd 6642, 1945; and Cmnd 6860, 1946. The first two were concerned with the Law Reform (Contributory Negligence) Act 1945 which was then under consideration. On the last see P. Bartrip, *Workmen's Compensation in Twentieth Century Britain* (Aldershot, 1987), ch. 10. It is not clear what effect abolition of the rule of election and the introduction of apportionment for contributory negligence had on the incidence of tort actions against employers.

50 Cmnd 6860, para. 32. In fact, the distinction between voluntary and compulsory insurance is not very relevant: a property owner cannot keep both tort damages and property insurance proceeds even though such insurance is not compulsory. Again, occupational pensions are not set off whether the pension scheme is voluntary or compulsory.

the committee had recommended. Instead of providing for full deduction of the value of social security benefits, the 1948 Act provided for the deduction from damages for loss of earnings resulting from personal injuries of half the value of certain (but not all) benefits received or likely to be received during a period of 5 years from the date of the injury. The justification[51] for deducting only half the value of benefits was that in respect of industrial benefits the employee was paying nearly half the cost (five-twelfths) and so was entitled to receive half the benefit without affecting a tort claim. In fact, only in the case of industrial injuries was five-twelfths of the cost paid by employees, yet the half-deduction rule was applied to all benefits. Moreover, that workers paid for half of their industrial benefits is false because contribution rates were not risk-related, which meant that workers in some occupations were heavily subsidized by workers in others.[52] There also appears to have been no justification for the 5-year limitation. Although few tort victims received social security benefits for more than 5 years, it simply meant that where common law damages were at their highest, the amount of duplication was the greatest. Finally, the provision only applied to court awards and not to settlements which, of course, greatly limited its impact.

The 1948 legislation only covered specified benefits. The rules about benefits other than those specified in the Act were not uniform. State retirement pension was not deducted at all;[53] but attendance and mobility allowance,[54] family income supplement,[55] income support,[56] statutory sick pay[57] and unemployment benefit,[58] at least in respect of payments received before trial, were deducted in full.[59]

In 1989 a new system for recovery of social security benefits was set up under the Social Security Act 1989. The provisions of the 1948 Act continued to apply to cases in which the value of any compensation awarded was £2,500 or less. In the case of compensation payments over £2,500 (whether made in pursuance of a court order or by way of a settlement out of court) the relevant rules were contained in the 1989 Act (subsequently re-enacted as Part IV of the Social Security Administration Act 1992). The Act provided, in effect, that the party paying the compensation had to deduct from it the full value of specified social security benefits received by the payee in respect of the injury in a period of 5 years after the date of the injury[60] (or in the period from the date of the injury to the date of the

51 Which was specifically rejected by the Monckton Committee.
52 13.1.2.
53 *Hewson* v. *Downs* [1970] 1 QB 93.
54 *Hodgson* v. *Trapp* [1989] AC 807. These benefits have now been replaced by disability living allowance.
55 *Gaskill* v. *Preston* [1981] 3 All ER 427. The current equivalent of this benefit is working tax credit.
56 Formerly supplementary benefit: *Lincoln* v. *Hayman* [1982] 1 WLR 488.
57 *Palfrey* v. *Greater London Council* [1988] ICR 437.
58 *Nabi* v. *British Leyland (UK) Ltd* [1980] 1 WLR 529. The current equivalent of this benefit is job-seeker's allowance.
59 No deduction was made in respect of benefits for which the claimant could have applied but had not: *Eley* v. *Bedford* [1972] 1 QB 155.
60 Or, in the case of diseases, the date on which the claimant first claimed a relevant social security benefit as a consequence of the disease.

compensation payment, if this was less than 5 years),[61] and had to pay the amount deducted to the DWP. The recoupment scheme was (and is) administered by the Compensation Recovery Unit (CRU) within the DWP, decisions of which are subject to appeal to a social security appeals tribunal and thence, on a point of law, to a Social Security Commissioner.

In effect, the 1989 Act achieved what the Monckton Committee recommended. But the mechanism by which it was achieved was quite different from that used in the 1948 Act. Under the 1948 Act, the value of the social security benefits was deducted from the tort damages on the ground that the injured person should not be compensated twice for the same need. However, the beneficiary of this deduction was not the source of the deducted payments but rather the tortfeasor. By contrast, under the 1989 Act it was not the compensation payer but the taxpayer who benefited. From one point of view, this difference is not of great importance because, at the end of the day, compensation for personal injuries and social security benefits are both paid for by a large section of members of the public. But the distinction between public expenditure and private expenditure is of political importance, and the main motivation for the 1989 provisions was to reduce public spending. From the government's point of view, the 1989 scheme also had the advantage of casting the administrative cost of recoupment on to defendants and their insurers.

The 1989 scheme was criticized on a number of grounds. First, it was said that since National Insurance benefits are paid for wholly by employers and employees, these benefits, at least, should not be deducted; but this is a weak argument because National Insurance contributions are, in effect, a tax. Secondly, it was argued that in practice, many tort claimants do not receive full compensation, and that this problem would be made worse by deduction of social security benefits; but there is no good reason why tort defendants should be subsidized by the taxpayer. Thirdly, it was initially suggested that the total costs of recoupment (administrative costs, increased delays in the settlement process and so on) might be greater than the resulting benefit to the public purse; but this has proved not to be the case. In the year to March 1998, the CRU recovered amounts equivalent to benefits of some £177 million at an administrative cost of less than £4 million. Fourthly, certain details of the scheme and its operation caused much consternation. One was the provision that social security benefits were to be deducted in full from compensation payments even if the compensation was reduced on account of contributory negligence, and even though contributory negligence is ignored in assessing social security benefits. Another was the provision that social security benefits were to be deducted from the total compensation and not just from that part which 'performed the same function' as the relevant benefit. For instance, income

---

61 Because the recoupment period ends when the claim is settled, it is unnecessary to take account of social security benefits in calculating compensation for future loss. Receipt of compensation for future loss may, however, affect entitlement to social security benefits after the date of settlement. As in the case of the 1948 Act, there was no principled justification for the 5-year limitation.

replacement benefits could be deducted not only from compensation for loss of income but also from compensation for non-pecuniary loss. People were also outraged by the fact that after deduction of benefits, a claimant might end up with little or no compensation. Moreover, it was alleged that the level of settlements was being depressed as insurance companies put pressure on injury victims to accept £2,500 or less in order to avoid the operation of the recoupment provisions. If we view the 1989 scheme as designed to prevent over-compensation and not merely to reduce public spending, the concerns about the failure to set like off against like and the alleged behaviour of insurers certainly have some force.

The recoupment scheme was re-enacted and amended in 1997.[62] The £2,500 threshold was removed,[63] and social security benefits are now deducted only from compensation[64] which performs a like function.[65] There is no deduction from damages for non-pecuniary loss. Nevertheless, the 1997 Act makes it clear that the relevant social security payments are to be deducted in full even if the result is that the injured person ends up with no compensation (because, for instance, the compensation has been reduced for contributory negligence).[66] Leaving these amendments aside, the 1997 scheme is the same as the 1989 scheme, which it replaces.

One notable feature of both the 1948 and the 1997 provisions is that they (did) do not apply to damages or settlements awarded under the Fatal Accidents Act 1976. Indeed, under this Act no benefits accruing from the death of the deceased are deducted from the damages awarded. Such generosity is hard to justify. Criminal injuries compensation is exempt from recoupment because awards under the CICS are reduced to take account of the receipt of benefits.[67] Payments under criminal compensation orders are exempt presumably because they are typically made by individuals, not insurers.

Apart from social security benefits, we saw in chapter 14 that there are many other social welfare services of which injured persons might be able to take advantage. Few of these are taken account of by the tort system.[68] Following the recommendations of the Monckton Committee,[69] the availability of treatment under the NHS is ignored in assessment of tort damages, so that a person may have private

---

62 Social Security (Recovery of Benefits) Act 1997 and Social Security (Recovery of Benefits) Regulations 1997.
63 But the Minister has power to make regulations to exempt 'small payments' from the operation of the scheme.
64 And interest: *Griffiths* v. *British Coal Corporation* [2001] 1 WLR 1493. This case also held that compensation for the value of gratuitous care constitutes 'compensation for cost of care incurred' for the purposes of off-setting care-related social security benefits.
65 But note that disablement benefit (13.4.3.2) is deducted from compensation for loss of income. Statutory sick pay is not set off, but will be taken into account in calculating loss of earnings.
66 The defendant must repay all the benefits even if greater than the compensation.
67 The 1997 Act expressly provides (in s. 17) that benefits covered by the recoupment scheme are to be disregarded in assessing damages.
68 But see Administration of Justice Act 1982, s. 5 (13.4.3.2 n. 101). See also *Cunningham* v. *Harrison* [1973] QB 942, 954, 957; *Taylor* v. *Bristol Omnibus Co.* [1975] 1 WLR 1054, 1058, 1063.
69 Cmnd 6860, para. 56. Although, it seems, contrary to Beveridge's inclinations: Beveridge Report, para. 262.

medical treatment and recover tort damages to cover the cost.[70] Private medical insurance is also ignored in the assessment of tort damages, so that a person can have private treatment and recover the cost of this twice over.[71]

15.5   Criminal injuries compensation

The value of any present or future entitlement to social security benefits is deducted in full from compensation under the CICS (other than the standard amount of compensation),[72] and the CICA may refuse to make an award until reasonable steps to claim social security benefits have been made. With certain exceptions – notably, private health insurance – the Board ignores the proceeds of insurance policies taken out and paid for by the victim.[73] Unlike the position at common law, the value of an occupational pension received as a result of the injuries is taken into account in assessing compensation for loss of earnings or dependency. If the pension is not taxable, its whole value is deducted; if it is taxable, half of its value is deducted.[74] This latter rule is rather generous, but may to some extent compensate for the fact that the pension may have been contributory. Personal pensions are ignored.

---

70 The Pearson Commission recommended that the cost of private medical treatment should be recoverable only if it was *medically* reasonable to incur it: Pearson Report, vol. 1, para. 342. The Chief Medical Officer has recently recommended that the cost of private medical treatment should not be recoverable in claims against the NHS: 6.2.3 n. 73.

71 BUPA tries to avoid this by requiring members to inform it of any negligence claim made and to include medical expenses in any such claim. Since in practice the expenses will usually need to be paid long before any damages are received, the member is expected to reimburse BUPA when damages are recovered. It seems probable, nevertheless, that many members secure double recovery.

72 The rules are complex. See D. Miers, *State Compensation for Criminal Injuries* (London, 1997), 232–5.

73 Ibid., 235–7; but the cost of private medical treatment will not be awarded unless the treatment and its cost were both reasonable (2001 Scheme, para. 35(c)).

74 Ibid., 237–9.

16

The cost of compensation and who pays it

In this chapter we examine what the various compensation systems we have considered cost, and how those costs are paid. The Pearson Commission provided a lot of information about the costs of the tort system in particular. There are two different types of costs, private costs and social costs. The main function of compensation systems is to transfer money from some people to others; the sums so transferred are a (private) cost to those who have to pay them, but they are not a social cost. They do not reduce society's resources as a whole. In economic terms, they are transfer payments. So far as transfer payments are concerned, the questions of interest concern the total value of the payments and the way the burden is distributed. In the context of compensation for personal injuries, social costs are, in essence, the administrative costs of making transfer payments. Administrative costs are social costs because they are the measure of the administrative resources consumed in making the transfer payments. The question of how much ought to be paid out in compensation is answered by reference to the goals of the compensation system in question; but the question of how much ought to be spent in making the compensation payments is purely a matter of efficiency. The lower the administrative costs of a system as a proportion of compensation paid out under the system, the more efficient the system is as a compensation system, whatever its goals.[1] As we shall see, some compensation systems are much more expensive to administer than others. Higher relative costs can be justified only if the system in question delivers desired benefits additional to the amount of compensation paid out,[2] and if the higher administrative costs are referable to those additional benefits.

16.1 The cost of tort compensation

The Pearson Commission estimated that in the years 1971–6 total tort compensation payments (at 1977 currency values) averaged some £202 million per annum, of which £69 million (about 34%) was paid out in industrial injury cases and

---

1 Unless, perhaps, one of the goals of the system is to keep a certain number of people in employment as administrators.
2 Or, in other words, only if the system has some goal other than and additional to compensation.

£118 million in road accident cases.[3] The total costs of the system are nearly double the amounts paid out in compensation because the tort liability insurance system is so staggeringly expensive to operate. The Pearson Commission estimated that the administrative cost of making the annual payments of £202 million averaged some £175 million during this same period, 1971–6 (again in terms of 1977 currency values). To translate these figures into 2005 currency values, they would need to be multiplied by about four, producing a figure of about £1.5 billion. However, we have also seen that the annual number of successful tort claims has approximately trebled since the 1970s (8.1.4), suggesting a total cost of the tort system in the region of £4.5 billion. This is very much less than estimates in the region of £10 billion per annum made, for example, by the Institute of Actuaries in 2002.[4] However, simply scaling up the Pearson figures in line with inflation and to take account of the increase in claims would produce an underestimate because general levels of compensation payments may (for various reasons) have increased at a faster rate than general inflation.[5] Advances in medical technology enable increasing numbers of seriously disabled people (including children born disabled) to be kept alive for long periods at great financial cost;[6] several new heads of damages have been introduced since 1977; the discount rate (6.4) has been halved, and levels of damages for non-pecuniary loss (6.5) have been significantly increased, in recent years; the schemes for recovery of social security benefits paid to claimants and NHS hospital costs (15.3) has increased the total cost of tort compensation. There is also some evidence to suggest that the Woolf reforms may have significantly increased legal costs by what is called 'front-loading' – i.e. by making it necessary to spend at an early stage in the settlement process amounts the expenditure of which would formerly have been deferred until later. The earlier costs have to be incurred, the larger the proportion of cases in which they have to be incurred, and so the greater the legal costs of the system overall.[7]

But even if the cost of the tort system has doubled in real terms (taking account of inflation and increased claiming), it is still much less than the most recent guesstimates, which go as high as £14 billion or more. According to a

3 Pearson Report, vol. 1, tables 158, 159.
4 In *The Cost of the Compensation Culture*.
5 For example, the EU Working Time Directive, which limits working hours to 48 per week, is said to have increased the cost of care: Department of Health, *Making Amends: A Report by the Chief Medical Officer* (2003), 67. According to a large-scale survey of motor accident claims, the cost of personal injury claims (compensation plus costs) increased by nearly 10% per annum in the decade up to 2003 as a result of increasing numbers of claims (3% per annum) and increasing average cost of claims (6.7% per annum). Inflationary pressures are apparently greatest in relation to high-value claims. Legal costs as a proportion of total cost have remained steady at around 30%: International Underwriting Association of London, *Third UK Bodily Injury Awards Study* (London, 2003).
6 According to the *Third UK Bodily Injury Awards Study* increasing use of prosthetics (such as artificial limbs) has added significantly to medical costs in motor accident cases.
7 P. Fenn and N. Rickman, *Cost of Low-Value Employers' Liability Claims, 1997–2002* (DCA, 2003); J. Peysner and M. Seneviratne, *The Management of Civil Cases: The Courts and the Post-Woolf Landscape* (DCA Research Series 9/05, November 2005), p. 71. Note that the abolition of legal aid for most personal injury claims transferred costs from the public to the private sector but did not itself increase costs. The uplifts associated with CFAs and the cost of ATE insurance represent new real costs.

government report published in 2004, the cost of the tort system in the UK in 2000 was about 0.6% of GDP, which gives a figure in the region of £6 billion;[8] and a more recent official document puts the cost in 2004 at £7.2 billion.[9] We might then, with some confidence, estimate the total annual cost of the tort system at between £6 and £8 billion. This is obviously a very large figure; but it is important to maintain a sense of proportion. For instance, estimated total current (as opposed to capital) expenditure on the NHS in 2002–3 was more than £64 billion, whereas the amount paid out in tort compensation and costs by the National Health Service Litigation Authority (NHSLA) in 2004–5 was about £528 million – i.e. about 0.8% of total NHS current account expenditure.

The aggregate Pearson figure (£377 million in 1977 currency values) included legal costs paid by insurers and self-insurers to claimants in settlements (as well as those awarded in cases tried); legal costs paid by insurers and self-insurers to their own legal advisers; other disbursements paid by insurers and self-insurers to claimants (e.g. to cover the cost of medical reports); and the general administrative costs of the insurers,[10] or in the case of self-insurers, of their claims departments. But this figure does not include anything for the costs of running the courts, which hear the very small proportion of cases that go to trial or appeal. Thus according to the Pearson figures, the administrative expenses of the system as a whole amount to about 85% of the value of the sums paid out, or about 45% of the total costs of the system.[11] So (if we ignore insurers' investment income) we can say that about 55 pence of the insurance premium pound is paid out to injured victims, and 45 pence is swallowed up in administration.

As we shall see later, no other compensation system is anything like as expensive to operate as the tort system. The social security system, for instance, runs at a cost of about 12% of the total amounts paid out;[12] although it should be noted that this figure does not include the cost of raising the revenue out of which social security payments are made. The great expense of the tort system seems to be largely due to two factors: first, most insurance companies pay large sums of money to brokers and advertising agencies to sell their insurance policies; and, secondly, the tort system requires a detailed examination of every claim for personal injury damages.

This processing of claims is very expensive not because of the high cost of litigation (only a very small minority of claims are litigated), but for several other reasons. First, it is necessary (in theory, at least) to ascertain in every case who, if

---

8 Better Regulation Task Force, *Better Routes to Redress* (2004), 15. This figure is low by international standards.
9 Compensation Bill Final Regulatory Impact Assessment (2005), para. 2.10. The predicted cost in 2008–9 is £10.2 billion.
10 Including the cost of selling insurance, buying reinsurance and meeting claims.
11 Ibid., para. 261.
12 Pearson Report, vol. 2, para. 158. Some benefits are more expensive to administer than others depending e.g. on the difficulty of establishing the conditions of eligibility. The administrative costs of the New Zealand accident compensation scheme are about 7% of the amounts paid out: G. Palmer, 'New Zealand's Accident Compensation Scheme: Twenty Years On' (1994) 44 *U. of Toronto LJ* 223, 227.

anyone, was at fault and whether that fault caused the claimant's injuries. These are
very difficult questions to answer in many cases, and the process of investigation
may be time-consuming (and time is money); it requires expertise (which costs
money); and it may require the interviewing of witnesses, the taking of statements,
the commissioning of technical or medical experts to analyse the evidence and so
on (all of which can be very expensive). Secondly, the compensation payable in a
tort case depends on the medical condition and other circumstances of the particular claimant; there are no rigid tariffs or formulae for assessing tort compensation –
every case is different. Thirdly, because of the adversarial nature of the tort process,
both parties will employ advisers to make the same inquiries about the causes and
consequences of the accident. This duplication itself accounts for a considerable
proportion of the total cost.

The Pearson Commission estimated that fees (i.e. legal costs) paid by insurers
amounted to about 20% of compensation payments.[13] As compensation payments
totalled £202 million, this means that fees paid to claimants must have totalled
about £40 million.[14] If we assume that insurers had similar costs of their own in
dealing with the claim itself, this would account for about £80 million of the estimated total of £175 million. The Civil Justice Review estimated that average (legal)
costs incurred in cases tried in the High Court are between 50% and 75% of the
amount recovered (depending on the basis of calculation); and in the county court
costs are (staggeringly) between 125% and 175% of the compensation awarded
(again, depending on the basis of calculation). These figures also show that in relative terms, the smaller the claim the higher the costs: in the Civil Justice Review
survey the amount awarded in 89% of the county court cases was less than £3,000,
while only 41% of the High Court cases were disposed of for less than £3,000. Of
course, these figures represent a maximum because they relate to cases that went to
trial. But the bulk of the costs of a personal injury action will be expended before
trial and will, moreover, need to be incurred whether or not proceedings are commenced. Clearly then, a major part of the total cost of the system consists of legal
costs – 30% according to a recent survey.[15] And it is the nature of the system that
renders these legal costs necessary, because it is almost indispensable for a person
claiming damages to have the assistance of a solicitor. By contrast, a person claiming for damage to a car under a comprehensive policy would very rarely need to
consult a solicitor. Yet many such claims are more substantial than many personal
injury damages claims.

Who pays for all this? So far, we have contented ourselves with the general answer
that the 'public' pays. But it is now necessary to delve a little further into this ques-

13 Pearson Report, vol. para. 526.
14 In fact fees as such were paid in only 75% of cases, but presumably in other cases the claimant
received a sufficient sum in settlement to pay their own fees. In relation to claims closed in 2004–5
by the NHSLA, defence costs were about 14% of damages paid and claimant costs were about
21%.
15 International Underwriting Association of London, *Third UK Bodily Injury Awards Study*.

tion to see how the burden of payment is distributed. In a recent report, the Law Commission suggested that the government is probably the largest single payer of personal injury compensation in England and Wales; and in this sense, the public, in the form of the taxpayer, bears a significant proportion of the costs of the tort system.[16] According to recent figures,[17] more than half of all personal injury compensation claims arise out of road accidents, around one-quarter out of workplace accidents and illness, about one-fifth out of accidents in public places ('public liability') and a very small proportion out of clinical negligence and all other types of liability, including product liability. In the case of workplace claims the cost is, in the first instance, paid for by employers, mostly in the form of premiums for employers' liability insurance. These premiums are business expenses and are therefore tax deductible. In this way part of the cost is borne by the taxpayer. The rest of the burden is distributed by employers in the same way in which they distribute all their costs, that is by passing them on to employees (in the form of lower wages), customers (in the form of higher prices) and shareholders (in the form of lower dividends). But how any particular cost is distributed between these groups is impossible to say. One effect of liability insurance is that the cost of injuries in one business will be paid for partly out of premiums paid by other businesses. As between different classes of businesses, insurance rates are principally adjusted according to the risk they present (this is called 'feature rating' or 'classified rating'). Businesses in an industry with a higher injury rate will pay higher premiums than businesses in an industry with a lower injury rate. Hence consumers, employees and shareholders of more dangerous industries will pay rather more; though the differences are in most cases likely to be so small when spread among these groups that they will not be perceptible at all. As between different enterprises within a single industry, the scope for variation according to risk is limited by a number of technical considerations. Although it might be thought that an employer with a bad injury record would have to pay a higher premium than an employer with a good record, the use of such 'experience rating' is in fact quite restricted because it is actuarially unsound to base premiums on the past record of a business unless it is quite large.[18]

In the case of road accidents, the cost, though still largely met by means of liability insurance, is spread in different ways. That part of the cost attributable to commercial vehicles is distributed in much the same way as the cost of industrial injuries, while the cost of accidents caused by publicly owned vehicles (of which there are about 1 million in Britain) falls on the taxpayer. About four-fifths of vehicles on the road are cars and motorcycles, and most of them are privately owned; so insurance costs in this area cannot be distributed beyond the vehicle owner. The car owner pays for liability insurance with no tax relief, and cannot spread the cost

16 Law Com. No. 287, *Pre-Judgment Interest on Debts and Damages* (2004), para. 7.30.
17 *The Recovery of National Health Service Costs in Cases Involving Personal Injury Compensation: A Consultation* (2002), para. 2.7.
18 P.S. Atiyah, 'Accident Prevention and Variable Premium Rates for Work-Connected Accidents' (1975) 4 *Industrial LJ* 1 and 89; but for a rather different view see J. Phillips, 'Economic Deterrence and the Prevention of Industrial Accidents' (1976) 5 *Industrial LJ* 148. See also 17.7.2.2.

any further. In the workplace context, the cost of liability is paid by a large class consisting of employees, shareholders and consumers for the benefit, generally speaking, of a subset of that class, namely employees. By contrast, in the road traffic context the cost of liability is largely borne by a subset of the class of beneficiaries, namely private motorists, for the benefit, generally speaking, of all road users, including pedestrians and cyclists as well as motorists themselves.

As between motorists, the burden is distributed basically according to accident-causing potential. In practice, insurers classify motorists into quite broad groups according to certain factors which have been shown to be statistically significant in accident involvement; in particular age, claims record, place of residence and type of vehicle. A person who is a member of a high-risk group pays a larger premium than a person who belongs to a low-risk group, despite the fact that the former may in fact be a more responsible and careful driver than the latter and might have had fewer accidents. In this way, some members of a risk group with a claims record better than the average for that group may be subsidizing other members with a worse-than-average claims record. The main reason why insurers classify motorists into risk groups rather than according to the risk presented by each individual motorist is that increased sub-classification would be expensive and complex to administer.[19] On the other hand, it may not be thought fair that a person should have to pay a higher premium simply by virtue of being *statistically* more likely to be involved in an accident despite the fact that they have a very good accident record. However, the force of this argument is somewhat reduced by the fact that the typical motor accident insurance policy incorporates a no-claims bonus based entirely on the claims record of the policy holder. Also, insurers cannot afford to allow the risk-variation within an insurance group to become too large because, if it does, it may cause the less risky members to terminate their insurance and seek lower-cost cover from another insurer. In other words, competition between insurers encourages a certain amount of risk-differentiation.

Just as subsidisation may occur within risk groups, so too an insurer may decide to let one risk group be subsidised by another. For instance, if an insurer thought that the premiums chargeable to young drivers on strictly statistical principles were so high that few young drivers would be able to afford them, it might be tempted to undercharge young drivers and to compensate for this by overcharging older drivers. Once again, there are limits to which this is possible in a competitive insurance market, although it is a common feature of non-competitive (or 'mutual') insurance, such as that organized for the benefit of professional groups including doctors and lawyers: for professional reasons, premiums for such insurance are often much lower for newly qualified professionals than is statistically justified on the basis of risk.

We must also consider the costs of road accidents caused by uninsured motorists. As we have seen, the MIB meets the cost of liability in cases of this kind

---

19 Moreover, as sub-categories are multiplied, they become smaller and less reliable statistically.

as well as in other similar cases, such as where a person is injured by a 'hit-and-run' driver. The MIB collects its income from its constituent members, who are themselves insurers engaged in road traffic business in the UK, and all such insurers are now required to be members of the MIB. This has the curious result that disqualified motorists who still drive but cannot get insurance and motorists who simply fail to insure, are having their insurance paid for them by other motorists who are insured with members of the MIB.

So far as public liability claims are concerned, the bulk of these are made against local authorities, and so their cost is borne ultimately by taxpayers. Concerning the cost of medical negligence liability, general practitioners insure with one of the three medical defence societies, the best known of which is the Medical Defence Union. These societies are mutual insurance organizations funded by subscriptions from members. Such subscriptions are in effect paid by the Department of Health because they are taken into account in fixing remuneration levels. The societies also offer members a range of claims-related services. Most medical negligence claims are made against NHS hospital doctors for whose negligence, in most cases, a health authority is vicariously liable. Until relatively recently, hospital doctors paid subscriptions to one of the defence societies to cover the risk of liability, and the cost of liability was shared between the doctor (that is, the defence society) and the hospital authority (that is, the taxpayer). But in the 1980s subscriptions for hospital doctors increased very rapidly; and there were plans to change the traditional practice of fixing subscriptions according to the number of years each doctor had been in practice and to introduce risk classifications according to the nature of the work done. As a result, doctors in high-risk specialties, such as obstetrics and neurosurgery, would have paid much higher subscriptions than doctors in lower-risk specialties. The first response to rising subscriptions was that the government agreed to pay doctors' medical-defence subscriptions, whereas previously doctors had paid them personally. Later, in response to fears that high, risk-related subscriptions would have an adverse effect on patterns of medical practice,[20] the government decided to introduce what is called 'Crown (or NHS) indemnity'. Under this arrangement, hospital doctors no longer paid for liability insurance, and the whole cost of liability was to be borne by hospital authorities out of their own resources, and hence, by the taxpayer. Now there is a central fund, the Clinical Negligence Scheme for Trusts (CNST), administered by the NHSLA, into which NHS hospital trusts make risk-related annual payments in the nature of insurance premiums to cover compensation awards against them.

Finally, it must be remembered that in the case of injuries not caused by anyone's fault, or injuries for which the victim is partly to blame (and so for which they receive only partial compensation), the cost of the injuries may be borne partly by the victim personally. But part of it, at least, is likely to be met in other ways, such as by the NHS, the social security system, social services and also by friends and

20 For a further discussion see 17.7.1.1.

family. The same is often true even in the case of fault-caused injuries, because many victims of such injuries receive no tort compensation or an amount inadequate to meet their needs.

16.2   Costs not paid through the tort system

16.2.1   The cost of social services

The cost of social services is paid predominantly by payers of central and local government taxes. For example, the cost of medical treatment for injuries and diseases falls mainly on the NHS, which is largely paid for out of central government taxes. This is so regardless of whether the injury or disease was due to anyone's fault, and regardless of whether the victim recovers any tort compensation. A proportion of the costs to the NHS of negligently caused road accidents is recovered from payers of tort compensation under the Road Traffic (NHS Charges) Act 1999 (15.3). In 2000, it was estimated that the total cost to the NHS of treating road accident victims was £500 million;[21] but this figure relates to all road accidents, not just to those in relation to which compensation is paid. In 2002–3 about £100 million was recovered under the NHS recoupment scheme, but the total cost to the NHS of treating compensated victims of road accidents is unknown. From October 2006 the cost-recovery scheme extends to all personal injuries (but not diseases) for which tort compensation is paid, regardless of cause, and to ambulance as well as hospital costs.[22]

Legal aid is paid for out of general taxes. However, since 2000 only a few categories of personal injury claims qualify for legal aid; and the proportion of the legal aid budget spent on such claims is very small. For present purposes, the most important category is medical negligence claims. The great majority of legally aided medical negligence claims end in payment of compensation to the claimant, and this means that the claimant's costs will be paid by the defendant rather than by the Legal Services Commission. Any costs not recovered by the Commission from the defendant will be recovered from the claimant out of the damages received. However, since the defendant in the typical medical negligence case will be the NHS, the taxpayer will bear the legal costs of most such successful claims whether they are legally aided or not. Other relevant social services paid for by taxpayers or ratepayers include the police, rehabilitation units, local authority welfare services and so on. Part of the costs of these services is certainly attributable to road and industrial injuries, but premium payers make no direct contribution to meeting it.

The Pearson Commission made a rough estimate that the annual total cost of 'public services' provided to tort victims was around £525 million (in 1977

---

21 Royal College of Surgeons of England, *Better Care for the Severely Disabled* (2000), para. 4.3.
22 In 2000 it was estimated the ambulance costs associated with road accidents were about £20 million. In 2002 it was estimated that the annual cost to the NHS of treating 'accidental injury and poisoning' was £2.2 billion (not including expenditure on rehabilitation): Department of Health, *Preventing Accidental Injury – Priorities for Action* (2002), 6.

currency values, say £2.1 billion in 2005).[23] A significant proportion of this large total is externalized and not paid directly by the tortfeasors responsible for the accidents or diseases, or by their insurers. Prior to the availability of the Pearson statistics, it was estimated that in 1970, 42% of the cost of road accidents and 76% of the cost of industrial accidents was borne by 'external' sources, such as the social security system, the NHS, private insurance and sick pay arrangements.[24] Now, of course, as a result of the schemes for recouping the cost of social security benefits and NHS care, a smaller proportion of the costs of tort-caused injury and disability is externalized.

However, paying liability insurance premiums is not the only way in which vehicle owners contribute to the social costs of road transport, including road accidents. They also make an indirect contribution by paying excise taxes on fuel and vehicles, which raise many billions of pounds a year. Similarly, even if industry does not directly pay the full cost of industrial injuries, it no doubt makes a substantial indirect contribution in the form of taxation.

16.2.2   The cost of the social security system

The Pearson Commission estimated the total annual cost of social security payments to victims of tortiously caused personal injuries at £421 million (at an administrative cost of £47 million – both in 1977 currency values); but there have been so many changes in the social security system since then that it is very difficult to assess the contemporary validity of such figures. It is probably safe to say, however, that the equivalent amount in 2005 would not have been less than the current value of the Pearson figure – say about £1.7 billion. The total cost of industrial injuries benefits in the late 1970s was around £259 million per annum (1977 currency values); the administrative cost of the IIS was some £28 million.[25] The cost of the IIS (and of other contributory benefits) is borne by employee and employer National Insurance contributions, which are effectively a form of taxation. The cost of non-contributory benefits is met by the general taxation.

Although the industrial injuries system is still often treated as a species of national insurance, the insurance element in the system is minimal. In the first place, there are no 'contribution conditions'; every employed person who earns more than the contributions threshold is entitled to the same benefits irrespective of contributions paid. Secondly, National Insurance contributions are not related to the risk that the employee contributor will make a claim or that the contributing employer's business will precipitate a claim.[26] This means, in effect, that the 'good risks' subsidize the 'bad risks'. There are obviously sound reasons for not

23 Pearson Report, vol. 2, table 158.
24 D. Lees and N. Doherty, 'Compensation for Personal Injury' (April 1973) *Lloyds Bank Review* 18, 20.
25 These figures are no longer identifiable in the statistics; those given are based on the Pearson Report, vol. 2, table 158, and *Social Security Statistics 1978*. Note that only a proportion of recipients of industrial injury benefits would be victims of tortiously caused injury and illness.
26 See T.H. Marshall, *Social Policy in the Twentieth Century*, 2nd edn (London, 1967), ch. 4.

adjusting employee premiums according to the risk of illness and incapacity. Quite apart from the administrative complexity of doing so, the result would be that those in the most serious need – the chronically sick – would either be required to pay unaffordably high premiums or would be given uselessly small benefits. Apart from the subsidy inherent in contributions unrelated to risk, the other main source of subsidy in the National Insurance system for those most in need of assistance derives from the fact that National Insurance contributions are earnings-related.

Beveridge gave some thought to whether, in the IIS, contribution rates could be varied (as were rates for worker's compensation insurance, which industrial injuries was replacing) with the extent of the risk or the accident rate of the industry in question.[27] The trades unions (particularly the Mineworkers' Federation) were strongly opposed to variable premiums. They thought that miners' wages were depressed by the cost of mining accidents, and they argued that nearly all industries were dependent on coal and so ought to pay their share of the cost of coal mining accidents through flat-rate premiums.[28] Beveridge accepted these arguments, though he wished to impose a special levy on industries with a particularly high accident rate, primarily to encourage accident prevention. The government was unimpressed by the suggestion that risk-related premiums deterred accidents, and therefore rejected the idea for a special levy and adopted a uniform rate for contributions.[29]

One has only to compare the rate of reported accidents in different industries to get some indication of the extent of the subsidy involved in the uniform-rate principle. In 2002–3 in the construction industry, for every 100,000 employees there were 4 reported fatal accidents, 1,166 reported accidents causing injury leading to more than 3 days off work (including 'major injuries'); whereas in the service sector the corresponding figures were 0.3 and 487 respectively.[30] Another element of subsidy inherent in the uniform-rate principle is that employees injured at work receive higher benefits (under the IIS) than other disabled employees. The Robens Committee called for an urgent re-examination of the uniform-rate principle,[31] but a majority of the Pearson Commission reaffirmed it, mainly on the ground that the cost of risk-related contributions would outweigh the benefits.[32]

A third respect in which the industrial injuries system does not work on insurance principles is that while National Insurance contributions are earnings-related, with only very minor exceptions industrial injury benefits are not.

27 Beveridge Report, paras. 86–9.
28 But the price of coal itself would have included some amount representing the cost of coal mining accidents, and so industries dependent on coal were already contributing in this way to the cost of coal mining accidents.
29 Cmnd 6551, para. 30.
30 *Health and Safety Statistics Highlights 2002/3*, supplementary tables 10 and 12. These figures relate to reported injuries (1.4.1 n. 22 for an explanation).
31 *Robens Committee Report*, para. 447.
32 See further 17.7.2.2.

Perhaps the major respect in which the social security system is based on insurance principles is that in respect of a few benefits, certain conditions relating to the amount of contributions paid have to be satisfied before the benefit is payable. But even here, the contribution conditions are not usually actuarially determined.

On the whole, then, the social security system is, in very many respects, based not on insurance principles, but on welfare principles. This is most obviously true of benefits entitlement to which is not subject to contribution conditions and which are not funded by contributions but entirely by general taxation.

16.2.3   Other sources of compensation

Other sources of compensation and provision for tort victims include contractual sick pay, occupational pensions, personal accident and private health insurance and medical services provided by employers. The Pearson Commission estimated that tort victims annually received 'other payments' (omitting life insurance payments, but including criminal injuries compensation: see 16.3) of some £204 million (in 1977 currency values); and 'private services' worth some £50 million (1977 values). There is really no way of knowing how meaningful these estimates are; but no other more recent estimates are available.

16.2.4   Costs in perspective

The Pearson Commission estimated the annual combined total value of *all* compensation payments made to, and *all* services provided for, tort victims (and relatives in fatal cases) at some £1.45 billion – around £6 billion in 2005 currency. Although there is no way of reliably testing this figure, we can say with some confidence that the actual total in 2005 was probably no less than this, and that it may have been considerably more. Indeed, taking account of the fact that the there are about three times as many tort claims per annum now as in the 1970s, and that the cost of compensation and other benefits to tort victims has probably increased faster than the general rate of inflation, the actual total might be as high as £20 billion.

In attempting to make some sense of such a figure, several points in particular should, perhaps, be borne in mind. First, according to the Pearson Commission, only about a quarter of compensation payments to tort victims are made by tortfeasors and liability insurers; and compensation payments represent only about 60% of the combined total. In other words, even taking account of the social security and NHS recoupment schemes,[33] it is probably the case that significantly less than 20% of the combined total cost of compensation payments and services provided to tort victims is internalized to (i.e. paid by) tortious activities. The rest is spread, by various mechanisms, such as taxation and the cost of goods and services, widely across society. It is in this sense that it can be said (and is frequently said in

---

33 Which together bring in nearly £300 million a year and will yield perhaps £100 million more when the NHS scheme is extended in 2006.

this book) that no matter how or by whom the various benefits are provided in the first instance, ultimately they are paid for by the public or, in other words, by society as a whole.

Secondly, the benefits provided to tort victims (and their relatives) represent only a proportion of the total social costs of the death, illness and injury they suffer. For example, in calculating the 'value' of preventing road accidents, the Department for Transport adopts a willingness to pay methodology[34] that takes account not only of 'loss of output' and medical expenses (which may be the subject of tort compensation) but also costs which the tort system ignores, such as the cost of policing and insurance administration, and 'human costs' representing 'pain, grief and suffering' not only to the victim but also to relatives and friends; and in relation to fatal casualties, 'the intrinsic loss of enjoyment of life over and above the consumption of goods and services'.[35] Application of this method produces an *average* value of preventing a fatal road accident of almost £1.5 million (in 2002 currency values), and an *average* value of preventing a personal-injury accident (whether serious or slight) of about £73,000. On the basis of such figures, it is calculated that the total cost of road accidents in 2002 was more than £17.7 billion.

Thirdly, the combined total of the cost of benefits provided to tort victims represents only a relatively small proportion of all the benefits in money and kind provided in respect of death, illness and injury: most such benefits are provided to people who receive nothing from the tort system (including many tort victims). On the other hand, fourthly, the group of beneficiaries of tort compensation no doubt receives a disproportionately large share of the combined total of benefits in respect of death, illness and injury.

16.3   The cost of criminal injuries compensation

Compensation payments under the old CICS amounted to some £190 million in 1996–7. The number of claims and the amounts paid out increased greatly after the Scheme was first introduced.[36] The administrative cost of the Scheme in 1996–7 was 8.8% of total expenditure. In 2002–3, more than £160 million was paid out in compensation under the new CICS. One of the main justifications for introducing the new enhanced-tariff scheme in 1996 was to reduce the cost of criminal injuries compensation, including administrative costs. The former aim has been achieved but, surprisingly, the cost of administering the new, supposedly simpler, Scheme is significantly greater than that of administering the old Scheme: 13.5% of total expenditure in 2002–3. Although the CICS requires (like the tort system) an analysis of the circumstances of each case to ascertain the cause and gravity of the

---

34 6.5.1.
35 Highway Economics Note No. 1 (2002).
36 £400,000 was paid out in the first full year of operation. The total compensation paid out between the date the Scheme started (on 1 August 1964) and 31 March 1997 was about £1.6 billion. Almost a third of this sum was paid out in the years 1994–7.

injuries, it is very much cheaper than the tort system to operate. In the first place, the cost of raising the money to pay for the compensation is hidden in the cost of the taxation system from which it is funded. The cost of raising the money to pay compensation is a very substantial item in the tort system because of the high costs of insurance brokerage and advertising. Secondly, the criminal injuries system is cheaper than the tort system because it eliminates the adversary process and therefore involves only one set of costs rather than two. Legal aid is not available for applications to the CICS, nor for appeals to the CICAP; and the costs of claimants who are represented are not paid by the CICA.

Almost the whole cost of the CICS falls on the taxpayer, though it is in some respects a mistake to look at the Scheme in isolation from other compensation systems. It is by no means true that the whole cost of criminal injuries is met by the Scheme. As we have seen, social security benefits are deducted in full from awards under the CICS. In 2002–3 the CICA recovered about £730,000 from the proceeds of compensation orders and damages awards in favour of recipients of CICS awards; and in an attempt to increase this figure, the CICA now has power to recover directly from convicted criminals. The main reason why the scheme is financed by taxation and not by any form of insurance is simply that the risk of being injured by criminal attack is so small that the cost of administration would be out of all proportion to the size of the premium which it would be necessary to levy.[37]

One feature of the scheme, which may be thought to bear on the question of its financing, is that a proportion of claimants receive injuries from assaults or attacks which are in some sense related to their occupation. For example, police officers, security guards, bartenders, wages clerks, bus conductors and post office workers are all particularly vulnerable to criminal attack. It could be argued that employers ought to be made responsible for compensation awards when the offence is related to the claimant's occupation on the basis that assaults of this kind should be a charge on the business in question and not on the taxpayer. In practice, however, this would probably create more problems than it would solve. In any event, a substantial proportion of those whose occupations are relevant to the offence are public officials of one sort or another – police officers, customs officials and so on.

37 Cmnd 1406, para. 13(a).

17

The functions of compensation systems

17.1 Compensation

17.1.1 Some preliminary questions

So far in this book the word 'compensation' has been used loosely and in various contexts. We must now consider more carefully what is meant by the term, and ask why we compensate the victims of injury and disease. One possible answer to this second question is that widely held notions of justice and fairness demand it. Unfortunately, however, we have very little evidence concerning what people think about compensation for death and personal injury. Attempts have sometimes been made to ascertain common views by survey questionnaires, but the results are not particularly helpful. One writer concludes that 'there seems to be rather little evidence that when asked, people actually do express consensus support for a fault-based compensation system'.[1] Several (now rather old) surveys[2] found that an overwhelming proportion of those questioned were in favour of damages being awarded for pain and suffering; but when it is appreciated that those questioned were themselves recent victims of road accidents, what is surprising is not the majority of affirmative replies, but the substantial minority who did not favour such awards – some 20% in one and around 30% in another. One US survey devoted to pain and suffering found widespread misunderstanding about the way damages are calculated and about the likelihood of receiving damages for pain and suffering.[3] In England, a former trade union claims official once said that people injured in industrial accidents sometimes 'can hardly be convinced' that they are entitled to claim disablement benefit when they have suffered no loss of earnings.[4] On the other hand, debates following disasters, such as fires in public places and rail crashes, often reveal a considerable demand for increased damages

---

1 S. Lloyd-Bostock, 'Fault and Liability for Accidents: the Accident Victim's Perspective' in Harris 1984 Survey, 143, referring to US and Canadian surveys; see also Ison, *The Forensic Lottery*, 217 (England).
2 Conard, *Automobile Accident Costs and Payments*, 265; *Osgoode Hall Study*, ch. VIII, section E. See also J. O'Connell and R.J. Simon, *Payment for Pain and Suffering – Who Wants What, When and Why?* (Champaign-Urbana, Ill., 1972).
3 O'Connell and Simon, *Payment for Pain and Suffering*.
4 J. Bell, *How to Get Industrial Injuries Benefits* (London, 1966), 78. But attitudes may have changed.

for non-pecuniary loss and even for exemplary damages. However, if people were asked whether they would be willing to pay premiums sufficient to cover increased compensation for pain and suffering, it is not clear that they would answer affirmatively.

A major difficulty, in basing any justification for compensation on widespread beliefs, is that most people simply know too little about the way compensation systems operate in detail to have any relevant views on the matter. Compensation systems are extremely complex sets of rules, institutions and practices, and only those with expert knowledge of the way they work are likely to have considered views about them. Public debates about compensation are often characterized by widespread, basic ignorance not only of the way compensation systems work and interact, but also of the vigorous debates, about their strengths and weaknesses and about options for reform, that have taken place around the world in the past forty-odd years. Another difficulty arises from the fact that to the extent that ordinary people have views about the justice of compensation systems, they are probably conditioned by their contact with such systems, whether directly as claimants or defendants or indirectly through the media or the experiences of colleagues and friends. There is evidence that the attitudes of personal injury victims to questions of fault, responsibility and compensation are heavily influenced by what they know of the relevant legal rules.[5] More generally, there is probably a good deal of inter-action between the law, on the one hand, and ideas of justice and equity held by members of the community at large, on the other.

Even when Members of Parliament (who might be thought to represent com-mon views in some sense) discuss compensation systems, the discussion is usually limited to one compensation system or one aspect of a system, and does not concern itself with the complex network of systems we have surveyed in this book. The debates on the CICS illustrate the defect of this sort of selectivity only too well. Asked to approve a scheme for compensating the victims of crimes of violence, both Houses gave almost unanimous approval; but the question of whether the claims of victims of violent crimes rank higher (say) than those of accident victims who receive social security benefits was not discussed. This problem of narrowness of view is vividly illustrated by the fact that with the exception of off-setting of social security payments against tort damages and recoupment of NHS costs from tortfeasors, the wide-ranging investigation conducted by the Law Commission in the 1990s into various aspects of compensation law has focused on the tort system to the exclusion of the larger picture of interrelated systems of provision for the injured and disabled. Discussion of no-fault compensation schemes tends to be limited to areas such as medical mishaps, without consideration of larger questions about the interrelationship of such schemes with either the tort system or the social security system.

5 Lloyd-Bostock, 'Fault and Liability for Accidents' in Harris 1984 Survey; see also H. Genn, 'Who Claims Compensation: Factors Associated with Claiming and Obtaining Damages' in the same volume, esp 65–70.

Even if we could say that the web of compensation systems we have conforms to widespread ideas of justice, we might still want to ask whether the whole structure operates efficiently, and whether the various parts of it fit together in a consistent and coherent way. We can do this only when we have decided what purposes are served by individual compensation systems and by the structure as a whole. The first thing to note in this regard is that paying compensation is a two-sided process: money is transferred from one person or group of people to another. There are three important questions we can ask about this process, namely who should be paid?, what should they be paid? and who should pay? These questions are interrelated. Take exemplary (or 'punitive') damages, for example. These are rarely awarded in a tort action, and their main aim is to penalize the tortfeasor's conduct and to deter such conduct in the future; they do not make good any loss suffered by the injured person. So why should they be paid to the claimant? If they are, will not the claimant enjoy an undeserved windfall? And who should pay such damages? For example, should exemplary damages ever be awarded against a person who is vicariously liable for the tort that attracts the damages?[6] Should a person be allowed to insure against liability for punitive damages so that he or she does not pay them personally? If the aim of such damages is primarily to punish, the proper answer would seem to be negative in both cases; and if it is to deter, then the answer should be negative in the case of insurance, and also in the case of vicarious liability, unless it is thought that the vicariously liable person ought to exercise some control over the conduct of the tortfeasor so as to prevent the tortious conduct.[7]

Or take the case of damages for non-pecuniary loss (pain and suffering and loss of amenities): if we ask whether injury victims ought to be paid such damages, the answer may very well depend on who will pay them. If they will be paid by a person who was seriously to blame for the accident, we are more likely to feel that such damages should be awarded than if they will be paid by the taxpayer or by some large group of persons in no way responsible for the accident (such as insurance premium payers). For example, the Working Party on Compensation for the Victims of Crimes of Violence[8] expressed grave doubts about the idea of the State paying compensation for non-pecuniary loss except as part of a contributory scheme.

When we turn to damages for financial loss, we may not be too concerned about who will pay; our main concern may be that the victim is actually paid by someone and that what is paid represents all, or a substantial proportion of, the losses suffered. In this context, once we know that any compensation will be financed by quite small payments from each of a large group of people (taxpayers or insurance premium payers) we may become even less concerned about who pays and focus

6 P.S. Atiyah, *Vicarious Liability in the Law of Torts* (London, 1967), ch. 39.
7 For a recent discussion of all of these issues see Law Com. No. 247, *Aggravated, Exemplary and Restitutionary Damages* (1997), Parts IV–VI. The Commission answered both of the questions posed in the text affirmatively.
8 Cmnd 1406 (1961), para. 48.

our attention almost entirely on who and what is paid. This has happened to a large extent in the social security system, but in the tort system, much attention is still given to the question of who pays: the complex rules of tort liability ensure this.

In answering the question of what will be paid, there can be no doubt that the types of misfortune which a society is willing to treat as compensatable, and the amount of compensation it is willing to award, will depend to a significant extent on the wealth of that society. A very poor society in which people die of starvation or malnutrition and many live in conditions of great need is unlikely to be willing or able to devote much of its resources to compensation for illness and injury. Even in wealthy societies, the amount we are prepared to spend on compensation systems is limited. For this reason, if for none other, it is of vital importance to ensure that money available for compensation is spent in the best possible way.

17.1.2   The meaning of 'compensation'

The legal notion of 'compensation' is a complex one.[9] Lawyers usually talk about compensation 'for loss'; but as we will see, not all forms of compensation are concerned with 'loss' in any common sense of that word. To compensate a person is to make good an undesirable aspect of their circumstances or situation in life which falls below some pre-determined benchmark of acceptability. A useful distinction can be drawn between two different types of compensation according to the benchmark they use. We shall call these respectively 'corrective compensation' and 'redistributive compensation'.

17.1.2.1   Corrective compensation

Corrective compensation takes as its benchmark the situation in which the person to be compensated was at some earlier stage of their life. This is the sort of compensation tort law provides. As we saw in chapter 6, tort law compares the position the injured person was in immediately before the tort occurred with their position after the tort, and aims to restore them to that earlier position. Corrective compensation is essentially backward-looking. It seeks to protect people from the effects of adverse changes in their circumstances and to maintain continuity and stability in their lives. Tort law provides corrective compensation because its concern is to hold people responsible for injuries caused by their acts and omissions. Tort compensation is backward-looking because tort liability is backward-looking.

17.1.2.2   Redistributive compensation

By contrast, the benchmark used by redistributive compensation is not some position which the person to be compensated formerly occupied, but rather the position that other people now occupy. Redistributive compensation does not compare earlier and later positions of the same person, but contemporaneous positions of different people. This is the main sort of compensation provided by the

9 R.E. Goodin, *Utilitarianism as a Public Philosophy* (Cambridge, 1995), chs. 11–13.

social security and social welfare systems.[10] The basic aim of these systems is to reduce differences between individuals by transferring resources from the more to the less affluent, from the healthy to the sick, from the fortunate to the unfortunate. Redistributive compensation is essentially forward-looking. It is not concerned with making up for the past but with improving people's lives in the future. The social security system, for instance, is not concerned with how a person came to be in the position they are in but with whether fairness and humanity demand amelioration of that position.

Another useful distinction can be drawn between what we might call 'equivalent compensation', on the one hand, and 'substitute/solace compensation', on the other. This distinction is based on the fact that the compensation provided by the tort system is in the form of monetary payments, but that not all of the adverse changes for which tort law compensates are financial in nature. When tort law gives monetary compensation for adverse financial changes in a person's life, we can say that the compensation is equivalent to that which is being compensated for; but this is not the case when those changes are not financial.

17.1.2.3   Equivalent compensation

There are at least three different types of equivalent compensation. First, a person may be compensated for having been deprived of money or some other asset that can be fully replaced with money. A person loses wages when away from work as a result of an accident; or a person's car is wrecked in an accident and they need to buy a replacement; or a house is destroyed by fire and the owner must rebuild or buy a new house. In such cases, monetary compensation can give the person back exactly what they have 'lost' or enable them to acquire an exactly similar replacement.

The second type of equivalent compensation is designed to meet costs incurred by a victim of injury or damage. Such costs may take various forms from medical expenses to the cost of hospital visits or the cost of modifying a house to make it easier for the victim to live in. Here again, money can make good the adverse change in the claimant's position, namely the need to incur expense which was formerly unnecessary.

The third type equivalent compensation is concerned with lost expectations, chiefly the expectation of being able to earn in the future. This is compensation for loss of the capacity to earn as opposed to compensation for earnings lost in the past. We might ask why a person should be compensated for loss of earnings when that person will never render the services for which the earnings are payment. One good answer is that the person has been deprived of the choice whether or not to exercise their earning capacity. In many cases the best evidence available of the value of this capacity is what the person was earning before being incapacitated. But in some

---

10 However, there are pockets of corrective compensation in cause-based schemes such as the IIS and the CICS.

cases (e.g. children) the court has to speculate about what the victim's capacity would have enabled them to earn had they not been injured. If an injured person has never worked, and it is clear that they would never have worked even if they had not been deprived of the capacity, no compensation for loss of future earnings would be awarded. Another good reason for compensating for loss of future earnings is to provide stability and continuity in people's lives. This partly explains why tort law adopts the earnings-related principle for the assessment of damages: it aims to protect people from changes in their life circumstances.

Although equivalent compensation is similar in nature to that which is compensated for, it is not necessarily equal in financial value. Both the tort system and the social security system provide equivalent compensation; in other words, equivalent compensation may be either corrective or redistributive. But whereas the tort system is committed to the 'full compensation' principle in relation to loss of income (for instance), the social security system is not.

17.1.2.4   Compensation as substitute and solace

Tort law compensates not only for financial changes in a person's life, but also for adversities such as pain and suffering and loss of amenities which cannot, in any meaningful sense, be valued in money. In relation to such adversities, the compensation the law provides is obviously different in nature from that which is being compensated for. The object of such compensation is to enable the injured person to obtain a substitute source of satisfaction or pleasure (where some 'amenity' has been lost), or alternatively to comfort the victim or provide him or her with solace for what has happened (as in the case of pain and suffering). This type of compensation is most commonly awarded in cases of personal injury (although damages for inconvenience and mental distress are increasingly being awarded in cases involving claims arising out of property damage or financial loss).

There is only one situation in which tort law explicitly awards damages as a solace, namely when it awards damages for bereavement under the Fatal Accidents Act 1976. But in some other types of case – where, for example, a person loses their sense of smell – it is difficult to think of anything that would count as a substitute. Even where substitute pleasures can be found, they are almost bound to be only partial. So compensation for lost amenities is often wholly or partly solace for what has been lost. Damages for pain and suffering can really only be understood as providing solace.

Few compensation systems provide substitute/solace compensation. For example, cover under personal accident insurance policies is usually limited to medical expenses or income losses; and though disability payments are often made under comprehensive road accident insurance policies, they are usually very small. Apart from the tort system and the CICS, the only system that gives significant substitute or solace compensation is the industrial injuries scheme; and this is the sole instance of such compensation in the social security system.

It might be thought that substitute compensation requires much greater justification than equivalent compensation. There is, for one thing, the difficulty of fixing the level of compensation. What is a reasonable substitute for a pleasure foregone? How can we measure the amount of pleasure or happiness a person derives from this or that activity? Should we make some estimate in money of the subjective value to the victim of various forms of activity, or should we look at objective costs? Should we deduct, from the value of the pleasure foregone, the cost of obtaining it?

Solace compensation, it might be thought, is even harder to justify than substitute compensation. If such compensation were actually paid by the tortfeasor personally, it might be supportable on grounds of fairness. But since such compensation will usually be paid out of insurance premiums by a substantial section of the public, one is forced to ask whether there are not other claims on society's resources that deserve priority. This point applies to both substitute and solace compensation, but more so to the latter. It is hard to justify compensation for mental distress and deprivation of pleasure when many disabled people receive little or no compensation even for income losses. On the other hand, it might be thought that physical pain does deserve legal recognition in its own right, at least if it is severe.

17.1.3   Compensation and compensation systems

There are, perhaps, three main criteria for judging the success of a system as a mechanism for compensating for personal injuries and death. First, how many of those who are entitled to compensation according to the rules of the system actually receive compensation and in the amount to which they are entitled? Secondly, how many people, by fraud or abuse of the system, receive compensation to which they are not entitled? Thirdly, what are the administrative costs of the system? As regards this last criterion, we have seen that the administrative costs of the tort system are very high relative to the costs of the social security system and the CICS. As for the second criterion, the reader should refer to the discussion in 13.8.

Concerning the first criterion, it is difficult to judge how successful the tort system, the CICS or the social security system is because we lack reliable information about how many potential recipients of compensation from the various systems make no claim or about how many good claims are rejected. There is reason, however, to think that all of these systems fail to reach a significant proportion of those entitled under them. As for the amount of compensation, we have seen that one result of the process of settling tort claims is that very many claims are settled for less than they are worth according to the rules of the system, and that a significant proportion are probably settled for more than they are worth. By contrast, the CICS and the social security system are, subject to administrative errors, much more likely to deliver to claimants the 'correct' amount of compensation. On the other hand, it might be thought that, in theory at least, the tort system is 'better' than the CICS or the social security system because unlike those systems, it aims to provide 'full compensation' for death and personal injuries.

17.2   Distribution of losses

17.2.1   What should be distributed?

Compensation is, by definition, one of the functions of compensation systems. But they may have others. A common suggestion is that the distribution of losses is an important function of compensation systems. But to say this begs at least three important questions. The first is that of how we are to define 'loss'. A 'loss' is not something that exists or occurs outside the law and for which the law simply provides compensation. It is the law itself that defines what is meant by 'loss'. In some respects, the law's use of the word 'loss' is odd. Outside the law, for instance, we would probably describe the suffering of pain as 'harm' rather than 'loss'. In tort law, 'loss' refers broadly to adverse changes in a person's life circumstances. However, the legal meaning of 'loss' is not simply a question of proper linguistic usage but also of policy. For example, it is only relatively recently that English common law has recognized that a domestic carer who is rendered incapable of providing such care has suffered a loss for which damages may be awarded; again, the loss caused by bereavement was recognized for the first time by English law in 1982. A striking example is provided by the need of an injured person to be nursed: if a relative or friend does the nursing gratuitously, the law treats the victim as having suffered a loss (assessed as the reasonable value of the nursing services) for which damages can be awarded; but if the victim is nursed for free in an NHS institution, no damages are awarded for the value of the nursing. It is, therefore, not possible to define what is meant by 'loss' – all one can do is to describe the losses which the law recognizes as proper subjects of damages awards.

A second important question begged by speaking of the goal of the law as loss distribution is how we are to value losses. We have seen, for example, that tort law adopts the 'full-compensation' and 'hundred-per cent' principles in relation to pecuniary losses, and a tariff system for the assessment of non-pecuniary losses. On the other hand, for example, social security systems never compensate for income losses in full. A different type of valuation issue arises in relation to compensation for loss of ability to keep house or for gratuitous nursing services. Suppose the domestic carer or nurse gives up a job or foregoes the opportunity of working in order to work in the home or to nurse. Should the services be valued at what it would cost to employ someone to perform them, or at what the person doing them could have earned at work? Tort law has not explicitly committed itself to either of these measures of value but awards what, in the particular case, the court considers to be the 'reasonable value' of the services.

The third and most fundamental question begged by speaking of loss distribution as a goal of a compensation system is whether it is 'losses' with which the system should be concerned. The idea that losses should be our concern is to some extent a corollary of the fault principle and of the individualistic nature of tort law. Social security systems tend to be concerned essentially with meeting basic financial 'needs' by means of flat-rate benefits. The idea that losses should not always be the law's focus has been the subject of some debate in the tort system: in one case Lord Denning argued unsuccessfully that an injured person in a state of (almost) total incapacity who has no dependants should not be awarded damages for loss of income in addition to adequate damages for the cost of care because, in effect, the person did not need and could not use them, and they would be simply a windfall to her relatives.[11]

17.2.2   How should it be distributed?

Compensation for loss can be said to involve shifting the loss from one person to another. But where the loss is not of money or money's worth (e.g. pain and suffering), the process of making some person compensate the victim for the misfortune is very inaccurately described as 'shifting the loss'. Losses of this kind cannot be shifted from one person to another in any meaningful sense. It may be possible to minimize pain and suffering, for example, by medical treatment, and it may be possible to make someone else pay for this medical treatment; and this may, perhaps, be regarded as 'shifting a loss'. But when all has been done to minimize the pain and suffering by medical means, any residual pain and suffering cannot be shifted: it remains with the victim, no matter what compensation is paid to that person by others.

The shifting of a loss – or making one person compensate another for some misfortune – involves an alteration of the status quo; and so it involves administrative expense. Therefore (it is usually asserted), the onus is on those who wish to shift a loss to justify the shift. Unless there is some good reason for shifting a loss, it should be left to lie where it falls. Tort law mostly attempts to justify the shifting of losses by reference to the fault principle, but this has become increasingly unattractive to many people. Tort lawyers have searched for something to put in its place, and some have found their answer in the idea of 'loss distribution'. The effect of the tort system is not, in general, merely to shift a loss from one person to another; the loss is normally distributed over a large number of people, and over some period of time. It is true that this distribution is not normally achieved by rules and practices which are regarded as part of tort law; but the combined practical effect of tort law, liability insurance and the operation of the market is, in practice, to distribute losses among a large group of people and over a period of time.

There is no doubt that the distribution of losses is an important and usually desirable result of successful tort claims. Losses that may be crushing if imposed on an individual can be borne easily when distributed amongst a large group of people; this is clearly in the interests of those who are themselves at risk, as well as of society as a whole. There is also a great gain in security and peace of mind when the fear of crushing losses from sudden disaster is displaced by knowledge that the loss will be spread. But to advocate loss distribution as an end in itself invites as an obvious retort: loss distribution among whom? There are many ways in which

---

11 *Lim Poh Choo v. Camden AHA* [1979] 1 All ER 332.

losses can be distributed; and – which is merely saying the same thing in another way – there are many ways in which money can be raised from members of the public. Tort law, interwoven as it is with liability insurance, provides one way. First-party insurance provides another way. Social security provides still another way of distributing losses, financed as it is by a mixture of insurance and taxation.

These are not the only ways of distributing losses. All sorts of permutations and combinations are possible. For example, compensation for road accidents could be financed by a fund contributed to solely by motorists, but by flat-rate contributions instead of by variable insurance premiums as at present; or it could be financed by a special tax on petrol, so that (in general) motorists who used the roads more would pay more; or the fund could be contributed to by all road users, including cyclists and pedestrians – though this large group is so nearly co-incident with the entire population that it would be tantamount to an ordinary tax. Or again, a special levy could be imposed on motor manufacturers and perhaps also on highway authorities, which could be paid into the fund. Much would no doubt depend on how compensation was to be assessed. If it involved paying variable compensation for income losses, it might be thought equitable to make people pay contributions to the fund according to their income. Alternatively the whole process could be financed out of general taxation, and no special tax imposed for the purpose. Because there are so many ways of distributing losses, it cannot be said that loss distribution as such is a rational and desirable goal of the law. Any loss distribution system must be judged according to the way it distributes particular losses. For example, few would find acceptable a system which distributed the costs of road accidents entirely amongst non-motorists or the costs of smoking-induced cancer entirely amongst non-smokers.

Two things about the tort system seem clear, however. The first is that loss distribution cannot be the sole purpose or justification of the tort system, because both in theory and in practice tort law allows recovery for only a small proportion of personal injury losses.[12] Secondly, it seems clear that there are much cheaper and more efficient ways of distributing the losses the tort system does deal with than the present combination of liability rules and liability insurance.

How, then, are we to choose between methods of loss distribution? Or, to put the question differently, how ought a system of loss compensation to be funded? There seem to be three broad options: first-party loss insurance (whether private or State-run (National Insurance)), which spreads the loss amongst potential victims; third-party liability insurance, which spreads the loss amongst those likely to inflict it; and general taxation. Each of these mechanisms can be used alone or in combination with other methods. Just as important as the method of funding is the question of whether the compensation paid out, on the one hand, and the contributions to the fund, on the other, are to be the same for all beneficiaries or contributors (i.e.

---

12 For the same reason, it makes no sense to say that compensation for death and personal injury is *the* goal of the tort system because even in theory, tort law only compensates for death and personal injury which comes about in certain ways.

flat-rate) or variable in some way (e.g. income-related).[13] A third important question, which cuts across the first two, is whether losses ought to be distributed by free market mechanisms (which would make people pay for what they enjoy and for the losses they cause), or by State-run schemes or by a mixture of the two. State-run schemes can be used to achieve other ends in addition to loss distribution, such as income redistribution in favour of the poor.

Another criterion relevant to choosing between methods of distribution is efficiency. There are several aspects to the question of efficiency. One is the administrative cost of the process; and as we have seen, the administrative costs of the social security system and of the CICS are much lower than those of the tort system. The comparisons are slightly misleading because a significant part of the cost of the tort system is attributable to the cost of collecting the money used to pay compensation, while the cost of collecting social security payments and criminal injuries compensation is borne partly by employers (in the case of National Insurance contributions and income tax) and partly by the tax system, and so it does not figure in the administrative costs of providing benefits or compensation. But even making allowance for this, it is clear that, on cost alone, the tort system is extremely inefficient.

17.3   The allocation of risks

Another commonly suggested purpose of the law is to allocate the risk of the occurrence of certain events between various parties rather than to decide whether one person has caused injury to another by fault or whether one person should compensate another for a wrong. The idea of risk allocation seems particularly appropriate to cases of strict liability in tort law and to many areas of the law of compensation outside the tort system, such as the industrial injuries scheme. For example, the basis of the principle in *Rylands* v. *Fletcher* is that a person who collects dangerous substances on land should bear the risk of their escape whether or not the escape was that person's fault.

It was in the field of workers' compensation that the idea of risk allocation first made a powerful impact. It was felt to be unjust that the whole burden of accidents should lie on the injured worker, and that it was immaterial that the accidents were or were not caused by fault. These risks were felt to be risks of the business.[14] Similarly, the vicarious liability of an employer for the wrong of its employees has often been justified by invoking the idea that the employer should take the risk of its employees causing injury or damage.[15] This is why strict liability is often referred to as 'enterprise liability'.

---

13 It should be noted that flat-rate levies are 'regressive' in the sense that they place a greater relative burden on those who are poorer; by contrast, income-related levies bear less heavily on the poor.

14 P.S. Atiyah, *Vicarious Liability in the Law of Torts* (London, 1967), 22–4.

15 Ibid.

Of course, saying only that the law is concerned with allocating risks does not answer the question of to whom particular risks ought to be allocated or why certain risks are allocated in a particular way. This question alerts us to the fact that although the language of risk allocation is often associated with strict liability in tort law, the difference between fault-based and strict liability is not that the latter allocates risks of injury but the former does not, but that they allocate risks of harm in different ways. When, for instance, a pedestrian is injured on the road without fault on anyone's part, why should the risk of such injury rest on the pedestrian rather than on motorists? Or if a person is injured as a result of an explosion of gas escaping from a fractured main, should the risk of such injury be borne by the gas undertaker whether or not negligence can be proved?[16] Underlying many judgments about how risks should be allocated lies the notion that a person who 'creates' a risk should be made to bear the cost of the risk; and the idea of 'creating' a risk is often based on causal concepts. A gas board whose leaking pipes result in an explosion that destroys a house is thought of as having 'caused' the destruction of the house, and so to have 'created' the risk of such damage. But in the absence of fault, there may be no greater reason for saying that the destruction of the house was 'caused' by the presence of the gas pipes than by the presence of the house itself. And if the house was built after the pipes were laid, there may be no more reason to say that the risk was 'created' by the gas board than by the house owner. If we are to justify allocation of risk to one party or the other, we need some better criterion. In tort law, the rule in *Rylands* v. *Fletcher*, for instance, is based on the idea that people who carry on very dangerous activities should bear the risks of those activities; and vicarious liability rests on the idea that people who carry on activities for profit should bear the risks of those activities. Another possible approach is to impose liability on the party in the better position to minimize the risk, so as to give that party an incentive to do so. A different approach would be to ask which party would be in a better position to distribute the loss if the risk materialized.

So, as with loss distribution as a goal of the law, risk allocation as such makes no sense as an objective of a compensation system. A scheme of risk allocation must be judged according to how risks are allocated.

17.4   Punishment

Punishment of wrongdoers (and by this means expressing disapproval of what they have done) is widely accepted as a legitimate function of the criminal law; but the 'conventional wisdom' is that punishing tortfeasors is not the reason why they are obliged to pay damages for injury and damage inflicted by their torts.[17] The House of Lords has, therefore, defined narrowly the circumstances in which 'punitive damages' (i.e. damages designed to punish the tortfeasor rather than to compensate

16 See *Dunne* v. *NW Gas Board* [1964] 2 QB 806.
17 *Rookes* v. *Barnard* [1964] AC 1129; *Broome* v. *Cassell* [1972] AC 1027.

the injured person) are recoverable in a tort action.[18] Unless there is express statutory authority, punitive damages can be awarded in only two situations: first, where a person or body exercising governmental powers has been guilty of arbitrary, oppressive or unconstitutional conduct; and, secondly, where the wrongdoer has sought to make a profit out of the tort. These two grounds for awarding punitive damages were not seen by the Law Lords as based on a rational foundation; indeed, the judges would probably rather have held that punitive damages were never available in a tort action, but they felt compelled by earlier cases to reach the decision they did.

Not all would agree with this restrictive approach to punitive damages. In the USA, for instance, punitive damages are sometimes awarded against corporate defendants, especially in unfair competition, product liability and environmental pollution cases; and some in this country have urged that punitive damages should be more widely available in personal injury actions, particularly those in which corporate or governmental defendants have been responsible for what is seen as seriously culpable inattention to the safety of members of the public. The main arguments used against punitive damages are that they amount to a criminal fine, but one which is imposed without the procedural safeguards for defendants which are built into the criminal process; and that damages which do not represent any loss suffered by the claimant are a 'windfall', and so unjustifiable.

Apart from the two grounds already mentioned on which punitive damages can be awarded, there are certain other situations in which the law of torts might be seen as performing a punitive function. First, courts are sometimes prepared to award what are called 'aggravated damages' in cases where the tortfeasor's conduct towards the victim was particularly outrageous or humiliating; such damages are said to be 'compensatory', not punitive, but they are awarded over and above ordinary compensation and are really indistinguishable from punitive damages.[19] Such damages may be awarded even if the tort victim suffers no compensatable loss, but only humiliation, outrage or indignity. It is doubtful whether wilfully or intentionally inflicting outrage or indignity on a person is tortious in itself (although it is in the USA);[20] but even in England such conduct would be actionable where the defendant has been guilty of conduct falling under one of the traditional heads of tort liability such as fraud, battery or libel. So, for example, if a person commits a battery by spitting at another, it is inconceivable that a judge would send the victim away with nothing but nominal damages. Another part of the law of torts that may be seen as performing a partly retributive function is the tort of defamation, although in theory this tort is designed to compensate for 'loss of reputation'.

The Law Commission has recently given detailed consideration to the law of punitive damages. Its main recommendation was that punitive damages should be

---

18 *Rookes* v. *Barnard* [1964] AC 1129.
19 But see Law Com. No. 247, *Aggravated, Exemplary and Restitutionary Damages* (1997), Part II.
20 *Prosser and Keeton on the Law of Torts*, 5th edn (St Paul, Minn., 1984), 57ff.

available in cases where the wrongdoer has shown 'deliberate and outrageous dis-regard of the claimant's rights'. Such a case could, in theory anyway, be a case of death or personal injury; but it is likely that the proposal would have no impact on the vast majority of personal injury claims. On the other hand, it would make punitive damages available in some types of case in which they cannot currently be awarded: where, perhaps, an employer deliberately cuts corners on safety for the sake of profit.

17.5   Corrective justice

As we have seen, punishment can rarely be a feature of a personal injury action. Because damages for personal injuries aim to be compensatory we may, perhaps, describe the function of the law in terms of corrective justice – by awarding compensation the law aims to restore and redress the balance of fairness or justice which the tortfeasor has upset by negligence or by creating a risk of injury. There is a huge modern literature on corrective justice in tort law, and it contains many different definitions of the concept. However, the basic idea behind it is fundamental to understanding tort law. Personal injury tort claims involve one individual seeking damages from another individual on the basis that the latter is responsible in some sense for the former's injuries. In tort law, a person will be responsible for another's injuries only if they 'caused' those injuries in the sense of 'cause' adopted by tort law. Normally, too, responsibility for personal injuries in tort law rests on fault. The realization of whatever other functions we may attribute to tort law or look to it to achieve is necessarily constrained by the fact that tort liability for personal injuries depends on responsibility for those injuries. For instance, tort law compensates people for losses, but only if responsibility for those losses can be pinned on some other individual. Again, we may hope that tort law will reduce accident levels; but its ability to do so is limited by the fact that it is only concerned with accidents that result in injuries for which someone other than the victim is responsible. And even if we accept punishment as a proper function of tort law, performance of that function is necessarily restricted to people responsible for causing injury to others.

In short, tort law is based on ideas of personal responsibility for the adverse effects of a person's conduct on others; and one of its functions is to express and give effect to such ideas. In this respect, it is quite different from the social security system (as well as from first-party insurance). Social security benefits are not claimed from individuals but from the State; and the basis of entitlement is not that the State is responsible for the claimant's plight. Nor is the obligation of citizens to 'contribute' to social security funds based on such responsibility. One might say that the social security system involves compensation without responsibility. A major theme of this book has been that the requirement of responsibility in tort law is one of the main sources of the gross inefficiency of the tort system of compensating for personal injuries. In this context, at least, the cost of corrective justice may be unacceptably high. Ironically, at the same time the development of liability insurance has seriously undermined the ability of tort to operate as a corrective justice system.[21]

Further doubt is cast on the capacity of the tort system to achieve the corrective justice aspirations of tort law by the fact that only a small proportion of accident victims secure compensation through the system and the fact that there is no direct relationship between accident victims' decisions to make tort claims and notions of responsibility.[22] In short, while the rules and principles of *tort law* are based on ideas of corrective justice, 'the notion that the *tort system* adjusts the relationship between victim and harm-doer is a fiction'.[23]

17.6   Vindication or satisfaction

Tort victims (and their relatives and friends) are often angry and resentful. Compensation can go some way to removing such feelings, as can punishment of the wrongdoer (whether by an award of aggravated or punitive damages, or by some other penalty). Often such feelings arise out of ignorance about what happened, which may be accompanied by refusal on the part of the tortfeasor to admit any responsibility.[24] In such circumstances a formal or informal inquiry aimed at finding a convincing explanation of what went wrong can often do much to assuage feelings of anger and resentment. It may be a great satisfaction to a personal injury victim (and to other interested parties) to be able to demand an 'official' inquiry into what happened. Such demands may be met by the setting up of a public inquiry. Inquiries of this sort may take place even when legal liability is not contested, so as to expose the wrongdoer to public scrutiny,[25] to apportion blame (and praise) formally and to explore ways of preventing similar occurrences in the future.[26] Such public inquiries are designed to ascertain facts and, sometimes, to ascribe responsibility for them. They do not award damages or grant any other legal remedy, although the findings of public inquiries often greatly assist the process of evidence-gathering for the purposes of the settlement or trial of legal claims. Indeed, tort claimants whose claims are investigated by a public inquiry may be put in a much stronger bargaining position than other claimants, and may have many of the costs of constructing their claims met by the taxpayer.

Ordinary litigation, which is usually conducted in public and which may attract a certain amount of media attention, can also satisfy the desire that wrongdoers be

---

21 For further development of this argument see P. Cane, *The Anatomy of Tort Law* (Oxford, 1997), ch. 7.
22 Lloyd-Bostock, 'Fault and Liability for Accidents' in Harris 1984 Survey, 160.
23 Ibid.
24 A. Simanowitz, 'Accountability' in C. Vincent, M. Ennis and R.J. Audley eds., *Medical Accidents* (Oxford, 1993), ch. 14.
25 Otherwise the wrongdoer may settle the claims with a minimum of publicity and without having to consider their future conduct.
26 For a discussion of public railway inquiries see B. Hutter, 'Public Inquiries: the Case of the Railway Inspectorate' (1992) 70 *J. of Public Administration* 177.

made publicly accountable. Indeed, it has been argued that tort law can play a role as a public grievance mechanism similar to an ombudsman, especially in cases against public authorities or large corporations (such as drug companies or transport undertakings) whose actions have caused widespread damage or injury to many people.[27] In such cases a tort action may serve as much to establish responsibility and to vindicate feelings of outrage and grief as to obtain compensation. As compared with a public inquiry, tort has the attraction that the citizen can set the system in motion and does not have to wait for the government to act. If the tort system of compensation for personal injuries were ever abolished entirely, it might be thought desirable to institute some procedure for citizen-initiated inquiries of this type.

However, the potential of the tort system for affording public vindication is limited. Most tort actions attract very little publicity even if they go to trial; and the vast majority are settled out of court by private agreement. The real defendant is usually an insurance company, not a tortfeasor, and the purpose of most tort claims is simply to unlock the door to an insurance fund. It is not uncommon for settlement agreements to contain clauses by which the claimant agrees not to publicize the grounds or terms of the settlement.[28] Furthermore, settlements are typically made 'without admission of liability' on the part of the tortfeasor. The low value which the tort system law places on vindication is further shown by the fact that if the defendant offers sufficient compensation to the claimant by way of settlement of the claim but the claimant rejects the offer and insists on a trial out of a desire for public vindication, they will normally have to pay the costs of the hearing (10.4). So far as the legal system is concerned, settlement out of court is better than trial in court. Even so, there is empirical evidence that some people view the very making of a tort claim as an aggressive act, and this may partly explain why tort claims are very rarely made, for instance, against friends, relatives and even employers.[29] From this point of view, whatever vindicatory capacity the tort system has does not support but interferes with its compensatory capacity.

Public vindication is not provided at all by compensation systems, such as personal insurance and social security, in which entitlement to compensation does not depend on establishing legal wrongdoing, where the compensation is sought from and paid by persons in no way responsible for the loss suffered, and where entitlement to compensation is determined by an administrative process conducted in private. Appeal hearings before tribunals and Criminal Injuries Compensation Appeals Panel adjudicators normally attract no publicity at all; indeed, criminal injuries appeal hearings are held in private.

27 A. Linden, *Canadian Tort Law*, 5th edn (Toronto, 1993), 20–7.
28 But if a case is settled after a draft judgment has been sent by the court to the parties, they cannot prevent its being delivered in open court: *Prudential Assurance Co. Ltd* v. *McBains Cooper* [2000] 1 WLR 2000.
29 Lloyd-Bostock, 'Fault and Liability for Accidents' in Harris 1984 Survey, 155.

17.7   Deterrence and prevention

One of the most important of the suggested functions of personal injuries com-pensation law is deterrence of potentially injury-causing conduct and the preven-tion of injury-causing incidents such as accidents. A distinction is sometimes drawn between specific and general deterrence. Specific deterrence involves the express prohibition or regulation of dangerous conduct or activities by means of statutes or regulations, typically backed up by criminal sanctions for non-compliance, in order to reduce the number of injuries and injury-causing inci-dents. General deterrence involves the use of compensation rules to provide indirect incentives to people to behave safely – the basic idea is that the prospect of having to pay damages for injuries caused by particular conduct will deter people from engaging in conduct of that type.

This idea of general deterrence can be given a more or less precise interpreta-tion. The less precise version says that by establishing rules and standards of con-duct and by attaching the sanction of damages (or, in the case of victims, a reduction of damages) for failure to satisfy those standards and rules, the law can provide incentives to safe conduct. This version also sees the law as performing an educational function. The more precise interpretation, which is based on economic principles, says, broadly, that if the cost of injuries inflicted by an activity is required by law to be paid by those who engage in that activity, they will take precautions to prevent inflicting injuries, provided the cost of precautions is less than the cost of the injuries (i.e. the damages they have to pay); and that in this way the optimum or efficient level of precautions (and, conversely, of injuries) will be reached. If the cost of precautions exceeds the cost of the injuries, so the theory goes, precautions will not be taken; but because those who engage in the activity are required to bear the cost of the injuries, the activity will become more costly. This will deter people from engaging in it, at least on the same scale as before, and will, consequently, reduce the number of accidents or injuries caused by it. This more precise version is sometimes called 'market deterrence', but more commonly 'general deterrence'; and in what follows the term 'general deterrence' will normally be used to refer to the more precise version.

In this book we are primarily concerned with the two versions of general deter-rence because they are about the way compensation systems can be used to promote safety. It should be noted that compensation systems are not the only, or even the most important, means of deterrence and injury prevention. In the two main fields in which personal injuries are compensatable by common law damages, that is road accidents and workplace injuries, other methods are at least as important. On the road, reliance is placed on a combination of criminal penalties – fines for reckless, careless, dangerous and drunken driving and disqualification from driving; and improved road and vehicle design. In the case of workplace injuries, reliance is placed on the criminal law and on education and publicity. On the other hand, it may be that compensation law is more effective as a deterrent in the latter case than in the former, because in these cases the potential tortfeasor will very often be a business concern, and business concerns are probably more sensitive to the incentives that tort law provides than are individuals. This will be discussed in greater detail later.

17.7.1   Rules and standards of behaviour

The less precise version of general deterrence has two aspects: first, that of deterring people from conduct which may injure others;[30] and secondly that of deterring people from conduct which may injure themselves.

17.7.1.1   Causing injury to others

If we make people pay for damage or injury they cause to others, they may try to cause less damage or injury. The effectiveness of the tort system as a deterrent depends crucially on the ability of the potential tortfeasor to take steps in advance to prevent the damage or injury occurring. There are several aspects to this. One, as we saw earlier (7.6), is that by allowing victims free choice as to who is and is not sued and by concentrating on the parties to the action, tort law tends to ignore other factors which may be responsible for accidents in many cases, such as the state of roads. In order to reduce accidents and injuries it is necessary to study their causes very carefully.

> If we try to find out why a particular accident occurred, we can seldom pinpoint a single cause. Nearly always, it might have been prevented if any one of a variety of things about the road, the vehicles, or the people involved had been different.[31]

When the causes of road accidents are carefully investigated, it may be found that deterring drivers from negligent conduct is not the easiest or cheapest way to avoid a certain type of accident. For example, the most effective way of preventing people driving into the car in front of them at night may be to require the rear end of vehicles to be better lit. Clearly the deterrent value of tort law is thrown into doubt if courts regularly ignore important causes of injuries. It is also the case that the less we know about the causes of particular injuries, the less will we be able to use tort law as a means of establishing standards of safety. This problem is particularly acute in respect of diseases.[32] Furthermore, the standard-setting function of tort law is

---

30 See generally D. Dewees, D. Duff and M. Trebilcock, *Exploring the Domain of Accident Law: Taking the Facts Seriously* (New York, 1996).

31 *Road Safety – A Fresh Approach* (Cmnd 3339, 1967), para. 7. See also J.T. Reason, 'The Human Factors in Medical Accidents' in Vincent, Ennis and Audley, *Medical Accidents*, ch. 1; C. Vincent, M. Ennis and R.J. Audley 'Safety in Medicine' in ibid., ch. 15. But see Pearson Report, vol. 2, table 42 summarizing findings of a Road Research Laboratory study that found 65% of road accidents may be the result of human error alone. See also C.J. Bruce 'The Deterrent Effects of Automobile Insurance and Tort Law: A Survey of the Empirical Literature' (1984) 6 *Law and Policy* 67, 68–73. A survey by a firm of insurance brokers in 1989 showed that 80% of traffic accidents occur in fine weather, 72% in good visibility and 70% on dry roads: *Financial Times*, 5 September 1989.

32 J. Stapleton, *Disease and the Compensation Debate* (Oxford, 1986), ch. 4; D.N. Dewees and R. Daniels, 'Prevention and Compensation of Industrial Disease' (1988) 8 *International R. of Law and Economics* 51.

unlikely to be of much importance in relation to the design of new products or drugs, where manufacturers and designers are operating at the edge of known technology.[33]

Another aspect of this point is that it is easier to deter deliberate conduct by the threat of a tort action for damages than it is to deter merely negligent conduct.[34] The risk of tort liability is more likely, for instance, to deter a surgeon from operating on a patient without his or her consent than to deter the surgeon from making a negligent mistake in the course of the operation. Again, the risk of liability is no doubt a factor in deterring newspapers from publishing material that they realise might be defamatory;[35] and there is some US evidence that the risk of tort liability may discourage vendors of alcohol from serving obviously intoxicated customers.[36] Road and workplace accidents, with which the tort system is in practice chiefly concerned, are often caused by inadvertent failure of observation and perception, by faulty judgment, by lack of basic skills and other factors which the threat of liability is unlikely to deter.[37] For example, the fear of liability will not induce a motorist to stop at a stop sign he or she has not seen – even if the driver ought to have seen it. Furthermore, given that negligent drivers put themselves as well as others at risk by their carelessness, it is perhaps unlikely that they will be deterred from carelessness by the prospect of having to pay a fine or damages if they are not deterred by fear for their own safety.[38]

It does not follow, however, that we can never hope to deter people from negligent conduct by threats of liability. For instance, we may not be able to deter a drunk from dangerous driving once behind the wheel, but we may be able to deter a person from getting drunk before driving. We cannot induce a driver to stop at a stop sign he or she has not seen, but we can try to bring pressure on drivers to look for stop signs rather more carefully.[39] Drivers can be discouraged from speeding,[40] drinking before

---

33 In this context, disclosure to consumers of product-risk information and enforcement by regulatory bodies of minimum safety standards are likely to be important: P. Burrows, 'Products Liability and the Control of Product Risk in the European Community' (1994) 10 *Oxford Review of Economic Policy* 68, 78–82.

34 For a general theoretical discussion of this issue see H. Latin, 'Problem-Solving Behaviour and Theories of Tort Liability' (1985) 73 *California LR* 677. The empirical literature on the causation of accidents distinguishes between (unintended) 'errors' and (deliberate) 'violations'.

35 E. Barendt *et al., Libel and the Media: The Chilling Effect* (Oxford, 1997); U. Cheer, 'Myths and Realities About the Chilling Effect: The New Zealand Media's Experience of Defamation Law' (2005) 13 *Torts LJ* 259.

36 F.A. Sloan *et al.,* 'Liability, Risk Perceptions and Precautions at Bars' (2000) 43 *J. of Law and Economics* 473.

37 The idea that some people are accident prone plays a part here. See C. McManus and C. Vincent, 'Selecting and Educating Safer Doctors' in Vincent, Ennis and Audley, *Medical Accidents*, 80–5.

38 There is evidence that people do learn from accidents independently of whether their accident-causing conduct was penalized: Transport and Road Research Laboratory (TRRL), Survey Report 750 (1982); A. Quimby and K. Watts, *Human Factors and Driving Performance* (TRRL, Laboratory Report 1004, 1981).

39 By seeing accidents or being involved in them people may learn how they are caused and how to avoid them. Simulated accidents and defensive driving courses are thought to be helpful: TRRL, Survey Report 750 (1982).

40 On the strong correlation between speeding and accidents see D.J. Finch *et al.,* 'Speed, Speed Limits and Accidents', Transport Research Laboratory (TRL), Project Report 58 (1994). On the

driving and driving when overtired[41] (all major causes of road accidents) and from consciously taking other unreasonable risks.[42] Pedestrians can be discouraged from crossing against red lights and going out on the roads when drunk.[43] Tort liability may also have some deterrent effect where the potential defendant is a business concern or an institution, such as a health authority, which will weigh the relative costs of paying damages and preventing injuries; and where the injuries are caused by defective products or premises or by unsafe working conditions which can be made safer by conscious design and which may be unsafe exactly because of a conscious decision to skimp on safety.[44]

Even so, there are serious limitations on the effectiveness of the risk of tort liability as a means of preventing injuries. Trying to deter people from dangerous conduct by bringing pressure to bear before they get themselves into the dangerous situation is only likely to be effective to the extent that people recognize dangerous situations. For example, one of the reasons why so many people drive while drunk is because, despite the introduction of drink-driving laws[45] and extensive educational campaigns, they still do not fully appreciate the risks involved.[46] Another reason why the risk of tort liability is likely to be a relatively ineffective deterrent is that it probably does not present itself as a very serious possibility to many people. This may be partly a result of the same ignorance of the law we noted when discussing claims consciousness,[47] and partly because of the prevalence of liability insurance. People are more likely to be deterred from careless driving (for instance) by fear for their own safety or by a significant risk of incurring a fine or driving disqualification[48] than by the risk of tort liability. Important, too, are social attitudes to particular types of careless behaviour. For example, it has been found that social disapproval of drunk driving plays an important part in reducing its

relationship between personality and speeding accidents see R. West, J. Elander and D. French, 'Decision Making, Personality and Driving Style as Correlates of Individual Accident Risk' (TRL Contractor Report 309, 1992).

41 It has been estimated that tiredness is a contributory factor in about 10% of car accidents: G. Maycock, 'Tiredness as a Factor in Car and HG Accidents', (TRL Report 169, 1995); and of 15–20% on 'monotonous roads, especially motorways': J.A. Horne and L.A. Reyner, 'Sleep Related Vehicle Accidents' (1995) 310 British Medical Journal 565. But hard evidence is lacking: J. Connor et al., 'The Role of Driver Sleepiness in Car Crashes: A Systematic Review of Epidemiological Studies' (2001) 33 Accident Analysis and Prevention 31.

42 See also Bruce, 'The Deterrent Effect of Automobile Insurance and Tort Law', 68–73, 78–81; Dewees, Duff and Trebilcock, Exploring the Domain of Accident Law, 20–1.

43 A third of pedestrians killed on UK roads are under the influence of alcohol.

44 Some businesses may be more susceptible to external incentives than others: H. Genn, 'Business Responses to Regulation of Health and Safety in England' (1993) 15 Law and Policy 219.

45 On the effect of such laws see J.R. Snortum, 'Another Look at "The Scandinavian Myth" ' (1984) 6 Law and Policy 5. One researcher found that the proportion of injured road users with blood alcohol concentrations above the legal limit was highest in groups not subject to the constraint of such laws: J.T. Everest, 'Drinking and Driving' in Papers on Vehicle Safety, Traffic Safety and Road User Safety Research (TRRL, 1991).

46 Drink Driving: The Effects of Enforcement (Home Office Research Study 121, London, 1991), 33. About 20% of drivers and motorcycle riders killed in road accidents are over the legal alcohol limit: TRRL, Research Report 266 (1990).

47 8.2.3.

48 Drink Driving: The Effects of Enforcement, 46.

incidence;[49] and it has been suggested that seat-belt laws are more effective than drunk-driving laws because they are 'morally neutral'.[50]

One of the reasons why fines (etc.) for driving offences are more likely to achieve deterrent effects than tort liability is that the standards of conduct prescribed by the criminal law (in the form of traffic and industrial safety rules and regulations) are usually much more precise than those laid down by the law of tort. If we are to take deterrence seriously, we must give people detailed guidance as to how to behave.[51] For example, because people like to think they are careful drivers, general exhortations to drive with care or at a reasonable speed are less likely to deter carelessness than specific rules such as that a car must not cross a double unbroken centre line or must not be driven at more than a stated speed.[52] It also appears to be important that rules should be clear and unambiguous:[53] it is better to establish a clear rule for right of way at roundabouts than to tell driver to take care at roundabouts.[54] The common law of tort does not typically give detailed guidance but only requires people to take reasonable care according to all the circumstances of the situation they are in. What is reasonable care will only be decided by a court after an injury has occurred, and courts usually refuse to give specific guidance for the future on the ground that the exact circumstances of each particular case are crucial in deciding how the defendant ought reasonably to have behaved. The courts fear that if they lay down detailed rules of conduct, such rules may turn out to be 'under-inclusive' by failing to deal with a particular set of facts which the court did not contemplate but which it thinks gives rise to a good claim for compensation.[55] The disadvantage of this approach is that many decisions that a particular defendant was negligent do not have much deterrent potential.

On the other hand, if a case deals with a frequently recurring situation, and if the nature of the negligence is identified in some detail, even court decisions may influence future conduct.[56] For example, in one case it was decided that a local authority had been negligent in using untoughened glass only one-eighth of an inch thick in school doors instead of toughened glass, because of the risk of

49 Ibid., 46–7.
50 J.S. Legge Jr, 'Reforming Public Safety: An Evaluation of the 1983 British Seat Belt Law' (1987) 9 *Law and Policy* 17, 33.
51 Also, this guidance needs to be well publicized through the media or educational programmes.
52 On the other hand, excessively detailed rules and regulations may be counter-productive in safety terms: Robens Committee Report, paras. 28–9. The deterrent effect even of specific rules is affected by how rigorously they are enforced. For instance, over a 6-year period in Victoria, a campaign of rigorous enforcement of speed limits reduced the proportion of drivers exceeding the limit from 23% to 1.8%; and rigorous enforcement of drink-driving laws reduced drink-related fatal accidents by 50%: *The Times*, 11 January 1999.
53 D.R. Harris, 'Evaluating the Goals of Personal Injury Law: Some Empirical Evidence' in P. Cane and J. Stapleton eds., *Essays for Patrick Atiyah* (Oxford, 1991), 304.
54 M. Austin, *Accident Black Spot* (Harmondsworth, 1966), 68–9.
55 The courts are more concerned to maximize the efficacy of tort law as a compensation mechanism than as a deterrence mechanism.
56 Data about settled cases is bound to be much less influential because the nature of the negligence will often not be clearly identified, and records of settled claims may not provide the required information. Also, of course, the fact that a negligence claim is settled favourably to the claimant

accidents to pupils.[57] It would not be surprising if this decision was treated as laying down a rule that glass in all school doors should be toughened, and if local authorities proceeded to act on the decision by replacing glass which did not conform to the rule. Even relatively non-specific rules can have some effect. For example, it has been suggested that replacing a rule that doctors need give patients only such information about their treatment as doctors think reasonable with a rule that doctors must, as a general rule, give patients all 'material' information and answer all their questions, can have an effect on doctors' behaviour, even though no two patients and no two situations are likely to be identical in all respects.[58] It is still probably true to say, however, that other things being equal, the more specific a rule of conduct, the greater its deterrent potential is likely to be.

We might summarize the discussion so far by saying that there are reasons to doubt the effectiveness of tort law as a deterrent to negligent conduct and as an effective mechanism for reducing accidents and injuries. But there is also some reason to think that fear of tort liability may sometimes actually be counter-productive in terms of accident prevention. A suggestion sometimes made is that by focusing attention on accidents which generate compensation claims, the tort system diverts attention away from the majority of accidents which do not, and so discourages the formation of systematic and thorough accident-prevention strategies.[59] In another direction, however, it is sometimes said that the fear of liability may make potential defendants unwilling to investigate or discuss injury-causing incidents lest evidence of tortious conduct should emerge. Even worse, they may tamper with documentary or other evidence in order to protect themselves. In the workplace context, the injured person's fellow workers, too, may be reluctant to discuss what happened for fear of prejudicing their colleague's claim for damages. Moreover, potential defendants may be unwilling to take remedial measures before any claim is settled for fear that this may be interpreted as an admission that adequate precautions were not taken before.[60]

It has often been suggested that the fear of tort liability can also be counter-productive by encouraging excessive caution and unnecessary precautions on the part of potential defendants; in other words, it may be said that tort law over-deters. This suggestion has been made in a variety of contexts, but most commonly in

does not mean that the defendant's conduct was tortious. Indeed, claims are typically settled without admission of liability. For a discussion of the difficulties of using data about medical negligence claims as a basis for risk management programmes see R. Dingwall and P. Fenn in R. Dingwall and P. Fenn eds., *Quality and Regulation in Health Care* (London, 1992), ch. 1.

57 *Reffell* v. *Surrey CC* [1964] 1 WLR 358.
58 For a medical practitioner's view see W.A. Ollbourne, 'The Influence of Rogers v. Whitaker on the Practice of Cosmetic Plastic Surgery' (1998) 5 *J. of Law and Medicine* 334.
59 E.g. M. Brazier, 'NHS Indemnity: The Implications For Medical Litigation' [1990] *Professional Negligence* 88, 90; H. Genn and S. Lloyd-Bostock, 'Medical Negligence – Major New Research in Progress' [1990] *J. of Medical Defence Union* 42, 43. Concerning shortcomings of studies of litigated medical mishaps as aids to accident prevention see C. Vincent, 'The Study of Errors and Accidents in Medicine' in Vincent, Ennis and Audley, *Medical Accidents*, 21–3.
60 E.A. Webb, *Industrial Injuries: A New Approach* (London, 1974), 11.

relation to medical treatment.[61] For instance, it is widely said that in the USA, where the number of medical malpractice actions is thought to be relatively high, doctors are encouraged to practise 'defensive medicine', that is to prescribe or refuse to provide treatment, procedures (such as Caesarian sections) or medical tests not because this is in the patient's best interest but merely to safeguard themselves from possible legal liability. Other suggestions are that fear of being sued leads people to leave or not to enter high-risk specialties (such as obstetrics) and may cause certain medical services to be unavailable.

There are several problems with such suggestions. First, such empirical evidence as there is does not really establish any clear connection between the incidence of tort liability and the various effects ascribed to fear of being sued.[62] One explanation may be (as we saw earlier: 8.3.3) that apparently only a small proportion of events of medical negligence results in tort claims.[63] Furthermore, evidence suggests a significant lack of fit between success or failure in a tort claim for medical negligence and presence or absence of negligence (respectively).[64] Secondly, the concepts of 'over-deterrence' and 'defensive medicine' are themselves problematic because the amount of care which it is appropriate to take is, to some extent at least, a value-judgment.[65] Thirdly, in England, as a general rule, a doctor will be held to have been negligent only if no body of reputable medical opinion (regardless of how small the minority may be which holds the opinion) can be found to support

---

61 For a careful discussion see R. Dingwall, P. Fenn and L. Quam, *Medical Negligence: a Review and Bibliography* (Oxford, 1991), 41–56. See also M.A. Jones and A.E. Morris, 'Defensive Medicine: Myths and Facts' (1989) 5 *Journal of Medical Defence Union* 40; D. Tribe and G Korgaonkar, 'The Impact of Litigation on Patient Care: An Enquiry into Defensive Medical Practices' [1991] *Professional Negligence* 2; Dewees, Duff and Trebilcock, *Exploring the Domain of Accident Law*, 96–112; B. Dickens, 'The Effects of Legal Liability on Physicians' Services' (1991) 41 *U. of Toronto LJ* 168; *Factors Influencing Clinical Decisions in General Practice* (Office of Health Economics, London, 1991); M. Ennis, A. Clark and J.G. Grudzinskas, 'Change in obstetric practice in response to fear of litigation in the British Isles' (1991) 338 *The Lancet* 616.

62 Dewees, Duff and Trebilcock, *Exploring the Domain of Accident Law*, 112. In Britain, a survey by the Royal College of Obstetricians and Gynaecologists reported in 1992 showed that although 85% of British obstetricians are or have been involved in litigation, this is less of a deterrent to recruitment than long working hours, resident conditions and the job prospects of junior hospital doctors: P. Saunders, 'Recruitment in Obstetrics and Gynaecology: RCOG Sets Initiatives' (1992) 99 *Brit. J. of Obstetrics and Gynaecology* 538; see also F.A. Sloan *et al.*, 'Tort Liability and Obstetricians' Care Levels' (1997) 17 *International Rev. of Law and Economics* 245. It is sometimes suggested that fear of liability discourages doctors from acting as Good Samaritans; but see K. Williams, 'Doctors as Good Samaritans: Some Empirical Evidence Concerning Emergency Medical Treatment in Britain' (2003) 30 *J. of Law and Society* 258. This is not to say that there is no evidence of defensive medical practices. See e.g. D. Kessler and M. McClellan, 'Do Doctors Practice Defensive Medicine?' [1996] *The Quarterly Journal of Economics* 353; K. Clark, 'Litigation: A Threat to Obstetric Practice?' (2002) 9 *J. of Law and Medicine* 303. But there is little evidence that it contributes significantly to health spending: G.F. Anderson *et al.*, 'Health Spending in the United States and the Rest of the Industrialized World' (2005) 24 *Health Affairs* 903.

63 M.M. Mello and T.A. Brennan, 'Deterrence of Medical Errors: Theory and Evidence for Malpractice Reform' (2002) 80 *Texas LR* 1595.

64 Ibid., 1618–20.

65 So some would argue that exposure to tort liability might have a beneficial effect on medical practice: R. Bowles and P. Jones, 'Medical Negligence and the Allocation of Health Resources' [1988] *Professional Negligence* 111.

what the doctor did as reasonable. This means that a doctor is unlikely to be held negligent for doing what other doctors do or for failing to do what other doctors do not do.[66]

There is no doubt that the prevalence of liability insurance greatly reduces the deterrent potentiality of tort law. For example, a motorist who is not deterred from doing something foolish by fear for his or her own safety or that of passengers in the car, nor by fear of the criminal law, nor by fear of being disqualified from driving, is not likely to be deterred by the fear of being sued in a tort action in which the damages will be paid by an insurance company. There is no real evidence that fear of the loss of a no-claims bonus or of having to pay the excess under a policy has any significant effect on the incidence of accidents.[67]

It has sometimes been suggested that motorists should not be permitted to protect themselves by unlimited liability insurance but that they should, for instance, be required to pay a certain amount of any claim personally.[68] This might jeopardize the accident victim's chances of receiving full compensation, and it would be a high price to pay for the additional deterrent value of such a scheme. A variant, which would overcome this problem, would allow or require the insurer to recover the designated sum from the insured after it had been paid to the victim. But the administrative cost of such a scheme would probably be unacceptably high. If the threat of having to pay large sums of money is a valuable deterrent against dangerous driving, a more satisfactory approach would be to introduce much larger criminal fines for driving offences. This would not jeopardize accident victims' compensation and it would have the desirable effect of giving incentives to be careful to offending motorists who do not cause accidents as well as to those who do.

In workplace-accident cases the problem is similar. Here also, liability insurance is compulsory and this means that the immediate financial consequences of an accident are not felt by the employer.[69] It is true that employers shoulder considerable indirect or incidental costs arising from accidents, such as disturbance of production, consumption of management time and effort in dealing with the accident

66 There is US evidence that doctors greatly overestimate the risk of being sued: M. Ennis and C. Vincent, 'The Effects of Medical Accidents and Litigation on Doctors and Patients' (1994) 16 *Law and Policy* 97, 100. If this is true, the better (partial) explanation of defensive medicine may be unrealistic fear of incurring tort liability rather than the incidence of tort liability as such. The way to cope with such fear is better education of doctors about the law. Assessing the impact of (the fear of) tort liability is further complicated by the fact that a doctor who has a medical mishap may face disciplinary proceedings or, in extreme cases where the patient dies, prosecution for manslaughter. 'Seriously negligent treatment' can amount to 'serious professional misconduct' for which a doctor can be disciplined: *McCandless* v. *General Medical Council* [1996] 1 WLR 167. There is some evidence that defensive practice may result from medical accidents even in the absence of actual or threatened litigation: Ennis and Vincent, ibid., 101–3. On the impact of accidents more generally see B.M. Hutter and S. Lloyd-Bostock, 'The Power of Accidents' (1995) 30 *Brit. J. of Criminology* 409.
67 But it may have an effect on claims under first-party policies.
68 J.J. Leeming, *Road Accidents: Prevent or Punish?* (London, 1969), 210–11.
69 The effectiveness of liability insurance in accident prevention is examined later (17.7.2).

and claims arising from it and so on. Such incidental costs represent a significant proportion of total accident costs. These are not normally covered by insurance,[70] but they will be passed on to the extent that the employer is able to do this; so they will not hit any individual sufficiently hard to provide an effective incentive to take accident avoidance measures. Even in the industrial field, the role of tort law as a deterrent will be limited so long as the primary aim of the law remains the compensation of the injured.

17.7.1.2   Avoiding injury to oneself

It seems unlikely that tort law provides people with significant incentives to take care for their own safety. The law attempts to do this through the doctrine of contributory negligence; but (as was argued above in the context of causing injury to others) if a person's instinct for self-preservation does not deter them from dangerous conduct, it is unlikely that a denial of monetary or other assistance will do so. If people are not deterred from smoking by knowledge of the health risks, it is unlikely that they would be deterred by a refusal of treatment under the NHS for disease caused by smoking, or by the possibility of being met by a defence of contributory negligence or *volenti non fit injuria* in a tort action against the cigarette manufacturer. Similarly, it seems unlikely that a person with an irrational fear of, or a religious objection to, receiving certain medical treatment which is medically advisable following an accident, will be induced to have it because, as a result of the doctrine of mitigation of damage, they may be deprived of damages for refusing treatment. This is not to say that a serious risk of incurring a fine or other criminal penalty might not have some deterrent effect, or to deny the importance of social pressures not to engage in dangerous conduct; but it does cast doubt on the deterrent impact of tort law.

The case of failure to wear a car seat-belt illustrates this. The common law treats such failure as contributory negligence, and a claimant's damages may be reduced on this ground. However, research has shown that during the period 1973–80 only about 30% of drivers and front-seat passengers wore seat-belts despite the risk of receiving reduced damages if injured while not wearing a seat-belt. In 1983 when, subject to limited exceptions, it became a criminal offence for a driver or front seat passenger not to wear a seat-belt if provided, the compliance rate rose to 95% for cars and over 80% for vans.[71] This dramatic change is perhaps partly attributable to the greater deterrent effectiveness of the criminal over the civil law; partly to the fact that the new provision was much better publicized and known than the common law rule; and partly because of the confirmed efficacy of seat-belts in reducing injuries – it is estimated that there are now some 20–25% fewer fatal and serious injuries to drivers and front-seat passengers than there would have been

---

70 It has been estimated that the ratio of insured to uninsured losses resulting from work accidents is between 1:8 and 1:36 depending on the type of industrial operation in question: *The Costs of Accidents at Work* (HMSO, 1993).

71 *Road Accidents Great Britain 1983* (HMSO, 1984), table 11.

without compulsory belt-wearing.[72] Social attitudes may also be important. Like smoking in public, failure to wear a seat-belt is widely frowned upon. By contrast, attempts to reduce speed-related accident rates may be hampered by 'the ethos of speed' that 'permeates discourse on driving' and 'has infiltrated all aspects of modern life'.[73]

17.7.2   Accident prevention via insurance

Because insurance (whether third party or first party) weakens incentives to prevent the loss insured against, insurers use various techniques to overcome what they call the 'moral hazard' generated by insurance.[74] There are two main types of technique. One is to encourage or require insured parties to take loss prevention measures; and the other is the use of risk-related premiums, excess payments (or 'deductibles'), ceilings on cover, and so on.

17.7.2.1   Encouraging or requiring loss prevention measures

Because insurance involves the pooling of a large number of risks, the insurer may find it worthwhile to take steps to reduce or eliminate risks that no individual risk-bearer would take. For example, fire brigades in England were originally established and maintained by insurers; not until 1865 was responsibility for fire-fighting transferred to local authorities. No individual householder would find it worth-while to maintain adequate fire-fighting facilities, because the value of any partic-ular house multiplied by the risk of its being burned down is far less than the cost of such facilities. But if an insurer sells fire policies to 100,000 house-owners, the risk the insurer bears may make it profitable for it to maintain a fire brigade. Similarly, insurers employ inspectors to survey plant, equipment and premises and to advise insured parties how to minimize risks and avoid losses. In the USA, for instance:[75]

> . . . regulation of the design safety of aircraft was initiated by insurers . . . Underwriters Laboratories, at the request of the National Aircraft Underwriters' Association, formed an aviation department in 1920 to certify the airworthiness of aircraft and develop

72 Ibid., para. 3.10. See also Legge, 'Reforming Public Safety', 31–2. For research showing the overall pattern of reductions and increases in particular types of injuries following the introduction of compulsory seat-belts see TRRL, Research Report 239 (1989). On the other hand, it has been suggested that seat-belts (and other aspects of car design provided as 'safety features') give drivers a false sense of security which may lead them to take risks with their own and other people's safety which they might not otherwise have taken. For evidence that improvements in road design may have similar effects see R.B. Noland, 'Traffic Fatalities and Injuries: The Effect of Changes in Infrastructure and Other Trends' (2003) 35 *Accident Analysis and Prevention* 599. But for a deeply sceptical view of the validity of such research see R. Elvik, 'To What Extent Can Theory Account for the Findings of Road Safety Evaluation Studies?' (2004) 36 *Accident Analysis and Prevention* 841.

73 Department for Transport, 'The Effects of Speed Cameras: How Drivers Respond (No 11)', 8.

74 C. Parsons, 'Moral Hazard in Liability Insurance' (2003) 28 *Geneva Papers on Insurance and Risk* 448.

75 J. Braithwaite and P. Drahos, *Global Business Regulation* (Cambridge, 2000), 454. This may be seen as an example of the efficacy of liability-cum-liability-insurance as a 'regulatory mechanism'; in

airworthiness standards . . . a function ultimately taken over by the Federal Aviation Administration.

In this country insurers have traditionally played their largest loss minimization role in connection with engineering and fire insurance.[76] For example, they maintain (in conjunction with fire authorities) a joint fire research organization which investigates fire causation and prevention. No insurer would take on any significant fire risk without surveying the premises. Employers' liability insurers may also survey premises and operations, and persuade or require the employer to take various precautions before the risk is accepted.[77] On the other hand, Stapleton argues, in relation to the prevention of diseases and health hazards (as opposed to traumatic accidents) that, 'loss minimization by insurers via the direct action of inspecting and advising policy holders is virtually impossible because of the much greater scientific expertise required in this area'.[78]

Potentially even more efficient than the efforts of insurers to prevent losses are community-wide accident-prevention techniques. Fire brigades maintained by insurers for the benefit of their policyholders are better than no fire brigades at all; but fire brigades maintained by the State for the benefit of all are better still. Similarly in the area of industrial safety, it is, in principle at least, more efficient for the Health and Safety Commission and the various government safety inspectorates to monitor and promote safety in industry generally by inspection, research, education and the enforcement of safety regulations,[79] than for the various employer's liability insurers to attempt to do so. In any event, when the insurance market is highly competitive, insurers have little incentive to spend money on loss-prevention: it has to be paid for out of premium income, and an insurer who chooses to spend little or nothing on loss prevention may be able to undercut insurers who spend significant amounts trying to reduce losses. Unless insurers undertake this loss-prevention activity jointly (as in the fire insurance industry) not much can be achieved; but joint activity, in turn, may attract accusations of illegal

other words, as a means of influencing human behaviour in order to promote socially desirable objectives, such as safety. By contrast, it has been argued that in relation to nuclear power generation, tort law was prevented from performing a regulatory function because governments protected the nuclear power industry from full tort liability, which would have been uninsurable: Braithwaite and Drahos, ibid., 308. On the relationship between tort law and regulation see P. Cane, 'Tort Law as Regulation' (2002) 31 *Common Law World Review* 305; J. Stapleton, 'Regulating Torts' in C. Parker *et al.* eds., *Regulating Law* (Oxford, 2004).

76 Sansom (1965) 62 *Journal of the Chartered Insurance Institute* 97.
77 See the evidence of the Association of British Insurers to the Robens Committee, Robens Committee Report, vol. 2, 43ff. One of the initiatives taken to address the recent 'crisis' in employers' liability insurance was to encourage insurers to offer lower premiums to employers who could demonstrate that they had devoted additional resources to safety. But as of mid-2005, employers' organizations were complaining of lack of progress in this regard: e.g. R. Tyler, 'Liability pledge a waste of time', *Telegraph*, 28 July 2005.
78 Stapleton, *Disease and the Compensation Debate*, 128.
79 Public regulatory techniques are beyond the scope of this book. For a discussion see R. Baldwin, 'Health and Safety at Work: Consensus and Self-Regulation' in R. Baldwin and C. McCrudden eds., *Regulation and Public Law* (London, 1987), 132–58.

restrictive practices and price-fixing.[80] Even in the USA, where the insurance industry has played an important role in promoting safety in industry, it has not done much, if anything, to further accident prevention on the roads.[81] One notable illustration is the failure of the insurance industry to force motor manufacturers to install seat-belts in cars once it became clear that they could play a major role in reducing the gravity of injuries: action in this field had to be taken (both in the USA and in this country) by legislation.[82]

17.7.2.2 Risk-related premiums and similar techniques

Excess (or 'deductible') provisions, under which the insured is obliged to pay the first £X of any claim, are designed both to encourage the insured to take measures to minimize the possibility of insured events occurring and to discourage small claims, which are disproportionately expensive to process. Deductibles are a common feature of first-party insurance; and compulsory motor insurance policies in respect of third-party property damage were, until recently,[83] not required to cover the first £300 of loss.[84] Exclusions from cover can also serve a deterrent function. For example, some insurers will not meet first-party road accident claims (or will seek to recover from the insured amounts paid out in respect of third-party liability claims) which result from the insured driving with a blood alcohol content above the legal limit.

Insurance companies can, in principle, set premiums in such a way as to encourage the insured to take loss-prevention measures and to reduce the severity of losses that do occur. For example, fire insurers may set different premiums for the insurance of buildings that have adequate sprinkler installations and those which do not.[85] In some contexts, differential premiums may prove unacceptable. For example, premiums for professional liability insurance under non-profit ('mutual') schemes run by the professions themselves often subsidize younger practitioners at the expense of the more experienced, even though the former might be expected to present a greater risk. Again, the threat of the introduction of medical negligence liability premiums related to the riskiness of different medical specialties, in place of flat-rate premiums, was a major catalyst for the introduction of Crown indemnity.[86] In the case of liability insurance in respect of road accidents and workplace injuries, it has proved difficult to devise premium structures that have a significant effect on accident costs and rates.

80 See e.g. *Report of the Monopolies Commission on Fire Insurance* (HMSO, 1972).
81 R.E. Keeton and J. O'Connell, *After Cars Crash* (1968), 95.
82 Insurers may be unduly sceptical of their ability to influence vehicle design: *Report of the British Columbia Royal Commission on Automobile Insurance* (1968), citing Swedish experience.
83 See 9.9 n. 107.
84 Ceilings on cover are also a common feature of liability insurance, including compulsory employers' liability insurance (£5 million per incident) and compulsory motor insurance in respect of third-party property damage (€1 million). Ceilings are not designed to deter insured events but to limit the insurer's exposure and so keep premiums down.
85 *Report of the Monopolies Commission on Fire Insurance* (HMSO, 1972), para. 106.
86 16.1.

So far as concerns road accidents, the general picture is well enough known. Liability insurance premiums depend on a variety of factors which have, in the past, been shown statistically to be associated with high claims experience; such factors include age,[87] sex,[88] vehicle type and level of usage. 'Feature-rating' on the basis of such factors does not take account of the claims record of the individual insured but is based on the aggregate claims record of the group(s) to which the particular insured belongs. On the other hand, the typical no-claims bonus system takes account of each particular insured's claims record (and so it may be called a system of 'experience rating'). A person with a history of accidents (or, more accurately, of accidents which give rise to claims) will pay substantially more for liability insurance than a person who has made few or no claims in recent years, regardless of which risk-category each belongs to. Drivers with a certain number of points on their licence may also be charged higher premiums.

Despite appearances, however, there is reason to doubt that the premium structure of motor liability insurance is based on sound scientific or statistical principles. For example, probably only some 3 to 4% of drivers are involved in a personal injury road accident in any one year, whereas six or seven times this number may be involved in accidents resulting in property damage alone. As a result, the claims record of most drivers is based largely on property damage accidents only; but this claims record also affects the size of that part of the premium which covers third-party personal injury risks. Unfortunately, however, there is no evidence of a significant correlation between involvement in property-damage accidents and involvement in personal injury accidents.[89] Moreover, except in relation to youth and inexperience, there is no firm evidence showing any significant correlation between past accident experience and likely future involvement in accidents, all other things being equal.[90] Nor is it easy to believe that fear of loss of a no-claims bonus plays a significant role in making drivers drive more carefully,[91] although

87 For evidence that the risk of being involved in an accident is greatest amongst young drivers and motorcycle riders see e.g. TRRL, Research Report 27 (1986); Research Report 135 (1988); Contractor Report 146 (1990) and Research Report 315 (1991). There is a strong correlation between lack of driving experience and accident involvement amongst young drivers: E. Forsyth, G. Maycock and B. Sexton, 'Cohort Study of Learner and Novice Drivers: Part 3, Accidents, Offences and Driving Experience in the First Three Years of Driving', TRL Project Report 111 (1995); D.D. Clarke, P. Ward and W. Truman, 'In-Depth Accident Causation Study of Young Drivers', TRL 542 (2002).

88 For a discussion of the ethical basis of such classifications see W.A. Wiegers, 'The Use of Age, Sex and Marital Status as Rating Variables in Automobile Insurance' (1989) 39 U. of Toronto LJ 149. Women typically pay lower premiums than men, especially amongst young drivers. Young women have many fewer accidents than young men partly because they are 'safer' drivers and partly because they drive less.

89 Although there is some evidence that drivers who engage in risky driving behaviour – and who, for that reason, might more likely to be involved in property-damage accidents – are more likely to suffer personal injury while driving: S. Blows et al., 'Risky Driving Habits and Motor Vehicle Driver Injury' (2005) 37 Accident Analysis and Prevention 619.

90 Pearson Report, vol. 2, para. 202.

91 Sansom, (1965) 62 Journal of the Chartered Insurance Institute 97, 107–8. But see Bruce, 'The Deterrent Effects of Automobile Insurance and Tort Law', 84–7.

it may well reduce willingness to claim (which is, indeed, a major purpose of the no-claims bonus system).

With regard to industrial injuries, employers' National Insurance contributions are not risk-related. By contrast, liability insurance covering employers' tort liability does operate according to market principles; accordingly, employers who present higher risks may pay higher premiums.[92] However, the great majority of employers pay premium rates based on certain features of the insured's business and not by reference to the individual insured's own claims experience. The main reason for this is that an employer's own pattern of claims is not a statistically reliable indicator of likely future claims unless the employer has quite a large workforce. It is impractical to take account of a firm's own experience unless it employs at least one hundred workers, and a firm would not be fully rated on its own experience unless it employed a great many more than this – perhaps 500 employees or more. This rules out the great majority of employers, because 99% of all firms[93] in manufacturing industry have a workforce of fewer than 500. However, the other 1% of firms in manufacturing industry together employ about 50% of the total manufacturing workforce, and for this group, experience rating may be valuable.

There are other problems with experience-rating which reduce its value for loss-prevention purposes.[94] First, it is not simple to define what is meant by the 'experience' of a firm. Does this mean the number or the cost of the accidents and injuries that have occurred? Should the experience take account of costs which are not paid by the employer's insurer; and if so, how are these to be estimated? What is to be done about one very large claim that could distort the employer's claims experience for years? And so on. Secondly, there is a time-lag problem. Experience-rating is always based on conditions which are to a greater or lesser extent out of date. For example, a firm's premium in 2006 must be fixed some time in 2005, and must therefore be based on the experience of 2004 and earlier years. One year's experience is unreliable statistically, so a 'moving average' of 3 years' experience is usually used, but this means that the premium for 2006 will depend in part on the experience of 2002. During this period, many relevant factors may have altered the reliability of that previous experience as a guide to likely future experience. Thirdly, the total cost of an employer's liability insurance represents only a very small proportion of the employer's total wage bill, on the one hand,[95] or its total

---

92 In 1995 London Transport set up its own 'captive' insurance company to handle its liability insurance. The reason given for this move was frustration at the high premium rates and tough policy terms set by its commercial insurers. LT believed that insufficient account was being taken of safety improvements achieved in its operations.

93 There are about 300,000 in total.

94 For more detail see P.S. Atiyah, 'Accident Prevention and Variable Premium Rates for Work-Related Accidents' (1975) 4 *Industrial LJ* 1 and 89.

95 According to one estimate, employers' liability insurance premiums in the UK represent only 0.23% of the total wages/salary bill: Health and Safety Executive, *Changing Business Behaviour: Would Bearing the True Cost of Health and Safety Performance Make a Difference?*, Contract Research Report 436/2002. The authors of this report suggest that the figure would need to

insurance costs (and especially fire insurance costs), on the other. It would not be uncommon for an insurer to refrain from imposing a risk-justified addition to an employer's liability insurance premium because (e.g.) of the insurer's desire to retain the fire insurance account. Fourthly, premium variation is virtually unknown in relation to clerical and office staff, whose risks of injury are very small compared with those of manual or manufacturing workers; but there are, nevertheless, many thousands of accidents among such employees every year.[96]

On the whole, it seems unlikely that experience rating of employers has a significant effect in reducing or minimizing accident costs.[97] On the other hand, it may have some beneficial effect, and provided the costs of doing so did not outweigh the benefits,[98] there might be a case for introducing an element of *experience* rating into the funding of the IIS, at least for firms employing more than 500 workers.[99] The case for introducing *feature* rating into the funding of the IIS is a different one. Accident rates in different industries vary widely. For example, the rate of reported fatal accidents per 100,000 workers in 2002–3 was 4 in the construction industry, but only 0.3 in the services sector; and the rate of reported injuries resulting in an absence from work of more than 3 days (including 'major injuries') was 1,166 per 100,000 employees in construction but only 487 in the services sector.[100] Seventeen industries with an average fatal injury rate of more than 2 per 100,000 employees in the 6 years up to 1991–2 accounted for two-thirds of reported fatalities but less than one-sixth of employment.[101] The case for

increase at least fivefold to motivate employers to improve health and safety. They also suggest that discounts for good health and safety performance would need to be at last 25% of basic premium to be motivational.

96 T.G. Ison, 'The Significance of Experience Rating' (1986) 24 *Osgoode Hall LJ* 723, makes several other arguments against experience rating in the industrial context: (a) it encourages employers to suppress claims rather than to improve safety; (b) it is unlikely to encourage additional safety measures because the cost of claims is only a proportion of the total cost of accidents to employers; and (c) it is of no relevance to cases of disease with long latency periods. Indeed, both experience and feature rating are impossible if the symptoms of a disease do not appear until years after the insured events that caused them (*Stapleton, Disease and the Compensation Debate*, 130–3).

97 For a similarly negative conclusion in relation to experience rating of individual medical practitioners see M.M. Mello and T.A. Brennan, 'Deterrence of Medical Errors: Theory and Evidence for Malpractice Reform' (2002) 80 *Texas LR* 1595, 1616–18. In Britain, NHS doctors do not pay medical indemnity insurance premiums (16.1) and so the issue does not arise. The authors argue that for effective deterrence, doctors need to be aggregated into larger responsible entities (such as hospitals) that can influence safety. This is the effect of the British system under which the cost of liability is sheeted home to NHS trusts. The ABI admitted to the Robens Committee that 'broadly speaking, the system of employers' liability insurance is not (designed to be) a major incentive to the adoption of safe working practices': Robens Committee Report, vol. 2, 55. For a contrary conclusion see H. Kötz and H.-B. Schäfer, 'Economic Incentives to Accident Prevention: An Empirical Study of the German Sugar Industry' (1993) 13 *International R. of Law and Economics* 19.

98 This is a very important proviso.

99 But this might be thought undesirable because it would redistribute costs away from large businesses and on to small businesses.

100 *Health and Safety Statistics Highlights 2002/03*, supplementary tables 10 and 12.

101 *Health and Safety Commission Annual Report 1991/2*, 86. According to the *Health and Safety Statistics 1997/8* the top ten riskiest occupations have injury rates which are more than twice the overall rate and together represented 30% of all reportable injuries in 1996–7.

a differential rating system which recognizes such variations depends partly on arguments of fairness and partly on the idea that only if industries bear all the costs of the accidents they cause will the level of accidents be reduced to the economically optimal level. It is to this latter type of argument that the following sections are devoted.

17.8   General deterrence
17.8.1   The basic idea

General deterrence[102] is a theory about who should bear the costs[103] of 'accidents'. It is not a theory about who should be paid compensation; indeed, by itself it does not even require that compensation be paid to anyone. General deterrence is based on economic theory about how competitive markets work. A competitive market is a mechanism by which people can express their preferences about what goods and services they want and can give expression to their views about the prices they are prepared to pay for them. In conditions of 'perfect competition' consumers are faced with a choice between competing goods and services about which they have full information, and there are no constraints to the free exercise of choice as between the various competing goods and services.[104] Perfectly competitive markets produce what economists call the 'optimal allocation of resources' which means that society's resources are used in the most efficient way possible to produce the maximum wealth attainable given the resources available. One precondition of the optimal allocation of resources is that prices of goods and services that are exchanged in the market accurately reflect the costs of producing them. If the price of a commodity is too low because it does not accurately reflect the costs of production, demand for the commodity will be too high and resources will be used in producing it which, if it were properly priced, might be used to produce something else which people wanted more. According to economic theory, in a perfectly competitive market prices will accurately reflect production costs.

One of the costs of producing a commodity is the cost of raw materials. Another is the cost of harm, injury or damage caused by the commodity or the process of producing it. Both need to be reflected in the price if the use of resources is to be optimized. Suppose, for example, that two firms are producing almost identical products, but that firm A uses more expensive raw materials than firm B, with no corresponding gain in the utility or appeal of the product. The

102 What follows is largely an attempt to explain the views of Guido Calabresi as expounded, most accessibly, in *The Costs of Accidents* (New Haven, Conn., 1970), with the addition of some critical comments. There is an enormous literature on this topic, but a few of the more straightforward contributions are R. Bowles, *Law and Economy* (Oxford, 1982), ch. 7; A.M. Polinsky, *An Introduction to Law and Economics*, 2nd edn (Boston, 1989), chs. 6 and 7; R.A Posner, *Economic Analysis of Law*, 6th edn (New York, 2003), ch. 6.
103 Including injury costs and administrative costs.
104 Or, in other words, there are no 'transaction costs', which means that the only cost of purchasing a good or service is the price of the good or service itself.

result is that firm *A*'s product will be more expensive than firm *B*'s, and firm *B*'s will be bought in preference to firm *A*'s. Hence, the unnecessary use of a more expensive raw material will be brought to an end. Now suppose that both firms use the same raw material but a different process of manufacture; and that *A*'s process is apt to cause a certain number of injuries to workers which *B*'s process does not. Again, it is desirable that the price of *A*'s product should reflect the cost of the injuries to workers, but it will only do this if the cost is shifted from the workers to *A*, perhaps in the form of higher wages for workers at risk of injury. If this does not happen, *A*, who is using a method of manufacture which is more costly (in that it causes injuries), will be able to sell its product at the same price as *B*. *A* will, therefore, be able to compete with *B* on equal terms instead of being squeezed out by competition (thus reducing the incidence of injuries to workers). Suppose, further, that *A*'s process is also quicker than *B*'s and therefore, in this respect, cheaper. If the cost of the injuries it causes is not reflected in the price of *A*'s products, *A* may be able to sell its product at a lower price than *B*'s. It will then be *B* who is squeezed out by competition, with a consequential misallocation of resources.

The same basic idea can be applied to the use of goods and services as opposed to their production. Take driving, for example. Other things being equal, the more it costs to drive, the less people will do it. Amongst the costs of driving are the costs of road accidents. According to the theory of general deterrence, if the costs of driving accidents are not included in the 'price' of driving, then driving will, relative to other transport activities, such as taking a bus or a train, be too cheap and will be engaged in at a higher than optimal level.

One aspect of the optimal allocation of resources is the minimization of resource-wasting events. Accidents consume resources that could be used in other ways. In conditions of perfect competition, therefore, accidents and accident costs are minimized by the operation of market forces. The level of accidents in conditions of perfect competition (the 'optimal level of accidents') is the level reached when the costs of reducing the level of accidents any further would exceed the savings in accident costs[105] that the further reduction would produce.

To summarize so far, in conditions of perfect competition, resources are allocated to their most productive use; the prices of goods and services accurately reflect their production costs, including their accident costs; activities are engaged in at the optimal level; and accidents are reduced to the optimal level.

However, in the real world, conditions of perfect competition do not exist. This means that if we want to produce the effects that a perfectly competitive market would, the real market cannot be left alone to do it. Governments therefore intervene in the operation of markets to correct imperfections in the hope, thereby, of generating the effects of a perfectly competitive market. One way of doing this is by

---

105 These include not only costs to the accident victim but also e.g. lost production and use of management time borne by producers as a result of accidents.

law; and this is where the theory of general deterrence comes in. According to that theory, if accident costs are allocated[106] in the way they would be in conditions of perfect competition, the optimal level of accidents will be reached. For this reason, general deterrence theorists say that the law should allocate the costs of an accident (that is, should impose liability for injury, death, disease and so on caused by the accident) to the party able in the future to avoid accidents of that type most cheaply. In this way, the optimal level of accidents will be reached because the person who bears the accidents' costs will take steps to avoid accidents of that type in the future to the point where any further accident-avoidance measures would cost more than the costs of the accidents they would prevent.

Alternatively, even if such accident prevention measures are not taken, the imposition of liability will cause the costs of accidents to be reflected in the prices of the relevant commodities or activities with the result that equivalent but safer commodities and activities will be preferred by consumers to less safe ones. In this way, the scale on which various activities are engaged in and various commodities produced will be optimized.

It should be noted that the notion of the optimal level of accidents allows that in a perfectly competitive world some accidents might be tolerated because the cost of preventing them would exceed the costs they inflict on the victims. In reality, too, some accidents cannot be prevented because we lack the knowledge or ability to do so or because we are unable to foresee them. The theory of general deterrence says that the costs of such accidents ought to be reflected in the prices of activities and commodities because only if this is done will consumers be able to choose rationally between alternatives on the basis of their relative safety.

To summarize briefly so far, whereas the common law of tort basically says that accident costs should be borne by the person who *caused* the accident, the theory of general deterrence says that they should be borne by the person who can most cheaply avoid accidents of that type in the future.

What is the possible scope for applying this notion of general deterrence in fashioning the law relating to compensation for personal injury, disease and so on? There are at least three conditions that must be satisfied if the idea of general deterrence is to provide guidance in individual cases as to how injury costs ought to be allocated. First, it must be possible to identify the party to which particular injuries or losses ought to be allocated; secondly, it is necessary to quantify the injury costs;[107] and, thirdly, the party to whom accident costs are allocated must, to some extent at least, be sensitive to increased costs. We will consider the second of these conditions first.

---

106 Whether by a liability rule externalizing them from the victim or a no-liability rule (e.g. a contributory negligence rule) internalizing them (wholly or partly) to the victim.
107 Costs in this context are costs to society as a whole ('social costs'), not costs to the persons whom tort law allows to recover damages ('private costs'). In any particular case, social costs may be greater or less than private costs, in which case tort law will only partially achieve the goal of correct cost allocation.

17.8.2   Ascertaining the costs of an accident

Accident costs can be usefully divided into primary costs, such as loss of income, loss of faculty, medical expenses and so on; and secondary costs, that is the administrative costs of allocating the accident costs to the party who ought to bear them.[108] General deterrence is concerned with both types of cost: the main aim is to allocate primary accident costs to the cheapest cost avoider, but also to minimize the sum total of the two types of cost. So there may come a point where the cost of identifying the cheapest primary accident cost avoider may be so high that it would be better to place those costs on a party less good at avoiding them, because the additional costs which the cheapest primary cost avoider could prevent would be less than the additional secondary cost involved in identifying that person.

So far as primary costs are concerned, for economic purposes costs are 'net costs'. The net costs of an 'accident' are the costs minus any benefits accruing from the accident-causing activity. It may be possible to identify and calculate economic costs and benefits relatively easily; but an activity may cause non-economic losses, which need to be assessed, and non-economic gains, which must be set off against the losses. For instance, an activity may create noise or smoke which is a source of irritation, rather than damage; it may destroy a beautiful view which thousands have admired daily; or it may maim and injure, causing pain and suffering. Is it possible to place an economic valuation on such gains and losses? This question has proved a source of extensive controversy among economists, as it has among lawyers. We have already discussed the legal aspects of the assessment of damages for 'pain and suffering' and we referred briefly to the approach of economists in that context.[109] On the whole, economists have tended to be more interested in the difficulties of valuing lives than in the problem of valuing disabilities, whereas with lawyers it has usually been the other way round. There is no need to explore this question at length because at the end of the day there is almost universal agreement that for purposes of cost-benefit analysis, economists must either ignore non-economic losses or place some fairly arbitrary conventional valuation upon them, because the cost of 'accurate' valuation of non-economic losses itself outweighs any benefit (in terms of deterrence) which would accrue from the exercise. As Calabresi says, 'resource allocation even in theory is an exercise in doing the best possible and not achieving perfection'.[110]

17.8.3   Allocation of costs to activities

As we have seen, the basic general deterrence idea is that primary net accident costs should be allocated to the cheapest cost avoider. But we have also seen that if the

108 But this is not the way Calabresi uses these terms. For him, general deterrence is an approach to 'primary accident cost avoidance'; compensating accident victims is a means to 'secondary accident cost avoidance'; and minimizing administrative costs is a means to 'tertiary accident cost avoidance'.

109 6.5.

110 'The Decision for Accidents: An Approach to Non-Fault Allocation' (1965) 78 *Harvard LR* 713, 724 n. 17.

cost of doing this is too great, it may be better to allocate the costs to a party who may not be the most efficient in avoiding accident costs, so as to minimize the sum of accident avoidance costs and costs of allocation of primary accident costs. The first step may be to rule out parties who clearly could not satisfy the description of 'cheapest cost avoider'. So, for example, the costs of accidents involving citizens should not be allocated to the State (e.g. in the form of an entitlement of injury victims to receive social security benefits in respect of their injuries) because it is highly unlikely that a party not involved in the accident would ever be the cheapest avoider of costs of that type of accident.

In the language of general deterrence, to allocate a cost to the wrong party is to 'externalize' it from the party who should bear it onto another party. Externalization of costs is to be avoided because it results in under-deterrence of accident costs. Another example of externalization would be the placing of the costs of road accidents on all 'drivers' equally when it was clear that young male drivers as a group caused proportionately more road accidents than the whole class of drivers as a group. This example shows that the principles of general deterrence are relevant even when the party to whom the costs of an accident are allocated is insured, provided the cost of insurance is related to the risk that the insured will generate accident costs.[111] It also shows that the process of categorization for insurance purposes and the process of allocating risks for general deterrence purposes are not dissimilar. For example, general deterrence theorists do not want to deter motoring but only to deter motor accidents; so the aim is to identify that class of drivers whose conduct is most closely related to motor accidents.

But having ruled out parties who are obviously not the cheapest cost avoider, it may be more difficult to choose from between the remaining parties the one who is the cheapest cost avoider. Calabresi gives some guidelines for performing this task. The first is that costs should be allocated to the party best able to assess the relevant risks of injury and the probable injury costs, on the basis that this party is in a better position to take injury-reduction steps, or to shift the costs to another party better able to take cheap avoidance action, than the party who is less well able even to assess the risks and costs. For example, a consumer who cannot assess the risks presented by various competing products will not be in a good position to choose safer products in preference to less safe products and in this way give the manufacturer of the less safe products an incentive to take steps to improve their safety. On the other hand, a consumer is in a better position than a manufacturer to assess risks arising from the consumer's peculiar personal characteristics, which may be unknown to the manufacturer.

If it is not possible to identify either the cheapest cost avoider or the cheapest cost assessor, a second guideline suggested by Calabresi is to allocate injury costs to the party who can most cheaply insure against the risk of their occurrence.

---

111 G.T. Schwartz, 'The Ethics and the Economics of Tort Liability Insurance' (1990) 75 *Cornell LR* 313, 336–59. We have already noted difficulties in making insurance accurately reflect risk: 17.7.2.2.

> If the loss is placed on the party for whom insurance is less available or more expensive, a false cost – the excess cost of his insuring – will in effect be made part of the price of the goods.[112]

Furthermore, if, for example, injury costs resulting from defective products are placed on consumers even though manufacturers are cheaper insurers, the losses may end up being borne, for instance, by the State in the form of social security payments. But according to general deterrence criteria, the State is a totally inappropriate loss bearer.

There is, however, a further complication, which must now be introduced. The fact that accident costs are allocated to a particular party does not mean that that party will ultimately bear them. Take a simple illustration: if the costs of injury caused by defective products are imposed on manufacturers in the first instance, they may be shifted by manufacturers to consumers in the form of increased prices. Economic theory says that in conditions of perfect competition it does not matter on whom accident costs are initially imposed, because the operation of market forces will reallocate those costs to the cheapest cost avoider because a perfect market produces an optimal allocation of resources. In the real world, however, although parties may have the ability to shift costs from themselves to another, accident costs may not end up on the cheapest cost avoider as they would, by definition, in a perfect market. Even if accident costs are placed by law on one party because that party is thought to be the cheapest cost avoider, the cheapest risk-assessor or the cheapest insurer, that party may be able to transfer them to another party who is a less good cost avoider (etc.) than the party on whom the costs were originally imposed. This process Calabresi calls 'externalization by transfer'. Since externalization is, by definition, undesirable, the decision as to who should bear accidents costs in the first place must be made taking into account the ability of that person to transfer costs to another less suitable cost bearer.

Conversely, however, in a situation where it is difficult to identify the cheapest cost avoider, the next best thing to do may be to place accident costs on what Calabresi calls the 'best briber', by which he means the party who is best able to identify the cheapest cost avoider and can, at least cost, transfer the costs to that person. Parties vary in their ability to transfer costs: for example, a monopoly manufacturer of goods with no substitutes would be able to transfer the costs of accidents resulting from the use of its goods easily and cheaply by increasing the price of its goods without taking any measures to make them safer. On the other hand, a pedestrian injured by a driver on the road will find it difficult to transfer the accident costs to the driver (which might be desirable in deterrence terms), and may find it much easier to transfer them to the State by claiming social security benefits (which would, in deterrence terms, be a bad thing).

112 Calabresi, *The Costs of Accidents*, 164.

This process of post-allocation transfer[113] can be easily illustrated by the case of *Sturges* v. *Bridgman*[114] in which a doctor sued his neighbour, a confectioner, in nuisance, complaining that the noise and vibration made by the confectioner's machinery made it impossible for him to use a consulting room, which he had built at the bottom of his garden. The court held that the doctor was entitled to an injunction to restrain the confectioner from using his machinery so as to prevent the doctor's use of the consulting room. The award of the injunction would not have prevented the confectioner negotiating with the doctor to be able to continue with his business, although it did give the doctor a very strong bargaining counter in any such negotiations. Suppose the net value to the confectioner of the use of his machinery was £50,000 a year, while the net value to the doctor of the use of his consulting room was £20,000 a year; it would plainly have been in the interest of both parties (although not necessarily of the wider community) for the confectioner to pay the doctor anything between £20,000 and £50,000 a year to release him from the injunction. If this had happened, it would have shown that the court had allocated the costs of the nuisance to the wrong party, but also that the parties were able to correct the misallocation by negotiating a transfer.

This sort of post-allocation bargaining may be very difficult in certain types of case. Suppose the costs of certain sorts of road accidents are wrongly placed on drivers when they should be placed on cyclists who could easily avoid accidents of that type by wearing luminous items. It would, in practice, be very difficult for the costs of this type of accident to be shifted by drivers back onto cyclists. Where desirable post-allocation bargaining is unlikely to take place, it is very important for accident costs to be correctly allocated in the first instance; and where externalization by transfer is likely to occur, the relevant question is whether the transferee (rather than the transferor) is a better cost avoider than the other party on whom the costs could initially be placed.

It should be clear from this discussion that it may be difficult to identify with any confidence the person on whom accident costs should be placed according to the principles of general deterrence. The problem is likely to be particularly acute in the case of diseases (as opposed to traumatic injuries) because we know so little about how a great many diseases are caused.[115] On the other hand, we can see that the application of general deterrence ideas may produce surprising results, quite different from those which an application of the rules of tort law would produce. Suppose that property of people who live near a factory, which produces explosive chemicals, is damaged as the result of an explosion in the factory. At first sight it might seem sound from a deterrence point of view to impose the explosion costs on the factory owner. But if it turned out that the result of placing the accident costs on the factory owner would be the closure of the factory with the loss of many jobs,

---

113 The most famous discussion is by R.H. Coase, 'The Problem of Social Cost' (1960) 3 *J. of Law and Economics* 1.
114 (1879) 11 Ch D 852.
115 Stapleton, *Disease and the Compensation Debate*, 124, 127.

the better solution might be to leave the costs on the neighbours and so encourage them to insure against such costs or to move house to a safer place. Another illustration may be found in the case of *Miller* v. *Jackson*[116] where home-owners complained of the playing of cricket on adjoining land as a result of which the occasional ball landed in their garden. Apparently Mrs Miller was a very sensitive person who was greatly disturbed by the risk of being hit. In such circumstances, it would probably be better in an economic sense for the home-owners to be refused a remedy, and thus encouraged to sell the house and move elsewhere, than to be awarded damages or an injunction in respect of the cricket playing.

17.8.4   Responsiveness to price mechanism

Even if we have decided on general deterrence grounds that a particular activity should bear particular accident costs, we may not be able, for some reason or other, to make that activity bear the costs. Take the case of lung cancer, which is significantly attributable to the activity of smoking. Smoking is not a good candidate for general deterrence measures because the only way of preventing smoking-related diseases is to stop smoking; and the level of smoking would not be substantially affected by increased costs (as is demonstrated every time the taxes on cigarettes and tobacco are raised), unless the increase was so great that it would be politically unacceptable. Or take the example of road accidents: some accidents are preventable at reasonable cost; and as for the rest, increasing the cost of motoring, or some types of motoring, could have some effect on the amount of motoring. On the other hand, increasing the 'cost' of pedestrianism (especially if this increase merely takes the form of refusing damages to injured pedestrians) might encourage pedestrians to be more careful, but is less likely to reduce the amount of walking.

Activities that are most likely to be amenable to control through the price mechanism are those which, in economists' jargon, have a high elasticity of demand. Elasticity of demand for a commodity or activity depends partly on how many sources of supply there are and partly on whether there are any substitutes for it. Increasing the cost (and so the price) of a commodity produced by a monopoly and for which there is no alternative is less likely to affect demand for the commodity than increasing the cost of a commodity marketed by several producers and which can be given up for some (near) equivalent. Many drugs, for example, have low elasticity of demand so that increasing their price may have little impact on consumption. For this reason, government control of the availability of a dangerous drug may be the only way of reducing consumption and hence of reducing the incidence of adverse side-effects.

In trying to identify activities with a high elasticity of demand, the way activities is described is of great significance. For example, it may well be that motoring as a whole has a low elasticity of demand, so that the total amount of motoring does

116 [1977] QB 966.

not respond appreciably to increases in the cost of motoring – as is demonstrated by the fact that little change follows from the regular increases in petrol prices. But we could perhaps break motoring down into categories which would be responsive to price variations. Within the activity of motoring we could distinguish between driving different types of vehicle – old vehicles and new ones, vehicles of different colours or power; between driving at night and in the day; in the town and in the country; and so on. If more of the costs of road accidents were placed on some of these sub-categories of driving and less on others, we might find an appreciable reduction in the number and costs of road accidents as people switched from more dangerous types of motoring to safer ones.

Elasticity of demand is not the only factor relevant to the amenability of commodities or activities to general deterrence techniques. For instance, disease-causing products and activities are likely to be less amenable to such techniques than products and activities which cause traumatic injuries because, for example, diseases often take a long time to develop, by which time the person responsible for the activity which caused the disease may no longer be engaged in the activity.[117]

Sensitivity to the imposition of accident costs is undoubtedly weakened by insurance against the risk of incurring such costs, even if the premiums for such insurance are risk-related, simply because insurance reduces the impact of accident costs on the individual by spreading them over time and amongst a large group of people. It may be, too, that different types of party vary in their sensitivity to the imposition of accident costs. A well-run company will, for instance, be aware of the value of taking safety measures which are less costly than the damage they prevent. By contrast, the ordinary motorist, for example, who pays for some road accident costs through insurance premiums, makes a payment once a year and then tries to forget about it until the following year. Such a person probably does not even calculate the cost of motoring in the same way that a company would calculate its costs.

The motorist is apt to look at the marginal cost of motoring in deciding how much to drive, and in practice this cost will probably be perceived as little more than the cost of petrol, all other costs (including insurance costs) being perceived as overheads. So increasing the cost of insurance might not have much effect on the amount of motoring done. By contrast, corporations are more likely to take account of the average rather than the marginal cost of their activities in deciding what to do. Since the average cost would be increased by increasing insurance premiums, the amount of commercial driving might be more affected by such a move than the amount of private driving. However, even this conclusion may be open to doubt if motoring is an activity with low elasticity of demand. One group of researchers concluded that in the case of auto accidents, 'there are no adequate grounds for believing that the proper cost allocation would either reduce accidents or change the total amount of driving appreciably'.[118]

117 Stapleton, *Disease and the Compensation Debate*, 126–8.
118 Conard, *Automobile Accident Costs and Payments*, 127.

17.8.5   Applying general deterrence criteria in practice

These, then, are the criteria recommended by general deterrence theory for deciding who should pay the costs of accidents, injuries, diseases and so on. But it must be said that they may be very difficult to apply in practice. For example, very little is known about the causes of many diseases and illnesses, and the less that is known about causation of a disease, the more difficult it will be to identify the party which could most cheaply prevent the disease. Or take the case of road accidents. It is probably the case that some types of road accidents would be most cheaply prevented by drivers, some by other road users, others by car manufacturers and yet others by road designers. However, it may be extremely difficult to decide what proportion of the costs of road accidents should be imposed on each of these groups in order to give them the correct incentives to take accident-avoiding action. Nor will such incentives be effective unless the various groups involved properly understand the accident risks their conduct entails. Moreover, each of these groups may be able to externalize some or all of the accident costs imposed on them. For example, drivers' liability insurance may be imperfectly related to risk; pedestrians and cyclists may claim social security benefits rather than suing drivers; road authorities may fund accident costs by taxation and not take avoidance action; and car manufacturers in an imperfectly competitive market may be able to pass costs on to car-buyers without improving car safety. Taking proper account of such opportunities for externalization might be very difficult indeed.

17.8.6   General deterrence and existing systems

In this section we shall inquire how far the various methods of compensation for which the law at present provides embody or give effect to general deterrence principles. But first we should repeat that general deterrence is not primarily concerned with compensation but with deterrence, whereas the prime concern of the systems we have surveyed is compensation. We must bear in mind the possibility that compensation and deterrence may not be compatible goals in all situations.

17.8.6.1   The tort system

First, let us consider the tort system. Because the tort system links liability to pay compensation with responsibility for causing accidents, it may, to some extent, further the goals of general deterrence. Application of the tort concepts of fault and causation may often lead to the imposition of liability to pay compensation on the cheapest cost avoider or cost assessor, or on the cheapest insurer or the best briber.

The idea that damage is compensatable only if it falls within the 'risk' that a particular rule is designed to guard against (5.3.2) is explicable in general deterrence terms. For instance, by saying that an unlicensed driver is not liable for an accident merely by virtue of being unlicensed, the law is in effect refusing to treat that accident as a cost of the activity of 'unlicensed driving'.[119] Some of the rules relating to remoteness of damage (5.3.3) are also explicable in general deterrence terms. If the consequence of a negligent act is altogether too freakish or unforeseeable the law exonerates the negligent party from liability; the general deterrence explanation of this is that the negligent party is unlikely to be the cheapest avoider of unforeseeable or freakish injuries. For example, suppose that a negligent motorist collides with the car in front and damages some exceptionally valuable paintings in its boot. It is possible that in such a case the courts would hold the loss unforeseeable and therefore refuse to hold the negligent motorist liable for the damage to the paintings. Hence, the owner of the paintings (or, more probably, an insurer) would have to bear the cost. This would probably be a sound result from the point of view of general deterrence because the owner of the paintings would most likely be able to protect the paintings from such damage more easily (by arranging safer transportation) than the driver.

Some argue that certain fundamental principles of tort law give effect to the economic notion of optimal resource allocation which underlies general deterrence. The negligence formula, as propounded, for example, in the famous Learned Hand calculus,[120] may be seen as based on the economic principle that liability for injury should be imposed where the cost of avoiding injury is lower than the sum of primary accident costs multiplied by the probability that the accident would occur, but not where the avoidance cost is higher than this latter sum. The doctrine of contributory negligence may also be seen as based on general deterrence ideas: if the injured persons could have avoided the accident more cheaply than the injurer, then the injured person should be required to bear some or all of the accident costs as an incentive to take accident-avoiding action in the future. There has been controversy about the extent to which the detailed rules of the law of negligence and contributory negligence can be said to promote optimal allocation of resources,[121] and there has also been controversy about whether strict liability may in some circumstances be more efficient in the economic sense than fault liability.[122] But in a broad sort of way, it does not seem necessary to dissent from the idea that there is some connection between the basic principles of tort law and general deterrence ideas.

However, the general deterrence potential of tort law is limited.[123] First, because most tort compensation is paid for via liability insurance, the deterrent effect of tort

119 But there is some evidence of a correlation between unlicensed driving by older drivers and suffering injury while driving: S. Blows *et al.*, 'Risky Driving Habits and Motor Vehicle Driver Injury' (2005) 37 *Accident Analysis and Prevention* 619. More strongly, Department for Transport research estimates that unlicensed drivers are between 2.7 and 8.9 times more likely than 'all drivers' to be involved in an accident: Road Safety Research Report No. 48, *Research into Unlicensed Driving: Final Report* (2003).
120 2.4.2.
121 See e.g. G.T. Schwartz, 'Contributory and Comparative Negligence: A Reappraisal' (1978) 87 *Yale LJ* 697.
122 Stapleton, *Disease and the Compensation Debate*, 122–3.
123 G.T. Schwartz, 'Reality in Economic Analysis of Tort Law: Does Tort Law Really Deter?' (1994) 42 *UCLALR* 377.

liability is inevitably weakened. Indeed, this is simply an illustration of a more general point: insurance spreads accident costs over time and over groups of people so that even if it is properly risk-related (with the result that it does not externalize accident costs), it can have the psychological effect of reducing incentives to avoid insured events. Insurers refer to this effect by the term 'moral hazard'. Loss spreading furthers compensatory goals by making it much more likely that compensation payments will be forthcoming; but it tends to be inimical to the furtherance of deterrence goals because it weakens to deterrence incentives felt by any particular individual insured party.

Secondly, application of the legal concept of 'causation' is much more likely to lead to the imposition of accident costs on some parties than on others, regardless of their relative ability to avoid costs cheaply. For example, we have seen that road accidents are much more likely to be attributed by tort law to the actions of drivers than to the actions of car or road designers, regardless of whether any particular type of accident could be more cheaply avoided by drivers, car designers or road designers. Again, the costs of property damage caused by gas explosions are much more likely to be imposed on gas suppliers regardless of whether the cheapest way to avoid such damage is to make gas pipes more leak-resistant or to make property more damage-resistant. To some extent, such problems are lessened by the fact that tort law is deficient as a mechanism for compensating injury victims. Because, in theory, tort law does not generally impose liability for accidents not caused by the fault of someone other than the victim, and because in practice many accident victims receive no tort compensation, everyone must take into account the fact that they may suffer personal injury or property damage in circumstances in which no tort compensation will be available. Incentives to avoid loss can be provided as much by not being relieved of accident costs as by having them imposed. Because general deterrence is not a theory of compensation, it is concerned only with ensuring that the right party is given accident-avoidance incentives, regardless of whether this is done by shifting a loss or letting it lie where it fell.

So the ultimate theoretical issue is whether tort law distributes the costs of accidents between victims and causers of accidents in the way general deterrence theory would require. There is good ground for thinking that it does not.[124] There are too many cases in which an activity does contribute (in a statistical sense) to accident causation, but in which the law's concepts of fault and cause operate in such a way that one 'causer' of an accident may be charged with too high a proportion of the costs, and another 'causer' with too small a proportion. For example, a person who parks a car in a street undoubtedly creates a risk both to the car and to others; this risk is sufficiently obvious to justify a higher comprehensive motor premium for cars regularly garaged in a public road. But in the event of a collision between a moving and parked vehicle, the entire fault, and hence cost of the accident, will

---

124 G. Calabresi, 'Does the Fault System Optimally Control Primary Accident Costs?' (1968) 33 *Law and Contemporary Problems* 429.

nearly always be attributed to the driver of the moving vehicle. The result of this may be that too high a proportion of the cost of such collisions is borne by the third-party liability insurance and too little by first-party property insurance. Consequently, there may be too much pressure on drivers to avoid such accidents and too little pressure to arrange off-street parking; too much pressure to develop cars that do less damage in collisions and too little pressure to develop cars that better resist damage.

It should also be remembered that general deterrence aims at the minimization of the sum of primary and secondary accident costs. The administrative costs of the tort system are relatively very high, and it may be that such deterrence as the tort system achieves is not worth the price paid for it. It may be that the compensatory goals of the tort system could be achieved equally well by some other system (such as first-party insurance with risk-related premiums) with little or no loss of deterrence but at a much lower administrative cost. Even from a general deterrence viewpoint, the fact that such an alternative system was no better a deterrent than the tort system would not matter if the cost of achieving that level of deterrence was less under the alternative system (although some other system which achieved better deterrence at similar cost would be even better from this perspective, regardless of how well it achieved compensatory goals).

It must next be observed that the tort system does not, in fact, impose all the costs of accidents on those whom it identifies as the proper parties to bear such costs. For instance, despite the scheme for recoupment of NHS costs from tortfeasors (15.4.5), it is probably still the case that a significant proportion of the cost of medical services required by tort victims is borne by the NHS, which is largely paid for by taxpayers, thus relieving motorists as such of a financial burden which would otherwise have to be paid for in tort damages, and hence in premiums. Similarly, the cost of police activity following road accidents is not charged to accident causers but to taxpayers. Many of the other costs of compensating accident victims are borne by the social security system,[125] sick-pay schemes and other forms of compensation. Furthermore, the off-setting of certain collateral benefits against tort damages relieves tortfeasors of some of the social costs of their torts.

Finally, tort damages are intended to compensate for the private losses of injury victims and their dependants; they do not take account of social loss. The social loss involved in the death of a young unmarried adult, for instance, may be high, especially if the person has received advanced education at public expense; but tort damages for the death of such a person will be very low. If no dependency can be proved, the only damages recoverable will be a small amount in respect of losses suffered by the victim between the date of the accident and the date of death (assuming they are different), which clearly bears no relationship to the loss of society's investment in the individual or its expectation of gain from that person's activities.

---

125 Despite the scheme for recovery of social security benefits from tortfeasors: 15.4.5.

17.8.6.2   The social security system

Next, let us consider the social security system. It is apparent that in so far as the social security system is financed out of general taxation it flies in the face of the precepts of general deterrence. So far as concerns those benefits entitlement to which depends on the payment of National Insurance contributions, there is no particular relationship between contributions paid and benefits received. Nor are contributions either feature-rated or experience-rated; but this is not surprising in the case of many benefits. It would be both impractical and politically unacceptable to make the chronically sick pay premiums for incapacity benefits according to risk, and there is no reason to suppose that doing so would have any significant effect on the incidence of sickness even if we did. The cost of industrial injuries and diseases could be made to fall more heavily on those industries which present greater risks by feature-rating some element of employer's National Insurance contributions. Doing this would bring the IIS more into line with general deterrence principles (although it would still not guarantee that the costs of industrial accidents were borne by the cheapest cost avoider). Whether feature-rating would be worthwhile would, of course, depend partly on how much it would cost and how effective it turned out to be in reducing the costs of industrial injuries. It is, perhaps, unlikely that it would be worthwhile attempting to introduce experience-rating into the calculation of employer's National Insurance contributions, given the cost and complexity of doing so.

Furthermore, it would probably be unacceptable to introduce either feature-rating or experience-rating into the calculation of employee's National Insurance contributions since the aim of the IIS is seen as being to provide basic benefits to all eligible claimants on the basis of need. The conduct of the claimant is, in certain cases, relevant in the IIS, but on the whole, the system does not aim to give workers incentives to avoid industrial injuries.

The cost of criminal injuries compensation awarded by the CICA is borne entirely by the taxpayer, though even in this field there is scope, in theory, for the operation of general deterrence. Criminals are most likely to be the cheapest avoiders of the costs of crime. On the whole, it would be impractical, though desirable, to charge criminals with the injury costs of crime in the hope of reducing crime; although criminal compensation orders (which are designed to compensate victims, not to deter criminals) may have some deterrent effect. Some deterrent effect might also be achieved by requiring employers of workers who, by reason of their occupation, are under a higher than normal risk of being subjected to criminal violence, to pay contributions towards criminal injuries compensation, given that a significant proportion of applicants for criminal injury compensation are engaged in high-risk occupations – police officers, post deliverers, wages clerks, night watchmen and so on.

17.8.6.3   First-party insurance

Finally, let us consider first-party insurance. There is some room for the operation of general deterrence by the charging of risk-related premiums for various sorts of loss insurance. For example, businesses that install fire sprinklers in commercial buildings may pay lower premiums on that account; people in hazardous occupations may have to pay higher life insurance premiums, and so forth. In the case of property damage insurance, there is probably considerable scope for risk-related premiums, and this might be an effective way of reducing insured losses. But feature-rating and experience-rating are administratively more expensive than flat-rating, and there comes a point where the gains to be achieved from more accurate risk differentiation in terms of claims and loss reduction are outweighed by the costs of greater differentiation. Furthermore, provided an insurer's total income is sufficient to cover claims and administrative expenses and provide a profit, the only incentive the insurer has for reducing the level of losses and claims further is competition – so that its premiums can be lower than those of its competitors. Thus the competitiveness of the insurance market is an important factor in determining the degree to which premiums will be risk-related. Also, there may be other less costly ways of reducing premiums; for example, by cutting administrative costs or increasing investment income.

17.8.7   An assessment of the value of the general-deterrence approach

An assessment of the value of the theory of general deterrence must take account of its limitations. First, deterrence is only one of a number of objectives that we may seek to achieve in relation to accidents and injuries. For example, no society tolerates any and every injury-causing activity even if those taking part are prepared to pay the injury costs. Some activities are the subject of outright prohibition. Thus we permit people to drive cars if they pay for the cost of accidents caused by their fault, but we do not permit them to drive while drunk, even if they are prepared to pay for the cost of accidents they cause while in that state. General deterrence may be an acceptable response to some accidents but not to others. Again, for example, although a prime aim of general deterrence is to avoid externalization of accident costs, a society may be prepared to contemplate a degree of externalization in order to achieve some income redistribution. This is, for example, exactly what we do at present in the industrial injuries scheme by not relating National Insurance contributions to risk. One result of this is that those who participate in low-risk industries (whether as consumers, workers or shareholders) in a sense subsidize those who participate in high-risk industries.

Furthermore, a large part of our social life is not even organized along market lines. Despite attempts in the last 25 years to inject competitive and market elements into its operation, much of the public sector does not operate according to the classical theories of free enterprise by seeking to maximize profits, nor is it always exposed to the harsh winds of competition: in the public sector, accident prevention and the minimization of accident costs is just as likely to be achieved by a sense of public responsibility and by humanitarianism as by market forces. Even in the private sector, it is wrong to suppose that businesses pursue profit maximization at all costs. Public opinion, as much as competition, restricts the level of profits which may be decently earned over a period of time: if profits seem excessive, public demands for price reductions may in due course become irresistible, quite apart from competition. Conversely, business people may also be sufficiently humanitarian to wish to reduce accident costs even at the expense of higher profits. It is thus unrealistic to suppose that accident costs can always or often be best minimized by use of the market mechanism.

Another way of making the same point is to observe that one of the assumptions underlying general deterrence theory (and welfare economics, of which general deterrence theory is an application) is that people know what is best for them. In theory, general deterrence and the optimal allocation of resources to accident prevention are achieved by the choices of consumers between differently priced goods and services available in the market. The theory must, therefore, assume that these choices are sound if the resulting allocation of resources is to be regarded as optimal. This does not mean that individual theorists believe that everyone knows their own best interests and spends their money in such a way as to further those interests. An economist may, for example, be in favour of imposing high taxes on smoking so as to discourage purchase of cigarettes partly on the ground that people who smoke are not acting in their own best interests. The point is that in taking this view, the economist would be acknowledging that consumer preferences as expressed in the market are not the only acceptable criterion for judging how resources ought to be used. General deterrence theory gives no guidance as to when criteria, other than the ones it recommends, should be adopted.

A second limitation arises from the fact that the concept of general deterrence is in conflict with the concept of loss distribution. The latter notion, as we saw earlier, suggests that losses should be spread over as wide a segment of the population as possible. General deterrence, on the other hand, suggests that losses should be concentrated on the person who can best avoid or minimize them. The most extreme form of general deterrence would be to place the entire cost of a loss on that person. Clearly, the incentive to avoid or minimize a loss would then be much greater; but equally clearly, this could lead to very serious consequences in the absence of liability insurance. It cannot even be assumed that the consequent gains in accident prevention would outweigh the costs in terms of bankrupted tortfeasors.

This conflict between general deterrence and loss distribution can be reduced by the use of risk-related insurance premium rates. But as we have seen, risk differentiation costs money, and so the question arises of how to identify the optimum degree of risk-differentiation; for if extra risk-differentiation costs too much, the extra cost may outweigh any consequent gains in accident cost reduction. Calabresi's ingenious answer to this difficulty is to say that this can be left to the operation of the market.[126] The point is that under the pressure of competition, insurance companies will seek to set premiums lower than those of their competitors. Inadequate risk differentiation stands in the way of this goal because it gives

---

126 'The Decision for Accidents', 733–4.

high-risk insureds inadequate incentives to avoid inflicting insured losses; and it also may lead low-risk insureds to seek insurance from another insurer who will charge premiums which are better related to the risks they present. So in theory, at least, insurers in a competitive market have an incentive to achieve the economically optimal level of risk differentiation.

However, this answer is open to doubt.[127] Although it might in fact be profitable for an insurer to differentiate further between risks, it may be reluctant to do so because the additional administrative cost is certain to follow, while the additional benefit from further differentiation may be somewhat uncertain at the outset. Moreover, the fact is that (outside the life insurance field) the role played by statistical methodology (which is essential to accurate risk differentiation) in premium-fixing is surprisingly small. The main reason for this is that insurers do not have much reliable data concerning the effect of individually significant factors on different risks. Furthermore, the greater the level of risk differentiation, the smaller each risk group becomes and so the less statistically reliable. Premium-fixing depends much more on the insurer's judgment and much less on statistical information than is commonly thought. In practice, risk-related premiums are used more in some areas than others: more in relation to fire insurance, for example, than in relation to employers' liability insurance.

Ironically, if insurance premiums were risk-related to the most efficient extent possible, this would produce a different conflict between the purposes of general deterrence and the purposes of loss distribution. This is because the further insurance companies go in varying premium rates according to risk, the greater the difference will be between the premiums payable by the most serious and the least serious risks. Losses are not well distributed if (e.g.) one person has to pay a premium of £200 per annum and others pay only £20 or £30 towards the same loss. The objective of distributing the cost of accidents widely, so that too heavy a burden does not fall on any one person, would be jeopardized by high levels of risk differentiation.

A third factor limiting the value of general deterrence theory is the assumption of perfect competition on which it rests. In reality, of course, there are great divergences from perfect competition in the operation of the market produced, for example, by the fact that consumers lack full information about the operation of the market and about the true costs of goods and services available in it; and by government taxes on, or subsidies to, various groups of producers and consumers. Besides these distortions, those produced by misallocation, through tort law, of the cost of injuries and even of diseases pale into insignificance. We have, for instance, commented on the misallocation that may result from the fact that employers' National Insurance contributions are not risk-related and that employers' liability insurance premiums are not experience-rated. But the total of industrial injury

---

127 C.A. Kulp, 'The Rate-Making Process in Property and Casualty Insurance – Goals, Technics and Limits' (1950) 15 *Law and Contemporary Problems* 493, 494.

insurance premiums and National Insurance contributions is a very small proportion of the employer's total wage bill, and an insignificant figure beside the employer's tax bill. Or consider the example of motoring. We have seen that the rules of tort law certainly do not impose all of the costs of individual road accidents on those responsible for them, as general deterrence would demand. Moreover, damages may well be too low on the basis of the sorts of valuation methods used by economists.[128] On the other hand, it has been estimated that through compulsory third-party liability insurance premiums and taxes on fuel, motorists as a class pay enough to cover the total social costs of road accidents plus at least a significant proportion of other costs associated with motoring, such as pollution and congestion.[129] In this light, one might doubt that the 'inefficiency' of tort law is of any great social significance.

The theory of general deterrence does not easily lend itself to empirical verification or refutation because no system in existence bases liability for accident costs on general deterrence criteria. But in 1972 the American National Commission on State Workmen's Compensation Laws attempted to test the theory by studying the industrial accident levels in States with very different levels of workers' compensation benefits. On the basis of economic theory, it might have been supposed that in States where the benefits and therefore the premiums were higher, employers would take more care (and spend more money) to minimize accident costs by keeping the accident levels as low as possible. However, no systematic relationship was discovered between accident levels and benefit levels. Even when comparisons were made between States with similar industrial backgrounds, there was no observable correlation between accident levels and benefit levels. For example, Virginia, Georgia and Alabama had similar benefit levels but widely different accident levels; while Pennsylvania and New Jersey had very similar accident levels but vastly different benefit levels. The Commission concluded that the evidence suggested that workers' compensation insurance rates were not the strongest force affecting the frequency of accidents.

As we saw earlier, there is a certain amount of empirical evidence about the effects of tort liability on accident and injury levels. However, as we have also seen, the tort system in many respects does not embody or give effect to general deterrence principles; and so such evidence is not directly relevant to assessing the theory of general deterrence. On the other hand, it does provide some clue to the deterrent effectiveness of liability to pay the costs of accidents. Almost all writers who have considered the matter have come to the conclusion that there is no reliable evidence that liability to pay tort damages has any significant effect on the level of accidents or accident costs; although logically, of course, the absence of evidence does not prove that liability to pay the costs of accidents has no substantial deterrent effect.

---

128 6.5.1.
129 M.W. Jones-Lee, 'The Value of Transport Safety' (1990) 6 *Oxford Review of Economic Policy* 39, 50–2.

17.8.8   Conclusions about general deterrence

Much of the literature on this subject is based on strong assumptions about the value of markets and of individual choice. For example, it is often taken for granted in the general-deterrence literature that there is only one 'rational' way of approaching the problem of safety and accident prevention – namely in terms of cost-benefit analysis.[130] It is assumed that the only rational course of action for an individual, an enterprise and a society is to spend as much, but only as much, on protecting health and safety as the value of the lives thereby saved and the injuries prevented. While it is important not to underestimate the value of these economic considerations, and of the proper use of cost-benefit analysis in injury prevention measures, other considerations may also be thought relevant. Decisions about how much to spend on preventing particular types of injuries and diseases may be made on political or moral grounds, or on grounds of public interest, which bear little relation to immediate cost-benefit equations. For example, because people make greater demands on health-care resources the older they become, it might make sense in purely financial terms not to spend large amounts of money to prevent people dying prematurely from smoking-related diseases, for example. But in moral terms, such an attitude to human life would be totally unacceptable. Again, while insurance premiums related to risk are clearly required by deterrence theory, they may not be introduced, for reasons unrelated to considerations of accident and harm prevention.[131]

Another limitation of the general-deterrence approach arises from the fact that because the cost of compensating for personal injury and death represents a very small proportion of the total costs of economic activity, other factors – such as rates of taxation and of government support, and the cost of labour and materials – are likely to have much greater impact on levels of activity in particular sectors of the economy than differences in compensation costs as between different activities. For instance, it is probably the case that forms of public transport – trains and buses – are, relatively, responsible for less personal injury and death than private motor transport; but levels of public investment in the road system relative to government investment in public transport more than counteract whatever safety advantage public transport may have over the private car. If governments support relatively unsafe activities, safer but unsupported activities may be unable to compete on the basis of the safety advantage.

Another problem with giving practical effect to the general-deterrence approach is that it depends on detailed and accurate calculation of the relative costs and benefits of activities, which will often be impossible because of lack of relevant information.

It is worth noting, too, that the general-deterrence approach is much more popular in the USA than in Britain; and this may be because it fits in better with US

---

130 But for evidence that 'ordinary Americans' do not think in terms of 'optimal deterrence' see C.R. Sunstein, D. Schkade and D. Kahneman, 'Do People Want Optimal Deterrence?' (2000) 29 *J. of Legal Studies* 237.
131 17.7.2.2.

than with British traditions and points of view. For instance, the common law of products liability, backed by the constraints of liability insurance costs, in practice plays a much more significant role in the USA than in the UK in regulating the safety of products:[132] in this country, administratively enforced statutory regulation is the primary mechanism. In general, it is probably fair to say that, in Britain, tort law functions, and is assessed, primarily as a compensation system, and only secondarily as a tool of health and safety regulation. In the USA, by contrast, lawyers and citizens alike put much more faith in tort litigation as a regulatory mechanism: witness such modern morality plays as *A Civil Action* and *Erin Brokowich*. This difference perhaps reflects deeper differences between the two societies.[133]

Considerations such as these perhaps cast doubt on the value of the general-deterrence approach as a way of understanding and evaluating the role of tort law in Britain. Although it would be wrong to overlook altogether the possibility that in some contexts tort law might play some part in limiting or reducing accident costs, the detailed application of general-deterrence ideas seems to depend too much on inappropriate and impractical 'fine tuning'. Thus, the idea that an elaborate system, requiring the allocation of carefully calculated accident costs to particular activities, would be justifiable or reasonably practicable, seems quite problematic. But once it is conceded that as a general-deterrence device, tort law can operate in only a rough-and-ready way, it is not easy to see why – in the field of personal injuries and disease – its compensation and loss distribution functions should not be transferred to a social security system paid for out of taxation, or a first-party insurance system, or a combination of the two, rather than to a liability system funded by third-party liability insurance. Although such a change might potentially externalize injury costs, this result could be avoided by designing any alternative system in such a way as to take account of general deterrence. Thus the Pearson Commission proposed that its road accident compensation scheme should be financed by a special levy on the price of petrol. Similarly, first-party insurance premiums could take into account the harm-causing potential of particular activities and the claims history of particular individuals and groups in the same way that comprehensive motor insurance premiums currently do. There is no reason to think that the sort of general-deterrence effects that could be achieved in a non-tort compensation system would be significantly less than those achieved by the tort system.

In summary, then, even if we accept that tort law's general-deterrence potential provides an argument in its favour, this argument does not seem strong enough, by itself, to justify retention of the tort system, at least in relation to personal injury and death, given its other serious weaknesses.

132 This is one reason why general product recalls are more common in the USA than in Britain.
133 See e.g. R.A. Kagan, *Adversarial Legalism: The American Way of Law* (Cambridge, Mass., 2001), esp. ch. 7.

Part 6

The future

18

Accident compensation in the twenty-first century

18.1 Where we are now and how we got here

Serious dissatisfaction with the operation of the tort system, as a mechanism of compensating for personal injury and death, first received widespread expression in the late 1960s. Terence Ison's book, *The Forensic Lottery*, was published in 1967, followed by D.W. Elliot and H. Street's *Road Accidents* in 1968, and the first edition of this book in 1970. At about the same time, the famous Thalidomide affair was coming to a head. In the late 1950s and early 1960s, a large number of children around the world were born with disabilities of varying degrees of severity as a result of their mothers' having taken the drug Thalidomide during pregnancy. Tort actions mounted against manufacturers of the drug came to the attention of the public in 1972 when *The Sunday Times* ran a series of articles in which one of the manufacturers, the Distillers Company, was heavily criticised for the way in which it was defending the actions. As a result, the proprietors of *The Sunday Times* were prosecuted for contempt of court, and the case eventually found its way to the European Court of Human Rights. By the early 1970s, then, there was a vigorous public debate in the UK about the shortcomings of the tort system as a compensation mechanism. Fuel was added to this debate by the enactment in New Zealand in 1972 of a general accident compensation scheme. The genesis of this scheme was a crisis in the New Zealand workers' compensation scheme in the mid-1960s. A Royal Commission was appointed under the chairmanship of Sir Owen Woodhouse, and in its 1967 report it recommended the abolition of the tort system so far as it dealt with personal injuries, and its replacement by a State-run compensation scheme covering all accidents and some diseases.

It was against this background that in December 1972 the UK government announced the establishment of the Royal Commission on Civil Liability and Compensation for Personal Injury, to be chaired by Lord Pearson. Besides receiving evidence and submissions from a large number of individuals and organizations, the Commission conducted the first large-scale survey of the practical operation of the tort system, the results of which have been referred to frequently in this book. The picture painted by the Pearson Commission seems broadly to be as accurate today as it was when it reported in 1978. The Report came as a disappointment to many. Instead of recommending a comprehensive compensation scheme, the Commission made separate proposals for dealing with road accidents, product liability, medical injuries and so on. The only area for which it recommended a non-tort compensation scheme was road accidents. In other contexts, the tort system was to remain in place, although the Commission did suggest various reforms to the rules about assessment of damages and about the relationship between tort compensation and social security benefits.

For the time, energy and money spent on the work of the Royal Commission, it produced very little by way of reform of the tort system. The Congenital Disabilities (Civil Liability) Act, which was a response to the doubt raised by the Thalidomide litigation as to whether tort liability could arise in respect of injuries suffered in the womb, was enacted in 1976; although the Commission did suggest some amendments to it. The Commission recommended the introduction of strict product liability, but the effective catalyst for the scheme contained in Part I of the Consumer Protection Act 1987 was a European Directive, not the Commission's proposal. Some of its recommendations regarding assessment of damages were enacted in the Administration of Justice Act 1982, but that was about all. The Commission's proposal for a non-tort road-accident compensation scheme received no serious consideration. In the late 1980s there was considerable pressure, mainly from doctors, for a no-fault scheme for medical injuries, but (not surprisingly) it subsided with the introduction of NHS indemnity.[1] In 1991 the Lord Chancellor's Department made fresh proposals for a non-tort scheme covering minor road accident cases,[2] but these were not pursued.

A number of factors contributed to this disappointing outcome. One was the fragmentary nature of the Commission's proposals. Also important was the change of political climate precipitated by the election of the first Thatcher Conservative government in 1979. For reformers who had lived in the post-War Welfare State, the model of an alternative to the tort system was the social security system. In the 1980s, by contrast, further extension of the social security system became political and economic anathema. Conservative ideology stressed the value of self-reliance and deprecated the 'nanny state'. The idea of dismantling the tort system not only ran counter to the new economic orthodoxy. Tort law and the tort system, based as they were on ethical principles of personal responsibility, also seemed to be in tune with the moral underpinnings of Thatcherism. To replace the tort system with a social security scheme would not only have required a vast increase in public expenditure, but would also have increased the individual's dependence on the State, to the benefit of those who ought to have been held accountable for their injury-causing conduct. Conservatives opposed both of these moves.

Around the world, many jurisdictions have adopted non-tort compensation schemes, especially to deal with road accidents. In Britain, pressure to replace the tort

1 16.1.
2 *Compensation for Road Accidents: A Consultation Paper* (May 1991).

system is now all but non-existent. Indeed, the recent extension of the scheme for recovering the costs of NHS care from payers of tort compensation (15.4.5) can be seen as entrenching the tort system more firmly than ever in the political economy of provision for the disabled. This is certainly not because the defects of the tort system have disappeared. It is as costly and inefficient as it was 40 years ago. What has changed over the last 25 years are people's ideas as to what should be done about it. The Woolf reforms,[3] introduced in 1999, were designed to address concerns about the cost and 'delays' of litigation. They were, of course, general in their operation and not targeted at the tort system; but they have produced perhaps their most dramatic results in that context. The years immediately following the introduction of the new procedural system also saw the coming-of-age of new arrangements for funding personal injury claims: conditional fees (introduced in 1995), abolition of legal aid for personal injury claims (except medical negligence claims and a very few others), the development of ATE insurance and introduction of the rule that the success fee and ATE premium payable by a successful claimant were recoverable from the defendant.[4] There was also a significant increase in the cost of settling low-value personal injury claims associated with aspects of the Woolf reforms designed to encourage early settlement.

This new environment gave a boost to the activities of non-legally qualified claims handlers, and by 2005 calls[5] for statutory regulation of their activities had been accepted by government.[6] The complexity of the conditional fee system, coupled with the new liability for the success fee and ATE premium of a successful claimant, provoked insurers to challenge the validity of individual CFAs in an attempt to avoid costs liability. Such challenges were unsuccessful, but eventually led to the radical simplification of the conditional fee regime. Concern about rising costs also led to the negotiation and enactment of fixed legal fees for low-value road accident claims, and fixed success fees for road accident and work accident claims. An insurance crisis, especially in relation to employers' compulsory liability insurance, has increased pressure on liability insurers to strengthen the relationship between premiums and the risk presented by individual insureds; but even assuming this can be done, it will not produce any short-term changes in the distribution of the costs of the liability system. The upshot of the changes of the past decade and the attendant turmoil seems to be that the tort system remains

---

3 Based on *Access to Justice, Final Report* (HMSO, 1996).
4 On all this see further 10.2.
5 Precipitated, inter alia, by aggressive marketing tactics and the collapse of the two largest claims management companies in 2002 and 2003 respectively. For the official rationale for regulation see Compensation Bill Final Regulatory Statement (2005), paras. 2.21–2.30.
6 Legislation to enable the establishment, by delegated legislation, of a regulatory regime – the Compensation Bill – was introduced into Parliament in November 2005. See also DCA, *Regulation of Claims Management Services: Policy Statement and Model Rules for Authorised Persons* (March 2006). It is possible that the regulator will be a private sector, non-profit company called the Claims Standards Council, members of which include claims managers, insurance companies and law firms. See Boleat Consulting, *The Claims Standards Council* (December 2005); Claims Standards Council, *Response to the Boleat Report* (January 2006).

firmly in place as a major source of compensation for victims of road accidents, work accidents and, to a lesser extent, accidents in public places. Most other accidents (with the exception of medical misadventure) and most diseases (with the exception of adverse reactions to drugs and medical devices) remain, in practice, outside the tort system. Much has changed in the past 40 years; but the situation the Pearson Commission uncovered in the 1970s remains, in its essentials, unchanged.

Although cases of medical negligence represent only about 1% of all personal injury claims, they have a very high public profile, partly because the most expensive medical negligence claims are very expensive indeed; partly because the most expensive medical negligence claims are made on behalf of children who suffer birth injuries; and partly because all the most expensive medical negligence claims are paid out of public funds, and are handled by a single body, the NHS Litigation Authority, which publishes regular reports of its activities and detailed statistics of claims and payments. In 2003 the Chief Medical Officer published a major report about the handling of medical negligence claims.[7] The report rejected the option of further reform of the tort system for various reasons, including: proving fault is a 'lottery'; the tort system is insufficiently integrated with the NHS complaints system; it provides inadequate incentives for improved safety; it undermines the relationship of trust between doctor and patient; and the only remedy it provides is money.[8] It proposed the establishment of an NHS Redress Scheme, which would be in some way integrated with the NHS Complaints Scheme. Victims of medical negligence would not be required to use the Scheme in preference to making a tort claim,[9] partly because it is anticipated that the Redress Scheme would only handle claims up to a certain value;[10] but a person who accepted a 'package' under the Redress Scheme would be required to waive their right to make a tort claim. In most cases, criteria for access to the Redress Scheme would be that there were serious shortcomings in the standard of care provided; the harm inflicted could have been avoided; and adverse outcome was not the result of the natural progression of an illness. The extent to which the application of these criteria would produce outcomes different from those arising from application of the concept of fault used in tort law depends on their detailed elaboration. In cases involving children damaged at birth, the access criteria would be that the birth took place under NHS care and that the child suffered severe neurological impairment resulting

---

7 *Making Amends* (Department of Health).
8 See 8.2 for a discussion of why people make medical negligence claims.
9 Medical negligence claims would continue to be eligible for legal aid, but the availability of the Redress Scheme would be taken into account in deciding whether legal aid should be granted.
10 In most cases, the maximum financial compensation available under the scheme would be £30,000 plus the 'notional cost of the episode of care or other amount as appropriate at the discretion of the local NHS Trust'. Most medical negligence claims settle for less than this amount. According to the Legal Services Commission, in 1999 the median medical negligence claim was settled for £6,500: Response of the Legal Services Commission to *Making Amends*, para. 3.9.

from or related to the birth. A claim would have to be made within 8 years of the birth.[11] The claimant would not have to prove that the harm was a result of negligence; but the maximum financial compensation payable in such a case would be up to £100,000 per annum for care, up to £50,000 for home adaptations and equipment and £50,000 for non-pecuniary loss.

Leaving aside the departure from the fault principle in the scheme for disabled children, the main differences between the tort system and the proposed Redress Scheme are that the latter would be more integrated with the NHS Complaints system, and that long-term care for victims of medical negligence would be provided by the NHS. The suggested advantages of the first difference is that treating claims also as complaints will facilitate the provision of redress in the form of explanations and apologies, and make it more likely that steps will be taken to prevent similar events in the future. Concerning the second difference, under current law, in assessing long-term care costs, the basic measure is the cost of providing the care privately. The fact that the care is available from the NHS does not prevent the claimant recovering the cost of procuring the care in the private sector. This rule was criticized earlier, and its abolition in relation to claims against the NHS was one of the Chief Medical Officer's proposals. Under the Redress Scheme, the basic idea is that the cost of care will be paid only if appropriate care is not available from the NHS.

Legislation to enable the establishment (in delegated legislation) of an NHS Redress Scheme – the NHS Redress Bill – was introduced into Parliament in November 2005. What is the likely impact of the introduction of such a scheme on the total compensation bill for medical negligence? Removal of the requirement to prove fault in birth-injury cases can be expected to result in increased claiming; and it is unclear whether the benefits on offer will significantly reduce tort claims in such cases. Moreover, the Legal Services Commission says that few medical negligence claims worth less than £5,000 are made because such claims do not generally qualify for legal aid, and CFAs are relatively rare in the medical negligence area. For these reasons, the Commission anticipates that introduction of the Redress Scheme will result in a large increase in small claims.[12] Whether provision of long-term care through the NHS and abolition of the right to recover damages for the cost of care available through the NHS will lead to significant cost savings is hard to say. Relevant in this regard is the fact that the most serious cases, in which long-term care costs are likely to be highest, will not fall within the Redress Scheme. Finally, it is impossible to predict how claim-handling costs under the Scheme will compare with those in the tort system.

Another recommendation made by the Chief Medical Officer is for the wider use of mediation in medical negligence claims made outside the Redress Scheme. Increased recourse to mediation and other forms of ADR is a basic principle of the

11 This is a much shorter limit than under the tort system.
12 LSC, Response of the Legal Services Commission to *Making Amends*, paras. 1.2, 3.10–11.

Woolf procedural reforms, but very little progress has been made in this direction. The use of mediation in legally aided medical negligence cases is extremely limited even though, according to the Legal Services Commission, it is beneficial in 83% of cases in which it takes place.[13]

At the time of writing, the precise details of the NHS Redress Scheme are yet to be settled: the NHS Redress Bill is only enabling legislation. In broad terms, the aims of the Chief Medical Officer's proposals are no doubt admirable. However, schemes such as this, running in parallel with the tort system, inevitably increase the complexity of arrangements to provide for the disabled and add a new element of differential treatment according to the cause of disability. Moreover, so long as recourse to the tort system remains available, the alternative is only likely to compete successfully with it if the benefits available under the latter are obviously superior to those on offer from the former. It is not clear at this stage whether this can be said of the proposed Redress Scheme.

Although the Chief Medical Officer described the proposals as radical, we might well question whether they are radical enough. Recall a few basic facts. As a personal injury compensation mechanism, the tort system is extraordinarily expensive both in absolute terms (85p to deliver £1 of tort compensation) and relative to the social security system (between 8p and 12p to deliver £1 of benefit). Its benefits in terms of accident and injury prevention are at best limited, and there are good reasons to think that a significant proportion of injury victims who would, according to the rules of tort law, be entitled to compensation receive nothing from the tort system. This is true not only in relation to injuries caused by traumatic accidents but even more in relation to illness and disease.[14] The main perceived benefit of the tort system is that it embodies and gives some effect to a set of principles of personal responsibility for the adverse consequences of individuals' conduct and to the idea of 'corrective justice'. The question we really need to ask ourselves is whether this benefit is worth more than 70 pence in the pound. No doubt some injury victims who receive compensation through the tort system feel better than they would if they received the same amount from the State, for instance. And no doubt the behaviour of some people is affected for the good by being a defendant to a tort claim or by seeing others undergoing that experience. On the other hand, we know that many victims find that the process of making a tort claim adds insult to injury; and the impact of liability insurance drastically reduces the potential impact of the tort process on individual defendants. Anyway, what we need to consider from a public policy point of view is not whether the tort system has benefits, but whether those benefits are worth the costs of the system. If you think they are not, then for you, the case for radical reform of the tort system remains strong. The fact that radical reform is currently off the political agenda does not reduce, and perhaps even increases, the importance of a careful consid-

13 Ibid., para. 5.7.
14 J. Stapleton, *Disease and the Compensation Debate* (Oxford, 1986).

eration of possible directions of development, if and when pressure for change builds up again.

The main aim of this chapter is, therefore, to discuss options for radical reform of the tort system of compensating for personal injuries. In the first part of the chapter we will discuss a number of basic issues of principle and policy relevant to reform of the law, and then we will discuss more specifically some of the proposals for reform which have been made in Britain and elsewhere, and some non-tort compensation schemes which have actually been put into effect.

18.2   Basic issues

18.2.1   Strict liability or no-fault?

Proposals involving abolition of the fault principle take two basic forms. Some involve its replacement by strict liability, that is liability without proof of intention or negligence. The reform of product liability law enacted in Part I of the Consumer Protection Act 1987 is a manifestation of the move towards strict liability. The main impetus for this reform was the Thalidomide tragedy. The legal aftermath of this affair demonstrated, amongst other things, the difficulties of proving negligence against manufacturers of drugs in respect of the testing of new products to ensure safety, and of proving a causal link between the alleged negligence and the claimant's injuries. One of the main advantages claimed for strict liability over negligence lies in the fact that the claimant need not prove fault in order to obtain compensation. In practice, however, most strict liability proposals (including those enacted in Part I of the Consumer Protection Act 1987) contain fault elements (such as retention of the defence of contributory negligence and definition of 'defective product' in terms of a negligence-type test) which reduce their claim to be radical reform measures.[15]

Moreover, strict liability schemes do nothing about two of the major drawbacks of the tort system – the need to prove a causal link between act and injury and the need to find a responsible defendant. In economic terms, strict liability is sometimes said to have the edge on negligence in respect of accident prevention because, by imposing liability for injuries which were unavoidable given knowledge and technology at the time of manufacture,[16] it forces manufacturers to spend more on research and development in the attempt to discover defects in products before they are manufactured in quantity and marketed. The force of this argument depends on the extent to which liability rules have a significant impact on manufacturers' behaviour, and about this there is considerable dispute.

Reform proposals of the second type – so-called 'no-fault' proposals – eliminate the need both to find a responsible defendant and to prove a causal link between a

15 In Australia, the Commonwealth Law Reform Commission did propose a very strict scheme of products liability, but it was rejected on the advice of the Industry Commission, and legislation along the lines of the 1987 Act was enacted in 1992: see F.A. Trindade and P. Cane, *Law of Torts in Australia*, 3rd edn (Melbourne, 1999), ch. 15.
16 The 1987 Act does not impose such liability: 4.8.

specific act or omission and the victim's injuries. No-fault schemes concentrate on the injuries rather than on the way the injuries were caused. For example, a no-fault road accident scheme will provide compensation for injuries suffered in a road accident regardless of whether those injuries were caused by another road user or by the injured person; and regardless of fault.[17]

However, in practice no-fault schemes do not eliminate all problems of proving causation because such schemes tend to be limited in scope rather than comprehensive. For example, a person claiming no-fault road accident compensation would have to prove that the injuries arose 'out of or in connection with the use of a motor vehicle', or something like that. A person claiming no-fault compensation for drug-related injuries would have to prove that the injuries were the result of the drug and not, for example, of 'natural causes'; and this may not be easy because many adverse drug reactions are indistinguishable from other illnesses.[18] Moreover, the concept of 'cause' used in this context tends to be infected with notions of fault: it is more like 'legal cause' than 'factual cause', and so its use derogates from the aim of providing 'no-fault' compensation. The only way of eliminating causal issues entirely is to base entitlement to compensation solely on the need of the claimant for compensation. At present, not even the most extensive no-fault scheme in operation (that in New Zealand) compensates entirely regardless of cause.[19] Under that scheme, two causal issues are particularly problematic: that of proving that the injury was caused by an 'accident' (itself a difficult term to define); and, in cases of medical misadventure, that of proving that the injury was the result of medical misadventure and not of the condition being treated.[20]

There is no discernible principle according to which reform in some areas takes the form of strict liability and in others, no-fault compensation. Legal tradition probably plays a part in some countries;[21] the influence of strong pressure groups was undoubtedly important in moulding the shape of product liability proposals; and the political and economic environment is extremely important to no-fault reforms, as the fate of the Pearson Commission proposals showed.

17 But there may be exceptions – e.g. under the New Zealand scheme a person who suffers personal injury in the course of committing an offence for which the person is convicted and imprisoned may be refused compensation: Injury Prevention, Rehabilitation and Compensation Act 2001, s. 122.
18 J. Stapleton, 'Compensating Victims of Disease' (1985) 5 Oxford J. Legal Studies 248, 250–2, 255–7. About 25% of unsuccessful claims made in the first 2 years of the Swedish no-fault drug injuries scheme failed because of lack of proof of causal link: J. Fleming, 'Drug Injury Compensation Plans' (1982) 30 American J. of Comparative Law 297, 303 n. 37. See also T.G. Ison, 'Etiological Classifications in Compensation Systems' (1985–6) 10 Adelaide LR 86.
19 This statement is slightly misleading because it ignores the general disability and income-support elements of the social security system, under which entitlement to benefits does not depend on establishing that the disability giving rise to the need for benefits had any particular cause. Here we are dealing with schemes which are seen as reforms of the tort system, rather than as developments of the social security system.
20 See generally K. Oliphant, 'Defining "Medical Misadventure": Lessons from New Zealand' [1996] Medical LR 1.
21 As in the case of the drug injuries compensation scheme in Germany: Fleming, 'Drug Injury Compensation Plans', 300.

18.2.2   Limited or comprehensive reform?

This book is about personal injuries. Physical disablement is only one type of misfortune which people suffer, and which generates needs for financial support; and it is not necessarily the most important of such misfortunes. Unemployment, for example, is an important source of financial dislocation and need. Some would argue that the basic problem which the State ought to seek to relieve is poverty and financial need, and that to the extent that disabled people suffer, as a result of their disabilities, from low income, they should be treated in the same way as other poor people. The disabled may well have additional needs generated by their physical condition, and these should be separately met. But so far as provision of income is concerned, the disabled should not be singled out for special treatment.

The course of action required by this line of argument might be to leave all victims of personal injuries to rely on the social security system in the same way as others in need. Unfortunately, this apparently simple solution would not really work because the social security system itself is far from perfect in the way that it deals with the disabled; and, perhaps more importantly, the social security system does not dispense benefits solely on the basis of financial need. Not only do different groups of the disabled receive different treatment in respect of exactly the same needs, but also different sources of need, such as disablement and unemployment, are treated differently. The social security system does not provide a minimum income and uniform provision for those with special physical needs. Before this proposal could be seriously considered, the social security system itself would have to be overhauled. Since this is a matter totally beyond the scope of this book, the rest of the discussion will concentrate purely on reform of the law concerning provision for the physically disabled in general, and victims of personal injury (including disease) in particular.

Perhaps the most radical type of reform of the law concerning compensation for personal injuries involves abolishing the tort system entirely and incorporating no-fault compensation for victims of personal injuries into the social security system. According to the most thoroughgoing version of this approach, all those who suffer disabilities (of whatever nature) for which society accepts responsibility should receive financial and other support from the State according to the same criteria of need, regardless of the source or nature of the disabilities.[22] This position, however, only expresses an ideal. As the writer of a study of disability income systems in Britain concluded more than 20 years ago: 'reasonably equal treatment of people with equal needs is not a notable feature of the present arrangements whether inside or outside the State schemes' (of compensation).[23] Again, the New Zealand Accident Compensation Scheme, which is often held up as a model for reform of the law of compensation for personal injuries, is very far from the ideal. It covers personal

---

22 For a discussion of some possible approaches see Stapleton, *Disease and the Compensation Debate*, 158–69.

23 J.C. Brown, *Disability Income*, vol. 2 (London, 1984), 342.

injury by accident, 'medical misadventure',[24] occupational diseases[25] and criminal injuries,[26] but not other sources of personal injury;[27] and it treats the victims of personal injury more generously than other social security claimants.[28] Many jurisdictions have no-fault compensation schemes for road and industrial accidents (and, often, some occupational diseases), which provide better benefits for claimants than general social welfare provisions. Various jurisdictions have limited compensation schemes for the victims of violent crimes, vaccination damage, medical experiments, drug injuries and so on.

In fact, a common pattern of reform is to institute limited no-fault schemes to deal with particular classes of injured persons whose claims are pressed by politically powerful groups, or whose plight for some reason attracts public attention and sympathy. The basic question raised by this limited and piecemeal approach is that of how the preference for the groups of injured who are singled out for special treatment under a no-fault scheme (or, in the case of product liability, e.g., a strict liability scheme) is to be justified in comparison with the position of less favoured groups of injured persons. It may be that good (or at least popularly acceptable) reasons for treating some groups of the disabled differently from others can be adduced, but serious attempts to do this are very rare. Even so, it seems that the likely direction of future reform measures will be towards limited rather than comprehensive schemes. In New Zealand, early intentions to extend the accident scheme quickly to other sources of personal injury are unlikely ever to be fulfilled;[29] and in Australia, where the path to comprehensive reform was seen as lying via transport accident schemes, no such comprehensive reform seems likely.

One possible argument in favour of limited schemes is that by focussing on one injury-causing activity (e.g. motoring), the scheme enables the cost of the activity to be fully internalized to that activity. But even in a comprehensive scheme the funding sources could, to some extent, anyway, be organized to achieve this objective.

Another important respect in which no-fault schemes are often limited is that even in the area in which they operate (e.g. road accidents) they do not always entirely supersede the tort system but leave the common law to operate side-by-side with the

---

24 'It is difficult to fit the concept of "medical misadventure" into the framework of what is essentially a workers' compensation scheme': M.A. Vennell and J. Manning, 'The Accident Rehabilitation and Compensation Insurance Act 1992' [1992] *New Zealand Recent LR* 1, 5–6.

25 More precisely 'gradual process, disease or infection arising out of the course of employment'.

26 Although these fit somewhat uneasily within the scheme: Vennell and Manning, 'The Accident Rehabilitation and Compensation Insurance Act 1992', 4.

27 T.G. Ison, *Accident Compensation* (London, 1980), 18–19; G. Palmer, *Compensation for Incapacity* (Wellington, 1979), ch. XV. But care needs to be taken in reading these sources because the scheme has been considerably altered in recent years. For an up-to-date account see S. Todd *et al.*, *The Law of Torts In New Zealand*, 4th edn (Wellington, 2005), chs. 2 and 3.

28 B. Rea, 'Accident Compensation: A Cuckoo in the Sparrow's Nest of Social Welfare?' (1982) 4 *Auckland ULR* 235; Palmer, *Compensation for Incapacity*, 322–3; R. Stephens, 'Horizontal Equity for Disabled People: Incapacity from Accident or Illness' (2004) 35 *Victoria U. of Wellington LR* 783.

29 Indeed, the scope of the accident scheme was reduced in 1992.

no-fault scheme. Sometimes tort and no-fault rights run in parallel, with set-off provisions to prevent double recovery. Indeed, we have already seen that under the present law in Britain, there are rules determining when and to what extent no-fault, first-party insurance and social security benefits are to be set off against tort damages. The proposals for an NHS Redress Scheme discussed earlier provide for such a type of 'dual system'.

Another type of dual system provides for no-fault benefits up to a ceiling, and then tort rights are available to top the compensation up to the level of 'full compensation'. Such dual systems have several disadvantages. First, they require the whole structure of tort law and third-party liability insurance, with all its inefficiencies and costly waste, to remain in existence. US experience shows that schemes which limit rights to sue in tort cut costs much more effectively than schemes containing no such limitation.[30] Secondly, since the no-fault benefits are subject to a ceiling, those who suffer most from the faults of the retained tort system are the long-term seriously disabled, who must rely on the common law to bring their compensation up to an adequate level. Conversely, those best off under a dual system are the less seriously injured, who can expect to receive compensation for most or all of their economic losses under the no-fault scheme, and who also enjoy the option of using the tort system to secure compensation for non-economic losses. The long-term disabled, by contrast, may have difficulty obtaining adequate compensation even for financial loss, despite using both elements of the dual system. Dual systems, therefore, tend to be costly, to preserve all the flaws of the tort process and to disadvantage those most in need relative to those less in need.

A case in favour of a dual system might be based on arguments about 'justice'. From this perspective, a dual system has the advantage that it embodies principles both of individual and of social responsibility.[31] Thus a dual system might be constructed which would ensure the victim adequate financial support from a no-fault fund, but also allow them to sue the tortfeasor for damages for intangible loss as an expression of the latter's individual responsibility. The desirability of retaining the element of individual responsibility is established, it is said, by the fact that criticism of the fault principle is not directed at the validity or acceptability of the ideals or objectives it embodies, but at the law's inability to achieve those objectives.[32] There may also be a political case in favour of dual systems. In New Zealand, the 'price' of the abolition of tort rights was that benefits under the Accident Compensation Scheme were to be broadly commensurate with those in tort, at least so far as financial losses were concerned. The high level of benefits

---

30 US Department of Transportation study, *State No-Fault Automobile Insurance Experience 1971–77* (Washington, 1978); J. O'Connell, 'Update on the Surveys on the Operation of No-fault Auto Laws' [1979] *Insurance LJ* 129.

31 L. Klar in F.M. Steel and S. Rodgers-Magnet eds., *Issues in Tort Law* (Toronto, 1983). See also L. Klar, 'The Osborne Report: "No" to No-Fault' (1989) 68 *Can BR* 301; R. Mahoney, 'Trouble in Paradise: New Zealand's Accident Compensation Scheme' in S.A.M. McLean, *Law Reform and Medical Injury Litigation* (1995), 32–4.

32 Klar in Steel and Rodgers-Magnet, *Issues in Tort Law*, 33.

both creates anomalies with other social security benefits and makes the scheme expensive; and the expense has inhibited the extension of the scheme to disease. The retention of tort might make it possible to introduce a more comprehensive no-fault scheme with relatively low flat-rate benefits. This would give all the disabled a floor of support but also enable those who wished (and were lucky enough to be able to make a successful tort claim) to gain higher tort benefits.

On balance, however, the case for a dual system is not convincing. The fact that the objectives of the tort system might be thought desirable does not justify retention of a system which achieves those goals so inefficiently, and in many respects not at all. The political point could be met by a two-tier, no-fault system in which relatively low flat-rate benefits were financed by compulsory levies and contributions and higher benefits for those who desired them could be bought by higher voluntary contributions, or by the purchase of insurance in the commercial market.

The basic policy choice between comprehensive and limited reform is a choice between viewing the position of victims of personal injuries in terms of social welfare, on the one hand, or in terms of legal rights and duties, on the other.[33] The first perspective leads to attempts to integrate compensation for personal injury into the social welfare system of compensating for those misfortunes for which the State takes some responsibility. It by no means follows that all victims of misfortune will be treated in the same way by the social welfare system, and that no distinctions will be drawn on the basis of type and source of misfortune. But the comprehensive approach does involve opting for social welfare techniques, and espousing as an ultimate goal an integrated system of social welfare to deal with all cases of 'social misfortune' on the basis of need. The second perspective, on the other hand, tends to start with the existing pattern of legal liability for personal injuries, and to concentrate on improving existing legal mechanisms so that they deliver compensation to more of those for whom it is intended (e.g. the 95% of accident victims (more or less) who at present receive no tort compensation). This approach may lead simply to procedural reforms, or to reform of the rules governing assessment of damages, or it may lead to no-fault schemes, such as road accident schemes, designed to use the resources presently poured into compensating personal injury victims more efficiently to provide more victims with tort-type benefits.[34] The two approaches are quite different, and the second is much more prevalent than the first.

18.2.3 Preferential treatment

An important feature of the present law, of avowedly limited reform proposals, and even of proposals and schemes designed by reformers with comprehensive reform as their ultimate goal, is that some groups of disabled people receive better treat-

---

33 Palmer, *Compensation for Incapacity*, 93.
34 This last approach favours those disabled people who already benefit from the tort system and does nothing for victims of disease, for example: Stapleton, *Disease and the Compensation Debate*, 143–52.

ment than others. The extreme egalitarian position would be that the only criterion of compensation should be need, and that like needs should be treated alike whatever their source. We have seen at various points how, in practice, particular groups receive preferential treatment despite the fact that their needs are no different from those of less favoured groups. We have, for example, noted the industrial preference in the social security system; in chapter 1 we discussed the preferential treatment accorded to the victims of injuries attributable to human as opposed to natural causes. The commitment of tort law to the principle of full compensation and to the hundred-per cent principle produces a preference in the law for the victims of injuries as opposed to other misfortunes such as unemployment. We have also noted that, in practice, tort law makes it easier for the victim of traumatically caused injuries to recover compensation than for the victim of illness and disease attributable to human causes – what one writer has called the 'accident preference'.[35]

This last preference is also present in the New Zealand accident compensation scheme,[36] and in that context the preference is partly the result of the fact that diseases are a much more common source of physical incapacity than accidents; and so the cost of a scheme which covered the former as well as the latter would be very much greater than that of a scheme covering accidents only. For example, the Australian Committee of Inquiry into a national compensation scheme found that a scheme covering accidents, congenital incapacity and sickness would cost about five times as much as one covering accidents only.[37] On the other hand, this estimate takes no account of the cost of existing schemes which compensate disease victims (such as occupational sick pay and personal insurance) and so does not represent the additional cost of a disease scheme.[38] Moreover, the proposed Australian scheme provided high-level, earnings-related benefits, which added considerably to the cost of the scheme. Nevertheless, the argument based on cost is a potent political weapon available against the introduction of comprehensive compensation schemes covering illness and disease as well as accidents. Opposition to the abolition of tort rights tends to be bought off by providing generous benefits, but when applied to the sphere of disease as well as accidents, the high benefits generate new opposition because they make the scheme very expensive. Thus it can be seen that the shape of reform can be influenced as much by political pressures as by rational arguments of principle or policy.[39]

Finally, it is worth noting the point that every proposal or scheme for strict liability or no-fault compensation in a limited area creates a preference in favour of some victims of personal injury against others. The purpose of pointing out that the law and most reform proposals contain such preferences is not to show that

35 Stapleton, 'Compensating Victims of Disease'.
36 And is likely to remain so: Sir Geoffrey Palmer, 'The Future of Community Responsibility' (2004)
35 *Victoria U. of Wellington LR* 905.
37 *Australian Committee Report*, para. 483.
38 Ison, *Accident Compensation*, 30–1.
39 Palmer, *Compensation for Incapacity*, 204–5, 338.

preferential treatment of selected groups is necessarily unjustifiable. It may be possible to produce more or less convincing arguments in favour of preferential treatment of various groups. The point to make is simply that it is important to recognize and to seek to justify preferential treatment, in order to ensure that any scheme proposed or put into effect reflects an acceptable set of priorities for the use of social resources. For example, some good reason might be found for compensating injury victims for financial loss more generously than victims of redundancy, but we should be clear what that reason is before we institute or continue a system which gives effect to that preference.

18.2.4   Assessment of compensation

As we have seen, the tort system seeks in theory to compensate claimants for 100% of their financial losses, and to provide monetary compensation for a wide variety of non-economic losses; it also purports to provide compensation for the full period of the claimant's incapacity or the full period during which they suffer loss. In other words, the tort system attempts to restore the claimant to the financial position they were in before the injuries were suffered (*restitutio in integrum*). To this end it provides fully earnings-related income replacement ('standard of living' benefits) for earners, and income for some non-earners (e.g. domestic carers) on the basis of the notional market value of their services; and full compensation for expenses incurred as a result of the injuries. The tort system also provides compensation for the disability itself – pain and suffering and loss of amenities. In order to do all this the tort system of assessment has to be highly individualized, and so it is costly and slow.

The features of the tort system of assessment represent a maximum, and reform proposals usually involve some sort of trade-off under which more people are compensated than by the tort system, but at a lower level of benefits. For example, one of the reforms recommended by the Pearson Commission was that no damages ought to be awarded for non-pecuniary loss suffered in the first 3 months after injury. Since the vast majority of accident victims recover fully in this period without suffering any financial loss, this proposal, if implemented, would remove from the tort system a large number of minor cases, and free considerable resources to compensate the more seriously injured or those who suffer permanent disability but currently receive no, or inadequate, tort damages. Again, social security systems usually begin paying income-replacement benefits only after the claimant has been off work for a fixed number of days. One writer has criticized the New Zealand accident compensation scheme for concentrating too heavily on short-term disabilities by paying generous income-related benefits for merely temporary or short-term incapacity.[40]

The common law's willingness to compensate for non-pecuniary losses is usually not shared to the same extent by other compensation systems.[41] The disability pen-

---

40 Ison, *Accident Compensation*, 31, 74–5, 188.
41 The Pearson Commission estimated that two-thirds of all tort payments are for non-pecuniary loss. Under the New Zealand scheme for the year ended 31 March 1978, compensation for non-pecuniary loss amounted to NZ$18.1 million, while total compensation paid was NZ$89.1 million

sion available under the industrial injuries scheme is a form of compensation for non-pecuniary loss, but it is peculiar to that scheme and is part of the industrial preference. The unemployed, for example, are not compensated for the pain and anguish of being out of a job for a long time. And when compensation is given for non-pecuniary loss, it is usually calculated on a tariff basis so as to reduce administrative costs. The major arguments against compensating for disability as such are that when resources are limited (as they always are), it is more important to compensate for pecuniary than for non-pecuniary loss; and that disability is not necessarily related to income loss. For example, a university professor who loses a leg may suffer no income loss, whereas a police officer similarly injured might suffer considerable income loss. The second objection is particularly important when disability is used as a measure of compensation for future pecuniary loss[42] (the main advantage of doing this is that it removes the need to calculate future pecuniary loss which, as we have seen, is a very difficult and speculative operation). But even if compensation for disability is additional to compensation for loss of income, the low earner might feel aggrieved if, in addition to receiving earnings-related compensation for lost earnings, the higher earner also receives the same amount as the low earner for disability.

Non-tort systems of compensation often impose quantum limitations on recovery for pecuniary loss. For example, most social security systems compensate for only a proportion of lost earnings in order to encourage return to work. At the other end of the scale, first-party insurance policies often require the insured to bear the first £X, or a certain proportion, of their financial loss, in order to discourage small claims. Strict liability schemes sometimes impose ceilings on the amount individual claimants can recover, and on the aggregate amount which can be recovered from a particular defendant in relation to a particular incident or a particular period of time – such provisions are designed to prevent very risky but socially desirable activities, such as the development and marketing of drugs, from being burdened with such a level of liability that they cease altogether, or are reduced below a socially desirable level.[43]

In relation to income replacement, non-tort systems of compensation are often less committed to providing income-related benefits than is the common law, although many people would now subscribe to the view that the State has a vital role to play in providing income-related insurance schemes.[44] The chief reason for this attitude to income-related benefits is that they are regressive in effect (that is, they distribute wealth from the poor to the rich) unless such benefits are funded

(Palmer, *Compensation for Incapacity*, 243). In 1991 more was paid out in non-pecuniary loss (NZ$259 million) than for medical and hospital treatment combined: G. Palmer, 'New Zealand's Accident Compensation Scheme Twenty Years On' (1994) 44 *U of Toronto LJ* 223, 249. Compensation for non-pecuniary loss under the NZ scheme was abolished in 1992 and was replaced by a modest pension related to degree of disability.

42 Stapleton, *Disease and the Compensation Debate*, 166–7.
43 Fleming, 'Drug Injury Compensation Plans', 311–12.
44 Ison, *Accident Compensation*, 187–8, 189.

in a fully income-related way – which may not be politically feasible. In this respect the tort system is highly regressive because third-party liability premiums are not at all related to income, while tort benefits are fully income-related. On the other hand, the fact that the social security system has elements of income-relatedness in it shows that earnings-relation is not perceived as being inconsistent even with a social security scheme of compensation. Indeed, income-relation is one of the basic principles of the New Zealand Accident Compensation Scheme. Hostility to earnings-related social security benefits is based on cost as much as on the ideological consideration that earnings-related benefits ought to be bought by individuals in the private insurance market.

Other expressed objections to income-related benefits are that they divert resources from areas of greatest need, and that even if they are progressively funded, they reflect existing inequalities in patterns of remuneration in society.

Another respect in which social security systems restrict entitlement to benefits is by means-testing. If the basis of entitlement is need, then collateral sources of income are relevant. The common law, on the other hand, compensates for losses, and the fact that even though a person's income has been reduced, they are not actually in need, is irrelevant in assessing common law compensation. Benefits under the New Zealand scheme are not means-tested, and this has led one writer to observe that the scheme is not designed to meet need or to help the poor, but to protect against financial inconvenience even people who are in no real sense in need.[45]

A final point to note is that the question of assessment of benefits is separate from that of the basis on which benefits are paid. For example, negligence as the basis of entitlement could be replaced by a strict liability or no-fault regime in a particular area without tort principles of assessment being abandoned in that area. Thus, additional compensation under the CICS and compensation under Part I of the Consumer Protection Act 1987 are assessed according to tort principles.[46] Indeed, the whole basis on which the New Zealand Accident Compensation Scheme was designed was that community expectations generated by the principles of assessment at common law ought to be met in the no-fault scheme by providing benefits broadly commensurate with those available in tort. This approach was taken partly to increase the popular and political acceptability of the reform; and also because it was perceived that the tort system had created 'vested rights'. The argument based on 'vested rights' is a very weak one for a number of reasons. In the first place, relatively few injured people actually receive tort compensation. Secondly, the rights in question are only 'inchoate' or potential rights to claim and be awarded compensation in the event that an injury is suffered. The use of the word 'vested' tends to conceal this fact. Finally, the 'vested rights' argument, carried to its logical conclusion, would rule out any reform of the law which deprived anyone of a potential right to some benefit or to compensation.

45 J.A. Henderson, 'The New Zealand Accident Compensation Reform' (1981) 48 *U. of Chicago LR* 781, 788–9.
46 But total compensation payable under the CICS is capped at £500,000.

In the result, some of the cost savings which could be achieved by introducing flat-rate benefits and less individualized assessment rules are not realized in schemes which are so designed as to preserve 'vested tort rights'. And, contrary to what might at first be expected, even a commitment to a State-run comprehensive scheme is not always accompanied by a commitment to flat-rate income replacement and abolition of compensation for non-pecuniary losses.

18.2.5   Funding

We have noted several times throughout this book that the question of how a system of compensation is funded can be decided quite separately from the question of what benefits it provides and to whom. So, for example, it is possible to design the benefits side of a system to give effect to some notion of 'just compensation for losses' and to design the funding side to achieve goals such as accident prevention or income redistribution.

A number of basic funding issues deserve mention. The first is a question of approach: one approach is to construct an ideal scheme and estimate its cost, leaving it to politicians to decide whether the cost is worth the benefits. A danger here is that if a scheme is indivisible, and thought too expensive, it may fail completely. To meet this eventuality it may be possible to construct the ideal scheme in steps, which could be implemented separately as funds became available. For example, the original intention in New Zealand was eventually to extend the accident compensation scheme to diseases. The risk in this course is that once the first step has been implemented, the momentum for reform will decrease and the later stages might never be implemented.[47] This sort of global approach tends to be associated with comprehensive reforms which aim to cover areas not previously covered by an effective compensation scheme.

A very different approach involves designing a scheme that seeks to rationalize and make better use of already available resources, and even of present funding mechanisms. For example, the short-lived New South Wales transport accident[48] scheme was seen by its designers as particularly attractive because it was planned to cost no more than the existing tort-cum-liability-insurance system, and the funds could be collected in exactly the way they were under the tort system, that is, by liability insurers. Such an approach sees the reform task as being to streamline and improve the present system rather than to look at the issue of injury compensation in terms of wider social issues about the community's responsibility for the injured.

---

47 One of the aims of 1992 amendments to the New Zealand scheme was 'to prevent creep in coverage towards disease': Palmer, *Compensation for Incapacity*, 243, 245–6.

48 The scheme was not a no-fault scheme but a fault-based scheme in which the issue of fault was decided administratively by a government agency. In other words, in terms of decision-making, the scheme was rather like the Industrial Injuries Scheme. The attraction of such a fault-based scheme is that by reducing administrative costs a greater proportion of accident victims can be compensated without an increase in total expenditure. At the same time, perceived advantages of a fault-based over a no-fault system are not sacrificed.

A second major funding issue is whether the scheme is to be State-run or based on the market. The chief importance of this choice is that a market-based system will be funded on the simple principle that a person should pay for the damage they cause (if a liability scheme is in issue), or that a person should insure against their own losses (if a no-fault or first-party insurance scheme is in issue); whereas a State-run scheme can accept this insurance principle or modify it to achieve other social objectives, such as redistribution of resources to the poor. So, whereas in a market-based system insurance premiums would ideally be based on a person's injury record (in a no-fault system), or on a person's safety record (in a liability system),[49] in a State-run system contributions could be based on income in such a way as to be distributionally regressive, neutral or progressive, according to the wishes of the political framers of the scheme.

A third issue is whether the scheme is to be fully funded or funded on a pay-as-you-go basis. In a fully funded scheme the contributions in any one financial year have to be sufficient to cover all claims made in that year in full (even if the claim will be paid out periodically over a period of years, or in one lump sum but not for several years' time). In a pay-as-you-go scheme, contributions in any one year need only be sufficient to cover amounts actually paid out in that year. Thus in a fully funded scheme, but not in a pay-as-you-go scheme, substantial reserves have to be built up. In theory, premiums under a fully funded scheme can be lower than under a pay-as-you-go scheme because the reserves can be invested to produce income out of which future payments can be partly met. But when there is significant inflation this advantage is often illusory because returns on investments may not keep pace with inflation.[50]

The choice between these two methods of funding is not unrelated to the last point, because the realities of the private insurance market and the legal accounting requirements placed on insurance companies require them to run fully funded schemes. They cannot deliberately run on a deficit one year and make it up by increased premiums the next year. In other words, only a State-run scheme can be pay-as-you-go. A pay-as-you-go scheme is desirable if benefits for financial losses are to be periodical, at least where inflation rates are high or unpredictable and liable to considerable variation. A system in which security of periodical payments depends on prudent investment of reserves may prove too risky in the long term.

From a general-deterrence point of view a fully funded scheme is, in theory, more efficient than a pay-as-you-go scheme. Under the latter, sums collected this year are used in part to pay for injuries inflicted by activities carried on in the past, whereas under a fully funded scheme the premiums paid in any one year are sufficient, and only sufficient, to meet obligations arising out of activities carried on in that year.

49 Leaving aside the complication introduced by the distinction between feature rating and experience rating: see 17.7.2.2.
50 Palmer, *Compensation for Incapacity*, 338–9. On funding methods see further Ison, *Accident Compensation*, 135–6.

In reality, however, even under a fully funded scheme new premiums are often used to make up deficits (caused e.g. by inflation) incurred in previous years.

18.2.6   Goals of the system

Many of the issues we have discussed so far in this chapter can only be resolved if the goals of a system for dealing with personal injury and death are made clear. Three main goals can be distinguished: compensation, deterrence (or injury prevention) and fairness (or corrective justice). An important ancillary goal, which is not strictly a goal of a compensation system but is an end such a system can be used to further, is achieving a particular pattern of social wealth distribution or redistribution.

Compensation is, of course, the principle underlying the assessment of tort damages. Even so, there is a sense in which compensation is a subsidiary goal of tort law, in that personal injury attracts compensation in tort only if a responsible defendant can be found to pay it. Tort law focuses primarily on the obligation of the defendant to pay rather than the entitlement of the claimant to be paid compensation. The fundamental goal of tort law (as opposed to the tort system, of which tort law is only a part) is corrective justice or fairness – in other words, the aim is to redress the balance of fairness or justice between the parties, which has been upset by the tortious behaviour of the defendant. In a negligence regime that conduct is, of course, carelessness; in a strict liability regime, the appropriate conduct is causing damage by creating a risk of injury which then materializes. As we have seen, there are strong reasons to doubt that the tort system is very effective as a deterrent or accident-prevention mechanism, and while economic analysts of law (such as Calabresi) see deterrence as the main function and rationale of tort law, the practical barriers to the fulfilment of the deterrence function are so substantial that it is unsatisfactory to attempt to justify the tort system in terms of the goal of deterrence. Finally, as we have noted, the tort system does have important wealth-distribution effects, in some areas at least. For example, the fact that third-party motor insurance premiums are calculated without reference to the insured's income while tort damages are income-related, means that the wealthy get much more out of the tort system than they put in relative to the poor.

So far as goals are concerned, there are some important differences between negligence-based and strict liability. In theory, at least, strict liability performs the compensation function better, simply because more people will recover compensation if fault does not have to be proved. As for deterrence, there has been much discussion of the relative efficacy of negligence and strict liability, and of whether strict liability will induce higher levels of safety than negligence liability. There is reason to think that the only respect in which strict liability is superior is that, by placing the costs of injuries not caused by fault on the defendant rather than on the injured party, the former might be encouraged to initiate research and development to reduce or eliminate the risks of such accidents. The corrective-justice principle underlying strict liability is clearly different from that underlying the fault principle – strict liability is based on the idea that the person who reaps the benefit of engaging in a risky activity ought in fairness to bear the cost of any loss or damage caused by the activity.

In terms of wealth distribution, strict liability coupled with liability insurance could be just as regressive in effect as negligence liability if, for example, liability for motor accidents were strict. But in practice, proposals for strict liability tend to be made in respect of entrepreneurial activities (such as manufacturing); in such cases, the costs of liability will be passed on to consumers in increased prices. This may be regressive if consumption by the poor is equal to or greater than that by the rich, but the amounts involved per consumer will perhaps be so small that this element of distribution in favour of the better-off might be thought by some to be tolerable.

How well do no-fault schemes fulfil the goals stated above? So far as compensation is concerned, the 'success' of any system depends entirely on who is entitled to receive benefits under it,[51] on the level of benefits and on how many members of the eligible groups in fact receive compensation.[52] We have already discussed the issue of limited versus comprehensive reforms, and touched on the issue of how close to the tort principles of full and hundred-per cent compensation no-fault benefits ought to be. Since no-fault schemes are all the result of legislative action, these issues can be decided as a matter of principle and policy. In practice, justification of no-fault schemes always involves being able to compensate more injured persons at no extra cost, or compensating more people by removing conditions of entitlement to compensation other than that of having suffered loss or being in need. A commitment to wide entitlement rules is basic to a commitment to no-fault. Similarly, the wealth-distributional effects of a no-fault scheme can be designed in advance to meet desired political goals; and they depend on the relationship between benefits and contributions.

No-fault schemes are often criticized because of their failure to further the goals of deterrence and corrective justice. Because no-fault systems do not involve an individual causer of injury paying an individual victim of injury, they clearly do not embody the principles of justice and fairness (or further the associated goals of retribution and vindication) which are a feature of the tort law and the tort system. Rather, no-fault systems embody a principle of social justice and community responsibility for those in need.

What is the basis of the idea of social or community responsibility? The simplest basis is to say that everyone is entitled to a basic standard of living and to have certain

51 For a feminist critique of the New Zealand Accident Compensation Scheme see L. Delany 'Accident Rehabilitation and Compensation Bill: A Feminist Assessment' (1992) 22 *Victoria U. of Wellington LR* 79.

52 This has two aspects: the question of take-up (what proportion of eligible claimants actually seek benefits) and the problem of manufactured or exaggerated claims. Regarding the latter, M.J. Trebilcock argues that differential benefit rates for different classes of claimants (based on the causes of their disabilities) should be used to reduce moral hazard under no-fault schemes: 'Incentive Issues in the Design of No-Fault Compensation Systems' (1989) 39 *U. of Toronto LJ* 19. By contrast, the social security system deals with moral hazard mainly by requiring claimants for disablement and invalidity benefits to undergo medical examinations.

basic material needs met, and that inequalities in society are only acceptable once everyone has been brought up to a minimum level of material well-being. This argument, however, will not justify a system which provides earnings-related benefits or (perhaps) compensation for non-pecuniary loss; nor a system in which people with like needs are treated differently according to the source of their needs (e.g. a system in which accident victims receive earnings-related benefits but the unemployed receive basic flat-rate benefits).

Another approach (which underlay the report on which the New Zealand scheme was based)[53] is to argue that because the activity of individuals in society is the cause of many personal injuries, society as a whole ought to take responsibility for these injuries. The nature of modern social life, it is said, generates an increasing amount of personal disability, and so society as a whole should bear the financial burden of these disabilities. This approach suffers from serious conceptual difficulties. In the first place, it assumes that for the purposes of society's responsibility to provide compensation, there is a relevant difference between disability caused by human action and disability resulting from natural causes. As was argued earlier (1.2), this distinction is not easy to justify, and many would question the idea that society (as opposed to individuals) has any more or less responsibility in the one case than in the other. Secondly, by utilizing the notion of causation, the approach makes it difficult to justify compensating for disabilities the cause of which is not known with any certainty; and it also introduces into the debate many of the ambiguities and value-laden uncertainties of the notion of causation.

Thirdly, even if we accept the link between individual causation of disability and social responsibility in the abstract, we might have doubts about its applicability to cases such as disabilities caused by criminal conduct. Many would vigorously deny that social conditions (as opposed to the free choice of the criminal) are the real cause of criminal activity. On the other hand, community responsibility might seem clearer in the case, for example, of victims of government-backed vaccination programmes or of volunteers in drug-testing programmes, because their injuries are the result of taking part in activities which are specifically designed for the benefit of all. Finally, the notion of social responsibility by itself goes very little way towards determining exactly what society ought to do to help the disabled whose incapacity is society's responsibility. Should benefits be basic flat-rate or earnings-related? Should intangible losses be compensated for (do they generate 'needs')?

The choice of justification also has ramifications for the issue of funding. The 'needs' justification might be seen as justifying funding by progressive taxation, whereas the 'causal responsibility' approach might seem more congenial to funding, as far as possible, by levies on disability-causing activities proportional to the risks created by them.

---

53 But note that the scheme as it now operates contains significant elements of first party insurance: R.S. Miller, 'An Analysis and Critique of the 1992 Changes to New Zealand's Accident Compensation Scheme' (1992) 5 *Canterbury LR* 1.

The choice between individual and social responsibility is, of course, of great importance; but it is hardly a valid criticism of either the tort system or of no-fault schemes that they do not embody the fundamental justice ideas of the other. On the other hand, it is valid to ask how well each type of system fulfils the justice goals it sets for itself; and there are, as we have seen, several compelling grounds for believing that the tort system does not give proper effect to the principle of individual responsibility embodied in the fault principle. So far as no-fault systems are concerned, the idea of social responsibility, as we have noted, is open to so many interpretations that individual no-fault schemes can only be assessed according to the values of the assessor, and according to how well the system achieves its expressed aims.

As for deterrence, a no-fault system clearly does not perform the function which tort law aims at when it sets up standards of conduct. However, this educational function could (and would probably have to) be performed by an agency charged with responsibility for promoting health and safety.[54] In addition, it may be desirable to strengthen the role of the criminal law, of health and safety inspectorates and regulators and of disciplinary procedures (e.g. within the medical profession)[55] in order to provide improved incentives for those whose activities are a potential source of claims.[56] There is some evidence that accident rates in New Zealand increased after the introduction of the Accident Compensation Scheme.[57] But there is no reason in theory why a no-fault system should not achieve as much by way of general deterrence as the tort system. Contributions to the scheme could be related to the risk of injury created by the contributor on the basis of feature-or experience-

---

54 Ison, *Accident Compensation*, ch. 8.
55 M.A. McG. Vennell, 'Medical Injury Compensation Under the New Zealand Accident Compensation Scheme: An Assessment Compared With the Swedish Medical Compensation Scheme' [1989] *Professional Negligence* 141.
56 Such moves might be desirable even in the absence of no-fault schemes, given doubts about the deterrent efficacy of tort law. S.A. Rea argues against the total abolition of fault-based liability on the ground that non-tort mechanisms of deterrence are better developed in some contexts than in others: 'Economic Analysis of Fault and No-Fault Liability Systems' (1986–7) 12 *Canadian Business LJ* 444, 471.
57 Klar, in Steel and Rodgers-Magnet, *Issues in Tort Law*, 37–8. C. Brown shows that the level of injuries and deaths in road accidents has fallen in New Zealand since the introduction of the Scheme as a result, probably, of new safety legislation and of enforcement measures by the police. What is not clear is whether the fall would have been greater if tort had not been abolished: 'Deterrence in Tort and No-Fault: The New Zealand Experience' (1985) 73 *California LR* 976. See also J. O'Connell and S. Levmore, 'A Reply to Landes: A Faulty Study of No-Fault's Effect on Fault?' (1983) 48 *Missouri LR* 649. Increases in deaths and injuries resulting from road accidents following the introduction of a no-fault scheme in Quebec has been attributed to the fact that the scheme covers more injured people than the tort system did, and the fact that premiums are flat-rate: J. O'Connell and C. Tenser, 'North America's Most Ambitious No-Fault Law: Quebec's Auto Insurance Act' (1987) 24 *San Diego LR* 917, 928; see also R.A. Devlin, 'Some Welfare Implications of No-Fault Automobile Insurance' (1990) 10 *International R. of Law and Economics* 193; J.D. Cumins, R.D. Phillips and M.A. Weiss, 'The Incentive Effects of No-Fault Automobile Insurance' (2001) 44 *J. of Law and Economics* 427 (introduction of no-fault results in an increase in fatalities, at least if funding is not risk-related).

rating.[58] We have seen that there are difficulties both with the general theory of economic incentives (17.8) and with classification and experience rating in particular (17.7.2). But these difficulties are no greater in a no-fault system than in the tort system.[59] Indeed, in a no-fault system administered by a central agency, useful statistics could gradually be gathered on which a more sophisticated system of rating could be based.

In New Zealand the accident scheme is funded from four sources: employers, earners, motor vehicle owners and health professionals. Some additional funding is provided by a petrol levy. All premiums can be experience-rated, but 'it is unlikely that the scheme proposed will achieve its intended aim of fairness and equity between premium payers'.[60] We have already seen that there are great problems with experience rating, not least its expense. Also, many accident-causing activities are subject to no levies at all, so that such activities receive no economic safety incentives from the scheme.[61]

It may be apparent from what has been said already that, although a no-fault scheme can be funded in such a way as to meet a variety of social goals, choices between these goals may well be necessary, since it would not be possible to pursue them all simultaneously. In particular, if a no-fault compensation scheme were seen basically as a social security programme to fulfil society's responsibility to the disabled, the most justifiable funding mechanism would be a general progressive tax – and this would be so whether the benefits were basic flat-rate or earnings-related. This method of funding would involve at least partial abandonment of the deterrence goal, which would require for its fulfilment a set of levies, on disability-causing activities, which would internalize the costs of disabilities to the activities that caused them. Disabilities not caused by human activities could then still be paid for by general taxation. It may be that a mix of taxation and levies based on risk provides the best possible funding pattern.

Finally, it is worth noting that a major advantage called in aid to justify the change from tort liability to no-fault compensation is that the administrative costs of a no-fault system are usually much less than those of the tort system. For example, the Pearson Commission found that under the tort system the administrative cost of delivering £1 of compensation was around 85 pence, while the cost of delivering £1 of social security benefits was only around 11 pence. The cost of handling claims under the New Zealand Accident Scheme is about 7% of the

---

58 Ison, *Accident Compensation*, 124–34. There is some evidence that where a no-fault scheme replaces an effective fault-based one and the level of benefits under the no-fault scheme is lower than under the fault-based scheme, this may encourage care: R.I. McEwin, 'No-Fault and Road Accidents: Some Australian Evidence' (1989) 9 *International R. of Law and Economics* 13.

59 But for a pessimistic assessment see C. Brown, 'Deterrence and Accident Compensation Schemes' (1978) 17 *U. of Western Ontario LR* 111.

60 Vennell and Manning, 'The Accident Rehabilitation and Compensation Insurance Act 1992', 9; see also ibid., 7.

61 Furthermore, the deterrent effect of the levies, especially those on manufacturers, is further diluted if the levies are spread via the price mechanism.

benefits paid.[62] It does not follow from this that the tort system is too expensive, because it may be argued that the tort system serves goals and values which by their nature are expensive to secure – for example, the highly individualized nature of the damages assessment process in the tort system is inherently expensive. But since such a relatively small number of injured people receive compensation under the tort system, and given that the administrative cost is so substantial, it is necessary to ask very seriously whether the tort system is worth what it costs. It is difficult to answer this question other than negatively.

18.3   Proposals and schemes

18.3.1   Road accident schemes

The majority of no-fault schemes so far enacted have been limited to road accidents,[63] although there are quite a few criminal injuries schemes,[64] and some drug injuries schemes. The industrial injuries scheme in this country is, of course, a no-fault social security scheme, but in most countries which have specialized industrial injuries schemes, compensation is given on the basis of strict employer liability funded by compulsory insurance. In US and most Canadian jurisdictions, the insurance fund from which no-fault road accident compensation payments are made is operated by the same private insurance companies as offer standard third-party liability insurance. In some jurisdictions, such as Victoria and Saskatchewan, the fund is operated by a government insurance agency, but this does not alter the essential nature of the scheme. In systems where the no-fault scheme is financed solely by premiums paid by vehicle owners, claims made by others injured on the road will be third-party, not first-party, claims (i.e. they will be made against the insurer of the vehicle by which the person was injured).

Traffic accident schemes fall into three broad categories.[65] First, there are 'add-on' schemes, which typically provide limited no-fault benefits for pecuniary losses arising from personal injury, but no no-fault benefits for non-pecuniary losses or property damage. Under such schemes the tort action remains intact, but there are provisions requiring no-fault benefits to be set off against tort damages to prevent double recovery.[66]

The second type of no-fault scheme can be called the 'modified' scheme. Under modified schemes the no-fault benefits are similar in type to those available under add-on schemes, although sometimes greater in amount. However, the right to sue

---

62 Palmer, *Compensation for Incapacity*, 227.
63 J.G. Fleming, *The American Tort Process* (Oxford, 1988), 166–74.
64 Such schemes are not strictly no-fault schemes: they are run along administrative, not judicial, lines; payment is made out of a fund, usually provided from general taxation; and the claimant does not have to identify the wrongdoer. But the claimant must establish that the injuries were the result of a violent crime, and so in this respect such schemes are fault-based.
65 But many schemes do not fall exactly into any one category.
66 An example of such a scheme is that in operation in Tasmania. For more details of this and other Australian schemes see R. Balkin and J. Davis, *Law of Torts*, 3rd edn (Sydney, 2004), 422–7.

for tort damages for non-pecuniary loss is abolished in less serious cases. In some jurisdictions, the right to sue in tort in respect of pecuniary losses is not affected, but set-off provisions prevent double recovery; in other jurisdictions, this right is abolished to the extent that the claimant is entitled to recover no-fault benefits. Quite a few US States have adopted modified no-fault schemes.[67] In a couple of States, the no-fault scheme gets very close to abolishing tort altogether – no-fault benefits for pecuniary losses are high, and the right to sue in tort is abolished to the extent of these benefits; tort damages for non-pecuniary loss can be recovered only in very serious cases.

The third category of scheme comprises what might be called 'pure' no-fault schemes.[68] Under such schemes the tort action is abolished entirely. The chief example of a pure scheme is that in New Zealand,[69] which has been in operation since 1974 and covers accidents of all types, not just road accidents. In broad terms, modified no-fault schemes are designed to deal with less serious cases on a no-fault basis, and to restrict use of tort to more (or the most) serious cases. Under a pure no-fault scheme, since tort is abolished more or less entirely, the benefits under the no-fault scheme have to be generous enough to provide adequate compensation even in the most serious cases. Thus benefits for loss of earnings tend, subject to certain thresholds and ceilings, to be standard-of-living benefits; in addition, limited benefits for non-pecuniary loss are usually available on a tariff basis according to the type or degree of disability. The tort concept of full compensation (*restitution in integrum*) forms the basis of the benefit scales in such schemes.

No-fault schemes generally cover personal injury only, but in a couple of US States there have been signs of a movement to no-fault property damage compensation as well. State-run pure no-fault schemes are unlikely ever to embrace property damage. Pure no-fault schemes tend to place considerable emphasis on rehabilitation as well as compensation, and facilities may be provided for this purpose.[70]

In Britain the road accident scheme proposed by the Pearson Commission did not fall neatly into any of the above categories. The proposal involved an extension of the industrial injuries scheme (itself extended to cover the self-employed) to road accidents – loss of earnings benefits would have been less than those available in tort, and compensation for disability would have replaced damages for non-pecuniary loss. As

---

67 Many of the US schemes were inspired by R.E. Keeton and J. O'Connell, *Basic Protection for the Accident Victim – A Blueprint for Reforming Automobile Insurance* (Boston, 1965). The scheme in Victoria is best described as a modified scheme. For details see I. Malkin, 'Victoria's Transport Accident Reforms – In Perspective' (1987) 16 *Melbourne ULR* 254.

68 The scheme in operation in the Northern Territory of Australia is close to a pure scheme. The Quebec scheme is also pure: O'Connell and Tenser, 'North America's Most Ambitious No-Fault Law'.

69 Although even here, the right to sue in tort for exemplary damages in suitable cases has been held to have survived the enactment of the scheme. Also, tort actions are only abolished in cases covered by the no-fault scheme. The scheme never covered diseases (except occupational diseases) which were not the result of an accident, and in 1992 its coverage was further reduced as part of a wide-ranging review of the social welfare system designed to reduce public expenditure.

70 Ison, *Accident Compensation*, ch. 7; Palmer, *Compensation for Incapacity*, 391–9.

in the case of industrial injuries, the tort action would not have been abolished (thus allowing recovery in serious cases of the difference between no-fault and tort benefits), but benefits obtained under the no-fault system would have been set off in full against tort damages. The Commission also recommended that damages for non-pecuniary loss should not be recoverable in tort where the claimant completely recovered within 3 months. The aim of these proposals was to eliminate many minor tort claims, to transfer the bulk of the remainder to the social security system and to relegate the tort action to cases of serious and lasting disability, especially those involving high earners. In essence, therefore, the proposals were for a modified no-fault scheme. No-fault road accident proposals put forward by the Lord Chancellor's Department in 1991 were, in effect, for an add-on scheme under which claims worth no more than £2,500 would have fallen within the no-fault scheme.

Which of the three types of no-fault scheme is to be preferred? We have already noted that dual schemes, which retain the tort action wholly or partly, appear to suffer from two major disadvantages: they require the retention of the apparatus of third-party liability insurance in addition to the new first-party insurance mechanism; and, secondly, they subject to the defects of the tort system those most in need – the seriously disabled.[71] This second disadvantage appears even more significant when it is recalled that the tort system tends to over-compensate in minor cases and to under-compensate in serious cases (10.6).

At the end of the day the success of any reform depends on how well it eliminates the faults of the old system. The main defects of the tort system, which no-fault schemes aim to ameliorate or eliminate are: the high volume of litigation generated by the need to decide complex issues of fault and assessment of damages; the high administrative costs (legal fees and insurance company overheads) of the tort system; the fact that the majority of road accident victims receive no compensation from the tort system, and that of those who do, the less seriously injured tend to be over-compensated while the more seriously injured are often under-compensated; the delay in obtaining compensation; the fact that the dynamics of the settlement process lead many claimants to accept considerably lesser sums than they would be awarded by a court. US research suggests that add-on schemes do very little to eliminate these defects, while modified schemes fare considerably better.[72] If partial abolition of tort can achieve improvements in the above respects, one can be confident that its total abolition improves matters even more.

Another crucial issue is that of cost. Two questions arise: does the no-fault system cost more or less than the old system would have cost for the same period; and is the

71 A third suggested disadvantage is that dual schemes which offer generous no-fault benefits actually encourage tort litigation: J. O'Connell, 'Reforming New Zealand's Reform: Accident Compensation Revisited' [1988] New Zealand LJ 399, 400.
72 See n. 28; J. O'Connell, 'Operation of No-Fault Auto Laws: A Survey of the Surveys' (1977) 56 Nebraska LR 23 and The Lawsuit Lottery (New York, 1979), ch. 8; R.A. Henderson, 'No-Fault Insurance for Automobile Accidents: Status and Effect in the United States' (1977) 56 Oregon LR 287.

no-fault system more efficient in the sense that a greater amount of its total cost is paid out in compensation (as opposed to administrative costs) than under tort? As for the first point, reformers usually perceive it to be politically prudent to design a road accident scheme which costs no more than the existing tort system, and reform proposals are often accompanied by actuarial calculations and costings to show that this aim has been achieved. The way it is achieved consistently with compensating many more people is by reducing the levels of compensation for lost earnings and for non-pecuniary loss, and by reducing administrative costs. US evidence on the cost of dual systems is equivocal. But it seems quite clear that the administrative costs of a pure no-fault scheme would be dramatically less than the administrative costs of the tort system; so provided benefits were not pitched too high, it would not be difficult to compensate many more people at no extra cost. Of course, commitment to no extra expenditure is quite easily satisfied in the road accident sphere because so much is currently spent on compensating victims of road accidents. The extension of no-fault schemes to areas where very few people currently receive tort damages would probably require considerable new expenditure, if benefits greater than basic and generally available social security benefits were to be paid.

Finally, it is worth noting again that limited no-fault schemes, such as road accident schemes, invariably create (or entrench, or extend) a preference for one group of the disabled over others. The justification for limited road accident schemes appears not to be that road accident victims deserve preferential treatment. The catalysts for such limited reform are the fact that the problem of road accidents is an old and easily recognized, not to say glaring, one; and the fact that it has been at the centre of criticism of the tort system because it is a major area of effective tort liability which has not previously been encroached upon by strict liability or social security schemes (as the industrial injuries area has) which have, to some extent, diverted attention from the defects of the tort system. The concentration on road accidents is looking increasingly anachronistic in the light of our growing realization of the role of human activities in producing all sorts of non-traumatic injuries. Moreover, road accident victims are already relatively well catered for by the tort system. If extra money is to be made available for extension of, or improvements in, the social security system, what is the case for injecting this money into those corners where victims already do relatively well? As one MP was moved to comment in the debate on the Pearson Commission Report in 1978: 'The arguments about improvements and alterations to the tort system are irrelevant. They are arguments about the distribution of the icing, when more than 90 per cent of the victims are not getting any of the cake.'[73]

18.3.2   Other schemes

The variety amongst no-fault road accident schemes is partly a result of the fact that the tort system is much used in this area. This has generated various solutions to the

---

73 Bruce Douglas-Mann, *Hansard*, HC Debs, vol. 958, col. 838 (17 November 1978).

problem of the relationship between tort and no-fault schemes. A similar variety exists in the way industrial injuries are dealt with in different jurisdictions – industrial injuries are, of course, the other main area of effective tort liability. One might have thought that in areas where successful tort actions are much less common, there might be less variety in the approach to the preservation of tort liability; but a survey of drug injury compensation schemes shows this not to be the case.[74] The West German scheme is based on strict liability-cum-liability insurance. The Swedish scheme[75] has three components: basic losses are met by social security, and further losses are dealt with by a voluntary (i.e. non-statutory) first-party insurance scheme (analogous to the Motor Insurers' Bureau scheme in England), set up by the pharmaceutical manufacturers and importers with major insurance companies; tort liability continues to exist, but all benefits received from social security or the insurance scheme must be set off against tort damages, and neither of these funds has a right of recourse against the tortfeasor. In Japan the tort remedy continues to exist and, indeed, no-fault benefits are not payable if it appears that someone's negligence was responsible for the injury.

The Swedish idea of using private first-party insurance to cover top losses rather than basic losses is a flexible one, because it could be combined either with a social security system, offering flat-rate income benefits or earnings-related benefits up to a ceiling; or with a tort system made subject to a damages ceiling – this would utilize the acknowledged fact that the tort system compensates generously for minor injuries, but inadequately for serious cases of large losses.[76]

18.4   The way ahead

18.4.1   A social welfare solution

In the third edition of this book it was argued that what was needed was a single comprehensive system for assisting the disabled, based on the existing social security system, but with benefits as large as society can afford. In particular, it was suggested that the most practicable and desirable direction of movement was the progressive abolition of tort actions[77] for personal injury accompanied by a gradual

---

74 Fleming, 'Drug Injury Compensation Plans'.

75 There is a similar scheme covering injuries caused by medical treatment (other than drugs): M. Brahams, 'The Swedish No-Fault Compensation System for Medical Injuries' [1988] *New LJ* 14 and 31. There are two similar schemes in Finland: M. Brahams, 'No-fault in Finland: Paying Patients and Drug Victims' [1988] *New LJ* 678; see also W. Wadlington and W.J. Wood III, 'Two No-fault Compensation Schemes For Birth Defective Infants in the United States' [1991] *Professional Negligence* 40. The steam was taken out of English proposals for a no-fault medical injuries scheme (see [1989] *New LJ* 101, 109, 119 and 124; Royal College of Physicians, *Compensation for Adverse Consequences of Medical Intervention* (London, 1990)) by the introduction of Crown indemnity in 1990. As we saw in 18.1, the Chief Medical Officer has recently proposed a limited no-fault scheme for birth injuries.

76 C. Morris and J.C.N. Paul, 'The Financial Impact of Automobile Accidents' (1962) 100 *U. of Pennsylvania LR* 913.

77 For a spirited defence of the tort system see A. Burrows, *Understanding the Law of Obligations* (Oxford, 1998), ch. 6.

extension of the industrial injuries scheme, with any necessary modifications, first to all accidents and, ultimately, to disease and illness, whether caused by human action or the result of natural causes.[78]

The main argument in favour of such a comprehensive scheme lies in the unfairness produced by lack of integration of the various presently existing schemes for assisting the disabled. Not only is the element of over-compensation, created by the overlap of systems, a waste of resources, but it is indefensible to compensate some people twice over while others go without any compensation at all. For example, how can we justify paying compensation twice over to a person who loses an eye in an industrial accident merely for the disability itself,[79] while we refuse any compensation for the disability itself to a person who is blinded by a disease resulting from natural causes? How can we justify giving social security benefits to people who continue to receive full wages while they are off sick[80] when the level of long-term sickness benefits is still so low?

Then there is the difficulty of justifying payments made under one system but refused by another. How can we justify giving damages for loss of support to a young, childless widow, for example, when the social security system provides no assistance at all to a childless widow under 45 unless she is destitute or incapable of work. Surely society must decide whether it thinks a widow is entitled to support irrespective of her capacity for work, and regulate its compensation systems accordingly. Finally, there is the whole problem of justifying the various preferences in favour of particular groups of disabled people embodied in the present set-up.

On the other hand, it must be admitted that there are very considerable difficulties facing the sort of comprehensive reform being suggested.[81] In the first place, it has been argued that the adoption by the EC of the Directive on Product Liability, which requires Member States to provide citizens with a remedy in tort, and which was implemented in Part I of the Consumer Protection Act 1987, would prevent a UK government introducing any personal injuries compensation scheme which involved the abolition of tort actions for victims of injuries falling within the terms of the Directive; or even a scheme which provided victims of such injuries with an entitlement to non-tort compensation in addition to the remedy required by the Directive.[82] If the argument is correct, then the more tort-based remedies the EC requires Members States to provide for their citizens, the more

---

78 But this sequence of development might be controversial. Stapleton, *Disease and the Compensation Debate*, argues that disease ought to be the first reform priority.
79 Social security benefits are set off against tort damages only in respect of a maximum period of 5 years after the accident.
80 It is up to the employer whether to set SSP off against contractual sick pay.
81 See especially Brown, *Disability Income*, chs. 12 and 13.
82 J. Stapleton, 'Three Problems with the New Product Liability' in P. Cane and J. Stapleton eds., *Essays for Patrick Atiyah* (Oxford, 1991), 276–87. On the other hand, the decision in *Matthews* v. *Ministry of Defence* [2003] 1 AC 1163 suggests that the European Convention on Human Rights would not stand in the way of abolition of tort liability for personal injuries, although it would affect the design of the administrative process.

difficult it becomes for any Member State to reform its law of personal injuries in a comprehensive way.

Secondly, the sort of proposal made in the third edition of this book assumes that the disabled should be treated as a separate group within the social security system not only in respect of the special needs of the disabled as contrasted with the able-bodied, but more generally. This assumption may not go unchallenged. Even if it were universally accepted, it remains the fact that the disability income system is extraordinarily complex, and the project of reforming it in a comprehensive way would be very difficult, time-consuming and expensive. The fragmented nature of the proposals made by the Pearson Commission perhaps provides a warning against being too optimistic about the prospects for comprehensive reform. Nevertheless, the fact that a comprehensive accident scheme has been in operation in New Zealand since 1974, and that a national scheme covering disease and illness as well as accidents reached the stage of draft legislation in Australia before being shelved after a change of government, shows that given vision and energy, plus a determination that broad principles should not be swamped by a mass of detail, a comprehensive scheme of assistance for the disabled need not be unattainable.

Another major obstacle in the way of comprehensive reform is the inevitable opposition from special interest groups, which, naturally, seek the preservation of schemes, arrangements and preferences that benefit them. One of the important arguments in favour of comprehensive reform is that justice requires that people with similar needs should receive similar assistance. But justice is a very slippery concept, and it is possible to make an argument, based on a more or less plausible concept of justice, in favour of many of the preferences for particular groups embodied in the present law. So comprehensive reform requires a firm adherence to a particular notion of social justice, and the political will to disregard the pleas of those who receive special treatment under present arrangements. Recent history does not give much cause for optimism on this score. But the importance of standing firm is clear when one remembers that only a very small proportion of disabled people benefits from especially generous schemes.

A related difficulty is that experience suggests that in a democratic system, large-scale reform is, on the whole, harder to effect than small-scale or incremental change. This is no doubt one reason why, in the past, pressure groups have been able to secure the enactment of specific preferential schemes (such as those to compensate vaccine-damaged children and people infected with HIV from contaminated blood products). Since any reformer must accept the realities of the political process, there may be an argument for aiming at comprehensive reform via limited reform – the development of more and more special schemes might generate pressure for rationalization into a comprehensive scheme; or, alternatively, special schemes might eventually cover virtually the whole field of disablement.

A major argument made against proposals for large-scale reform is that of cost. In the case of some limited reforms, such as no-fault road accident schemes, this objection can be met simply by designing a system which, by effecting various savings and trimming certain benefits slightly, costs no more than the scheme being replaced. Comprehensive reform will almost certainly require new money because it would involve compensating many disabled persons who receive little or nothing under present arrangements. One of the advantages of reform by extension of a currently existing scheme is that by choosing a scheme (the IIS) with relatively generous benefits, the end result might be a general upgrading of provision for the disabled. The danger in this course is that the objection of cost might lead to a general downgrading of benefits in the existing scheme before its coverage is extended. There is, then, a basic dilemma facing the comprehensive reformer – is it better to compensate more people at lower levels, or fewer people at more generous levels? In the end, a compromise is most likely which involves, for example, compensating the more seriously disabled quite generously at the cost of relatively low benefits for those with only minor or short-term disabilities – in this way a large number of the disabled receive some assistance, but the more seriously disabled are relatively better catered for.

Crucial to the issue of cost is that of whether the income-replacement element of benefits (as opposed to the element designed to meet the special needs of the disabled arising out of their physical condition) is to be flat-rate and means-tested – that is, designed to provide a level of reasonable subsistence; or earnings-related and regardless of means – that is, designed to compensate for income loss. We have seen that income-relation is a basic principle of the New Zealand Accident Compensation Scheme, and those who support special schemes for disabilities identified by cause (e.g. industrial disabilities) usually argue that those whose disabilities arise from a particular source deserve compensatory benefits, even if social security benefits generally are flat-rate and means-tested. Clearly the cost of an income-related scheme would be much greater than that of a flat-rate scheme, and as a matter of principle it is reasonable to ask to what extent it is the obligation of the State to maintain people in their accustomed way of life, as opposed to providing them with a reasonable floor level of support. It is clear that very few would argue that a State-run system should compensate relative to income, however high that income is. But some reformers would argue that, up to a certain maximum, benefits ought to be income-related, at least if the income loss lasts for more than a relatively short time (a qualifying period for income-related benefits would save money, and might encourage rehabilitation).

On the other hand, if the demand for income-relatedness were seen as a major obstacle to comprehensive reform, it might be worthwhile giving more thought to some sort of dual system under which flat-rate, means-tested benefits at a reasonable level would be available through the social security system, leaving it to individuals to take out private insurance if they wanted benefits above the State-provided level.

A related question concerns the future of tort law. One of the factors which has led reformers to propose earnings-related benefits is that the tort system provides such benefits (in theory at least) whatever the income of the injured person; and in order to defuse opposition to the abolition of tort it has seemed expedient to provide benefits under the new system broadly comparable to those available under tort. This might suggest that at least some, if not most, of the opposition to the introduction of a scheme under which all the disabled received flat-rate income replacement, plus provision for special needs, could be defused by leaving the tort system in existence so as to provide a source of earnings-related benefits for those who wanted them. Such a proposal would avoid some of the criticisms of dual systems noted earlier. Since all the special needs of the disabled would be met by social security, it could not be argued that those most in need (i.e. the severely disabled) were being relegated to an inferior remedy – their basic needs would be met by the State. It is true that such a dual system would be administratively expensive, but one might expect that the tort system would not be heavily used if the State benefits were reasonable in amount (ideally based on average weekly earnings).

On the other hand, such a dual system suffers from what is really a fatal disadvantage. The tort system would provide earnings-related benefits for only a proportion of the disabled, as indeed at the moment it only covers a small proportion of the disabled. It would be difficult to justify special treatment for some of the high-earning disabled, when the removal of special treatment is a major justification for comprehensive flat-rate benefits. A much more satisfactory solution would be to abolish tort and leave all high earners to insure themselves for income-related benefits if they wished.

Finally, it might be argued that the model for any comprehensive reform should be the non-industrial incapacity benefits scheme rather than the industrial injuries scheme on the basis that provision for compensation for permanent disability, regardless of income loss, is unjustified while so many are without adequate income. Even if there is a genuine public demand for disablement benefits over and above adequate income replacement benefits, there is a strong case for restricting these benefits to serious cases in which the disability threatens to destroy a person's normal mode of life. The emphasis in a comprehensive disability-benefits scheme should be firmly on income replacement and provision for the special needs of the disabled. On the other hand, the fact that the IIS is in some respects more generous than the non-industrial incapacity scheme makes it a desirable starting point with a view to encouraging the setting of benefits for all the disabled at higher rather than lower levels.[83] Whatever scheme provides the basis for development, better provision should be made than under present arrangements for those who suffer partial loss of earnings, especially in cases of long-term disability. Working tax credit is not an adequate response to this problem.

Given that the present political and economic climate is uncongenial to comprehensive reform, should lawyers support and press for whatever limited reform (such as a road accident scheme or a drug injuries scheme) seems politically feas-

83 Leaving aside questions of relativities with other groups of social security beneficiaries.

ible? The answer must be 'yes'. The waste and inefficiencies of the tort system are continuing realities, and there is only so much that tinkering with the tort system can achieve. Even if all we can realistically hope for is that the funds currently tied up in the tort system as it now operates will be better used, this is enough to justify a limited reform, even at the cost of creating or perpetuating anomalies between road accident victims and other social welfare recipients. And in the process the public mind might be sufficiently weaned off the idea of tort rights and on to the notion of no-fault welfare rights, to lead eventually to more comprehensive reform.

18.4.2   A private insurance solution

The approach we have been discussing might be thought, at the turn of the twenty-first century, to be anachronistic and unrealistic. Surely there is simply no prospect of reforms involving increases in public expenditure and expansion of the social security system. If this is true, what should be done to meet the undeniably strong case for radical reform of the way we as a society deal with compensation for injury and disability? Patrick Atiyah has argued that the way ahead lies in 'the spread of more first party insurance'.[84] As a first move, he would abolish the tort-cum-liability-insurance system in relation to road accidents and replace it with compulsory 'first-party' insurance paid for by car owners. The insurance would cover not only the car owner but, for instance, passengers in the car and pedestrians injured by it. Coverage would, of course, be on a no-fault basis. The element of compulsion would only extend to coverage for medical expenses and a basic level of income replacement, plus (perhaps) some compensation for nonpecuniary loss in cases of very serious injuries.

In relation to all other injuries and diseases theoretically covered by the tort system, Atiyah favours the abolition of tort liability, and leaving people to buy such insurance as they want to provide protection against risks of personal injury and illness over and above that already provided by the social security and social welfare systems. Given the limited coverage of the tort system (largely confined in practice to injuries suffered on the roads, at work, in hospital and in public places), the only contexts in which this proposal would represent a radical reform are those of occupier's liability claims, medical mishaps and work-related injuries. In the longer term, however, the logic of Atiyah's position seems to contemplate a possible, gradual replacement of the social security and social welfare system with private, first party insurance arrangements.

Those interested in understanding Atiyah's ideas better are encouraged to read *The Damages Lottery*. Here I will make just a few comments so as to indicate the differences of opinion between us. First, Atiyah's reason for dealing with road accidents in a special way seems to be the pragmatic one that the amounts currently spent on compulsory third-party liability insurance could easily be switched to

84 P.S. Atiyah, *The Damages Lottery* (Oxford, 1997), ch. 8.

first-party loss insurance. Even in the case of the other major areas of the practical operation of the tort system – accidents in public places, work injuries and medical mishaps – the mechanism of change would not be so obvious or straightforward because at present, people generally do not take out insurance to cover themselves against injuries suffered in these contexts.[85] However, there is no good reason of principle why injuries caused in road accidents should receive different treatment from injuries caused in any other way.

A second reservation about Atiyah's approach concerns its voluntary nature. It is only in the context of road accidents that Atiyah proposes that insurance should be compulsory. But the reason he gives for compulsion – that otherwise 'too many people would probably end up without any cover' – applies as much to other contexts as well. Under a voluntary system, the people least likely to be adequately insured are the poor, the ill-educated and the vulnerable. The protection of such people provides one of the strongest arguments for State provision of social services and social security benefits according to need. Compulsory redistribution of income and wealth from those who are strong, rich and well-educated to those who are less well-off is one of the marks of a humane society. The freedom to be inadequately insured against personal injury and disability is no freedom at all. I certainly support a two-tier system in which cover for losses and expenses above a certain minimum would be voluntary. But up to that minimum level, people should not be left to the vagaries of the 'free market'.

In my view, there is a strong case for abolishing tort law and the tort system as a mechanism for compensating victims of personal injuries, illness and disability. However, I also believe that the State has an obligation to guarantee an agreed minimum level of support for those in need as a result of suffering injury, illness and disability. This will inevitably involve a certain amount of wealth redistribution, and probably the simplest way of achieving this is through the tax system. Whether the provision of minimum support is administered by government agencies or private organizations should be decided in terms of who can do the job most efficiently.

Another problem with Atiyah's proposals is that they depend on a considerable expansion in the availability of a variety of first-party disability insurance products. It is by no means clear that it is realistic to expect such a development. One study in the late 1990s concluded that the private insurance industry is probably also unlikely to be able to provide affordable and comprehensive disability cover for sickness and illness, especially for those on low incomes and in high-risk groups.[86] Even in the USA, where there is much less social provision for the disabled than in Britain, dis-

---

85 In the case of work injuries, employers are required to insure against tort liability to their employees. There would be technical problems in replacing this with loss insurance purchased by employers for the benefit of their employees (9.7); and it is not clear that employers would have any incentive to compensate employees for the abolition of third-party insurance in the form of higher wages which would enable employees to purchase their own loss insurance.

86 T. Burchardt and J. Hills, *Private Welfare Insurance and Social Security* (York, 1997).

ability insurance is relatively uncommon.[87] A recent Home Office consultation paper concluded that it would not be practical to require members of the public to insure themselves against the risk of being a victim of crime, and that take-up of voluntary insurance would probably be low.[88] It must be admitted, however, that a related problem may also afflict any proposal to replace tort liability with social security. For instance, in 2004 the IIAC concluded that work-related stress should not be a prescribed illness for the purposes of the IIS, partly because of the difficulty of diagnosing the condition accurately without the detailed examination of individual cases characteristic (and responsible for much of the expense) of the tort system.[89] This suggests that there may be practical limits to the feasible coverage of a high-volume, low-cost social security system of disability compensation. In short, there may be certain misfortunes for which the tort system is the most feasible compensation mechanism.

If this is a valid conclusion, the goal of total abolition of tort liability for personal injuries and death, however desirable in principle, may be unrealistic in practice. Perhaps comprehensive reform in either a welfarist or a market-oriented direction, is a pipe-dream given the complexity of the human and social problems of injury, illness and disability.

18.5   Damage to property

If tort law were completely abolished as a mechanism for dealing with personal injuries, a question would arise about the fate of the law relating to property damage. Except in the very special case of ships, actions for property damage are now in practice almost invariably confined to cases of damage to vehicles (and such like) in road accidents. Outside this sphere, few tort actions are ever brought, and those that are brought rarely serve a useful social function. The practice of insuring property is so much more widespread than the practice of insuring one's own earning power that no hardship would probably be caused by total abolition of the tort action for damage to property, even if nothing else were put in its place.[90] The deliberate infliction of damage would, of course, remain a criminal offence, as would careless and dangerous driving. There is no doubt that this would save a great deal of money for motorists in the long run, since it would be much cheaper for them to insure their own cars against damage than to be compelled to go on carrying personal and liability insurance policies, even if they were restricted to property damage.

However, it is possible that people would find this inequitable in certain circumstances. For one thing, the fact that comprehensive insurance is not usually full

---

87 K.S. Abraham and L. Liebman, 'Private Insurance, Social Insurance and Tort Reform: Toward a New Vision of Compensation for Illness and Injury' (1993) 93 *Columbia LR* 75.
88 *Compensation and Support for Victims of Crime* (2004), paras. 42–5.
89 IIAC Position Paper 13.
90 Although this conclusion must be subject to arguments about the loss-prevention effect of tort liability especially in cases of bailment (e.g. carriage and warehousing).

insurance but involves an excess of £100 or more (not to mention loss of a no-claims bonus) means that a motorist whose car was damaged entirely by fault of another might well be dissatisfied if the law gave no redress against the other in respect of uninsured losses and increased premiums.[91] One possible answer to this – though a limited one – would be to make it a regular practice for criminal courts to make appropriate awards of compensation on the conviction of a motorist for a driving offence which caused damage to another vehicle. Alternatively, it might be possible to abolish tort liability for property damage except for (say) the first £300 of damage, and then to prohibit people from insuring against this liability. This would leave the property owner with insurance in the case of really serious damage, while still being able to claim the loss of the excess or no-claims bonus from another motorist at fault, and the fault principle would be given a reality it does not now possess by ensuring that there was no liability insurance, and that therefore the person at fault actually paid for the damage.[92] On the other hand, the inordinate cost of pursuing small tort claims might by itself be enough to rule this out as an acceptable approach.

18.6   The role of the insurance industry and the legal profession

If actions for damages for personal injuries were eliminated, a large proportion of the third-party liability insurance cover provided by the insurance industry would no longer be required. Although no industry is likely to welcome the disappearance of a substantial amount of business – especially captive business such as third-party liability insurance – there are reasons to think that insurers do not find this a particularly profitable line of business. In any event, the insurance industry has no real reason to fear the abolition of tort liability for personal injuries, especially if it were replaced by a private loss insurance system. Even if the social welfare route were taken, it is reasonable to expect increased demand for personal accident insurance and income protection insurance on the part of high salary earners. In this way, private insurance against loss through sickness or accident could supplement the social security system for the more affluent in precisely the same way as it does in relation to retirement pensions.

And if – though this seems less likely to win public acceptance – legal liability for negligent damage to property was also abolished (at least in some spheres), there can be little doubt that there would in consequence be a great expansion of property loss and damage insurance. It is true that the protection afforded the property owner by legal liability of others is limited, and not very valuable in comparison

---

91 There is a considerable and growing market for 'uninsured loss recovery' products and services, as revealed by searching 'uninsured loss recovery' on an internet search engine.
92 Professor Linden found it 'paradoxical' to contemplate the total abolition of actions for personal injury, but drew back from abolition of actions for property damage: 'Book Review' (1971) 49 *Canadian Bar Review* 146, 151. The explanation is that an adequate and universal replacement for the former is contemplated, but only a voluntary replacement for the latter.

with the much more extensive protection afforded by loss insurance; and therefore the elimination of legal liability would not be a particularly good reason for deciding to invest in property insurance if the property owner had done without it before. But it might be expected that the psychological effect of a change in the law of this nature would be immense, and insurance companies would be well placed to take advantage of this fact. Indeed, they would have to do so if the change were to have any real prospect of success, because the main reason for proposing this change so far as property damage is concerned is the belief that loss insurance is a cheaper, simpler and more effective form of protection for the property owner.

Clearly, the abolition of the tort action for personal injuries would have serious implications for the legal profession.[93] It is important that proposals for reform should grasp this nettle, and not dismiss the problem with an airy reference to 'vested interests'. The concerns of lawyers cannot be allowed to determine the shape of the law relating to compensation for personal injuries; law is a social service, and in the long run the interests of the consumers and not the administrators must prevail. Moreover, abolition of tort actions would clearly be a slow process with a long transitional period, if only because of the backlog of old cases waiting to be disposed of when the legislation took effect.

One obvious way in which the effects on the legal profession of eliminating all personal injury litigation could be cushioned would be to make legal aid available for social security tribunals. These tribunals already deal with far more cases than the tort system, and although the average case probably involves less money than the average tort case, many social security cases involve entitlement to long-term benefits the value of which over a period may be many thousands of pounds. The law relating to these benefits is also extremely complex and yet it is administered in the first instance by non-lawyers, and even social security appeal tribunals rarely have the assistance of legal representatives for the claimant. There is a great deal to be said even now for extending legal aid to some cases before these tribunals; plainly, the case would be stronger if the social welfare route for reform of compensation law were taken. The danger in this course of development is that social security law would become as dogged by delay, technicality, formality and excessive rigidity as the tort system; and this would open tribunals to the same criticisms as are currently levelled at the courts. There is an argument for preserving tribunals as 'lawyer-free zones'.[94]

At all events, this 'obvious' solution for the legal profession is highly unlikely to materialise. Governments of all political persuasions are keen to cut the amount

93 It has been said that one reason why fixed costs for road-accident claims were agreed relatively easily in 2003 is that lawyers feared the introduction of cheaper, non-tort alternatives of compensating for personal injuries suffered on the road: J. Peysner, 'Finding Predictable Costs' (2003) 22 *CJQ* 349, 365.

94 Empirical evidence shows that claimants who are represented enjoy greater success before social security (and other) tribunals than claimants who are not. However, the research also shows that non-legal representatives can do just as well or even better for the 'clients' as lawyers.

spent on legal aid. Legal aid is no longer available for most personal injury claims; and it is unlikely that conditional fees arrangements would have any place in a tribunal-based social security system of personal injury compensation. If the private insurance reform route were taken, there would undoubtedly be a certain amount of litigation arising from disputes about policy coverage, but nothing like the current volume of personal injury litigation. So far as the legal profession is concerned, we may have to face up to the fact that without the tort system, society would need fewer lawyers!

Index

accident insurance 292, 293
Accident Line 262, 263
accidents
    definition 3
    see also individual topics
actions see claims
actuarial tables 157–8
administration
    costs 27–8, 194, 324, 451, 483
    Criminal Injuries Compensation Scheme
        324–6
    income support 360
    industrial injuries scheme 351–5
    social security system 260–1
after-the-event (ATE) insurance 223, 224, 264,
    265, 463
aggravated damages 420
agreement not to sue 61–2
alcohol, duty of care and 80
alternative dispute resolution (ADR) 273–4
amenities, loss of 161
animals 72
    damage caused by 101
    road accidents and 216
    vicarious liability for 93, 248
annuities, structured settlements and 141
appeals
    Criminal Injuries Compensation Scheme
        324, 326
    social security tribunals 352, 353–4
arbitration 274
asbestos mesothelioma 20, 113, 193, 212, 231,
    241
assault, consent to 62
Association of Personal Injury Lawyers 194, 269
attachment of earnings order 226

attendance allowance 348
Australia
    corporate defendants 231
    insurance claims crisis 195–6, 197, 242
    proposed national accident insurance
        scheme 16, 470, 473

balance of probabilities 114, 117
bankruptcy, defendants 225, 230–1, 246–7
banks 82
barristers, duty of care 69
before-the-event (BTE) insurance 223, 263, 264
behaviour see conduct
benzodiazepine cases 219
bereavement
    benefits 350–1
    damages for 89–90, 162, 169, 413
Beveridge Report 331–3
blame culture 192–8, 269
Brandeis brief 42
British Coal 221, 286
British Nuclear Fuels 278
burden of proof 271
    shifting 94–5
'but-for' see factual causation

Canada, duty of care in 79
cancer
    asbestos mesothelioma 20, 113, 193, 212,
        231, 241
    delay in diagnosis 114
    statistics 20
capital
    adequacy 13
    human 163
captive insurers 228–9

care *see* duty of care; standard of care
carer's allowance 349
causation 3, 6–11, 110, 129
  contributory negligence and 54–5
  egalitarianism and problem of drawing line
    10–11
  factual causation 111–18
    causing and increasing risk of harm
      112–15
    limits on liability of factual causes 118–29
    multiple causation 116–18
    omissions 115–16
    proving 111–12, 188
  general deterrence theory and 450
  legal causation 118–25
  mixed systems in mixed society 11–18
  protecting reasonable expectations 9–10
  society's responsibility for human causes 8–9
  strict liability and 93
ceiling on benefits 296
charities, over-compensation and 389–90
children and young people
  abuse 82
  congenital defects 72, 246
    compensation for 16
    contributory negligence 57
    statistics 21
  Criminal Injuries Compensation Scheme
    and 313, 316
  duty of protection 79
  duty to control 81
  life insurance for 295
  responsibility for actions 92
choice
  of compensation system 378–80
  consumers 454
Citizens Advice Bureau 262
Citizens' Charter 194
civil partnerships 350
claimants 201
  conduct *see* conduct
claims
  actions commenced 203–4
  all tort claims 204–5
  cases reaching trial 201–3
  cases set down for trial 203
  costs of tort compensation 395–402, 405–6
  criminal injuries compensation 300–1
  defendants *see* defendants

funding *see* funding issues
  group claims 212, 221, 267
    negotiation 274–8, 286
  industrial injuries and illnesses 216–18
  medical injuries 219–21
  negotiation 260, 261, 268–78
    breakdown of 278–81
    claims assessors (CAs) 262, 272
    group claims 274–8, 286
    individual claims 269–74
    time taken 281–4
  public liability 218–19
  reasons for (not) making claims 206–14
    alternative remedies 207–9
    claims consciousness 209–14, 326–7
    research findings 206–7
  road accidents 214–16
  settlement *see* out of court settlements
claims assessors (CAs) 224–5, 262, 272
claims management companies (CMCs) 193–4,
    224, 262
class actions 276
cohabitation, claims for fatal injuries and 134–5
collection of evidence 270, 275
collective liability 179–80
common employment doctrine 36, 245, 328
common law, impact of liability insurance
    248–55
communitarianism 12
  collective liability 179–80
  social responsibility 8–9, 478–84, 480–2
compensation for accidents 3–6, 408–11, 461–6
  definition of compensation 4, 411–14
  see also individual topics
compensation neurosis 131
Compensation Recovery Unit (CRU) 204–5
competition 453
  perfect 439, 440, 455
complications 130–1
compulsory insurance 12, 14, 36, 96, 234, 246
compulsory purchase 185–6
conciliation 274
conditional fee arrangements (CFAs) 213, 214,
    223, 263–7, 463
conduct 53–4, 183–5
  contributory negligence 36, 53, 54–61, 245,
    251, 432, 449
    assessment 58–9
    differences from negligence 56

family cases and 57–8
fault system and 54, 59–60
usefulness of doctrine 60–1
volenti non fit injuria (voluntary
assumption of risk) and 62–4
Criminal Injuries Compensation Scheme
and 317–19
duties to control the conduct of others 81–3
illegality 53–4, 65–7
legal causation and 122–3
rules and standards of behaviour
avoiding injury to self 432–3
causing injury to others 425–32
volenti non fit injuria (voluntary assumption
of risk) 53, 61–5
agreement not to sue and 61–2
contributory negligence and 62–4
standard of care and 64–5
congenital defects 72, 246
compensation for 16
contributory negligence 57
statistics 21
consciousness of claims 209–14
Criminal Injuries Compensation Scheme
326–7
consent
consent orders 142
defence to trespass/assault 62
constant attendance allowance 348
consumer choice 454
contact sports 62
contractors, vicarious liability and 229–30, 248
contracts
contractual duties 99–100
exclusion clauses 61, 62
insurance 234
privity 71
undertakings 78
contribution, joint liability and 102
contributory negligence 36, 53, 54–61, 245, 251,
432, 449
assessment 58–9
differences from negligence 56
family cases and 57–8
fault system and 54, 59–60
usefulness of doctrine 60–1
volenti non fit injuria (voluntary assumption
of risk) and 62–4
coroners' inquests 270

corporations
corporate defendants and intangible losses
172
defunct 253
insurance 228–9, 230, 232
reorganization plans 231
as tort defendants 228–32
vicarious liability 93, 95, 102–3, 222, 229–32
see also industrial injuries/diseases
corrective compensation 411
corrective justice 421–2, 479
cost-benefit analysis 163
costs
administrative 27–8, 194, 324, 451, 483
criminal injuries compensation 406–7, 452
externalization of costs 443, 453
general deterrence theory *see* general
deterrence
industrial injuries 395, 399, 403–4, 452
insurance 399, 400
legal *see* legal costs
medical negligence claims 399, 401
no-fault compensation schemes 486–7
production costs 439–40
public liability 401
reforms 490–1
road accidents 396, 399–401, 443, 446, 447,
448–9
social security 403–5
social services 402–3
tort system 395–402, 405–6
usage costs 440
county courts 201, 202, 203, 204, 281
courts
actions commenced 203–4
cases reaching trial 201–3
cases set down for trial 203
county courts 201, 202, 203, 204, 281
court orders 225–6
criminal injuries compensation 301–3
Crown Courts 302
group litigation orders (GLOs) 276–7
High Court 201, 202, 203, 204, 281
litigation procedures 269–70
payment into court 280
representative actions 276
crime
compensation for criminal injuries 303–4
compensation orders 301–3

crime (*cont.*)
  compensation for criminal injuries (*cont.*)
    costs 406–7, 452
    over-compensation 394
    tort claims 300–1
    see also Criminal Injuries Compensation
      Scheme
  criminal proceedings 270
  illegality and negligence 53–4, 65–7
  prevention of 52–3, 82
  statistics 19
  violent 310–13, 409
    domestic violence 315–16
Criminal Injuries Compensation
    Board/Authority (CICB/CICA) 300
Criminal Injuries Compensation Scheme 4–5,
    6, 7, 14, 27, 36, 53, 301, 379–80, 409
  administration 324–6
  awards 303
  claims consciousness 326–7
  comparison with tort liability 316–24
    assessment of compensation 319–24
    conduct of claimant 317–19
    mental distress/nervous shock 316–17
  costs 406–7, 452
  hundred-per-cent principle 156
  justification for 304–9
  over-compensation 394
  scope 309–16
    accidental injuries 314–15
    crimes of violence 310–13, 409
    exclusions 315–16
  subrogation rights 383
crisis in insurance 195–7, 242–3, 463
critical illness insurance 292
Crown Courts 302
Crown indemnity 17
culture of compensation/blame 192–8, 269
cumulation 377

Dalkon Shield 212
damage to property 4, 62, 207
  insurance and 5
  war property damage compensation 10, 117
damages 23, 24, 239–40, 410–11
  aggravated damages 420
  for bereavement 89–90, 162, 169, 413
  contributory negligence and 58–9
  full compensation 143–52

commitment in practice 157–61
  general damages 144
  interest 145–6
  lost earnings and support 146–9, 152–61
  medical and other expenses 149–52
  special damages 144
  instalment payments 225
  intangible losses 286, 410
    assessing intangible losses 161–6
    justification 171–3
    subjective factors 170–1
    tariff system 166–70
  lump sum
    alternatives to lump sums 139–43
    fatal cases 132–5
    personal injury cases 130–2
    suitability of lump sums 137–9
    variation of awards after trial 135–7
    workers' compensation claims 329–30
  maxima 173
  negotiation on 270–1
  out of court settlement 284–7
  over-compensation *see* over-compensation
  periodical payments 140, 142–3
    arguments against 139
  punitive damages 172, 173–4, 410, 419–21
  structured settlements 141–2
dangerousness, strict liability and 105–6
deceased persons
  claims against 245
  contributory negligence 57
  negligence by 36
  see also fatal injuries
deductibles (excess) 296, 435
defamation 212–13
defective premises 72
defective products *see* product liability
defendants 222
  bankruptcy 225, 230–1, 246–7
  corporations/employers 228–32
  enforcement of judgments against 225–7
  individuals 222–7
  repeat 269
  see also funding issues
delays 283
  interest on damages awards and 145–6
  postponement of trial/settlement 131–2
demand, elasticity of 446–7
Denmark, subrogation rights 385

dependants
    claims for fatal injuries 132–5
    loss of earnings and 146–7
dependency culture 192
design, negligence in 50–3, 191
deterrence 479
    as function of compensation systems 424–58,
        482–3
    general deterrence 424, 439–58
        allocation of costs to activities 442–6
        application in practice 448
        ascertaining costs of accident 442
        assessment of value of general-deterrence
            approach 453–6
        basic idea 439–41
        conclusions on 457–8
        insurance and 443–4, 452–3, 455
        responsiveness to price mechanism 446–7
        social security system and 452
        tort system and 448–51
    punitive damages as 174
    rules and standards of behaviour 425–33
        avoiding injury to self 432–3
        causing injury to others 425–32
development risk defence 104
disability 468–9, 474–5
    causation 7
    costs of social services 402–3
    discrimination on grounds of 368–9, 370
    effects on income 21–2
    employment and 21–2, 366–9
    housing and residential accommodation
        370–1
    mobility schemes 369–70
    other social services 371–2
    protecting reasonable expectations 9–10
    responsibility for human causes 8–9
    social security and 6, 7, 335–6, 355–8
        income support 359
        long-term incapacity from industrial
            injuries 344–50
        preferences in State system 356–8
        reform proposals 488–93
        social services 402–3
    social services and 365–72
    statistics on 21–2
    tax reliefs 364
    unemployment and 367, 369
disclosure of evidence 270

discount rate 158–9, 396
discrimination
    disability and 368–9, 370
    preferential treatment 472–3
disease 3, 6
    causation 6–7
distributional issues 12
    distribution of losses 415–18, 454
        how should it be distributed 416–18
        what should be distributed 415–16
    redistributive compensation 411–12
    strict liability and 479–80
domestic violence 315–16
double compensation 161
Dow-Corning 212
drugs
    elasticity of demand 446
    product liability 103–4, 219, 467
    side effects 114, 220
    Thalidomide case 16, 20, 105, 285, 461, 467
    vaccine damage 107–8
dual systems 470–2, 491–2
duties
    breach of statutory duty 95–9, 126
    care see duty of care
    contractual duties 99–100
    duty of care 34, 69–70
        distinction between acts and omissions
            72–84
        control over property 83–4
        duties of physical protection 78–81
        duties to control the conduct of others
            81–3
        undertakings 77–8
        situations where duty of care has been
            imposed 70–2

earnings see wages and salaries
economic torts 34
efficiency, distribution of losses and 418
egalitarianism 10–11
elasticity of demand 446–7
emergency services, duty of care and 79
employment
    common employment doctrine 36, 245, 328
    disability and 21–2, 366–9
    duty of care 78, 80
    employers as defendants 228–32
    negligence of employees 36

employment (*cont.*)
  sick pay 209, 293–4, 343–4, 379
    over-compensation and 387–8
  vicarious liability 93, 95, 102–3, 222, 229–32
  see also industrial injuries/diseases
enforcement of judgments 225–7
equality 472
  fault principle and 177–9
equivalent compensation 412–13
European Convention on Human Rights 194
evidence
  collection of 270, 275
  disclosure 270
  problems with 271
ex gratia compensation schemes 107–9, 307
  hepatitis C 108–9
  HIV infection 108
  vaccine damage 107–8
  variant CJD 109
excess 296, 435
exclusion clauses
  contracts 61, 62
  insurance 61, 62, 248
exemplary (punitive) damages 172, 173–4, 410, 419–21
expectations
  equivalent compensation and 412–13
  protecting reasonable expectations 9–10
expenses, full compensation damages and 149–52
expert evidence, nervous shock 85
externalization of costs 443, 453

facts of the case 36–9
factual causation 111–18
  causing and increasing risk of harm 112–15
  limits on liability of factual causes 118–29
    damage not within the risk 125–7
    foreseeability 125, 127–9
    legal causation 118–25
    multiple causation 116–18
    omissions 115–16
    proving 111–12
faculty, loss of 161–2
failure to act *see* omissions
fairness 408
  fair hearing right 70
family cases
  negligence 89–91

contributory negligence and 57–8
  see also spouses
fatal injuries
  bereavement benefits 350–1
  bereavement damages 89–90, 162, 169, 413
  Criminal Injuries Compensation Scheme 320, 322–3
  full compensation damages 143–4, 149
  inquests 270
  intangible losses 162, 163, 171
  loss of earnings and 146–7
  lump sum damages 132–5
fault 3, 14, 35–6, 235, 250–1
  appraisal of fault principle 175
  avoidance of responsibility 192–8
  compensation bears no relation to degree of fault 175–7
  compensation bears no relation to means of tortfeasor 177–9
  contribution to culture of blame 192–8, 269
  difficulty of adjudicating allegations of fault 187–91
  fault principle pays little attention to conduct or needs of victim 183–5
  justice may require compensation without fault 185–6
  legal liability without moral culpability and vice versa 179–83
  moral culpability without legal liability 182–3
  contributory negligence and 54, 59–60
  definition 180–2, 187
  departures from fault principle
    breach of statutory duty 95–9, 126
    contractual duties 99–100
    ex gratia compensation schemes 107–9
    joint liability 101–2
    procedural devices 94–5
    product liability 103–5
    proposals to extend strict liability 105–6, 467–8
    Rylands v. *Fletcher* rule 100–1
    strict liability 92–4, 105–6, 467–8
  proof of 94, 187–8
  see also negligence
finance *see* funding issues
fires 207, 208

fire brigades 433, 434
insurance 4, 295
legal causation 125
multiple causation 116
statistics 19
first-party insurance 235–8, 378, 475
for benefit of others 244–5
compared with tort liability 295–9
compensation reform proposals 493–5
general deterrence theory and 452–3
over-compensation and 388–9
types 291–5
Fisher Committee 361
foreseeability 47–8, 68–9, 125, 127–9
Forum of Insurance Lawyers 269
fraud
social security 360–1
tort system 361–2
front-loading 270, 281, 396
full compensation damages 143–52
commitment in practice 157–61
general damages 144
lost earnings and support 146–9
earnings-related principle 152–5, 475–6
hundred-per-cent principle 156–7
justification 152–7
medical and other expenses 149–52
special damages 144
functions of compensation systems
allocation of risks 418–19
corrective justice 421–2
criteria for success 414
definition of compensation 4, 411–14
deterrence 424–58, 482–3
general deterrence 424, 439–58
rules and standards of behaviour 425–33
distribution of losses 415–18, 454
how should it be distributed 416–18
what should be distributed 415–16
preliminary questions 408–11
prevention 424–39
punishment 419–21
vindication or satisfaction 422–3
funding issues 223–5, 261–8, 483
legal aid 17, 213, 223, 247, 263, 264, 275
costs and 278–9
costs of 402
Criminal Injuries Compensation Scheme
325

no-win-no-fee 263, 264
claims assessors (CAs) 224–5, 262, 272
claims management companies 224, 262
conditional fee arrangements (CFAs) 213,
214, 223, 263–7, 463
Criminal Injuries Compensation Scheme
325
reform proposals 477–8
trade unions 213, 261–2, 279
see also insurance
future of compensation system see reform
proposals

general damages 144
general deterrence 424, 439–58
allocation of costs to activities 442–6
application in practice 448
ascertaining costs of accident 442
assessment of value of general-deterrence
approach 453–6
basic idea 439–41
conclusions on 457–8
insurance and 443–4, 452–3, 455
responsiveness to price mechanism 446–7
rules and standards of behaviour 425–33
avoiding injury to self 432–3
causing injury to others 425–32
social security system and 452
tort system and 448–51
Germany 488
goals of system see functions of compensation
systems
government and the State
compensation schemes and 11–12, 13, 477–8
war property damage compensation 10
legal system 13–14
public sector 453
see also social security
group claims 212, 221, 267
negotiation 274–8, 286
group litigation orders (GLOs) 276–7

haemophilia, HIV infection and 108
health and safety 98
see also industrial injuries/diseases
health insurance 292
hedonic value of life 162
hepatitis C infection 108–9
High Court 201, 202, 203, 204, 281

highways, failure to repair 72
hit-and-run accidents 36, 255–9
HIV infection 108
home accidents 207–8, 211
homicide, statistics 19
hotels, duty to control conduct of others 81–2
household services, fatal injury awards and
   147–8
housing 370–1
human capital 163
human rights issues 70, 82–3, 194

identification doctrine 57
ignorance of law 210–11, 427
illegality, negligence and 53–4, 65–7
incapacity benefit 6, 336
income see wages and salaries
income distribution see distributional issues
income support 14, 22, 337, 358–60
   administration 360
indemnities 232, 254
   Crown indemnity 17
individualism 12–13, 192
individuals
   negotiation of individual claims 269–74
   as tort defendants 222–7
industrial injuries/diseases 111, 216–18, 413
   asbestos mesothelioma 20, 113, 193, 212,
      231, 241
   breach of statutory duty 95–9
   cases reaching trial 202, 203
   claims consciousness 213
   costs 395, 399, 403–4, 452
   damage not within the risk 126
   deterrence 431–2
   insurance 234, 246
      risk-related insurance premiums 437–9
   multiple causation 117–18
   omissions 115–16
   over-compensation and 388–9
   social security and 6, 332–3
      accidents and disease 340–2
      administration 351–5
      benefits 342–51
      bereavement benefits 350–1
      long-term incapacity 344–50
      scope of system 338–40
      short-term incapacity 343–4
      tort system compared 355

workers' compensation 328–30, 331–3,
   390, 456
statistics 19, 193, 205, 216–18
inequalities 11
   earnings-related principle and 155
inflation 241–2, 331
   social security and 334
information disclosure 270
inquests 270
instalment payment of damages 225
insurance 5, 11, 13–14, 59, 178–9, 186, 222, 233
   accident insurance 292, 293
   accident prevention and 433–9
      encouraging/requiring loss prevention
         measures 433–5
      risk-related premiums and similar
         techniques 435–9
   after-the-event (ATE) 223, 224, 264, 265, 463
   captive insurers 228–9
   claims crisis 195–7, 242–3, 463
   compensation reform proposals 493–5
   compulsory 12, 14, 36, 96, 234, 246
   corporations 228–9, 230, 232
   costs 399, 400
   earnings-related principle and 154–5
   excess (deductibles) 296, 435
   exclusion clauses 61, 62, 248
   fire insurance 4, 295
   first-party insurance 235–8, 378, 475
      for benefit of others 244–5
      compared with tort liability 295–9
      compensation reform proposals 493–5
      general deterrence theory and 452–3
      over-compensation and 388–9
      types 291–5
   general deterrence theory and 443–4, 452–3,
      455
   impact of liability insurance on the law 245–55
      common law 248–55
      statutory provisions 245–8
   industrial injuries 234, 246
      risk-related insurance premiums 437–9
   'knock-for-knock' agreements 238, 385
   legal expenses (before-the-event) insurance
      223, 263, 264
   Motor Insurers' Bureau (MIB) scheme 36,
      255–9, 279, 315, 379, 400–1
   mutuals 228
   nature of liability insurance 234–8

New Zealand national accident insurance
    scheme 16, 461, 469, 470, 471, 473, 475,
    476, 477, 481, 483, 485, 491
no-claims bonuses 436–7
over-compensation and 388–9
problems of liability insurance 239–43
property 5, 291, 298–9, 495–6
    fire insurance 4, 295
reform proposals and insurance profession
    496–8
road accidents 154, 234, 235–6, 246
risk-related insurance premiums 436–7
self-insurance 228
solvency of insurance companies 13
intangible losses 286, 410, 474–5
assessing intangible losses 161–6
insurance and 297–8
justification 171–3
subjective factors 170–1
tariff system 166–70
intention 35
interest
damages awards and 145–6
discount rate 158–9, 396
Investigative Help 263
investment
lump sum damages 137–8
real rates of return 159
structured settlements and 141

joint liability 101–2
Journal of Personal Injury Law 194
judgments, enforcement 225–7
justice 408, 410, 490
corrective justice 421–2, 479
dual systems and 471
no-fault compensation and 185–6

'knock-for-knock' agreements 238, 385

last opportunity rule 55
Law Society 269
lead cases 277
legal advice scheme 213
legal aid 17, 213, 223, 247, 263, 264, 275
costs and 278–9
costs of 402
Criminal Injuries Compensation Scheme 325
legal causation 118–25

legal costs 213, 239, 278–81, 397, 398
losing party 223, 278–9
legal expenses (before-the-event) insurance
    223, 263, 264
legal profession see barristers; solicitors
Legal Services Commission (LSC) 263
legal system 13–14
    see also common law; statutory law; tort law
level crossing accidents 40
life expectancy 162
full compensation damages and 148
intangible losses and 165
life insurance 291, 295
litigation procedures 269–70
local authorities 82
residential accommodation 371
    see also social services
Lockerbie bombing 212
long-tail liability 240–1
long-term care insurance 292
loss
definition of 4, 415
distribution of losses 415–18, 454
    how should it be distributed 416–18
    what should be distributed 415–16
intangible see intangible losses
social loss 451
valuation 415
loss of earnings 132, 146–9
fatal injuries 132
full compensation damages 146–9
    earnings-related principle 152–5, 475–6
    hundred-per-cent principle 156–7
    justification 152–7
insurance against 292, 293, 294–5, 296
lump sum damages 137
road accidents 379
lump sum damages
alternatives to lump sums 139–43
    arguments against abandoning lump-sum
        system 139–40
    early proposals 140–1
    periodical payments 140, 142–3
    structured settlements 141–2
fatal cases 132–5
personal injury cases 130–2
suitability of lump sums 137–9
variation of awards after trial 135–7
workers' compensation claims 329–30

Macfarlane Trust 108
magistrates' court, criminal injuries
    compensation orders 301–3
malingering 131
Malta 254
manufacturers, liability of *see* product liability
marginal utility of money 162, 163
market system 11
mass torts 212
means testing 337, 358, 476
mediation 274
medical expenses
    conditional fee arrangements (CFAs) 267
    full compensation damages and 149–52
medical negligence 38–9, 42, 69, 176, 219–21,
        252, 464
    claims consciousness and 210
    costs of tort compensation 399, 401
    defensive medicine and 430–1
    foreseeability of injury 129
    legal aid for claim 263
    legal causation 121–2, 124
    NHS Redress scheme proposal 464–6, 470
    reasons for claiming 206–7
    res ipsa loquitur and 95
    statistics 19, 20, 27, 193, 205, 208, 219–21
        actions commenced 203, 204
        cases reaching trial 201, 202, 203
medical profession 429
    defensive medicine 430–1
    duty of care 78
    expert evidence 85
    negligence *see* medical negligence
medical technology 194–5, 210, 396
mental illness, Criminal Injuries Compensation
        Scheme and 313
mental injury *see* psychiatric damage
mesothelioma 20, 113, 193, 212, 231, 241
misfeasance 72–3
mistake 176, 185
mitigation of loss 157
mobility schemes 369–70
Monckton Committee (1946) 98, 390
morality, fault principle and popular morality
        183
mortgages, insurance 291, 295
Motability 369–70
Motor Insurers' Bureau (MIB) 36, 255–9, 279,
        315, 379, 400–1

motor vehicles
    construction and use 96
    see also road accidents
multi-party claims *see* group claims
multiple causation 116–18
multiple defendants 230
multiplier/multiplicand 146, 157

National Health Service (NHS) 17, 149–51, 206,
        209, 248, 252, 365–6
    complaints scheme 263, 464, 465
    expenditure 397
    Redress scheme proposal 464–6, 470
    subrogation/recoupment rights 382, 396,
        451, 463
National Insurance 14, 298, 330–1, 334, 336
negligence 33, 34, 35, 36–53, 175–6, 180,
        249–50, 297, 449
    as basis of liability 34
    conduct of claimant 53–4
        contributory negligence 36, 53, 54–61, 245
        illegality 53–4, 65–7
        volenti non fit injuria 53, 61–5
    contributory negligence 36, 53, 54–61, 245,
        251, 432, 449
        assessment 58–9
        differences from negligence 56
        family cases and 57–8
        fault system and 54, 59–60
        usefulness of doctrine 60–1
        volenti non fit injuria (voluntary
            assumption of risk) and 62–4
    damage not within the risk 125–7
    in design 50–3, 191
    deterrence 426–32
    duty of care 34, 69–70
        distinction between acts and omissions
            72–84
        situations where duty of care has been
            imposed 70–2
    family cases 89–91
        contributory negligence and 57–8
        foreseeability 47–8, 68–9, 125, 127–9
        joint liability 101–2
        medical *see* medical negligence
        nature of 40–2
        negligence formula 41, 46–7
            likely magnitude of harm 43–4
            probability of harm 42–3

value of activity and cost of precautions
  needed to avoid harm 45–6
nervous shock 84–9
in operation 50
punitive damages and 174
question of fact 36–9
standard of care 48–50
negotiation 260, 261
  breakdown of 278–81
  claims assessors (CAs) 262, 272
  course of 268–78
    group claims 274–8, 286
    individual claims 269–74
    time taken 281–4
    transfer of costs and 445
neighbour principle 68
nervous shock see psychiatric damage
New Deal 366–7
New Zealand
  earnings-related principle in 153
  hundred-per-cent principle in 156
  national accident insurance scheme 16, 461,
    469, 470, 471, 473, 475, 476, 477, 481,
    483, 485, 491
no-claims bonuses 436–7
no-fault compensation schemes 17, 93–4,
    185–6, 409, 462
  costs 486–7
  dual systems 470–2, 491–2
  goals of system 480–4
  New Zealand 16, 461, 469, 470, 471, 473, 475,
    476, 477, 481, 483, 485, 491
  reform proposals 467–8, 469–70
  road accident scheme proposals 484–7
nonfeasance see omissions
non-pecuniary losses see intangible losses
not-for-profit organizations 372
no-win-no-fee 263, 264
  claims assessors (CAs) 224–5, 262, 272
  claims management companies 224, 262
  conditional fee arrangements (CFAs) 213,
    214, 223, 263–7, 463
  Criminal Injuries Compensation Scheme 325
nuisance 100–1

occupiers' liability 36, 72, 205, 218–19, 248
Ogden tables 158, 159
omissions (failure to act) 72–84
  control over property 83–4

duties of physical protection 78–81
duties to control the conduct of others 81–3
factual causation and 115–16
legal causation 124
undertakings 77–8
operation, negligence in 50
opinions on compensation 408–9
Opren 267–8
out of court settlements 260–1
  amount of compensation 284–7
  negotiation 260, 261, 268–78
    breakdown of 278–81
    claims assessors (CAs) 262, 272
    group claims 274–8, 286
    individual claims 269–74
    time taken 281–4
  Part 36 offers 279–81
  time taken to achieve 281–4
  workers' compensation claims 329
over-caution 429–31
over-compensation 377–8
  criminal injuries compensation 394
  general principles 385–7
  subrogation and recoupment 156, 204, 380–5
  tort damages and charitable payments
    389–90
  tort damages and personal insurance 388–9
  tort damages and sick pay 387–8

Part 36 offers 279–81
payment into court 280
Payne Committee 226
Pearson Royal Commission 15, 17, 461–2
pensions 294, 334
perfect competition 439, 440, 455
periodical payments 140, 142–3
  arguments against 139
permanent health insurance 292
persistent vegetative state 170–1
personal accident insurance (PAI) 292, 293
personal injury lawyers 194–5
physical protection, duties of 78–81
Piper Alpha 212, 276
post-traumatic distress disorder (PTSD) 88,
    172, 278, 341–2
predictions, lump sum damages and
  fatal cases 132–5
  personal injuries 130–2
preferential treatment 472–3

prevention of accidents 5–6, 45–6, 189–90
    as function of compensation systems 424–39
    general deterrence theory and 441
    insurance and 433–9
        encouraging/requiring loss prevention
            measures 433–5
        risk-related premiums and similar
            techniques 435–9
    road accidents 12, 44
prevention of crime 52–3, 82
prices, general deterrence theory and 446–7
prisons
    duty of care towards prisoners 79
    negligence in design 51–2
    suicide in 67
privity of contract 71
probability 188–9
    balance of probabilities 114, 117
product liability 71, 99–100, 103–5, 111, 211,
        458
    drugs 103–4, 219, 467
    legal causation 124
    res ipsa loquitur and 94–5
production costs 439–40
professionals, duty of care 78
profit, public opinion on 453–4
proof
    burden of 271
        shifting 94–5
    of fault 94, 187–8
    problems with 271
    proving factual causation 111–12, 188
property 178
    bankruptcy and 225
    compulsory purchase 185–6
    control over 83–4
    damage to 4, 62, 207
        insurance and 5
        reform proposals 495–6
        road accidents 207, 495–6
        war property damage compensation 10,
            117
    defective premises 72
    insurance 5, 291, 298–9, 495–6
        fire insurance 4, 295
    see also occupiers' liability
protection, duties of 78–81
psychiatric damage (nervous shock) 84–9
    compensation neurosis 131

Criminal Injuries Compensation Scheme
    and 316–17
    post-traumatic distress disorder (PTSD) 88,
        172, 278, 341–2
    railway suicides and 310–12
public inquiries 40, 111, 275
public interest 40
public liability 218–19
    costs of claims 401
public opinion
    on compensation 408–9
    on profit 453–4
public policy 40, 125
public sector 453
public transport, duty to control conduct of
    others 82
public vindication, as function of
    compensation systems 422–3
punitive (exemplary) damages 172, 173–4, 410,
    419–21

Queen's Bench Division 201

railway accidents 40, 106
    Criminal Injuries Compensation Scheme
        and 311–12
reasonableness, reasonable persons 37–8, 39
recklessness 35
recoupment *see* subrogation and recoupment
redistributive compensation 411–12
reduced earnings allowance (REA) 347
reform proposals 195, 196, 467–98, 470–2,
        491–2
    basic issues 467–84
        assessment of compensation 474–6
        funding 477–8
        goals of system 478–84
        limited or comprehensive reform 468–72
        no-fault schemes 467–8, 469–70
        preferential treatment 472–3
        strict liability 105–6, 467–8
    other schemes 487–8
        private insurance solution 493–5
        property damage 495–6
        road accident schemes 484–7
        role of insurance industry and legal
            profession 496–8
        social welfare solution 488–93
remoteness of damage 118, 127

repeat defendants 269
representative actions 276
res ipsa loquitur 94–5, 103, 112
rescuers 74, 83–4
residential accommodation 371
responsibility, avoidance of 192–8
retailers, liability of 99
retroactive legislation 240
risks
  allocation of 418–19
  attitudes to 48
  damage not within the risk 125–7
  foreseeability 47–8, 68–9, 125, 127–9
  risk-related insurance premiums 435–9
  volenti non fit injuria (voluntary assumption
    of risk) 53, 61–5
    agreement not to sue and 61–2
    contributory negligence and 62–4
    standard of care and 64–5
road accidents 61–2, 176, 189, 214–16
  cases reaching trial 202, 203
  contributory negligence and 55, 56, 57, 58,
    432–3
  costs 396, 399–401, 443, 446, 447, 448–9
  Criminal Injuries Compensation Scheme
    and 315
  deterrence 426–8
  driving ability and 176–7
  duty of care and 79
  enforcement of judgments 226
  fatal injuries, lump sum damages 134
  full compensation awards 160
  hit-and-run accidents 36, 255–9
  imposition of duty of care 70–1
  insurance 154, 234, 235–6, 246
    risk-related insurance premiums 436–7
  intangible losses 164
  joint liability 101–2
  legal causation 119, 120, 121–2, 123, 124, 125
  loss of earnings 379
  multiple causation 116
  negligence in design 50–1, 52, 191
  negotiation of claims 270
  no-fault compensation schemes 484–7
  prevention 12, 44
  property damage and 207, 495–6
  society's responsibility 8
  statistics 19, 188–91, 193, 205, 214–16
  strict liability and 93

subrogation rights 382
uninsured drivers 36, 247, 255–9
Robens Committee 16
Royal Commission on Legal Services 213
rules and standards of behaviour 425–33
  avoiding injury to self 432–3
  causing injury to others 425–32
Rylands v. *Fletcher* rule 100–1

salaries *see* wages and salaries
satisfaction, as function of compensation
  systems 422–3
self-insurance 228
services, liability for 94, 104
settlements
  out of court *see* out of court settlements
  structured settlements 141–2
sick pay 209, 293–4, 343–4, 379
  over-compensation and 387–8
sickness benefits 6, 209, 293–4, 330–1, 336
silicone breast implants 278
Skipton Fund 109
smoking tobacco 231, 278, 432, 446
Social Fund (SF) 358
social loss 451
social responsibility 8–9, 478–84, 480–2
social security 6, 7, 11, 14, 16, 236, 378–89, 462,
  469
  administration 260–1
  Beveridge Report and 1946 Acts 331–3
  compensation for criminal injuries and 303,
    304
  compensation reform proposals and 488–93
  costs 403–5
  dependency culture 192
  developments since 1946 333–7
  disability and 6, 7, 22, 335–6, 355–8
    income support 359
    long-term incapacity from industrial
      injuries 344–50
    preferences in State system 356–8
    reform proposals 488–93
  earnings-related principle 153–4, 334–5,
    475–6
  flat-rate principle 153
  foundations of system
    National Insurance 330–1
    workers' compensation 328–30, 331–3,
      390, 456

social security (*cont.*)
  fraud and abuse 360–2
  general deterrence theory and 452
  hundred-per-cent principle 156
  income support 14, 22, 337, 358–60
    administration 360
  industrial injuries and 6, 332–3
    accidents and disease 340–2
    administration 351–5
    benefits 342–51
    bereavement benefits 350–1
    long-term incapacity 344–50
    scope of system 338–40
    short-term incapacity 343–4
    tort system compared 355
    workers' compensation 328–30, 331–3,
      390, 456
  means testing 337, 358, 476
  pensions 294, 334
  recovery of benefits 156, 204, 381, 384,
    390–4, 396
  redistribution and 411
  sickness benefits 6, 209, 293–4, 330–1, 336
  taxation and 364
  tribunals 352, 353–4, 497–8
social services 365–72
  costs 402–3
  employment-related 366–9
  housing and residential accommodation
    370–1
  mobility 369–70
  other services 371–2
society
  collective liability 179–80
  mixed society 11–18
  social responsibility 8–9, 478–84, 480–2
  see also government and the State
solace, compensation as 412, 414
solicitors 262–3, 268–9
  negotiation by *see* negotiation
  reform proposals and 496–8
  reluctance to consult 213
special damages 144
sports 62, 64
spouses
  bereavement benefits 350–1
  bereavement damages 89–90, 162, 169, 413
  fatal injuries claims 132–5, 147, 149
    remarriage and 133–4

negligence and 57–8, 72
  suing other spouse 245–6, 253–4
standard of behaviour *see* rules and standards
  of behaviour
standard of care 48–50
  volenti non fit injuria (voluntary assumption
    of risk) and 64–5
State *see* government and the State
state-of-the-art defence 104
statistics 18, 455
  accidents causing personal injury/death
    18–20
  actions commenced 203–4
  cases reaching trial 201–3
  cases set down for trial 203
  death and disability from other causes
    20–1
  distribution and sources of compensation
    22–5
  effects of disability on income 21–2
  home accidents 208
  industrial injuries 19, 193, 205, 216–18
  medical negligence 19, 20, 27, 193, 205, 208,
    219–21
    actions commenced 203, 204
    cases reaching trial 201, 202, 203
  prevalence of disability 21
  road accidents 19, 188–91, 193, 205, 214–16
  seriousness 25–9
  tort claims 192–3
  use of lump sum damages awards 138
statutory duty, breach of 95–9, 126
statutory law
  impact of liability insurance 245–8
  retroactive legislation 240
stress 341
  post-traumatic distress disorder (PTSD) 88,
    172, 278, 341–2
strict liability 71, 92–4, 235, 475, 479–80
  breach of contractual duties 99–100
  breach of statutory duty 95–9, 126
  joint liability 101–2
  product liability 99–100, 103–5
  proposals to extend 105–6, 467–8
    dangerous things and activities 105–6
    railway accidents 106
  Rylands v. *Fletcher* rule 100–1
  vicarious liability 102–3
structured settlements 141–2

subrogation and recoupment 380–5
    National Health Service (NHS) 382, 396,
        451, 463
    social security benefits 156, 204, 381, 384,
        396
substitute, compensation as 412, 413–14
success fees 223, 265–6
suicide, Criminal Injuries Compensation
    Scheme and 310–12
survival actions 132–3, 147
Sweden 488

tariff system
    Criminal Injuries Compensation Scheme
        320–4
    intangible losses 166–70
taxation 363–5, 452
    earnings-related principle and 153
    periodical payments and 142
    State compensation schemes and 12
taxis, duty of care and 79
test cases 277
Thalidomide 16, 20, 105, 285, 461, 467
third party debt orders 225–6
time limits 283
tobacco 231, 278, 432, 446
tort law 4, 5
    conceptual basis 33–4
    see also individual topics
trade unions 390
    funding of claims by 213, 261–2, 279
tranquillizer cases 219
trespass 72
    consent to 62
tribunals, social security 352, 353–4, 497–8

undertakings 77–8
unemployment 468, 474
    disability and 367, 369
unfair terms in contracts 61, 62, 248
uninsured defendants
    enforcement of judgments 225–7
    funding of legal action 224–5
    uninsured drivers 36, 247, 255–9, 315, 379,
        400–1
United States of America
    accident prevention in 433–4
    Brandeis brief 42
    claims consciousness 210

class actions 276
corporate defendants 231
defensive medicine 430
full compensation awards 159
general deterrence theory in 457–8
insurance claims crisis 243
intangible losses 166, 168–9
medical negligence 208
no-fault compensation 185, 484, 485
product liability in 458
public opinion on compensation 408
punitive damages 174, 420
tobacco industry claims 278
tort reform 195
workers' compensation in 456
unpaid work, full compensation damages and
    149
usage costs 440
utility companies, strict liability and 93

vaccine damage 107–8
valuation of loss 415
variant CJD sufferers 109
variation of awards
    lump sum damages 135–7
    periodical payments 142
vicarious liability 93, 95, 102–3, 222, 229–32
    animals 93, 248
    contractors 229–30, 248
vicissitudes principle 117–18
victims of accidents 201
vindication, as function of compensation
    systems 422–3
violent crime 310–13, 409
    domestic violence 315–16
Vioxx 219–20
volenti non fit injuria (voluntary assumption of
    risk) 53, 61–5
    agreement not to sue and 61–2
    contributory negligence and 62–4
    standard of care and 64–5
voluntary organizations 372

wages and salaries
    attachment of earnings order 226
    bankruptcy and 225
    disability and 21–2
    earnings-related principle in social security
        153–4, 334–5, 475–6

wages and salaries (*cont.*)
  income protection insurance (IPI) 292, 293,
    294–5, 296
  loss of *see* loss of earnings
  pensions 294, 334
  sick pay 209, 293–4, 343–4, 379
    over-compensation and 387–8
war 69
  insurance risks and 295
  war property damage compensation 10, 117
warranties 99
wealth
  compensation bears no relation to means of
    tortfeasor 177–9

distribution *see* distributional issues
  intangible losses and 164
welfare system *see* social security; social services
widows *see* bereavement
willingness to pay 162, 163
Winn Committee 382
witnesses
  difficulties with 187, 271
  nervous shock 87–9
Woolf reforms 463
workers' compensation 328–30, 331–3, 390, 456
working tax credit (WTC) 347–8, 358

young people *see* children and young people